Exam 70-238: *PRO: Deployir with Microsoft Exchange Ser*

S

MW00487617

Objective

Objective	
Planning Microsoft Exchange Server 2007 Upgrades and Migrations	
Plan the Exchange Server 2007 upgrade implementation.	Chapter 3, Lesson 1
Plan the Exchange Server 2007 migration implementation.	Chapter 3, Lesson 2
Plan interoperability with Exchange in separate organizations.	Chapter 4, Lesson 1
Plan coexistence with Exchange 2000 Server and Exchange Server 2003 in a single organization.	Chapter 4, Lesson 2
Plan interoperability with third-party messaging systems.	Chapter 4, Lesson 3
Planning for High Availability Implementation	
Plan a backup solution implementation.	Chapter 5, Lesson 1
Plan a recovery solution implementation.	Chapter 5, Lesson 2
Plan the service's high availability implementation.	Chapter 6, Lesson 1
Plan a data redundancy implementation.	Chapter 6, Lesson 2
Planning the Exchange Topology Deployment	
Plan the storage group deployment.	Chapter 2, Lesson 1
Plan the server role deployment.	Chapter 1, Lesson 1
Plan the deployment of required Exchange services.	Chapter 2, Lesson 2
Plan the deployment of optional Exchange services.	Chapter 2, Lesson 3
Planning Messaging Security and Compliance Implementation	
Plan the antivirus and anti-spam implementation.	Chapter 7, Lesson 1
Plan the network layer security implementation.	Chapter 7, Lesson 2
Plan the transport rules implementation.	Chapter 8, Lesson 1
Plan the messaging compliance implementation.	Chapter 8, Lesson 2
Planning for Messaging Environment Maintenance	
Plan for Exchange infrastructure improvements.	Chapter 9, Lesson 2
Plan for configuration changes.	Chapter 9, Lesson 2
Plan for change management.	Chapter 9, Lesson 1
Plan for patch and service pack implementation.	Chapter 9, Lesson 2
Plan for monitoring and reporting.	Chapter 10, Lesson 1

NOTE   Exam objectives

The exam objectives listed here are current as of this book's publication date. Exam objectives are subject to change at any time without prior notice and at Microsoft's sole discretion. Please visit the Microsoft Learning Web site for the most current listing of exam objectives: *http://www.microsoft.com/learning/exams/70-238.mspx.*

Microsoft

MCITP Self-Paced Training Kit (Exam 70-238): Deploying Messaging Solutions with Microsoft® Exchange Server™ 2007

Nelson Ruest
Danielle Ruest

PUBLISHED BY
Microsoft Press
A Division of Microsoft Corporation
One Microsoft Way
Redmond, Washington 98052-6399

Library of Congress Control Number: 2008927280

Printed and bound in the United States of America.

1 2 3 4 5 6 7 8 9   QWT   3 2 1 0 9 8

Distributed in Canada by H.B. Fenn and Company Ltd.

A CIP catalogue record for this book is available from the British Library.

Microsoft Press books are available through booksellers and distributors worldwide. For further information about international editions, contact your local Microsoft Corporation office or contact Microsoft Press International directly at fax (425) 936-7329. Visit our Web site at www.microsoft.com/mspress. Send comments to tkinput@microsoft.com.

Microsoft, Microsoft Press, Access, Active Directory, ActiveSync, Entourage, ESP, Excel, Forefront, Hotmail, Hyper-V, Internet Explorer, OneNote, Outlook, PowerPoint, SharePoint, SmartScreen, SQL Server, Visual Studio, Windows, Windows Media, Windows Mobile, Windows NT, Windows PowerShell, Windows Server, Windows Server System, and Windows Vista are either registered trademarks or trademarks of Microsoft Corporation in the United States and/or other countries. Other product and company names mentioned herein may be the trademarks of their respective owners.

The example companies, organizations, products, domain names, e-mail addresses, logos, people, places, and events depicted herein are fictitious. No association with any real company, organization, product, domain name, e-mail address, logo, person, place, or event is intended or should be inferred.

This book expresses the author's views and opinions. The information contained in this book is provided without any express, statutory, or implied warranties. Neither the authors, Microsoft Corporation, nor its resellers, or distributors will be held liable for any damages caused or alleged to be caused either directly or indirectly by this book.

Acquisitions Editor: Ken Jones
Developmental Editor: Laura Sackerman
Project Editor: Maureen Zimmerman
Editorial Production: S4Carlisle Publishing Services
Technical Reviewers: Rodney Buike and Rozanne Whalen; Technical Review services provided by Content Master, a member of CM Group, Ltd.
Cover: Tom Draper Design

Body Part No. X14-71511

This book is dedicated to the IT professionals who take the time to become messaging professionals. We hope you will find this guide useful in your studies and in your efforts to improve messaging systems everywhere.

—Danielle Ruest and Nelson Ruest

About the Authors

Danielle Ruest

Danielle is passionate about helping people make the most of computer technology. She is a Senior Enterprise Workflow Architect and Consultant with more than 20 years of experience in IT project implementations. Her customers include governments and private enterprises of all sizes. Throughout her career, she has led change-management processes, developed and delivered training, provided technical writing services, and managed communications programs during complex technology implementation projects. More recently, Danielle has been involved in the  design and support of test, development, and production infrastructures based on virtualization technologies. She is familiar with most components of the Windows Server System as well as security implementations, Active Directory Domain Services, Exchange Server, interoperability, manageability, and virtualization. In addition, one of her best talents is communications through illustration, portraying complex concepts graphically and therefore, facilitating the understanding of these concepts. She is a Microsoft Most Valuable Professional for the virtual machine product line.

Nelson Ruest

Nelson Ruest is passionate about doing things right with Microsoft technologies. He is a Senior Enterprise IT Architect with more than 25 years of experience in migration planning and network, PC, server, and overall solution design. He was one of Canada's first MCSEs and Microsoft Certified Trainers. In his IT career, he has been computer operator, systems administrator, trainer, help desk operator, support engineer, IT manager, project manager, and now IT architect. He has also taken part in numer-ous migration projects where he was responsible for everything from project to systems design in both the private and the public sectors. He is very familiar with all versions of Windows and the Windows Server System as well as security, Active Directory Domain Services, Exchange Server, systems management, intra- and extranet configurations, collaboration technologies, office automation, and interoperability solutions. He is a Microsoft Most Valuable Professional for the Windows Server product line.

In 2007, Danielle and Nelson released a free e-Book: *The Definitive Guide to Vista Migration* (*www.realtime-nexus.com/dgvm.htm*) and finished *Windows Server 2008, The Complete Reference* (McGraw-Hill Osborne); *The Deploying and Administrating Windows Vista Bible* (Wiley); and *MCTS Self-Paced Training Kit (Exam 70-640): Configuring Windows Server 2008 Active Directory* (Microsoft Press). Nelson and Danielle are delivering a multi-city tour called Virtualization: Controlling Server Sprawl (*http://events.techtarget.com/virtualization2008*), which is designed to help organizations make the most of a virtual infrastructure.

Together, they are co-authors of *Preparing for .NET Enterprise Technologies* (*www.Reso-Net.com/EMF*), which, despite its name, focuses on implementing and managing locked-down desktops; *Windows Server 2003: Best Practices for Enterprise Deployments* (*www.Reso-Net.com/WindowsServer*), a step-by-step guide for the implementation of an enterprise network; and *Windows Server 2003 Pocket Administrator* (*www.Reso-Net.com/PocketAdmin*), a guide for managing a network on a day-to-day basis. Both are also involved as freelance writers for several IT publications, produce white papers for various vendors (*http://www.reso-net.com/articles.asp?m=8*), and deliver webcasts and conferences (*http://www.reso-net.com/presentation.asp?m=7*).

Danielle and Nelson work for Resolutions Enterprises (*www.Reso-Net.com*), a consulting firm focused on IT infrastructure design. Resolutions can be found at *www.Reso-Net.com*.

Contents at a Glance

Table of Contents

What do you think of this book? We want to hear from you!

Microsoft is interested in hearing your feedback so we can continually improve our books and learning resources for you. To participate in a brief online survey, please visit:

www.microsoft.com/learning/booksurvey/

What do you think of this book? We want to hear from you!

Microsoft is interested in hearing your feedback so we can continually improve our books and learning resources for you. To participate in a brief online survey, please visit:

www.microsoft.com/learning/booksurvey/

Introduction

This training kit is designed for IT professionals who plan to take the Microsoft Certified IT Professional (MCITP) Exam 70-238: Deploying Messaging Solutions with Microsoft Exchange Server 2007. The primary objective of this exam is to certify that architects know how to deploy an efficient messaging solution. We assume that before you begin using this kit, you have spent at least two years as a messaging systems administrator. We also assume that you have been involved in multiple phases of messaging deployment projects, including design, deployment, and post-production/maintenance. The Preparation Guide for Exam 70-238 is available at *http://www.microsoft.com/learning/exams/70-238.mspx*. The practice exercises in this training kit will use Microsoft Exchange 2007 Enterprise Edition. A 180-day evaluation edition is included on the companion DVDs. If you do not have access to this software, you can download a 180-day trial of Microsoft Exchange 2007 at *http://technet.microsoft.com/en-ca/exchange/bb330843.aspx*.

By using this training kit, you will learn how to do the following:

- Plan Microsoft Exchange Server 2007 upgrades and migrations.
- Plan for high availability implementations.
- Plan Exchange topology deployments.
- Plan messaging security and compliance implementations.
- Plan messaging environment maintenance programs.

Hardware Requirements

We recommend that you use a test workstation, test server, or staging server to complete the exercises in each practice. However, it would be beneficial for you to have access to sample e-mail accounts. If you need to set up a workstation to complete the practice exercises, the minimum system requirements follow:

- Personal computer with an Intel Pentium or compatible 800-megahertz (MHz) or faster 32-bit processor (for testing and training purposes only; not supported in production)

- 2 gigabytes (GB) of RAM or more
- 1.2 GB free hard disk space for the Exchange 2007 installation
- A second disk for storing data for certain server roles
- Disks formatted in NTFS format
- DVD-ROM drive, local or network accessible
- Super VGA (800 x 600) or higher-resolution video adapter and monitor
- Keyboard and Microsoft mouse or compatible pointing device

Software Requirements

Note that you will need Exchange Server 2007 to complete the practice exercises included with each chapter. Although this product can be installed on a production server, it is not recommended that you do so. Instead, install these products and execute the practices in each chapter on a single computer. The following software is required to complete the practice exercises:

- One of the following operating systems:
    - Windows Server 2003, Standard Edition SP2
    - Windows Server 2003, Enterprise Edition SP2
    - Windows Server 2003, Datacenter Edition SP2
    - Windows Server 2003 R2, Standard Edition SP2
    - Windows Server 2003 R2, Enterprise Edition SP2
    - Windows Server 2003 R2, Datacenter Edition SP2
- Microsoft .NET Framework version 2.0
- Microsoft .NET Framework version 2.0 update
- Microsoft Windows PowerShell
- Microsoft Management Console (MMC) 3.0 if the operating system is not R2
- Exchange Server 2007. For instructions on downloading and installing Exchange Server 2007 Enterprise Edition, see the "Installing Exchange Server 2007" at *http://www.msexchange.org/tutorials/Installing-Exchange-2007-Part1.html* or refer to Chapter 1, "Plan the Exchange Topology Deployment."

Create Your Virtual Machine Environment

You can also use virtual machines to perform the exercises in this guide. In fact, virtual machine environments are ideal because they let you create several different computers, which is a requirement for most of the exercises. You can use two virtual machine environments.

IMPORTANT   Exam focus

The original release of this exam is focused on the original or RTM release of Microsoft Exchange 2007. Therefore, you should create an environment that runs Windows Server 2003 and Exchange 2007 without Service Pack 1.

First, obtain the fully configured Exchange Server 2007 virtual machine from Microsoft at *http://technet.microsoft.com/en-us/bb738372.aspx*. This will help you review many of the operations discussed in each chapter without having to set up a new environment. Note that this machine runs a 32-bit installation of Exchange 2007.

Then, build an environment according to the following configurations for the more advanced practices in this guide:

1. Set up a computer with sufficient RAM and processing power to run Microsoft Virtual Server 2005 R2, Windows Server 2008 Hyper-V, or VMware Server so that you can create and run virtual machines. Ideally, this computer will be running an x64 operating system (Windows XP Professional x64, Windows Server 2003 x64, Windows Vista x64, or Windows Server 2008 x64). Note that if you choose to use Microsoft Virtual Server 2005 R2, you will be limited to 32 bit versions of Exchange 2007.

2. Create four virtual machines and install an x64 version of Windows Server 2003 R2 with SP2. You should not need to activate these machines because you have a 60-day trail.

   ❑ Begin by creating a core machine and use P@ssw0rd as the administrative password.

   ❑ When the machine is installed, rename the Administrator account to **EXAdmin**.

   ❑ Change to the DVD drive in Windows Explorer and open the Support\Tools folder. Double-click Deploy.cab. In Deploy.cab, select the four executables and copy them to the clipboard. Move to the C:\ drive and create a new folder called **Sysprep**. Paste the four executables into this folder.

   ❑ Update the machine using Microsoft Update. Reboot the machine as required.

   ❑ Next, install the three Exchange prerequisites, .NET Framework 2.0, Windows Powershell, and MMC 3.0. Insert the Exchange installation media into the DVD drive or attach the Exchange installation ISO file to this media in the virtual machine and run through each of the first three installation steps on the Setup screen. If Setup does not launch automatically, use Windows Explorer to open the DVD drive and double-click Setup.exe.

❑ Install Internet Information Services and ASP.NET. Enable ASP.NET in IIS when the installation is complete.

❑ Update the machine using Microsoft Update again. Reboot as required.

❑ Move to the C:\Sysprep folder and double-click SetupMgr.exe to create a new Sysprep installation file. Do not use a fully automated setup: Type in the administrator password and choose defaults for both network settings and for the machine name. Save the file with the default name.

❑ Double-click Sysprep.exe, leave all defaults, and click Reseal. The machine is now ready for duplication.

❑ To duplicate the machine, copy the folder that contains the virtual machine files, rename the copied folder and the files within it, and add the new machine to your virtual environment.

3. Use one of the machines to create an Active Directory forest. Assign a static IP address—for example, 192.168.1.90. Change the DNS address to point to itself. Name it **TreyDC** and use DCpromo.exe to create the TreyResearch.net forest. Make sure the forest is in Windows Server 2003 Functional Mode.

4. Create a machine called **ExchangeOne**. Assign a static IP address—for example, 192.168.1.91. Change the DNS address to point to the DC—for example, at 192.168.1.90. Make ExchangeOne a member of the treyreasearch.net domain. Add two additional disks to this machine: a D: drive with 10 GB and an E: drive with 4 GB. The machine is ready.

5. Create a machine called **ExchangeLCR**. Assign a static IP address—for example, 192.168.1.92. Change the DNS address to point to the DC—for example, at 192.168.1.90. Make ExchangeLCR a member of the treyreasearch.net domain. Add four additional disks to this machine: a D: drive with 10 GB, an E: drive with 4 GB, an F: drive with 10 GB, and a G: drive with 4 GB. The machine is ready.

6. Create a final machine called **ExchangeETOne**. Assign a static IP address—for example, 192.168.1.93 and change the DNS address to point to the DC—for example, at 192.168.1.90. Make ExchagneETOne a member of the TREYREASEARCH workgroup. Install Active Directory in Application Mode with SP1 into this machine. Obtain the update from *http://go.microsoft.com/fwlink/?linkid =71063*. Make sure the machine's DNS suffix is set to TreyResearch.com. Do this by right-clicking My Computer in the Start Menu, choosing Properties, clicking the Computer Name tab,

clicking Change, and then clicking More. Type in the DNS suffix and close all dialog boxes. Reboot the computer. The machine is ready.

You will use these four machines to run through the practices in each chapter.

MORE INFO **Creating virtual applications**

For detailed procedures for creating the virtual machines required for these exercises, look up the "Create Virtual Applications" series of articles at *http://itmanagement.earthweb.com/entdev/ article.php/3718566*. In addition, for information on how to build and manage a virtual laboratory, see "Build a Virtual Laboratory Parts 1 and 2" at *https://mcp.microsoft.com/mcp/resources/ resources.mspx*. Note that you need to be an MCP to view the latter articles.

Prepare for your Microsoft Certification Exam

Use the following checklist to see whether you are ready for your exam. This compilation stems from the experience we have gathered from the more than 40 exams we have taken ourselves.

- **Be ready** It is useless to try an exam if you do not think you are ready. Perform lots of practices and ensure that you are familiar not only with the technology itself, but also with how it interacts with other Microsoft technologies.

- **Practice** New exams include software simulations. This simulates the activity you perform in the actual software program. If you do not have the opportunity to practice with this tool, you will never be able to answer the questions.

When actually taking the exam, remember the following:

- **Mark your questions** Several questions are very detailed. If you see that a question is too time-consuming, mark it and move on to the next one.

- **Mark your time** Make sure you have enough time for the exam. It would be unfortunate not to pass because you did not have enough time to at least read every question.

- **Read each question attentively** Questions often include a lot of clutter—information included to confuse you. Make sure you carefully read each question from beginning to end before you answer.

- **Return to previous questions** An exam often includes several questions on the same subject. One question can often provide the answer to another.

- **The first answer you're inclined to choose is right most often** If you do not know the answer, follow your intuition.

- **It is better to answer something than leave blanks**   Blank answers are worth nothing. Wrong answers are also worth nothing, but even a guess may be right in the end.

- **Do not stress yourself**   After all, it is just an exam and if you know your stuff, you will not find it too challenging.

Using the CD and DVD

A companion CD and an evaluation software DVD are included with this training kit. The companion CD contains the following:

- **Practice tests**   You can practice for the 70-238 certification exam by using tests created from a pool of approximately 200 realistic exam questions. These questions give you many different practice exams to ensure that you are prepared to take the real thing.

- **An eBook**   An electronic version (eBook) of this book is included for times when you do not want to carry the printed book with you. The eBook is in Portable Document Format (PDF), and you can view it by using Adobe Acrobat or Adobe Acrobat Reader, available from *http://www.adobe.com*.

The evaluation software DVD contains a 180-day evaluation edition of Exchange Server 2007 Enterprise Edition, which you need to run the practice files in this book.

> **Digital Content for Digital Book Readers:** If you bought a digital-only edition of this book, you can enjoy select content from the print edition's companion CD.
> Visit *http://go.microsoft.com/fwlink/?LinkId=117357* to get your downloadable content. This content is always up-to-date and available to all readers.

How to Install the Practice Tests

To install the practice test software from the companion CD onto your hard disk, perform the following steps:

1. Insert the companion CD into your CD drive and accept the license agreement. A CD menu appears.

   NOTE   If the CD menu does not appear

   If the CD menu or the license agreement does not appear, AutoRun might be disabled on your computer. Refer to the Readme.txt file on the CD-ROM for alternate installation instructions.

   ---

2. Click Practice Tests and follow the instructions on the screen.

How to Use the Practice Tests

To start the practice test software, follow these steps:

1. Click Start, click All Programs, and then click Microsoft Press Training Kit Exam Prep. A window appears that shows all the Microsoft Press training kit exam prep suites installed on your computer.

2. Double-click the practice test that you want to use.

Practice Test Options   When you start a practice test, you can choose whether to take the test in Certification Mode, Study Mode, or Custom Mode.

- **Certification Mode**   Closely resembles the experience of taking a certification exam. The test has a set number of questions, the test is timed, and you cannot pause the test or restart the timer.

- **Study Mode**   Creates an untimed test in which you can review the correct answers and the explanations after you answer each question.

- **Custom Mode**   Gives you full control over the test options so that you can customize them as you like. You can click OK to accept the defaults, or you can customize the number of questions you want, how the practice test software works, which exam objectives you want the questions to relate to, and whether you want your lesson review to be timed. If you are retaking a test, you can select whether you want to see all the questions again or only those questions you missed or did not answer.

In all modes, the user interface you see when taking the test is essentially the same but with different options enabled or disabled, depending on the mode.

After you click OK, your practice test starts.

- To take the test, answer the questions and use the Next, Previous, and Go To buttons to move from question to question.

- After you answer an individual question, if you want to see which answers are correct—along with an explanation of each correct answer—click Explanation.

- If you prefer to wait until the end of the test to see how you did, answer all the questions and then click Score Test. You will see a summary of the exam objectives you chose and the percentage of questions you answered correctly overall and per objective. You can print a copy of your test, review your answers, or retake the test.

When you review your answer to an individual practice test question, a "References" section lists where in the training kit you can find the information that relates to that question and provides links to other sources of information. After you click Test

Results to score your entire practice test, you can click the Learning Plan tab to see a list of references for every objective.

How to Uninstall the Practice Tests

To uninstall the practice test software for a training kit, use the Add Or Remove Programs option in Control Panel.

Microsoft Certified Professional Program

The Microsoft certifications provide the best method to prove your command of current Microsoft products and technologies. The exams and corresponding certifications are developed to validate your mastery of critical competencies as you design and develop, or implement and support, solutions with Microsoft products and technologies. Computer professionals who become Microsoft-certified are recognized as experts and are sought after industry-wide. Certification brings a variety of benefits to the individual and to employers and organizations.

MORE INFO **All Microsoft certifications**

For a full list of Microsoft certifications, go to *http://www.microsoft.com/learning/mcp/default.mspx.*

Technical Support

Every effort has been made to ensure the accuracy of this book and the contents of the companion CD. If you have comments, questions, or ideas regarding this book or the companion CD, please send them to Microsoft Press by using either of the following methods:

E-mail: tkinput@microsoft.com

Postal Mail:

Microsoft Press
Attn: MCITP Self-Paced Training Kit (Exam 70-238): Deploying Messaging Solutions with Microsoft Exchange Server 2007, *Editor*
One Microsoft Way Redmond, WA 98052-6399

For additional support information regarding this book and the CD-ROM (including answers to commonly asked questions about installation and use), visit the Microsoft Press Technical Support Web site at *http://www.microsoft.com/learning/support/books.* To connect directly to the Microsoft Knowledge Base and enter a query, visit *http://support.microsoft.com/search.* For support information regarding Microsoft software, please visit *http://support.microsoft.com.*

Evaluation Edition Software Support

The 180-day evaluation edition provided with this training kit is not the full retail product and is provided only for the purposes of training and evaluation. Microsoft and Microsoft Technical Support do not support this evaluation edition.

Information about any issues relating to the use of this evaluation edition with this training kit is posted to the Support section of the Microsoft Press Web site at *http://www.microsoft.com/learning/support/books.* For information about ordering the full version of any Microsoft software, please call Microsoft Sales at (800) 426-9400 or visit the Microsoft Web site at *http://www.microsoft.com.*

Chapter 1
Plan the Exchange Topology Deployment

For many organizations, Microsoft Exchange Server has become *the* mission-critical application. Users cannot live without access to their e-mail and must always be in contact with their messaging service so that they can be in contact with the world both inside their organization and outside the boundaries of their offices.

Microsoft Exchange Server 2007 makes this possible through the support of multiple platforms for e-mail delivery: e-mail clients such as Microsoft Office Outlook, Web interfaces such as Outlook Web Access (OWA), mobile platforms such as smart phones or Windows mobile devices, and for the first time, normal telephones through the new Unified Messaging feature.

As a messaging professional, your job is to ensure that the design and deployment of Exchange Server 2007 in your organization covers the various access methods your users require, as well as ensuring that the service used to deliver the messages users send is always available to them, no matter which access method they use. Traditionally, your skills have been focused on Information Technology (IT)—working with server and client platforms from personal computers to mobile devices. With the arrival of Unified Messaging in Exchange Server 2007, you also need additional skills—skills that have traditionally been separate from the IT skill set because they focus on telephony. It made sense: Telephony was mostly an analog world through the use of Private Branch Exchanges (PBX), while IT focused on digital services. But Exchange changes this by bridging the gap between telephony and IT through software—software that can either create a link between servers and the PBX or replace the PBX altogether with Voice over IP (VoIP) services.

Because Exchange 2007 brings together IT and telephony skills, you need to update your skill set to properly understand how Exchange Server 2007 must be deployed. Another reason is that with Unified Messaging, you should be able to reduce your total communications costs, using existing hardware with new software to provide a more complete communications experience to users. There are many other reasons to update your skill set: Exchange Server 2007 includes better availability technologies and enhanced features at multiple levels, it provides a simpler and better experience for users, and much more.

With this in mind, this chapter focuses on one very important aspect of Exchange Server deployment: the Exchange Server topology you will deploy in your organization. It also covers the various roles your Exchange servers can play in this topology. The chapter then goes on to describe how you can configure different topologies based on your organization's size and structure. Armed with this knowledge, you should be able to properly plan an Exchange Server 2007 deployment in organizations of any size or complexity.

Exam objectives in this chapter:
- Plan the server role deployment.

Before You Begin

To complete the lesson in this chapter, you must have the following:

- Use the Exchange Server 2007 virtual machine from Microsoft to review the configuration options for pre-installed computers.

- Use the newly created virtual environment you set up based on the instructions in the Introduction to test the deployment and installation process for each of the Exchange server roles.

Lesson 1: Deploy Exchange Server Roles

Estimated lesson time: 80 minutes

When you prepare to deploy Exchange server roles, you must address the deployment in a structured manner:

- First, you must become familiar with the standard and supported topologies Microsoft recommends for Exchange.

- Next, you must be familiar with the different server roles supported in Exchange 2007.

- Finally, you must become familiar with the prerequisites for each server role before you can deploy it.

This is the structure of this lesson.

Understand Exchange Topology Concepts

Microsoft Exchange Server 2007 topologies can be as simple as having almost everything run on a single server to having highly complex distributed environments with multiple Exchange servers, each running specific functions to produce a complete messaging service. In fact, you must consider four different topologies when preparing your Exchange 2007 deployment design:

- The Logical Topology focuses on the structure of the directory services that will host the Exchange 2007 systems.

- The Physical Topology focuses on the structure of your organization's geographical distribution and office locations.

- The Organization Topology focuses on the distribution of Exchange services within your IT infrastructure among a single or multiple servers.

- The Administrative Topology focuses on how your organization intends to manage and administer Exchange once it is in place.

You must consider each of the four topologies when you create your Exchange Server overall topology. It is very unlikely that you will be working in an organization that has no e-mail service at all, although creating a new Exchange Server topology from scratch is of course the ideal situation. This means that when you do create your topology, you will most likely need to take existing e-mail services into consideration. Keep in mind that there is no upgrade path from previous versions of Exchange to Exchange Server 2007. There are, however, both transition and migration paths. You will need to consider which path to take when you are ready to begin the implementation of new services based on Exchange Server 2007.

Exchange Server Roles

Exchange Server 2007 includes five server roles:

- **Edge Transport Server (ET)**   This server role is designed to provide protection against spam and other unwanted malware that may be picked up by your messaging system. Edge Servers are not connected to Active Directory because they are deployed to perimeter networks, although they can rely on Active Directory in Application Mode (ADAM) when working with Windows Server 2003 to filter recipients.

- **Hub Transport Servers (HT)**   These are routing servers that direct mail to appropriate back-end servers. When Edge Servers are deployed, they link directly to internal Hub Transport Servers.

- **Client Access Servers (CAS)**   These are sometimes called Front-End Servers; they provide the interface for client services such as Outlook Web Access, Exchange ActiveSync, and Web Services.

- **Mailbox Servers (MB)**   These are sometimes called Back-End Servers; they support the mail store and provide configuration and policy services for messaging. They also provide access for Microsoft Office Outlook when inside the internal network.

- **Unified Messaging Servers (UM)**   UM Servers link up to either voice over IP or private branch exchanges to integrate voicemail and faxing to the Exchange messaging infrastructure.

MORE INFO   The Exchange Server role documentation roadmap

For more information on the various server roles, see the Exchange Server 2007 Server role documentation roadmap at *http://technet.microsoft.com/en-us/library/aa996319.aspx.*

All of the roles except the Edge Transport Server role can run on the same computer if necessary, but most typically, these roles will be separated to some degree. But Exchange Server does not live in a vacuum. It also relies on additional services to operate, including:

- A fully functioning TCP/IP infrastructure that links servers and client systems together. Clients can rely on the Dynamic Host Control Protocol (DHCP) for automatic addressing, but servers will more often rely on static IP addresses. This infrastructure requires proper subnetting—groupings of IP addresses by location or by machine categories—and if multiple sites are included in your IT infrastructure, it will also require proper switching and routing between locations. Finally, because Exchange is used to communicate both internally and externally, your IP infrastructure will also require proper routing to the Internet as well as protection through at least one firewall.

Exam Tip   The original version of Exchange Server 2007 will only work with an IPv4 addressing scheme. To support IPv6, you need to deploy Exchange Server 2007 with Service Pack 1 and run it on Windows Server 2008. Make sure you take this into consideration when planning your network topology for Exchange. Most organizations will deploy Exchange initially on Windows Server 2003 with IPv4. Note that the original exam does not include questions about SP1 features.

- A fully functioning domain name system (DNS) with proper zone structuring. Typically, an organization will implement an internal DNS infrastructure and link it to the outside world, either through root hints or DNS forwarding.

- A fully functioning Active Directory infrastructure including at least one forest and a domain. Active Directory topologies can be much more complex and include either multiple domains or multiple forests. This Active Directory topology will be tightly linked to the DNS infrastructure, using dynamic updates of server and client records. It will also include a distribution of domain controllers as well as global catalog servers. If your organization includes more than one geographic location, Active Directory will also include a site and site link infrastructure to control replication traffic between sites. Active Directory should also include a proper logical structure using forest, domain, and organizational units to manage Active Directory objects.

Exam Tip   Active Directory can use two different transport technologies for inter-site replication: IP and Simple Mail Transfer Protocol (SMTP). SMTP is used when physical site connections do not provide high speeds. Therefore, it is used more rarely than IP as a transport. Exchange Server 2007 will only work with the IP replication transport and does not support SMTP for Active Directory replication. If your organization uses SMTP site links in Active Directory, you will need to convert them to IP and possibly upgrade the physical site connections before you can implement Exchange 2007.

- Fully functioning security services such as antivirus, anti-spam, anti-spyware, and general anti-malware.

In addition, your Exchange Server topology will include various Exchange components:

- Exchange servers: any server with Exchange services installed on it.
- Mail connectors: connectors that are used to route e-mail throughout the Exchange topology both inside and outside the organization's own boundaries.
- Exchange database: an Extensible Storage Engine (ESE) database that stores mailboxes and public folders.
- Mailboxes: a selection of private folders used to store information associated with a particular user. Mailboxes are contained within the Exchange database.
- Public folders: a hierarchical folder structure that contains information that is not restricted to a single user.
- Distribution lists: collections of users, computers, contacts, and security or distribution groups that are used to address e-mail.
- Organization: the logical container that brings all of the Exchange resources together for a given implementation. These resources share a single security context. Because of this, there can be only a single Exchange organization per Active Directory forest.

Together, each of these elements makes up a complete Exchange topology (see Figure 1-1).

Exchange Organization Definitions

Exchange deployments are usually contained within four different organization types:

- **The Simple Organization**   This represents the most basic topology for Exchange deployment. It usually consists of one single Exchange server running on a 64-bit operating system and also hosting the Active Directory domain controller service or a server running a version of Small Business Server (SBS) that includes Exchange Server 2007. Because most roles are hosted on the same server, this topology hosts both the Service Delivery Location (SDL) and the Client Service Location (CSL) in the same location. The SDL is the location that provides all of the Exchange services; the CSL is the location that provides client access to Exchange services. However, because of the differing needs of small and medium organizations, this topology includes two subsets.

MORE INFO   Exchange and SBS

The version of SBS which includes Exchange 2007 is based on Windows Server 2008. Because of this, it is released after the official launch of Windows Server 2008.

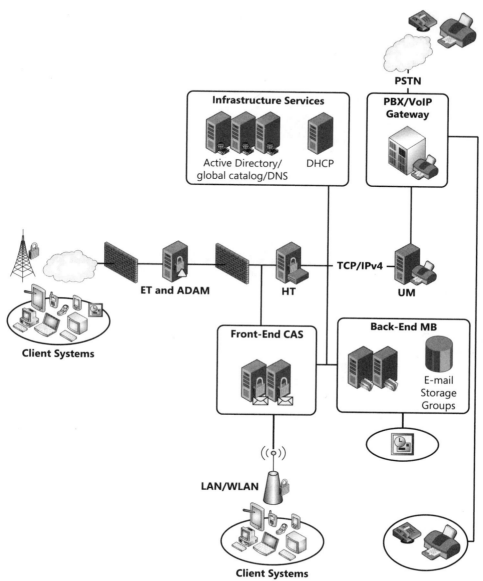

Figure 1-1   A typical Exchange Server topology

- **The Single-Server Simple Organization**   This configuration has all of the Exchange server roles except the Edge Transport Server hosted on the same server. Because of this, the Hub Transport Server role is directly connected to the Internet through the use of a firewall (see Figure 1-2). Microsoft recommends using this configuration only if you are using SBS.

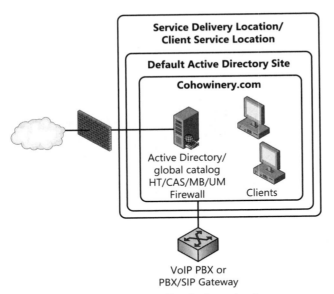

Figure 1-2   A Single-Server Simple Organization

IMPORTANT   **Protect your Single Server**

Because the Single-Server Simple Organization includes only a single server, the Mailbox Server role also faces the Internet. Make sure you deploy a proper firewall between the Exchange server and the Internet to protect this critical Exchange server role.

- **The Multiple-Server Simple Organization**   This configuration still runs the four internal Exchange server roles on a single server that is also an Active Directory domain controller, but it also includes an additional server running the domain controller role as well as one other server running the Edge Transport Server role. In this case, the ET is connected to the Internet through a firewall. The ET is also connected to the HT for internal mail delivery (see Figure 1-3). Microsoft recommends using this configuration only if you are using Windows Essential Business Server 2008 (WEBS)—a new point solution designed for medium-sized businesses (25 to 250 computers). WEBS is built on Windows Server 2008.

NOTE   **Installing Exchange 2007 on Windows Server 2008**

You cannot install the original release of Exchange Server 2007 on Windows Server 2008 as it is not supported. Support for Windows Server 2008 is only available in Exchange 2007 Service Pack 1. In addition, no upgrade path is available for a server running Exchange 2007 on Windows Server 2003 to a server running Exchange 2007 SP1 on Windows Server 2008. You must perform new installations.

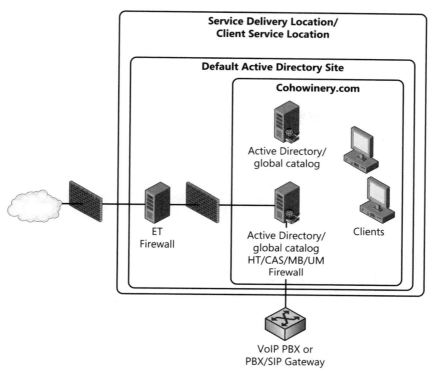

Figure 1-3 A Multiple-Server Simple Organization

- **The Standard Organization** This configuration represents the most typical topology for Exchange deployment. Here, the internal Exchange server roles are not deployed on a domain controller, but rather on member servers. This organization type remains standard, however, because the Service Delivery Location and the Client Service Location, while not necessarily being on the same server, will be within the same local area network (LAN) or physical site (see Figure 1-4). In a pure Exchange Server 2007 organization, this topology will include a single routing group because routing groups are no longer required in version 2007. If non-Exchange Server 2007 servers exist in the organization, multiple routing groups will have to be used. The standard organization is hosted within a single Active Directory forest.

- **The Large Organization** This configuration represents a topology for Exchange deployment that is still hosted within a single Active Directory forest but the forest includes more than five Active Directory sites. It may also include more than five routing groups if older versions of Exchange are present. Also, the SDL and CSL are hosted in multiple sites and may even be separated to reside on different servers. Several Active Directory domains may exist within the forest, but the external messaging presence and the client namespace are common among all locations.

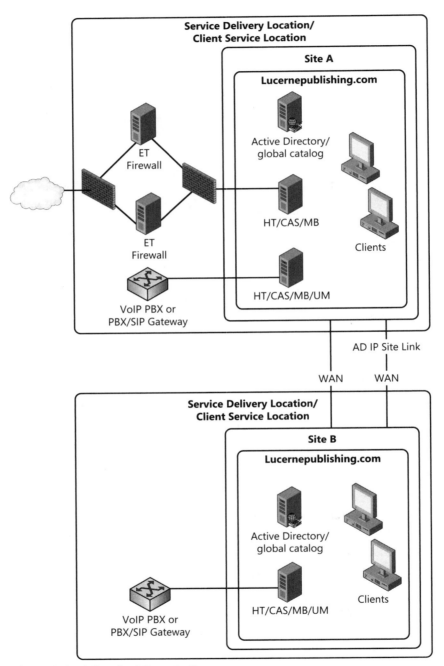

Figure 1-4   A Standard Organization

This means that messages transfer to and from the Internet in a single location and are then routed to multiple points throughout the internal network infrastructure. It also means that while your different domains will have different fully qualified domain names (FQDN), all of them use the same root. For example, The Phone Company has sites in different parts of the United States and in Europe. Each area has its own domain to allow for different security strategies. While each domain has its own name, all domains use a common root: thephone-company.com (see Figure 1-5).

■ **The Complex Organization**   The last deployment topology for Exchange is designed for organizations that host multiple Active Directory forests. Because of this, you need to synchronize multiple Exchange Global Address Lists (GALs). The best way to do this is to rely on Microsoft Identity Integration Server (MIIS) or its updated successor, Microsoft Identity Lifecycle Manager (MILM). Complex organizations usually stem from partnerships, acquisitions, or mergers where each of the parties involved in the organization has its own identity and therefore its own Active Directory forest. There are several models of Complex Organizations:

❑ If you have multiple forests, but you have complete control of each of the forests—for example, when the forests are created within the same organization, but are used to segregate business units—you should use an **Exchange Resource Forest Topology.** This allows you to maintain the strict boundaries between each forest. The Exchange Resource Forest uses a one-way trust towards the account forest(s), or the forests that contain the user accounts for each business unit. The Resource Forest contain duplicates of each user account within the account forests, but these duplicates are disabled. They are, however, linked to the user's mailbox. Mailbox creation is performed only in the Exchange Resource Forest and account creators in each of the account forests will not usually have the right to create these mailboxes unless that right has been specifically delegated to them. Additional account information such as phone numbers or office locations must be added separately to the accounts in the Exchange Resource Forest.

NOTE   **Using the Exchange Resource Forest topology**

Beware of choosing the Resource Forest topology—it has very high administrative overhead because it does not rely on synchronization technologies to keep the data in each forest in sync.

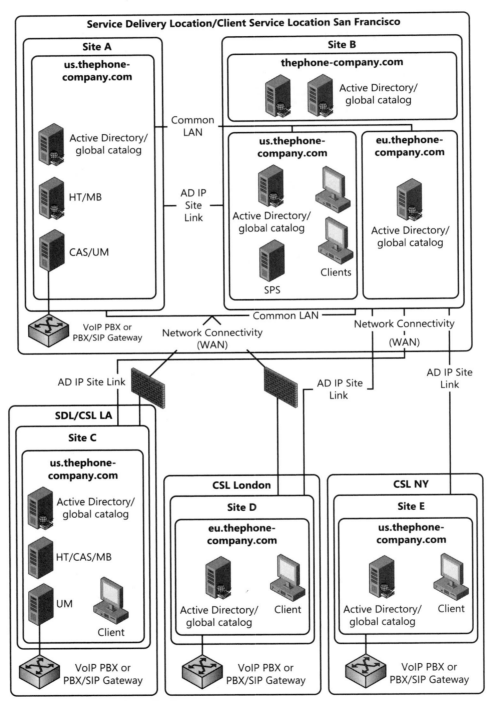

Figure 1-5 A Large Organization

❑ In situations where you must work alongside existing Active Directory forests that may already contain their own Exchange organizations, you must use a **Multiple Exchange Forest Topology**. Because this topology includes multiple Exchange repositories, you must also synchronize information between the forests. This means synchronizing directory objects as well as replicating free/busy data (see Figure 1-6). Two solutions are available for object synchronization:

- **Identity Integration Feature Pack (IIFP)**, which is freely available but provides simpler synchronization services. Find IIFP at *http:// go.microsoft.com/fwlink/?linkid=41606.*

- **Microsoft Identity Integration Server** or its updated successor, **Microsoft Identity Lifecycle Manager,** which provide a complete commercial solution for object synchronization. Find both at *http:// go.microsoft.com/fwlink/?linkid=21271.*

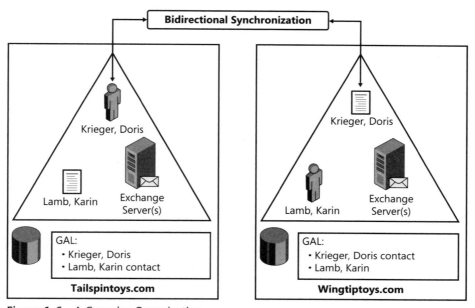

Figure 1-6   A Complex Organization

In addition to synchronizing objects between directories, you also need to synchronize free/busy data by using one of the following tools:

- In Exchange Server 2007, this is performed through the **Availability Service** so long as all organizations use Office Outlook 2007.

- If other versions of Outlook are in use, you must keep at least one server running Exchange Server 2003 in each forest and then use the **Inter-Organization Replication** (IORepl) tool to synchronize both free/busy data as well as public folder information.

Exam Tip   IORepl is deprecated in Exchange Server 2007 and is only available in Exchange Server 2003.

When using the Multiple Exchange Forest topology, you will be faced with the following limitations:

- If your distribution lists include members whose mailboxes are in a different forest, you will not be able to view membership lists.
- You will not be able to add a user from a different forest to a distribution list.
- You will not be able to nest membership lists from different forests.
- You cannot move a distribution list from one forest to another.
- If you move a mailbox from one forest to another, you will lose its delegation properties if they exist.
- You cannot move public folders from one forest to another.
- You cannot send signed or encrypted messages from one forest to another if they are using self-signed certificates.

Keep the following in mind when using Complex Organizations:

- If you work with multiple Exchange Organizations and you want to share the Global Address List, you must have some form of directory synchronization. You should also consider solutions for free/busy calendaring information synchronization.
- Complex Organizations often have complex requirements for firewall configurations because they most often have multiple access points to the Internet.
- Complex Organizations should rely on high availability solutions to ensure that the e-mail service is always available.
- When you configure the Client Access Service, make sure you use unique URL namespaces for each forest.

Exam Tip   When planning your own organization structure, rely on these four typical organization models. Using a custom organization topology other than one of the four listed here is unsupported by Microsoft.

No matter which organization model you choose to deploy, you will soon see that Exchange 2007's new deployment and installation model makes it easier than ever to install. Each role is contained within distinct Windows Installer packages, which provide the best settings as default configurations. In addition to a smarter installation, Microsoft has backed the Exchange Best Practice Analyzer (BPA) into Exchange 2007. This means that all of your installation choices are validated against Exchange best practices before you even run the installation.

The Mailbox Server Role

The Mailbox Server is designed to host Exchange data in the form of user mailboxes contained within mailbox databases. The MB role can also host public folders. It integrates with the directory service provided by Active Directory to provide access to user information stored within the database(s). In addition, the MB role provides calendaring, resource management, and offline address book downloads.

MB roles also provide services that calculate e-mail address policies and address lists for recipients as well as enforcing managed folders. They interact with:

- Domain controllers
- Hub Transport Servers
- Client Access Servers
- Unified Messaging Servers
- Microsoft Outlook clients

To do so, the MB role relies on several communications protocols—protocols that are used whether the server role is hosted uniquely on a server or whether it coexists with other roles on a server. The only difference is whether the communications are internal to a server or external over your network to other servers. Communications use the following protocols for each component with which it interacts:

- The MB uses the Lightweight Directory Access Protocol (LDAP) to obtain recipient, server, and organization configuration from Active Directory domain controllers.
- The MB acts as a repository for messages. Therefore, the Hub Transport Server relies on its Store driver to take messages from the transport pipeline and place them in the appropriate mailbox on the MB. Similarly, it captures messages in the Outbox of any sender on the MB to place them into the transport pipeline. Communications between the HT and the MB are performed through MAPI.Net over Remote Procedure Calls (RPC). The .NET Framework's Mail application programming interface (API) includes built-in SMTP functionality, making it the ideal transport for these communications.

- Communications between most clients and the MB are managed through the Client Access Server. These communications include messages, free/busy data, and client profile settings. Once again, these communications are performed through MAPI.Net over RPC. In addition, the CAS will rely on NetBIOS file sharing to obtain offline address book files from the MB.

- The Unified Messaging Server obtains e-mail and voice mail messages as well as calendaring information from the MB to provide them through Outlook Voice Access. It also relies on the MB to obtain storage quota information. These communications are performed through MAPI.Net over RPC.

- Outlook clients that are on the intranet (inside the firewall) or the Internet (outside the firewall) will also be able to communicate directly with the MB to send and retrieve messages. Outlook relies on MAPI RPC over TCP when on the intranet and MAPI RPC over HTTP—or rather, RCP over secure HTTP or HTTPS—when on the Internet. To retrieve calendaring information from the MB, Outlook clients must communicate through a Client Access Server.

- Administrative consoles running only the administrative components of Exchange Server 2007 will rely on domain controllers to communicate with the Exchange Active Directory Topology service. This service will give them access to the Active Directory topology for Exchange as well as e-mail address policies and address list information. These communications rely on Remote Procedure Calls.

As you can see, while the MB role is critical to any implementation, Exchange also depends on other roles, especially the HT and the CAS, to provide full e-mail functionality to end users.

IMPORTANT   The Exchange Server 2007 Store

The MB role is the core role that maintains all Exchange databases, or the Exchange 2007 Store. Before you can deploy this server role, you should have a clear understanding of its logical components and its file structure. Both are covered in Chapter 2, "Planning Deployments."

Exam Tip   The MB role is the only role that can be installed and configured on a Windows Server 2003 Failover Cluster. All other roles must use different high availability methods and cannot be installed onto Failover Clusters. Note that combining the MB with any other server role automatically disqualifies it from being installed into a Failover Cluster.

The Hub Transport Server Role

The second critical role for any Exchange Server 2007 implementation is the Hub Transport Server role. It is an internal role that is designed to handle all mail flow within the organization. It also applies the transport rules and journaling policies and handles message delivery to and from a user's mailbox. When an Edge Transport Server is present, the HT relies on the ET for all connections to the Internet. If no ET is present, the HT is responsible for Internet communications. If so, install the ET agents on the HT to properly handle spam and virus protections. In either case, make sure that a firewall is configured between the HT and its method of communication with the Internet.

As with the MB, HT configuration information is stored within Active Directory. This includes the transport rule and journaling settings as well as connector configurations. Because of this, configuring the settings once in Active Directory automatically applies them to every HT server in the network.

Exam Tip In multi-site organizations, you must install at least one HT in each site that includes an MB. Placing more than one HT in each site provides redundancy for the service in that site.

Every single message that transits through your Exchange Organization will transit through an HT, without exception. The HT has four ways to pick up a message for transmission:

- The message can be delivered through SMTP to the Receive connector from either an ET residing in the perimeter network, another HT inside the organization, or directly from the Internet.
- The message can be waiting in the Pickup or Replay directory that is located on the HT.
- The message can be picked up from an Outbox by the Store driver that communicates directly with Mailbox Servers and places messages in the Submission queue.
- The message can be submitted by an Exchange Server agent.

Each message is processed by the Exchange categorizer, a component that determines what to do with a message based on the information about its intended recipients. The categorizer can expand distribution lists as well as identify alternative recipients and forwarding addresses. After the categorizer obtains the required information about recipients, it applies the appropriate policies, routes the message, and converts content if required. At this point, messages are either delivered through the Store driver directly to a user's mailbox or through SMTP to another transport server. Messages that must exit your organization are picked up by the Store driver and delivered to the Submission queue that is hosted on the HT.

The HT uses two agents—the transport rules agent and the journaling policies agent—to apply messaging policy and transport rules. Transport rules are used to apply your organization's compliance scenarios. Journaling is used to enforce message retention according to your internal policies.

Transport Architectures   In Exchange, the transport architecture is called the transport pipeline. On the internal network, this pipeline is made up of a collection of server roles, connections, components, and queues that all work together to route messages to the categorizer on a Hub Transport Server. On external networks, the transport architecture consists of the Receive connector on the Edge Transport Server, which then routes the message to an internal HT.

A typical transport pipeline will include the following steps:

- The SMTP Receive connector located on the Edge Transport Server or the Hub Transport Server first determines message validity. On the ET, anti-spam and antivirus agents filter the connections as well as the content of a message. They are also used to identify the sender and the recipient addresses to see whether the message will be accepted or rejected. If these agents are also found on the HT, they will provide an additional layer of protection. If a message passes all of the conditions of the SMTP Receive, it is placed into the Submission queue.

- The Submission queue relies on the categorizer to examine each message in the queue to determine where a message should be sent. On the ET, categorization is basically a forwarding process for approved messages to an appropriate HT. On the HT, categorization is more complex. It involves:

  - Recipient resolution including top-level addressing, expansion, and bifurcation
  - Routing resolution
  - Content conversion

  Categorization also involves the application of all of the mail flow rules. After the message is categorized, it is either placed into the local mailbox through the Store driver or sent to a remote recipient through the Send connector.

- Delivery is deemed local if the destination mailbox store is located in the same AD site as the HT. This is performed by the Store driver.

- Delivery is deemed remote if the destination mailbox store is in another Active Directory site, on a server running a previous version of Exchange Server, or the message must be sent through the Internet. This is performed by the SMTP Send connector.

- Clients can access their messages through a variety of means. Because of this, they do not interact directly with the transport pipeline. For example, Outlook 2003, Outlook Web Access, Outlook by Phone, and Exchange ActiveSync rely on the Client Access Server, the Unified Messaging Server, and the Mailbox Server to access their mailboxes. When messages are sent, they are placed into the sender's Outbox by Outlook or the CAS on behalf of the sender. When a message is in the Outbox, the Store driver is alerted by the Exchange Mail Submission service and retrieves the message to place it in the pipeline.

Together, these different components make up the transport pipeline, interacting at different levels to manage e-mail transport (see Figure 1-7).

The Client Access Server Role

The Client Access Server role is designed to provide front-end services to client access points. These include accessing e-mail through a Web browser with Outlook Web Access, accessing mail through a Windows Mobile Device through Exchange Active-Sync, or accessing Exchange Web Services. The CAS role also provides the access point for the Post Office Protocol (POP) version 3 and Internet Message Access Protocol version 4 revision 1 (IMAP4) messaging formats if they are in use. Finally, the CAS role is the access point for the new Exchange Autodiscover service–the service that lets Outlook clients automatically create connections to their Exchange Server.

Several features have been enhanced in this version of Exchange. OWA, for example, includes several improvements, such as smart meeting bookings, integration with Windows SharePoint Services, and integration with Universal Naming Convention (UNC) file sharing. It also includes improvements in reminders as well as the address book. OWA comes in two versions: Premium OWA provides a full-featured experience, while OWA Light is designed for slower connections or connections through mobile devices.

Mobile devices can also rely on ActiveSync, a service that is compatible with devices which run either Pocket PC 2002, 2003 or Windows Mobile 5.0 or 6.0. ActiveSync supports Direct Push–keeping the device continuously synchronized with the Exchange server–if the mobile device is running Windows Mobile 5.0 along with the Messaging and Security Feature Pack (MSFP) or Windows Mobile 6.0. ActiveSync will synchronize the following:

- E-mail messages
- Calendar items

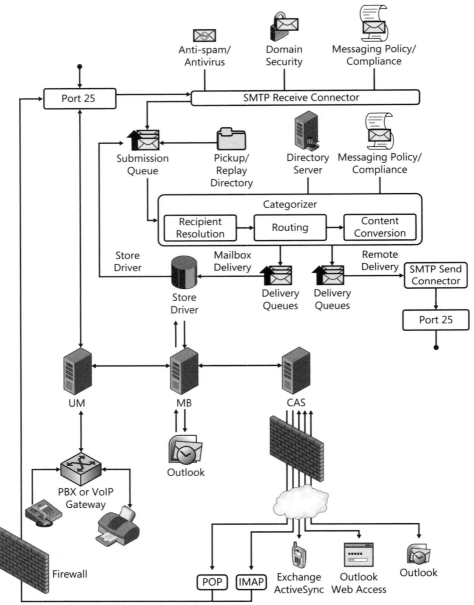

Figure 1-7 A typical transport pipeline

- Contacts
- Tasks

But it will not synchronize Notes in Outlook.

Because of the features it offers, CAS requires the installation of Internet Information Services version 6.0. Communication between Exchange and endpoints is encrypted. The Secure Sockets Layer (SSL) is required on all virtual directories and a self-signed certificate is installed.

Clients for the POP3 or IMAP4 protocols can either be Outlook Express or Eudora. Non-Windows mobile devices can also rely on the POP3 or IMAP4 protocols to connect to Exchange Server.

The Unified Messaging Server Role

The Unified Messaging Server role is a new Exchange Server 2007 role that combines voice messaging, fax, and e-mail into one Inbox that can be accessed from either the telephone or the computer. This role integrates Exchange 2007 with the telephony network in your organization. Because of this, it covers concepts that may not be familiar to the messaging professional. Because the traditional way to manage voice and e-mail messaging was to use two completely separate infrastructures, this role may be the most difficult to implement in your network.

The UM combines voice messaging, fax, calendaring, and e-mail messaging into a single store. When this role is deployed, end users can access each of these services through all of the classical e-mail clients, but also through the telephone. Users gain the following features:

- **Call Answering**   Users have access to traditional voice messaging services such as call answering on their behalf, personal greetings, message recording, and voice message delivery to the e-mail Inbox. When messages are delivered, users can either listen to the messages through the computer system or redirect them to their telephones through the Play on Phone feature.

- **Fax Receiving**   Faxes are received in the user's Inbox.

- **Subscriber Access**   Users can access their e-mail Inboxes through the telephones using Outlook Voice Access. This can be done through either voice inputs or the telephone keypad (also called DTMF input). Users can access voice-mail, manage e-mail messages, hear calendar information, access contacts or global address lists, control meeting requests, set Out-of-Office messages, and set security or personal options, all through the telephone.

- **Auto Attendant**   The Exchange UM role includes a set of voice prompts, known as the UM Auto Attendant, that can help users navigate through its services through a telephone. The UM Auto Attendant interacts with users to let them use telephone keypads or voice input to navigate the menu, place a call to a user, or locate a user and then place a call to that user. The Auto Attendant is configurable and administrators can create customizable menus and define formal or informal greetings, holiday schedules, directory search instructions, and operator access. The UM role supports more than one Auto Attendant.

IMPORTANT   Using machine virtualization

Microsoft does not support running the UM role as a virtual machine inside a machine virtualization environment such as Microsoft Virtual Server or Windows Server Hyper-V. Note that Hyper-V is the ideal platform for virtualizing other Exchange Server 2007 roles since it supports the creation of 64-bit virtual machines.

When installed, the UM role relies on custom objects created within Active Directory. These objects include:

- Dial Plan objects
- IP Gateway objects
- Hunt Group objects
- Mailbox Policy objects
- Auto Attendant objects
- Unified Messaging Server objects

Each object you create and configure in Active Directory controls the corresponding function in UM. Like other Exchange server roles, the UM role relies on the HT to deliver messages to their intended recipients.

The Edge Transport Server Role

The Edge Transport Server role is a stand-alone server designed to minimize the attack surface because it is located in your perimeter network. As such, it has no direct access to Active Directory; all configuration and recipient information is stored in Active Directory Application Mode. This role handles all Internet-facing mail flow and acts as an SMTP relay and smart host for the Exchange organization. The Send and Receive connectors on the ET perform all e-mail processing.

Exam Tip   The ET role can be hosted by application service providers (ASPs) and therefore can provide Edge Transport Services to organizations that do not have their own perimeter networks.

The ET is the role that protects your organization from unwanted or malicious e-mail. As such, it relies on the following series of agents to filter out spam and, therefore, potential viruses:

- **Attachment Filter Agent**   This agent filters messages based on attachment filenames, filename extensions, or MIME content type. It can block the entire message, strip out attachments, and send on the message or simply delete both message and attachment.

- **Connection Filter Agent**   This agent controls the IP Block and the IP Allow lists, blocking or allowing e-mails sent from specific IP addresses.

- **Content Filter Agent**   This agent relies on SmartScreen technology to assess message content. It uses the Exchange Intelligent Message Filter to learn the distinguishing character of legitimate e-mail versus spam.

- **Recipient Filter Agent**   This agent examines the RCPT TO: SMTP header of messages to determine whether recipients are allowed or blocked.

- **Sender Filter Agent**   This agent examines the MAIL FROM: SMTP header of messages to determine whether senders are allowed or blocked.

- **Sender ID Agent**   This agent examines the RECEIVED: SMTP header of messages as well as the DNS service of the sending system to determine whether senders are allowed or blocked.

In addition, the ET supports two message policy and compliance agents to assist organizations in implementing their regulatory policies for messages going to and from the Internet:

- **Address Rewrite Agent**   This agent rewrites the sender or recipient address to help hide internal domains, let multiple organizations appear as a single organization, or integrate services that are provided by a third-party organization.

- **Edge Rules Agent**   This agent uses rules to control the flow of messages to and from the Internet. Rules apply specific actions to messages that meet specific conditions. These transport rules are configured on each server. Rule conditions are based on specific data such as keywords or text patterns in the header, subject, body, From address, attachment type, or even the spam confidence level (SCL) of a message. When messages meet specific conditions, the Edge Rules Agent can quarantine the message, drop or reject it, append additional recipients, or simply log an event. Rules also support exceptions to exclude specific messages from rule processing.

IMPORTANT **ET agents and the HT**

You can also load the ET agents on an HT server. Do this in one of two situations: Add the ET agents to an HT when no ET is present, as with the Simple Organization. Add the ET spam and antivirus agents to an HT when you want to include a second layer of protection for messages coming from the Internet.

The ET communicates directly with an HT inside your network. You should ensure that this communication passes through a firewall. The HT will rely on EdgeSync—a collection of processes that establish one-way replication of recipient and configuration information from Active Directory to ADAM—to ensure that the Edge Transport Server has up-to-date information for message processing.

Plan Exchange Server Role Deployment

Now that you understand the different roles Exchange Server 2007 can play and the basic transport pipeline it needs to rely on, you can begin to explore possible Exchange deployment scenarios. First, you must understand the various Exchange Server editions as well as the core hardware and software requirements for deploying Exchange. Each edition has its own feature set. Table 1-1 outlines the differences between the two Exchange Server 2007 editions: Standard and Enterprise.

Table 1-1   Standard and Enterprise Edition Features

Feature	Standard Edition	Enterprise Edition
Storage Group Support	5 storage groups	50 storage groups
Database Support	5 databases	50 databases
Database Storage Limit	16 terabytes per database	16 terabytes per database
Single Copy Clusters	Not supported	Supported
Local Continuous Replication	Supported	Supported
Cluster Continuous Replication	Not supported	Supported

The Enterprise Edition is designed to operate in Large or Complex Organizations. The Standard Edition is useful for Simple or Standard Organizations or as specific server roles within more complex implementations.

It is also important to properly understand how clients will be able to access Exchange Server because different Client Access Licenses (CALs) will grant different features to Exchange users. Table 1-2 outlines the various features supported by different CALs.

Table 1-2   Standard and Enterprise CAL Features

Feature	Standard CAL	Enterprise CAL
E-mail, shared calendaring, contacts, tasks, and management	Included	Included
Outlook Web Access	Included	Included
Exchange ActiveSync	Included	Included
Unified Messaging		Included
Per-User/Per-Distribution List Journaling		Included
Managed E-mail Folders		Included
Exchange Hosted Filtering		Included
Forefront Security for Exchange Server		Included

The Standard CAL must be used along with the Enterprise CAL in order to obtain the full Exchange client feature set. In addition, the last two items in Table 1-2, Hosted Filtering and Forefront Security, are only available through Volume Licensing Agreements and are not available through retail purchases.

Processor Requirements per Role

Exchange server roles can be installed together (not including the ET role) or separately. Each role has its own memory and processor requirements. Microsoft recommendations for processor core requirements are outlined in Table 1-3. Multi-core processors should be used in all server scenarios.

Table 1-3   Processor Core Requirements for Exchange Server Roles

Server Role	Recommended number of cores	Maximum number of cores
Edge Transport Server	2	4
Hub Transport Server	4	8
Client Access Server	4	4

Table 1-3   Processor Core Requirements for Exchange Server Roles

Server Role	Recommended number of cores	Maximum number of cores
Unified Messaging Server	4	4
Mailbox Server	4	8
Combined Roles (HT, CAS, MB, and/or UM)	4	4

As you can see, two roles, MB and HT can run on a maximum of eight processor cores, either four dual-core processors or two quad-core processors. Keep in mind that a multi-core processor uses one single processor socket and modern servers include several processor sockets. When you combine roles, you are limited by the lowest maximum number of cores for the roles you include. This means that when you deploy multiple roles including the Client Access Server role, you are limited to its maximum number of cores, which is four.

Exam Tip   Carefully consider your processor core selections, especially if you intend to use new quad-core processors from AMD or Intel—several roles will only work with four cores as a maximum or one single quad-core processor, as outlined in Table 1-3.

Memory Requirements per Role

You should also consider the memory allocations you will assign to each server. Table 1-4 outlines the recommended memory configurations for each server role. Memory is closely tied to the processor core recommendations.

Table 1-4   Memory Recommendations per Server Role

Server Role	Recommended	Maximum
Edge Transport Server	2 GB	16 GB
Hub Transport Server	4 GB	16 GB
Client Access Server	4 GB	8 GB
Unified Messaging Server	4 GB	4 GB

Table 1-4   Memory Recommendations per Server Role

Server Role	Recommended	Maximum
Mailbox Server	4 GB plus 2 to 5 megabytes (MB) per mailbox	32 GB
Combined Roles (HT, CAS, MB, and/or UM)	4 GB plus 2 to 5 MB per mailbox	8 GB

Mailbox memory allocation depends on the type of users you have. Light users only require 2 MB per mailbox; average users require 3.5 MB; and heavy mailbox users will require 5 MB of RAM for each mailbox. It might be a good idea to identify where your own users fit so that you can take this into consideration when you design your server configurations.

MORE INFO   Calculating mailbox memory allocations

For more information on how to calculate mailbox memory allocations go to *http://msexchangeteam.com/archive/2004/11/03/251743.aspx*.

Storage groups and storage group configurations will also have an impact on the amount of memory the server requires. Storage groups are discussed Chapter 2.

NOTE   Configuring paging file sizes

The amount of RAM has an impact on the size of your paging file. Microsoft recommends that the minimum paging file size should be equal to the amount of RAM in the server plus 10 MB.

Exchange Server 2007 runs on x64 platforms, not Itanium (IA64). The x64 platform is an extension of the x86 platform and provides backward compatibility for 32-bit applications. The IA64 platform is a custom 64-bit platform designed for high-load environments. Microsoft has, however, released both an x64 and an x86 (32-bit) version of Exchange Server 2007 in the original release. Future releases will only be in x64 versions. Production systems should run x64 installations; x86 installations are made available for testing and training purposes as well as to provide support for the installation of Exchange administration tools on 32-bit client operating systems such as Windows XP. You can also rely on Windows XP x64 Edition to install the 64-bit administration tools. Exchange administration tools do not run on any version of Windows Vista. If you want to manage Exchange from Windows Vista, you need to install the administration tools on a server and then use a Remote Desktop Connection to access them on the server.

MORE INFO   x64

For more information on x64, look up "Move to the Power of x64," a webcast at *http://www.reso-net.com/presentation.asp?m=7* or the following article *http://www.msexchange.org/tutorials/Why-64-Bit-Good-E12.html.*

Exchange requires a minimum of 1.2 GB on the drive where it will be installed. An additional 200 MB is required on the system drive. Each language pack you install for the UM role requires an additional 500 MB on the drive where Exchange is installed. Make sure all disk partitions are formatted as NTFS file systems, which simplifies installations. In any case, Exchange Server 2007 does not support running on any other partition type.

NOTE   Exchange Server 2007 and disk space

Planning for adequate disk space is one of the most important aspects of server sizing for Exchange. The MB role, especially, requires lots of space to store the Exchange database. Skimping on space at installation is definitely not a best practice.

Operating System Requirements

Exchange Server 2007 will run on several operating systems. For production installations, this includes:

- Windows Server 2003, Standard x64 Edition
- Windows Server 2003, Standard x64 Edition, with the Multilingual User Interface Pack (MUI)
- Windows Server 2003, Enterprise x64 Edition
- Windows Server 2003, Enterprise x64 Edition, with MUI
- Windows Server 2003, R2 Standard x64 Edition
- Windows Server 2003, R2 Standard x64 Edition, with MUI
- Windows Server 2003, R2 Enterprise x64 Edition
- Windows Server 2003, R2 Enterprise x64 Edition, with MUI
- Windows Server 2003 SP2, Standard x64 Edition
- Windows Server 2003 SP2, Standard x64 Edition, with MUI

- Windows Server 2003 SP2, Enterprise x64 Edition
- Windows Server 2003 SP2, Enterprise x64 Edition, with MUI

For testing and training environments, or to install the 32-bit administration tools, this includes:

- Windows Server 2003 with SP1, Standard Edition
- Windows Server 2003 SP1, Standard Edition, with MUI
- Windows Server 2003 SP1, Enterprise Edition
- Windows Server 2003 SP1, Enterprise Edition, with MUI
- Windows Server 2003 R2, Standard Edition
- Windows Server 2003 R2, Standard Edition, with MUI
- Windows Server 2003 R2, Enterprise Edition
- Windows Server 2003 R2, Enterprise Edition, with MUI

IMPORTANT   Windows Server 2008 and Windows Vista

The original release of Exchange Server 2007 does not run on Windows Vista or Windows Server 2008, but Exchange 2007 with Service Pack 1 supports both platforms. You will need the x64 Standard, Enterprise, or Datacenter Editions of Windows Server 2008 to perform the installation.

Exam Tip   Exchange Server 2007 provides several high availability features, including the Single Copy Cluster (SCC) and Cluster Continuous Replication (CCR). If you plan to use either feature, you must use an Enterprise Edition of Windows Server 2003 as well as an Enterprise Edition of Exchange Server 2007. A third availability feature focused on data availability, Local Continuous Replication (LCR), will work with either the Standard or Enterprise Editions of Windows Server 2003, and Exchange 2007. (See Chapter 6, "Business Continuity," for more information.)

Exam Tip   The list in the following section outlines a series of updates and hotfixes required for the installation of Exchange Server 2007. It is important for you to know what they correct, but you do not need to know the specific number of the hotfix for the exam.

Prerequisites to Exchange Installation

When you prepare your servers to host Exchange server roles, they will need certain prerequisite installations first. These include:

- The Microsoft .NET Framework version 2.0 for x64 systems. You can obtain a copy of this version of the .NET Framework at *http://www.microsoft.com/downloads/ details.aspx?FamilyID=b44a0000-acf8-4fa1-affb-40e78d788b00&displaylang=en*.

Then you should update it to the latest version. Obtain the update from *http://go.microsoft.com/fwlink/?linkid=74465*.

- You will also require the Microsoft Management Console (MMC) version 3.0. For download information, see Microsoft Knowledge Base (KB) article 907265 at *http://go.microsoft.com/fwlink/?linkid=3052&kbid=907265*. Note that the R2 Editions of Windows Server 2003 already include this component.

- The Microsoft Windows PowerShell scripting language, which is required for the Exchange Management Shell because every command generated by this shell is transformed into a PowerShell script. For download information, see Microsoft Knowledge Base article 926139 at *http://go.microsoft.com/fwlink/?linkid=3052&kbid=926139*.

These initial requirements are part of the default Exchange Server 2007 installation screen (see Figure 1-8).

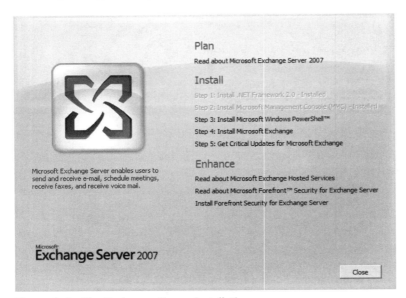

Figure 1-8   The Exchange Server installation screen

NOTE   **Installing isolated servers**

If your staging area is isolated from the Internet, you must review each of the prerequisites for each server role, download the required components from another computer, and then have them on hand as you perform your Exchange server build. You should, however, need to connect the server to the Internet once it is built so that you can access any available updates for Exchange 2007.

In addition, you will need the following prerequisites:

- Each x64 server or workstation that will run any server role or run the administration tools will require a TCPIP.SYS update. More information is available through Knowledge Base Article 898060 at *http://support.microsoft.com/?kbid=898060*. You can obtain a copy of this hotfix at *http://go.microsoft.com/fwlink/ ?linkid=59272*. If you have SP2 for Windows Server 2003, this hotfix is not required.

- If you intend to install the Mailbox Server role, you also need these two hotfixes:
    - ❑ The first corrects issues with applications that run on x64 computers and use the Interface Remoting components of Microsoft Data Access Components (MDAC) version 2.8. You can find this hotfix at *http://go.microsoft.com/ fwlink/?linkid=73962*. If you have SP2 for Windows Server 2003, this hotfix is not required.
    - ❑ The second provides a fix for the Exchange Object Linking and Embedding (OLE) database component. More information is available through Knowledge Base Article 918980 at *http://support.microsoft.com/?kbid=918980*. You can find the hotfix at *http://go.microsoft.com/fwlink/?linkid=74467*. If you have SP2 for Windows Server 2003, this hotfix is not required.

- In addition, the MB requires some components from Internet Information Services (IIS) 6.0 to be installed on the server before installation can proceed. Select the components in the Application Server role in Add/Remove Windows Components in Add or Remove Programs in the Control Panel to install IIS with the following components:
    - ❑ Internet Information Services with the World Wide Web Service
    - ❑ Network COM+ access

Exam Tip   MB does not require IIS because all of the functions that depend on IIS have been removed from this server role. The installation logic for this role, however, has not been updated. Because of this, the installation will fail if IIS is not present on the computer.

- If you intend to install the Client Access Server role, you also need to install the following components:
    - ❑ IIS 6.0 with the World Wide Web Service
    - ❑ ASP.NET
    - ❑ RPC over HTTP Proxy (from Windows Networking Services)

- If you intend to install the Unified Messaging Server role, you also need three additional components on the server operating system:
  - Windows Media Encoder and the Windows Media Audio Voice Codec must be installed prior to installing the role. Obtain the latest x64 version of the Encoder at *http://go.microsoft.com/fwlink/?linkid=67406* and the Codec at *http://go.microsoft.com/fwlink/?linkid=67407*. Note that a Genuine Windows Validation will be required to obtain the Media Encoder download.
  - Microsoft Core XML Services 6.0 must be installed prior to installing the role. Obtain the latest x64 version at *http://go.microsoft.com/fwlink/?linkid=70796*. Make sure you obtain the x64 version of the installation file.

- If you intend to install the Edge Transport Server role, you also need to pre-install ADAM with Service Pack 1. ADAM SP1 can be downloaded from *http://go.microsoft.com/fwlink/?linkid=71063&clcid=0x409*. Install ADAM with all the defaults. It will be properly configured when you install the ET role.

- Also, you cannot change the name of the server once the Edge Transport Server role is installed. Make sure that you configure a proper DNS name along with its suffix for the server before you install ET. More information can be found at *http://technet.microsoft.com/en-us/library/bb123528.aspx*.

- If you intend to install the Mailbox Server role onto Failover Clusters, you will need two hotfixes:
  - The first is an update to the cluster service in Windows Server 2003. It adds the ability to create a File Share Witness instead of relying on a Quorum disk. It also allows you to configure cluster heartbeats. You can obtain this update from *http://go.microsoft.com/fwlink/?linkid=69785*. If you have SP2 for Windows Server 2003, this hotfix is not required.
  - The second updates the driver for volume mount points on Windows Server 2003. You can obtain this update from *http://support.microsoft.com/kb/898790*. This hotfix is not required if you already have Service Pack 2 for Windows Server 2003.

Exam Tip   You must make sure that the Network News Transfer Protocol (NNTP) service or the Simple Mail Transfer Protocol (SMTP) services provided with Windows Server 2003 are not installed on a server where you intend to run either the Hub Transport Server or the Edge Transport Server roles.

- If you intend to install the Exchange Management Tools on an x86 version of Windows XP, you must install Windows Installer 3.1 first. For more information,

see Microsoft Knowledge Base article 893803 at *http://go.microsoft.com/fwlink/
?linkid=3052&kbid=893803.*

IMPORTANT **Preparing server builds**

If you intend to install anything but the Simple or Standard Organization, you might consider creating custom server builds for Exchange Server 2007 to simplify the process. Each build can include a standard installation of your x64 operating system, the required hotfixes and any required prerequisites for the server role you intend to run on it. Then use the System Preparation (Sysprep) tool in Windows to depersonalize the installation. Copy this installation for each server you need to create. For more information on Sysprep, go to *http://technet2.microsoft.com/WindowsServer/en/library/c03a5469-ef71-4545-b970-ce2add5e715c1033.mspx?mfr=true.*

Alternatively, you can create a standard server build and then create custom scripts that install required prerequisites based on intended server role. Whichever method you use, relying on standard server builds will both simplify and speed the deployment of Exchange server roles.

Prepare Dependent Services

When you have determined which platform to use to run your Exchange server roles, you can move on to ensuring that dependent services are ready to receive the different server roles. As seen earlier in Figure 1-1, a complete Exchange Server topology requires the proper operation of several networked components, including:

- Active Directory
- Domain Name System name resolution
- Network configuration based on TCP/IP version 4

In fact, each is already dependent on the other. Your network must have a properly configured TCP/IP implementation for it to function and Active Directory must have a proper DNS implementation to function properly.

NOTE **Learn about Active Directory implementation**

For more information on implementing Active Directory, download Chapter 3 of *Windows Server 2003 Best Practices for Enterprise Deployments* by Ruest and Ruest from *www.reso-net.com/documents/007222343x_ch03.pdf.*

Then make sure your network meets the following conditions:

- Make sure you are running the appropriate version of Windows Server 2003 on your directory servers. One domain controller in particular, the Schema Operations Master—the server managing the structure of the Active Directory database—must be running at least Service Pack 1, R2, or Service Pack 2. Ideally, it would be running R2 with Service Pack 2 to be as up to date as possible. In addition, if your forest includes more than one site, you must make sure that at least one domain controller in each site will be running either on Windows Server 2003 R2 or with one of the service packs. If this is not the case, update the DCs first. Either upgrade the DCs to R2 or update them with SP2.

Exam Tip   If any DCs in your network have not been updated to at least SP1 for Windows Server 2003, you will have to use the command-line version of Setup.com along with the */DomainController* switch to specify which DC does have at least SP1. To make it easier on yourself, update all of your DCs, ideally to SP2. You should do so as a best practice for security anyway.

Note that R2 is not a requirement in terms of the exam. However, it is highly recommended that you use the very latest server operating system in your network.

- There must be at least one Global Catalog server in each site where you plan to deploy Exchange Server 2007 roles.

- The functional level of each domain in your Active Directory must be at least Windows 2000 Server-native or higher. Ideally, your functional level will be at its highest possible level.

- If you are running a multilingual operation where some of your DCs are installed on a non-English version of Windows Server 2003 and you intend to use OWA, you must apply a hotfix to the DC. For more information and to access this hotfix, look up Knowledge Base article 919166 at *http://support.microsoft.com/ ?kbid=919166*. This hotfix resolves issues between the DC and OWA when they are using different locales.

- If you want to use a Large or Complex Organization installation that involves more than one forest and you want to share selected free/busy data as well as perform cross-forest administration, each forest must be at the Windows Server 2003 functional level and you need to establish a trust relationship between each forest.

- If you plan to install Exchange Server 2007 in an existing organization running on either Exchange Server 2000 or 2003, you must ensure that no Exchange Server 5.5 servers are in the organization before installing Exchange 2007 server roles.

- DNS must be configured properly to support Active Directory operation. Ideally, the DNS service will be stored within Active Directory partitions and will be found on each DC in your network. For more information on Exchange dependencies on DNS, go to *http://technet.microsoft.com/en-ca/library/bb124896.aspx*.

- If you are using a *disjointed namespace*—a namespace where the computer's DNS suffix is not the same as the domain name it resides in—you must make sure that the Exchange DNS Suffix Search Order includes every possible DNS namespace that Exchange may be involved in. This should include computers, servers, third-party applications, and any other applicable namespace.

- If you have more than one site, the connection points in your network must have at least 64 kilobits per second (Kbps) of available bandwidth.

- Active Directory sites are configured correctly and will support message routing. If you are deploying only Exchange Server 2007 messaging services, you need to do nothing more than install the HT role. If your network includes older versions of Exchange Server, you must plan your routing strategy carefully. More information is available at *http://technet.microsoft.com/en-ca/library/aa996299.aspx*. This topic is covered in depth in Chapter 3, "Upgrades and Migrations," and Chapter 4, "Interoperability."

Exam Tip   The fact that Exchange Server 2007 can finally rely only on existing Active Directory site structures for replication and that it does not need custom replication groups is one of its very best features. This greatly simplifies purely Exchange 2007 deployments; all you need to do is make sure your Active Directory replication structure is already in place and you are ready to go. This information is bound to be on the exam.

- Update the Active Directory schema for Exchange Server 2007. Exchange more than doubles the Active Directory schema to create all of the objects it manages. This update affects both the forest as a whole and each domain it contains. This task is performed on the schema master. The schema master runs on one of the domain controllers in the forest root domain. The easiest way to identify it is to use the Schema Management snap-in. Go to *http://technet2.microsoft.com/windowsserver/en/library/3ed42e38-a1d9-41f9-87d3-43c6e4f834671033.mspx?mfr=true* for more information. Microsoft has also made a white paper available for the preparation of the schema for Exchange: "Preparing Active Directory for Exchange 2007" at *http://technet.microsoft.com/en-us/library/bb288907.aspx*.

- If you plan to install Exchange server roles onto a domain controller, this domain controller must run an x64 version of Windows Server 2003. You should, however, aim to install Exchange server roles on member servers, which will provide better performance than when it has to share resources with the DC role. Also, installing on a DC is not supported by Microsoft.

You are now ready to deploy Exchange in your network.

Define Role Implementation Strategies

The division of Exchange Server 2007 into five different roles is more than just cosmetic. Even though you can deploy four of the five roles—MB, HT, CAS, and UM—onto the same server, they will still need to be administered separately. That is because each of the roles is defined in such a way that it regroups features and components into logical collections that are designed to perform a specific function within the Exchange topology. This is also why you can deploy each of the roles individually on different servers. Remember that the ET role is always deployed on stand-alone servers in perimeter networks and cannot coexist with other server roles.

If you do plan to implement multiple roles on the same server, you can install the MB, HT, CAS, and/or UM roles in any combination. Base your configuration on required performance. Rely on Tables 1-3 and 1-4 to create your server configurations for combined role installations.

If you want to deploy server roles on more than one server and you are installing Exchange Server 2007 into an existing Exchange 2000 or 2003 organization, install the server roles in the following order:

- Client Access Server
- Hub Transport Server
- Mailbox Server
- Unified Messaging Server

The Edge Transport Server can be deployed at any time and does not require existing installations of other roles before installation. It does, however, require the installation and configuration of a Hub Transport Server before you can finalize its configuration.

You start with the CAS because previous versions of Exchange front-end servers (2000 or 2003) cannot act as front-end servers for the Exchange 2007 MB role. In addition, your Exchange 2007 servers will not be able to send or receive mail until a Hub Transport Server is installed in the same site. This is why you should begin with the CAS role, follow with HT, and then install the MB role.

The Unified Messaging Server role can be installed on its own; you will need to have access to existing installations of CAS, HT, and MB. This is why this role is usually the last of the four coexisting roles to be installed.

Actual installations of Exchange Server are performed in one of two ways:

- You can rely on the Exchange Server 2007 Setup Wizard. This wizard guides you through the setup steps. In addition, it gives you access to the Exchange Best Practices Analyzer, which can validate configurations prior to installation.

- You can rely on the Setup.com command. This command allows you to create unattended installations of Exchange components on servers. This command is most often used in either Large or Complex Organization deployments.

When the installation is complete, you will need to perform post-installation tasks. These tasks will help complete the configuration of the role or roles you selected during installation.

Exam Tip   When you have at least one role installed on a server, you can no longer use the Setup Wizard to modify your Exchange Server installation. Instead, you must rely on Add Or Remove Programs from Control Panel or the Setup.com command.

In core installations of Exchange Server in Exchange 2007 only organizations really require two server roles—HT and MB—but you should aim to install at least three roles in your organization: CAS, HT, and MB. In fact, you must install both HT and MB in each Active Directory site if you want mail flow to work correctly. And, if you want client access to work properly, you must install a CAS role in each site that has an MB role. Basically, you should install the CAS, HT, and MB roles in each Active Directory site. Use this as a rule of thumb for your installations.

When installing Exchange Server 2007 for the first time, you must use an account that belongs to the Enterprise Administrators group in the forest root domain or that has permissions to modify the Active Directory schema. If, however, you have already updated the Active Directory schema though Setup.com, you must use an account that belongs to the Exchange Organization Administrators group.

IMPORTANT   Administrator accounts with non-ASCII characters

By default, Exchange will create a mailbox for the system administrator account. When it does so, Exchange automatically changes non-ASCII characters to underscores. If you are in a multilingual organization, you may end up with a mailbox account that has only underscores because Exchange could not read the characters of the account. To correct this, make sure your administrator account has a predefined user principal name that uses ASCII-only characters before installation.

When all prerequisites have been met, Exchange will offer two basic installation modes during setup (see Figure 1-9):

- **Typical Exchange Server Installation** This option will install the CAS, HT, and MB roles onto a single computer along with the Exchange Management Tools.

- **Custom Exchange Server Installation** This option lets you select which roles you want to install on a one-by-one basis. It also lets you select a stand-alone installation of Exchange Management Tools.

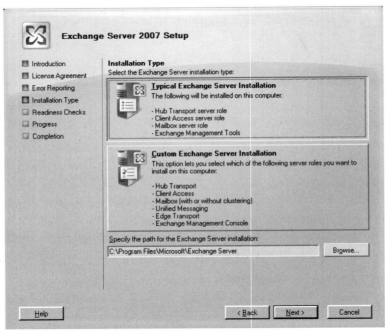

Figure 1-9 The Installation Type Page of the Exchange Setup Wizard

---

IMPORTANT Exchange Organization names

Be careful what you name your Exchange Organization. The name should be representative of your organization, use only normal ASCII characters, and not include spaces at the beginning or the end. Use a common-sense name that is representative but not overly complicated. You cannot rename Exchange Organizations after you create them, so make sure you get it right the first time.

If you select a custom installation, you will have the opportunity to install cohabitable roles singly or together, install the Edge Transport Server role, install the MB role into a cluster or install only the management tools (see Figure 1-10).

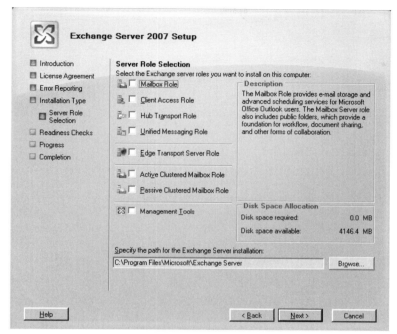

Figure 1-10   Using a custom Exchange setup

IMPORTANT   Entering a product key

One of the first tasks you should perform when the installation is complete is to enter a product key to license the installation. By default, Exchange installs as a trial edition only. If you do not add a product key in time, Exchange will stop working after 120 days. When you open Exchange Management Console, it will display all of the unlicensed servers in your network as well as the number of days remaining in their trial. Add the product key in the console under Server Configuration, then Server Name and click Product Key.

To perform an unattended installation of an Exchange server role, use the following command, where **serverrole** is the name of the server role or roles you want to install and **newExchangeorg** is the name of the new organization you want to create:

```
setup.com/mode:install/roles:serverrole/OrganizationName:newExchangeorg
```

Use the /*OrganizationName* switch only if you are creating a new organization. Server roles can be provided in a comma-separated list. Appropriate names for each role are:

- ClientAccess or CA or C
- HubTransport or HT or H

- Mailbox or MB or M

- UnifiedMessaging or UM or U

- EdgeTransport or ET or E

- ManagementTools or MT or T

Remember that the ET role cannot be installed with any other role.

MORE INFO   **The Setup.com command**

A lot of other switches are supported by this command. For more information, see *http://technet.microsoft.com/en-us/library/aa997281.aspx.* In addition, Microsoft has made available a white paper on the topic called "Description of the Parameters Used With the Exchange 2007 Setup.com Tool." You can find it at *http://technet.microsoft.com/en-us/library/bb288906.aspx.*

Define Server Role Configurations

As you have seen, each different server role has its own requirements and prerequisites. Each is also used to support specific feature sets within your Exchange Organization. Server role configurations are examined in depth as you move through the topics of the 70-238 exam in this guide. When you complete the guide, you will have a clear understanding of the functions of each role in your organization, how you can deploy and protect it, and how you should design your overall Exchange Organization structure for optimal operation.

Practice: Prepare Active Directory for Exchange Server Deployment

In this practice, you will prepare Active Directory for Exchange server role deployments and then install your first Exchange server. This practice consists of two exercises. The first exercise lets you see how you need to prepare Active Directory to host Exchange server roles. The second guides you through the installation of your first Exchange server using a typical installation of three of the four server roles that can coexist together: HT, CAS, and MB.

▶ **Exercise 1: Prepare Active Directory for Exchange**

In this exercise, you will update Active Directory to prepare for Exchange deployment. This is an Active Directory forest that has never hosted any previous version of Exchange and is running in Windows Server 2003 fully functional mode, but will now be used for your first Exchange 2007 implementation. You prepared this Active Directory based on the instructions outlined in the Introduction as you created your initial virtual environment. You will continue to rely on this virtual infrastructure as you move through practices in other chapters.

1. Begin by identifying the Schema Master in your Active Directory. Type the following command on a computer that includes the Windows Server 2003 administrative tools:

    ```
    dsquery server -hasfsmo schema
    ```

    The response should give you the name of the Schema Master domain controller.

2. Next, because Exchange binaries are in x64 format, you must log onto a 64-bit installation of Windows Server 2003 to run the Active Directory preparation commands. Log on to the ExchangeOne.treyresearch.net computer using forest root domain credentials. The account you use must be a member of the Schema Administrators group.

3. Load the Exchange 2007 installation media into the DVD reader of the server, open a Command Prompt window, and move to the DVD reader drive. Make sure that the core prerequisites for Exchange—.NET Framework 2.0, MMC 3.0, and PowerShell—are already available on this computer.

4. Type in the following commands. Wait for the completion of each command and verify its results before moving on to the next one.

    ```
    setup /PrepareSchema
    setup /PrepareAD /OrganizationName:"Trey Research"
    setup /PrepareDomain
    ```

    In the PrepareAD portion of Setup, you must indicate the name of the Exchange Organization you are preparing; otherwise, the command will fail. If your Organization name includes spaces, make sure you enclose it in double quotes.

5. If more than one domain in your network will host Exchange server roles, you must repeat the last command in each domain.

Your Active Directory is ready to run Exchange. Now you can proceed to actual server installations. Note that since your Active Directory does not include a legacy Exchange installation, you do not have to use the */PrepareLegacyExchangePermissions* switch with the Setup command.

▶ Exercise 2: Perform a Typical Exchange Server Installation

Now that your Active Directory is ready to host Exchange services, you can install your first Exchange server. You perform this installation on the x64 virtual machine you created as a member server of the Active Directory for Trey Research. This virtual machine should be called ExchangeOne.treyresearch.net.

1. Log on to the ExchangeOne.treyresearch.net virtual machine using local administrator credentials.

2. Load the Exchange 2007 installation media into the DVD reader of the server. Exchange Setup will launch the Installation screen. If not, use Windows Explorer to locate Setup.exe on the DVD and double-click it.

3. Verify that the three core prerequisites have been installed. They should be displayed as such in the Auto Launch Screen of Setup. These prerequisites were installed during your server preparation in the Introduction.

4. Click Step 4: Install Microsoft Exchange. This opens the Introduction screen. Click Next.

5. Accept the License Agreement and click Next. Choose how you want to report errors to Microsoft and click Next.

6. On the Installation Type screen, click Custom Exchange Server Installation. You will actually perform a typical installation to install the Hub Transport, Client Access Server, and Mailbox Server roles as well as Exchange Management Tools, but selecting Custom Exchange Server Installation lets you view all of the installation options. Click Next.

7. Review all of the available setup options. Select the three server roles to install: Mailbox Role, Client Access Role, and Hub Transport Role. You will notice that Management Tools is selected automatically as soon as you select any role. Install the Exchange application binaries to the default location on the C: drive. Click Next.

8. On the Client Settings page, select No, because you will not have Outlook 2003 clients, and click Next. This will not set up public folders for the Availability Service but rely on the new structure of this service to make free/busy data available to your clients.

9. Exchange then runs the readiness checks for each role you are installing. If any test fails, cancel the installation and then confirm the cancellation. Perform the corrective action and re-launch Setup. Follow steps 1 through 9 again. If no test fails, click Install.

10. Exchange begins the installation and displays progress information in the graphical interface. Click Finish. Notice that Finalize Installation Using The Exchange Management Console option is selected. This will automatically launch the console. You can use it to review your settings when you are done with Setup and close the console when done.

11. Return to the Setup window and click Step 5: Get Critical Updates For Microsoft Exchange. This launches Microsoft Update. Click Custom to obtain the list of applicable updates. Apply the proposed updates.

12. Close the Internet Explorer window when done and also close the Setup window. You may have to restart the system if updates were available.

Congratulations, your first Exchange server has been installed into a new Exchange 2007 Organization. You will notice that Exchange tells you how long you have before you need to install a license on this server when you move to the console. You may not want to add a license to this system because it is a learning system only.

Quick Check

1. After looking over information about Exchange Server 2007 roles, you decide that you are ready to implement your own solution for messaging. Fortunately, this is a brand-new network and it does not have any messaging services deployed yet. You know all users will be working with Office Outlook 2007, so you decide to install only the two core server roles that are required for messaging: Hub Transport Server and Mailbox Server. After your deployment, users complain that they cannot use the calendaring functions in Outlook. What could be the problem?

2. Your organization has decided to put together a brand-new network that will use the very latest in technologies. As such it decides to deploy Windows Server 2008 as its base server operating system. In addition, it has decided to be proactive and meet the U.S. Federal Government's edict on having an IPv6 plan for June 2008 by putting in place a network based purely on IPv6. (See *http://www.whitehouse.gov/omb/memoranda/fy2005/m05-22.pdf#search=%22omb%20ipv6%22* for more information.) Now it wants to deploy Exchange Server 2007. What do you need to do?

3. You prepare your servers for Exchange deployment. You have fully configured the base prerequisites, installing the .NET Framework version 2.0 and Windows PowerShell on each. You do not need to install the Microsoft Management Console version 3.0 because you are running Windows Server 2003 R2 on each server. Now you are ready to install the Mailbox Server role, but it will not install. What could be the problem?

4. You prepare a new server that will host the MB, CAS, and HT roles. You have just acquired the latest and the greatest server hardware that is running two

quad-core processors. You go to install the roles and you find that you cannot. What could be the problem?

5. You prepare a server to host the Edge Transport Server role. You join it to the domain so that the base server Group Policy will apply to the server to secure it. Next you proceed to install the ET role on the server and you place it in the perimeter zone. Some time later, you verify the server and you discover that its event log is full of Group Policy errors. What could be the problem?

Quick Check Answers

1. Your strategy is right. In a pure Exchange Server 2007 environment, only two roles are required to provide basic mail delivery services: the Hub Transport Server and the Mailbox Server, especially if all users are relying on Office Outlook 2007. This solution does indeed give them access to e-mail functionality. It does not, however, give them access to calendaring functions. To provide calendaring functionality, you must install a Client Access Server. The CAS role is the one that supports free/busy scheduling in Exchange Server 2007. Install this role to resolve the issue.

2. While it is commendable for your organization to want to rely on the latest and often the greatest technologies for its new network, this network will unfortunately not support Exchange Server 2007 in its original format. Exchange Server 2007 does not run on Windows Server 2008. It does not support Active Directory Domain Services and it does not support IPv6 unless you are deploying Exchange Server 2007 with SP1.

3. Although the MB role no longer has any requirement for Internet Information Services, its former prerequisite requirements for installation have not been updated. Because of this, you need to pre-install IIS with the World Wide Web service and network COM+ access to install the MB role.

4. Although the MB role on its own supports up to eight processing cores, what is available on your server, the CAS role, has a maximum of four cores. When installing multiple roles on a server, you need to go to the lowest common denominator—in this case, the CAS requirement. Remove one processor and the installation will proceed.

5. Microsoft recommends that ET servers be stand-alone servers that are members of a workgroup instead of Active Directory. This makes sense, because most organizations do not open Active Directory ports on their firewalls for

> good reason. The server's event log is full of errors because it can no longer communicate with Active Directory to update its Group Policy settings. To correct this issue and have a proper ET server design, remove the server from Active Directory and join it to a perimeter workgroup.

Chapter Summary

- Exchange Server 2007 divides each major functionality area into different server roles. For the first time, one of these roles supports integration of e-mail messaging with voice mail.

- Five server roles are available with Exchange Server 2007: Client Access Server, Hub Transport Server, Mailbox Server, Unified Messaging Server, and Edge Transport Server.

- Of the five server roles, four can be installed together and one must be isolated. The four that can coexist on the same server are CAS, HT, MB, and UM. The ET role must be deployed on a stand-alone server that is member of a workgroup because it will be located in a perimeter network.

- Exchange Server supports four organization types: Simple, Standard, Large, and Complex. Any other organization topology is not supported by Microsoft.

- Production Exchange servers must run an x64 operating system from the Windows Server 2003 family. Ideally, this platform will be an x64 Edition of Windows Server 2003 running SP2 to be as up to date as possible. Note that R2 is not a requirement while the service pack is.

- Active Directory domain controllers should run at least Service Pack 1 for Windows Server 2003. Ideally all of your domain controllers will run at least this service pack level or newer, but if not, at least one DC in each site must have this service pack as well as the DC running the Schema Operations Master role.

- There are several prerequisites to server installation prior to being able to host any Exchange Server role. The most common prerequisites include the .NET Framework version 2.0, Windows PowerShell, and the Microsoft Management Console version 3.0. In addition, each server role has its own particular prerequisites.

- Exchange Server 2007 can coexist with older versions of Exchange in existing organizations. It cannot, however, coexist with Exchange 5.5. All Exchange 5.5 servers must be removed from the organization before you can introduce Exchange Server 2007 servers.

Case Scenarios

In the following case scenarios, you will apply what you have learned about Exchange deployment. You can find answers to the questions in this scenario in the "Answers" section at the end of this book.

Case Scenario 1: Build a Plan for a Multi-site Server Role Deployment

Lucerne Publishing needs to prepare its Exchange 2007 implementation. Lucerne Publishing wants to deploy every server role within its organization because it wants to take advantage of every Exchange Server feature. In addition, Lucerne Publishing has its own perimeter network so it will be installing its own Edge Transport Server infrastructure. Your job as a messaging professional is to help Lucerne Publishing plan their server deployments and identify where each server role should be installed. Lucerne Publishing is a growing organization. Their network is currently running Active Directory directory services and the replication topology has been tested and is working well. Lucerne has offices in various parts of the country. Some offices are very large, such as the head office, which has 1,000 users. Others are quite small, often with fewer than 10 users. The size and location of each office is displayed in Table 1-5. This table also displays information about their site links and available bandwidth.

Table 1-5   Lucerne Publishing Site Topology

Site Name	Link Speed	Number of Users	Site Link Cost	Available Bandwidth
Headquarters (New York)	T1	1,000	1	512 Kbps
Site 2 (Los Angeles)	T1	600	100	512 Kbps
Region 1 (San Remo)	256	50	400	128 Kbps
Region 2 (Philadelphia)	512	75	150	256 Kbps
Region 3 (Dallas)	128	9	500	32 Kbps
Region 4 (Newark)	64	5	1,000	32 Kbps
Total		1,739		

Lucerne Publishing's site topology is based on the following information:

- Open replication schedules are available for all sites.
- The Knowledge Consistency Checker—the service that controls Active Directory replication—is on by default in all sites.

- All site link costs decrease as they get closer to the headquarters office, so replication is prioritized towards this office.

- Replication is only performed with RPC over IP.

- Every site has a backup replication route at a higher cost.

- Everything is based on calculated available bandwidth.

Lucerne has turned to a messaging professional, you, to help them devise their configuration. They tell you that they have a single PBX system and it is in the New York office. They also tell you that they have their own perimeter network, which is also located in New York. Their network topology is illustrated in Figure 1-11.

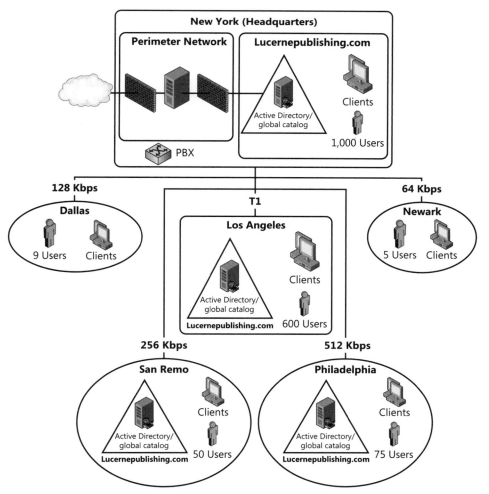

Figure 1-11   The Lucerne Publishing network topology

They want to use the full breadth of Exchange Server 2007's features, and cost is no object—rare in any project. Your job is to determine the placement of different server roles throughout the network and determine how users will connect to their Exchange mailboxes. Your solution should include a table outlining the server roles deployed to each site as well as an illustration that displays the Exchange Server topology for Lucerne's network. At this stage, you do not need to determine whether the server roles will coexist on a server—you only need to name the role to deploy.

To facilitate this exercise, a table for case scenario 1 has been prepared for you and is available on the companion CD. Fill out the values in this table as you prepare your answer. Identify the server roles to deploy in each site. Also identify how users will connect to their mailboxes in each site. Then use Figure 1-12 to identify server roles in each site.

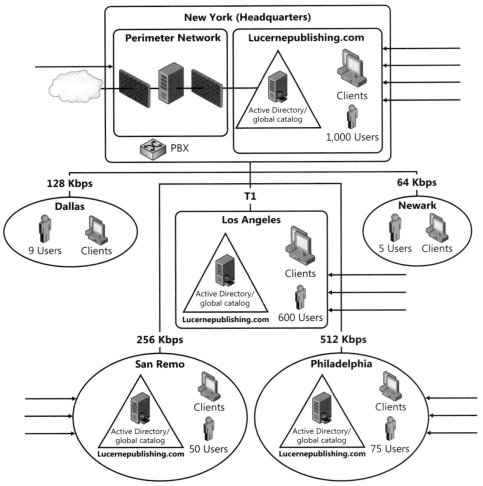

Figure 1-12   Identify Exchange Server role positions

Case Scenario 2: Deploying Unified Messaging

As a leader in the field, The Phone Company (TPC) wants to deploy unified messaging with Exchange Server 2007. Your job as a messaging professional is to design a plan for multiple server role implementation using the least number of servers possible within the TPC network. TPC uses a multi-domain network because they have operations in the United States as well as in Europe. The network is mostly centralized network because it only has four locations: San Francisco, which is the headquarters; Los Angeles; New York; and London. Each location has its own PBX. TPC also has their own perimeter network, located in San Francisco. The TPC network is illustrated in Figure 1-13.

Because TPC has some understanding of the new Exchange Server 2007 features, they have asked you specific questions for which they want answers. You try to provide the simplest answers possible.

TPC wants answers for the following questions:

1. Given that it has a PBX in each office, how should TPC deploy the Unified Messaging Server role?

2. Which roles should TPC have coexist on the same servers?

3. TPC wants to cluster their storage locations for Exchange so that they can provide high availability for users. Which roles should TPC run on Failover Clusters?

4. How should TPC configure the entry point for Internet mail?

5. Which client access licenses should TPC purchase?

Suggested Practices

You can perform several practices to prepare for this section of the exam. First, you should review some reference information to complement what you have seen in this chapter. Second, you should take a practice test. Do not take the entire test. Instead, concentrate on the objective in this chapter.

In addition, it is difficult to practice the deployment of Exchange features without access to a full infrastructure, but you can do so if you prepare a virtual environment as outlined in the "Before You Begin" section at the beginning of this chapter. Ideally, you would prepare your Active Directory for Exchange deployment, then you can run through the installation of each of the different roles. You do not have to install each role—simply run through the installations to see what kind of configurations are required.

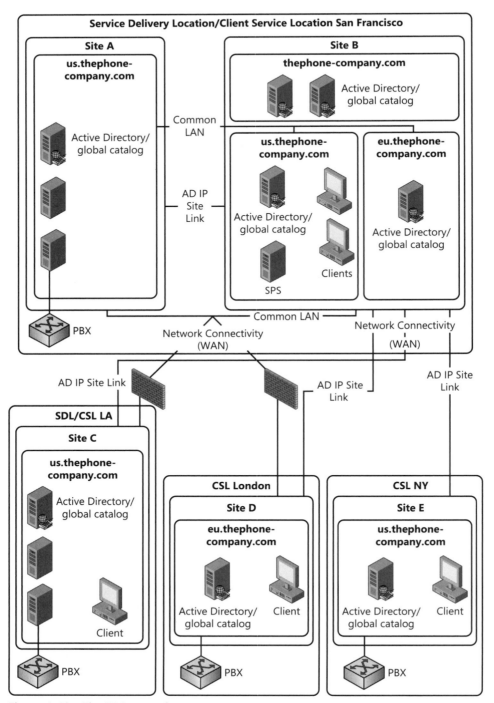

Figure 1-13   The TPC network

To view and examine the various settings for the Exchange roles, you should download and open the Microsoft Exchange Server 2007 Virtual Hard Drive from *http://technet.microsoft.com/en-us/bb738372.aspx*. This includes a fully functional Exchange environment and will let you see many of the settings discussed in this chapter.

Chapter 2
Planning Deployments

Now that you understand the basic structure of the services and server roles in Exchange Server 2007, you need to begin looking at the various subcomponents that make up each server role. Mailbox Server (MB) roles are designed to store information your users create and generate with the various e-mail engines they use. The Client Access Server (CAS) role is designed to support these various engines, but because each engine has its own requirements, you will need to make sure you properly configure the underlying services of each CAS. The Hub Transport Server (HT) role bridges every other Exchange server role by enabling e-mail routing to each and every part of your infrastructure. Therefore, you will need to make sure you properly understand Exchange connectors—especially connectors to the Edge Transport Server (ET) role. Finally, the Unified Messaging Server (UM) role brings the telephone and e-mail together into one integrated experience.

This chapter focuses on the examination of the different components that make up these server roles, helping you finalize your overall deployment choices before you move on to the actual implementation of Exchange.

Exam objectives in this chapter:
- Plan the storage group deployment.
- Plan the deployment of required Exchange services.
- Plan the deployment of optional Exchange services.

Before You Begin

To complete the lessons in this chapter, you must have the following:

- A virtual machine setup as outlined in the Introduction under "Virtual Machine Environments."
- Use the Exchange Server 2007 virtual machine from Microsoft to review the configuration options for pre-installed computers, in this case the Mailbox Server role as well as the Client Access Server role.

■ Use the newly created virtual environment you set up to test the deployment of different storage configurations, as well as both the required and the optional services. For the exercises in this chapter, you will need access to the Active Directory server, the all-in-one Exchange server, and the member server that will host the Edge Transport role.

Lesson 1: Plan the Storage Group Deployment

Estimated lesson time: 40 minutes

When it comes to the Mailbox Server role, Microsoft Exchange Server is nothing more than a database application. The Exchange store—the collection of Exchange databases and transaction logs—is designed to provide a single repository for managing multiple types of information in one infrastructure. The Exchange store is designed to work in conjunction with the distributed Active Directory database to contain all information pertaining to Exchange Server systems. Active Directory will store configuration information for the different Exchange server roles along with administrative groups, storage groups, and database locations. The Exchange store, on the other hand, captures all Exchange data—the information generated by users of the Exchange system.

Exchange Storage Concepts

When planning for Exchange storage, you must take three different factors into account:

- The transactional input and output (I/O) rate or Input/Output Per Second (IOPS). This factor is focused on storage performance, which is the I/O latency factor for your chosen storage technology. This is why disk structure and random array of independent disks (RAID) structure is so important to Exchange storage. The calculation of user I/O per second is part of the mailbox profile you need to calculate before you deploy your MB roles.

- The backup and restore throughput, or the speed at which you can perform a backup or restore operation. This factor is based on the speed at which you can move data to and from your backup medium. One reason that so many organizations are opting for disk-based backup technologies for Exchange is that tape is so slow.

- The capacity, or the space you must calculate for each user's mailbox to be stored within the various mailbox databases. While Exchange storage is often placed within direct-attached storage (DAS), it is also placed within storage area networks (SAN). Using SANs often means that you must first configure the proper RAID structure, and then ensure that the logical unit (LUN) used for the Exchange store has sufficient free space to allow for database growth over time. Of course, you need to ensure that you have corresponding free space in your backup medium as well.

The Exchange store is first divided into logical components. These logical components have different representations within the file structure of a Windows Server disk. And, because the Exchange store is a database, it must rely on transaction logging to control how objects are stored and retrieved from within it.

The Logical Components of an Exchange Store

The Exchange store is designed to contain three different logical components:

- **Storage groups**   The logical containers for Exchange databases as well as their associated system and transaction log files.

- **Mailbox databases**   The containers of data, data definitions, indexes, checksums, flags, and any other information that make up a mailbox in Exchange. The data contained in a mailbox database is private to an end user. Data in the mailbox is structured through folders and is represented as a set of folders to the user through the various interfaces used to access Exchange.

- **Public folder databases**   The containers of data, data definitions, indexes, checksums, flags, and any other information that make up a public folder in Exchange. Public folders contain information that can be shared between end users. As shown in Table 2-1, each edition of Exchange Server can only contain a single public folder database per server.

Storage groups are containers that are used to divide and structure the various databases you store on a Mailbox Server. They provide the basic unit for backup and restoration operations. Of course, you can restore a single database from within one group, but you rely on the storage group to structure your backup schedules. In addition, the databases in a storage group share transaction log files. Therefore, the simplest representation of a storage group is a folder with one database and one set of transaction files.

You can create a recovery storage group (RSG) on an MB server. This RSG is used to mount mailbox databases and extract data from within them. This is how you would recover a single user's mailbox or a single message from within a mailbox. By using this offline method for recovering objects, you do not disturb user access to existing data in production databases. Unlike normal mailbox databases, an RSG will not be visible within the Exchange Management Console. RSGs must be managed either through the Exchange Management Shell (Windows PowerShell) or through the Exchange Server Disaster Recovery Analyzer tool.

Remember that the two Exchange Server Editions, Standard and Enterprise, have different storage features.

Table 2-1   Standard and Enterprise Edition Storage Features

Feature	Standard Edition	Enterprise Edition
Storage Group Support	5 storage groups	50 storage groups
Mailbox Database Support	5 databases	50 databases
Database Storage Limit	16 terabytes per database	16 terabytes per database
Public Folder Database Support	1 database	1 database
Single Copy Clusters	Not supported	Supported
Local Continuous Replication	Supported	Supported
Cluster Continuous Replication	Not supported	Supported

The File Structure of an Exchange Store

Though you manage Exchange through its logical structure through storage groups and databases, these all translate to a series of specialized files in the Windows disk structure. The Exchange file structure consists of:

- **Storage group files**   Each storage group is represented by a single instance of the Extensible Storage Engine (ESE). Each storage group is regrouped at the file system under a specific folder or directory. This directory contains the database and log files that make up the contents of the storage group (see Figure 2-1).

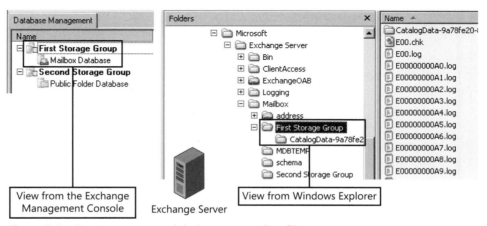

Figure 2-1   Storage groups and their corresponding file structure

- **Database files**   Database files have an .edb extension. They are the repository of the mailbox data. Access to the database contents is performed through the ESE using a balanced or B-tree structure that provides high efficiency and quick access. Because of this structure, users can access any page in the database within four I/O cycles. Each database includes multiple B-trees with ancillary trees that work with the main tree to contain indexes and views.

Exam Tip   In Exchange 2003, databases were split between .edb and .stm or stream files. Exchange 2007 no longer uses the .stm file format and stores all data within the .edb file.

MORE INFO   ESE architecture

For information on the ESE architecture and its internal structure, go to *http://technet.microsoft.com/en-us/library/bb310772.aspx*.

- **Log files**   Because the Exchange store is a database, when users perform operations such as creating or modifying a message, all data is initially written into transaction log files (.log), verified, and then committed to the proper database. Using log files protects data against service failures. All databases in a storage group share the same log files. Each log file is named with a consecutive number, such as E0000000001.log, E0000000002.log, and so on.

- **Checkpoint files**   Each time a transaction is successfully saved to the database, an entry is written to the checkpoint file (.chk). Checkpoint files are used by the ESE to replay all transactions in the event of a potential inconsistence within a database resulting from a service interruption. When the ESE finds the last correct transaction, it begins writing logs back to the database to repair it.

Like all previous versions of Exchange, Exchange 2007 relies on the Joint Engine Technology (JET) database engine. There are also two versions of JET: JET Red is used by Microsoft Access and JET Blue is used by Exchange. JET powers the ESE. In Exchange 2007, JET has been enhanced to reduce its I/O rate. Running Exchange on an x64 operating system allows the JET database engine to use a much larger cache than ever before. In previous versions running on 32-bit operating systems, the cache was limited to 900 megabytes (MB). Now the cache can be sized up to dozens of gigabytes (GB), all depending on the size of available memory. Remember that the MB role is one of the roles that requires the largest amounts of RAM.

Because Exchange 2007 runs on an x64 OS, cache operations have been optimized. For example, I/O coalescing has been increased from 64 kilobytes (KB) to 1 MB, letting the JET engine read and write larger I/O blocks. These and other improvements make I/O a lot faster and more efficient in Exchange 2007. In fact, because it runs on an x64 platform, Exchange 2007 has access to significantly more actual and virtual memory than ever before. Ideally, operations will be performed strictly from cache, therefore limiting the impact of I/O speeds on your MB.

IMPORTANT   Configuring storage groups

Exchange Server 2007 Enterprise Edition will support up to 50 databases and/or 50 storage groups on the same server. However, each storage group is limited to a maximum of five databases. If you create a storage group with a single database within it, all transactions might actually be stored in cache, reducing I/O requirements and speeding up database access. Consider this a best practice.

File Structure and Disk I/O

Several mailbox activities affect I/O. Table 2-2 outlines how each file type or activity affects I/O performance.

Table 2-2   Mailbox Activity versus I/O Performance

Activity	Comment
Mailbox database (.edb)	Because all data is stored within the ESE database, you should rely on standard database disk structures. Ideally, the database will be stored on separate disks from the transaction logs to improve recoverability and performance.
Transaction log files (.log)	Transaction logs use sequential writes to disks. Each write varies from 512 bytes to the entire log buffer size.
Content indexing	Indexing is a random operation, but because it is performed against the database, the index should also be placed on the same LUN or disk set as the database to improve performance. Indexes are typically about 5 percent of the size of the database. Because indexing is performed as each message arrives, the impact on performance is minimal.

Table 2-2 Mailbox Activity versus I/O Performance

Activity	Comment
Paging and paging files	Operating systems rely on page faults to access data. If a page of memory is requested and it is not available, a page fault automatically occurs. A soft page fault occurs if the page is elsewhere in memory. A hard page fault, which produces I/O, occurs if the page is not in memory and must be retrieved from disk. Hard page faults also have an impact on processing. If your systems incur a lot of hard page faults, the system has insufficient memory.
Content conversion	Exchange Server 2007 has the ability to transform content to make it readable for end users. Most content conversion is performed either on the CAS or the HT roles. In pure Exchange 2007 setups, this has no impact on MB I/O. But in legacy environments where Exchange 2003 servers exist, content conversion for OWA is performed on the Mailbox Server within its TEMP folder. Because of this, the TEMP folder should be stored on a different disk structure or LUN than the database.
Database maintenance	You must run several different maintenance tasks against the mailbox database on an ongoing basis. A hard content deletion and database defragmentation are both activities that impact I/O. When messages or mailboxes are older than the configured retention policy, they are deleted from the system. Then, when items have been deleted, the database should be defragmented. You must plan a proper defragmentation window: If a backup operation begins during defragmentation, defragmentation will stop and the database will be left in a fragmented state.

Table 2-2   Mailbox Activity versus I/O Performance

Activity	Comment
Backup and Restore	Because a backup requires a complete read of both the database and transaction logs, it will have a negative impact on I/O and the user experience. This is one more reason why backups should be performed during non-business hours or at least non-peak hours if you are running a 24/7 operation.
Data protection	Exchange Server 2007 includes two continuous replication scenarios: Local Continuous Replication (LCR) and Cluster Continuous Replication (CCR). Both have a high impact on I/O because they rely on transaction log shipping. Using the built-in continuous replication requires you to make changes in the way you configure the hardware for your mailbox servers. In previous releases, Exchange Server was mostly focused on writing to transaction logs and not reading them; read/writes were focused on the actual database with reads taking up most of the I/O. With Exchange 2007 built-in replication, transaction logs are written and read, creating much more I/O than with previous releases (see Figure 2-2).

IMPORTANT   **Using the Volume Shadow Copy Service**

Windows Server 2003 relies on the Volume Shadow Copy Service (VSS) to perform backups of Exchange databases. Basically, VSS takes a snapshot of an active database and then performs the backup against the snapshot. VSS reduces the impact of backup I/O on production databases, but the ideal scenario is to perform a backup from replica media using either LCR or CCR. Using the replica for backups has no impact whatsoever on I/O against the production databases.

Mailbox Server Role Storage Calculations

One of the most demanding jobs the messaging professional will face is calculating storage requirements for MB roles. Fortunately, Microsoft has put together a storage

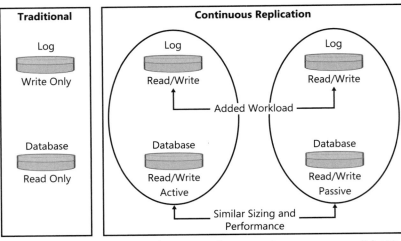

Figure 2-2 Using Exchange data protection scenarios means more disk I/O

calculator that allows you to automatically calculate your storage requirements. This calculator is broken into five categories:

- Server Configuration
- Storage Requirements
- Disk Structure or LUN Requirements
- Backup Requirements
- Log Replication or Data Protection Requirements

MORE INFO **Obtain and use the Exchange Storage Calculator**

The Exchange Storage Calculator is an automated Excel 2007 spreadsheet that assists you in your storage estimates. You can obtain it from *http://msexchangeteam.com/files/12/attachments/entry438481.aspx*. More information on the Storage Calculator can be found at *http://msexchangeteam.com/archive/2007/01/15/432207.aspx*.

The calculator spreadsheet is outlined in such a way that all you need to do is fill in the blue text in each of the boxes. The first part of the calculator deals with the server configuration (see Figure 2-3).

If you need more information on each entry, just look at the notes within each cell of the calculator. This section deals with the following items regarding your configuration:

- **Server configuration** This part of section one deals with items such as continuous replication, content indexing, standby continuous replication and log replay

Storage Requirements Input Factors - Server Configuration	
Step 1 - Please enter in the appropriate information for cells that are blue and choose the appropriate drop-downs for cells that are red concerning your server configuration.	

Exchange Server Configuration	
Source Continuous Replication (CR) Model	CCR
Number of SCR Targets	0
SCR Log Replay Delay (Days)	1
Content Indexing?	Enabled
Dedicated Maintenance / Restore LUN?	Yes
LUN Free Space Percentage	20%

Exchange Data Configuration	
Deleted Item Retention Window (Days)	14
Data Overhead Factor	20%
Mailbox Moves / Week Percentage	10%

IOPS Configuration	
I/O Overhead Factor	20%
Additional I/O Requirement	0.00

Database Configuration	
Use Recommended Maximum Database Sizes?	Yes
Maximum Database Size (GB)	0

Figure 2-3   Using the server configuration portion of the Exchange Storage Calculator

delay, usage of dedicated restore LUNs, and free space requirements. You can change each section or only change the section in blue if the default settings are those in your configuration. Note that you can move your cursor over each item to get more information from the spreadsheet.

Exam Tip   Standby Continuous Replication (SCR) is a new feature introduced in Exchange Server 2007 Service Pack 1. It adds to the data protection provided by LCR and CCR and, as its name implies, replicates data to a standby recovery server. Unlike CCR or LCR, Standby Continuous Replication can have more than one target for each storage group. SCR copies the transaction logs to the standby server, and then SCR replay determines when Exchange will replay the transaction logs on this server. By default, this replay period is one day, but you can specify up to seven days. More on LCR, CCR, and SCR is covered in Chapter 6, "Business Continuity."

SCR will not be a part of the 70-238 exam unless Microsoft updates the base set of questions after the release of Exchange Service Pack 1. You must, however, consider the continuous replication modes in real life when structuring your storage requirements for MB roles.

- **I/O per second (IOPS) configuration**   This section covers I/O latency. It includes extra overhead for I/O spikes and any additional third-party device overhead that is not part of a default Exchange configuration.

- **Exchange data configuration**   This section deals with how you configure Exchange settings. Settings include Deletion Item Retention Window (Days), which is 14 days by default; Data Overhead Factor; and Mailbox Move/Week Percentage.

- **Database configuration**   Microsoft recommends that databases be no larger than 100 GB when there is no replication and no larger than 200 GB when replication is in use. You should use Microsoft's recommendations unless you have a compelling reason not to do so.

The second section of the calculator deals with the storage requirements and mailbox configuration (see Figure 2-4). It allows you to configure your storage based on mailbox

Storage Requirements Input Factors - Mailbox & Client Configuration

Step 2 - Please enter in the appropriate information for cells that are blue and choose the appropriate drop-downs for cells that are red concerning your mailbox population. If this server will house multiple mailbox types, then please enter that information in the Tier-2 and Tier-3 User Mailbox tables. Otherwise, only use the Tier-1 User Mailbox table.

Tier-1 User Mailbox Configuration	
Number of Tier-1 User Mailboxes / Server	1200
Send/Receive Capability / Mailbox / Day	20 sent/80 received
Average Message Size (KB)	50
Tier-1 User Mailbox Size Limit (MB)	2048
Predict IOPS Value?	Yes
Tier-1 User IOPS / mailbox	0.00
Tier-1 Database Read:Write Ratio	50%
Outlook Mode (Majority of Clients)	Cached Mode

Client Configuration	
User Concurrency	100%

Tier-2 User Mailbox Configuration	
Number of Tier-2 User Mailboxes / Server	0
Send/Receive Capability / Mailbox / Day	20 sent/80 received
Average Message Size (KB)	50
Tier-2 User Mailbox Size Limit (MB)	2048
Predict IOPS Value?	Yes
Tier-2 User IOPS / mailbox	0.00
Tier-2 Database Read:Write Ratio	50%
Outlook Mode (Majority of Clients)	Cached Mode

Tier-3 User Mailbox Configuration	
Number of Tier-3 Mailboxes / Server	0
Send/Receive Capability / Mailbox / Day	20 sent/80 received
Average Message Size (KB)	50
Tier-3 User Mailbox Size Limit (MB)	2048
Predict IOPS Value?	Yes
Tier-3 User IOPS / mailbox	0.00
Tier-3 Database Read:Write Ratio	50%
Outlook Mode (Majority of Clients)	Cached Mode

Figure 2-4   Using the storage requirements portion of the Exchange Storage Calculator

types. Three different mailbox types are supported. For each tier, you must provide the following information:

- The number of mailboxes to be deployed on this server along with the amount of mail you expect users to send and receive.

- Average message size and mailbox limits or quotas.

This section can also predict the IOPS values for this server based on responses. If you want to map your storage requirement to a specific IOPS value, override the default. You can also override the default database read-write ratio. This section also looks at how your Microsoft Office Outlook clients will operate. By default, Outlook clients operate in cached mode. Finally, the section looks at the number of expected users to operate concurrently. Normally, you should expect that 100 percent of your clients will run Outlook at the same time.

Section three looks at backup requirements (see Figure 2-5). It requests the backup and restore rates in MB per seconds, backup frequency, and the time you can wait before log truncation. Log truncation occurs when you perform a full backup. It also looks at your backup methodology. Several are available: hardware VSS, software VSS, streaming, or VSS backup only. Each has an impact on the configuration of your LUNs.

Storage Requirements Input Factors - Backup Configuration

Step 3 - Please enter in the appropriate information for cells that are blue and choose the appropriate drop-downs for cells that are red concerning how your server will be backed up.

Backup Configuration	
Backup Rate (MB/s)	20
Restore Rate (MB/s)	20
Backup Methodology	Software VSS Backup/Restore
Backup Frequency	Weekly Full / Daily Incremental
Backup Failure Tolerance	2

Figure 2-5   Using the backup configuration portion of the Exchange Storage Calculator

The final step looks at log replication or data protection requirements (see Figure 2-6). If you choose to use either LCR or CCR, you need to enter values for the number of generated logs per hour. Fortunately, default values are filled in for you. This section also requests the recovery point objective you intend to aim for. This value is in number of hours.

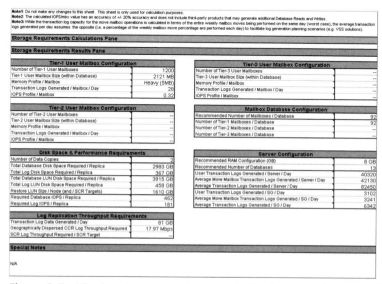

Storage Requirements Input Factors - Log Replication Configuration

Step 4 (Optional) - If this server will replicate data between physical locations, then please enter in the appropriate information for cells that are blue concerning your log generation frequency on an hourly basis. Also, choose the appropriate red variable for the acceptable amount of lag time between the production site and the SCR site. This data will help determine the appropriate log bandwidth requirements for both geographically dispersed CCR and SCR configurations.

Log Replication Configuration

Hours in the Day	Number of Logs Generated / Hour
1	1949
2	1244
3	2737
4	2281
5	3401
6	4852
7	3940
8	3567
9	5060
10	8087
11	6138
12	5558
13	5848
14	4479
15	5184
16	3401
17	1908
18	1825
19	1535
20	1327
21	4023
22	1949
23	1244
24	912

Recovery Configuration

Recovery Point Objective (Hours)	24

Figure 2-6 Using the server configuration portion of the Exchange Storage Calculator

After you enter all the values, move through the different tabs of the spreadsheet. The second tab, storage requirements, outlines how you must configure your storage (see Figure 2-7). It lists the recommended server configuration as well as the disk space and performance requirements. If you select log shipping, it also includes the throughput requirements for optimal performance.

Note1: Do not make any changes to this sheet. This sheet is only used for calculation purposes.
Note2: The calculated IOPS/mbx value has an accuracy of +/- 20% accuracy and does not include third-party products that may generate additional Database Reads and Writes.
Note3: While the transaction log capacity for the move mailbox operations is calculated in terms of the entire weekly mailbox moves being performed on the same day (worst case), the average transaction logs generated per day assumes the opposite (i.e. a percentage of the weekly mailbox move percentage are performed each day) to facilitate log generation planning scenarios (e.g. VSS solutions).

Storage Requirements Calculations Pane

Storage Requirements Results Pane

Tier-1 User Mailbox Configuration

Number of Tier-1 User Mailboxes	1200
Tier-1 User Mailbox Size (within Database)	2121 MB
Memory Profile / Mailbox	Heavy (5MB)
Transaction Logs Generated / Mailbox / Day	28
IOPS Profile / Mailbox	0.32

Tier-3 User Mailbox Configuration

Number of Tier-3 User Mailboxes	---
Tier-3 User Mailbox Size (within Database)	---
Memory Profile / Mailbox	---
Transaction Logs Generated / Mailbox / Day	---
IOPS Profile / Mailbox	---

Tier-2 User Mailbox Configuration

Number of Tier-2 User Mailboxes	---
Tier-2 User Mailbox Size (within Database)	---
Memory Profile / Mailbox	---
Transaction Logs Generated / Mailbox / Day	---
IOPS Profile / Mailbox	---

Mailbox Database Configuration

Recommended Number of Mailboxes / Database	92
Number of Tier-1 Mailboxes / Database	92
Number of Tier-2 Mailboxes / Database	---
Number of Tier-3 Mailboxes / Database	---

Disk Space & Performance Requirements

Number of Data Copies	2
Total Database Disk Space Required / Replica	2983 GB
Total Log Disk Space Required / Replica	367 GB
Total Database LUN Disk Space Required / Replica	3915 GB
Total Log LUN Disk Space Required / Replica	458 GB
Restore LUN Size / Node (and / SCR Targets)	1610 GB
Required Database IOPS / Replica	462
Required Log IOPS / Replica	181

Server Configuration

Recommended RAM Configuration (GB)	8 GB
Recommended Number of Databases	13
User Transaction Logs Generated / Server / Day	40320
Average Move Mailbox Transaction Logs Generated / Server / Day	42130
Average Transaction Logs Generated / Server / Day	82450
User Transaction Logs Generated / SG / Day	3102
Average Move Mailbox Transaction Logs Generated / SG / Day	3241
Average Transaction Logs Generated / SG / Day	6342

Log Replication Throughput Requirements

Transaction Log Data Generated / Day	81 GB
Geographically Dispersed CCR Log Throughput Required	17.97 Mbps
SCR Log Throughput Required / SCR Target	---

Special Notes

N/A

Figure 2-7 Viewing storage requirements in the Exchange Storage Calculator

The third tab lists recommended LUN requirements (see Figure 2-8). Note that storage groups are divided into groups of five per LUN. Both database and log LUNs are listed.

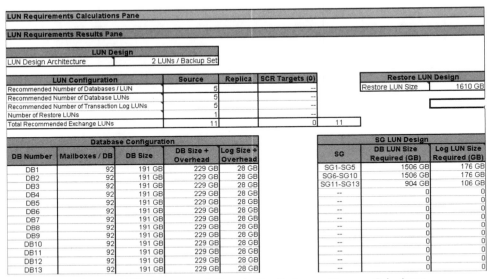

LUN Requirements Calculations Pane							

LUN Requirements Results Pane

LUN Design	
LUN Design Architecture	2 LUNs / Backup Set

LUN Configuration	Source	Replica	SCR Targets (0)		Restore LUN Design	
Recommended Number of Databases / LUN	5		--		Restore LUN Size	1610 GB
Recommended Number of Database LUNs	5		--			
Recommended Number of Transaction Log LUNs	5		--			
Number of Restore LUNs	1		--			
Total Recommended Exchange LUNs	11	0	11			

Database Configuration						SG LUN Design		
DB Number	Mailboxes / DB	DB Size	DB Size + Overhead	Log Size + Overhead		SG	DB LUN Size Required (GB)	Log LUN Size Required (GB)
DB1	92	191 GB	229 GB	28 GB		SG1-SG5	1506 GB	176 GB
DB2	92	191 GB	229 GB	28 GB		SG6-SG10	1506 GB	176 GB
DB3	92	191 GB	229 GB	28 GB		SG11-SG13	904 GB	106 GB
DB4	92	191 GB	229 GB	28 GB		--	0	0
DB5	92	191 GB	229 GB	28 GB		--	0	0
DB6	92	191 GB	229 GB	28 GB		--	0	0
DB7	92	191 GB	229 GB	28 GB		--	0	0
DB8	92	191 GB	229 GB	28 GB		--	0	0
DB9	92	191 GB	229 GB	28 GB		--	0	0
DB10	92	191 GB	229 GB	28 GB		--	0	0
DB11	92	191 GB	229 GB	28 GB		--	0	0
DB12	92	191 GB	229 GB	28 GB		--	0	0
DB13	92	191 GB	229 GB	28 GB		--	0	0

Figure 2-8   Viewing LUN recommendations in the Exchange Storage Calculator

This calculator also gives you a recommended backup schedule, which is found on the fourth tab. The fifth tab lists the requirements for log replication based on your choices. The last tab lists the changes that have been made to the calculator in its different iterations.

Rely on this calculator when determining your configurations and calculations. Because of the intelligence included in its calculations, it will save you a lot of time. If the Microsoft Exchange team does not know how to recommend storage structures, no one will.

Disk Configurations for Exchange Server 2007

Exchange performance is closely tied to three critical components of a server configuration: processor type, memory, and disk structure. As you have seen earlier in this chapter, planning storage for MB roles is a complex operation that requires multiple factors. One thing is certain, though: You must provide some form of redundancy for your storage as the first step in your recovery plan. This means using a series of redundant disks through some form of RAID configuration.

Prepare Your Exchange Server Disks   Storage decisions are always based on the same requirements. First, you need to make sure you have enough space for growth. Next, you need to make sure your disk structure will provide an acceptable rate of latency and a responsive user experience. The key to this value is the transactional I/O your storage delivers. The last factor focuses on the non-transactional I/O and making sure it has time to complete and sufficient disk throughput to meet your service level agreements (SLAs). Ideally, you will be able to balance each of these factors in your storage solution. Keep the following in mind when selecting storage:

- **Obtain high-performance disks**   In Exchange, smaller disks with faster speeds are better than larger disks with lower speeds. For example, you are better off choosing 73-GB drives that run at 15,000 revolutions per minute (rpm) than choosing 300-GB drives that run at 10,000 rpm. Of course, you will need a lot more of the 73-GB drives to create large LUNs, but your I/O throughput will be much faster.

- **Choose performance before capacity**   In Exchange, you are better off creating multiple smaller storage areas than creating one large storage area with a very large capacity. Once again, performance is more important than large storage areas because you can split databases through the proper structure of storage groups.

- **Align your disks**   When disks are formatted, especially through the graphical Windows interface, their tracks are not sector-aligned. By default, Windows creates the partition starting at the sixty-fourth sector of a disk, misaligning the partition with the structure of the disk. You can increase performance by as much as 20 percent when you create partitions that are sector-aligned because you are therefore aligning the partition with the disk structure.

  The only way to create partitions that are sector-aligned is through the Diskpart.exe tool. In Windows Server 2003, you will find Diskpart.exe in Support Tools. Diskpart.exe is a command interpreter, which means that you enter the Diskpart.exe command prompt after you type the command. Use the following commands to align your partitions. Begin by opening a command prompt. Make sure you have at least local administrative privileges. The command in the following example assumes that the disk you want to prepare is disk 2 and that it has no partitions on it. The result will be an aligned disk that is assigned to the letter D:

```
diskpart
list disk
select disk 2
create partition primary align = alignmentvalue
assign letter D
format label = disklabel
exit
```

Alignmentvalue is a either 32 or 64, depending on the type of disk you are working with. The disk manufacturer will tell you what this value should be. If the storage vendor does not have a recommendation, use 64. *Disklabel* is the label you want to assign to the disk.

MORE INFO **Find out more about Diskpart.exe and sector alignment**

To find out more about the Diskpart.exe command, go to *http://technet.microsoft.com/en-ca/library/bb124518.aspx*. To find out more about sector alignment, go to *http://technet.microsoft.com/en-us/library/aa995867.aspx*. For information on aligning sectors on multiple disks, go to *http:// support .microsoft.com/kb/929491*. To test disk performance using the Winsat.exe utility, go to *http://technet2 .microsoft.com/windowsserver2008/en/library/d51ea641-c258-4f6c-aba1-7031cce09e571033 .mspx?mfr =true*. Note that Microsoft corrected the disk formatting and alignment issue in Windows Vista and Windows Server 2008. This means that in these versions, you no longer need to use the Align option with the Diskpart.exe command and you can properly format disks in the graphical interface.

Consider Your Choice of RAID Given the previous considerations, it is important for you to determine which RAID configuration you will use in your servers. You can choose from among several RAID types, each with its own overhead and performance capabilities. The three most common RAID configurations are RAID 5, RAID 6, and RAID 10. RAID 5 consists of a set of disks that distribute parity among them. You can recover from the failure of one disk with impacts on performance but with no downtime. RAID 6 consists of a set of striped disks with double parity distributed among them. As with RAID 5, disk failures have an impact on performance but do not require downtime. RAID 10, also called RAID 1+0, consists of a set of striped disks that are mirrored as a whole (see Figure 2-9). Because the disks are striped, they provide faster performance. Because they are mirrored as groups, they provide better fault tolerance. Of course, RAID 10 requires more disks than the other configurations. See Table 2-3 for a comparison of each of the three popular RAID types.

Exam Tip Microsoft recommends that you use RAID along with a battery-backed controller in all your Exchange Server storage configurations.

Table 2-3 Comparison of RAID solutions

RAID type	Speed	Capacity utilization	Rebuild performance	Disk failure performance	I/O performance
RAID10	**Best**	Poor	**Best**	**Best**	**Best**
RAID5	Good	**Best**	Poor	Poor	Poor
RAID6	Poor	Good	Poor	Poor	Poor

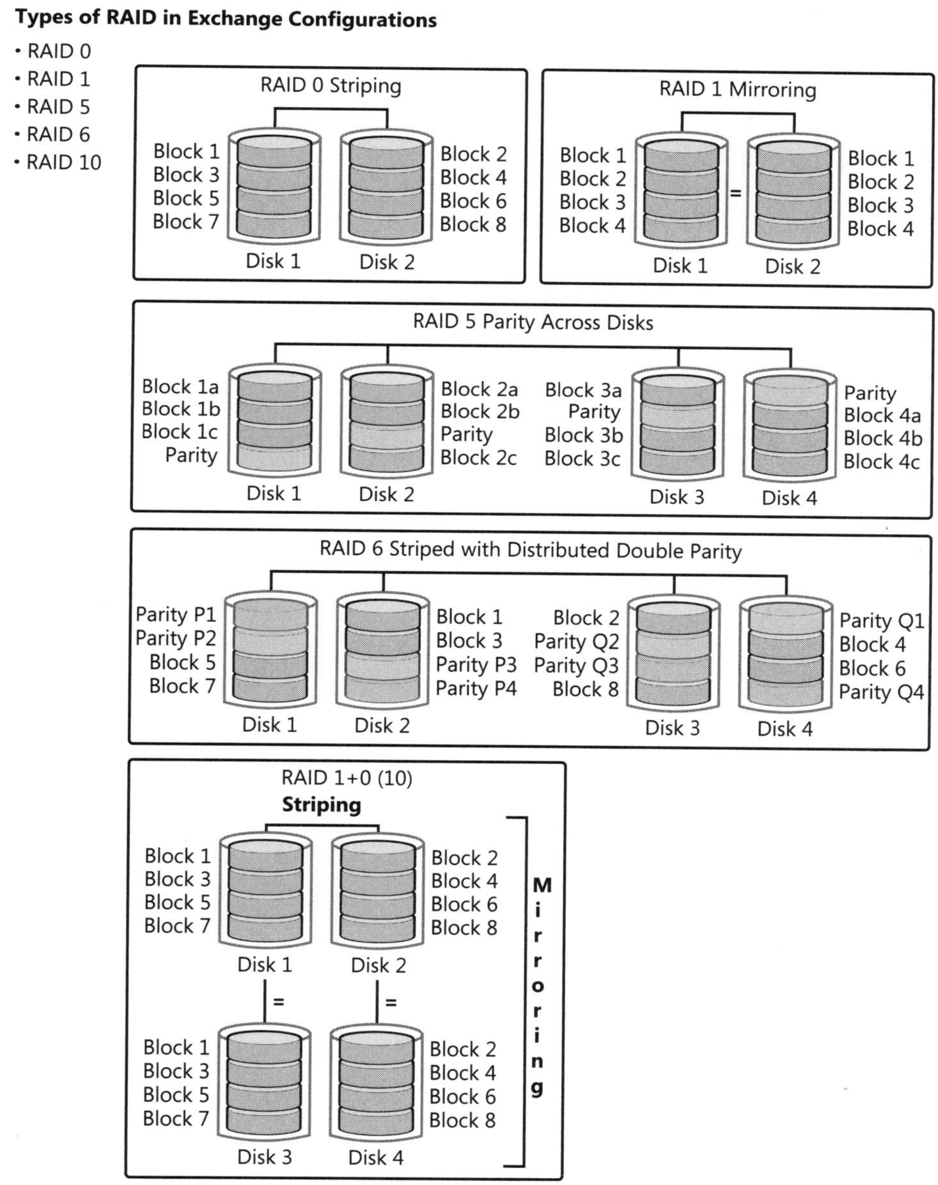

Types of RAID in Exchange Configurations

- RAID 0
- RAID 1
- RAID 5
- RAID 6
- RAID 10

RAID 0 Striping

Block 1
Block 3
Block 5
Block 7

Block 2
Block 4
Block 6
Block 8

Disk 1   Disk 2

RAID 1 Mirroring

Block 1
Block 2
Block 3
Block 4

=

Block 1
Block 2
Block 3
Block 4

Disk 1   Disk 2

RAID 5 Parity Across Disks

Block 1a
Block 1b
Block 1c
Parity

Block 2a
Block 2b
Parity
Block 2c

Block 3a
Parity
Block 3b
Block 3c

Parity
Block 4a
Block 4b
Block 4c

Disk 1   Disk 2   Disk 3   Disk 4

RAID 6 Striped with Distributed Double Parity

Parity P1
Parity P2
Block 5
Block 7

Block 1
Block 3
Parity P3
Parity P4

Block 2
Parity Q2
Parity Q3
Block 8

Parity Q1
Block 4
Block 6
Parity Q4

Disk 1   Disk 2   Disk 3   Disk 4

RAID 1+0 (10)
Striping

Block 1
Block 3
Block 5
Block 7

Block 2
Block 4
Block 6
Block 8

Disk 1   Disk 2

=   =

Block 1
Block 3
Block 5
Block 7

Block 2
Block 4
Block 6
Block 8

Disk 3   Disk 4

M i r r o r i n g

Figure 2-9 Popular RAID configurations

When you plan storage for your Exchange servers, you should consider the function of that server and the acceptable I/O latency for that function. Table 2-4 outlines some RAID configuration recommendations based on function.

Table 2-4   RAID Configuration Recommendations

Data	RAID
Logs	RAID 1 or RAID 10
Databases with large-capacity disks	RAID 10
High-speed and smaller-capacity disks	RAID 5
To meet capacity requirements with fewer physical disks	RAID 10

In short, transaction logs are the most important data set. Because of this, you should invest in good write latency to obtain optimal server performance. Remember that your database location should be on a different set of disks than the transaction logs.

In Exchange 2007, Microsoft shifted the number of database writes as a percentage of database I/O. Because of this, RAID 5 configurations perform worse in Exchange 2007 than they did in Exchange Server 2003. If you are moving from an Exchange Server 2003 configuration to an Exchange 2007 configuration, you should rethink your database storage strategies, especially if they are based on RAID 5. Another negative factor for RAID 5—and this is similar for RAID 6—is the rebuild performance. When a disk crashes, you can replace it and have the RAID system rebuild it from parity data. The problem is that this has a very heavy impact on performance. If this occurs during daily Exchange usage, your end users will take a significant performance hit and—you guessed it—you will be getting all of the irate telephone calls. To avoid this, rethink your RAID strategies for Exchange Server 2007.

MORE INFO   The Microsoft Exchange Solution Reviewed Program (ESRP)

Because storage is so critical to the proper operation of Exchange, Microsoft has put together a testing and solution publishing program for Exchange. The program uses a testing engine (Jetstress) along with solution guidelines to validate third-party storage solutions. Each solution that passes this test is listed in the ESRP. For a list of available solutions, go to *http://technet.microsoft.com/en-us/exchange/bb412164.aspx*.

Select Disk Sets for Exchange   Finally, when you select disk sets for Exchange Server 2007, keep the following factors in mind:

- Serial ATA disks are much less expensive than SCSI disks, but should only be used in Exchange configurations that have low volume and a minimal number of users. If you want the best in performance, do not use this type of disk.

- Serial Attached SCSI (SAS) disks support high-performance disks. Smaller disk sizes will provide the best speeds and may be ideal for Exchange Server 2007.

- Internet SCSI (iSCSI) is the only network-based storage that is supported by Exchange 2007. Make sure you completely isolate all iSCSI traffic from all other network traffic. iSCSI is network-based, but it is focused on disk traffic, not network traffic.

- Fibre Channel provides high-speed access to remote storage, but to make the most of Fibre Channel with Exchange Server 2007, you may need to request assistance from your storage vendor to ensure that it is properly configured to give you the best performance levels.

With Exchange 2007, Microsoft removed all support for network-attached storage (NAS) devices. NAS was supported for Exchange Server 2003, which could mean a redesign of your storage strategy if you are upgrading from Exchange 2003 to Exchange 2007.

Plan for Exchange Storage Groups

Storage groups are the first units of storage that you need to deal with on a Mailbox Server role. Storage groups contain the databases and transaction logs that store user data within mailboxes. In Exchange 2007, the Standard Edition can contain up to 5 storage groups, while the Enterprise Edition can contain up to 50 storage groups. Each storage group can contain up to five databases. Databases within one storage group all share the same transaction logs.

NOTE Microsoft recommendation

Although a storage group can contain up to five databases, Microsoft recommends that you use one database for each storage group. In some cases, using one single database per storage group can speed I/O by storing all data in cache.

Storage Groups and Memory Requirements   Storage groups are used to segregate databases and logs into discrete administrative units. They are also designed to be used as the unit to back up and restoration operations. You design the number of storage groups you require based on the memory capacity of your server along with the number of databases you need. Table 2-5 outlines how many storage groups you should create based on the available memory on a server.

Table 2-5   Memory Requirements Per Storage Group

Number of storage groups	Required RAM
1–4	2 GB
5–8	4 GB
9–12	6 GB

Table 2-5   Memory Requirements Per Storage Group

Number of storage groups	Required RAM
13–16	8 GB
17–20	10 GB
21–24	12 GB
25–28	14 GB
29–32	16 GB
33–36	18 GB
37–40	20 GB
41–44	22 GB
45–48	24 GB
49–50	26 GB

IMPORTANT   MB role coexistence

The requirements of Table 2-5 assume that only the MB role is deployed on a server. If more roles are deployed, more RAM is required.

Storage groups are created and managed through the Exchange Management Console (EMC) or the Exchange Management Shell. Once created, groups can be moved to new disk sets. For example, when you first install Exchange Server 2007 you may or may not position the first storage group within the appropriate disk set. If you do not, you can correct the placement through the administrative tools. Use the same administrative tools to create new storage groups and position them in the right location (see Figure 2-10).

Plan Exchange Database Quantities

Determining the number of databases to generate is one of the most important decisions you will make when structuring the MB role. As time goes by, users will fill their mailboxes and reach the maximum quota you set for them. This means you need to delete an equivalent amount of mail from the mailboxes if users are to continue to receive mail. Deleted mail is moved to the database dumpster—a component that is

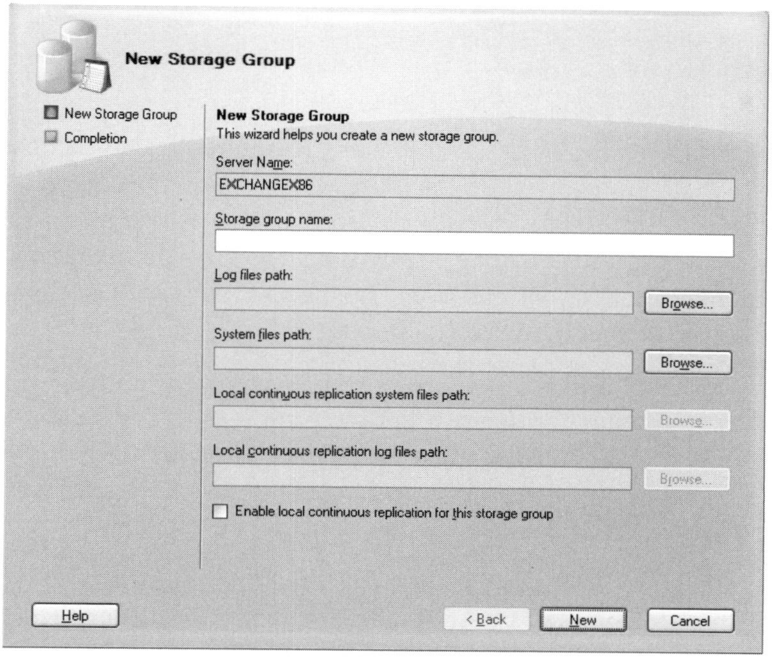

Figure 2-10   Creating and positioning a new storage group

designed to store deleted items for a period of 14 days. This also includes items that are removed from the Deleted Items folder in a user's mailbox. Because items are kept for 14 days, you need to accommodate this when you plan your database sizes and corresponding storage areas. When users reach their quota, it puts pressure on the dumpster because in addition to storing normally deleted items, it must also store the offset used to reduce mailbox sizes to fit under the quota. The dumpster will not be emptied until you perform maintenance on the database.

For example, take the following scenario. You have assigned a 500-MB mailbox to a user. The user receives 60 MB of mail per week. In a two-week period, the dumpster would contain 120 MB of mail. In addition, you will have white space—extra space that is within the database until defragmentation. White space accounts for about 10 percent of the mail you move in the dumpster. The user's total mailbox size will then be 644 MB. A database in the storage group that contained 100 of these mailboxes would therefore need 64.4 GB of space.

Formula for Database Sizing Calculations   Use the following formula when calculating database size:

```
Mailbox Size = MailboxQuota + Whitespace + (WeeklyIncomingMail*2)
```

For example:

```
MailboxSize = 2048MB + (12MB) + (60MB*2)
2180MB = 2048MB + 12MB + 120MB or 7% larger than the quota
```

Smaller databases are always better. Remember the non-replicated database recommendation of 100 GB. But using small databases can increase the complexity of your storage solution. Temper your decisions with acceptable performance and acceptable administrative overhead. You will not gain anything if you design a solution that gives the very best performance to your end users, but also requires your Exchange administrators to work day and night to keep it running.

Once you have determined your actual mailbox size using the preceding formula, you can move on to determining how many users you want to store per database. The easiest way to do this is to take the recommended database size (100 GB non-replicated or 200 GB replicated) and divide it by the average mailbox size. This gives you the number of users per database. Then, take the total number of users and divide it by the number of users per database. This gives you the number of databases you require.

Keep in mind that the smaller a database is, the faster it will be backed up and restored. This should also be a consideration in your final recommendations. Also, make sure that whatever you do, you size your storage areas or LUNs with sufficient space to store the database and allow for growth. Planning appropriate LUN capacity is absolutely critical: If the database reaches the maximum LUN size, it will automatically dismount. That will be cause for a few irate phone calls because all of the mailboxes within this database will become unavailable.

Plan Exchange Transaction Logs

Transaction logs are closely tied to databases. Each storage group has a single set of transaction logs no matter how many databases it contains. Transaction logs are used to record each operation performed by the database engine in Exchange Server. All transactions are written to the logs first, and then afterward written to the database. This is why you want your transaction log storage to be as fast as possible. Transaction logs in Exchange Server 2007 are now 1 MB in size; in previous versions, they were 5 MB. Having smaller logs makes it easier to replicate the data from one location to another to protect data.

Formula for Transaction Log Sizing Calculations You can estimate the number of transaction logs that will be generated on a per-mailbox basis. The number of transaction logs per mailbox depends on the expected load the mailbox use will generate on the server. Table 2-6, which is based on average message size of 50 KB, outlines the impact of different mailbox loads.

Table 2-6   Number of Transaction Logs per Mailbox

Mailbox Load	Message Traffic	Estimated Logs per Mailbox per Day
Light	5 sent/20 received	7
Average	10 sent/40 received	14
Heavy	20 sent/80 received	28
Very Heavy	30 sent/120 received	42

If your average message size is greater or smaller than the 50 KB estimate here, the number of logs will generally increase or decrease in parallel with the size of the message. For example, if your average message size is 100 KB, your increase will be about 1.9 times the numbers displayed in Table 2-6, and if the average message size is 200 KB, the number of transaction logs will be about 3.8 times the number listed in Table 2-6.

Best Practices for Transaction Log Disk Sizing   Use the following practices when sizing disk sets or LUNs for transaction logs:

1. Estimate how many transaction logs you will need.

   ❑ Determine the number of mailboxes in this storage group.

   ❑ Determine the traffic load and identify the number of transaction logs per mailbox per day.

   ❑ Determine how many days of transaction logs you intend to keep. Transaction logs are not cleared until a backup operation truncates them. For example, if you perform a full or incremental backup each night, the logs will be truncated each night. To be safe, you might reserve at least three days of space for logs in the event of an issue with a backup operation on one day. If you use differential instead of incremental backups, logs will not be truncated until a full backup is run. Keep this in mind in your estimates.

   ❑ If you move mailboxes from one storage group to another, you will need to reserve space for the operation. If you are migrating from an older Exchange structure to Exchange 2007, you will need to reserve additional space as well, because any move operation must be written to a transaction log before it is committed to the new database. Make sure you allocate enough space for this type of operation.

❑ Estimate an additional 20 percent over and above the number of transaction logs you expect to store on an ongoing basis.

2. Make sure the transaction logs are placed on a disk set that is separate from the database(s) in the same storage group.

3. Make sure that you use fast disks and the appropriate RAID strategy. The ideal RAID strategy is RAID 10.

The speed at which Exchange will read and write transaction logs will be the speed at which your servers will respond to end user requests. The faster the I/O on transaction log disk sets, the faster your end users' experience will be.

Plan Exchange Database and Transaction Log Locations

After you have designed and calculated the amount of storage you need for each mailbox in your network, you can create the databases and transaction log disk sets you will be using to store them. Remember that if possible, you should store a single database per storage group. This is why the Enterprise Edition supports 50 databases and 50 storage groups—one database per storage group. In addition, if you use a standard naming practice with your storage groups and databases, your administrators will have an easier time figuring out which files belong to which storage group.

Database and transaction log locations can be specified at the time that you create a new store. Remember that databases and transaction logs should be on their own disk sets for optimal performance. If for some reason, you did not assign a database or transaction log to the appropriate location when you created them, you can always move them at a later time through the Management Console (see Figure 2-11) or through the Exchange Management Shell.

Naming Practices for Storage Groups   When you create storage groups, you should endeavor to pair filenames with the group names. In very large Exchange environments, you will need to use multiple disk sets or LUNs to store all of the required storage groups. Because you will quickly run out of drive labels, you should rely on volume mount points to connect all of these disk sets. In this case, you should also use a naming convention for the mount points. Table 2-7 outlines how you can link storage groups, database, and mount points in an integrated naming strategy. It assumes that you will be using the M: drive as the anchor point for databases and the L: drive as the anchor point for logs.

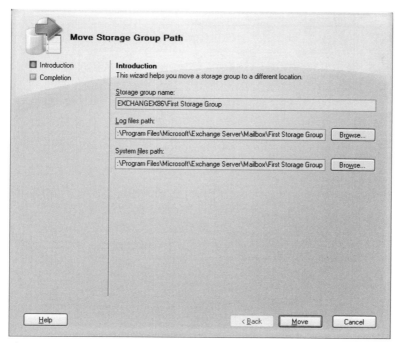

Figure 2-11   Moving a database and transaction log location in the Exchange Management Console

Table 2-7   Nomenclature for MB Storage

Storage Group	Database	DB Mount Point	Log Mount Point
StorageGroupOne	SGOneDB	M:\Storage GroupOne	L:\Storage GroupOne
StorageGroupTwo	SGTwoDB	M:\Storage GroupTwo	L:\Storage GroupTwo
StorageGroupThree	SGThreeDB	M:\Storage GroupThree	L:\Storage GroupThree

Each mount point links to a different drive set. This strategy will give you the ability to create up to 50 disk sets as long as your storage device supports this number of disk sets.

Best Practices for MB Storage and Disk Preparation   Table 2-8 outlines the best practices for planning MB role storage and preparing disks.

Table 2-8   Best Practices for MB Storage and Disk Preparation

Item	Configuration
Boot and System Disk Partitions	Boot and system partitions should be formatted with Master Boot Record (MBR) partitions. Other partition types are not supported.
Dedicated Disk Partition Creation	All dedicated x64 data disks should use MBR partitions.
Shared Disk Partition Creation	All shared x64 data disks should use GUID Partition Tables (GPT). GPT partitions can exceed 2 terabytes in size and can contain up to 128 primary partitions. GPT partitions also add some level of reliability.
Partition Alignment	All partitions should be created with the Diskpart.exe tool so that they can be sector-aligned on the disks. Use the storage vendor's recommendation for track boundary recommendation. If a recommendation is not available, use 64 KB.
Database Disk Partitions	Use NTFS volumes with an NTFS allocation unit size of 64 KB. This provides performance improvements on large sequential reads.
Transaction Log Partitions	Use the default 4-KB NTFS allocation unit size on transaction log disks because no benefit is seen from larger units.
Disk Set or LUN Assignment	Assign one disk set for databases and another for transaction logs. If you store one database per storage group, you have two disk sets per storage group. Create only one aligned partition per disk set.

Table 2-8   Best Practices for MB Storage and Disk Preparation

Item	Configuration
Drive Letter Assignment	If you assign two disk sets per storage group and you want to use the maximum 50 storage groups, you will exceed the number of available drive letters. Rely on volume mount points instead.
Database Disk Set Capacity	Always allocate at least 20 percent more space in your database disk set than your best database size estimate.
	Allocate five percent more for content indexing.
	Allocate the database size plus ten percent for database maintenance such as compaction.
	Calculate the database dumpster size based on your message delivery rates and add the required amount of space to your disk set.
Direct-attached Storage (DAS)	If you plan to implement Exchange Server 2007's high availability features, such as Cluster Continuous Replication, you may be able to increase performance by using direct-attached storage rather than any form of storage area network because DAS often provides better performance.
Storage Groups	Create storage groups as you need them, but store only a single database per storage group if possible. This facilitates administration and can help speed performance.

Plan Storage for non-MB Roles

Other roles also need storage because each role has its own particular storage requirements. Remember that transport servers—both Edge and Hub—are designed to transfer mail in and out of the organization and in and out of the MB, and to transfer voice messages from UM to mailboxes. Client Access Servers act as the access point for client protocols, especially Internet protocols. Unified Messaging Servers are designed to support Outlook Voice Access and incoming faxes.

If you install each of these roles on different servers, you will need to plan appropriate storage for each role. If you install these roles on the same server as the MB role, you need to plan additional storage for each role.

When installed on a different server, the CAS role is designed to offload tasks from the MB. It also provides a single namespace for all users to connect to no matter which MB holds the mailbox. Basically, CAS is a broker that links client connections to the appropriate mailbox. Its highest requirements are on CPU, memory, and network throughput. As such, it has little need for storage, but these can impact performance. For example, the CAS can log all protocols. You may decide to enable protocol logging for specific protocols, for example, to identify whether you are experiencing attacks from the Internet. Protocol logging is a sequential write. If you enable protocol logging, it should be directed to a separate disk set.

CAS servers can also perform content conversion. All content is converted within the server's TMP folder within a pure Exchange 2007 environment. If your mailboxes are located on Exchange Server 2003, conversion is performed on the mailbox server and its configuration should take this into account. If you are using the CAS to convert content, move the TMP folder to a separate disk set than the paging file and the operating system.

Transport servers are the Exchange Server gateways. Their role is to manage all SMTP transmissions. Although both Edge and Hub Transport Servers manage message traffic, they each have their own roles. The ET is designed to provide message hygiene, stopping all spam and virus-infected mail at the gate and ensuring that only appropriate messages enter your network. The HT is the message router, categorizing all clean mail and delivering it to the proper MB and the proper mailbox. Their storage requirements depend on the amount of mail they need to manage. Both have the same requirement types.

All mail is stored within an ESE database within a mail.que file. Ideally, this database will be on a separate disk set from the transaction logs. Transaction logs will use a sequential write and need the fastest disk structure you can provide for them. Rely on the recommendations for MB transaction logs to prepare disk sets for the Transport server role. This server role can also perform protocol logging as well as message tracking. Agents, which are .NET Framework code designed to customize transport rules, can also log events. Rely on the preceding recommendations for the CAS role to position these logs.

The Hub Transport Server role also performs content conversion because every message that comes in from the Internet is converted to MAPI prior to delivery. This occurs in the server's TMP folder. Rely on the recommendations for the CAS role to position this folder on a separate disk set.

The Edge Transport Server role, because of its exposure to the Internet, can log much more information than the HT. Therefore, you should ensure that you have considerably more space for log storage on this server than on the HT server.

The Unified Messaging Server role does not have quite the same requirements as the other roles in terms of storage, but it does perform content conversion. Each call that comes through the UM is transformed through the voice mail storage codec (for coding and decoding of digital data into an audio or streaming audio file format). The UM uses two different types of codecs: One is used between the IP gateways and one is used to encode voice messages. The Windows Media Audio (WMA), Group System Mobile (GSM), and G.711 Pulse Code Modulation (PCM) linear audio codecs are used to create .wma or .wav audio files for voice messages. The WMA codec creates audio files in .wma format; the other two use the .wav format. Creating these files means writing to disk and then reading from the disk to pick up the voice message and transfer it to the appropriate mailbox. When planning for UM storage, you should use the same strategies as described earlier to move the TMP folder to a faster disk system to ensure that this translation is performed as fast as possible.

Practice: Plan Storage Group Configurations

In this practice, which consists of a single exercise, you will learn how to move and otherwise control mailbox databases and logs. Using the best practice, you will store only one database per storage group.

▶ Exercise: Move a Mailbox Storage Group

When you first install Exchange Server, it automatically creates the First Storage Group in the default path where the Exchange binaries are installed on drive C:. This is obviously not a best practice. Therefore, you need to move the database and log files to proper disk partitions. You move databases either through the Exchange Management Shell or through the Exchange Management Console. In this exercise, you will use the Exchange Management Console.

To complete the exercise, follow these steps:

1. Log on to the ExchangeOne.treyresearch.net server using local administrator credentials.

2. Launch the Exchange Management Console by clicking Start | Menu | All Programs | Microsoft Exchange Server 2007 | Exchange Management Console.

3. Expand the Server Configuration section in the tree pane of the console.

4. Click Mailbox.

5. Once the mailbox section has been updated in the details pane, right-click First Storage Group and select Move Storage Group Path to open the Move Storage Group Path dialog box.

6. Note that you cannot change the name of the storage group. Move to the Log Files Path section and click Browse. Navigate to the E: drive and click Make New Folder. Call the new folder **FSGLogs** (for First Storage Group Logs) and click OK.

7. Move to the System Files Path and click Browse. Navigate to the D: drive and click Make New Folder. Call the new folder **FSGTemp** (for First Storage Group Database) and click OK.

    You have now moved the temporary database files and are ready to move the storage group.

8. Click Move. The Console will generate the PowerShell script required for the move and perform the actual move.

9. Exchange warns you that moving the database and logs will automatically render them inaccessible for a temporary period. Click Yes.

10. When the operation is complete, Exchange will display the actual Windows PowerShell script used to move the storage group contents. Copy this script by pressing Ctrl+C.

11. Launch Notepad by clicking Start | Menu | All Programs | Accessories | Notepad. Paste the cmdlet into Notepad and save it in your my Documents folder. Call it **Move Storage Group.txt.**

12. In the Move Storage Group Path dialog box, click Finish.

    You are now ready to move the actual database files.

13. Right-click the Mailbox Database in the details pane and select Move Database Path to open the Move Database Path dialog box.

14. Click Browse, navigate to drive D:, and click Make New Folder. Name the new folder **FSGDB**. After you create the folder, select it and click Open.

15. Click Save to save the database into this path.

16. Click Move to move the database.

17. Exchange warns you that moving the database will automatically render it inaccessible for a temporary period. Click Yes.

18. When done, Exchange will display the actual Windows PowerShell script used to move the storage group contents. Copy this script by pressing Ctrl+C.

19. Paste the cmdlet into Notepad at the end of the previous cmdlet and save it again. Close Notepad when you are finished.

20. Click Finish to close the Move Database Path dialog box.

    You can reuse this cmdlet if you have to move the First Storage Group and database on other servers.

Note that the details pane now displays the new database path.

Quick Check

1. How many databases should you host per storage group?

2. What kind of partition table should you use with partitions that will host storage groups?

3. Which tool should you use to prepare partitions if you want to maximize performance for Exchange?

4. Should databases and transaction logs share disk sets?

5. In large implementations, how should you configure access to multiple disk sets?

Quick Check Answers

1. Ideally, you will host a single database per storage group because the storage group provides a unit of administration as well as backup and recovery.

2. Exchange 2007 is an x64 application. As such, it runs on x64 operating systems, which can work with different partition types and larger disk sets. The partition you use depends on the type of storage. Dedicated or direct-attached storage should use Master Boot Record partitions. Shared partitions should use GUID Partition Tables because they give access to larger partition sizes.

3. All partitions should be prepared with Diskpart.exe to properly align the partitions' sectors with those on the disk. Formatting with the graphical

Disk Management tool does not support sector alignment. Sector-aligned disks can increase performance by up to 20 percent.

4. Transaction logs and databases should not share disk sets. Transaction logs require frequent reads and writes—therefore, they need very fast sequential access disks. Databases only write after the transaction logs are committed to them. To improve performance each should be assigned to separate disk sets. With the practice of one database per storage set, you will have two disk sets per storage group.

5. Disk sets should be accessed through volume mount points because there are not enough drive letters for complex storage implementations. Exchange Enterprise Edition can host up to 50 storage groups. With two disk sets per storage group, this could mean more than 100 disk sets. Using drive letters would be insufficient to meet the requirements.

Lesson 2: Plan the Deployment of Required Exchange Services

Estimated lesson time: 50 minutes

Now that you understand how to store mailboxes, you need to identify how mail will transit from server to server. In addition, you need to identify how Outlook clients will connect to their mailboxes. Another key aspect of client connections is calendaring; it is important to understand how users can access this important feature. In previous versions of Exchange Server, this feature was mostly called free/busy data, but has been renamed in Exchange Server 2007.

Exchange Additional Service Overview

Connectivity features deal with all of the server roles; client connectivity deals specifically with the Client Access Server role. Mail flow and transport are the cornerstone of any messaging system, which is why connectivity is an important aspect of this exam.

Review Client Access Server Features

The Client Access Server role is designed to provide front-end services to client access points, including:

- Accessing your Exchange profile through a Web browser with Outlook Web Access.

- Accessing mail and other Exchange features through a Windows Mobile device through Exchange ActiveSync. If your clients are running Windows Mobile 5 and the Messaging and Security Feature Pack (MSFP), or if they are using Windows Mobile 6, you can also configure ActiveSync for Direct Push—keeping the device continuously synchronized with the Exchange server.

- Accessing programmatic messaging services through Exchange Web Services.

- Providing the access point for the Post Office Protocol (POP) version 3 and Internet Message Access Protocol version 4 revision 1 (IMAP4) messaging.

- Accessing the Autodiscover service—the service that lets Outlook clients automatically create connections to their Exchange server and mailbox.

- In pure Exchange Server 2007 environments, Autodiscover also supports the Availability Service—the service that provides free/busy data to end users.

Of all of these services and features, two are required in any Exchange implementation: Autodiscover and Availability. All other services and features are optional and are implemented only if they are required in your organization.

IMPORTANT   Install Internet Information Services

Because of the features it offers, CAS requires the installation of Internet Information Services (IIS) version 6.0. Several of the CAS features are actually Web features that must be configured in IIS to operate properly.

Implement the Autodiscover Service

The Autodiscover service is based on a virtual directory that is created in IIS under the default Web site. This service is designed to respond to requests from Outlook 2007. In fact, when clients are using Outlook 2007, they rely on this service to automatically locate their server and configure their settings from both within and outside of the internal network if the service is published to the Internet. To do this, clients use the Auto Account Setup Wizard in Outlook 2007 (see Figure 2-12). During this process, the client connects to the Autodiscover Web site based on Domain Name Service (DNS) records it locates and then uses the information provided by the Web site to automatically configure the Exchange Server settings on the client. The DNS lookup is based on the user's e-mail address—which is also the e-mail domain name—as entered in the Auto Account Setup dialog box.

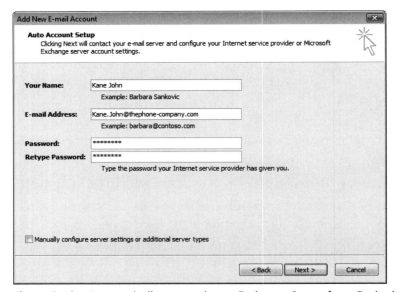

Figure 2-12   Automatically connecting to Exchange Server from Outlook 2007

Auto Account Setup begins by performing an encrypted search for connection settings. If the encrypted communication does not work, Setup tries an unencrypted lookup. Of course, if the user mistypes her e-mail address, the service will not work and the client will get an error message (see Figure 2-13). This will also occur if the Autodiscover service is misconfigured. In this case, the user has two choices: either review the settings she typed and correct the error if it is on her end, or manually configure the service by selecting a check box in the dialog box.

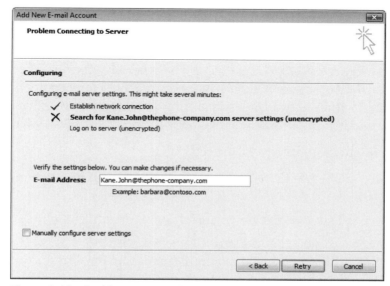

Figure 2-13   Problems connecting to the Exchange server

Autodiscover is a boon when it is properly configured because it saves you from having to provide complex settings to users to connect to the server. It also greatly facilitates the connection process to the point where most users can do it themselves without additional assistance.

When properly configured, Autodiscover will provide the following information to systems running Outlook 2007:

- User display name
- Separate connection settings for internal and external connectivity
- Location of the user's Mailbox Server
- Uniform Resource Locators (URLs) for various Outlook features that control free/busy information, unified messaging, and offline address book
- Outlook Anywhere server settings—the connection type that allows secure communication between clients and servers over HTTP

If any of the user settings are changed, such as if the user's mailbox is moved from one MB to another, Autodiscover will automatically update the user's profile.

IMPORTANT   Outlook and Autodiscover

Autodiscover only works with Outlook version 2007. If your users are running an earlier version of Outlook, they will have to use manual service configurations. Autodiscover will also work with some mobile devices—mostly those running Windows Mobile version 6.

Autodiscover Requirements   To be able to rely on the Autodiscover service, you must have at least one CAS role deployed in your Exchange organization. This is one reason why the minimal Exchange installation to support an organization running e-mail depends on three key roles: MB, HT, and CAS. The other two roles are often deemed optional. Because the Autodiscover service relies on a service connection point that is created and stored within Active Directory during installation, the Active Directory schema must be updated prior to the installation of the first CAS role in your network.

Autodiscover configuration has several aspects:

- Autodiscover can be used internally for all client configurations running Outlook 2007.
- Autodiscover can support Exchange organizations spanning multiple forests.
- Autodiscover can support moving mailboxes from one MB to another, from one site to another, from one domain to another, and from one forest to another.
- Autodiscover can be used externally to configure clients automatically.

Each configuration builds on the settings of the base configuration to work.

Autodiscover is based on three key services: DNS, Active Directory, and IIS. DNS is used to locate the e-mail domain and identify the configuration file for the Exchange settings. Active Directory contains the Service Connection Point (SCP) that will contain the URLs for Autodiscover operation. IIS hosts the Autodiscover Web site and makes it available for users when needed.

Connect to the Autodiscover Service   In the internal network, DNS plays a slightly different role. It is used to locate Active Directory servers that contain the SCP object. The SCP object contains the *ServiceBindingInfo* attribute that includes the FQDN of the CAS location. For example, in Figure 2-12 earlier in this chapter, this location would be in the form of *https://CAS01.thephone-company.com/autodiscover/autodiscover.xml* given that the CAS role's name was CAS01. Then, once Active Directory is located, the Autodiscover process can proceed (see Figure 2-14). Note that connection settings are returned through a secure HTTP connection (HTTPS). This means that

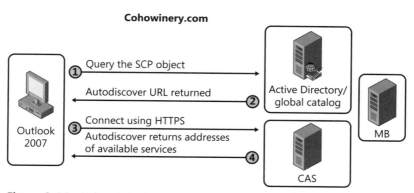

Figure 2-14   Using Autodiscover in an internal network

you must have a valid Secure Sockets Layer (SSL) certificate on the Web server host-ing the CAS role. This certificate must be trusted by the Outlook clients for the oper-ation to work. The entire operation is performed using the client's authentication credentials to perform the initial lookup in Active Directory.

This process is slightly different when connecting to Autodiscover from the Internet (see Figure 2-15). Once again, the client tries to locate the SCP in Active Directory, but because the client is outside the firewall and cannot contact the directory service, this query will fail. The fallback query is to identify the location of the Autodiscover Web site from a DNS server. Because this query is to DNS, it is unencrypted. The query includes the cli-ent's e-mail domain. For example, in Figure 2-12, the e-mail domain is *thephone-company .com*. DNS responds with the address of the Autodiscover service, which in the case of Figure 2-12 would be either *https://thephone-company.com/autodiscover/autodiscover .xml* or *https://autodiscover.thephone-company.com/autodiscover/autodiscover.xml*.

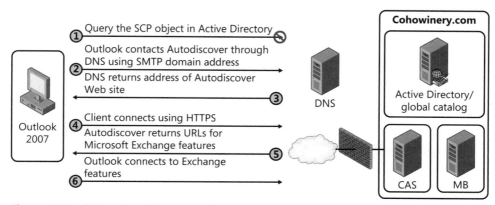

Figure 2-15   Using Autodiscover on the Internet

Configure Autodiscover for Internal Networks   As you can see, several critical compo-nents make this process work. First, the appropriate entries must be found in DNS for both internal and external connections. Second, in internal connections, the SCP must be properly configured. In an ideal scenario, you would include more than one CAS role in your network to support failures and provide high availability. Third, you must make sure users have the access rights to read the SCP object in Active Directory. This is performed by applying read permissions to the Authenticated Users group to this object. Fourth, you must have the appropriate certificate on the CAS role. This certificate must be trusted by your client systems—both internal and external. Ideally, this will be a certificate purchased from a public certificate authority (CA) so that it is automatically trusted by all clients. By default, Exchange uses self-signed certificates that are not trusted by your clients. And finally, your Exchange services must be properly configured on the CAS role otherwise clients may be able to access their mailbox, but will not be able to access any additional service such as the Availability Service.

The process becomes even more complex when you want to configure Autodiscover in more complex environments. For example, in a Standard or Large Organization, both of which will include multiple Active Directory sites, you will need to configure site affinity—identifying which sites clients should connect to based on their current location.

All configuration changes to the SCP object are performed through a standard Exchange cmdlet: **Set-ClientAccessServer**. For example, if you wanted all of the clients in site A to connect to this site and all clients in site B to connect to site B at Lucerne Publishing, you would use the following commands either on a CAS computer or on a computer running the Exchange Management Tools; CAS roles are named by site:

```
Set-ClientAccessServer -Identity "CASSiteA" -AutodiscoverServiceInternalURI
"https://lucernepublishing.com/autodiscover/autodiscover.xml"
AutodiscoverSiteScope "SiteA"
Set-ClientAccessServer -Identity "CASSiteB" -AutodiscoverServiceInternalURI
"https://lucernepublishing.com/autodiscover/autodiscover.xml"
AutodiscoverSiteScope "SiteB"
```

In short, the two values you need to modify in the command are the server names and the site names. This command must be performed with appropriate credentials. You must be a member of the Exchange Server Administrators group as well as have local administrative access to the CAS roles you want to include in the affinity.

If you do not configure affinity, Outlook will randomly select the CAS and may obtain information over slower connections instead of through faster LAN connections.

MORE INFO   Affinity configuration

For more information on affinity configuration, go to *http://technet.microsoft.com/en-ca/library/aa998575.aspx.*

If your Exchange organization is a Complex Organization that spans multiple forests, you need to properly configure the Autodiscover service in every forest. If you rely on an Exchange Resource Forest, you must create the SCP pointer in the Active Directory forest that includes the user accounts. This pointer will include the URL of the Resource Forest. To do so, you need to rely on the **Export-AutoDiscoveryConfig** cmdlet. Run it in the Resource Forest to obtain the proper settings to implement in your user account forest.

IMPORTANT Exchange Resource Forest

Do not use an Exchange Resource Forest if you can help it. Resource Forests have very heavy administrative overhead because they do not include any synchronization mechanism with the User Account Forest.

If you rely on a multiple trusted forest topology, you must configure Autodiscover in each of the forests. Once again, you run the **Export-AutoDiscoveryConfig** cmdlet in each forest that includes Exchange Server 2007 and use the exported information to properly configure the settings in each user account forest. For example, to run the command in Forest A to enable access to Forest B, you would use the following command. Make sure you use an account that is a member of the local administrators group on each CAS role as well as a member of the Exchange Server Administrators group in each forest. This command assumes that the domain controllers are named after the forest they reside in and that the command is performed with Forest A as the source forest.

```
Export-AutoDiscoverConfig -DomainController DCForestA -TargetForestDomainController DCForestB
```

If you intend to move mailboxes and user accounts from one forest to the other, you will need to make sure the Autodiscover service is properly configured in each forest first. Then, when you perform the move, you will need to create a mail contact in the source forest. This contact will have the same name as the original user account in the source forest. When the client tries to access mail in the new forest with the new account, it will be redirected to the mail contact in the original forest. At this point, Autodiscover will reconfigure Outlook 2007 on the client computer to obtain mail from the new forest.

MORE INFO Multi-forest mailbox moves

For more information on multi-forest mailbox moves, go to *http://technet.microsoft.com/en-ca/library/bb201665.aspx*.

When you configure Autodiscover for Internet access, you must use a valid and trusted SSL certificate on the CAS role. This server certificate must have two key values: a common name and a subject alternative name. For example, for Lucerne Publishing, the names would be:

■ The common name should be mail.lucernepublishing.com.

■ The subject alternative name should be autodiscover.lucernepublishing.com.

You must also make sure your additional Exchange services are properly configured before Autodiscover can provide external URLs to access them. Finally, if your internal services use different names than the external services, you must include them in the certificate as well.

Configure Autodiscover for External Networks   If you give users access to your CAS from outside your network, you should configure a separate Web site to host the Autodiscover service. This segregates it from your other Exchange services and does not use the same site as the mail access provided by the CAS. This is also recommended when your external Web site address is the same as your e-mail domain (for example, lucernepublishing.com) and the Web site has fairly heavy traffic. Use the following steps to prepare this second site:

1. Move the Autodiscover service to a new site. Do this with the **New-AutodiscoverVirtualDirectory** cmdlet. See *http://technet.microsoft.com/en-us/library/aa99 6418.aspx* for detailed steps for this operation. You use the following basic cmdlet structure:

   ```
   New-AutodiscoverVirtualDirectory –Websitename Websitename –BasicAuthentication:$true
   –WindowsAuthentication:$true
   ```

2. Obtain and configure a server SSL certificate with both a common name and a subject alternative name.

3. Update the SCP object in Active Directory to point to the alternative Web site you created in step 1. Use the **Set-ClientAccessServer** cmdlet.

4. Configure additional Exchange services such as the Offline Address Book and the Availability Service. (See the instructions in the "Configure the Availability Service" later in this chapter.)

Configure Autodiscover for Hosted Environments   Autodiscover is also available externally for Simple and Standard Organizations that do not have their own perimeter networks or even for organizations that do not have their own networks at all. This is done through hosted environments (see Figure 2-16). In hosted environments, multiple e-mail services are hosted within the same servers. Because of this, you must create multiple Autodiscover Web sites on the IIS server and redirect the appropriate service to the appropriate e-mail domain name.

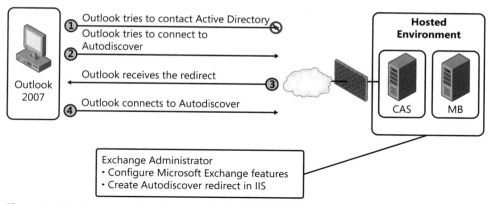

Figure 2-16   Accessing Autodiscover through a hosted service

In hosted environments, you do not need to use SSL certificates for redirected sites because all communication is performed on port 80, which is unencrypted. Use IIS Manager to configure the redirection for each e-mail domain. When you configure redirection, you must use anonymous access and disable authenticated access. Do not configure other options such as The Exact URL Entered Above, A Directory Below URL Entered, and A Permanent Redirection For This Resource. Configuring redirection in this manner ensures that the Outlook 2007 client will receive an HTTP 302 response.

This is because at first, Outlook tries to make an encrypted connection. Because there is no SSL certificate and therefore no connection on port 443, the connection fails (see Figure 2-17). When this happens, Outlook tries to obtain the information over

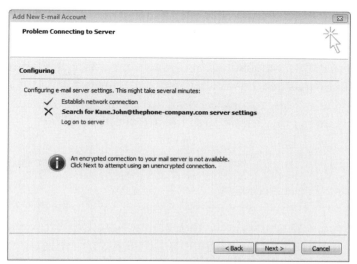

Figure 2-17   Encrypted connection failure with hosted environments

port 80 in unencrypted format (see Figure 2-18). No user information is sent over this open connection. IIS will then redirect the request and send the appropriate HTTPS response. At this point, the communication will be encrypted and will rely on the SSL certificate to provide configuration information to the endpoint.

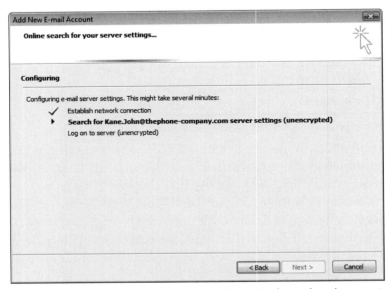

Figure 2-18   Unencrypted connection attempt to hosted environment

As you can see, there is a close link between DNS, Active Directory, IIS, and the Autodiscover service no matter which scenario you deploy them in.

Availability Service

In pure Exchange Server 2007 and Outlook 2007 environments, calendaring information or information known as free/busy data is provided through the Availability Service. This is a significant change from previous incarnations of Exchange Server because free/busy data was provided through the use of public folders.

Exam Tip   Note that in a pure Exchange Server 2007 and Outlook 2007 environment, you do not need public folders to provide free/busy data. It is provided by the Availability Service linked with Autodiscover. This is sure to be on the exam.

Accessibility is provided to Outlook clients through the Autodiscover service. In fact, the Availability Service is one of the additional Client Access Server services that must be configured once Autodiscover has been configured for the type of Exchange

Organization you intend to run. When the Availability Service is properly set up, clients access the Exchange Calendar directly and do not need to perform public folder lookups to locate free/busy information.

The Availability Service at Work   When Outlook 2007 clients access the Availability Service, several events occur:

- First, the client locates the Autodiscover service and this service returns the URL for the Availability Service.

- When Outlook has the URL, it connects to the CAS that provides the service.

- If the target mailbox is in the same Active Directory site, the CAS uses MAPI over RPC to obtain the free/busy data from the MB that holds the mailbox.

- If this is a multi-site organization and the target mailbox is in another site, the CAS makes an HTTPS connection to the CAS in the other site. In the remote site, the CAS will use MAPI over RPC to obtain the free/busy data from the target mailbox on the MB where the mailbox resides, then send this information back to the original CAS over HTTPS.

- The original CAS then provides the data to Outlook.

Users can rely on the Availability Service to share calendaring information at multiple levels. They control how much information will be provided to the Availability Service when other users request it. They can share:

- Nothing
- Only free/busy data
- More detail, including subject, location, and time of a meeting
- Full calendar details

Though the Availability Service is server-based, it is users who control just how much information the service can access when others request it.

Accessing the Availability Service   The Availability Service can be accessed directly through Outlook 2007 or through the Outlook Web Access Scheduling Assistant. When accessed, the service provides the following abilities:

- Retrieve live free/busy data for Exchange 2007 mailboxes
- Retrieve live free/busy data from Exchange servers in other forests
- Access legacy free/busy data from public folders in organizations running older versions of Exchange Server or for clients using older versions of Outlook

- View attendee working hours
- Show meeting time suggestions

IMPORTANT Outlook versions and free/busy data

Only Outlook 2007 and OWA 2007 can access the Availability Service. All other versions of Outlook or OWA must access free/busy data from public folders.

If your organization should have the need to run either older versions of Outlook or older versions of Exchange in a coexistence mode—Exchange Server 2007 with older versions or Outlook 2007 with older versions—you will still be able to access free/busy data for all systems. Exchange 2007 mailboxes using the Outlook 2007 client will publish free/busy data to both the Availability Service (for new systems) and to a public folder (for legacy systems).

Accessing Free/Busy Data in Mixed Topologies   Table 2-9 outlines how Exchange and Outlook can work together to provide free/busy data in mixed client or server topologies running in a single forest.

Table 2-9   Accessing Free/Busy Data in Mixed Topologies

Client	Logged in Mailbox	Target Mailbox	Free/Busy Retrieval
Outlook 2007	Exchange 2007	Exchange 2007	The Availability Service reads free/busy data from the target mailbox.
Outlook 2007	Exchange 2007	Exchange 2003	The Availability Service uses HTTP connections to the /public virtual directory of the Exchange 2003 mailbox.
Outlook 2003	Exchange 2007	Exchange 2007	Free/busy data will be published in local public folders.
Outlook 2003	Exchange 2007	Exchange 2003	Free/busy data will be published in local public folders.

Table 2-9   Accessing Free/Busy Data in Mixed Topologies

Client	Logged in Mailbox	Target Mailbox	Free/Busy Retrieval
Outlook Web Access 2007	Exchange 2007	Exchange 2007	OWA 2007 uses the Scheduling Assistant to call the Availability Service API to read free/busy data from the target mailbox.
Outlook Web Access 2007	Exchange 2007	Exchange 2003	OWA 2007 uses the Scheduling Assistant to call the Availability Service API to make an HTTP connection to the /public virtual directory of Exchange 2003 mailbox.
Any Client	Exchange 2003	Exchange 2007	Free/busy data is published in local public folders.

Exam Tip   Learn Table 2-9 well. The exam is bound to have questions about accessing free/busy data in mixed topologies.

Configure the Availability Service   The Availability Service is a Web Service that is installed and activated by default on Exchange Server 2007 installations. In fact, it is installed when you deploy the CAS role in your organization. Outlook 2007 uses the Autodiscover service to discover the URL that links it to the Availability Service. Depending on your deployment of the Autodiscover service, you may or may not have both an internal and an external URL listed and available through Autodiscover. If you do deploy both internal and external access, you should use different URLs for each to increase the security of the service.

You can—though this is not recommended—configure the external and internal addresses of the Availability Service to use the same Web site. In this case, your internal and external DNS server entries must point to this single Web site. For example, at Lucerne Publishing, Web site addresses for both the CAS and for Autodiscover would be mail.lucernepublishing.com and autodiscover.lucernepublishing.com respectively.

You cannot configure the Availability Service through the Exchange Management Console in multiple forest topologies. Instead, you must use the **Set-WebServices VirtualDirectory** cmdlet. In most cases, the only time you need to use this command is if you want to provide high availability for the service, such as making a member of a server farm running the Network Load Balancing (NLB) service—a service that allows multiple identical Web sites to respond to the same requests.

Exam Tip   Be sure to remember that you must use the Exchange Management Shell, not the Console to configure the Availability Service in multiple forest topologies.

Configure the Availability Service for Multiple Forest Access   Another instance where you need to modify the configuration of the Availability Service is when you use a Complex Organization that links multiple forests together. If all forests rely only on Exchange Server 2007 and Outlook 2007, the Availability Service is the only method of accessing free/busy data. In this topology several configurations are possible:

■ Forests can be trusted or untrusted.

■ Free/busy data can be on a per-user or per-organization basis.

■ Per-user free/busy data is only available between fully trusted forests.

■ When configured on a per-user basis in trusted forests, the Availability Service can make free/busy data requests across forests on behalf of a particular user.

■ When configured on a per-user basis in trusted forests, users in one forest can grant detailed free/busy data or even delegate access to a calendar to a user in another forest.

■ In untrusted forests, you configure the Availability Service on a per-organization basis.

■ With organization-wide free/busy data, the Availability Service can only make cross-forest requests on behalf of an organization as a whole. This returns only default free/busy data. Free/busy data cannot be configured to provide more extensive information.

■ Before you can use the Availability Service in any cross-forest configuration, trusted or untrusted, you must configure Global Address List (GAL) Synchronization using the GALSync feature of either Microsoft Identity Integration Server or the Identity Integration Feature Pack.

- If any clients use legacy versions of Outlook, such as Outlook 2003, you must also configure Inter-Organization Replication (IORepl) to synchronize free/busy data between forests.

- To configure the Availability Service to provide cross-forest information, you must have Exchange Organization Administrator access rights.

Once you have decided which configuration you want to use, you can proceed to the modification of your Availability Service configuration. Two commands are required in either situation. In the case of trusted forests—Wingtip Toys and Tailspin Toys in this example—use the following commands to configure per-user availability. To configure bidirectional availability, you run two command sets: you run the first set on a CAS in the target forest (Wingtip Toys) and you run the second set on a CAS in the source forest (Tailspin Toys).

Run these commands in the Wingtip Toys forest:

```
Get-ClientAccessServer | Add-ADPermission -Accessrights Extendedright -Extendedrights
"ms-Exch- EPI-Token-Serialization" -User "TailspinToys.com\Client Access servers"
Add-AvailabilityAddressSpace -Forestname TailspinToys.com -AccessMethod PerUserFB
-UseServiceAccount:$true
```

Run these commands in the Tailspin Toys forest:

```
Get-ClientAccessServer | Add-ADPermission -Accessrights Extendedright -Extendedrights
"ms-Exch- EPI-Token-Serialization" -User "WingtipToys.com\Client Access servers"
Add-AvailabilityAddressSpace -Forestname WingtipToys.com -AccessMethod PerUserFB
-UseServiceAccount:$true
```

In untrusted forests, you must use slightly different commands. Once again, the commands must be run in both forests. In this case, Wingtip Toys does not trust Adventure Works. First, you must set an account that will have forest-wide access rights, then you must tell the forest to use this account to access data. In this case, the service account's name is CASAvailability in both forests. Run the first command set in the source forest, then repeat the operation in the target forest.

Run these commands in the Adventure Works forest:

```
Set-AvailabilityConfig -OrgWideAccount "Adventure-Works.com\CASAvailability"
$a = get-credential "WingtipToys.com\CASAvailability"
Add-AvailabilityAddressspace -Forestname WingtipToys.com -Accessmethod OrgWideFB
-Credential:$a
```

Run these commands in the Wingtip Toys forest:

```
Set-AvailabilityConfig -OrgWideAccount "WingtipToys.com\CASAvailability"
$a = get-credential "Adventure-Works.com\CASAvailability"
Add-AvailabilityAddressspace -Forestname Adventure-Works.com -Accessmethod OrgWideFB
-Credential:$a
```

MORE INFO   Configuring cross-forest availability

For more information on configuring cross-forest availability data, go to *http://technet.microsoft.com/en-us/library/bb125182.aspx.*

You can again see the value of running a pure Exchange and Outlook 2007 environment. In these environments, you only need to configure two base services—Autodiscover and Availability—to provide your users with complete access to Exchange's features.

Exchange Connectors Overview

Exchange Server processes e-mail through the transport pipeline. This pipeline is based on two components: the communication protocols used to exchange information between the various server roles, and connectors—special transport mechanisms that are used to control message flow within an Exchange Organization. Both are essential to the proper operation of Exchange in your organization. Keep in mind that the transport mechanisms or communications protocols used to exchange information between the various server roles are always used, even if all the roles—or at least the four roles that can coexist on one server—are installed on the same server.

To process e-mail, Exchange relies on connectors. Exchange Server 2007 has three connector types:

- Receive connectors are incoming connection points for SMTP traffic.
- Send connectors represent logical gateways through which all outgoing messages are sent.
- Foreign connectors are used to link to other messaging services that do not support SMTP traffic.

Each plays an important role in the messaging pipeline (see Figure 2-19). These connectors are part of the Transport Server roles, both Edge and Hub. After you finish installing a Transport Server role, you must configure its connectors to support its transport function. You can also add additional connectors to a server to provide multiple paths for messaging flow both within and outside of your organization.

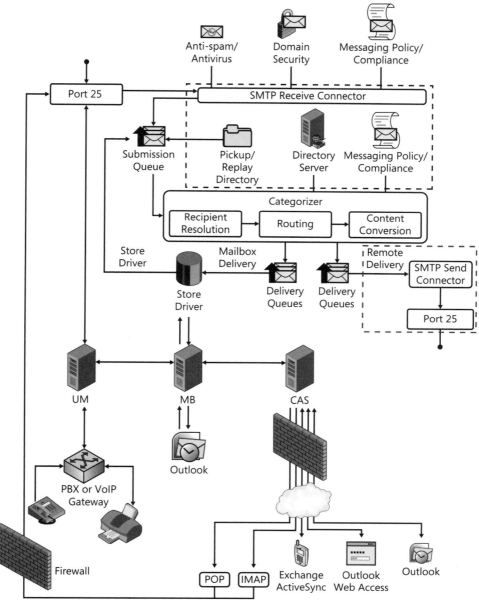

Figure 2-19   The Exchange Server 2007 transport pipeline

Work with Hub Transport Server Connectors

Hub Transport Server roles rely on both Send and Receive connectors to control message flow within an organization. When linked to the Internet, HT roles will connect to an Edge Transport Server role to relay messages. On the internal network, especially one with multiple Active Directory sites, HT roles will connect to other HT roles to route messages to their recipients.

Send Connectors and HT Roles   Send connectors are configured either through the Exchange Management Console or the Exchange Management Shell. In the Exchange Management Console, they are configured under the *Organization Configuration* node (see Figure 2-20).

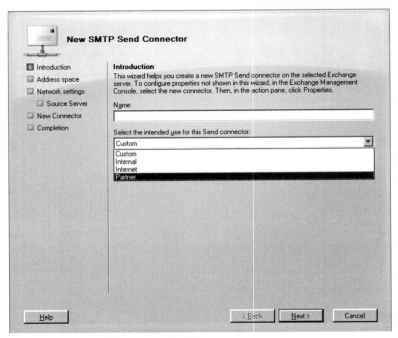

Figure 2-20   Creating a new Send connector

Once configured, information about the Send connector is stored within Active Directory as a configuration object. Send connectors contain an address space within them to support the transmission of messages to specific e-mail domains. They also contain source servers or the servers that should be used to route messages to this e-mail domain. When a message is transported by an HT, it verifies the e-mail address of the recipient, selects the appropriate Send connector for that e-mail domain, and routes the message to the appropriate source server for delivery. If the connector includes more than one source server, the HT will load-balance message routing for this address space on all of the servers listed. If, however, you have multiple Send connectors for the same address space, no load balancing will occur.

Exam Tip   If you want to load balance routing to a specific e-mail domain, you must configure more than one source server in the same connector. Configuring multiple Send connectors to the same address space will not achieve the same result.

There are four types of Send connectors in Exchange 2007:

- Custom Send connectors are used to route mail to non-Exchange servers.
- Internal Send connectors are used to route mail to known servers within your organization. They are also used to send mail to Edge Transport Servers. Known servers are called smart hosts.
- Internet Send connectors are used to route mail directly to the Internet. They rely on DNS Mail Exchanger (MX) records to route the mail.
- Partner Send connectors are used to route mail to partner domains. They rely on Transport Layer Security (TLS) certificates for the SMTP domains listed in the connector.

Create Edge Subscriptions   To send messages to the Internet, you would ideally rely on an Edge Transport Server because it provides automatic protection to your network. To do so, you need to create a Send connector to the ET computer. But, unlike with other Send connectors, you do not do this by creating a new Send connector. Instead, you do this by using an Edge Subscription along with the Exchange Edge-Sync service, described by the following steps:

1. Install the HT role on a server in your network.
2. Install an ET role on a server outside your network.
3. On the ET computer, export the Edge Subscription file. If you (rightly) created more than one ET computer, you need to export this file from each computer.
4. On the HT computer, import the Edge Subscription file from each of the ET computers you intend to use. Use the New Edge Subscription command in the *Organization Configuration* node.

   Server synchronization will begin after the files have been imported and the configuration has been integrated in the HT.

You can force replication by using the following cmdlet on an HT computer that is part of the Edge Subscription:

```
Start-EdgeSynchronization
```

Routing will be based on the Internet Send connector. This connector's configuration settings are stored within the Active Directory in an Application Mode instance that is stored on the ET computer. The ET will serve as the source server for this connection. The connector will rely on DNS MX record entries to route the messages to the internal HT computers. Whenever HT computers receive messages destined for the Internet, they will automatically route them to an ET computer.

You can also configure the Internet Send connector manually if you do not want to rely on EdgeSync. If you do so, you need to create a new Send connector with the following properties:

- Type of Connector: Internal.
- Address Space: * (for all domains).
- Smart Host: Enter the IP address or FQDN of the ET computer(s).
- Smart Host Authentication: Use Basic or Externally Secured.
- Source Server: The current HT is entered by default; add more if you need to.

Then, you also need to configure the appropriate connector on the ET computers.

IMPORTANT Smart Host authentication

If you do not plan to use IPsec as your authentication method, at the very least use Basic authentication over TLS. This will encrypt the transmission that sends the user name and password to the ET computer. Make sure that each computer has the appropriate certificate installed to support TLS.

Receive Connectors and the HT Role   Like Send connectors, Receive connectors are configured through either the Exchange Management Console or the Exchange Management Shell. In the Exchange Management Console, Receive connectors are configured under the Server Configuration node. Receive connector configurations are also stored in Active Directory, but they are stored as child objects of the HT server object. By default, two Receive connectors are automatically configured when you install the HT role:

- A default Receive connector that is designed to accept messages from all remote IP addresses through SMTP port 25. This connector is designed to provide transport for any source within the internal network. It does not, however, accept connections from anonymous senders. It will also accept connections from Edge Transport Servers to receive messages from the Internet.
- A client Receive connector that is designed to receive messages from all remote IP addresses through SMTP port 587. This connector is designed to support all

non-MAPI clients—POP or IMAP connections—for e-mail transport. Once again, its intended use is internal.

Both of these connectors are installed and configured by default when you install an HT role. In organizations where multiple HT roles are deployed, as in the Standard, Large, or Complex Organization topologies, you do not need to configure connectors—either Send or Receive—between different HT computers. Implicit connectors are automatically computed and configured based on the Active Directory site topology and all internal HT computers are connected through them.

The two default connectors, along with the automatic connections between all HT computers are all you need in terms of Receive connectors. However, you must make sure that the default configuration of these connectors is not modified. For example, you want to ensure that the Default Receive connector has the Exchange Server authentication mode enabled (see Figure 2-21), otherwise Edge Transport Servers will not be able to use it to route messages from the Internet into your internal network.

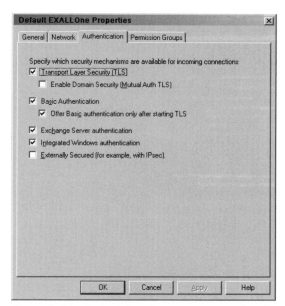

Figure 2-21   Default Receive connector authentication modes

IMPORTANT   Exchange Server 2007 SP1

With Service Pack 1, you can also configure connectors to support IPv6 if the HT computer is running Windows Server 2008. In this configuration, you can support IPv4, IPv6, or both.

Note that questions regarding SP1 are not in the original version of the 70-238 exam.

When you create custom Receive connectors, you can create the same four types of connectors as with Send connectors—Custom, Internal, Internet, and Partner—but there is also one additional connector type: Client. Client Receive connectors are used to receive mail from Exchange users. Only authenticated Exchange users will be allowed to send mail to this connector.

Configure the SMTP Banner   Whenever a server connects to either an HT or an ET through the Receive connector, a default SMTP response is provided by the server hosting the connector. You control the contents of this banner by using the Exchange Management Shell. In fact, you rely on the Banner parameter in the Set-ReceiveConnector or the New-ReceiveConnector cmdlets. By default, the Banner value is empty and will return the following message to the connecting server:

```
220 <Servername> Microsoft ESMTP MAIL service ready at <RegionalDay-Date-24HourTimeFormat>
<RegionalTimeZoneOffset>
```

You can change all of the contents of this message, except for the initial 220 value. This value is defined in request for comment (RFC) 2821 and is used to tell the connecting server that the SMTP service is ready. To modify an existing connector—in this example, a Receive connector at Lucerne Publishing that is named Internet Reception—use the following command:

```
Set-ReceiveConnector "Internet Reception" -Banner "220 Lucerne Publishing"
```

From then on, connecting servers will receive the "220 Lucerne Publishing" message when they initiate a connection.

IMPORTANT   Configuring SMTP banners

As a best practice, you should always configure the SMTP banner of your Exchange Server environment. This way, you will not be telling the world over that you are using a Microsoft product to manage e-mail, which may help increase the security of your configuration.

Work with Edge Transport Server Connectors

While the ET role relies on the same type of connectors as the HT role, it does not configure any connectors by default. Instead, you must use Exchange EdgeSync or manually configure each connector to integrate message flow through your ET computers. Your ET computers need to have at least three of the following connectors and one optional connector configured to operate:

- A Send connector that will route messages to the Internet. This connector should use an address space of "*"to route messages to all Internet domains. Using EdgeSync will automatically create and configure this connector.

- A Receive connector that will accept messages from the Internet. Typically, this connector will accept messages from anonymous senders using any IP address range. The type for this connector is Internet and it is bound to the external facing network interface card(s) on the server.

- A Send connector that will route messages to HT computers in your Exchange Organization. The address space for this connector can either be "--" which means any domain, or you can specify which domains to route to. Make this connector type Internal and add each HT in your domain as smart hosts. Using EdgeSync will automatically create and configure this connector.

- An optional Receive connector that will accept messages from the HT computers in your Exchange Organization. This connector should be configured as an Internal type and set to accept connections from the IP address range assigned to your HT computers and it should be bound to the internal facing network interface card(s) on the server.

The last Receive connector is optional because by default ET computers are designed to accept all messages—from the Internet and from internal HT computers—on the same Receive connector. In addition, using EdgeSync automatically configures authentication types on this Receive connector. Because of this, using a second Receive connector for internal traffic is usually performed only when EdgeSync is not used.

IMPORTANT   Using Exchange Server 2007 SP1

When you use Exchange Server 2007 with Service Pack 1, you can configure the Receive and Send connectors to operate with IPv6. Microsoft strongly recommends against configuring Receive connectors to accept anonymous connections from unknown IPv6 addresses. If you configure a Receive connector to accept anonymous connections from unknown IPv6 addresses, the amount of spam that enters your organization is likely to increase. Currently, there is no broadly accepted industry standard protocol for looking up IPv6 addresses. Most IP Block List providers do not support IPv6 addresses. Therefore, if you allow anonymous connections from unknown IPv6 addresses on a Receive connector, you increase the chance that spammers will bypass IP Block List providers and successfully deliver spam into your organization.

Note that questions regarding SP1 are not in the original version of the 70-238 exam.

Working with Exchange EdgeSync

The Exchange EdgeSync service provides an easy way to configure subscriptions between internal HT and external ET roles in your organization. Because ET computers are not part of your Active Directory service—and they should not be because they are outside your firewalls—they do not profit from Active Directory replication and Active Directory configuration storage as do other Exchange server roles.

They can however, subscribe to an Active Directory service. This subscription associates the ET computers with the Exchange Organization hosted by the Active Directory service and allows these computers to regularly obtain information from Active Directory and store it in their local ADAM instance. Because the EdgeSync service resides on internal HT computers, these computers have the ability to periodically initiate a one-way replication process to the ADAM instance on the ET computers. This one-way replication transmits data about recipients and organization configuration. The configuration information includes data about anti-spam configuration tasks as well as data about the Send connector configuration required to route mail to and from internal HT computers. This replication is performed on a schedule to ensure that the information in ADAM is current.

The major advantage of using an Edge Subscription, besides automating the configuration process, is that you do not have to connect to the Edge Transport Servers to perform most administration tasks. These tasks are performed on an internal HT computer and then replicated to the ET through EdgeSync. In addition, using an Edge Subscription will automatically configure the two required Send connectors and the required Receive connectors on the ET computers.

When data is sent to ADAM, it is sent over an encrypted channel using Secure Lightweight Directory Access Protocol (Secure LDAP). In addition, the Safe Senders lists and recipient information is hashed to further protect the data. Access to ADAM is controlled through the credentials stored within the Edge Subscription file generated by the Edge Server. Data sent over this subscription includes:

- Send connector configuration
- Accepted domains
- Remote domains
- Message classifications
- Safe Senders Lists
- Recipients

Edge Subscriptions are automatic when first created. Each HT computer that exists within the Active Directory site at the time you create the subscription will be able to participate in it. But, if you add more HT servers after the subscription has been created, you need to remove the subscription from both the ET computers and the HT computers in the Active Directory site and recreate it for the new HT computers to participate in EdgeSync replication.

Exam Tip   The addition of new HT computers in a site that already contains an Edge Subscription is bound to be on the exam. Make sure you take note of the procedure required to add these new servers to the subscription.

CAUTION   Configuring HT computers before an Edge Subscription

Because Edge Subscriptions are not dynamic and do not update new HT servers, you should carefully plan HT computers before you create your Edge Subscription. This way, you will not have to add new HT computers and reset the subscription.

Work with Foreign Connectors

When Exchange communicates with systems that do not accept SMTP traffic, you need to use a Foreign connector. One example of a Foreign connector is a third-party fax gateway, which does not rely on SMTP to transmit faxes. Foreign connectors control outbound connections from the HT computer to the foreign gateway server. Basically, the outbound message is placed into a Drop folder on the HT or in a network file share on another server. The foreign gateway server picks it up from this folder and processes the information. For this reason, each Foreign connector uses its own Drop folder.

As with other connectors, Foreign connector configurations are stored in Active Directory as objects in a connector's container. Whenever messages are sent to the domain contained within this connector, HT computers will automatically route it to the source servers. If you add multiple source servers to the connector, it will become fault tolerant. But, to enable fault tolerance, the Drop folder should be on a server that does not host the HT role so that it is available if one HT computer is down.

Foreign Send connectors must be configured through the Exchange Management Shell since there is no equivalent in the Management Console.

IMPORTANT   Foreign Send connectors

To find more information on Foreign connectors and their configuration, go to *http://technet.microsoft.com/en-us/library/aa996779.aspx.*

Practice: Prepare the Deployment of an Edge Transport Server

In this practice, you will prepare an Edge Transport Server for use with your Exchange topology. This practice consists of three exercises. In the first, you install the Edge Transport role. In the second, you prepare the Edge Subscription. In the third, you load and configure the Edge Subscription on an internal Hub Transport server.

▶ **Exercise 1: Install the Edge Transport Role**

Installing the Edge Transport server is slightly different than installing any other role. First, it must be performed on a server that is not a member of the internal Active Directory service; it must therefore be member of a workgroup. Second, it does not rely on Active Directory to store its configuration information, but rather on Active Directory in Application Mode, the junior cousin of Active Directory. And third, each Edge Transport server's configuration is independent from all of the others.

To complete the exercise, follow these steps:

1. Log on to the server you prepared to host the Edge Transport role, Exchange-ETOne. Use local administrator credentials with the EXAdmin account.

2. Load the Exchange installation media into the DVD drive. This should automatically launch Exchange Setup. If it does not, use Windows Explorer to change to the DVD drive and launch Setup.exe. When Setup is launched, you will see that all prerequisites have been met on this system.

3. Click Install Microsoft Exchange.

4. Click Next when the installation is launched.

5. Accept the license terms and click Next.

6. Set Error Reporting to your organizational standards and click Next.

7. On the Installation Type page, click Custom Exchange Server Installation, keep the installation folder default settings, and click Next.

8. On the Exchange Server 2007 Setup page, select Edge Transport Server Role. This automatically dims all other choices and selects Management Tools. Leave the installation path at the default path and click Next.

9. Exchange performs the role prerequisite checks. For example, the Edge Transport role cannot be installed if ADAM has not been installed first and if the DNS suffix for the computer has not been set. Click Install when the checks are complete.

10. Exchange Setup will copy the Exchange files and then configure the Edge Transport role. Click Finish to complete the installation.

11. When the Exchange Setup screen appears again, click Get Critical Updates For Microsoft Exchange. This launches Microsoft Internet Explorer and links you to the Microsoft Update Web site. Locate and apply the updates. There should be at least some anti-spam updates.

12. Close Internet Explorer and Exchange Setup when you are finished.

When you click Finish, Exchange Setup launches the Exchange Management Console. This prepares you for the next exercise. You may need to restart the computer depending on the required updates to Exchange.

▶ **Exercise 2: Prepare an Edge Subscription**

Exchange uses an Edge Subscription to synchronize configuration information between internal and external transport servers. Edge Subscriptions must first be exported from the Edge Transport server(s) and then imported into a Hub Transport server. Begin by exporting the subscription. Edge Subscription files are created through the Exchange Management Shell.

1. Open the Exchange Management Shell. Use Start Menu | All Programs | Microsoft Exchange Server 2007 | Exchange Management Shell.

2. Once the shell is open, change to your My Documents folder. Use the following command:

   ```
   cd "my documents"
   ```

3. You create the Edge Subscription file in your My Documents folder. Use the following command. Note that you must include your user name in the path to store the file in your profile.

   ```
   New-EdgeSubscription -file "c:\documents and settings\username\my documents\
   ExchangeETOne.xml"
   ```

4. Type **Y** and press Enter to generate the subscription file. Note that you have 24 hours to load this file into a Hub Transport server before the credentials used in the subscription expire.

5. Using Windows Explorer, copy the subscription file to the ExchangeOne.treyresearch.net Hub Transport server to prepare for the next exercise. Copy the ExchangeETOne.xml file to the clipboard. Then, in the Address bar, type **\\ExchangeOne\c$**. Navigate to C:\Documents and Settings\EXAdmin\EXAdmin's Documents. Paste the file. Close Windows Explorer.

Your subscription file is ready for import.

▶ **Exercise 3: Enable an Edge Subscription**

Each Edge Subscription must be imported into a Hub Transport Server to store it in Active Directory. To complete this exercise, follow these steps:

1. Log on to ExchangeOne.treyresearch.net with EXAdmin credentials from the domain.

2. Launch the Exchange Management Console if it is not already open. Use Start Menu | All Programs | Microsoft Exchange Server 2007 | Exchange Management Console if it isn't.

3. Move to the Organization Configuration, then Hub Transport node in the tree pane.

4. Click on New Edge Subscription in the action pane to launch the New Edge Subscription Wizard. Note that this also moves you to the Edge Subscription tab in the details pane.

5. On the New Edge Subscription page, select the Default-First-Site-Name as the Active Directory site and then click Browse to locate the ExchagneETOne.xml file. It should be in your My Documents folder. Make sure the Automatically Create A Send Connector For This Edge Subscription check box is selected and click New.

6. Copy the cmdlet to the clipboard and launch Notepad to save the script. Save the Notepad file as **NewSubscription.txt**.

7. Click Finish to complete the operation.

8. To force an EdgeSync to make sure data is synchronized between internal and external servers, begin by opening the Exchange Management Shell.

9. Use the following cmdlet in the Exchange Management Shell:

```
Start-EdgeSynchronization
```

10. Verify the results of the synchronization process as displayed in the Exchange Management Shell. Close both the Exchange Management Shell and the Exchange Management Console when you are finished.

Your Edge Subscription is now functional.

Quick Check

1. Your organization has deployed Exchange Server 2007. Clients are using Outlook 2003. Your IT administrators have set up the Autodiscover service so that all client configurations are performed automatically. Users report that the configuration does not work. What could be the problem?

2. What are the three key components that make the Autodiscover service work after the CAS role has been installed?

3. What is the Exchange Server 2007 service that provides free/busy data to users?

4. What is the Send connector's role in an Exchange Organization?

5. What is the purpose of an Edge Subscription in Exchange Server 2007?

Quick Check Answers

1. Autodiscover only works with Outlook 2007 or Outlook Web Access 2007. Clients running Outlook 2003 must configure their e-mail settings manually or receive an automated configuration file from the IT administrators. If your IT team wants users to run Auto Account Setup, they need to deploy Outlook 2007 or at the very least, set up OWA 2007 so that users can access all of the features of Exchange Server 2007.

2. The three core components are DNS, Active Directory, and IIS. DNS hosts the records that point to the Autodiscover service as well as the e-mail domain for the organization. Active Directory hosts the service connection point that contains the URLs for Autodiscover operation. IIS hosts the Autodiscover Web site and makes it available for users when they need it.

3. In Exchange Server 2007, the Availability Service provides free/busy data to Outlook 2007 or OWA 2007 users. In previous editions of Exchange, this was published through public folders. Public folders are still needed in Exchange 2007 if there are legacy clients such as Outlook 2003.

4. The Send connector's role is to contain an address space to support the transmission of messages to specific e-mail domains. They also contain source servers or the servers that should be used to route messages to this e-mail domain. When a message is transported by an HT, it verifies the e-mail address of the recipient, selects the appropriate Send connector for that e-mail domain, and routes the message to the appropriate source server for delivery. If the connector includes more than one source server, the HT will load balance message routing for this address space on all of the servers listed. If, however, you have multiple Send connectors for the same address space, no load balancing will occur.

5. Edge Subscriptions rely on the Exchange EdgeSync service to provide an easy way to configure subscriptions between internal HT and external ET roles in your organization. Because ET computers are not part of your Active Directory, they do not profit from Active Directory replication and Active Directory configuration storage as do other Exchange server roles. A subscription associates

the ET computers with the Exchange Organization hosted by the Active Directory service and allows these computers to regularly obtain information from Active Directory and store it in their local ADAM instance. Because the Edge-Sync service resides on an internal HT computer, this computer has the ability to periodically initiate a one-way replication process to the ADAM instance on the ET computers. This one-way replication transmits data about recipients and organization configuration.

Lesson 3: Plan the Deployment of Optional Exchange Services

Estimated lesson time: 40 minutes

As you have seen earlier, pure Exchange Server 2007 requires two core services provided by the Client Access Server role: Autodiscover and Availability. But the CAS role can support a considerable number of other features if you need them.

Overview of Optional Exchange Services

The first feature that comes to mind is Outlook Web Access. While optional, OWA is very useful if your users travel or ever need to access their e-mail from public computers outside the network. A second service that is optional but also very useful is Outlook Anywhere (formerly RPC over HTTPS), which provides access to a user's mailbox from Outlook through the Internet.

A third useful feature is the Search engine included in Exchange. Search lets your users locate information within their mailboxes and within public folders. If you have used Windows Vista at all, you know that you just cannot live without some form of search tool. ActiveSync lets your users have access to their e-mail through mobile devices. Other features allow users to access mail through non-Outlook tools such as Windows Vista's Windows Mail or third-party tools such as Eudora. This is done by providing mail through the POP or IMAP protocols, another optional feature of the CAS role. Another important feature is DSAccess. Among other things, DSAccess lets users query Active Directory for information—for example, to access the Global Address List stored in the directory service.

All of these features are useful at some point and, depending on the organization type you plan to deploy, may or may not be implemented. Understanding how these features work is important; you need to be comfortable with them if you require them.

Plan for Mobility

The CAS role supports many mobility features. Whether because you are on the road with no computer and you need to access your e-mail, or you are using a Windows Mobile device and want to access e-mail from it, or you are using a non-Windows Mobile device that has browser capability, you are never really disconnected when you implement the optional features of the CAS role correctly.

Outlook Web Access

Perhaps the most famous of the optional features is Outlook Web Access (OWA). OWA lets you use a Web browser to access most of the functions you normally find within the Outlook rich client. With version 2007 of Exchange, OWA comes in two versions: Outlook Web Access Premium and Light. The Premium version is usually used on high-speed connections. It supports the use of a public or private computer (see Figure 2-22). The public computer option provides faster time-outs while the private computer option lets you work longer without disconnecting. The Light version provides fewer features and faster performance (see Figure 2-23). It is useful when you are using a computer with strict security settings or using a non-Internet Explorer browser.

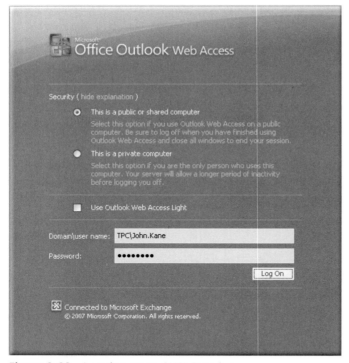

Figure 2-22   Logging on to OWA Premium

Compare OWA Premium to OWA Light   The browser requirements for Premium differ from those of the Light version. In addition, these requirements differ based on the operating system you are working with. Table 2-10 outlines the requirements for both.

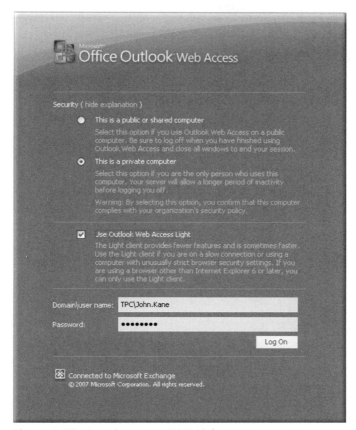

Figure 2-23 Logging on to OWA Light

Table 2-10 Web Browser Requirements for OWA Premium and Light

Operating System	OWA Premium	OWA Light, MS Browser	OWA Light, non-MS Browser
Windows 98	n/a	Internet Explorer 5.01, 5.5, 6, or later	n/a
Windows Millennium Edition	Internet Explorer 6 or later	Internet Explorer 5.5, 6, or later	n/a
Windows 2000 Server	Internet Explorer 6 or later	Internet Explorer 5.01, 5.5, 6, or later	n/a

Table 2-10   Web Browser Requirements for OWA Premium and Light

Operating System	OWA Premium	OWA Light, MS Browser	OWA Light, non-MS Browser
Windows XP	Internet Explorer 6 or later	Internet Explorer 6 or later	Mozilla Firefox 1.8, Opera 7.54
Windows Server 2003	Internet Explorer 6 or later	Internet Explorer 6 or later	Mozilla Firefox 1.8, Opera 7.54
Windows Vista	Internet Explorer 7	Internet Explorer 7	Mozilla Firefox 1.8, Opera 7.54
Mac OS 9	n/a	Internet Explorer 5.01	Netscape Navigator 7.1
Mac OS 10.3	n/a	n/a	Safari 1.2
Sun Solaris 9, x86	n/a	n/a	Mozilla Firefox 1.8, Netscape Navigator 7.1
Linux Red Hat Desktop (RHEL3)	n/a	n/a	Mozilla Firefox 1.8, Netscape Navigator 7.1
HP/UX 11i	n/a	n/a	Mozilla Firefox 1.8, Netscape Navigator 7.1

As you can see, OWA Light is designed to run with a simpler user interface and therefore runs on a wide variety of platforms and Internet browsers. OWA Premium only runs on Internet Explorer, but provides significantly more features. Both support accessibility features for the visually impaired. Table 2-11 outlines the differences between OWA Light and Premium.

Table 2-11   Differences between OWA Light and Premium

Feature	Light	Premium
Spell Checking	n/a	Available
Reading Pane	n/a	Available
Accessibility for the visually impaired	Available	Available
Notifications and Reminders	n/a	Available
Weekly Calendar Views	n/a	Available
Windows SharePoint Services and Windows file share Integration	n/a	Available
Compose Messages with HTML	Supports only plain text	Available
Calendar Options	Limited to the following: Show week numbers Set the first day of the week Select days of the week Set day start and end times	Available
Arrange By	Depends on folder type	Available
Right-Click	n/a	Available
Drag-and-Drop	n/a	Available
Explicit Logon	n/a	Available
Type-down Search	n/a	Available
Resource Mailbox Management	n/a	Available
Color Schemes	n/a	Available
Voice Mail Options	n/a	Available

IMPORTANT   OWA Premium in Exchange 2007 SP1

Microsoft added some additional features to OWA Premium with Service Pack 1 for Exchange Server. These include the ability to recover deleted items, the ability to view calendar months, and control personal distribution lists. There are a few more, but these are the most significant.

Keep in mind that the original exam has no questions on SP1.

In addition, some features that are available in the rich Outlook client are not available in OWA Premium despite its fuller feature set than OWA Light.

- Display of multiple calendars
- Propose new time for meetings
- To Do Bar
- Attach items to items
- Pasting inline images
- Hierarchical address book

Also, features that require local file storage on the client computer are not available, including: Cached Exchange Mode, offline access, offline address book (OAB), custom dictionaries, customizable views, .pst files, the ability to import or export data, and the ability to use Send to OneNote.

Despite this lack of some features, OWA Premium provides a very good experience to the end user because it provides a richer interface.

Preparing to Run the OWA Feature   The CAS role's load will increase as you add additional features to it. This is one reason why you should look to a Network Load Balancing (NLB) scenario for your CAS computers. NLB automatically distributes the load between one computer and the other to help provide a better response to clients. Given that CAS computers already run the Autodiscover and Availability services, which themselves have a certain load on the server, as well as Exchange Web Services, which provide access to the application programming interfaces (API) made available through the CAS role, you should first ensure that your servers have the ability to run additional features. For example, Table 2-12 first outlines the type of load you can expect from OWA on its own, then the type of load you can expect when running OWA on top of the core services provided by CAS computers. In most cases, the CAS will respond to four requests, either Web Services or Availability requests, per second from internal clients in addition to the values provided in Table 2-12.

Table 2-12 OWA Load on CAS Roles

Services used	Load at peak	Supported users per CAS computer
Outlook Web Access only	70 requests per second 4,500 concurrent users	18,000
Multiple services: 25 percent Exchange ActiveSync 5 percent Outlook Web Access 70 percent Outlook Anywhere	Exchange ActiveSync: 5 requests per second 500 concurrent users Outlook Web Access: 20 requests per second 100 concurrent users Outlook Anywhere: 40 requests per second 1,400 concurrent users	Exchange ActiveSync: 500 Outlook Web Access: 2,140 Outlook Anywhere: 1,980

The values in Table 2-12 stem from Microsoft's own deployment of CAS computers. Microsoft has more than 123,000 Exchange users and uses a Complex Organization topology.

IMPORTANT Microsoft's Exchange 2007 deployment

For more information on Microsoft's deployment of Exchange Server 2007 and their performance findings, go to *http://technet.microsoft.com/en-us/library/bb331971.aspx*.

Your own deployments might not be as complex, but you should still be aware of the impact OWA will have on your servers.

OWA relies on IIS to provide Web information to end users. In fact, you create a virtual directory in IIS to host OWA. When you do so, you can rely on the security features of IIS 6—and IIS 7 with Service Pack 1—to secure the transmission between the end user and the CAS computer. Three security methods are available. The first is configured through IIS itself and consists of using the Secure Sockets Layer. This means adding a Public Key Infrastructure (PKI) certificate to the server. Ideally, you would use a certificate from a trusted certificate authority—one that is already included in the trusted authorities of most client computers—so that you do not need to add the administrative overhead of deploying another certificate authority to end users. In fact, this is the ideal strategy for SSL with OWA because both versions of OWA are designed to work mostly with public computers, or computers that you have no control over.

The other two security configurations are managed through the Exchange Management Console or through the Exchange Management Shell. Standard authentication methods include Integrated Windows, Digest, and Basic authentication. Each has strengths and weaknesses. Integrated Windows authentication, as its name implies, only works with Windows systems. Basic authentication sends user names and passwords in clear text but can be protected through SSL tunnels. Digest authentication protects user names and passwords and also works with non-Windows platforms.

Forms-based authentication displays a logon page for OWA. It uses cookies to store encrypted user logon credentials and password information. When you configure multiple authentication methods, IIS will automatically try the most secure method first and go down the list until it finds one that works both with the server and the client trying to connect.

By default, when you install the CAS role, four OWA virtual directories are created in IIS under the default Web site. These four virtual directories, along with the default Web site, are all configured to require SSL—and therefore HTTPS—communications for access. Of course, you must still add the SSL certificate for these directories to work.

When you make OWA available to end users, you need to let them know how to access OWA from inside and outside the network. By default, the URL path to OWA consists of the public URL for the organization followed by */Exchange*. For example, at Lucerne Publishing, this URL would be *http://www.lucernepublishing.com/ Exchange*. You need to publish this URL to your users so they know how to log on to OWA when they do not have access to their own computers.

IMPORTANT   Accessing OWA from outside

When OWA is published outside your internal network, it exposes an internal service to outside users and can be a risk. OWA Web sites must be secured from tampering or other malicious behavior. This topic is discussed in Chapter 7, "Security Implementations."

IMPORTANT   Renaming the OWA Web site

You can rename the OWA Web site, but if it is installed into the default Web site as it normally is when you install a CAS role, you should be very careful about this procedure. If the default ActiveSync Web site is also installed in this Web site, you cannot rename it. Therefore, renaming the OWA Web site may damage the ActiveSync Web site.

You can also delegate access to a mailbox through OWA. For this to work, your installation must be modified to allow Explicit Logon. When enabled, Explicit Logon lets a user add the name of another mailbox he has access to at the end of the URL for OWA. For example, at Lucerne Publishing, David Jaffe can open the mailbox of conference room A through OWA by typing **http://www.lucernepublishing.com/Exchange/ conferenceA@lucernepublishing.com** and logging on with his credentials.

OWA will convert Office documents for viewing through HTML. OWA also works with Windows SharePoint Services (WSS 2.0 or 3.0). You can make the OWA Web Part available for your users for integration into their personal sites. You can also integrate OWA with SharePoint so that users will have read-only access to document libraries. This saves them from sending attachments because both are Web technologies. If you do not work with Windows SharePoint Services, you can do the same thing using universal naming convention (UNC) file shares.

Mobile Device Support

Exchange Server 2007 also provides support for mobile devices, both those that run Windows Mobile and those that do not. The first is provided through the ActiveSync feature. The second is provided through more conventional Internet technologies such as the POP or IMAP e-mail services. Different features are available to mobile clients based on the type of device and the back-end service they are using. These features are outlined in Table 2-13.

Table 2-13   Features Available to Mobile Clients

Component	Feature	ActiveSync	IMAP4	IMAP client for a non-Windows Mobile phone
Email	Push Email	Yes	Yes (through IDLE command)	No–pull e-mail only
	HTML e-mail formatting	Yes	Yes	Yes
	Attachment download	Yes	Yes	Yes (view only)

Table 2-13   Features Available to Mobile Clients

Component	Feature	ActiveSync	IMAP4	IMAP client for a non-Windows Mobile phone
	Search	Yes	Yes	No
Calendar	Calendar Sync	Yes	No	No
	Accept/Decline meeting requests	Yes	No	No
Contacts	Contact Sync	Yes	No	No
	Global Address List (GAL) lookup	Yes	No	No
Tasks	Task Sync	Yes	No	No
Out of Office	Out-of-office (OOF) settings	Yes	No	No
Document Access	File share and/or SharePoint Document Library Access	Yes	No	No
Security	Enforce security policies to protect data on device	Yes	No	No

Ideally, your end users will be working with Windows Mobile devices and you will be able to create a more secure infrastructure, but as you know, it is sometimes very difficult to enforce personal digital assistant (PDA) standards. Users often choose whatever they want, as they might when they see a non-Windows Mobile phone in action. Using different mobile platforms will provide variable experiences to your users and will make more work for you. Refer to Table 2-13 to demonstrate to them the value of using Windows Mobile. For example, the Touch Pocket PC provides a touch interface and runs Windows Mobile, and is also smaller than other phones. This makes a compelling argument for staying away from a phone that does not support all of your corporate mobile e-mail features.

Work with ActiveSync   ActiveSync stems from older versions of Exchange where users would link their mobile devices to their computers for synchronization of data and settings. Today ActiveSync has evolved to support complete synchronization over wireless connections and does not require the land connection through the computer. New features in ActiveSync 2007 include support for the following:

- HTML-formatted messages
- Follow-up flags
- Fast message retrieval
- Meeting attendee information
- Enhanced Exchange Search
- Windows SharePoint Services and UNC document access
- PIN reset
- Enhanced device security through password policies
- Autodiscover for over-the-air provisioning
- Out-of-Office configuration
- Task synchronization
- Direct Push of e-mail and data

Feature access is dependent on the version of the Windows Mobile operating system. During the development of Exchange Server 2007, Windows Mobile 5.0 was available. Many of the features in ActiveSync 2007 were actually developed for the next version of Windows Mobile, version 6, which was released after the release of Exchange 2007. In fact, to have access to many of the new features, Windows Mobile 5.0 must also use the Messaging and Security Feature Pack. Table 2-14 outlines the different features supported by both device operating systems.

Table 2-14   ActiveSync Features by Windows Mobile Operating System

Feature	Windows Mobile 6.0	Windows Mobile 5.0 with MSFP
Direct Push	Yes	Yes
E-mail, Calendar, and Contact Synchronization	Yes	Yes
Task Synchronization	Yes	Yes

Table 2-14 ActiveSync Features by Windows Mobile Operating System

Feature	Windows Mobile 6.0	Windows Mobile 5.0 with MSFP
HTML E-mail Support	Yes	No
Message Flags	Yes	No
Meeting Attendee Information	Yes	No
Out-of-Office Management	Yes	No
Exchange Search	Yes	No
Windows SharePoint Services and UNC document access	Yes	No
Inline Message Fetch	Yes	No
Exchange ActiveSync Policy Support	Yes	Yes
Remote Device Wipe	Yes	Yes
SSL Encryption	Yes	Yes
Device Certificate for Authentication Management	Yes	No
Recovery Password	Yes	No

ActiveSync is enabled by default when you install the CAS role. It relies on the basic settings requirements for the CAS role. These include the pre-installation of IIS and ASP.NET. ASP.NET must be allowed on the Web server. Once these conditions are met, ActiveSync and other CAS features are enabled by default.

Implement Direct Push Direct Push is an ActiveSync mode that keeps a remote device up to date through a cellular network connection. It basically notifies the remote device that new content is available for synchronization. To function, devices that support Direct Push will have to send a long-lived HTTPS request to the Exchange server. Because ActiveSync relies on HTTPS, port 443 must be open on the firewall and an SSL certificate must be available on the Exchange server running the CAS role. If you are already supporting OWA, your CAS computer will also support ActiveSync and Direct Push. Because the device uses Direct Push through a long-lived HTTPS request, you will need to ensure that this request can be as long-lived as possible. For example, some firewalls will time out this type of request. If the request time-out is too short, devices will continually resend the long-lived HTTPS request.

IMPORTANT   Device data plans

Make sure users of Direct Push in your organization have an unlimited data plan, otherwise Direct Push will quickly escalate their monthly costs. To reduce costs, consider configuring mobile device policies that limit the size of e-mail messages.

ActiveSync supports Autodiscover, and if your user devices support it, configuration will be automatic, as it is with OWA and Outlook 2007. If not, you will need to provide configuration details to your users.

You must, however, enable user mailboxes to support ActiveSync. This can be done in one of two ways: through the individual user's mailbox settings or through a mailbox policy. By default, all mailboxes are enabled for MAPI, which lets them link to the mailbox through Outlook, enabled for OWA, and enabled for ActiveSync. The only feature that is disabled is Unified Messaging. In the Exchange Management Console, controlling these features is performed through the Properties | Mailbox Features tab.

You can also set policies to control ActiveSync and other features. The Exchange Management Console lets you control some of the policy settings while the Exchange Management Shell lets you control all of their settings. Policies are managed and created in the Console through the Organization Configuration | Client Access node. Policy Control is relatively simple (see Figure 2-24). Policies let you control how devices can be used and which password settings should be enabled. After you create the policy, you can assign it to either existing or new mailboxes as they are created.

When using the Exchange Management Shell, use either the **New-ActiveSyncMailboxPolicy** or **Set-ActiveSyncMailboxPolicy** cmdlets. The power of ActiveSync becomes evident when you have policies in place and, when your users lose their devices, you can remotely wipe the device contents and protect your organization's information from within the comfort of your office.

Exam Tip   ActiveSync also relies on PKI certificates to validate connections and link users through HTTPS. However, if the CAS does not include a trusted certificate, clients will receive an error during the connection and they will not be able to connect. No error message will appear, so users will not know the error is because of the certificate. Watch out for this on the exam.

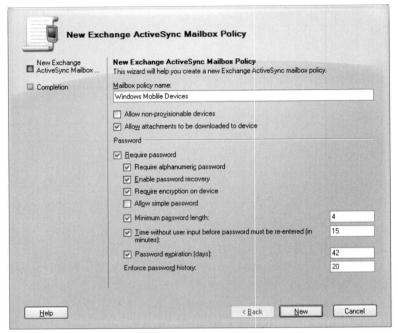

Figure 2-24   Creating a new ActiveSync policy

Prepare POP or IMAP Services   Both POP and IMAP are disabled by default in Exchange Server 2007 because Microsoft expects you to use the full Exchange feature set and therefore either use Outlook clients or Windows Mobile devices. But, if you do not want to rely on these features and you want to use something else, you will need to enable either POP or IMAP e-mail access. In the original version of Exchange Server 2007, you must rely on the Exchange Management Shell to control these protocols. In Exchange 2007 Service Pack 1, you can manage these items through the Exchange Management Console. Use the following commands to manage the items:

- Set-PopSettings
- Set-ImapSettings
- Set-CASMailbox

The first two commands let you enable the services while the third lets you configure mailboxes to use these features.

IMPORTANT   Set-CASMailbox options

For more information on the **Set-CASMailbox** options, go to
http://technet.microsoft.com/en-us/library/aa996347.aspx.

To use these protocols, you must first start the service you want, then configure SMTP settings for the service in Exchange. These services are installed as normal Windows Services. This means you need to use the Computer Management console in Windows Server 2003 or the Server Manager console in Windows Server 2008— which requires Service Pack 1 to run Exchange Server 2007. You can also use the **net start** command. After the services are started, use the Exchange Management Shell to enable the services.

Next, you rely on the **Set-CASMailbox** cmdlet to configure SMTP settings for mailboxes so that they can use these protocols. Table 2-15 outlines the different message retrieval format options you can set on either protocol. Use these settings to control the message retrieval formats for individual users.

Table 2-15   Message Retrieval Formats for POP and IMAP

Setting	Value
PopMessageRetrievalFormat	0:Text Only
	1:HTML Only
	2:HTML and Alternative Text
	3:Enriched Text Only
	4:Enriched Text and Alternative Text
	5:Best Body Format
ImapMessageRetrievalFormat	0:Text Only
	1:HTML Only
	2:HTML and Alternative Text
	3:Enriched Text Only
	4:Enriched Text and Alternative Text
	5:Best Body Format

To control these settings, you must be a member of the Exchange Server Administrators group and have local administrative rights to the CAS computer.

You can also manage time-out settings for each protocol, manage calendaring options, configure IP addresses and TCP/IP ports, and control message flow for these protocols.

Users of non-Windows Mobile devices can rely on these protocols to access their e-mail with a less rich experience than those who have a true Windows Mobile device, especially version 6.0. Refer to Table 2-13 for the differences in experience for these users.

You should make sure you have a full Exchange Server 2007 infrastructure if you deploy either POP or IMAP. If not—for example, if you have back-end servers running Exchange Server 2003—you will encounter physical and security limitations; you will have to place the CAS and back-end mailbox server in the same Active Directory site, potentially giving users access to this mailbox server.

Simplify Client Connectivity

Another very powerful service is the new Outlook Anywhere capability Exchange Server 2007 includes. Outlook Anywhere (formerly RPC over HTTP) allows users to traverse the firewall over common ports, most often port 443 with HTTPS, to access their mailboxes from Outlook 2007 or Outlook 2003. By default Outlook Anywhere is not enabled after a CAS installation. It is enabled through the Enable Outlook Anywhere Wizard (see Figure 2-25). This wizard is found under Server Configuration | Client Access in the Management Console. You can also use the **enable-OutlookAnywhere** cmdlet to do so.

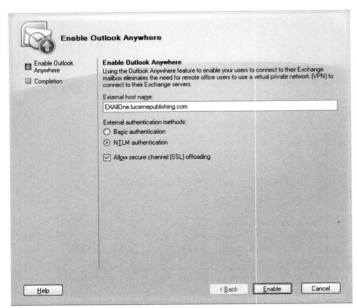

Figure 2-25   Enabling Outlook Anywhere on a CAS

NOTE **Microsoft recommendation**

Microsoft recommends enabling Outlook Anywhere on at least one CAS computer in each Active Directory site you manage.

Outlook Anywhere relies on IIS and SSL for operation. If you are using OWA or Active-Sync or both, you can use the same certificate and the same URL for Outlook Anywhere. The major advantage of Outlook Anywhere is that it provides a secure channel of communications with Exchange servers without requiring virtual private network (VPN) implementations. This greatly simplifies Exchange implementations.

Outlook Anywhere is the component that requires the installation of RPC over HTTP proxy along with IIS and ASP.NET for the CAS role. When enabling Outlook Anywhere, set it to NTLM or Integrated Windows authentication. You should also use an advanced firewall in the perimeter network. And, as already recommended, you should obtain a certificate from a trusted third-party certificate authority to simplify deployment.

Help Users Find Data

Locating data has always been a major issue for users. With Exchange Server 2007, users will be able to find and locate data like never before. The tool that allows them to do this is the indexing engine, or Search tool. In addition to finding content, users also need to find each other. A second tool that assists users at this level is the Directory Service Access tool that links Exchange to Active Directory, providing users with content such as the Global Address List. When either of these two components is not configured properly, users get frustrated because they cannot find anything. It is your job as the messaging professional to ensure that these components are properly deployed.

Plan for Exchange Content Indexing

Content indexing in Exchange is based on an index or catalog that is generated by the Search tool. Instead of searching the actual content, users search in the catalog, which provides much faster results. In version 2003, Exchange would generate a catalog or content index of users' mailboxes that was approximately 35 to 40 percent of the capacity of the mailbox database. This required significant space and was a disk-intensive activity.

In Exchange Server 2007, the index is no more than five percent of the database size and can therefore be placed on the same disk set as the database itself. This should be factored into the disk set sizing you perform for each storage group.

Indexing overhead is very low because all messages are indexed as they are received. This means that all messages are indexed all the time and usually within 10 seconds of arrival. Indexing is turned on by default and does not require any configuration. Because indexing is based on the MSSearch service, users only have access to the results in messages to which they have access rights. Both messages and attachments are indexed. Attachment indexing includes Office documents, text, and HTML.

To profit from attachment search, users must use either Outlook or OWA 2007 and must be online with Outlook for the search to work. To perform a search, users only need to use either Instant Search or Advanced Find. In Outlook 2003, users must be once again online and must use the Find or Advanced Find features. The same applies to Outlook 2000. For users of Outlook 2007 on versions other than Windows Vista, Windows Desktop Search 3.0 must be installed to support cached mode searching.

If your organization uses a language other than English, Search will only support searches within content that uses the same locale as the user's. For example, if a message contains two different languages, only the user's language or computer locale will be searchable.

IMPORTANT When Search does not work

Search will not index documents that are tagged with Digital Rights Management. If attachments do not have a file extension association, they will not be indexed.

Exam Tip   Remember that if your users are not using Windows Vista desktops, you need to deploy Windows Desktop Search 3.0 for Instant Search to work.

Directory Service Access Implementations

Exchange relies very heavily on Active Directory for storing configuration information and for maintaining the attributes of all its recipients. All Active Directory–Exchange interactions are performed through the Active Directory Driver. This driver uses the Exchange AD Topology service (MSExchangeADTopology) to run Directory Service Access (DSAccess) queries. These queries provide information on Exchange topology including the location of domain controllers and global catalog servers that Exchange can rely on to handle its requests.

DSAccess provides directory lookup for Exchange components, including SMTP, Message Transfer Agents (MTA), and the Exchange store. Clients or users rely on the DSProxy service for directory access. All exchanges are performed through LDAP queries, which are encrypted between Exchange servers and domain controllers. A major difference between DSAccess in Exchange 2007 and Exchange 2003 is that in Exchange 2003, directory information was stored in a cache to make it more readily available. In certain situations this cache could be compromised or outdated. With DSAccess, Exchange 2007 servers do not look up information from a cache, but rather through a direct Active Directory lookup. This provides more relevant results.

You can control how Exchange servers link to Active Directory through DSAccess through the **$AdminSessionADSettings** cmdlet variable. This lets you set preferred domain controllers, global catalog servers, or centralized data centers.

IMPORTANT   More information on *$AdminSessionADSettings*

For more information on this variable, go to *http://go.microsoft.com/fwlink/?linkid=89092*.

The services that rely on DSAccess include:

- The Exchange AD Topology (listed earlier)
- The Exchange Information Store
- The Exchange System Attendant
- The Word Wide Web Publishing Service

In each case, the services only rely on Active Directory data to have a consistent topology view through all of the Exchange services that are running on a server.

Note that in Exchange Server 2007, Edge Transport Servers—the servers that would be in your perimeter network—do not perform queries to Active Directory, but rather through Active Directory in Application Mode, protecting your internal directory from direct links with the perimeter.

Practice: Plan Mobility Services with Exchange Server 2007

In this practice, you will perform the preparation of Outlook Web Access to allow delegated mailbox access. This practice consists of a single exercise. The exercise lets you see the actual commands required to configure OWA to allow Explicit Logon.

▶ **Exercise: Prepare Outlook Web Access for Delegated Mailbox Access**

Enabling Explicit Logon is performed through the Exchange Management Shell, but first you must create new mailboxes to be able to delegate access to them.

To complete this exercise, follow these steps:

1. Log on to ExchangeOne.treyresearch.net with EXAdmin.
2. Open the Exchange Management Console. Use Start Menu | All Programs | Microsoft Exchange Server 2007 | Exchange Management Console.
3. Move to the Recipient Configuration | Mailbox node in the tree pane.
4. Click New Mailbox in the Action pane. This launches the New Mailbox Wizard.

5. Select User Mailbox and click Next.

6. Select New User and click Next.

7. Use the following values for the new user:

   Organizational Unit: Use the default

   First Name: **John**

   Last Name: **Kane**

   User Logon Name: **John.Kane**

   User Logon Name (Pre-Windows 2000): **JohnKane**

   Password: **P@ssw0rd**

   Confirm Password: **P@ssw0rd**

   User Must Change Password At Next Logon: Leave unchecked

8. Click Next. On the Mailbox Settings page, use the following values:

   Alias: **John.Kane**

   Server: **ExchangeOne**

   Storage Group: **First Storage Group**

   Mailbox Database: **Mailbox Database**

   Managed Folder Mailbox Policy: Leave unchecked

   Exchange ActiveSync Mailbox Policy: Leave unchecked

9. Click Next. Review your settings and then click New.

10. Copy the contents to the Clipboard and paste them into a Notepad file called **NewUser.txt**.

11. Return to the Console and click New Mailbox in the Action pane. This launches the New Mailbox Wizard.

12. Select Room Mailbox and click Next.

13. Select New User and click Next.

14. Use the following values for the new user:

   Organizational Unit: Use the default

   First Name: **Conference**

   Last Name: **Room A**

   User Logon Name: **ConferenceRoomA**

User Logon Name (Pre-Windows 2000): **ConferenceRoomA**

Password: **P@ssw0rd**

Confirm Password: **P@ssw0rd**

User Must Change Password At Next Logon: Leave unchecked

15. Click Next. On the Mailbox Settings page, use the following values:

Alias: **ConferenceRoomA**

Server: **ExchangeOne**

Storage Group: **First Storage Group**

Mailbox Database: **Mailbox Database**

Managed Folder Mailbox Policy: Leave unchecked

Exchange ActiveSync Mailbox Policy: Leave unchecked

16. Click Next. Review your settings and then click New.

17. Copy the contents to the Clipboard and paste them into a Notepad file called **NewConferenceRoom.txt**.

18. Launch the Exchange Management Shell. Use All Programs | Microsoft Exchange Server 2007 | Exchange Management Shell.

19. Allow explicit logon to EXAdmin for Conference Room A. You use EXAdmin so that you can test the results later. Use the following cmdlet:

```
Add-MailboxPermission -identity ConferenceRoomA -User EXAdmin -AccessRights FullAccess
```

20. After the cmdlet completes, test the access. Open Internet Explorer and type *https://ExchangeOne.treyresearch.net/Exchange/conferencerooma@treyresearch.net* to open OWA with the conference room mailbox. Click Continue To This Website when you see the Certificate Error page. This page is displayed because the self-signed certificate is not trusted.

21. Add the OWA Web site to the trusted sites.

22. On the OWA logon page, select This Is A Private Computer and log on as EXAdmin@treyresearch.net with the appropriate password and click Logon.

23. On the next Web page, select your language and your current time zone and click OK. This will open your conference room mailbox. As you can see, you can completely control this mailbox.

24. Close OWA.

Explicit Logon lets you control other mailboxes. Because it is run as a cmdlet, you can easily script this operation to grant delegated mailbox control to several users at once.

Quick Check

1. The Exchange CAS role supports many features. Which are required and which are optional?
2. What is the difference between Outlook Web Access Premium and Light?
3. How many OWA virtual directories are created by default when you install a CAS role?
4. What can happen if you rename the OWA Web site improperly?
5. What is required to support most Exchange Server 2007 features with Windows Mobile version 5.0?

Quick Check Answers

1. Required features include the Autodiscover and the Availability services. Optional features include Outlook Web Access, ActiveSync, Outlook Anywhere, and POP or IMAP mail protocols.
2. OWA Premium is designed for fast connections and requires the use of Internet Explorer version 6 or higher. OWA Light works on slower connections and, although it works with Internet Explorer version 5.01 and higher (depending on the Windows or Macintosh OS version), it also supports non-Microsoft browsers.
3. Four OWA virtual directories are created by default when you install a CAS role. Each directory is ready for operation but must be matched to an SSL certificate before users can link to them.
4. If you rename the OWA Web site improperly, you may cause an interruption of service with ActiveSync because you cannot rename its Web site.
5. To support most Exchange Server 2007 features with Windows Mobile version 5.0, you must deploy the Messaging and Security Feature Pack. The best support for Exchange Server 2007 is provided by Windows Mobile version 6.0.

Chapter Summary

- The Exchange Store contains three logical components: storage groups, which are containers for both mailbox databases and transaction log files; the mailbox database itself, which contains private user data; and the public folder database, which contains shareable Exchange data.

- Each storage group is composed of three sets of files: .edb files are databases; .log files are the transaction logs associated with the mailbox databases; and .chk files are checkpoint files used to replay all transactions in the event of a potential inconsistency in the database resulting from a service interruption.

- The ideal RAID configuration for Exchange Server 2007 is RAID 10 because it includes both disk spanning and disk mirroring. Disk spanning provides the best performance because Windows can access multiple disks at once through its multi-threaded disk engine. This provides the fastest reads and writes even though it is often the RAID configuration that requires the most disks to implement.

- Autodiscover is based on three key services: DNS, Active Directory, and IIS. DNS is used to locate the e-mail domain and identify the configuration file for the Exchange settings. Active Directory contains the Service Connection Point (SCP) that will contain the URLs for Autodiscover operation. IIS hosts the Autodiscover Web site and makes it available for users when needed.

- The Availability Service now provides free/busy data to end users in Exchange Server 2007. Public folders are no longer required unless using older versions of Outlook.

- There are three connector types in Exchange Server 2007: Receive, Send, and Foreign.

- By default, the installation of a Hub Transport Server will install three connectors: two Receive and one Send. This is normally all that is needed for the HT role to function.

- You use three security methods with OWA. The first is configured through IIS itself and consists of using the Secure Sockets Layer. The second authentication method includes Integrated Windows, Digest, and Basic authentication. The third is forms-based authentication, which displays a logon page for OWA.

- ActiveSync is enabled by default when you install the CAS role. In addition, mailboxes are enabled for ActiveSync by default. Direct Push is also enabled by default, but must be available on port 443 through the firewall to work.

■ Outlook Anywhere (formerly RPC over HTTP) allows users to traverse the fire-wall over common ports, most often port 443 with HTTPS, to access their mail-boxes from Outlook 2007 or Outlook 2003. By default Outlook Anywhere is not enabled after a CAS installation. It is enabled through the Enable Outlook Anywhere Wizard.

■ In Exchange Server 2007, the index is no more than five percent of the database size and can therefore be placed on the same disk set as the database itself. Indexing overhead is very low because all messages are indexed as they are received and within fewer than 10 seconds of arrival.

Case Scenarios

In the following case scenarios, you will apply what you have learned about Exchange deployment. You can find answers to the questions in these scenarios in the "Answers" section at the end of this book.

Case Scenario 1: Plan for a New Messaging System Implementation

Adventure Works is working on a deal for adventure toys with two partner firms: Wingtip Toys and Tailspin Toys. If the deal works out, these three firms intend to merge together, but since they each have their own Web presence and each has an existing forest, they want to move to Exchange Server 2007 and plan to perform a new implementation of the messaging system.

They have asked you as a messaging professional to assist them in planning their storage for the MB role. What they want is a standard server configuration so that they know what to purchase and implement when they need to add a new MB role anywhere in their multi-forest configuration.

Because they have multiple sites, the group intends to use Cluster Continuous Replication as a means of failover from one site to another. They give you the following specifications:

■ Servers will host a maximum of 20 databases each.

■ Each database disk set will be 200 GB in size.

■ Transaction logs will be split from databases onto their own disk sets.

■ Each server will host a recovery storage group with its corresponding transaction logs.

■ Each server will run the Enterprise Edition of Exchange Server 2007.

In your recommendation, they want:

1. Server processor type and speed

2. RAM sizing

3. Storage type

4. Storage sizing

5. Storage configuration

They also want justifications for each selection.

Case Scenario 2: Work with Transport Servers

You are working for Lucerne Publishing as a messaging professional. Lucerne is large enough to have its own perimeter network. Lucerne has decided to deploy Exchange Server 2007 internally and to use two external Edge Transport Servers to clear out messaging spam before it enters its network. You configure your Hub Transport Servers in the headquarters site of Lucerne's network. Next you configure the two ET computers. You export the Edge Subscription information from the two ET computers and import it into your HT computer in the headquarters site.

A month later, you notice that your HT workload has increased dramatically. You decide to add two more HT computers. You set them up and, because they are available, you decide to perform maintenance on the original HT computers you deployed. You take them both down. As soon as you do so, you see errors that start occurring in the Exchange Server Event Logs. What could be the problem and how can you fix it?

Case Scenario 3: Design a Storage Group Strategy in a SAN Environment

Lucerne Publishing has an existing Exchange Server 2003 environment. They are planning to deploy Exchange Server 2007, but because the storage requirements for 2007 differ so much from those of 2003, they intend to use a new storage structure for this implementation. The also intend to have recovery storage groups in each location that hosts MB roles to provide local restoration capabilities. Lucerne's mailbox requirements are outlined in Table 2-16.

Note that both Dallas and Newark do not have local servers. Their mailboxes are hosted in the New York site. Also, after some quick analysis, Lucerne tells you that in each site, mailbox usage and quotas are defined as illustrated in Table 2-17.

Table 2-16   Lucerne Publishing Exchange Storage Requirements

Site Name	Number of Users
Headquarters (New York)	1,000
Site 2 (Los Angeles)	600
Region 1 (San Remo)	50
Region 2 (Philadelphia)	75
Region 3 (Dallas)	9
Region 4 (Newark)	5
Total	1,739

Table 2-17   Lucerne Publishing Exchange Storage Requirements

Mailbox Profile	Number of Users	Quota	Amount of Mail Per Week
Light	50 percent	1 GB	60 MB
Heavy	25 percent	2 GB	100 MB
Very Heavy	25 percent	4 GB	150 MB

Your job is to define the following:

- Number of MB roles per location
- Number of storage groups per server
- Number of databases per storage group
- Number of mailboxes per database
- Disk set configuration for each server

Your results will be defined in a table format along with commentary for each selection. To facilitate this exercise, a table for case scenario 3 has been prepared for you and is available on the companion CD. Use this table to fill in the requirements for each blank portion of the table. Also, justify your selection in the bullet points following the table.

Case Scenario 4: Design a Deployment Strategy for the Autodiscover Service

Coho Winery is a small organization that wants to make use of the power of Exchange Server 2007 to unify their communications. Because they are small, it is easy for them to make sure that all of their users have access to the latest versions of technology; therefore, they have decided to deploy Outlook 2007 to all of their users.

But, because they are a small firm, they do not have the wherewithal or the capacity to host Exchange internally. Therefore, they have decided to turn to an ASP to host Exchange for them. Because they are using a hosted Exchange service, their users must connect through the Internet. Each user must use Outlook's Auto Account Setup to automatically configure their connection to the Exchange server.

But, once the service is launched, users report that Auto Account Setup does not work. Each user gets an error and cannot configure the mailbox. Coho Winery officials contact the ASP to resolve the issue, but nothing seems to be happening. They are getting upset because they are paying for the service, yet it does not work and the ASP insists that nothing is wrong on their end, so something must be wrong at Coho's end. In desperation, Coho turns to you, the messaging professional, to help resolve the issue. What could be wrong?

Case Scenario 5: Prepare the Design for a Mobility Solution

The Graphic Design Institute wants to implement a mobility solution. Their design teams are often on the road with clients and they need to be in constant communication with the office to ensure that they continue to win the best bids when opportunities arise. Because they are a small team of professionals, the staff of GDI knows that instant communication through their mobile devices will give them an advantage that their competitors will not have.

As graphic designers, many of the employees have obtained their own mobile devices. Some have the latest in Windows Mobile technologies, such as the Touch Pocket PC— a Pocket PC running Windows Mobile version 6.0. But, others have decided to go with a non-Windows Mobile phone.

Your job as a messaging professional is to provide GDI with three items:

- The configuration of their CAS server to support both phones.
- A list of the features they will be able to use with the selected Pocket PC which is a Touch Pocket PC.

MORE INFO Note that the Touch Pocket PC is used here only as an example and is by no means a recommendation.

- A list of the features they will be able to use with the other phone.

To facilitate your response, you have been given a table that will let you identify which phone supports which features. A table for this scenario is included on the companion CD to do this.

Suggested Practices

You can perform several practices to prepare for this section of the exam. First, you should review some reference information to complement what you have seen in this chapter. Second, you should take a practice test. Do not take the entire test. Instead, concentrate on the objectives in this chapter.

It is difficult to practice the deployment of Exchange features without access to a full infrastructure, but you can do so if you prepare a virtual environment as outlined in the "Before You Begin" section at the beginning of this chapter. At this point, you should have several roles installed in this environment.

This should let you view and examine the various settings for both the CAS and MB roles. In addition, you should be able to configure EdgeSync Subscriptions between at least one HT and one ET server. Try to run through each of the settings described in this chapter to view its results and become familiar with its requirements.

Chapter 3
Planning Exchange Server 2007 Upgrades and Migrations

Most Exchange Server 2007 implementations will very likely need to recover information and data from existing deployments. Exchange is after all, Microsoft's most popular server product and has been deployed to organizations of all sizes all over the world. For these organizations, it will be important to transform their existing installations into an Exchange Server 2007 implementation and do so with as little end-user disruption as possible. This is what this chapter is all about: helping you prepare for the implementation of an Exchange Server 2007 infrastructure with the objective of replacing an existing implementation of Exchange.

There is no direct or in-place upgrade path from a previous installation of Microsoft Exchange (2000 or 2003) to Exchange Server 2007. That is because Exchange 2007 is a native x64 application and because of this, requires a new installation. In fact, moving from an existing e-mail system to Exchange Server 2007 will take one of three paths:

- A *transition* is a move from Exchange Server 2000 or Exchange 2003 to Exchange Server 2007 through the upgrade of an existing organization. To do this, you introduce Exchange 2007 server roles into the existing organization, move the data from its original containers to the new MB servers, and then transition the other servers in the infrastructure to the other Exchange 2007 server roles.

- A *migration* is a move from an existing e-mail system to Exchange Server 2007 by moving the data from the existing system to a new Exchange Server 2007 organization. This migration can be from a third-party e-mail system or from an existing Exchange Server 2000 or Exchange 2003 organization that you do not want to recover. Instead, you just keep the data from the previous installation and move it to a new, pristine Exchange 2007 organization. In this case, you preserve only e-mail data and discard all configuration data.

- A *multi-step migration* is when you move from Exchange 5.5 to Exchange Server 2007. We call this a multi-step transition because there is no direct path from Exchange Server 5.5 to 2007. Instead, you must migrate from 5.5 to either Exchange 2000 or Exchange 2003 and then use the transition or migration process to move to Exchange 2007. This type of migration also applies when you move from a third-party messaging system to Exchange 2007.

Exam Tip There is no direct or in-place upgrade path from Exchange 2000 or Exchange 2003 to Exchange 2007. You must always install a new Exchange 2007 server and then use either a migration or transition to move the data.

Transitions occur in several phases. In each phase, you introduce new Exchange 2007 server roles and new transports. When each phase completes, you are in a stable state of coexistence with servers running older and newer versions of Exchange. Eventually, you decommission all older servers and run only Exchange 2007 server roles.

MORE INFO **Exchange coexistence scenarios**

Exchange coexistence scenarios are covered extensively in Chapter 4, "Planning Exchange Server Interoperability."

Transitions are supported from Exchange 2000, Exchange 2003, or even mixed Exchange 2000 and Exchange 2003 organizations. Migrations are supported from third-party e-mail systems such as Lotus Notes as well as from the same organization types as for the transition.

IMPORTANT **ActiveSync users**

During a transition from Exchange 2003 to Exchange 2007, ActiveSync cannot transition the synchronization state from a user's Exchange 2003 mailbox to the new Exchange 2007 mailbox. Users will be warned that they will lose all synchronization data from their last Exchange 2003 synchronization. When they are moved to an Exchange 2007 mailbox, however, all of the information in the users' mailboxes will be synchronized.

Table 3-1 outlines the possible migration or transition paths to Exchange 2007.

IMPORTANT **Migration from Exchange 5.5**

Though it is supported, when performing item 8 from Table 3-1, you should not use Exchange 2000 Server as an intermediary during the migration to Exchange 2007. If you need to perform this step, use Exchange Server 2003. This will let you set up many more features that you can simply transition, not migrate, to Exchange Server 2007. In this case, you perform scenario 8 along with scenario 2 to complete the process.

MORE INFO **Exchange migration white paper and poster**

If you need to move from Exchange 5.5 to Exchange Server 2003 before you can take advantage of Exchange 2007, consider the information in the white paper "A 10-Step Migration Survival Guide" and the poster "10 Fast Facts to Exchange Migration." You can find both on the companion CD.

Table 3-1 Supported Migration or Transition Scenarios to Exchange 2007

Upgrade Scenario	Starting Point	Action	Action	Midpoint	Action	Endpoint
1. Transition	Exchange 2000 Server	Install Exchange 2007 server role(s) into organization	Move mailboxes	Combined Exchange 2000/ Exchange 2007 organization	Decommission Exchange 2000 servers	Organization transitioned to Exchange Server 2007
2. Transition	Exchange Server 2003	Install Exchange 2007 server role(s) into organization	Move mailboxes	Combined Exchange 2003/ Exchange 2007 organization	Decommission Exchange 2003 servers	Organization transitioned to Exchange Server 2007
3. Transition	Combined Exchange 2000/ Exchange 2003 organization	Install Exchange 2007 server role(s) into organization	Move mailboxes	Combined Exchange 2000/ Exchange 2003/ Exchange 2007 organization	Decommission Exchange 2000/ Exchange 2003 servers	Organization transitioned to Exchange Server 2007
4. Migration	Exchange 2000 Server	Install Exchange 2007 server role(s) in new organization	Move mailboxes	none	Decommission Exchange 2000 servers	New Exchange Server 2007 organization

Table 3-1 Supported Migration or Transition Scenarios to Exchange 2007

Upgrade Scenario	Starting Point	Action	Action	Midpoint	Action	Endpoint
5. Migration	Exchange Server 2003	Install Exchange 2007 server role(s) in new organization	Move mailboxes	none	Decommission Exchange 2003 servers	New Exchange Server 2007 organization
6. Migration	Combined Exchange 2000/ Exchange 2003 organization	Install Exchange 2007 server role(s) in new organization	Move mailboxes	none	Decommission Exchange 2000/ Exchange 2003 servers	New Exchange Server 2007 organization
7. Migration	Exchange Server 5.5 organization	Install Exchange 2000 or Exchange 2003 server(s)	Migrate data	Exchange 2000 or Exchange 2003 organization	Use appropriate transition or migration process as outlined in scenarios 1, 2, 4 or 5	New or transitioned Exchange Server 2007 organization

Table 3-1 Supported Migration or Transition Scenarios to Exchange 2007

Upgrade Scenario	Starting Point	Action	Action	Midpoint	Action	Endpoint
8. Migration	Lotus Notes	Install Exchange 2007 server role(s) in new organization	Use Lotus Interoperability And Migration Tools to interoperate	Exchange Server 2007/ Lotus Notes interoperability	Use Lotus Interoperability And Migration Tools to migrate data and then decommission Lotus Notes servers	New Exchange Server 2007 organization
9. Migration	Novell GroupWise	Install Exchange 2003 server(s)	Migrate data with the GroupWise Connector	Exchange 2003 organization	Use appropriate transition or migration process as outlined in scenarios 2 or 5	New or transitioned Exchange Server 2007 organization

This chapter will rely on the various scenarios outlined in Table 3-1 to discuss the potential strategies you should consider to move to Exchange Server 2007.

MORE INFO   **Making the Exchange 2007 migration decision**

Deciding how to migrate or transition to Exchange 2007 involves several factors. Before you are ready to make this decision, you should consider the contents of the white paper "Making the Exchange 2007 Migration Decision," which you can find on the companion CD.

Exam objectives in this chapter:
- Plan the Exchange Server 2007 upgrade implementation.
- Plan the Exchange Server 2007 migration implementation.

Before You Begin

To complete the lessons in this chapter, you must have the following:

- A virtual machine setup as outlined in the Introduction under "Virtual Machine Environments."

- Use the Exchange Server 2007 virtual machine from Microsoft to review the configuration options for preinstalled computers.

- Use the newly created virtual environment you set up to test the deployment of different server configurations. For the exercises in this chapter, you will need access to the Active Directory server and the all-in-one Exchange server.

Lesson 1: Plan the Exchange Upgrade Implementation

Estimated lesson time: 90 minutes

Chapter 1, "Plan the Exchange Topology Deployment," outlined the various Exchange server roles and the general planning strategies you should take into consideration when preparing an Exchange Server 2007 implementation. Chapter 2, "Planning Deployments," focused on role-specific configurations, covering the storage requirements for each role, the transport requirements for the two transport roles, and the configuration of the various features of the Client Access Server role.

As you move toward the preparation for a transition or a migration, you need to review these strategies and requirements before you can proceed. Each scenario is based on the prior installation of Exchange 2007 server roles. This is the objective of the first part of this lesson. It will then move on to describe the various transition scenarios you can use to perform the update of an existing Exchange organization.

Message System Planning

When you prepare and plan your Exchange Server 2007 Organization, you must first consider the various server roles and how you will position them in your own organization. This positioning will depend on the size and needs of your organization and will usually fit within one of the four typical organization types supported by Exchange. Then you can proceed with the actual implementation. For this you'll need to prepare your Active Directory to host the new Exchange Server 2007 features, prepare the hardware to host Exchange server roles, prepare the prerequisites for Exchange on each server, prepare your client to work with Exchange Server 2007, and finish with a review of all of these components before you move on to the actual transition.

Exchange Server 2007 Roles and Organization Types

As you will remember from Chapter 1, there are five specific Exchange server roles: the Mailbox Server (MB), the Hub Transport Server (HT), the Client Access Server (CAS), the Unified Messaging Server (UM), and the Edge Transport Server (ET). Of these five roles, only the ET cannot coexist with the others.

Exam Tip Of the five server roles, only four are actually included on the exam: MB, HT, CAS, and ET. Keep this in mind when preparing for the exam. In your own implementations, however, you will most likely want to work with all five server roles.

In addition, supported deployments of Exchange Server 2007 fit into four different organization types. Table 3-2 lists the different organizations supported by Microsoft for Exchange Server 2007 along with the details of each organization type.

Table 3-2   Supported Organization Types for Exchange Server 2007

Organization	Characteristic	Requirement
Simple	The organization is deemed simple because all of the four internal roles coexist on the same server.	Roles are hosted on the same server. Hosts Service Delivery Location (SDL) and Client Service Location (CSL) in the same location.
Simple: Single server	One single Exchange server on a 64-bit operating system hosting the Active Directory domain controller service or one Small Business Server 2008 installation.	Host all the roles except ET on the same server. The HT is directly connected to the Internet through a firewall. Microsoft recommends this solution only for Small Business Server. The MB can be at risk because it also faces the Internet through a firewall.
Simple: Multiple servers	One single Exchange server on a 64-bit operating system hosting the four internal roles or one Microsoft Business Essentials Server 2008 installation.	The four internal roles are located on a single member server. The Active Directory domain controller is located on a different computer. A second domain controller server for redundancy. The ET role is running on a member server in a workgroup and is connected to the Internet through a firewall. The ET is connected to the HT for internal mail delivery. Microsoft recommends this solution only if you are using Centro, an upcoming medium organization server solution based on Windows Server 2008.

Table 3-2 Supported Organization Types for Exchange Server 2007

Organization	Characteristic	Requirement
Standard	Hosted in a single Active Directory forest.	Internal Exchange roles on member server(s). The SDL and CSL are within the same LAN or physical site. If Exchange 2007 is in a native implementation, there is a single routing group. If not, there are multiple routings groups.
Large	Hosted in a single Active Directory forest but includes more than five Active Directory sites. May have several Active Directory domains within the forest but the external messaging presence and client namespace are common among all locations. Also, different domains will have different FQDNs but use the same root name.	If older versions of Exchange exist, there may be more than five routings groups. The SDL and CSL are hosted in multiple sites and may reside on different servers. Messages are transferred to and from the Internet from a single location and routed to multiple points throughout the internal network.
Complex	Hosts multiple Active Directory forests. Need to synchronize multiple global address lists (GALs).	Synchronization usually relies on Microsoft Identity Integration Server (MIIS), now Identity Lifecycle Manager, or the Identity Integration Feature Pack (IIFP).

Table 3-2 **Supported Organization Types for Exchange Server 2007**

Organization	Characteristic	Requirement
Complex: Exchange Resource Forest	Strict boundaries are required between each forest, and the source schema cannot be changed.	The Exchange Resource Forest (ERF) has a one-way trust toward the account forest(s) or the forests that contain the user accounts for each business unit.
		The ERF contains duplicates of each user account within the account forests, but duplicates are disabled.
		Duplicates are linked to the user's mailbox.
		Mailbox creation is performed only in the Exchange resource forest.
		Account creators can create mailbox only if the right is delegated to them.
		Phone numbers or office location must be added separately to the accounts in the resource forest.
		Not recommended because of high administrative overhead.
Complex: Multiple Exchange Forests or Cross-Forest Implementation	Works with existing Active Directory forests that have their own Exchange organizations.	Multiple Exchange repositories, often one in each forest.
		Rely on MIIS or IIFP to synchronize information between forests.
		To replicate free/busy data from forest to forest, use Availability Service if only using Outlook 2007 or the Inter-Organization Replication (IORepl) tool if older Outlook clients exist. IORepl is only available from Exchange 2003.

The typical organizations listed in Table 3-2 are the basis for the transition or migration scenarios Microsoft supports. As such, they form the basis of this lesson and the next.

IMPORTANT Exchange Server and time synchronization

Exchange servers are very sensitive to time synchronization. In an Active Directory forest, the central time server is the PDC Emulator master of operations and all domain members are automatically linked to this DC for time synchronization. Workgroups, however, such as the workgroups required for the Edge Transport role, have no default time synchronization server. Make sure that you synchronize all server clocks in your Exchange Organization.

Active Directory Integration and Preparation

As with other Exchange releases, Exchange Server 2007 must modify the Active Directory schema before it can be installed. This is true whether you are installing a brand new instance of Exchange Server 2007 or installing an Exchange Server 2007 role into an existing organization. You can prepare Active Directory either through the graphical setup tool for Exchange or through the command line. Before you can prepare your directory, it must meet some prerequisites.

Active Directory Preparation Prerequisites   Table 3-3 outlines the Active Directory prerequisites for your directory and the domain controllers contained within it.

Table 3-3   Active Directory and Domain Controller Prerequisites

Component	Requirement
Computer from which the operation is performed	Install the .NET Framework 2.0. Install the Microsoft Command Shell (Windows PowerShell).
Domain Controllers	At least one DC in each site that will host an Exchange Server 2007 role must have Windows Server 2003 Service Pack 1 or later or Windows Server 2003 R2.
Non-English Domain Controllers	You must install the hotfix from Knowledge Base article 919166 to correct the Outlook Web Access link to the Global Address Book.
Domain Controllers running Windows 2000	You must run the Active Directory update through the command line and you must specify the /**Domain-Controller** with **Setup.com** to identify a DC with Windows Server 2003 SP1. If you are using Exchange Server 2007 with Service Pack 1, you no longer need to specify this parameter.

Table 3-3   Active Directory and Domain Controller Prerequisites

Component	Requirement
Domain Controller Operating System	If you can, you should run your DCs on an x64 operating system. Running DCs on 64-bit servers vastly improves performance. In fact, Microsoft recommends a four-to-one ratio of Exchange servers to Global Catalog servers, assuming they are of similar size and performance.
Schema Operations Master	You must have Windows Server 2003 Service Pack 1 or later or Windows Server 2003 R2.
Global Catalog Server	There must be at least one GC in each site and it must have Windows Server 2003 Service Pack 1 or later or Windows Server 2003 R2.
If there are existing Exchange Servers	You must run **Setup /PrepareLegacyExchange-Permissions** in the root domain and each child domain.
Directory Version	The original version of Exchange 2007 cannot run on Windows Server 2008, but it can participate in an Active Directory Domain Services (AD DS) directory. It must, however, be installed on a Windows Server 2003 computer running SP1 or later. You can install Exchange 2007 SP1, however, on Windows Server 2008. If you are installing from a Windows Server 2008 member server, you must install the AD DS management tools first.
Domain Functional Level	The domain functional level must be at least Windows 2000 Native to host Exchange 2007 server roles.
Forest Functional Level	The Forest functional level must be Windows Server 2003 in each forest that contains Exchange servers for advanced features such as forest-to-forest delegation and for a user to select the type of free/busy data available to users of another forest. If you do not require the Exchange Server 2007 advanced features, your forest functional level must be at least Windows 2000.

Table 3-3 Active Directory and Domain Controller Prerequisites

Component	Requirement
Forest Trusts	As with the forest functional levels, you must have a forest trust relationship to support both advanced features in a cross-forest topology.
	If you are using a Resource Forest, you need an external trust from the ERF to the account forest(s).
Exchange Server 5.5	There can be no Exchange Server 5.5 computers in the Active Directory domain or forest before you install an Exchange 2007 server role.
Disjoint Namespaces where computer DNS suffixes are different than the domain where they reside	The DNS Suffix Search Order list must include the suffixes for the DCs and Exchange servers, as well as the namespaces for other servers that Exchange may interoperate, such as monitoring servers or servers for third-party applications.
DNS	DNS must be configured correctly—as it should be to operate and support Active Directory.
Exchange Server Role Installation	Do not install Exchange server roles onto domain controllers unless you are using the Simple Organization. Exchange should be installed on member servers because it improves performance and security.
	Also, while you can turn a member server hosting Exchange to a DC or turn a DC hosting Exchange into a member server with the DCPromo.exe command, Microsoft does not support either operation.

Links to the listed prerequisites are listed in Chapter 1 under "Prerequisites to Exchange Installation" so they are not repeated here.

IMPORTANT Windows Server 2003 Service Pack 1

Windows Server 2003 SP1 is required because of several enhancements it includes. It supports Exchange 2007 service notifications, which are sent each time a configuration change occurs in Active Directory. Exchange server roles rely on these notifications to function. It lets Outlook Web Access 2007 users browse the GAL. It also performs more efficient lookups for distribution list memberships. Ideally, however, your servers would be running the latest available service pack.

Prepare Active Directory   When you use the graphical setup tool, you must be logged on with an account that has the right to modify the schema as well as prepare both the forest and the domain(s) where Exchange servers will reside. This account must be a member of the Enterprise Administrators group in the root domain of the forest. If you do not have the appropriate permissions, Setup will fail.

This is one reason why most messaging professionals prefer to rely on the command line to perform the required directory modifications. Using the command line lets you find out if each command works properly because it provides direct feedback as each command is executed.

To prepare Active Directory, complete the following steps. Make sure you are using a computer that meets the prerequisites listed in Table 3-3.

1. Log on with appropriate credentials.

2. If there are existing Exchange 2000 or 2003 servers or an existing legacy organization, run the following command first in each domain that hosts Exchange servers. You must be a domain administrator in each target domain to perform this task.

   ```
   setup /PrepareLegacyExchangePermissions
   ```

   You can shorten this command to **setup /pl**. You can also run it from a single location without having to log onto each domain, but you need Enterprise Administrator permissions to do so. When you do so, each domain in the forest will be updated. If the command cannot contact a domain, it will return an error code for that domain. To update a single domain, use the following command:

   ```
   setup /pl:FQDNofTargetDomain
   ```

   The *FQDNofTargetDomain* value is the fully qualified domain name of the target domain. For example, for Lucerne Publishing, it would be lucernepublishing.com.

   IMPORTANT   **Replication Latency**

   You must wait for replication to complete in all domains before you can continue. A good way to find out if it is complete is to monitor replication with the Active Directory Replication Monitor (replmon.exe), which can be found in the Windows Server 2003 Support Tools.

   ---

3. Now you are ready to prepare the schema. Using an account with Enterprise Administrators *and* Schema Administrators membership, use the following command:

   ```
   setup /PrepareSchema /DomainController:FQDNofSchemaMaster
   ```

This lets you run the command without having to log on to the actual schema master DC. Use the *FQDNofSchemaMaster* value to specify the FQDN of the DC holding the schema master role. In addition, you can shorten this command to **setup /ps**. It will perform several tasks, including the update of the schema to prepare Exchange objects. If you did not run the command in step number 2, this command will perform it automatically. It is better to run the command in step 2 separately because you immediately know whether it worked everywhere. Make sure you wait for replication to be completed before moving on to step 4.

IMPORTANT   Schema updates

Be sure you run the schema update only in forests in which you intend to host an Exchange organization; otherwise, the schema will be left in an unfinished state.

---

4. To prepare the Exchange organization, run the following command with Enterprise Administrators credentials. The computer from which you run this command must be in the forest root domain and must be in the same site as the schema master. This computer must also be able to contact all domains in the forest.

   ```
   setup /PrepareAD /OrganizationName:ExistingorNewOrganizationName
   ```

   Using the */OrganizationName* switch with the *ExistingorNewOrganizationName* value lets you rely on the same command to create a new organization or to update an existing one. You can also shorten this command to **setup /p**, but you always need to use the */Organization* switch. This command performs a series of steps, creating a new organization if one does not exist, updating an organization if it does, creating or updating Exchange containers in Active Directory, assigning permissions throughout the configuration partition of Active Directory, adding extended rights to install Exchange into Active Directory, creating the Microsoft Exchange Security Groups organizational unit (OU) in the forest root domain, creating Exchange universal groups and updating them, and creating the Exchange 2007 Administrative and Routing groups. It will also create the Unified Messaging Voice Originator contact that is used to forward all voice mail.

   Make sure you wait for replication to complete before you move on to step 5.

IMPORTANT   Exchange Administrative and Routing Groups

The preceding command creates the Exchange 2007 Administrative Group (FYDIBOHF-23SPDLT) and the Routing Group (DWBGZMFD01QNBJR). Microsoft does not support either renaming these groups or moving objects out of these groups in Active Directory.

---

5. In each of the child domains where you plan to host Exchange server roles or you plan to have mail-enabled users, run the following command. Make sure you use domain administrator credentials for the target domain.

`setup /PrepareDomain`

You can shorten this command can to **setup /pd**. You can also run it from a single location without having to log on to each domain, but you need Enterprise Administrator permissions to do so. Use the following command from a central location.

`setup /pd:FQDNofTargetDomain`

The *FQDNofTargetDomain* value is the fully qualified domain name of the target domain. For example, for Lucerne Publishing, it would be lucernepublishing.com.

If you want to update all of the child domains in your forest, shorten the command to the following. Make sure you have Enterprise Administrator credentials.

`setup /PrepareAllDomains`

You can shorten this command to **setup /pad**. When you do so, each child domain in the forest will be updated. If the command cannot contact a domain, it will return an error code.

This command will perform several tasks, including setting permissions on the domain container for Exchange objects, creating a new global group called Exchange Install Domain Servers, and assigning permissions in this domain for the Exchange Servers universal group created in step 4. Make sure you wait for replication to complete within the child domain before you proceed to any other step.

As you can see, preparing Active Directory is an intensive operation. This is one more reason why it is worthwhile to perform this step through the command line.

MORE INFO   **Find out more about Active Directory preparation**

Microsoft has released a white paper on Active Directory preparation for Exchange Server 2007 that you can find at *http://technet.microsoft.com/en-us/library/bb288907.aspx*.

Prepare Exchange Hardware

Chapter 1 provides several topics on the hardware required to run Exchange 2007. Table 3-4 provides a summary of these topics.

Table 3-4 Exchange Server Hardware Requirements Per Role

Role	Minimum Processor Cores	Maximum Processor Cores	Recommended RAM	Maximum RAM	Disk Structure
MB	4	8	2 GB plus 2 to 5 MB per mailbox	32 GB	One database per storage group. Two disk sets per storage group.
HT	4	8	2 GB	16 GB	TMP folder on a separate disk set.
CAS	4	4	2 GB	8 GB	If you enable protocol logging, place it on a separate disk set. If CAS is used to convert content from Exchange 2003, move the TMP folder to a separate disk set other than the paging file and the operating system.
UM	4	4	2 GB	4 GB	TMP folder on a separate disk set.
ET	2	4	2 GB	16 GB	ESE database on a separate disk set than transaction logs. Needs more space for log storage than HT.
Combined HT/CAS/ MB/UM	4	4	4 GB plus 2 to 5 MB per mailbox	8 GB	Use the same recommendations as for MB.

Rely on the values in Table 3-4 to prepare your servers. Remember that all servers must run an x64 operating system for production implementations. You can, however, run x86 operating systems for test and development implementations.

IMPORTANT   Running Exchange Server 2007 on x86 operating systems

Although you can run Exchange 2007 on x86 operating systems for test and development purposes, we strongly recommend that you run all implementations on x64 computers. This ensures that all your implementations are identical and all your tests provide the same results. You can, however, use x64 virtual machines to reduce costs.

Prepare Exchange Server Software

Chapter 1 provides several topics on the software required to run Exchange 2007. Table 3-5 provides a summary of these topics. You can also use this table as a checklist for prerequisite installation.

Table 3-5   Exchange Server Software Requirements Per Role

Server Role	Required Software	
All roles or Administrative Tools	.NET Framework 2.0.	☐
	MMC version 3.0 (on operating systems prior to Windows Server 2003 R2).	☐
	Windows PowerShell (KB 926139).	☐
	TCPIP.SYS update (KB 898060).	☐
	If you have Windows Server 2003 SP2, the TCPIP.SYS update is not required.	
MB	MDAC version 2.8 hotfix (KB 904639).	☐
	OLE database component hotfix (KB 918980).	☐
	Neither update is required if you have Windows Server 2003 SP2.	
	IIS 6.0 with WWW Service.	☐
	COM+.	☐
HT	Refer to requirements for all roles.	☐

Table 3-5   **Exchange Server Software Requirements Per Role**

Server Role	Required Software	
CAS	IIS 6.0: WWW Service.	☐
	ASP.NET 2.0–Enabled.	☐
	Distributed Transaction Coordinator service must be started.	☐
	RPC over HTTP Proxy (for CAS computers running Outlook Anywhere).	☐
UM	Windows Media Encoder.	☐
	Windows Media Audio Voice Codec.	☐
	Microsoft Core XML Services 6.0.	☐
ET	ADAM with SP1 with all the defaults.	☐
	Proper DNS name along with a proper DNS suffix.	☐
MB onto Failover Clusters	First update for the File Share Witness (KB 921181).	☐
	Second update Volume Mount Points (KB 898790).	☐
	If you have Windows Server 2003 SP2, these updates are not required.	
Windows XP for Administrative Tools	Windows Installer 3.1 (KB 893803).	☐

Note that no role supports the installation or operation of the NWLink IPX/SPX/NetBIOS–compatible transport protocol. If this protocol is installed on a server where you target an Exchange 2007 role, you must remove it before the installation of the role.

If you plan to integrate Exchange into an environment that has an existing organization, make note of the service pack levels for each version of Exchange:

- No Exchange 5.5 servers can exist in the forest.
- Exchange 2003 servers must be running at least Exchange Server 2003 Service Pack 2.

■ Exchange 2000 servers or any computer using the Exchange 2000 System Manager must be running at least Exchange 2000 Service Pack 3. They also require the Exchange 2000 Post-SP3 update rollup. This will allow the Exchange 2000 System Manager to work with Exchange 2007 objects. See KB article 870540 at *http://support.microsoft.com/?kbid=870540* for more information.

Exam Tip   After you have created a new Exchange 2007 organization, you will no longer be able to install either Exchange 2000 or Exchange 2003 servers into that organization. If you want to install a mixed organization, you must install the older versions of Exchange first.

Prepare Client Requirements

Client computers also have requirements, which are outlined in Table 3-6.

Table 3-6   Client Computer Software Requirements

Client	Required Software	
Rich Client	Microsoft Office Outlook 2007 provides the best experience.	☐
	Outlook 2003.	☐
	Outlook XP.	☐
Outlook Web Access Premium	Internet Explorer 6 and above.	☐
	Can also use Windows Integrated Authentication.	☐
OWA Light	Internet Explorer 5.01 and later.	☐
	Non-Internet Explorer Browser.	☐
Mobile Device	Windows Mobile 6.0 or later.	☐
	Windows Mobile 5.0.	☐
	Windows Mobile 5.0 with the Messaging and Security Feature Pack.	☐
	Non-Windows mobile devices compatible with ActiveSync.	☐
	Non-Windows mobile devices with integrated browser (POP/IMAP clients).	☐

Table 3-6 **Client Computer Software Requirements**

Client	Required Software	
Third-party POP or IMAP applications	POP3 application must meet POP requirements.	☐
	IMAP4 application must meet IMAP requirements.	☐
Microsoft Entourage	Macintosh computer. Read the *Microsoft Office 2004 for Macintosh Resource Kit version 2* at *http://go.microsoft.com/ fwlink/?linkid=85723*.	☐

MORE INFO **Deploying Outlook 2007**

Obviously, the best client experience is with Outlook 2007. You might consider deploying Windows Vista along with the Microsoft 2007 Office system. If you intend to do so, we recommend that you obtain the free e-Book *The Definitive Guide to Vista Migration* by Ruest and Ruest from Realtime Publishers (*www.realtime-nexus.com/dgvm.htm*).

Final Planning Review

Now that you understand the prerequisites for a migration or transition, it is time to make a final review of the considerations you need to keep in mind before you proceed with the actual Exchange Server 2007 implementation. Table 3-7 provides a planning checklist you can rely on to make this final preparation.

Refer to Chapters 1 and 2 as well as the tables listed in this lesson to complete the requirements outlined in Table 3-7.

Table 3-7 **Final Planning Review**

Planning Item	Requirements Review	
Active Directory	The schema master DC must have Windows Server 2003 SP1 or Windows Server 2003 R2.	☐
	At least one DC in each site must have Windows Server 2003 SP1 or Windows Server 2003 R2.	☐
	At least one DC in each site must be a Global Catalog and have Windows Server 2003 SP1 or Windows Server 2003 R2.	☐
	The Active Directory domain functional level must be at least Windows 2000 native.	☐

Table 3-7 **Final Planning Review**

Planning Item	Requirements Review	
	If multiple forests are involved, you need appropriate trusts in place.	☐
	If installing into an existing organization, run `Setup /PrepareLegacyExchangePermissions`	☐
Network and Name Resolution	DNS must be configured properly for Active Directory to work.	☐
	Sites including Exchange server roles must have at least 64 kilobits per second of available bandwidth.	☐
Existing Organization	Remove all Exchange 5.5 servers.	☐
	Convert the Exchange organization to native mode.	☐
	Exchange 2003 servers must run Exchange 2003 SP2.	☐
	Exchange 2000 servers must run Exchange 2000 SP3 plus the post-SP3 update rollup.	☐
Mailbox Server	Use x64 hardware.	☐
	Create all partitions as sector-aligned partitions.	☐
	Format all partitions with NTFS.	☐
	Install an x64 version of Windows Server 2003 (or Windows Server 2008 if using Exchange 2007 SP1).	☐
	Install MB prerequisites.	☐
Client Access Server	Use x64 hardware.	☐
	Create all partitions as sector-aligned partitions.	☐
	Format all partitions with NTFS.	☐
	Install an x64 version of Windows Server 2003 (or Windows Server 2008 if using Exchange 2007 SP1).	☐
	Install CAS prerequisites.	☐

Table 3-7   Final Planning Review

Planning Item	Requirements Review	
Hub Transport Server	Use x64 hardware.	☐
	Create all partitions as sector-aligned partitions.	☐
	Format all partitions with NTFS.	☐
	Install an x64 version of Windows Server 2003 (or Windows Server 2008 if using Exchange 2007 SP1).	☐
	Install HT prerequisites.	☐
Unified Messaging Server	Use x64 hardware.	☐
	Create all partitions as sector-aligned partitions.	☐
	Format all partitions with NTFS.	☐
	Install an x64 version of Windows Server 2003 (or Windows Server 2008 if using Exchange 2007 SP1).	☐
	Install UM prerequisites.	☐
	Install and configure at least one IP PBX or IP gateway. (For supported IP PBX gateways, see *http://technet .microsoft.com/en-us/library/aa996831.aspx*; for supported IP gateways, see *http://technet .microsoft.com/en-us/library/bb123948.aspx*.)	☐
Edge Transport Server	Use x64 hardware.	☐
	Create all partitions as sector-aligned partitions.	☐
	Format all partitions with NTFS.	☐
	Install an x64 version of Windows Server 2003 (or Windows Server 2008 if using Exchange 2007 SP1).	☐
	Install ET prerequisites.	☐
	Server is not a member of Active Directory, but in a stand-alone workgroup.	☐

Table 3-7   Final Planning Review

Planning Item	Requirements Review	
Exchange Clients	Rich or MAPI clients are running a supported version of Outlook.	☐
	OWA Premium clients are running a supported version of Internet Explorer.	☐
	OWA Light clients are running a supported Web browser.	☐
	Mobile devices are running a supported operating system.	☐

Exam Tip   When you prepare to install any Exchange server role, the Installation Wizard will automatically perform an Exchange 2007 Readiness Check using the Exchange Best Practices Analyzer. If you missed any of the prerequisites, this readiness check will identify and list them. In addition, it will stop the installation from proceeding. Correct the missing requirements and you will be able to proceed.

Transition Strategies from Different Organization Types

Now that you know how to get ready for a transition or migration to Exchange Server 2007, you can begin to consider how to proceed. Procedural instructions are different based on the organization type you are working with. There are five supported transitions:

- Single-forest to single-forest
- Cross-forest to cross-forest
- Single-forest to cross-forest
- Resource Forest to Resource Forest
- Single-forest to Resource Forest

Each type of transition requires specific procedures to succeed properly. Rely on the scenarios in Table 3-1 to identify which transition best suits your organization.

Single-Forest to Single-Forest

Single-forest organizations fit into three organization types: simple, standard, or large. Obviously each has its own requirements, but each generally follows the same process for transition from either Exchange Server 2000 or Exchange 2003 to Exchange Server 2007.

First, you need to determine whether you intend to perform a complete transition to Exchange Server 2007 and decommission all legacy Exchange servers at the end of the transition, or if you plan on continued coexistence with the legacy Exchange servers. You may decide to continue coexistence because several features available in previous releases are no longer available in Exchange 2007. Table 3-8 outlines the deprecated features from legacy Exchange versions to Exchange 2007.

Table 3-8   Deprecated Features in Exchange Server 2007

Exchange Version	Deprecated Feature	
Exchange Server 2003	Novell GroupWise connector	☐
	Network News Transfer Protocol	☐
	X.400 Connector	☐
	Connector for Lotus Notes	☐
Exchange 2000 Server	Microsoft Mobile Information Server	☐
	Instant Messaging Service	☐
	Exchange Chat Service	☐
	Exchange 2000 Conferencing Server	☐
	Key Management Service	☐
	Cc:Mail connector	☐
	MS Mail connector	☐

If you choose to continue to use some of the features listed in Table 3-8, you will have to plan for the continued existence of legacy Exchange servers in your 2007 organization. Coexistence is covered in Chapter 4.

The transition process for a single forest is very straightforward. It presupposes that you have prepared all of the prerequisites listed in the previous section. Once this is done, complete the following steps:

1. Begin by installing a new Exchange Server 2007 computer into the existing organization. This computer can host all four coexistence roles or you can use several computers to host each role individually. If you choose to install each role individually, install them in the following order:

    ❑ Client Access server to replace front-end servers

    ❑ Hub Transport server to replace bridgehead servers

❑ Mailbox server to replace back-end servers

❑ Unified Messaging server

The CAS role is required because an Exchange 2000 or Exchange 2003 front-end server cannot provide access to an Exchange 2007 Mailbox server. The MB also cannot send or receive e-mail unless an HT is installed onto the same site. This is why Microsoft recommends installing these roles first, before the MB.

In addition, as soon as you installed a CAS role, you can begin to remove the legacy Exchange front-end servers from the organization.

You can also install an Edge Transport server computer or computers at this point, but remember that they must be installed on separate servers and must be members of a workgroup, not an Active Directory domain or forest. They will replace any Internet message relay that was used in the legacy organization.

2. Prepare the target storage groups in your MB server(s). Keep in mind the recommendations in Chapter 2. Use a single database per storage group and use two disk sets per storage group, one for the database and one for the transaction logs.

3. Once the three core roles are installed—CAS, HT, and MB—you can begin to move mailboxes from your existing back-end servers to the new MB computer. Note the following for this process:

❑ To move the mailboxes, you must have the Exchange Recipient Administrator and the Exchange Server Administrator, and you must be a local administrator on both the source and target servers.

❑ When you move mailboxes, items in the dumpster will not be moved. However, items in the Deleted Items folder will be moved because they are part of the mailbox.

❑ In the original Exchange 2007 version, you must use the **move-mailbox** cmdlet to perform the moves. For example, to move John Kane's mailbox in The Phone Company into a storage group called StorageGroupOne, use the following command:

```
move-mailbox TPC\john.kane –TargetDatabase "StorageGroupOne\MailboxDBOne"
```

❑ You can also use the Exchange Management Console to move mailboxes. Go to the Recipient Configuration | Mailbox node, right-click the mailbox to move and select Move Mailbox. Follow the prompts in the wizard to perform the move. Note that you can only run one Move Mailbox Wizard at a time in the Exchange Management Console, but you can open multiple consoles if you want to perform multiple moves at the same time. You can also preselect multiple users and move them all at once as long as they are all moved to the same storage group and mailbox database.

❑ Obviously, if you have a lot of mailboxes to move, you might prefer to use the **move-mailbox** cmdlet and script the operation.

❑ In either case, if the target mailbox is smaller than the source mailbox, the operation will fail. Make sure your MB quotas are set properly before you perform this operation. You can also use the *PreserveSource* switch in the **move-mailbox** cmdlet to make the target mailbox the same size as the source mailbox.

❑ Note that Exchange 2007 will automatically apply any recipient policies you have set when you move a mailbox. This behavior is different than that of previous versions, which did not apply policies to existing mailboxes. If you do not want your policies applied, you must first go into Active Directory, select the user's name and clear the Automatically Update E-Mail Addresses Based On E-Mail Address Policy check box on the E-Mail Addresses tab of the user's Properties dialog box (see Figure 3-1).

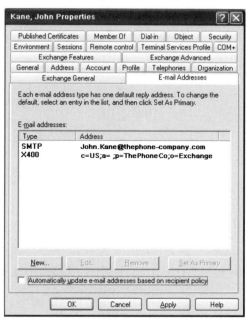

Figure 3-1   Preparing the user account before moving a mailbox

---

MORE INFO   Moving mailboxes

You can find more information on the move mailbox operation at
http://technet.microsoft.com/en-us/library/aa997961.aspx.

IMPORTANT   Moving contacts and distribution groups

You do not need to move your contacts or distribution groups because they are contained within Active Directory and are available to either the legacy Exchange servers or the new Exchange 2007 servers.

---

4. After the mailboxes are moved, you can remove the legacy Exchange 2000 or Exchange 2003 servers from the organization. Removing the servers one by one will let you generally control the transition. Use Add Or Remove Programs in Control Panel to uninstall Exchange from the legacy servers.

5. Before you remove the last legacy server in the organization, you must take special steps to ensure that all items have been transferred. This includes:

    ❑ Moving public folder replicas

    ❑ Removing the public folder database

    ❑ Moving the public folder hierarchy

    ❑ Moving the Offline Address Book (OAB)

    ❑ Moving the generation server

    ❑ Deleting the routing group connectors

    ❑ Deleting the recipient update service

    ❑ Verifying that all mail flow, protocols, and recipient policies are working correctly

Each of these items requires special attention. The overall process is covered in these five steps, no matter the size of your Simple, Standard, or Large Organization (see Figure 3-2).

Move Public Folder Content   To move public folder content from your legacy Exchange environment to the new Exchange Server 2007 environment, you need to perform several steps. First, determine whether you actually require the public folder content. In legacy Exchange organizations, free/busy data is provided to Outlook users through public folders, but in Exchange Server 2007, it is provided to Outlook 2007 clients through the Availability Service. If you use public folders only to provide free/busy data and you update all your clients to Outlook 2007, you will not need to move public folder content, but rather make sure you properly configure the Availability Service.

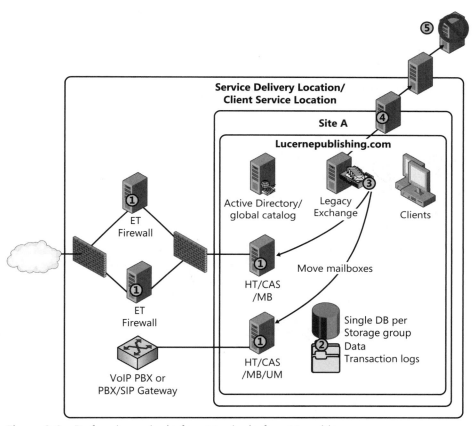

Figure 3-2   Performing a single-forest to single-forest transition

If you choose to continue using older versions of Outlook, you will have to maintain at least one public folder database to provide them with free/busy data.

To move public folder data from one database, make sure you have Exchange Server Administrator credentials and local administrative rights on both the source and target servers. Moving public folder content cannot be done in the Exchange Management Console; it must be done through the Exchange Management Shell.

- If you want to move all of the content from one public folder database to another, use the MoveAllReplicas.ps1 script. This script automatically replaces a legacy server with a new server in the replication list for all public folders, including system folders.

- If you want to move only a single tree from the public folder hierarchy, use the ReplaceReplicaOnPFRecursive.ps1 script. This script adds a new server name in the replication list for a public folder and its subfolders.

Both scripts can be found under C:\Program Files\Microsoft\Exchange Server\Scripts. Make sure the replication of all of the contents you wanted to move is complete before you remove the legacy public folder database.

MORE INFO   Reviewing scripted operations

You can find more information on both scripts at *http://technet.microsoft.com/en-us/library/aa997966.aspx.*

Move the Offline Address Book   The Offline Address Book (OAB) is often critical to users, especially when they are not connected. In Exchange Server 2007, the Client Access Server role can provide the OAB to end users in one of two ways: through Web-based distribution or through a public folder. The OAB can be generated from either Exchange Server 2003 or Exchange Server 2007, but if you decide to have it generated from Exchange 2003, you will have to use public folder distribution. For this reason, you should have the OAB generated by an Exchange 2007 server. This will give you more choices than using a legacy system to generate it. In addition, relying on Exchange Server 2007 to generate the OAB provides more functionality. This includes the ability to display OAB information in Japanese phonetic characters as well as rendering proper icons for objects in objects replicated throughout the forest.

You can use the Exchange Management Shell to move the OAB generation process to a new server.

1.   Use the Organization Configuration | Mailbox node.
2.   Click the Offline Address Book tab in the Details pane.
3.   Use the Move command in the Action pane.
4.   Step through the Move Offline Address Book Wizard.

You can also move the OAB with the Exchange Management Shell. For example, to move the OAB called OABOne to a server called EXMBOne, you would use the following command:

```
move-OfflineAddressBook –Identity "OABOne" –Server EXMBOne
```

Repeat this process for each OAB in the legacy organization.

When this is done, you can remove the legacy server running the OAB, as long as it does not have any other activated functions.

Remove Public Folder Databases   When the public folder mailbox and store is empty or at least replicated to a new server, you can remove it the from the legacy Exchange server. In either Exchange 2003 or Exchange 2000, you use Exchange System Manager to perform this task. Expand the server, expand the storage group that contains the public folder, right-click the public folder store, and select Delete. The Delete dialog box will notify you that it is the default store for one or more mailbox stores or users. Click OK. Then select a new public folder store on a new Exchange 2007 server and click OK.

Exchange Server 2003 SP2 will not allow you to perform this operation unless all replicas have been updated. This move process can take several hours or even days depending on the amount of content in the database. On Exchange 2000 Server, you must verify manually that all data has been replicated before you perform this process. You can do this by going to one of the target servers, using Exchange System Manager to expand the storage group that contains the public folder store, and then selecting Public Folder Instances. If the Details pane is empty, all replicas have been moved.

Verify Additional Exchange 2007 Components   Before you decommission all legacy servers you also need to make sure that other processes have been picked up by your new Exchange 2007 infrastructure. This includes the transport mechanism for the mail flow as well as the client components for user access. It also includes routing groups and e-mail address policies.

By default, Exchange Server 2007 does not route e-mail to the Internet. Before you remove your last legacy servers, you must make sure Internet mail flow is enabled and all required SMTP Send connectors are created. The best way to do this is to deploy an Edge Transport server—ideally at least two ET servers—and perform an Edge Subscription from the HT servers to the ET servers. If you are using a Simple Organization type, you either configure the HT to directly connect to the Internet or you use a hosted service for the Edge Transport Server role. The second option is the best because your HT does not directly face the Internet and acquires the additional protection an ET provides.

MORE INFO   Creating an Edge Subscription

See Lesson 2 in Chapter 2 for more information on creating an Edge Subscription.

Table 3-9 outlines a summary of the requirements for the Hub Transport Server role. Use it to review these requirements but use the information in Chapters 1 and 2 to supplement this information.

Table 3-9 Summary of Hub Transport Server Role Requirements

Component	Installed by default	Required Configuration
Hub Transport Server role		Should be the second role to install.
		You should configure a firewall between this role and its method of communication with the Internet.
		All HT configuration information is stored in Active Directory.
		Active Directory automatically applies settings to each new HT in the network.
		In multi-site organizations, you must install at least one HT in each site that includes an MB.
		Add ET agents onto HT facing Internet when no ET is present.
		Can also add ET anti-spam and antivirus agents to include a second layer of protection for messages from the Internet.
Send connectors	☑	Stored within Active Directory as a configuration object.
		Must be configured to link to Internet. Use Edge Subscription if possible.
		Configured either through the Exchange Management Console, under the *Organization Configuration* node or the Exchange Management Shell.
Receive connectors	☑	Two connectors (default and client) are automatically installed when installing HT.
		Do not modify the default configuration.
		Stored with Active Directory as child objects of the HT server object.
		Configured either through the Exchange Management Console, under the *Server Configuration* node, or through the Exchange Management Shell.

Table 3-9   Summary of Hub Transport Server Role Requirements

Component	Installed by default	Required Configuration
Foreign connectors		Stored in Active Directory as objects in a connector's container.
		Target Drop folders for pickup by a third-party service.
		To enable fault tolerance, the Drop folder should be on a server that does not host an HT role.
		Configured through the Exchange Management Shell.
SMTP Banner	☑	Default Microsoft message.
		Should be modified to change default.
		Do not remove 220 value from banner.

Table 3-10 outlines a summary of the requirements for the Edge Transport Server role. Use it to review these requirements but use the information in Chapters 1 and 2 to supplement this information.

Table 3-10   Summary of Edge Transport Server Role Requirements

Component	Installed by default	Required Configuration
Edge Transport Server role		Install on a stand-alone server.
		Can be installed at any time.
		Cannot be installed with any other role.
		Requires the installation and configuration of HT to finalize its configuration.
		All configuration and recipient information is stored in ADAM.
		A firewall should be configured between HT and ET as well as between ET and the Internet.
Send connector	☑	Two Send connectors are required: one for the Internet and one for internal connection to HT.
		Must be configured.

Table 3-10   Summary of Edge Transport Server Role Requirements

Component	Installed by default	Required Configuration
		Internal connector bound to internal-facing NIC.
		Internet connector bound to Internet-facing NIC.
		Connector's configuration settings are stored in ADAM.
		Connector relies on DNS MX record entries.
		Both connectors are automatically configured if using an Edge Subscription.
Receive connector	☑	Only one required.
		Automatically configured.
		Bound to Internet-facing NIC.
		Configured by default to accept all messages (from the Internet and internal HT) on the same Receive connector.
		You can add an optional Receive connector to accept messages from HT computers.
EdgeSync		Automates the configuration process.
		Subscription is generated from Edge server(s) and imported into HT.
		Automatically configures authentication types for the Receive connector.
		Edge subscriptions are automatic when first created, but must be re-created when new HT servers are added.

Next, you need to verify that all inbound services are also active and ready to replace those of the legacy organization. This includes all of the services that are available through the CAS role. Table 3-11 outlines a summary of each CAS role feature and its configuration requirements. Make sure all your client inbound connections will point to the new Exchange 2007 services.

Table 3-11   Summary of Client Access Server Role Requirements

Component	Installed by default	Requires Trusted SSL	Required Configuration
Client Access Server role			Should be the first role to install.
			Relies heavily on IIS version 6.0 (original Exchange 2007 release) or later (with Exchange 2007 SP1).
			Must have at least one CAS in the organization.
Autodiscover	☑	☑	Appropriate internal and external entries must be found in DNS.
			Service Connection Point in Active Directory must be properly configured.
			Give users access rights to read SCP object in Active Directory.
			Communicates with users over HTTPS.
			Use **Set-ClientAccessServer** cmdlet for all configuration changes to the SCP object.
			In Complex and Large Organizations, configure site affinity to reduce WAN connections.
			In a Complex Organization with multiple forests, properly configure SCP for all users in every forest.
			In an Exchange Resource Forest, create an SCP pointer in the Active Directory forest that includes the user accounts; use the **Export-AutoDiscoveryConfig** cmdlet.

Table 3-11 Summary of Client Access Server Role Requirements

Component	Installed by default	Requires Trusted SSL	Required Configuration
			In a multiple trusted forest topology, configure the service in each of the forests.
			To move mailboxes and user accounts from one forest to the other, configure the service in each forest first.
			Requires SSL certificate with a common name and a subject alternative name.
			For external networks, configure a separate Web site to host the feature.
			For hosted environments, create multiple Autodiscover Web sites on the IIS server and redirect the appropriate service to the appropriate e-mail domain name.
			Use IIS Manager to configure the redirection for each e-mail domain.
Availability	☑	☑	In pure Exchange 2007 and Outlook 2007 environments, the Availability Service replaces public folders to provide free/busy data.
			Configure after Autodiscover.
			If deployed internally and externally, use different URLs for each.
			Cannot be configured with Exchange Management Console. You need to use the **Set-WebServices-VirtualDirectory** cmdlet.

Table 3-11   Summary of Client Access Server Role Requirements

Component	Installed by default	Requires Trusted SSL	Required Configuration
			In multiple forests with trusts, configure at user level.
			In multiple forests without trusts, configure at organization level.
OWA	☑	☑	Four virtual directories are created in IIS under a default Web site.
			All required SSL and HTTPS communications for access.
			Add the SSL certificate for these directories.
			Can use Basic, Digest, or Integrated Windows Authentication or Forms-based authentication.
			OWA Web site must be secured through a firewall.
			Use Explicit Logon to support delegation.
			Supports access to Windows SharePoint Services or UNC file shares.
ActiveSync	☑	☑	Requires ASP.NET.
			Works with Windows Mobile 5.0, Windows Mobile 5.0 with Messaging and Security Feature Pack, Windows Mobile 6.0 or non-Windows devices that support ActiveSync.
			Supports Direct Push.
			Firewall must be open for port 443.

Table 3-11   Summary of Client Access Server Role Requirements

Component	Installed by default	Requires Trusted SSL	Required Configuration
			Firewall must support long-lived HTTPS requests.
			Clients need unlimited data plan.
			Mailboxes are enabled by default.
			Should configure an ActiveSync policy to centrally control all mailboxes.
POP/IMAP Services	☑	☑	Services must be set to automatic and started in Computer Management.
			Use the **Set-PopSettings** cmdlet for POP.
			Use the **Set-ImapSettings** cmdlet for IMAP.
			Use the **Set-CASMailbox** cmdlet for configure mailboxes.
Outlook Anywhere	☑	☑	Requires HTTP over RPC Proxy.
			Not enabled by default.
			Use the Enable Outlook Anywhere Wizard or the **enable-OutlookAnywhere** cmdlet to turn on.
			Enable in each site in Active Directory where a CAS computer is located.
			Set to NTLM or Windows Integrated Authentication.

As with the preceding tables, rely on Chapters 1 and 2 for more information on the contents of Table 3-11. Because so many of the services the CAS offers are Internet-facing services, you will have to integrate it with a firewall. This subject will be discussed in more detail in Chapter 7, "Security Implementations."

Remove the Last Legacy Server   When you have set up your core Exchange Server 2007 roles, you can proceed to the finalization of all other aspects of the transition. At this point, you need to ensure that your Exchange 2000 or Exchange 2003 recipient policies are removed and transferred to Exchange 2007.

Policies that are only Mailbox Manager policies—policies that do not have an E-mail Addresses (Policy) tab—can simply be deleted because they are not transferred. Verify that they are not e-mail address policies by selecting each and looking at its Properties sheet. If the E-mail Addresses tab is not present, select the policy and delete it.

Policies that are e-mail address policies require a different treatment. In fact, you want to retain e-mail address policies as often as possible. To remove the legacy policies, you simply select the policy, right-click it and choose Change Property Pages. In the New Policy dialog box, clear the Mailbox Manager Settings option (see Figure 3-3). Click OK. You do not want to delete the e-mail address portion of the policy because Exchange 2007 will automatically pick it up and apply it to new e-mail accounts when the Mailbox Manager portion is removed.

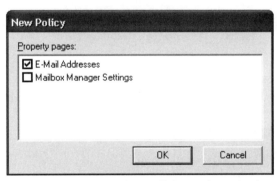

Figure 3-3   Clearing the Mailbox Manager Settings option on a policy

Now you can remove the last legacy server in the organization by completing the following steps:

1. Move the public folder hierarchy to Exchange 2007. In Exchange System Manager, expand Administrative Groups, right-click Exchange Administrative Group (FYDIBOHF23SPDLT), select New, and then choose Public Folders Container. Expand the administrative group that contains the public folder tree and then expand Folders. Drag the Public Folders container to Folders under the Exchange 2007 administrative group. This process will ensure that the Exchange 2007 public folder database will mount properly when you delete the Exchange 2000/ Exchange 2003 administrative group.

2. In Exchange System Manager, expand Recipients and select Recipient Update Services. Right-click each Recipient Update Service and select Delete. Click Yes to confirm each deletion.

3. One Recipient Update Service will remain, the Recipient Update Service (Enterprise Configuration). This cannot be deleted from System Manager. You must use the ADSIEdit console (ADSIEdit.msc) instead. This console is part of the Windows Server 2003 Support Tools. To launch the console, click Start, click Run, and type **adsiedit.msc**. Expand the tree to get to Configuration | CN=Configuration,CN=*domainname* | CN=Services | CN=Microsoft Exchange | CN=*organizationname* | CN=Address Lists Container | CN=Recipient Update Services. Select the Recipient Update Service (Enterprise Configuration) in the right pane, right-click it, and choose Delete. Click Yes to confirm deletion (see Figure 3-4). Close ADSIEdit when done.

4. Uninstall the last legacy Exchange server from your organization by using Add or Remove Programs from Control Panel.

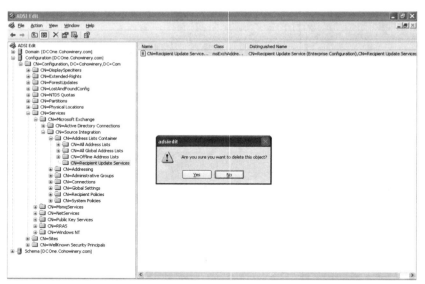

Figure 3-4 Deleting the last Recipient Update Service using ADSIEdit

IMPORTANT Legacy Administrative Groups

Do not delete any legacy administrative groups that have ever contained mailboxes, even if the mailboxes are moved to a new server. The LegacyExchangeDN property on a mailbox references these groups and they must remain for Outlook access to free/busy data to work properly. Also, all versions of Outlook rely on this property when a user delegates access to folders using the Outlook client. If these groups are deleted, Outlook 2003 and earlier will not be able to access free/busy data. In addition, no versions of Outlook will be able to find assigned delegated users.

You are done. Now you can begin to take advantage of all of the native features of Exchange Server 2007.

Transition the Simple Organization   Simple Organizations are often based on Microsoft Small Business Server (SBS). Version 2003 of SBS is a stand-alone product that integrates several Microsoft server components, notably Exchange Server 2003. Because SBS is designed to run only on a single server (and a 32-bit server at that), and because there is no upgrade path from Exchange 2003 to Exchange 2007, transitioning from Exchange 2003 to Exchange 2007 in SBS involves the installation of another server into your SBS domain.

IMPORTANT   Small business transitions

For many small organizations, introducing another server, especially a 64-bit server, will be cost-prohibitive because the addition of any new server is costly. Therefore, the transition will not occur until the release of SBS 2008 the 64-bit version of SBS that will be based on Windows Server 2008, or Windows Essentials Business Server 2008, the medium organization version that will support multiple servers. Neither is slated for release until the third quarter of 2008.

The new server must run a 64-bit operating system. If you did not upgrade your SBS server to SP1, your new server will also need to be a domain controller, because the Active Directory schema updates require a domain controller and global catalog server with Service Pack 1 installed. You then proceed with the same operation you use for a single-forest to single-forest transition.

MORE INFO   Obtain SP1 for SBS

For more information on Service Pack 1 for Small Business Server, go to *http://www.microsoft.com/windowsserver2003/sbs/downloads/sp1/default.mspx*.

Cross-Forest to Cross-Forest

When you use Complex Organizations—organizations that rely on multiple forests linked together to provide integrated e-mail services—you face both similar and different issues than when you transition in a single forest. Similar issues relate to how you actually transition in each of the forests. Different issues stem from the fact that your Exchange organizations must exchange information between the forests. In most cross-forest topologies, this exchange of information is performed through the use of a synchronization tool, either the Identity Integration Feature Pack (IIFP) or the Microsoft Identity Integration Server (MIIS). Both tools must be running Service Pack 2 to operate with Exchange 2007. But even then you face issues.

For example, IIFP and MIIS provide a tool—Global Address List Synchronization (GAL-Sync)—designed to synchronize recipients in each forest. But because the Exchange 2007 recipient object is different from previous Exchange recipient objects, and because both IIFP and MIIS were released before Exchange 2007, GALSync cannot support the new features included in Exchange 2007.

In addition, the GALSync process relies on the Recipient Update Service found in Exchange 2000 or Exchange 2003 to complete the synchronization process when data is copied from forest to forest. Because Exchange Server 2007 does not have this service, you must manually update recipients if you want to fully provision them.

Therefore, you will lose some functionality when you rely on GALSync to provision users from forest to forest. The missing features include:

- When users delegate their mailboxes to others, the delegation is lost.

- Contacts designed to represent rooms or equipment will not have detailed information about the resources they represent.

- Outlook will not recognize that a contact is from another forest. In fact, all contacts will appear the same in Outlook.

IMPORTANT   Exchange 2007 SP1

Exchange 2007 SP1 introduces a new cmdlet, **update-recipient**, to finish the provisioning process. This cmdlet is not available in the original version of Exchange 2007.

IMPORTANT   Microsoft Identity Lifecycle Manager 2007

You can replace both IIFP and MIIS with Microsoft Identity Lifecycle Manager 2007 with Feature Pack 1 (ILM FP1) and avoid all of these issues because ILM FP1 is designed to support Exchange 2007.

The overall transitioning process relies on the same prerequisites and will face the same limitations as the single-forest transition. The major difference is the presence of either IIFP or MIIS.

To complete a cross-forest transition, follow these steps:

1. Install Exchange Server 2007 roles on either a single or separate computer in each forest.

2. If you are not using Outlook 2007 and you want to make free/busy data available in each forest, you must install and configure the Inter-Organization Replication tool (IORepl). In most cases, this tool will already be installed because it is a legacy tool.

3. Use Active Directory Users And Computers to create an OU that will contain contacts from other forests. Perform this action in each forest.

4. Create a GALSync management agent for each forest with IIFP or MIIS. Alternatively, you can use ILM FP1 to do so. Once again, if you are running a Complex Organization type, this is most likely already done.

5. Enable GALSync.

6. Move the mailboxes from legacy Exchange back-end servers to MB computers.

7. Decommission the legacy Exchange servers in each forest. Use the same procedures as with the single-forest transition.

8. Complete the recipient provisioning process.

   ❑ If you are using ILM FP1, the process is already complete.

   ❑ If you are using IIFP or MIIS, you must create an Exchange Management Shell script that will update all of the address lists and address list policies in each organization. You should schedule this script to run once a day in each organization. Use Windows Scheduled Tasks to do so.

The most significant difference between this process and single-forest transition is the configuration of GALSync in each forest. You will need to work with either IIFP or MIIS to do so.

MORE INFO   **Configuring GALSync to support the transition**

For information on how to configure GALSync for cross-forest transitions, go to *http://technet.microsoft.com/en-us/library/bb124363.aspx.*

Single-Forest to Cross-Forest

The single-forest to cross-forest transition occurs when you need to move from a Simple, Standard, or Large Organization to a Complex Organization type. As such, it combines the single-forest and cross-forest transition processes. In fact, this process is extremely similar to that of the cross-forest transition, except that it begins with the creation of a new Active Directory forest because single forests are not Complex Organizations. You must also configure trusts between the forests. After you have created the second forest, you have two choices:

- You can use the new forest as the location for the installation of Exchange 2007 server roles, move all of the user accounts from the source forest to the new forest, and move all of the mailboxes from the source forest to the new forest. In the end, you can decommission not only the Exchange Organization in the source forest—you can decommission the source forest altogether.

- Alternatively, you can install Exchange 2007 server roles in the new forest and the source forest, move a certain number of accounts from the source to the new forest, and move their mailboxes as well. In this case, you must rely on the single-forest scenario to remove all of the legacy Exchange servers in the source forest. In this scenario, you end up with a Complex Organization type that has two forests, one with a new Exchange organization and one with an updated Exchange organization.

MORE INFO   Creating a new forest

For information on creating a new forest as well as migrating its contents from one forest to another, see *Windows Server 2008: The Complete Reference* by Ruest and Ruest (McGraw-Hill Osborne, 2008). This book outlines how to build a complete infrastructure based on Windows Server and migrate all contents from one location to another.

BEST PRACTICES   Creating a new Active Directory

For best practices on how to create an Active Directory forest, see Chapter 3, "Designing the Active Directory," from *Windows Server 2003, Best Practices for Enterprise Deployments* on the companion CD.

MORE INFO   Single- to cross-forest transition

For more information on this scenario, see *http://technet .microsoft.com/en-us/library/aa996926.aspx*. Note that this scenario only covers the first of the two choices listed previously, moving from a source to a new forest.

Resource Forest to Resource Forest or Single-Forest to Resource Forest

Performing a transition in an Exchange Resource Forest (ERF) relies on exactly the same process as the single-forest transition. This is because in this scenario, only the Resource Forest includes legacy Exchange servers. Because this is the case, all operations occur in one single forest, the Resource Forest.

IMPORTANT   Using Resource Forests

We recommend that you avoid using an Exchange Resource Forest as much as possible because there is no synchronization between the user account forests and the ERF, causing a high degree of administrative overhead. Using a different topology allows you to reduce this overhead significantly. We recommend that if at all possible, use the opportunit to move to Exchange Server 2007 to change the topology you rely on and move to either a single-forest or a cross-forest scenario.

Look up the details of the single-forest transition outline earlier to perform the ERF to ERF transition.

Moving from a single forest to an ERF is very similar to the single-forest to cross-forest scenario because it involves creating a new forest that will host all mailboxes. One advantage of this scenario—as with the single-forest to cross-forest scenario—is that you create a new, pristine forest that will host an Exchange 2007 organization. In this case, however, you do not need to move all of your user accounts from the source forest to the ERF, which actually simplifies this scenario.

MORE INFO   **Single-forest to Resource Forest transition**

For more information on this scenario, see *http://technet.microsoft.com/en-us/library/aa995896.aspx*.

Move Mailbox Commands

When it comes to moving mailboxes, you can use three cmdlets:

- **Move-mailbox**   Copies or moves a mailbox that is associated with an Active Directory account. The mailbox must be connected for the command to work. In this case, the mailbox is deemed active.

- **Export-mailbox**   Copies or moves content from an active mailbox to a folder inside another active mailbox. For example, you can copy the contents of the Inbox to another Inbox.

- **Restore-mailbox**   Recovers content from a mailbox within the Recovery Storage Group (RSG) to either an active mailbox or to a folder within an active mailbox. For example, you can use this cmdlet to recover an important message a user has lost.

These commands are designed to support mailbox moves in two different scenarios:

- Intra-organization or intra-forest moves involve situations in which you move a mailbox from one database or one server within the same Exchange Organization.

- Inter-organization, cross-organization, or cross-forest moves involve situations in which you move a mailbox from one Exchange Organization to another. Because there is only one Exchange Organization per Active Directory forest, this is considered a cross-forest move.

When you actually move mailboxes, you can script the operation with these cmdlets or you can perform the operation interactively with the Exchange Management Console. In the latter case, you locate the mailbox you want to move and right-click it to select the Move Mailbox command. This launches the Move Mailbox Wizard (see Figure 3-5). It is a good idea to run through this command at least once because it will show you the options available within it. For example, you can skip corrupted messages and create a move schedule, moving the mailbox during off hours. This shows you which options are available within the **move-mailbox** cmdlet. Remember that you can perform this operation once with the wizard and copy the resulting cmdlet to use as a source script.

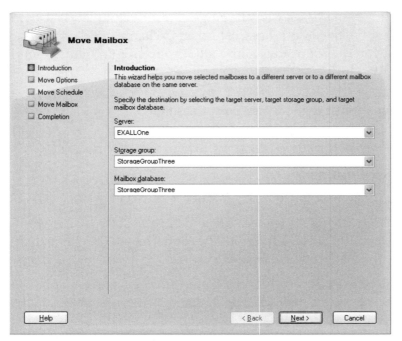

Figure 3-5   The Move Mailbox Wizard

These commands are the very basis of each of the transition scenarios discussed in this lesson.

Practice: Plan the Transition to Exchange 2007

In this practice, you will assist Lucerne Publishing (LP) in preparing a migration plan for a migration from Exchange Server 2003 to Exchange 2007. This practice consists of a single exercise. LP wants to deploy the Exchange 2007 server roles on dedicated member servers. They want to be able to decommission their existing Exchange servers as soon as possible because they want to use the Unified Messaging Server role, but not before they have removed Exchange Server 2003 computers. Your job as a messaging professional will be to help LP plan their transition.

▶ **Exercise: Plan the Transition from Exchange 2003 to Exchange 2007**

Lucerne Publishing runs a Standard Organization Exchange 2003 deployment. Their organization has two sites in a single Active Directory forest. They have deployed front- and back-end servers for protection. E-mail servers exist in each of the two sites (see Figure 3-6). They want to move to Exchange Server 2007 mostly because they want to use its unified messaging capabilities. They have their own Private Branch Exchange (PBX) and want to link it to their e-mail messaging system.

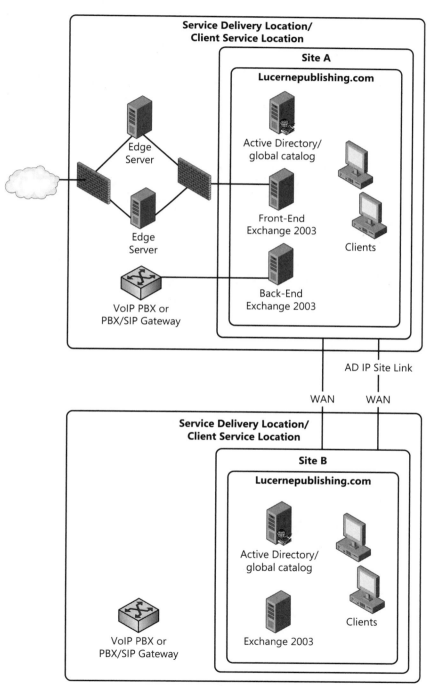

Figure 3-6 The existing Lucerne Publishing Organization

In addition, Lucerne has a small IT administration staff. They want the transition to occur as quickly as possible because they do not have the staff to support multiple e-mail systems at the same time.

Because they do not have the expertise to design their own transition plan, they turn to you, the messaging professional, to assist them in creating the appropriate plan for the transition.

Because Lucerne Publishing runs a Standard Organization, they can take advantage of the single-forest to single-forest transition scenario. This scenario involves the following steps, which you must include in the plan you prepare. Be sure to refer to the preceding pages in this chapter for clarifications on each step.

1. Perform an analysis of the existing Exchange organization at Lucerne Publishing. Look for items such as average mailbox size, number of storage groups, location of mailbox databases, and so on. This will help you size the replacement servers LP will need to bring in to host Exchange 2007 server roles.

2. Make sure all of the Exchange 2007 prerequisites are met within the LP Active Directory.

3. Install two new computers in Site A, the first Active Directory site at Lucerne. These two computers will run 64-bit operating systems, have all Exchange prerequisites, and will host the three first Exchange server roles: CAS, HT, and MB. Next, install one computer in Site B for the same reason.

4. Prepare the target storage groups in both MB servers. Size them appropriately so that they will be ready to host the transitioned mailboxes. Pay special attention to mailbox quotas so that you have sufficient space for the mailbox moves to occur.

5. Move the mailboxes. Perform the moves during weekends and off hours to minimize end-user downtime.

6. After the mailboxes are moved, begin decommissioning the Exchange 2003 servers.

7. Finalize the transition with the following steps:
    - ❏ Move and remove public folder replicas.
    - ❏ Move the Offline Address Book.
    - ❏ Delete routing group connectors.
    - ❏ Delete the recipient update service.
    - ❏ Verify that all mail flow is working properly.
    - ❏ Remove the last Exchange 2003 server.

When the internal migration is complete, you can finalize the implementation by adding Edge Transport servers to replace the Edge Services and implementing the Unified Messaging Server role to integrate voice into the e-mail system.

Quick Check

1. Your Exchange organization includes both Exchange 2000 Server and Exchange Server 2003 servers. You want to integrate some Exchange 2007 server roles into the organization, but first you must upgrade Active Directory. You try to run Active Directory update from the graphical setup tool but nothing happens. What could be the problem?

2. You are performing a single-forest to single-forest transition. You have moved the mailboxes to new Exchange 2007 servers and now you are ready to finalize the transition, but before you do so, you want to move all of the contacts and distribution lists. You search and search, but you cannot find a tool to perform this step in the transition process. What could be the problem?

3. You are performing a cross-forest migration. Your existing Exchange Server 2000 implementations rely on the Identity Integration Feature Pack (IIFP) and the Global Address List Synchronization (GALSync). You perform all of the steps for the transition and start using Exchange 2007. But as you begin to work, users complain that they are missing information in their new Exchange 2007 systems. What could be the problem?

4. Which transition scenario should you use when moving a Resource Forest to Exchange 2007?

5. You finish the transition from Exchange 2000 to Exchange 2007. At the end of the transition, you delete all remaining legacy administrative groups. Soon after, users start complaining that they cannot access free/busy data through Outlook or perform mailbox delegations. What could be the problem?

Quick Check Answers

1. Because your organization includes Exchange 2000 servers, it also includes Windows 2000 domain controllers. When this is the case, you must run Setup.com from the command line and you must specify the */DomainController* switch to point to a DC running Windows Server 2003 with SP1. If you are deploying Exchange 2007 with SP1, you can use the graphical setup tool because you no longer need to specify this parameter.

2. You do not have to move contacts or distribution lists during a single-forest to single-forest transition scenario because they are all contained within the

Active Directory. Because you are staying within the same Active Directory forest, there is nothing to move.

3. When you use IIFP or Microsoft Identity Integration Server (MIIS) to perform cross-forest synchronization with GALSync, you must finish the provisioning process manually. Both IIFP and MIIS are not designed to support Exchange 2007. If you want to have full support for Exchange 2007, move up to Microsoft Identity Lifecycle Manager 2007 instead.

4. Exchange Resource Forests are forests that are dedicated to hosting Exchange services. As such, you only need to transition in one single forest. Rely on the single-forest to single-forest transition scenario.

5. Do not delete any legacy administrative groups that ever contained mailboxes even if the mailboxes are moved to a new server. The LegacyExchangeDN property on a mailbox references these groups and they must remain for Outlook access to free/busy data to work properly. Also, all versions of Outlook rely on this property when a user delegates access to folders using the Outlook client. If these groups are deleted, Outlook 2003 and earlier will not be able to access free/busy data. In addition, all versions of Outlook will not be able to find assigned delegated users.

Lesson 2: Plan the Exchange Server 2007 Migration Implementation

Estimated lesson time: 30 minutes

Migration Strategies Overview

Migration is defined as the move from one existing Exchange or non-Exchange environment to a new implementation of Exchange 2007. Normally, you would choose a migration scenario over a transition scenario in three situations:

- If you are running Exchange 5.5, you need to migrate to another version of Exchange before you move to Exchange 2007. Ideally, you will move to Exchange 2003 first and then move to Exchange 2007.

- If you are unhappy with the current state of your Active Directory forest(s) and Exchange organization(s), or you are in a situation where you have been using a Complex Organization and you want to simplify it to a Large Organization, you would consider a migration scenario over a transition scenario.

- If you are not running an Exchange-based e-mail system and you want to take advantage of the features Exchange 2007 offers, you need to migrate to Exchange 2007. For example, if you are using Lotus Notes and you want to move to Exchange 2007, you must perform a migration.

Each of these situations calls for different approaches to the migration process.

Migrate from Exchange 5.5

As you have seen before, Microsoft does not provide a direct transition path from Exchange 5.5 to Exchange 2007. Instead, you must migrate from Exchange 5.5 to either Exchange 2000 or Exchange 2003 and then perform a transition to Exchange 2007. Because you need to use the intermediary step, and this step requires the installation of a new Exchange organization based on one of the intermediary versions, you have little reason to use Exchange 2000. Most organizations in this situation will therefore use Exchange 2003 as the intermediary because it provides the closest feature set to Exchange 2007 and will make the transition as simple as possible.

This migration requires some custom steps to move from Exchange 5.5 to Exchange 2003, but as soon as you are in an Exchange 2003 organization, you can rely on one of the transition scenarios covered in Lesson 1 to finalize the move to Exchange 2007.

Exchange 5.5 deployments did not rely on Active Directory, and for this reason many organizations are still using this version of Exchange. Their networks are based on the old domain model that was supported by Windows NT. As such, their migration will be a significant challenge because they will need to learn how to work with Active Directory before they can begin to work with Exchange Server.

BEST PRACTICES   **Creating a new Active Directory forest**

For best practices on how to create an Active Directory, see Chapter 3 from *Windows Server 2003, Best Practices for Enterprise Deployments* on the companion CD.

Considering the release schedule of Windows Server 2008, these organizations may be best to move directly from Windows NT Server to Windows Server 2008 and create new networks based on the very latest operating system Microsoft has to offer. This should stabilize their environments and last almost as long as their NT and Exchange 5.5 implementations have lasted. If these organizations decide to do this, they will need to implement Exchange 2007 with Service Pack 1 because the original release of Exchange 2007 does not run on Windows Server 2008.

MORE INFO   **Moving to Windows Server 2008**

For information on creating a new forest as well as migrating its contents from one forest to another, see *Windows Server 2008: The Complete Reference* by Ruest and Ruest (McGraw-Hill Osborne, 2008). This book outlines how to build a complete infrastructure based on Windows Server and migrate all contents from one location to another.

Exam Tip   Like the original version of Exchange Server 2007, the original version of the exam does not cover Windows Server 2008 content.

Whatever the choice, the migration will not be a simple operation and the most significant challenge these organizations will face will be IT staff skill upgrades so that they can become familiar with all of these new technologies.

Perform the Multi-Step Migration from Exchange 5.5

The best way to perform this migration is to move from Exchange 5.5 to Exchange 2003 and then to Exchange 2007. Keep the following in mind when performing this operation:

- Exchange 5.5 cannot reside on the same server as Exchange 2003. Similarly, Exchange 2003 cannot reside on the same server as Exchange 2007. This means installing new Exchange servers to host Exchange 2003 and new servers to host Exchange 2007. Depending on the size of the mailbox databases you need to migrate, you might seriously consider using virtual machines to run the Exchange 2003 intermediary step and only install Exchange 2007 on physical computers.

■ Because the Exchange 2007 computers must run a 64-bit operating system, you might consider using one or more of the target Exchange 2007 servers to host the virtual machines you use to run Exchange 2003. You can recover these servers to host Exchange 2007 after you have decommissioned the Exchange 2003 computers.

When you are ready, follow these steps to perform the migration. Run the project in phases.

1. In phase one, verify that the migration is possible. You will need to rely on the Exchange Server 2003 Deployment Tools to do so, which you can find at *http:// go.microsoft.com/fwlink/?linkid=25097*.

   ❑ Use the deployment tools to verify that your organization meets the specified requirements outlined within the tools.

   ❑ Run a diagnostics on your environment. Use the DCDiag tool to identify whether your NT domain meets requirements.

   ❑ Use the NetDiag tool to see whether your network will support the upgrade.

2. In phase two, prepare the new directory. You have two ways to perform this task. You can either upgrade the existing Primary Domain Controller to Active Directory, or you can install a new directory and move the users from Windows NT to the new directory. We strongly recommend the latter. Few organizations have had a great success with the first method because it carries over all of the content of the existing domain. Using a new directory lets you filter out unwanted objects and creates a pristine environment. Then, when you have completed the directory implementation, perform the following steps:

   ❑ Run ForestPrep and DomainPrep to update the Active Directory to host Exchange 2003.

   ❑ Install the Active Directory Connector and run it to connect to the Exchange 5.5 environment.

3. In phase three, install Exchange 2003. Then you can move your mailboxes to the new Exchange servers and prepare for the transition that will move you to Exchange 2007.

While this process seems simple, it is actually quite complex. One area you need to focus on is the design of the new directory. Because Exchange 5.5 and Windows NT do not have the concept of a forest, you should aim for the simplest Active Directory design that will meet your goals. If you are working with multiple NT domains, you do not have to have multiple forests. Ideally, you will be able to migrate to a single forest and then rely on the single-forest to single-forest transition scenario.

MORE INFO **Migrating Exchange 5.5 to Exchange 2003**

For more information on migrating Exchange 5.5 to 2003, go to *http://technet.microsoft.com/en-us/ library/84fd1f06-cf90-43fe-b836-f21b2fa88d4d .aspx*.

As you prepare for this operation, you might find that it is best to simply purchase a third-party migration tool. In some cases, these tools will let you move mailbox and other data from Windows NT and Exchange 5.5 directly to Exchange 2007, saving the intermediary step required in the Microsoft migration scenario. The cost of the tool may well be offset by the cost of the additional server hardware you need to transition through Exchange 2003.

MORE INFO **Exchange 5.5 migration tools**

For more information on tools designed to migrated Exchange 5.5 to newer versions of Exchange, go to *http://go.microsoft.com/fwlink/?linkid=96684*.

Migration from Lotus Domino

Like Exchange 5.5, Lotus Notes (now called Lotus Domino) includes its own directory service and does not necessarily rely on Active Directory. In these cases, migrating from a Lotus Notes environment becomes very similar to migrating from Exchange 5.5 because in addition to moving the data users generate, you must also find a way to migrate the contacts and distribution groups that make Lotus Notes work.

Microsoft offers several tools that help in the migration process:

- **Microsoft Transporter for Lotus Domino** The Transporter supports two scenarios:
    - ❑ It provides directory synchronization services and supports free/busy look-ups between Lotus Domino 6 or 7 and Exchange Server 2007 with Active Directory. It relies on the SMTP protocol to route mail between the versions of Domino and Exchange 2007. This scenario supports coexistence.
    - ❑ It migrates users, mail databases, and applications from Lotus Domino 5, 6, or 7 to a combination of Exchange Server 2007, Active Directory, and Windows SharePoint Services 3.0.

- **Exchange Server 2003 Connector for Lotus Notes**   Supports messaging and calendaring interoperability between Lotus Domino 5 and Exchange Server 2003 with Active Directory. While there is a connector that ships with Exchange and is updated with Exchange 2003 SP2, you should obtain the connector from the Microsoft Web site because it has been updated to provide more reliable mail transfers between Exchange and Domino. It also supports iNotes and Domino Web Access clients.

- **Application Analyzer 2006 for Lotus Domino**   Because Lotus Domino combines e-mail services with collaboration services, many organizations will have built applications that take advantage of both features within Domino. When you want to migrate from Domino to a Microsoft platform, you need to consider the applications as well as the e-mail system. Applications are normally transferred to Windows SharePoint Services 3.0, but before you can transfer them, you should inventory and analyze them. This is what the Application Analyzer 2006 for Lotus Domino does. It scans all Domino applications and generates a report with suggested strategies for migration.

MORE INFO   **Microsoft migration tools for Lotus Domino**

Obtain the Microsoft Transporter for Lotus Domino from *http://go.microsoft.com/fwlink/ ?linkid=82688*. Obtain the updated Exchange Server 2003 Connector for Lotus Notes from *http://go.microsoft.com/fwlink/?linkid=57194*. Obtain the Application Analyzer 2006 for Lotus Domino from *http://www.microsoft.com/downloads/details.aspx?familyid=d94c5719-570d-4adb-b449-70e1e42cbfc5&displaylang=en*.

MORE INFO   **Information resources for Domino migrations**

For more information and to locate information resources in support of a migration from Domino to Exchange, go to *http://technet.microsoft.com/en-us/interopmigration/bb403105.aspx*.

Plan Your Migration Approach

Migrating from a Lotus infrastructure to one including Exchange and Active Directory usually happens in three distinct phases:

1. Plan and prepare. This phase focuses on:
    - Collecting information about the current system. This information should include items like available network bandwidth, organization type, IT administration model, current issues, potential organizational growth, and general organizational topology.

❏ Identifying the strategy used to implement a similar and improved messaging system using Active Directory and Exchange.

❏ Identifying the tools Microsoft and others provide to coexist and migrate resources.

This phase is complete when you have outlined a strategy that defines the Active Directory you plan to create if one does not exist already, the Exchange 2007 implementation you need, and the items, if any, that you want to retain from the Domino configuration.

2. Set up the two environments so that they can interoperate. In this phase, you have users in both Exchange and Domino and your systems intercommunicate with each other. This means that you have moved some users to the Exchange platform, but the bulk of your users are still in Domino. Because users are in both environments, you must use the migration tools to synchronize directory information and support free/busy lookups. Mail is routed between both platforms through SMTP. You may, however, run into issues during this phase. Consider the following:

❏ Message routing must work properly. Users from either platform should be able to send and receive messages to each other and to the Internet.

❏ Contacts and distribution lists must be up to date at all times. This is why directory synchronization is so important. Users will not be able to send or receive e-mails properly if the contacts or distribution lists are out of date.

❏ Calendaring information is also crucial to the way organizations function. Free/busy data must be made available no matter which platform users work in.

3. Migrate content from Domino to Exchange and decommission the Domino service. You usually perform this migration in batches of users. Migrating in batches allows you to match user training programs with the migration process, making it easier for users to learn their new systems. You should try to group users together based on workgroups and/or location so that groups of users can continue to work together with little or no interruption in their productivity. Because you perform this migration in batches and you must continue to support the Domino environment during the migration, you must continue phase two throughout the end of phase three.

While this process appears to be a simple three-step process, it is quite complex and requires serious planning before proceeding.

The Microsoft Transporter Suite for Lotus Domino

Although Microsoft has produced several tools for Lotus and Exchange interoperability, the only connector that supports Exchange Server 2007 is the Microsoft Transporter Suite for Lotus Domino. This means that you should focus on this tool when planning the transformation of a Domino environment.

You may, however, run into situations where Exchange Server 2003 already coexists with Domino. In this case, you need to consider both the migration from Domino and the transition from Exchange 2003 at the same time as you plan your move to Exchange 2007.

MORE INFO   **Coexistence between Exchange and Domino**

Coexistence between Exchange and third-party environments is covered in Chapter 4.

The Microsoft Transporter Suite for Lotus Domino includes the following components:

- **Directory Connector**   Synchronizes users, distribution lists (or groups as they are called in Domino), and Domino mail-in database information from the Domino directory to Active Directory.

- **Free/Busy Connector**   Allows users of both environments to share free/busy data and perform lookups between the two systems.

- **Directory Migration**   Creates Active Directory accounts for Domino users.

- **Mailbox Migration**   Migrates mail, calendar, and task information from Domino databases to Exchange mailbox databases.

- **Application Migration**   Migrates Domino applications and their corresponding information from Domino to Windows SharePoint Services 3.0. Note that depending on the complexity of the application, additional programming with Microsoft Visual Studio may be required to render the applications fully functional.

The Transporter Suite also includes its own prerequisites, which are very similar to those of Exchange 2007, but while Exchange only runs on 64-bit platforms, the Transporter Suite can also run on 32-bit systems. The Transporter Suite requires:

- Windows Server 2003 Service Pack 2 or Windows Server 2003 R2 with Service Pack 2 in either 32-bit or 64-bit editions.

- Active Directory with proper schema updates.

- A service account in Active Directory that will be used to perform the migration of the mail. This account must have the right to write mail objects to an Exchange mailbox database.

- Exchange Server 2007 deployed in at least the three core roles: CAS, HT, and MB.

- A Hub Transport server that also includes the Exchange MAPI client. Note that the MAPI client is not part of the default Exchange Server 2007 installation.

MORE INFO   Obtain the MAPI Client

The MAPI client is included in the Microsoft Exchange Server MAPI Client and Collaboration Data Objects 1.2.1 download from Microsoft. Obtain it from *http://go.microsoft.com/fwlink/ ?linkid=68174*.

- Windows SharePoint Services 3.0 deployed in a manner that will support the hosting of transferred applications. Windows SharePoint Services requires SQL Server 2005 to store information about the applications it runs.

- A workstation running Windows XP with Service Pack 2. This workstation should include the Domino client as well as the Exchange Management Console. Because it requires the Exchange Management Console, it will also require the .NET Framework 2.0, MMC 3.0, and Windows PowerShell.

Two installation files are provided: Transporter32.msi for 32-bit systems and Transporter.msi for 64-bit systems. When you have obtained the proper Transporter installation file, you install it on a client workstation as per the preceding prerequisites. This console will be used to configure the different connectors included with the Transporter; therefore, it requires the Domino client to contact Domino servers. It also requires the Exchange Management Console to support the migration of mailboxes and users from one system to another.

You can also install the Transporter on a server, but because you only do so to interact with the two e-mail systems, it is best to install it on a workstation.

You must install the Directory Connector and Free/Busy Connector on a Hub Transport server. This server must include a MAPI client so that it can access free/busy data from Exchange mailboxes.

While the Lotus Notes Connector in Exchange Server 2003 relied on the Notes client installed on the server to transfer mail from one system to the other, the Transporter no longer has this requirement. It relies on SMTP to transfer mail between each system, letting each system route the mail to the appropriate destination.

The Transporter is very similar to the Exchange Management tools. It provides a Management Console that resembles the Exchange Management Console and it also adds several cmdlets to the Exchange Management Shell environment on the target computer. Both tools are used to support collaboration and migration.

Implement the Transporter Suite

Now you are ready to implement the Transporter Suite. First, assign account impersonation to the account you will use to transfer mail objects from Domino to Exchange. Impersonation allows the account to authenticate as another user to add information to that user's mailbox. Run this command on a Client Access server. For example, if your service account is named DominoTransfers and is located in the Exchange Servers OU in the domain, the command would be:

```
Add-ADPermission -Identity (get-exchangeserver).DistinguishedName -User
(Get-User -Identity [DominoTransfers@LucernePublishing.com] |
select-object).identity -extendedRight ms-Exch-EPI-Impersonation
```

Remember to remove this account from the directory when your migration is complete. Having an account that can impersonate other users could be a potential security risk.

Rely on the Transporter documentation to install and configure its components. Make sure you browse through the Release Notes for the tool and rely on the MTHelp.chm file for operations instructions.

MORE INFO   **Third-party migration tools**

Several non-Microsoft tools provide support for migration from Lotus Domino to Exchange 2007. Quest, for example, has an extensive series of migration tools, which you can find at *www.quest.com*. Casahl also offers powerful migration tools. In fact, Casahl's tools are the basis of Microsoft's own tools. You can find Casahl tools at *www.casahl.com*. To find other tools, use your favorite search engine to locate them on the Web.

Migration from Novell GroupWise

Few organizations still rely on Novell GroupWise for e-mail services, but for those that do it is still important to be able to migrate from this platform to Exchange Server 2007. Because Exchange 2007 cannot connect to Novell GroupWise, however, you cannot perform a direct migration. This means using the multi-step migration scenario, as with Lotus Domino.

You need to migrate all data from GroupWise to Exchange Server 2003 using the Exchange Server 2003 Connector for Novell GroupWise. Rely on this connector to perform the initial migration from Novell to Exchange 2003, and then rely on the appropriate transition scenario to move from Exchange Server 2003 to Exchange 2007.

As you can see, this migration is very similar to that of Exchange 5.5 because you need Exchange 2003 as an intermediary during the migration.

MORE INFO   **Migration from Novell GroupWise to Exchange 2003**

For more information about migrating from Novell GroupWise to Exchange 2003, go to *http://technet.microsoft.com/en-us/exchange/bb288526.aspx*.

Practice: Plan the Migration to Exchange Server 2007

In this practice, you will help two organizations that have been using a cross-forest Exchange 2003 implementation move to a single-forest implementation of Exchange 2007. Your job will be to help them plan the move to the single forest.

▶ **Exercise: Plan a Migration from Exchange 5.5 to Exchange 2007**

Tailspin Toys and Wingtip Toys have been working together for more than three years since the two companies merged together. A year ago, they created a joint venture, Adventure Works, and began moving forward toward using this new company as the single identity for all products produced by each member of the group. When the merger occurred, neither organization had the time to integrate the two systems together. Because both toy companies already had their own Active Directory and Exchange 2003 implementations, they decided to implement a cross-forest topology to minimize the impact of the merger.

Now both companies want to move to Exchange Server 2007. They do not need to continue running separate forests. In addition, they are ready to assume the identity of the new venture, Adventure Works, so they plan to use the new directory created for Adventure Works as the merged directory for the Exchange 2007 implementation. They turn to you to help them plan this migration. Your job is to provide them with a multi-step plan to perform the move.

Carefully consider their selection and their objective. You can determine that in actual fact, they are moving from one forest to another, new Exchange 2007 forest. This means implementing a new Exchange 2007 organization. It also means that both companies will move from a Complex Organization to a Large Organization, simplifying their day-to-day operations and integrating the best of both directories into a new, single management infrastructure.

Because of this, you should select the single-forest to cross-forest scenario. In fact, this is a classic case of the scenario as outlined by Microsoft, except that instead of moving from a single forest to a new forest, the companies will be moving from two single forests to a new forest. Therefore, your plan must include the following steps. Refer to the content of the chapter for additional information on each step.

1. Use the new Adventure Works forest as the location for the installation of Exchange 2007 server roles. Install at least two roles using the all-in-one model.

2. Implement forest trusts between each of the three forests using Active Directory Domains And Trusts. You will need credentials in all three forests to achieve this operation.

3. When the trusts are in place, move all of the user accounts from the source forests to the new forest. Use the Active Directory Migration Tool to move the accounts.

4. Now you are ready to move all of the mailboxes from the source forests to the new forest. Add additional Mailbox servers as required in the new Adventure Works forest.

5. When all of the mailboxes are moved, you can decommission not only the Exchange Organizations in the source forests—you can decommission the source forests altogether.

Quick Check

1. You want to migrate from Exchange 5.5 to Exchange 2007. What must you do?

2. Which tool must you use to perform a migration from Lotus Domino 7 to Exchange 2007?

3. You want to migrate from Novell GroupWise to Exchange 2007. What must you do?

Quick Check Answers

1. To migrate from Exchange 5.5 to Exchange 2007, you must use a multi-step migration process, first moving from Exchange 5.5 to Exchange 2000 or Exchange 2003 and then moving from Exchange 2000 or Exchange 2003 to Exchange 2007. This will involve the creation of an Active Directory and the transitory installation of Exchange 2000 or Exchange 2003 servers.

2. To migrate from Lotus Domino 7 to Exchange 2007, you must use the Microsoft Transporter Suite for Lotus Domino. This is the only tool from Microsoft that supports a direct migration path between the two platforms. All other Microsoft tools require Exchange 2003 as an intermediary.

> **3.** To migrate from Novell GroupWise to Exchange 2007, you must use a multi-step migration process, first moving from GroupWise to Exchange 2003 and then moving from Exchange 2003 to Exchange 2007. This will involve the creation of an Active Directory and the transitory installation of Exchange 2003 servers. You will rely on the Exchange Server 2003 GroupWise Connector to perform the initial migration to Exchange 2003.

Chapter Summary

- There is no direct or in-place upgrade path from a previous installation of Microsoft Exchange (Exchange 2000 or Exchange 2003) to Exchange Server 2007. That is because Exchange 2007 is a native x64 application and your current Exchange servers will not be running on this platform. In fact, moving from an existing e-mail system to Exchange Server 2007 will take one of three paths:
  - ❑ Transition is a move from Exchange Server 2000 or Exchange 2003 to Exchange Server 2007.
  - ❑ Migration is a move from an existing e-mail system to Exchange Server 2007 by moving the data from the existing system to a new Exchange Server 2007 organization.
  - ❑ Multi-step is when you move from Exchange 5.5 or a third-party messaging system to Exchange Server 2007.
- Transitions are supported from Exchange 2000, Exchange 2003, or even mixed Exchange 2000 and Exchange 2003 organizations. Migrations are supported from third-party e-mail systems such as Lotus Notes as well as from the same organization types as for the transition. Table 3-1 details the supported migration or transition scenarios to Exchange 2007.
- Five transition strategies are supported:
  - ❑ Single-forest to single-forest
  - ❑ Cross-forest to cross-forest
  - ❑ Single-forest to cross-forest
  - ❑ Resource Forest to Resource Forest
  - ❑ Single-forest to Resource Forest

- Simple Organizations are often based on Microsoft Small Business Server (SBS). Version 2003 of SBS is a stand-alone product that integrates several Microsoft server components, notably Exchange Server 2003. Because SBS is designed to run only on a single server (and a 32-bit server at that) and there is no upgrade path from Exchange 2003 to Exchange 2007, transitioning from Exchange 2003 to Exchange 2007 in SBS involves the installation of another server into your SBS domain.

- The single-forest to cross-forest transition occurs when you need to move from a Simple, Standard, or Large Organization to a Complex Organization type. As such, it combines the single-forest and cross-forest transition processes. In fact, this process is extremely similar to cross-forest transition, except that it begins with the creation of a new Active Directory forest because single forests are not Complex Organizations. You must also configure trusts between the forests.

- The best way to perform the migration from Exchange 5.5 is to move to Exchange 2003 and then to Exchange 2007. Keep the following in mind when performing this operation:

  ❑ Exchange 5.5 cannot reside on the same server as Exchange 2003. Similarly, Exchange 2003 cannot reside on the same server as Exchange 2007. This means installing new Exchange servers to host Exchange 2003 and new servers to host Exchange 2007. Depending on the size of the mailbox databases you need to migrate, you might seriously consider using virtual machines to run the Exchange 2003 intermediary step and only install Exchange 2007 on physical computers.

  ❑ Because the Exchange 2007 computers must run a 64-bit operating system, you might consider using one or more of the target Exchange 2007 servers to host the virtual machines you use to run Exchange 2003. You can recover these servers to host Exchange 2007 after you have decommissioned the Exchange 2003 computers.

- Migrating from a Lotus infrastructure to one including Exchange and Active Directory usually happens in three distinct phases:

  ❑ Plan and prepare.

  ❑ Set up the two environments so that they can interoperate.

  ❑ Migrate the content from Domino to Exchange 2007 and decommission the Domino service.

- Exchange 2007 cannot connect to Novell GroupWise; you cannot perform a direct migration. This means you must use the multi-step migration scenario, as with

Lotus Domino. Rely on the Exchange Server 2003 Connector for Novell Group-Wise to migrate from Novell to Exchange 2003, and then rely on the appropriate scenario to move from Exchange 2003 to Exchange 2007.

Case Scenarios

In the following case scenarios, you will apply what you have learned about Exchange deployment. You can find answers to the questions in this scenario in the "Answers" section at the end of this book.

Case Scenario 1: Create a Migration Lab

Tailspin Toys and Wingtip Toys have been running a Complex Organization in multiple forests for several years. They want to move to a new Exchange 2007 implementation but they want to perform a proof of concept first. They turn to you, the messaging professional, to create a testing lab that will help them stage an environment similar to theirs, and then let them prove that the transition will work as expected. This will also help them identify the exact steps they need to perform to make the transition.

To run this testing lab, the two organizations decide to use virtual machines. Because they want to simulate the correct environment as much as possible, they want to use Windows Server 2008 and Windows Server Hyper-V so that they can run 64-bit virtual machines to host Exchange 2007 server roles. You must provide the answers to the following questions as you help them set up their testing lab.

1. How should the lab set up the computers that will simulate the existing environment?

2. Which transition scenario should they rely on?

3. How should they set up their Exchange 2007 computers?

4. Which replication engine should they rely on?

Case Scenario 2: Move from Lotus Notes to Exchange Server 2007

The Graphics Design Institute has been working with Lotus Notes for several years. Their infrastructure is outdated, and although they could upgrade to Lotus Domino, they are not impressed by the fact that the upgrade requires a revamping of their entire Notes infrastructure. Therefore, they have decided to move to Exchange 2007 and begin to use mobile devices to give everyone access to information at all times through Direct Push.

They tell you that their current usage scenarios correspond to the information in Table 3-12. Your job as a messaging professional is to help them make the smoothest transition as possible to a new Exchange 2007 organization. In addition, they tell you that money is no object and that they are willing to purchase a migration tool if required. What do you do?

Table 3-12   Lotus Notes Usage Levels

User profile	Average mailbox size	Average attachment size	Attachment percentage	Schedules meetings
Low use	20 MB	1 MB	5 percent	No
Low to medium use	50 MB	2 MB	10 percent	Occasional
High to medium use	100 MB	Unknown	10 percent	Frequent
Power use	200 MB	>3 MB	25 percent	Frequent
Heavy use	500 MB	Unknown	30 percent	Frequent

Suggested Practices

It is difficult to practice either the transition or migration to Exchange Server without access to a full infrastructure, but you can do so if you prepare a virtual environment as outlined in the Introduction. Using this environment, add a second mailbox database to ExchangeOne and practice moving mailboxes from one database to another.

Also, rely on this environment to review the prerequisites and all other requirements for the installation of a new Exchange 2007 environment.

Chapter 4
Planning Exchange Server Interoperability

As mentioned in Chapter 3, "Planning Exchange Server 2007 Upgrades and Migrations," few organizations will have the opportunity to implement a new Exchange Server 2007 deployment without the need to recover data from existing systems. While most of these organizations will opt for a rapid transition or migration to Exchange 2007, some will opt to deploy a mixed environment, continuing to rely on the existing features of their e-mail systems while implementing some of the new features available from Exchange 2007. In this case, they will opt to implement an interoperability environment.

In fact, transitioning or migrating to Exchange Server 2007 relies on the same path as interoperability; the only difference between them is the duration of the interoperability phase. When you transition or migrate to Exchange 2007, you try to do it as fast as possible to minimize the potential interoperability issues that may arise. When you opt for a longer interoperability period, you must pay more attention to these potential issues and ensure that all systems will behave as expected for the duration of your interoperability period.

You may choose a longer interoperability period several reasons:

- You might find it cost-prohibitive to update all your Exchange servers to 64-bit hardware. Exchange Server 2007 only runs on 64-bit systems, and most organizations already running an e-mail system are most likely to have all of their e-mail servers on 32-bit systems. Whether this e-mail system is a Standard Organization running on a handful of servers or a Complex Organization running on multiple clustered servers, many organizations may find it cost-prohibitive to replace all servers at once.

- A second factor for the cost-conscious is client deployments. Perhaps an organization has the means to update all servers to a new platform, but the cost-prohibitive factor is updating all client systems to the latest version of Outlook. Therefore, the organization will need to learn the limitations their client platform will have.

■ A third factor for the cost-conscious is storage requirements. As you learned in Chapter 2, "Planning Deployments," the storage requirements for Exchange Server 2007 are considerably different from those of previous versions of Exchange Server. Therefore, organizations running legacy versions of Exchange may opt to continue to rely on their existing mailbox servers while implementing other features of Exchange Server 2007.

■ Finally, a consideration for coexistence that is unrelated to cost is the feature set provided by the different versions of Exchange Server, or even by third-party e-mail systems. Both Exchange 2000 Server and Exchange Server 2003 offer features that are not available in Exchange Server 2007. Conversely, Exchange 2007 offers features that are not available in previous versions. Therefore, some organizations may opt to keep some components of their legacy e-mail systems along with the implementation of selected Exchange 2007 components. Table 4-1 outlines the various features that have been deprecated from each previous version of Exchange in Exchange 2007.

Table 4-1   Supported Migration or Transition Scenarios to Exchange 2007

Exchange Version	Deprecated Feature	
Exchange Server 2003	Novell GroupWise connector	☐
	Network News Transfer Protocol	☐
	X.400 Connector	☐
	Connector for Lotus Notes	☐
Exchange 2000 Server	Microsoft Mobile Information Server	☐
	Instant Messaging Service	☐
	Exchange Chat Service	☐
	Exchange 2000 Conferencing Server	☐
	Key Management Service	☐
	cc:Mail connector	☐
	MS Mail connector	☐
Exchange 5.5	There is no possibility of interoperability between Exchange 5.5 and Exchange 2007.	

In each of these situations, interoperability will be a key factor and will require a closer look at the various considerations for continued operation of mixed e-mail environments.

Exam Tip   Learn the contents of Table 4-1 well. They will be important to know when you face exam questions related to interoperability. However, the exam is unlikely to include questions related to the cc:Mail and MS Mail connectors because both systems are very old and no longer in use.

Remember that when you transition or migrate to Exchange Server 2007, you must include a specific phase that includes a period of interoperability. Table 4-2 outlines the possible migration or transition paths to Exchange 2007 and emphasizes the interoperability aspects of these paths. Note that the interoperability phases of each path are in bold type to distinguish them from the migration or transition phases.

As you can see, Table 4-2 provides the same information as if you were transitioning of migrating from a legacy e-mail system to Exchange 2007. The only difference here is that the focus is now on the interoperability aspects of the processes you would use based on the source e-mail system.

This chapter will focus on three key aspects of interoperability:

- Interoperability with Exchange in separate organizations—creating a new organization and providing interoperability between two separate Exchange organizations, a legacy and an Exchange 2007 organization. This addresses scenarios 4, 5, and 6 in Table 4-2.

- Coexistence with Exchange 2000 Server and/or Exchange Server 2003 in a single organization—installing Exchange 2007 server roles into an existing organization and supporting interoperability between legacy and new Exchange servers. This addresses scenarios 1, 2, and 3 in Table 4-2.

- Interoperability with third-party messaging systems—installing a new Exchange 2007 organization and maintaining interoperability between two different e-mail systems, or using an existing organization to install new Exchange 2007 server roles because of the need to rely on legacy Exchange Server features to provide the interoperability features. This addresses scenarios 8 and 9 in Table 4-2.

Table 4-2 Supported Migration or Transition Scenarios to Exchange 2007

Upgrade Scenario	Starting Point	Action	Action	Midpoint	Action	Action	Endpoint
1. Transition	Exchange 2000 Server	**Install Exchange 2007 server role(s) into organization.**	Move mailboxes.	**Combined Exchange 2000/Exchange 2007 organization**	Decommission Exchange 2000 servers.		Organization transitioned to Exchange Server 2007
2. Transition	Exchange Server 2003	**Install Exchange 2007 server role(s) into organization.**	Move mailboxes.	**Combined Exchange 2003/ Exchange 2007 organization**	Decommission Exchange 2003 servers.		Organization transitioned to Exchange Server 2007
3. Transition	Combined Exchange 2000/ Exchange 2003 organization	**Install Exchange 2007 server role(s) into organization.**	Move mailboxes.	**Combined Exchange 2000/Exchange 2003/ Exchange 2007 organization**	Decommission Exchange 2000/ Exchange 2003 servers.		Organization transitioned to Exchange Server 2007
4. Migration	Exchange 2000 Server	**Install Exchange 2007 server role(s) in new organization.**	Move mailboxes.	**none**	Decommission Exchange 2000 servers.		New Exchange Server 2007 organization

Table 4-2 Supported Migration or Transition Scenarios to Exchange 2007

Upgrade Scenario	Starting Point	Action	Action	Midpoint	Action	Endpoint
5. Migration	Exchange Server 2003	**Install Exchange 2007 server role(s) in new organization.**	Move mailboxes.	**none**	Decommission Exchange 2003 servers.	New Exchange Server 2007 organization
6. Migration	Combined Exchange 2000/ Exchange 2003 organization	**Install Exchange 2007 server role(s) in new organization.**	Move mailboxes.	**none**	Decommission Exchange 2000/ Exchange 2003 servers.	New Exchange Server 2007 organization
7. Migration	Exchange Server 5.5 organization	Install Exchange 2000 or 2003 server(s).	Migrate data.	**Exchange 2000 or Exchange 2003 organization.**	**Use appropriate transition or migration process as outlined in scenarios 1, 2, 4 or 5.**	New or transitioned Exchange Server 2007 organization

Table 4-2 Supported Migration or Transition Scenarios to Exchange 2007

Upgrade Scenario	Starting Point	Action	Action	Midpoint	Action	Endpoint
8. Migration	Lotus Notes	**Install Exchange 2007 server role(s) in new organization.**	**Use Lotus Interoperability And Migration Tools to interoperate.**	Exchange Server 2007/ Lotus Notes interoperability	Use Lotus Interoperability And Migration Tools to migrate data and then decommission Lotus Notes servers.	New Exchange Server 2007 organization
9. Migration	Novell GroupWise	**Install Exchange 2003 server(s).**	**Migrate data with the GroupWise Connector.**	Exchange 2003 organization	**Use appropriate transition or migration process as outlined in scenarios 2 or 5.**	New or transitioned Exchange Server 2007 organization

In addition, this chapter will outline the impacts of relying on older Office Outlook clients to interact with a new Exchange 2007 implementation. For each scenario, you will need to focus on two key messaging factors:

- Message flow, which determines how messages are routed between e-mail systems
- Availability or free/busy data exchange to help users determine each other's schedules and coordinate meetings

As you will see, each scenario has different ways to address both factors.

IMPORTANT Scenario 7 in Table 4-2

Note that scenario 7 in Table 4-2 is not specifically addressed in this chapter because there is no coexistence path between Exchange 5.5 and Exchange 2007.

Exam objectives in this chapter:

- Plan interoperability with Exchange in separate organizations.
- Plan coexistence with Exchange 2000 Server and Exchange Server 2003 in a single organization.
- Plan interoperability with third-party messaging systems.

Before You Begin

To complete the lessons in this chapter, you must have the following:

- A virtual machine setup as outlined in the Introduction under "Virtual Machine Environments."
- Use the Exchange Server 2007 virtual machine from Microsoft to review the configuration options for pre-installed computers.
- Use the newly created virtual environment you set up to test the deployment of different server configurations. For the exercises in this chapter, you will need access to the Active Directory server and the all-in-one Exchange server.

Ideally, you will also have access to legacy installations of Exchange 2000 or Exchange 2003 or even Lotus Notes or Domino, but if you do not, make sure you look up all quoted references.

Lesson 1: Plan Interoperability with Exchange in Separate Organizations

Estimated lesson time: 30 minutes   •

As you know, only a single Exchange organization can exist within an Active Directory forest. When you plan to have e-mail systems coexist within separate organizations, you are basing your strategy on the Exchange migration scenarios, not the transition scenarios discussed in Chapter 3.

You could have multiple organizations running different versions of Exchange coexisting with each other in two situations:

- If you are unhappy with the current state of your Active Directory forest(s) and Exchange organization(s), you would consider creating a new organization. The intervening period where more than one organization exists is the coexistence period.

- If you are in a situation where you have been using a Complex Organization and you want to simplify it to a Large Organization, you would consider a migration scenario over a transition scenario. Once again, the intervening period where multiple organizations exist is the coexistence period.

A third coexistence situation using a new Exchange 2007 organization involves the migration from a third-party messaging system to Exchange 2007. This situation is discussed in Lesson 3 of this chapter.

Exam Tip   When you install a new Exchange 2007 organization, you cannot install any legacy version of Exchange into the same organization. Be sure to remember this; it is bound to show up on the exam.

As mentioned in the introduction, in each of these situations, you have two main concerns:

- Make sure messages flow from one organization to another.
- Ensure that free/busy data will be available between the organizations you manage.

Table 4-3 outlines how these concerns are addressed in the case of a new Exchange organization.

Table 4-3   Interoperability Concerns with a New Exchange Organization

Required Component	Strategy
Name Resolution	Use DNS forwarders from each forest to other forests.
Message Routing	Rely on SMTP protocol to route messages from one organization to another.
Global Address List	Rely on a synchronization tool to merge Global Address Lists between Exchange organizations.
Free/Busy Data	If all clients are Outlook 2007 clients, use the Availability Service in Exchange 2007. If you are running legacy clients, use the Inter-Organization Replication tool.

Plan Message Connectivity

Message flow is the simplest when it comes to separate organizations. That is because the exchange of messages between two different Exchange organizations—and therefore two different Active Directory forests—is very similar to message exchanges between a single organization and the Internet. Everything operates through the SMTP protocol, although through the internal network rather than the external network. Therefore, you need to ensure that everything required for the routing of SMTP messages is in place and working properly.

The more complex aspect of coexistence in this case deals with the exchange of free/busy data between the two Active Directory forests. In this case, you need to rely on some form of synchronization tool—a tool that will publish the information from one forest to the other and vice versa.

In addition, to make the exchange of information simpler for end users, you need to synchronize Global Address Lists. This takes user accounts from one forest and transforms them into e-mail contacts in the other and vice versa. Users from one forest can then locate any user from the other forest directly within the GAL for their own forest.

In fact, interoperability between Exchange organizations is very similar to the cross-forest transition scenario discussed in Chapter 3. It is also similar to the Complex

Organization implementation scenario for Exchange. In Complex Organizations, you must use synchronization tools to make both free/busy data and GALs available to each forest that makes up the Complex Organization (see Figure 4-1). Interoperability in this case will stem from the fact that there are too many components—Exchange servers or e-mail clients—to migrate all at once. Therefore, you will find yourself in a coexistence scenario and must ensure that all of the forests can interact with each other for the duration of the migration.

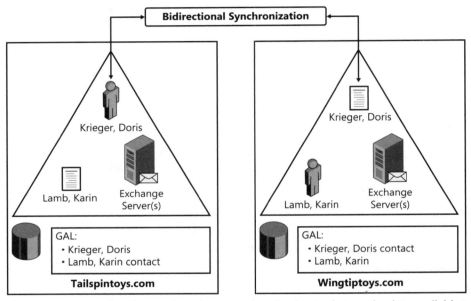

Figure 4-1   Cross-forest scenarios rely on synchronization tools to make data available to end users

Connect to Other Exchange Organizations

Connecting multiple Exchange organizations is very simple, no matter which version of Exchange is running in each organization. Mail transport will rely on the SMTP protocol and message routing will be treated exactly as if you were routing the messages from your internal organization to an external organization on the Internet.

As you know, proper message delivery relies on the Domain Name Service (DNS) entries found in your DNS servers. To link multiple forests together and ensure that message delivery operates properly, you must rely on DNS forwarders, which forward requests from one forest to the DNS servers of the other forest and vice versa (see Figure 4-2). For example, when a message is sent from Tailspin Toys to Adventure Works, the DNS service in the Tailspintoys.com domain forwards the name

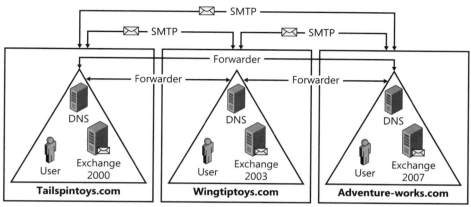

Figure 4-2   Relying on STMP and DNS forwarders to ensure proper message routing in Complex Organizations

resolution request to the DNS server in the Adventure-works.com domain. When the name is resolved properly, the message is transferred to the appropriate recipient through the SMTP protocol.

Synchronize Directories

When you use Complex Organizations—organizations that rely on multiple forests linked together to provide integrated e-mail services—each Exchange organization must exchange information between the forests. This exchange of information makes it easier for end users to communicate with their peers from one forest to the other. Users could rely on their own skills and manually write out recipient addresses in each message or manually create personal contacts for the recipients they work the most with in other forests, but this is a tedious task at best and is often unreliable. This is why you need to implement an automated information provisioning system.

In most cross-forest topologies, this exchange of information is performed through the use of a synchronization tool, either the Identity Integration Feature Pack (IIFP) or the Microsoft Identity Integration Server (MIIS). Both tools must be running Service Pack 2 to operate with Exchange 2007.

Both IIFP and MIIS provide a tool—Global Address List Synchronization (GALSync)—which is designed to synchronize recipients in each forest, converting user accounts from one forest into contacts in the other(s). But the Exchange 2007 recipient object is different from recipient objects in previous versions of Exchange. Both IIFP and MIIS were released before Exchange 2007, and therefore GALSync cannot support the new recipient object features included in Exchange 2007.

To complete the synchronization process when data is copied from forest to forest, the GALSync process relies on the Recipient Update Service (RUS) found in Exchange 2000 or 2003. Because Exchange Server 2007 does not have this service, you must manually update recipients if you want to fully provision them.

Relying on GALSync to provision users from forest to forest when your forests are running different versions of Exchange causes some functionality loss. The missing features include:

- Loss of delegations when users delegate their mailboxes to others.
- Loss of detailed information about the represented resources for contacts designed to represent rooms or equipment.
- All contacts appear the same in Outlook whether they are from the local or a remote forest.

These issues affect interoperability, so you should seriously consider whether interoperability is your best choice. If you do choose interoperability, you need to implement a strategy that will circumvent these issues.

Even when you have migrated all forests to Exchange 2007, you will still face cross-forest limitations, including:

- If distribution lists include members from different forests, users will not be able to view the distribution list membership.
- Users will not be able to add users from a different forest to a distribution list.
- Users will not be able to nest distribution lists across forests.
- You cannot move a distribution list from one forest to another.
- When you move mailboxes from one forest to another, you will lose any delegation properties assigned to the mailboxes.
- You cannot move public folders from one forest to another.
- If your forests rely on a Windows public key infrastructure (PKI) self-signed certificate to sign messages, you will not be able to send messages from one forest to another. To resolve this issue, use proper PKI certificates from a trusted certificate authority.

Despite these limitations, many organizations must rely on the Complex Organization model because of the very nature of their businesses. Organizations that are linked together through mergers or acquisitions and must maintain separate identities have little choice but to use the Complex Organization model, but if there is any way these organizations can blend together into a single organization, you should endeavor to move them toward a Complex to Standard Organization migration by relying on the cross-forest to single forest transition scenario described in Chapter 3.

MORE INFO **Configuring GALSync to support interoperability**

For information on how to configure GALSync for cross-forest interoperability, go to *http://technet.microsoft.com/en-us/library/bb124363.aspx.*

Plan Calendar Availability

The last aspect of interoperability for new Exchange organizations relates to free/busy data availability. This aspect of interoperability often includes both the availability of free/busy data as well as the availability of public folder content. In most cases, this means replicating information from one Exchange organization to another.

In Exchange 2007, free/busy data is made available through the Availability Service as long as the end-user systems rely on Outlook 2007. Note that the Availability Service does not provide public folder replication. To provide public folder replication if public folders are in use, you must rely on the Inter-Organization Replication (IORepl) tool that is available with Exchange 2000 or Exchange 2003 (see Figure 4-3).

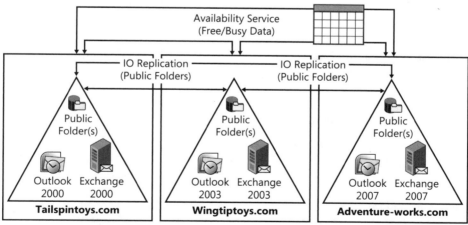

Figure 4-3   Replicating free/busy data and public folders when clients run Outlook 2007

Because IORepl stems from Exchange 2000 and 2003, you can install it on servers running either version of Exchange with no problems. You cannot install IORepl on a server running Exchange 2007. You can, however, install it on a system running the Exchange 2007 management tools without any other Exchange 2007 server role installed. But to do so, you also need to install the Exchange MAPI client libraries.

If your client systems are not using Outlook 2007 and are running a legacy version of Outlook (Outlook 2000 or Outlook 2003), you must rely on the IORepl tool only. This tool supports the coordination of meeting, appointments, contacts, and public folder information between separate Exchange organizations (see Figure 4-4).

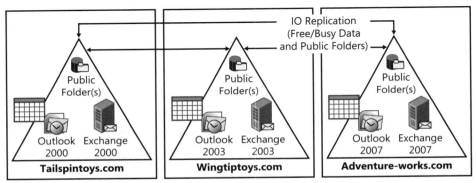

Figure 4-4 Replicating free/busy data and public folders when clients run legacy versions of Outlook

Potential Issues with Legacy Outlook Systems

Older versions of Outlook will present a significant set of limitations when you are working with an Exchange 2007 organization. Table 4-4 outlines the limitations your end users will face when working with legacy versions of Outlook.

Table 4-4 **Feature Limitations for Outlook 2000 or Outlook 2003 with Exchange 2007**

Feature	Limitation
Synchronization of free/busy data between forests	Must rely on Inter-Organization Replication tool.
Autodiscover	Must configure e-mail settings manually or send an automated configuration file to users.

Table 4-4   Feature Limitations for Outlook 2000 or Outlook 2003 with Exchange 2007

Feature	Limitation
Public Folders	Required to provide free/busy data. Cannot rely on the Availability Service.
Search	Users must be online and must use the Find or Advanced Find tools.
Legacy Administrative Groups	These groups are required to access free/busy data and to find assigned delegated users.
Unified Communications	Legacy clients do not support unified communications. Users must use Outlook Web Access 2007 to access these features.

Ideally, you will be able to upgrade your clients to the latest version of Outlook so that you can avoid these limitations. If not, you will need to address each limitation as you prepare to support interoperability.

MORE INFO   Upgrading from legacy versions of Outlook

For more information on upgrading clients from earlier versions of Outlook, go to *http://technet2.microsoft.com/Office/en-us/library/8a060469-bbe7-4f09-80f3-24201e6ac4ef1033.mspx?mfr=true*.

In addition, when you install Exchange 2007, you will be prompted about whether you have earlier versions of Outlook or Entourage (the Apple Macintosh e-mail client for Exchange) in your network. In some cases, you may click No to this question during Setup only to realize later that you do in fact have legacy Outlook clients. When you click No to this question during Setup, Exchange 2007 does not install support for legacy clients. In fact, it does not create any public folder structure. Public folders are required for legacy Outlook clients to access free/busy data.

To resolve this situation, you must modify the configuration of your Exchange 2007 installation, which you can do by following these steps:

1. Create a new public folder store.

2. Connect this public folder store to the existing mailbox store(s) that host user mailboxes.

3. Configure the Offline Address Book (OAB) to support legacy Outlook clients. Use the Configure Offline Address Book (OAB) Distribution For Outlook 2003 And Earlier Clients Wizard to perform this activity.

This will provide support for your legacy Outlook systems. See Knowledge Base article number 555851 at *http://support.microsoft.com/kb/555851* for more information.

Plan Availability Service Implementations

The Availability Service is a Web Service that is installed and activated by default on Exchange Server 2007 installations when you deploy the CAS role in your organization. Outlook 2007 uses the Autodiscover service to discover the URL that links it to the Availability Service. If all your clients run Outlook 2007, you have a few options for the configuration of the Availability Service between Exchange organizations.

First, you must determine whether your forests are trusted. If the forests are trusted and you have implemented forest trusts between them, you will be able to provide per-user free/busy data between the forests. Remember that forest trusts are only available between forests running Windows Server 2003. Forests running Windows 2000 Server must create explicit trusts between each domain in the forests.

If there are no trusts between the forests, you will only be able to share free/busy data on a per-organization basis. This limits the amount of information your users will have access to when trying to book cross-forest meetings.

MORE INFO **Cross-forest Availability Service configuration**

See Lesson 2 in Chapter 2 for more information on the configuration of the Availability Service in a cross-forest topology. In addition, you can find more information on configuring cross-forest availability data at *http://technet.microsoft.com/en-us/library/bb125182.aspx*.

Plan Inter-Organization Replication Implementations

As you can see, integration between forests is a lot easier when you have updated Outlook clients. But when you do not, or when you also want to replicate public folders, you need to work with the IORepl tool. IORepl relies on publisher and subscribers to replicate information from one forest to another. The publisher prepares information from the source forest and packages it to send to one or more subscribers based on a schedule. The subscriber is a computer running a version of Exchange that accepts and distributes information from a publisher within its own organization (see Figure 4-5).

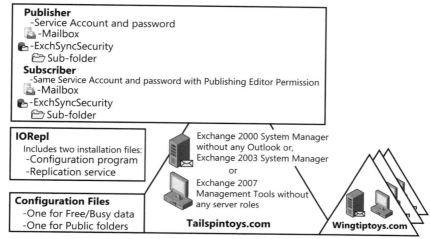

Figure 4-5   Configuring the IORepl tool with publishers and subscribers

Both publishers and subscribers rely on service accounts to operate. For the publisher, the service account must have an Exchange mailbox along with appropriate permissions to access all information you want to replicate. You must create the mailbox for this service account on a server that also hosts at least one public folder store. After you create the mailbox, you must use Outlook to create a public folder named **Exchsync-SecurityFolder** in the root of the public folder hierarchy for this account to use to replicate data. Then, you must use Outlook to assign this service account as owner of each public folder and subfolder you want to replicate. This will allow the service account to replicate Anonymous and Default permissions between organizations.

The subscriber must also have the same service account with (ideally) the same password to facilitate the replication between organizations. This service account also requires a mailbox and must be created on a server that hosts a public folder store. When this account is ready, you must use Outlook to create the top-level public folders for each folder you want to replicate; subfolders will be created automatically during replication. Then, you must grant the Publishing Editor permission for each replicated folder to the service account. Finally, you must also create the **Exchsync-SecurityFolder** in the root of the public folder hierarchy for this account to use to replicate data.

Make sure you assign publisher and subscriber information to the service account in each Exchange organization that will be part of the replication if you want bidirectional replication between each forest. After you create the service accounts and set them up in each forest, you can proceed to install the IORepl tool. This tool is made up of two installation files, one for the configuration program and one for the replication service. You must either use an Exchange server or install Exchange System Manager on the computer you want to use to run the IORepl tool.

IMPORTANT   IORepl on Exchange 2000

If you choose to install the IORepl tool on another computer that is not an Exchange 2000 server, you must ensure that Outlook was *never* installed on the computer or the installation will fail. Exchange 2003 and Exchange 2007 do not suffer from this limitation.

Finally, you create configuration files for replication. Two files are used: one for free/busy data and one for public folders. If you are using IORepl to replicate only public folders because you are relying on the Availability Service to replicate calendar information between forests, create only one configuration file to replicate public folders. If not, you must create both configuration files.

From this point on, you will need to monitor replication to ensure that all data is being made available to users in all of the Exchange organizations you want to synchronize.

MORE INFO   IORepl configuration

For detailed steps to configure IORepl, see Knowledge Base article number 238573 at *http://support.microsoft.com/?kbid=238573*.

Practice: Plan the Integration of Two Separate Exchange Organizations

In this practice, you will assist Tailspin Toys and Wingtip Toys to prepare a plan for interoperability between Exchange Server 2003 and Exchange 2007. This practice consists of a single exercise. Both companies want to deploy Exchange 2007 to take advantage of its new feature set, but they cannot afford to update all of their systems immediately. They have decided to use a new Exchange Organization for the deployment of Exchange 2007, called Adventure Works, so that they can eventually move from a Complex to a Large Organization topology. Your job as a messaging professional is to help them plan interoperability for the intervening period before they can complete their transition.

▶ **Exercise: Build an Exchange Interoperability Plan**

Tailspin Toys and Wingtip Toys have been working together for several years. They first joined forces through a merger in 2004 and are very pleased with the relationship to date. Tailspin Toys uses an Exchange 2000 organization along with Outlook 2000. Wingtip Toys uses Exchange 2003 with Outlook 2003. Because they plan to move to Exchange 2007 with Outlook 2007, they have decided to use a cross-forest to single forest transition. This will let them simplify their e-mail structure and finally bring all of their forces together into a single organization. The new organization will be called Adventure Works and will use Adventure-works.com as a domain name (see Figure 4-6).

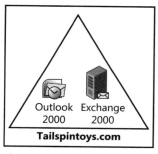 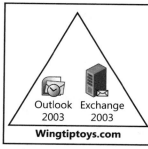 

Figure 4-6 The Tailspin Toys and Wingtip Toys organization along with the new Adventure Works organization

This transition will take time, however. As such, they have the resources to create the new forest, but do not have the resources to replace all of their servers and update their client systems right away. They turn to you to help them plan the interoperability between their organizations and help identify potential issues they will face. Specifically, they want to know:

- What are the critical aspects of the configuration for interoperability?
- Which tools should they use to synchronize all data?
- Which features will they lose because of their legacy clients?
- How should they configure free/busy data replication?

You work with their IT staff to get a better picture of their requirements and potential transition timelines and you come up with the following answers to their questions:

1. There are four critical configuration aspects to provide interoperability between organizations running Exchange 2000, Exchange 2003, and Exchange 2007; these are listed in Table 4-5. In addition, you will require two replication tools.

Table 4-5 Interoperability Preoccupations for Tailspin Toys and Wingtip Toys

Required Component	Strategy
Name Resolution	Use DNS forwarders from each forest to other forests.
Message Routing	Rely on SMTP protocol to route messages from one organization to another.
Global Address List	Rely on a synchronization tool to merge Global Address Lists between Exchange organizations. Because this is a short-term solution, you recommend the Identity Integration Feature Pack. which is free, to perform this replication.
Free/Busy Data	Because each forest includes legacy Outlook clients, the organizations need to use the Inter-Organization Replication tool for both free/busy data and public folders.

2. Because the organizations have both Outlook 2000 and Outlook 2003, you will lose some functionality. This information is listed in Table 4-6.

Table 4-6 Feature Limitations for Legacy Outlook Clients with Exchange 2007

Feature	Limitation
Synchronization of free/busy data between forests	The organizations must rely on the Inter-Organization Replication tool.
Autodiscover	This service is not available for legacy clients. The organizations must either configure e-mail settings manually or send an automated configuration file to users.
Public Folders	The organizations must use public folders to provide free/busy data.
Search	Users must be online and must use the Find or Advanced Find tools.

Table 4-6   **Feature Limitations for Legacy Outlook Clients with Exchange 2007**

Feature	Limitation
Legacy Administrative Groups	These groups are required to access free/busy data and to find assigned delegated users.
Unified Communications	Legacy clients do not support unified communications. Users must use Outlook Web Access 2007 to access these features.

3. Finally, to make free/busy data available in each forest, the organizations should use the IORepl tool and implement both publishers and subscribers in each forest. To simplify the installation, you should install IORepl on servers in both the Tailspin Toys and Wingtip Toys forests and install it on a workstation running both the Exchange 2007 Management Tools and the MAPI Client Libraries for the new Adventure Works forest. You should begin with a replication schedule that performs the task twice a day and then see whether this continues to meet their requirements.

Quick Check

1. Which Exchange Server 2003 features are deprecated when you are migrating to Exchange Server 2007? Mention at least three.

2. Which interoperability components need to be addressed in a new Exchange organization?

3. A Complex Organization with multiple forests needs to migrate to Exchange 2007. They ask you which limitations they will face. Name at least four.

4. If the client systems are running legacy version of Outlook (2000 or 2003), which tool should you rely on and what can this tool coordinate between separate Exchange organizations?

5. What are the limitations of the older versions of Outlook when working with Exchange Server 2007?

Quick Check Answers

1. Novell GroupWise connector, Network News Transfer Protocol, x.400 Connector, Connector for Lotus Notes.

2. Name resolution, message routing, Global Address List synchronization, and Free/Busy data synchronization.

3. There are several limitations:

   ❑ If distribution lists include members from different forests, your users will not be able to view the distribution list membership.

   ❑ Users will not be able to add users from a different forest to a distribution list.

   ❑ Your users will not be able to nest distribution lists across forests.

   ❑ You cannot move a distribution list from one forest to another.

   ❑ When you move mailboxes from one forest to another, you will lose any delegation properties assigned to the mailbox.

   ❑ You cannot move public folders from one forest to another.

   ❑ If your forests rely on a Windows public key infrastructure (PKI) self-signed certificate to sign messages, you will not be able to send messages from one forest to another. To resolve this issue, use proper PKI certificates from a trusted certificate authority.

4. The IORepl tool. This tool supports the coordination of meeting, appointments, contacts, and public folder information between separate Exchange organizations.

5. The limitations are focused on:

   ❑ Synchronization of free/busy data between forests

   ❑ Autodiscover

   ❑ Public folders

   ❑ Search

   ❑ Legacy Administrative Groups

   ❑ Unified Communications

Lesson 2: Plan Coexistence with Exchange 2000 Server and Exchange Server 2003 in a Single Organization

Estimated lesson time: 50 minutes

Chapter 3 outlined the various transition or migration strategies you could use to move to Exchange Server 2007. It pointed out the five supported transitions scenarios:

- Single-forest to single-forest
- Cross-forest to cross-forest
- Single-forest to cross-forest
- Resource Forest to Resource Forest
- Single-forest to Resource Forest

Of these five scenarios, three focus on reusing the existing Exchange organization you might already have in place. Single-forest to single-forest, cross-forest to cross-forest, and Resource Forest to Resource Forest all reuse the existing organization. Reusing the existing organization makes the transition from Exchange 2000 or Exchange 2003 to Exchange 2007 simpler in many ways because you do not need to create a new Active Directory forest and migrate all of the contents of your network—user accounts, computer accounts, file shares, printers, and more—to the new Active Directory and Exchange organization. On the other hand, reusing the existing Exchange organization does not let you change the way it functions. Therefore, you must be completely happy with the way you implemented the legacy Exchange organization.

Of the preceding scenarios for transition into an Exchange 2007 organization, only Large or Complex Organizations face long-term interoperability because of the duration of the transition from one e-mail system to another. Simple or Standard Organizations can often perform a fast-paced transition to Exchange 2007, minimizing the duration of the interoperability period and thereby avoiding many of its potential issues.

Plan Message Connectivity

When you have complex Exchange implementations with several different servers in several locations running different Exchange functions, moving all of the functions and content to Exchange 2007 takes time. Therefore, you must plan for interoperability. Once again, you must address four key aspects of interoperability. Table 4-7 outlines how you need to address these four key aspects when interoperating within the same Exchange organization.

Table 4-7   Interoperability Preoccupations Within an Existing Exchange Organization

Required Component	Strategy
Name Resolution	No modifications required.
Message Routing	Rely on the message transfer agents from Exchange 2000, Exchange 2003, or Exchange 2007 to properly route messages.
Global Address List	No change required because you are working with the same Active Directory forest.
Free/Busy Data	If all clients are Outlook 2007, use the Availability Service in Exchange 2007. If you are running legacy clients, use public folders.

Microsoft supports several coexistence scenarios for Exchange 2007 in existing organizations, including:

- Exchange 2007 and Exchange Server 2003
- Exchange 2007 and Exchange 2000 Server
- Exchange 2007 and a mix of Exchange 2000 Server with Exchange Server 2003

Fortunately, the procedures you use to manage interoperability in each of these scenarios are identical. Exchange 2000 Server has no special requirements that differ from those of coexistence with Exchange Server 2003, so coexistence is simplified no matter which version of Exchange you are moving from. Remember that there is no coexistence between Exchange 2007 and Exchange 5.5.

Connect Within the Same Exchange Organization

Coexistence between Exchange 2000, Exchange 2003, and Exchange 2007 has the following requirements:

- All Exchange 5.5 servers must be removed from the organization before you can install Exchange 2007 server roles.
- The Site Replication Service must be decommissioned before you can install any Exchange 2007 server roles.

- Exchange Active Directory connectors must be decommissioned.

- The Exchange Organization must be upgraded to native mode. This is done through the Exchange System Manager under the Organization's Properties | General Tab | Change Operations Mode.

Now you are ready to integrate Exchange 2007 server roles into the existing organization. Each role has its own particularities when coexisting with either Exchange 2003 or Exchange 2000 servers. Table 4-8 outlines these particularities.

Table 4-8   Exchange Server 2007 Server Roles in Coexistence Mode

Exchange 2007 Server Role	Supported Configuration
Client Access Server	Can be the only role deployed.
	Must be deployed in each site that also includes a Mailbox Server role.
	The version of Outlook Web Access displayed to end users depends on where the user's mailbox is stored. OWA displays the same version as the Exchange version running the mailbox store.
	You must update the ActiveSync Web site to Integrated Windows Authentication if user mailboxes are still on Exchange 2003; otherwise, they will not be able to connect. After this update, the Exchange 2007 CAS and the Exchange 2003 mailbox server can use Kerberos authentication together.
Hub Transport Server	Can be the only role deployed.
	Because this role manages message routing, you must create routing group connectors between the Exchange 2007 Routing Group (DWBGZMFD01QNBJR) and each Exchange 2003 routing group that will communicate directly with Exchange 2007. By default, the first connectors are created at installation of the HT role, but you should use the **New-RoutingGroupConnector** cmdlet to add more servers for redundancy. Before you do so, you must suppress minor link state updates on each Exchange 2003 or Exchange 2000 server. See *http://technet.microsoft.com/en-us/library/aa996728.aspx* for more information.

Table 4-8   Exchange Server 2007 Server Roles in Coexistence Mode

Exchange 2007 Server Role	Supported Configuration
Mailbox Server	If you deploy MB roles in any Active Directory site, you must also deploy an HT and a CAS.
Edge Transport Server	Because the ET is a role deployed outside the Active Directory, it can coexist with Exchange 2000 or Exchange 2003 infrastructures. In this case, you can use it as an SMTP relay and smart host server only.
Unified Messaging Server	If you deploy UM roles in any Active Directory site, you must also deploy an HT. Exchange 2000 and Exchange 2003 mailboxes cannot be Unified Messaging–enabled. Exchange 2000 and Exchange 2003 servers cannot interact with this role.

When the mixed infrastructure is in place, you can manage systems in the following manner:

- Exchange 2007 server roles must be managed through the Exchange Management Console or the Exchange Management Shell.
- Exchange 2000 and Exchange 2003 servers are managed through Exchange System Manager.
- Deprecated features in either Exchange 2000 or 2003 must be managed through the appropriate version of Exchange System Manager.
- Mailboxes stored on Exchange 2000 and Exchange 2003 servers can be managed through the Exchange 2007 Management Console.
- Mailboxes stored on Exchange 2000 and Exchange 2003 servers can be moved to Exchange 2007 MB systems with the **Move-Mailbox** cmdlet only.

As you would expect, routing group management is one of the most important aspects of coexistence operations when working with mixed organizations.

IMPORTANT Exchange Server 2007 Routing Group

By default, all Exchange 2007 HT systems are placed into the Exchange Routing Group (DWBGZMFD01QNBJR). Do not rename this group and do not move Exchange 2007 servers out of this group. This group is required to provide communications with servers running legacy versions of Exchange. Note that you cannot put Exchange 2000, Exchange 2003, and/or Exchange 2007 servers into the same routing group.

IMPORTANT Exchange Server 2007 Administrative Group

Exchange 2007 servers are all placed within the Exchange Administrative Group (FYDIBOHF23SPDLT). Do not rename this group and do not move Exchange 2007 servers out of this group. This group is used to store configuration data for Exchange 2007.

Exam Tip   It is easy to remember the bizarre names of both the Exchange 2007 Routing and Administrative groups. The Exchange Routing Group name is DWBGZMFD01QNBJR. The Exchange Administrative Group name is FYDIBOHF23SPDLT. Both are based on one key phrase: Exchange12Rocks. To find the Routing Group name, change the letters in Exchange12Rocks by moving back one. For example, E becomes D, X becomes W and so forth. To find the Administrative Group name, change the letters in Exchange12Rocks by moving forward one. For example, E becomes F, X becomes Y, and so forth.

Connect Exchange 2000 and Exchange 2007

As you will remember from Chapter 3, you cannot perform a direct upgrade from previous versions of Exchange to 2007. Therefore, if you want to maintain your existing implementation and simply change the existing infrastructure to an Exchange 2007 infrastructure, you need to install new servers running Exchange 2007 server roles. (Remember, all Exchange 2007 production systems use 64-bit hardware.)

When you install a new Exchange 2007 server into an existing organization, after you have performed the appropriate Active Directory modifications, Exchange will perform the following tasks:

- Create a new Active Directory universal security group called ExchangeLegacy-Interop. This group is given the appropriate permissions to allow Exchange 2000 or Exchange 2003 servers to send e-mail to Exchange 2007 servers.
- Create the Exchange Administrative Group (FYDIBOHF23SPDLT).
- Create the Exchange Routing Group (DWBGZMFD01QNBJR).

- Create a single two-way routing group connector between Exchange 2007 and a selected legacy Exchange bridgehead server (see Figure 4-7).

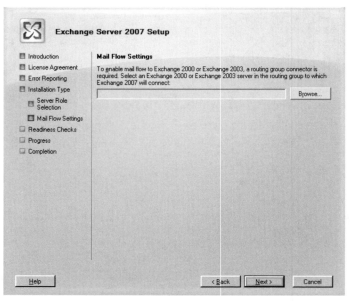

Figure 4-7   Selecting a legacy bridgehead server during the installation of Exchange 2007

If your legacy Exchange Organization has front-end servers, you typically begin with the installation of a Client Access Server role. In any event, you should begin with this role as a best practice. Your Exchange 2007 implementation will not be fully functional, however, until you have added an HT and an MB along with the CAS installation.

Installation of the new Exchange 2007 roles can be performed either through the graphical Setup.com program or through the command line. If you choose to use the command line, you should use a command similar to this:

```
setup /mode:Install /roles:ClientAccess,HubTransport,Mailbox
/LegacyRoutingServer:FQDNofBridgeheadServer
```

Of course, you select the roles you want to install and you must provide the fully qualified domain name (FQDN) of the bridgehead server you want to include in the routing connector. As mentioned in Table 4-8, you should add more routing connectors with the **New-RoutingGroupConnector** cmdlet. Once created, you can manage them with the **Set-RoutingGroupConnector** cmdlet.

As soon as you complete the installation of the first Exchange 2007, the Exchange System Manager (ESM) will display the new server, the new administrative and routing groups, and the new routing connector (see Figure 4-8). Remember that even though you can view Exchange 2007 objects in ESM, you must use the Exchange Management Console or the Exchange Management Shell to manage every Exchange 2007 object.

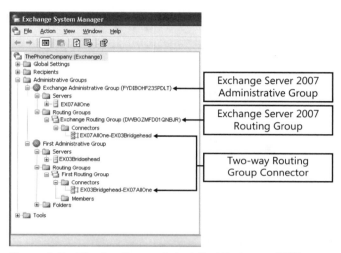

Figure 4-8   Viewing the newly installed Exchange 2007 server, administrative, and routing groups and routing connector in ESM

Create Additional Routing Connectors

The first routing connector is created by default as you install the first HT system in your existing organization. But, to provide redundancy and ensure that message routing is performed properly between legacy and 2007 Exchange systems, you should create additional routing connectors.

Remember that you use the **New-RoutingGroupConnector** cmdlet to create these routing connectors. When this cmdlet creates a routing connector, it automatically applies the appropriate permissions to enable mail flow between Exchange versions.

Unlike legacy versions of Exchange, Exchange Server 2007 does not use routing groups. For compatibility purposes, a special routing group, the Exchange Routing Group (DWBGZMFD01QNBJR) is created during installation of an Exchange 2007 HT role. Therefore, you cannot manage routing groups through the Exchange Management Console—you must use the Exchange System Manager to do so. Keep in mind that you cannot manage HT systems through ESM or the routing connectors you create with the **New-RoutingGroupConnector** cmdlet. Use ESM to manage legacy outing groups only.

Exam Tip   Remember that you cannot manage routing groups through the Exchange 2007 management tools and you must use the legacy Exchange System Manager to do so.

IMPORTANT   Viewing routing groups in ESM

You cannot view routing groups in Exchange System Manager by default. You must enable this option in the Properties dialog box of the Exchange Organization.

To create new routing connectors, your Exchange Organization must meet the following conditions:

- The Active Directory forest must be updated for Exchange 2007.

- At least one HT system must be installed into the organization.

- Minor link-state updates must be suppressed on all Exchange 2000 or Exchange 2003 servers.

- The user account you use must have Exchange Administrator permissions for Exchange 2000 or Exchange 2003 as well as for Exchange 2007. It must also be local Administrator on the target HT systems you intend to add to the routing connectors.

When you are ready, launch the Exchange Management Shell and apply the cmdlet that sets routing connectors. For example, in The Phone Company, you could create a routing connector named TPC_RGC_Two between servers EX07AllOne and EX03Bridgehead with the following cmdlet:

```
New-RoutingGroupConnector -Name "TPC_RGC_Two" -SourceTransportServers
"Ex07AllOne.thephone-company.com" -TargetTransportServers
"Ex03Bridgehead.thephone-company.com" -Cost 100 -Bidirectional $true -
PublicFolderReferralsEnabled $true
```

As you can see, this cmdlet enables public folder referrals on the connector. This allows users with mailboxes still residing on the legacy Exchange servers to access public folders stored within Exchange 2007 MB systems.

Suppress Minor Link-State Updates

Minor link-state updates are used in legacy Exchange servers to control routing costs and determine the route to use when transferring messages. When enabled, minor link-state updates allow legacy Exchange servers to mark connectors as down because they do not respond fast enough. When this happens, routing between Exchange 2007 and legacy systems does not work properly.

You suppress minor link-state updates to ensure that legacy Exchange systems will not mark connectors as down and will rely solely on least-cost routing to plan message transfer routes. This avoids routing loops and ensures that messages are transferred properly between all systems.

There is no interface for making this modification. You must be a member of the local Administrators group and use the Registry Editor to make this modification on every legacy Exchange server in the organization. Proceed as follows:

1. In the Registry Editor, locate HKEY_LOCAL_MACHINE\System\Current ControlSet\Services\RESvc\Parameters.

2. Create a new DWORD value and name it **SuppressStateChanges**.

3. Double-click the new *SuppressStateChanges* object and change the Value field to 1.

4. Close the Registry Editor and use Computer Management to restart the following services:

   ❑ Simple Mail Transfer Protocol (SMTP)

   ❑ Microsoft Exchange Routing Engine

   ❑ Microsoft Exchange MTA Stacks

5. Repeat these steps for each legacy Exchange server in the organization.

If you export the Registry values for the Parameters object into a .reg file, you can then make the modification automatically on each of your servers.

Only then can you create new routing connectors.

Message Routing in Coexistence Environments

Message routing is probably the most important aspect of coexistence you will face when running a mixed organization. Routing in an Exchange 2007 Organization and routing in legacy organizations are significantly different, as outlined in Table 4-9.

Table 4-9   Routing in Exchange 2007 and Legacy Versions

Exchange 2007	Exchange 2000 and Exchange 2003
Internal message routing is based on existing Active Directory sites. Only a single routing group is created for legacy compatibility purposes.	Custom routing groups are created to provide internal message routing.
Least-cost routes between HT systems are based on Active Directory IP site link costs.	Bridgehead servers are assigned in each site. Exchange uses routing group connector costs to determine the best route.
HT systems directly relay messages from one to another.	All message relay is performed through bridgehead servers.

Table 4-9   Routing in Exchange 2007 and Legacy Versions

Exchange 2007	Exchange 2000 and Exchange 2003
Exchange uses a *queue at point of failure* process when messages cannot be delivered to the appropriate HT system: All messages are transferred to the site that is closest to the actual destination and queued until a working connection is found.	Exchange determines an alternative path when the original route is no longer available.
Exchange uses *delayed fan-out* to keep messages destined to multiple recipients together as long as possible. When a fork in the routing path is reached, Exchange splits the message to deliver it to all of the recipients.	Messages that are destined to multiple recipients are split as soon as they are sent.
HT systems are responsible for obtaining their own data about routes and configuration changes from Active Directory.	Link state tables are used to store routing tables. The link state tables are distributed to other servers through minor link-state updates. Each routing group has a master who is responsible for retrieving these updates from Active Directory and propagating them to other members of the routing group.
Exchange 2007 uses a mapping between MAPI and MIME to transmit information about messages and recipients (metadata) that cannot normally be included in the message itself. Therefore, it does not require the X-EXCH50 verb. It can, however, propagate Exch50 data to legacy Exchange servers.	Exchange 2003 relies on the X-EXCH50 verb to transmit metadata about e-mail messages. This information is transmitted as a large Exch50 binary object. This metadata can include information such as spam confidence level, address rewriting information, and other MAPI properties that may not have a MIME representation. The X-EXCH50 verb is a proprietary Extended SMTP verb and therefore cannot be transmitted to non-Exchange servers.

Because of the differences in routing between Exchange 2007 and legacy versions, it is important to properly plan where your first HT installation will occur. Ideally, your legacy Exchange routing strategy will mirror your Active Directory replication strategy and will rely on a hub and spoke configuration, using a central site as a hub and relaying information to remote sites as on the spokes of a wheel. If this is the case, your first HT should be installed in the hub. If not, you should install the first HT in one of your most populous Active Directory sites so that it will connect with the legacy Exchange servers that handle the most mail.

After you have created the first HT, all messages to and from Exchange 2007 will be routed through the connector this installation creates. In Simple or Standard Organizations, this has little impact because the Exchange Organization structure is relatively flat. But in Large and Complex Organizations, this can create a routing bottleneck because messages destined to remote sites are routed through a central site before they are delivered. This is one reason why you will want to create additional routing connectors between Exchange 2007 and the legacy servers. Other reasons include redundancy and service continuity. Note that all routing connectors created between Exchange 2007 and legacy versions are set to transmit Exch50 data by default.

IMPORTANT   Modifying the Exchange Routing Group (DWBGZMFD01QNBJR)

If you make configuration changes to the default Exchange Routing Group (DWBGZMFD01QNBJR), it can take up to one hour for the legacy routing group masters to receive and propagate the information to their routing group members. The only way to speed this process is to restart the legacy routing group master servers.

There are also differences between the SMTP connectors in Exchange 2007 and legacy versions. These differences can affect how routing is performed. Table 4-10 outlines these differences and their impact on routing.

Exchange 2007 always uses the lowest-cost routing path when routing messages, whether those messages are intended for Exchange 2007 or legacy systems. Therefore, the Active Directory IP site link cost is only considered when two paths have the same cost.

Legacy systems consider the cumulative cost of the different routing group connectors required to send a message to an Exchange 2007 system. Therefore, the lowest-cost routing path is always used regardless of Active Directory IP site link costs.

Table 4-10 SMTP Connector Features Per Exchange Version

SMTP Connector Feature	Version of Exchange Server	Description
Per-user connector delivery restrictions	Exchange 2000/ Exchange 2003	Exchange 2007 will not recognize these restrictions and may route a message even though the legacy connector does not allow it.
Message priorities	Exchange 2000/ Exchange 2003	Exchange 2007 will not recognize priority restrictions set on legacy SMTP connectors.
Message type (system and non-system designations)	Exchange 2000/ Exchange 2003	Exchange 2007 will not recognize message type restrictions set on legacy SMTP connectors.
Connector scope	Exchange 2000/ Exchange 2003 and Exchange 2007	Legacy Exchange systems and Exchange 2007 define connector scope differently. A legacy connector can be limited to work with only servers within the same routing group. In Exchange 2007, this limitation is based on Active Directory sites. Legacy Exchange systems recognize all scoped restrictions, even those of Exchange 2007. Exchange 2007 bases this recognition on Active Directory sites. In all cases, messages that are routed through connectors that are out of scope will not be sent.
Maximum message size	Exchange 2000/ Exchange 2003 and Exchange 2007	Size restrictions set in any server version will be applied to all messages routed through the connector.
Enabled and disabled property setting	Exchange 2007	Legacy Exchange systems do not support this setting and will continue to route messages even if an Exchange 2007 connector is disabled.

Table 4-10   SMTP Connector Features Per Exchange Version

SMTP Connector Feature	Version of Exchange Server	Description
Integrated Windows Authentication	Exchange 2000 /Exchange 2003 and Exchange 2007 Receive connectors only	Exchange 2007 Send connectors do not support Integrated Windows Authentication. You must select an alternative authentication method if you modify or recreate Send connectors.

Exam Tip   Before Service Pack 1, Exchange 2007 did not support setting maximum message size limits on Active Directory IP site links or routing group connectors that rely on HT systems as either source or destination servers. Therefore, Exchange 2007 also does not recognize message size limits set on routing group connectors by earlier versions of Exchange. When a message is sent from Exchange 2007 to legacy versions of Exchange, it may be reevaluated for delivery by the legacy systems and, may be sent back to the Exchange 2007 server because of existing restrictions. This can cause message loops and result in the message never being delivered. Therefore, Microsoft recommends that all message size restrictions be removed from every routing connector in the organization when Exchange 2007 is installed. You can be sure that this item will be part of the exam.

Of course, this feature has been added to Service Pack 1 and can now be set through the **Set-RoutingGroupConnector** cmdlet.

IMPORTANT   **Non-SMTP connectors**
Before Service Pack 1, Exchange 2007 did not recognize non-SMTP connectors in routing connectors. They are always ignored when routing path calculations are made.

Exchange 2007 Server Role Considerations

Each server role in Exchange 2007 can interact with legacy Exchange Organizations to some degree. But because the organization has not been upgraded to Exchange 2007, there are limitations, including the following:

- **Client Access Server role**   As you saw in Chapter 2, the CAS provides access to a host of front-end features for e-mail clients. OWA, ActiveSync, POP3, IMAP4, Availability Service, and more are all features that can only be provided by this server role in Exchange 2007. In fact, the CAS role is often the first server role to introduce when you deploy Exchange 2007 into an existing organization. The CAS role does not require any other Exchange 2007 roles to operate in a legacy environment. When you do deploy the CAS, your users will experience the following:

❑ When using OWA, the user will see the version that is tied to his or her mailbox location. If the mailbox is on a legacy server, the user will see a legacy version. If it is on a 2007 server, the user will see OWA 2007.

❑ How users access OWA is also server dependent. If users' mailboxes are on legacy servers, they access OWA through a URL such as *http://www.tailspintoys.com/Exchange*. If their mailboxes are on an Exchange 2007 server, they could either use the same URL or use *http://www.tailspintoys.com/OWA*.

❑ When the Exchange Organization is using ActiveSync, the user will have access to the features supported by the server hosting the mailbox. For example, to have access to Direct Push, the mailbox must be hosted on either Exchange 2003 SP2 or Exchange 2007. Any user whose mailbox is hosted on a legacy server will not have access to new ActiveSync features such as GAL lookup or Search.

■ **Hub Transport Server role**   The HT role is often the second role you deploy. Much has been said about HT systems and routing interoperability. This is often the most important system to deploy when dealing with interoperability because it is so essential for Exchange 2007. For example, no messages can be routed to MB systems unless they are managed by an HT system. Therefore, plan your deployments well and ensure that you prepare your routing strategies accordingly.

■ **Mailbox Server role**   The first time you deploy a new MB server in a site or an organization, you must also deploy both a CAS and an HT. The CAS provides client access services while the HT will allow systems to route e-mail to and from the MB. Both the CAS and the HT must be deployed in each Active Directory site that contains an MB. Most organizations will deploy MB systems with the intention of moving the mailboxes from existing systems to the MB. This is performed through the Exchange 2007 **Move-Mailbox** cmdlet. If e-mail address policies are assigned to the mailboxes you move, they will automatically be updated with new e-mail addresses after the move is performed. If the mailbox has a separate SMTP address that is different from the e-mail address policy, this separate SMTP address becomes a secondary address and the one generated by the policy becomes the primary SMTP address for that mailbox. As you will remember, this behavior is the opposite of that of legacy Exchange systems because in both Exchange 2000 and 2003, e-mail address policies were not applied even if they existed. If you want to prevent this behavior, you must block the policy from being applied or use mailboxes that do not have policies. This is done in Active Directory Users And Computers and is an aspect of the Properties sheet of an e-mail account (see Figure 4-9).

Figure 4-9   Make sure your user accounts do not change SMTP addresses when moved to Exchange 2007

By default all routing connectors are set to enable public folder replication. To ensure public folders are replicated properly, you need to create appropriate replicas in the legacy Exchange systems using Exchange System Manager.

Exam Tip   You cannot use a legacy front-end server to access an Exchange 2007 MB system. You must always deploy CAS roles along with the MB.

- **Edge Transport Server role**   As mentioned earlier, the ET role can act as an SMTP relay and smart host for legacy Exchange Organizations, but with limited functionality. You can install the ET whether or not other Exchange 2007 roles have been deployed. Remember that the ET does not require Active Directory changes because it is deployed outside of the internal Active Directory. For example, if you are already using the Exchange Intelligent Message Filter from Exchange 2003, the ET will add an additional level of anti-spam as well as antivirus protection. If no Exchange 2007 HT servers are available, you will not be able to use Edge Subscriptions and will have to manually configure the ET systems. Access to the recipient lookup and safe-list aggregation features will not be available.

■ **Unified Messaging Server role**   This server role cannot interoperate with any legacy system because it is new to Exchange 2007. If you deploy UM roles, you will also require both HT and MB roles to support it. All UM messages must be routed through HT systems and all UM features are only available to users who have a mailbox located on an MB system.

As you can see, the integration of Exchange 2007 server roles into existing Exchange Organizations follows a specific order, as outlined in the following steps:

1. Begin with the deployment of CAS roles and aim to use them to replace all legacy front-end servers. Deploy CAS roles in each Active Directory site where you intend to host MB roles.

2. Next, deploy your HT roles, disable minor link-state updates on all legacy servers, and then configure routing connectors and Send and Receive connectors. Deploy HT roles in the Active Directory site where you intend to host MB roles.

3. When the HT systems are in place, deploy your MB systems. Then you can begin to move mailboxes from legacy to new MB systems.

4. You can deploy ET roles at any time, but they are easiest to deploy after the HT systems are in place because you can then rely on Edge Subscriptions for configuration automation.

5. UM roles are often the very last role to deploy because they offer such a new set of features and because messaging professionals are often unfamiliar with telephony in general.

IMPORTANT   **Decommissioning legacy front-end servers**

Your organization may have decided to customize some of the features of the front-end servers it deployed. Because CAS systems will be deployed on new computers (64-bit systems), you will not be able to recover any of these settings automatically; therefore, you should take note of any customizations—permissions, configurations, and so on—and ensure that they are deployed to the back-end servers before you decommission your front-end servers. If not, you will lose any customization you performed.

Cross-Forest Routing Considerations

As with Large Organizations, interoperability in Complex Organizations relies very heavily on message routing. The challenge is to ensure that both messages and message information is routed to the appropriate recipient no matter which forest they reside in. To do this, you need to implement cross-forest connectors. These connectors can be implemented to support Exchange 2007 to Exchange 2007 routing or routing from Exchange 2007 to legacy systems.

Keep in mind the access rights you need to perform these operations in Exchange 2007:

- To create Send connectors, you need to be a member of the Exchange Organization Administrators group.
- To create Receive connectors, you need to be a member of the Exchange Server Administrators group as well as have local Administrators rights to the computer.

Cross-forest Connectors between Exchange 2007 HT Systems   When you create cross-forest connectors between two Exchange HT systems, you can rely on several methods of authentication. If you use Basic Authentication, you should set the smart host authentication method to Basic Authentication Requires TLS or Transport Layer Security. This provides both confidentiality and authentication of the receiving server because the sending server validates the receiving server's certificate before sending data. If you set it only to RequiresTLS, you will not have server authentication and will only have messaging confidentiality. The certificate used in both cases must have the same name as the Receive connector and a domain account must be assigned to support Basic authentication in all forests.

You can also use external authentication. In this case, you use an IPsec connection or a virtual private network (VPN), or you create a trusted physically controlled network where you place all servers.

Use one of the three methods when you can route mail from forest to forest through newly added HT systems in each forest. This way, Exchange 2007 handles all cross-forest message routing.

MORE INFO   Configuring cross-forest Exchange 2007 connectors

For information on how to configure the required connectors, go to
http://technet.microsoft.com/en-us/library/bb123546.aspx.

Cross-forest Connectors between Exchange 2007 and Legacy Systems When you need to create cross-forest connectors between Exchange 2007 and legacy systems, the procedure is slightly different. In this case, cross-forest connectors will go from an HT or an ET system to a legacy bridgehead server. You will again need a domain user account in each forest for authentication purposes. Then, on the Exchange 2007 HT or ET system, create a Send connector that is set as Internal type. On the legacy Exchange system, create an SMTP connector.

Remember that legacy systems rely on X-EXCH50 verbs to transfer message metadata. By default, legacy SMTP connectors require authentication to provide this data. Because of this, you will need to change the properties of the SMTP connector to allow sending and receiving of Exch50 data anonymously. This is done through a registry hack. The registry key that must be modified is HKEY_LOCAL_MACHINE\ SYSTEM\CurrentControlSet\Services\SMTPSVC\XEXCH50.

MORE INFO **Configuring cross-forest Exchange 2007 and legacy system connectors**

For information on how to configure the required connectors, go to *http://technet.microsoft.com/en-us/library/bb123546.aspx.*

Plan Calendar Availability

Chapter 2 outlined how you could make free/busy data available to users of different versions of Outlook as well as different versions of Exchange. For this exam, it will be important for you to remember the following:

- If you have deployed CAS roles and all your users are running Outlook 2007, you can rely on the Availability Service to manage free/busy data in the mixed organization. You will still require public folders and public folder replication if the legacy organization has implemented public folders for purposes other than free/busy data availability, however.

- If you have not deployed CAS roles or your clients are not using Outlook 2007, you must rely on the traditional methods of free/busy data availability. In legacy versions of Exchange, this is performed through the replication and availability of public folders.

MORE INFO **Plan calendar availability**

Review the topics on free/busy data availability in Chapter 2 to get more information on this topic.

Interoperate Within a Single Organization

Managing interoperability is always more complex than managing homogeneous systems. If it turns out that your organization will be running a mixed Exchange environment for a long period of time, you will need to make sure all system operators are familiar with the strategies they must use to manage this mixed environment.

For example, as soon as you introduce any Exchange 2007 server role into the organization, you will have modified how the entire organization should be managed. Because you need to update Active Directory before you install any Exchange 2007 role, you introduce components that can no longer be managed by the legacy Exchange System Manager. From then on, any change that must be applied to the organization as a whole or any modification to organization-level settings must be performed through the Exchange Management Console or the Exchange Management Shell.

Different Administrative Approaches

As with routing, Exchange 2007 brings changes to the administration of its various services. In legacy versions, you used Administrative Groups to organize all Exchange objects and to support permission delegation. Exchange 2007 does not rely on this permissions model, but to provide legacy support all Exchange 2007 objects are placed within one single Exchange Administrative Group (FYDIBOHF23SPDLT). You can view this group in Exchange System Manager, but no administrative groups are displayed in the Exchange Management Console.

You can, however, use the Exchange Management Console to edit legacy Exchange objects, but you cannot create them. In addition, the Exchange Management Console will allow you to delete or remove legacy Exchange features.

You cannot manage Exchange 2007 features through the legacy Exchange System Manager.

Manage Through Exchange System Manager or 2007 Management Tools   Management occurs differently in different systems. Table 4-11 outlines the differences between Exchange System Manager and the Exchange Management Console.

Table 4-11   Managing Mixed Exchange Systems

Legacy Exchange Feature	Corresponding Exchange 2007 Feature	Manage in		Description
		Exchange 2007 Management Tools	Exchange System Manager	
Organizational Settings: Delegate Control	n/a	☞	☞	Legacy delegation rights must be managed from ESM.
Internet Mail Wizard	n/a	☞	☞	If ET servers exist, this feature will not work.
Stop Public Folder Content Replication	n/a	☞	☞	Only for Exchange 2003 SP2.
Internet Message Format	Remote Domains	☞	☞	Can be managed from both, but when it is modified in Exchange 2007, it is upgraded and can no longer be modified by ESM.
Message Delivery Properties: Sender or Recipient Filtering	Sender or Recipient Filtering	☞	☞	Replaced by new entries in 2007. On ET, manage through the Exchange Management Console. On HT, manage through the Exchange Management Shell.

Table 4-11   Managing Mixed Exchange Systems

Legacy Exchange Feature	Corresponding Exchange 2007 Feature	Manage in		Description
		Exchange 2007 Management Tools	Exchange System Manager	
Message Delivery Properties: Connection Filtering	IP Allow or Block Lists, IP Allow or Block List Providers	☞	☞	Replaced by new entries in 2007. On ET, manage through the Exchange Management Console. On HT, manage through the Exchange Management Shell.
Intelligent Mail Filter: Gateway Blocking Threshold	ET Content Filtering: Actions	☞	☞	Configurations are stored in different locations in Exchange 2007. Each threshold must be managed independently for both systems.
Intelligent Mail Filter: Store Junk E-mail Configuration Settings	**Set-Organization Config** *SCLJunkThreshold*	☞	☞	Can be maintained from both systems.
Sender ID Filtering	n/a	☞	☞	No interoperability. Must be managed independently for both systems.

Table 4-11 Managing Mixed Exchange Systems

Legacy Exchange Feature	Corresponding Exchange 2007 Feature	Manage in		Description
		Exchange 2007 Management Tools	Exchange System Manager	
Mobile Services	n/a	☞	☞	Features such as Always-up-to-date (AUTD) System Management Server SMS, Exchange ActiveSync, and Direct Push are now located in the appropriate section of the Exchange Management Console. Must be managed independently for both systems.
Recipient Details and Address Templates	n/a	☞	☞	Maintained as separate items.
GAL/Address Lists	n/a	☞	☞	Can be edited in either tool, but once it is modified in Exchange 2007, it is upgraded and can no longer be modified by ESM.

Table 4-11 Managing Mixed Exchange Systems

Legacy Exchange Feature	Corresponding Exchange 2007 Feature	Manage in		Description
		Exchange 2007 Management Tools	Exchange System Manager	
Offline Address Book	n/a	☞	☞	Can be edited in either tool, but to edit it in Exchange 2007, you must move it to an Exchange 2007 server. Once moved, it can no longer be edited by ESM.
Offline Address Book: Rebuild Action	Update-OfflineAdressBook	☞	☞	Can be managed from either tool.
Recipient Update Service	Update-AddressList and Update-Email AddressPolicy	☞	☞	This service does not exist in Exchange 2007. However, Exchange 2007 servers will appear in the list because the filter only looks for non-front-end servers. *Do not assign an Exchange 2007 server to this service.* If you do, it will break. Make sure you name your servers appropriately to avoid this issue.

Table 4-11 Managing Mixed Exchange Systems

Legacy Exchange Feature	Corresponding Exchange 2007 Feature	Manage in		Description
		Exchange 2007 Management Tools	Exchange System Manager	
Recipient Policies	E-mail Address Policy and Accepted Domains	☞	☞	Separated in Exchange 2007. If any mailbox is modified, either through Move-Mailbox or Set-Mailbox, policies are reapplied even though they were never applied in legacy systems. To avoid this, turn off automatic update on e-mail accounts (see Figure 4-7 earlier in the chapter).
Recipient Policies	Accepted Domains	☞	☞	Because they are separated in Exchange 2007, accepted domains must be added manually in both systems to make them routable. The Exchange Best Practices Analyzer can tell you whether objects are mismatched.

Table 4-11 Managing Mixed Exchange Systems

Legacy Exchange Feature	Corresponding Exchange 2007 Feature	Manage in		Description
		Exchange 2007 Management Tools	Exchange System Manager	
Recipient Policies	E-mail Address Policy	☞	☞	If modified in Exchange 2007, the policy is upgraded and can no longer be modified in ESM.
Recipient Policy: Apply this policy now	E-mail Address Policy or **Update-EmailAddressPolicy**	☞	☞	If the change is made in ESM, you must wait for the Recipient Update Service to process it. If it is made in Exchange 2007, it is applied immediately.
Mailbox Policy Manager	n/a	☞	☞	Does not take place in Exchange 2007 even though the property is applied to the mailboxes.
Queues	Queue Viewer	☞	☞	ESM will not be able to manage Exchange 2007 objects even though it displays them. If you try, you will receive an error message.

Table 4-11   Managing Mixed Exchange Systems

Legacy Exchange Feature	Corresponding Exchange 2007 Feature	Manage in		Description
		Exchange 2007 Management Tools	Exchange System Manager	
Storage Group	n/a	☞	☞	Must be managed through ESM.
Mailbox Store	n/a	☞	☞	Must be managed through ESM.
Public Folder Store	n/a	☞	☞	Must be managed through ESM.
X.400 Connectors and Mail Transfer Agent objects	n/a	☞	☞	Neither object exists in Exchange 2007. Must be managed by ESM.
SMTP Virtual Server	Receive Connector	☞	☞	This object does not exist in Exchange 2007. Must be managed by ESM.
SMTP Virtual Server: Resolve anonymous e-mail	Receive Connector	☞	☞	To provide the same functionality in Exchange 2007, configure a Receive connector on an HT and assign the Exchange Servers permission group as well as using Externally Secured as the authentication.

Table 4-11   Managing Mixed Exchange Systems

Legacy Exchange Feature	Corresponding Exchange 2007 Feature	Manage in		Description
		Exchange 2007 Management Tools	Exchange System Manager	
Routing Group	n/a	☞	☞	Exchange 2007 does not use routing groups. Placing mixed Exchange 2007 and legacy servers in routing groups is not supported.
Routing Group Connectors	Routing Group Connectors	☞	☞	Any routing group that contains an Exchange 2007 server must be managed in Exchange 2007.
SMTP Connectors	Send Connectors	☞	☞	Must be managed in the tool where they are created.

Keep in mind that you cannot modify Exchange 2007 objects such as servers in Exchange System Manager even though they are displayed through the console.

Manage Through Active Directory Users And Computers   Some objects and properties from legacy e-mail systems are also managed in Active Directory Users And Computers. Table 4-12 outlines which objects and properties can be managed in Active Directory Users And Computers in mixed Organizations. This applies to both User Accounts and *InetOrgPerson* objects. Operations applied to Contact and Group objects are listed at the end of the table.

Table 4-12   Managing Mixed Exchange Active Directory Objects

Legacy Active Directory Feature	Corresponding Exchange 2007 Feature	Manage in	
		Exchange 2007	Legacy Exchange
Outlook Mobile Access: Enable or Disable	ActiveSync	👎	👍
ActiveSync and Up-to-Date Notifications	ActiveSync	👎	👍
OWA, POP3, or IMAP4: Enable or Disable	n/a	👎	👍
Mailbox Rights	**Set-MailboxPermission**	👎	👍
Delivery Restrictions	**Set-MailboxPermission**	👎	👍
Delivery Options	**Set-MailboxPermission**	👎	👍
Storage Limits	**Set-MailboxPermission**	👎	👍
Establish E-mail Address	**Enable-Mailbox**	👎	👍
Enable Mailbox	**Enable-Mailbox**	👎	👍
Delete Mailbox	**Disable-Mailbox**	👎	👍
Configure Exchange Features	**Set-Mailbox** or **New-Mailbox**	👎	👍

Table 4-12   Managing Mixed Exchange Active Directory Objects

Legacy Active Directory Feature	Corresponding Exchange 2007 Feature	Manage in	
		Exchange 2007	Legacy Exchange
Remove Exchange Attributes	**Disable-Mailbox**	👎	👍
Contact: Establish E-mail Address	**Enable-MailContact**	👎	👍
Contact: Delete E-mail Addresses	**Disable-MailContact**	👎	👍
Contact: Remove Exchange Attributes	**Disable-MailContact**	👎	👍
Group: Add E-mail Addresses	n/a	👍	👍
Group: Delete E-mail Addresses	n/a	👍	👍
Group: Add Query-based Distribution Group to a Group	n/a	👍	👍
Group: Add Public Folder to a Group	n/a	👍	👍

MORE INFO   Mixed environment administration

For more information on system administration on mixed environments, go to *http://technet.microsoft.com/en-us/library/aa995972.aspx*.

Track Message in Mixed Environments

Message tracking is also completely different in Exchange 2007. Legacy Exchange systems rely on the Windows Management Instrumentation (WMI) to query message tracking logs. WMI is not supported in Exchange 2007. Therefore, the only way to track messages in Exchange 2007 is to use Exchange 2007 Management Tools. This means that when you must track and troubleshoot message routing in either the legacy system or in Exchange 2007, you must use their respective tools to view log information.

When you track messages sent from Exchange 2007 to legacy systems, you start the track in Exchange 2007 until you reach the legacy system. When you reach the legacy system, you switch to the legacy system Tracking Tool and continue message tracking.

Exam Tip   Keep an eye out for questions related to message tracking. Make sure you remember that you must use the respective tool to track messages in mixed environments.

Practice: Build a Plan to Integrate Exchange 2007 Services into an Exchange 2000 Organization

In this practice, you will assist The Phone Company (TPC), a large telecommunications vendor, to prepare a plan for interoperability between Exchange Server 2000 and Exchange 2007. This practice consists of a single exercise. TPC wants to deploy Exchange 2007 to take advantage of its new feature set, but because of the sheer size of their organization they cannot update all of their systems immediately. They have decided to install new servers into the existing Exchange Organization. Your job as a messaging professional will be to help them plan interoperability for the intervening period before they can complete their transition.

▶ **Exercise: Build a Plan to Integrate Exchange 2007 Services into Exchange 2000 Organizations**

The Phone Company is planning a move to Exchange 2007. They decide to implement Exchange 2007 systems in their existing Exchange 2000 Server Organization. Because they have multiple Active Directory sites, they plan to perform the upgrade on a site-by-site basis. Therefore, they turn to you, the messaging professional, to assist them with both their upgrade and interoperability plan. In fact, they want answers to three specific questions:

- First, they want to know in which order they should deploy the Exchange 2007 server roles.

- Next, they want to know where they should deploy the first Exchange 2007 servers.

- Finally, they need to know what to do to ensure that routing will work between each system for the duration of the migration.

As an Exchange 2007 messaging professional, you are happy to assist TPC in their transition planning.

▶ **Suggested Answers**

1. The first question is easy to answer. Exchange 2007 server roles can be deployed in several different orders, but the easiest is to start with the CAS role, followed by the HT and MB roles. The ET role can be deployed at any time, but is easiest to work with if HT systems already exist because you can use Edge Subscriptions. UM roles should be saved for last because legacy e-mail systems cannot use their features.

2. Next, you help them determine when and where to deploy Exchange 2007 servers. This is also relatively easy. TPC uses a hub and spoke routing configuration that follows their Active Directory IP site configurations. You help them plan to implement Exchange 2007 server roles in the hub site first, and then move to the other sites on a size basis.

3. Install the hub site and replace all of the central servers with Exchange 2007 server roles. Then, install each other site based on numbers of users and replace all of the legacy servers in the site. Move down the line until all sites have been replaced.

4. The final question requires structure because Exchange 2007 and legacy Exchange systems do not control message flow in the same manner. Begin by updating the Active Directory site to support the installation of Exchange 2007 server roles.

5. Next, install your first Exchange 2007 servers. When you install the first server, Exchange 2007 will prepare three groups:

   ❏ A universal security group called ExchangeLegacyInterop that is given the appropriate permissions to allow Exchange 2000 or Exchange 2003 servers to send e-mail to Exchange 2007 servers.

   ❏ The Exchange Administrative Group (FYDIBOHF23SPDLT).

   ❏ The Exchange Routing Group (DWBGZMFD01QNBJR).

6. In addition, the installation of an HT role will automatically create a single two-way routing group connector between Exchange 2007 and a selected legacy Exchange bridgehead server.

7. Next, you must disable minor link-state updates on all legacy Exchange servers. This is done through a registry hack on each legacy Exchange server. Log on with local administrator credentials.

8. In Registry Editor, locate HKEY_LOCAL_MACHINE\System\CurrentControlSet\ Services\RESvc\Parameters.

9. Create a new DWORD value and name it **SuppressStateChanges**.

10. Double-click the new *SuppressStateChanges* object and change the Value field to 1.

11. Close the Registry Editor and use Computer Management to restart the following services:

    ❑ Simple Mail Transfer Protocol (SMTP)

    ❑ Microsoft Exchange Routing Engine

    ❑ Microsoft Exchange MTA Stacks

12. Repeat on each legacy Exchange server in the organization.

13. Finally, you can use the **New-RoutingGroupConnector** cmdlet to create additional routing connectors. This will provide redundancy and also remove the bottleneck from the original routing connector created during the HT installation.

From then on, TPC will need to use mixed management practices to control both messaging systems.

Quick Check

1. What are the actions you must perform in a transition scenario from Exchange Server 2000/ Exchange 2003 to Exchange Server 2007?

2. What are the coexistence scenarios that Microsoft supports for Exchange 2007 in existing organizations?

3. What are the prerequisites for coexistence between Exchange 2000, Exchange 2003, and Exchange 2007?

4. What are the particularities for each Exchange 2007 server role when coexisting with Exchange 2000 or Exchange 2003?

5. You try to view the routing groups in the Exchange System Manager, and nothing appears. What is the problem?

Quick Check Answers

1. Install Exchange 2007 server roles into the organization, move the mailboxes, and decommission the existing Exchange 2000 and Exchange 2003 servers.

2. Exchange 2007 and Exchange Server 2003, Exchange 2007 and Exchange 2000 Server, Exchange 2007 and a mix of Exchange 2000 Server with Exchange Server 2003.

3. The prerequisites are:

   ❑ First, all Exchange 5.5 servers must be removed from the organization before you can install Exchange 2007 server roles.

   ❑ The Site Replication Service must be decommissioned before you can install any Exchange 2007 server roles.

   ❑ Exchange Active Directory connectors have been decommissioned.

   ❑ The Exchange Organization has been upgraded to native mode. This is done through the Exchange System Manager under the Organization's Properties | General Tab | Change Operations Mode.

4. See Table 4-8, "Exchange Server 2007 Server Roles in Coexistence Mode."

5. To be able to view the routing groups in Exchange System Manager, you must enable this option in the Properties of the Exchange Organization.

Lesson 3: Plan Interoperability with Third-Party Messaging Systems

Estimated lesson time: 30 minutes

Like all of the other scenarios discussed in this chapter, interoperability between Exchange Server 2007 and third-party messaging systems relies on four critical components, listed in Table 4-13.

Table 4-13 Interoperability Preoccupations with a Third-Party E-mail Systems

Required Component	Strategy	
Name Resolution	Use DNS forwarders from the Exchange forest to other systems.	
Message Routing	For Lotus Domino systems, rely on SMTP protocol to route messages from one organization to another.	
	For Lotus Notes systems, rely on the Exchange Server 2003 Connector for Lotus Notes for message transport.	
	For Novell GroupWise systems, rely on the Exchange Server 2003 Connector for Novell GroupWise for message transport.	
	For POP3 or IMAP4 systems, rely on SMTP protocol to route messages from one system to another.	
Global Address List	For Lotus Domino, rely on the Microsoft Transporter for Lotus Domino to provide directory synchronization between the Domino system and Active Directory.	
	For Lotus Notes, rely on the Exchange Server 2003 Connector for Lotus Notes for directory synchronization.	
	For Novell GroupWise systems, rely on the Exchange Server 2003 Connector for Novell GroupWise along with the Microsoft Directory Synchronization Services (MSDSS) for directory synchronization.	
	For POP3 or IMAP4 systems, there is no tool to synchronize directory information. Users must re-create their own address lists.	

Table 4-13   Interoperability Preoccupations with a Third-Party E-mail Systems

Required Component	Strategy
Free/Busy Data	For Lotus Domino, rely on the Microsoft Transporter for Lotus Domino to provide free/busy data synchronization.
	For Lotus Notes, rely on the Exchange Server 2003 Connector for Lotus Notes for calendar synchronization.
	For Novell GroupWise systems, use the Exchange Calendar Connector to synchronize free/busy data.
	For POP3 or IMAP4 systems, there is no tool to synchronize calendar information. Users must plan meetings through e-mail.

Plan Message Connectivity

As you can see, each third-party system requires a different approach to migration and coexistence. For example, Novell GroupWise, like Exchange 5.5, requires an intermediary path for both migration and coexistence—Exchange 2003. The same goes for Lotus Notes. That is because only Exchange 2003 offers support for both of these systems. If you are migrating from a POP3, IMAP4, or Lotus Domino system, you can perform both the migration and the coexistence directly with Exchange 2007.

Connect Exchange with Lotus Domino

Lotus Domino is perhaps the simplest third-party system to migrate from because support for this migration is implemented directly within Exchange Server 2007. This is because you can rely on the Microsoft Transporter for Lotus Domino to both perform a migration and to interoperate between the two systems. Interoperation usually occurs in the intervening period between the installation of interoperability tools and the decommissioning of the legacy e-mail system.

In this situation, you have users in both Exchange and Domino, and your systems intercommunicate with each other. Because users are in both environments, you must use the migration tools to synchronize directory information and support free/busy lookups. Mail is routed between both platforms through SMTP. Consider the following to ensure proper interoperability:

- Message routing must work properly. Users from either platform should be able to send and receive messages to each other and to the Internet.

- Contacts and distribution lists must be up to date at all times. This is performed through directory synchronization.

- Calendaring information is also crucial to the way organizations function. Free/busy data must be made available no matter which platform users work in.

Interoperability focuses on two key components of the Microsoft Transporter Suite:

- **Directory Connector** This is used to synchronize users, distribution lists (called groups in Domino), and Domino mail-in database information from the Domino directory to Active Directory.

- **Free/Busy Connector** This allows users of both environments to share free/busy data and perform lookups between the two systems.

To interoperate, you must have at least three Exchange 2007 server roles installed and running: Client Access Server, Hub Transport Server, and Mailbox Server (see Figure 4-10). In addition, you must install the Free/Busy Connector on an HT computer that also includes the MAPI Client libraries. The Directory Connector can be installed on any system, either 32 or 64-bit.

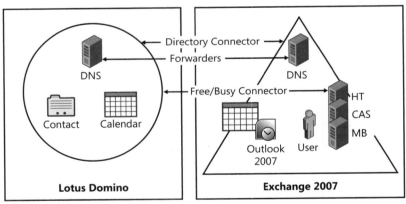

Figure 4-10 Interoperability between Lotus Domino and Exchange 2007

You will also need to determine how you intend to support interoperability for the Domino applications you have developed. In many cases, you can do this by deploying the Domino client to all systems along with Outlook. If you migrate these applications to Windows SharePoint Services, users can access them through Internet Explorer.

MORE INFO **Migrating from Lotus Domino to Exchange 2007**

For more information on migrating from Lotus Domino to Exchange 2007, see Lesson 3 in Chapter 3.

Connect Exchange with Lotus Notes

Because Exchange 2007 cannot work with Lotus Notes, you must use Exchange 2003 as an intermediary. You need to install Exchange Server 2003 into a new organization, install the Exchange Server 2003 Connector for Lotus Notes, and then install Exchange 2007 servers into the same organization as the Exchange 2003 servers. Lesson 2 of this chapter provides information for the configuration of the Exchange 2003 and Exchange 2007 components.

In fact, you only need a very few Exchange 2003 servers for this migration/coexistence scenario to work. Exchange 2003 is not going to be your main e-mail system; it is only required to provide transitional services between the legacy e-mail system and Exchange 2007 (see Figure 4-11).

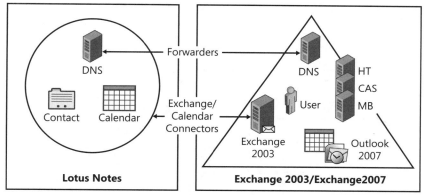

Figure 4-11 Interoperability between Lotus Notes, Exchange 2003, and Exchange 2007

To support interoperability, you will need to rely on both the Exchange Connector for contact and data synchronization as well as the Calendar Connector for free/busy data. Both of these components must be installed on the Exchange 2003 system.

MORE INFO **Microsoft migration tools for Lotus Notes**

You cannot rely on the components included in Exchange 2003 or even with Service Pack 2 for Exchange 2003. Instead, you must download the updated connector components. Obtain the updated Exchange Server 2003 Connector for Lotus Notes from *http://go.microsoft.com/fwlink/?linkid=57194*.

Connect Exchange with Novell GroupWise

Like Lotus Notes, interoperating between Novell GroupWise and Exchange 2007 requires an Exchange 2003 intermediary system. That is because Novell connectivity with Exchange only exists in Exchange 2003 and is not available in Exchange 2007. When interoperating between these systems, you need to rely on two key components of the connector:

- **Connector for Novell GroupWise** Supports bidirectional message transfer and directory synchronization between the systems.

- **Calendar Connector** Allows users to view free/busy data from one system to the other.

In addition, you can rely on the Microsoft Directory Synchronization Services (MSDSS) to perform initial directory synchronization between Novell Directory Services to Active Directory (see Figure 4-12). In this case, it is possible that your Active Directory site will contain duplicate items because they have been created by MSDSS and then possibly duplicated by the Connector for Novell GroupWise. If this is the case, you need to use the Active Directory Cleanup Wizard to remove these duplicates and merge them into a single account.

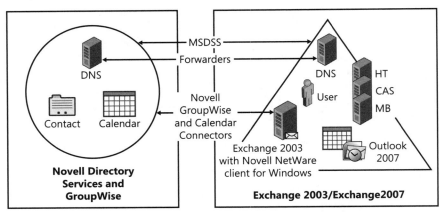

Figure 4-12 Interoperability between Novell Directory Services, Novell GroupWise, Exchange 2003, and Exchange 2007

The Connector for Novell GroupWise is used to convert and transfer messages between both systems. It relies on the Message Transfer Agents (MTA) in each system to perform this activity. Message formats are automatically converted to their corresponding types in each system. For example, e-mail messages are seen as e-mail messages, calendar invitations are seen as invitations, and so on. Delivery confirmations, read receipts, and non-delivery reports are processed appropriately. Certain non-supported message types are converted to simple e-mail messages. For example, the Novell phone message is sent as an e-mail message. However, the Connector does not support signed or encrypted messages because it must modify them by default to convert them. Because it cannot modify a signed message and it cannot read an encrypted message, it cannot convert them.

To provide free/busy data between each system, you must install and deploy the Calendar Connector. Microsoft recommends that you deploy this connector on the same server as the Connector for Novell GroupWise. Each connector has dependencies on the other and must therefore have high-speed access to the data the other connector provides to function properly.

Microsoft also does not recommend that you host this connector on a server that hosts mailboxes. Therefore, you should make sure your mailboxes are hosted on an Exchange 2007 Mailbox Server role and use the Exchange 2003 installation only to perform synchronization between the Exchange Organization and the GroupWise e-mail system.

Finally, you should make sure all systems are completely updated before you implement coexistence. This means applying Service Pack 2 to your Exchange 2003 installation and Service Pack 1 to Exchange 2007. You should also apply the appropriate updates for your Novell infrastructure. The Exchange 2003 server that will provide synchronization services must also include the Novell NetWare client for Windows so that it can talk to the Novell infrastructure.

MORE INFO **Migrating from Novell GroupWise to Exchange 2007**

For more information on migrating from Novell GroupWise to Exchange 2007, see Lesson 3 in Chapter 3. You can also look up more information on Microsoft TechNet at *http://technet.microsoft.com/en-us/library/aa998380.aspx*.

Connect with Other Messaging Systems

There are a number of other messaging systems you might wish to migrate from or interoperate with when moving to Exchange Server 2007, including Microsoft Mail, Lotus cc:Mail, Digital All-in-1, Verimation MEMO, IBM OfficeVision/VM, HP OpenMail, or simply POP3 or IMAP4 systems. In each case, you must consider the following to support interoperability or migration, especially when there is no direct connector between the two systems:

- **Name Resolution** You must ensure that DNS name resolution will occur properly between the two systems in support of message routing.

■ **Message Routing**   You must implement some reliable form of message routing. Ideally, you will be able to rely on SMTP and if so, you will only need to ensure that your Exchange 2007 infrastructure works properly to receive and send SMTP messages. If the messaging system you are connecting to does not support SMTP, it may support X.400 to route messages. If this is the case, you will need to install an Exchange 2003 intermediary server because there is no X.400 connector in Exchange 2007.

■ **Directory Synchronization**   Active Directory includes several tools that support manual or semi-automated directory synchronization. These include Ldifde.exe and Csvde.exe, which rely on comma-delimited lists to import or export data from Active Directory. You can also use the Active Directory Services Interface (ADSI) to create custom scripts and programs to automate the import and export of data.

■ **Free/Busy Information**   When no connector is available, you can use Outlook to publish free/busy information in a public location and give all users access to it. You can also use Collaboration Data Objects for Exchange (CDOEX) to develop a custom solution that will display free/busy data in an ASP.NET Web page.

■ **Data Migration**   In scenarios where there is no connector and therefore little possibility of coexistence, you can use the Exchange Migration Wizard that is part of Exchange 2003 to migrate data from certain legacy e-mail systems. This includes systems such as Microsoft Mail (both PC and AppleTalk networks), Lotus cc:Mail, and systems that support the Lightweight Directory Access Protocol (LDAP) and IMAP4. Of course, you will need to rely on Exchange 2003 as an intermediary toward Exchange 2007 to use this solution.

■ **Manual Data Imports**   You can also perform manual data imports. For example, Outlook 2007 supports the conversion of several different e-mail sources to an Outlook-supported format. It also includes both import and export tools that allow you to import e-mail data, calendar data, and address books.

MORE INFO   Interoperating with unsupported legacy systems

There is no topic for this subject in the Exchange 2007 technical library. There is, however, an extensive topic on this subject in relation to Exchange Server 2003. For more information, go to *http://technet.microsoft.com/en-us/library/bb124132.aspx*.

Practice: Plan Integration with Non-Exchange Messaging Systems

The Graphics Design Institute has been working with Lotus Notes for several years. Their infrastructure is outdated, and while they could upgrade to Lotus Domino, they are not impressed by the fact that the upgrade requires a revamping of their entire Notes infrastructure. They have decided to move to Exchange 2007. But they cannot perform this move as quickly as they would like because they need to translate some of their Notes applications to Windows SharePoint Services.

Therefore, they need a plan to interoperate between the two systems. They turn to you, the messaging professional, for help. In this practice, you need to assist the Graphics Design Institute in planning their integration of Exchange 2007 with Lotus Notes. This practice consists of a single exercise.

▶ **Exercise: Plan the Integration of Exchange 2007 with Lotus Notes**

Your job as a messaging professional is to help them make the smoothest transition possible to a new Exchange 2007 organization. You need to help them plan out their implementation and devise an interoperability plan for the duration of the transition. Fortunately, they already have an Active Directory site in place. What do you do?

Because Exchange 2007 has no support for Lotus Notes, you must provide a plan that relies on an Exchange 2003 intermediary system, as demonstrated in the following steps.

▶ **Suggested Answers**

1. Update their Active Directory to prepare it for both Exchange Server 2003 and 2007.

2. Install an Exchange Server 2003 system into a new organization.

3. Install at least three Exchange 2007 roles into the same organization: Client Access Server, Hub Transport Server, and Mailbox Server.

4. Install the Exchange Server 2003 Connector for Lotus Notes on the Exchange 2003 server. Make sure you obtain the Web version, which is the most up to date.

5. Configure both the Exchange Connector for contact and data synchronization and the Calendar Connector for free/busy data synchronization.

6. Train their operators on the operation of both connectors and ensure that they are ready to face mail transfer issues if they arise.

Quick Check

1. What are the two key components of the Microsoft Transporter Suite and what do they do?

2. You perform initial directory synchronization between Novell Directory Services to Active Directory. You notice that after the synchronization, your Active Directory site contains duplicate items. Why is this happening and what can you do?

3. Which agent is used by Novell GroupWise to convert and transfer messages between Exchange and Novell?

4. What are items you must consider if you migrate other messaging systems that do not have a direct connector between the two systems?

Quick Check Answers

1. The two connectors are:

   ❑ The Directory Connector is used to synchronize users, distribution lists (or groups as they are called in Domino) as well as Domino mail-in database information from the Domino directory to Active Directory.

   ❑ The Free/Busy Connector allows users of both environments to share free/busy data and perform lookups between the two systems.

2. Your Active Directory site will contain duplicate items because they have been created by MSDSS and then possibly duplicated by the Connector for Novell GroupWise. You need to use the Active Directory Cleanup Wizard to remove these duplicates and merge them into a single account.

3. The connector relies on the Message Transfer Agents in each system to perform this activity. Message formats are automatically converted to their corresponding types in each system.

4. The items you must consider are free/busy information and data migration.

Chapter Summary

- When using multiple organizations to run different versions of Exchange in a coexistence mode, you have two main areas of concern:

   ❑ You need to make sure messages flow from one organization to another.

   ❑ You must ensure that free/busy data will be available between the organizations you manage.

- In most cross-forest topologies, the exchange of information is performed through the use of a synchronization tool—either the Identity Integration Feature Pack (IIFP) or the Microsoft Identity Integration Server (MIIS). Both tools must be running Service Pack 2 to operate with Exchange 2007.

- In Exchange 2007, free/busy data is made available through the Availability Service as long as the end-user systems use Outlook 2007. Note that the Availability Service does not provide public folder replication. To provide public folder replication if public folders are in use, you must rely on the Inter-Organization Replication (IORepl) tool, which is available with Exchange 2000 or Exchange 2003.

- Forest trusts are only available between forests running Windows Server 2003. Forests running Windows 2000 Server must create explicit trusts between each domain in the forests. If there are no trusts between the forests, you will only be able to share free/busy data on a per-organization basis.

- When you install a new Exchange 2007 server into an existing organization, after you have performed the appropriate Active Directory modifications, Exchange will perform the following tasks:

    ❏ Create a new Active Directory universal security group called ExchangeLegacyInterop. This group has the appropriate permissions to allow Exchange 2000 or Exchange 2003 servers to send e-mail to Exchange 2007 servers.

    ❏ Create the Exchange Administrative Group (FYDIBOHF23SPDLT).

    ❏ Create the Exchange Routing Group (DWBGZMFD01QNBJR).

    ❏ Create a single two-way routing group connector between Exchange 2007 and a selected legacy Exchange bridgehead server.

- Even though you can view Exchange 2007 objects in Exchange System Manager, you must use the Exchange Management Console or the Exchange Management Shell to manage every Exchange 2007 object.

- If you have deployed CAS roles and all your users are running Outlook 2007, you can use the Availability Service to manage free/busy data in the mixed organization. You will still require public folders and public folder replication if the legacy organization has implemented public folders for purposes other than free/busy data availability, however.

- If you have not deployed CAS roles or your clients are not using Outlook 2007, you must use the traditional methods of free/busy data availability. In legacy versions of Exchange, this is performed through the replication and availability of public folders.

- To provide legacy support, all Exchange 2007 objects are placed within a single Exchange Administrative Group (FYDIBOHF23SPDLT).

- Novell GroupWise, like Exchange 5.5, requires an intermediary path for both migration and coexistence–Exchange 2003. The same is true for Lotus Notes. That is because only Exchange 2003 offers support for both of these systems. If you are migrating from a POP3, IMAP4, or Lotus Domino system, you can perform both the migration and the coexistence directly with Exchange 2007.

- To connect Exchange with Lotus Notes, you must use Exchange 2003 as an intermediary. You need to install Exchange Server 2003 into a new organization, then install the Exchange Server 2003 Connector for Lotus Notes, and then install Exchange 2007 servers into the same organization as the Exchange 2003 servers.

- To provide free/busy data between each system (Novell and Exchange), you must install and deploy the Calendar Connector. Microsoft recommends that you deploy this connector on the same server as the Connector for Novell GroupWise.

Case Scenario

In the following case scenario, you will apply what you have learned about Exchange interoperability. You can find answers to the questions in this scenario in the "Answers" section at the end of this book.

Case Scenario: Manage Exchange Server 2007

In an earlier practice, The Phone Company asked you as a messaging professional how to proceed with the implementation of Exchange 2007 server roles into their existing Exchange 2000 Server Organization. Now, they want to tell their administrators how to manage this new mixed Exchange environment. They turn to you once again and ask you to produce a table or set of tables that can assist their e-mail administrators in their day-to-day operational tasks. How many tables are required and what should they contain?

Suggested Practices

It is difficult to practice interoperability with Exchange Server without access to a full infrastructure, but you can do so if you prepare a virtual environment as outlined in the Introduction. If you also have access to either a legacy Exchange environment or a third-party e-mail system, you can run through each of the step-by-step procedures in this chapter. If not, you should at least run through the portions of the step-by-step procedures that address Exchange 2007.

Chapter 5
Plan for High Availability Implementation

As you know, e-mail systems have become one of the most important and often mission-critical systems in the enterprise, small and large. As such, you need to make sure that e-mail is always available, both as a service and as a data retention tool. Organizations of different sizes have different needs or different capabilities to implement high availability or business continuity solutions. Implementations for high availability and business continuity also differ based on the Exchange Organization type you are working with. But in any case, high availability is always concentrated on two aspects of the e-mail service:

- First, you need to make sure that the data that makes up your e-mail system is protected at all times. This involves both backup and recovery.

- Second, you need to make sure the e-mail service itself is always available. This means focusing on the various server roles and making sure that if one is not available for whatever reason, another will always be able to take up the role and continue to provide e-mail services to end users.

Fortunately, Exchange Server 2007 includes a host of new features specifically oriented to both data and service protection. Each of these topics will be covered in this chapter and the next. This chapter covers backup and recovery strategies, while Chapter 6, "Plan for Business Continuity," covers service availability strategies.

While the two protection strategies work hand in hand, you have no recourse other than restoring information from backup when you face a damaged or corrupted database. This is why backup and its corresponding aspect, recovery, are the first step in any disaster recovery or business continuity program. In fact, you need to cover three aspects of data protection:

- How to back up data.
- How to restore the data.
- How to recover data from corrupted databases when no backup is available.

But an Exchange 2007 architecture and implementation is more than just the data it stores and protects—it also includes the actual servers that provide the service and their configurations. In addition, much of the data that makes Exchange 2007 work is stored within the Active Directory database. This database is hierarchic and non-relational in nature. Because it is contained within the domain controllers that support the Active Directory service, it is also distributed and is found in various different locations. This database differs from the Exchange database. You must understand how both databases work, how Exchange interacts with Active Directory, and how the various components of an Exchange implementation work together to make the right data-protection decisions.

But you do not have to do it all yourself. Many Simple or Standard Organization types simply do not have the resources or the skills to fully protect the entire e-mail system. This is one reason why Microsoft has introduced a new Software as a Service (SAAS) strategy that offers these smaller Exchange implementations the opportunity to host key services outside their organization and access them on a subscription basis. Microsoft's Exchange SAAS (Microsoft Exchange Hosted Services) offers four levels of service:

- Filtering, which addresses malware issues and protects your organization from spam and viruses.
- Archiving, which is aimed at data retention for compliance purposes.
- Encryption, which lets you encrypt data for long-term protection.
- Continuity, which lets you access e-mail services in the event of a disaster or an e-mail-related emergency.

In many cases, gaining technical access to these services requires no more than a simple configuration on the DNS servers.

MORE INFO   Microsoft Exchange SAAS

Microsoft's Exchange Hosted Services are available directly from Microsoft. More information can be found at *http://technet.microsoft.com/en-us/exchange/bb288501.aspx*.

You may need to recover from several situations. One hopes that you will never run into any of them, but if you do, it pays to be well-prepared beforehand.

As you will also see, one of the most important aspects of disaster recovery is the actual recovery itself. Too many organizations have performed backups forever without ever taking the time to test their recovery strategy. When an actual disaster occurs, they try to recover data from their backup media only to find out that it does not work.

This is a significant issue and you should make sure it never happens to you. Sometimes this issue can be completely unplanned—for example, one of our customers stored their disaster recovery tapes in a room underneath a swimming pool. They never expected the pool to leak, but guess what? That is exactly what happened. The pool had a major leak and their tape room was completely flooded. All of the tapes were rendered completely useless. And, of course, this occurred during a service blackout that corrupted their e-mail databases. They were stuck between a rock and a hard place, having lost all data, but not having any backed-up data to recover from.

Not only should you perform recovery tests on an ongoing basis, but you should also ensure that the locations you select to store your protected data are secure at all times from both artificial and natural disasters.

Exam Tip   Remember that you should test the backup and restore solution before you deploy any data to your new Exchange servers. In fact, your disaster recovery solution should be available as soon as you begin installing server roles, but before they host any data. The last thing you want to do is move mailboxes to new Exchange 2007 servers without having first implemented a data protection strategy.

Exam objectives in this chapter:

- Plan a backup solution implementation.

- Plan a recovery solution implementation.

Before You Begin

To complete the lessons in this chapter, you must have the following:

- A virtual machine setup as outlined in the Introduction under "Virtual Machine Environments."

- Use the Exchange Server 2007 virtual machine from Microsoft to review the configuration options for pre-installed machines.

- Use the newly created virtual environment you set up in the Introduction to test the backup and restore operations. For the exercises in this chapter, you will need access to the Active Directory server and the all-in-one Exchange server, ExchangeOne.

Lesson 1: Plan a Backup Solution Implementation

Estimated lesson time: 40 minutes

Disasters occur when we least expect them. In Exchange 2007, with its various server roles, disasters can take several forms. While losing an entire server is a major disaster to a messaging administrator, sometimes losing a single message can be disastrous for an end user. Table 5-1 outlines the potential disasters—large and small—you can face with Exchange 2007.

Table 5-1   Potential Exchange 2007 Disasters

Lost Item	Description
E-mail item	A message has been permanently deleted.
Mailbox	The mailbox is corrupted or destroyed.
Database or storage group	The database is corrupted.
ET, HT, CAS or UM server	Mail databases are intact.
MB server	Mail databases and transaction logs are lost.
Highly available CAS server	Server Web farm running Network Load Balancing has lost one member.
Highly available MB server	Server node in a back-end Failover Cluster is lost.
Highly available database	The Failover Cluster is fine, but the database and transaction logs are gone.
Highly available mailbox storage	The entire Failover Cluster; server nodes and mailbox databases are lost.
Supporting services	These include domain controllers, global catalog servers, certificate authorities, DNS, and so on.
Entire site	All Exchange servers, databases, and supporting servers in a site are destroyed.

As you can see in Table 5-1, disasters can range from one single e-mail message to the massive destruction of an entire e-mail system. When you plan your disaster recovery strategy, you must begin by planning to protect against each and every one of these potential issues.

In addition, you must make sure that your backup strategy includes much more than just the e-mail data; it must also include all configuration settings, system components, and everything else you need to re-create an Exchange server, no matter which role it plays. Finally, you must also capture information from all of the supporting systems that make up your Exchange implementation—Active Directory, DNS, certificate authorities, and so on. Because these supporting systems also provide support for other services within the network, chances are very good that you will already have a backup strategy for them. However, it will be important for you to make sure you review these strategies with Exchange in mind to ensure that you are ready for disasters that are particular to the Exchange system and that all information is protected at all times.

Disaster Recovery Concepts

When you do create your backup strategy, you will need to plan for the following:

- Identify what you need to back up based on the type of system or data you are backing up.
- Select the appropriate backup solution for the content to back up.
- Plan backup schedules, backup types, and retention duration for each backup category.
- Plan for media management.
- Test the overall backup solution to ensure that it meets your objectives.
- Implement your backup solution in production.

Backup Solution Requirements

When you plan your backup solution, you need to identify the basic requirements, including:

- The potential service level agreements (SLAs) you intend to support
- How you intend to recover data based on your SLAs
- How you intend to recover systems based on your SLAs

Normally, disaster recovery service level agreements address two key factors:

- **Maximal Recovery Time (MRT)**   How long will it take to recover data or systems based on the SLA you put in place? You need to choose the appropriate backup hardware and software that will satisfy the commitment you make to users in the SLA.

- **Maximal Acceptable Data Loss (MADL)** How often do you need to perform backups? This factor identifies just how much data loss can be acceptable based on your SLAs. For example, if you have agreed with your end users that two hours is the maximal amount of time you can accept potential data losses resulting from the system being down, you need to back up your systems every two hours. If you decide that this time can be longer or shorter, you must schedule your backups accordingly.

To provide acceptable SLAs, you must also be cognizant of the amount of time it takes to restore data. If you agree that two hours is the MADL, but it takes four hours to restore a complete database, you must readjust your SLA to match the capacity of the systems you use.

As you can see, the backup software and hardware you select has a direct relationship with the SLA you can put in place. If you perform disk-to-disk backups, you will be able to restore data much faster than if you choose a disk-to-tape solution, especially if the tapes are offsite and must be returned to the main site before they can be restored.

Potential Backup Solutions

You can use several technologies for backup purposes. The technology you use depends on the strategy you plan to use in support of your backup SLAs. Of course, the technology you use will also depend on the amount of data you plan to protect, the Exchange Organization type you are running, and the budget you have to work with. Available technologies include:

- **Legacy Streaming Backup** This backup technology relies on the application programming interface (API) for the Extensible Storage Engine (ESE). For example, Microsoft Windows Server Backup—commonly referred to as NTBackup—is one of several programs that rely on this API to perform backups. These tools perform online storage group backups as well as system and overall server backups. Exchange 2007's new continuous replication feature—Local Continuous Replication (LCR) or Cluster Continuous Replication (CCR)—can create live copies of storage group data. For storage groups that are protected through LCR or CCR, streaming backups will only be able to work with the active copy of the data, not the passive copy. Because legacy streaming is the oldest technology that supports Exchange backups, it has limited scalability and performance.

- **Volume Shadow Copy Service (VSS)** VSS is a feature of Windows Server that automatically takes a copy or snapshot of content before a backup is performed and then performs the backup from the copy. In Exchange, VSS triggers a snapshot of the storage group that is being backed up and backs it up from the snapshot. This has less performance impact on Exchange than do legacy streaming backups. When used in conjunction with LCR or CCR, VSS can rely on either the active copy or the passive copy of the data being protected.

When performing restores, VSS supports restores to alternate storage groups and alternate servers. However, VSS only works with third-party backup software. Make sure you verify that the solution you choose offers support for VSS.

■ **Tape Backups**   Tape media has been the traditional choice for long-term data protection. Today's tape devices provide much faster performance than ever before. For example, Linear Tape Open (LTO) version 4 tapes can store up to 800 gigabytes (GB) of uncompressed data and write the data at 120 megabits per second (MBps). Older LTO-1 tapes stored only 100 GB of uncompressed data and wrote it at only 40 MBps.

Organizations often rely on tape libraries to increase speed and capacity. Libraries switch tapes automatically when needed and can stream data to multiple tapes at once to increase backup speeds.

IMPORTANT   Running Exchange 2007 on Windows Server 2008

You will not be able to use tape backups if you intend to use Windows Server Backup when you run Exchange 2007 server roles on Windows Server 2008. The version of Backup that is found on Windows Server 2008 does not support backup to tape and can only perform disk-to-disk backups.

■ **Disk-to-Disk Backups**   Many vendors offer disk-to-disk backup solutions. For example, Microsoft Data Protection Manager (DPM) is a solution that first relies on disk-to-disk backups and then transfers the backed-up data to tape. Disk-to-disk backups are much faster than tape backups. Serial Advanced Technology Attachment (SATA) disks can be much cheaper than small computer system interface (SCSI) disks. SATA disks, however, are slower than SCSI disks and should therefore only be used for backup purposes. Unlike tapes, though, disk-to-disk backup solutions cannot be stored offsite unless the backup tool includes a capability to backup to remote sites.

■ **Storage Area Network (SAN) Backups**   Storage Area Network backups also rely on snapshots to perform backups. They have the additional advantage of freeing the network for the backup operation. While all other technologies back up data over network connections, SANs back it up directly within the storage array. This creates faster, more reliable backups.

Determine Backup Solution Components

As you did when you were planning for storage requirements, you must consider capacity when you plan your backup strategy. What is the volume of data you need to back up? If you are updating an existing Exchange environment to Exchange 2007, you will already have this information in hand, but if you are deploying a new Exchange 2007 Organization, you will need to gather this information. Use the formulas outlined in Lesson 1 of Chapter 2, "Planning Deployments," to calculate required capacity.

When you know data volumes for your backups, you will need to combine them with your SLAs to determine your backup window. This determines how much time you need to back up the data and when you can perform the backup. Many organizations back up data during off hours such as at night and during weekends. But, when you are working with Large or Complex Organizations that have a worldwide presence, these low-activity windows become more difficult to identify. For these topologies, you need to use very fast backup technologies such as disk-to-disk or SAN-based backups. In fact, the best backup technologies to support these situations are technologies that will work in conjunction with data protection mechanisms such as LCR and CCR and use the passive replica or copy of the data because it does not affect the performance of an MB server at all.

Finally, if you do use tape backups, you will have to consider three additional elements:

- How will you rotate the tapes?
- Where will you store the tapes offsite?
- When will you retire tapes?

You must answer each of these questions before you implement your backup strategy. Tape rotation and reuse depends on how long you need to retain the data. The best practice is to permanently retain at least a monthly copy of all tapes. Tape storage must be in a protected location—a location that will be protected from both artificial and natural disasters. Finally, tapes deteriorate as you work with them. You must know the life expectancy and potential failure rates of the tapes you buy so that you can incorporate proper retirement timelines in your backup strategy.

Build Your Backup Strategy

Now that you have considered the various aspects of your backup strategy, you can begin to build it. Like a security strategy, a backup strategy must use multiple layers of protection to minimize risk as much as possible. Table 5-1 outlined the various potential disasters that could occur to both your data and your Exchange servers as well as to supporting services. Begin with your data protection strategy.

Protect Individual Messages

The first thing you need to do is teach users how to protect their own data. All users of Office Outlook should know that when they delete a message, it is moved to the Deleted Items folder and kept there until the Deleted Items folder is emptied. If they need to recover the item, they simply access this folder and move the item to another folder.

The Deleted Items folder can be emptied in several ways:

- The user can empty it interactively.
- It can be emptied when the user exits Outlook.
- It can be emptied through central policies that are assigned on the Mailbox server.

But even if the user empties the Deleted Items folder, its content is actually still retained on the Exchange MB system. This means that users can continue to recover items even if they have been deleted locally.

In Outlook, the user can first select the Deleted Items folder, and then go to Tools | Recover Deleted Items to view items that are available for restoration. Then, all the user has to do is select the item to recover and click Recover Selected Message. Recovered messages will then appear in the Deleted Items folder again.

Protect Data on the Exchange Server

Exchange administrators can determine the number of days Exchange will retain deleted items. By default, Exchange 2007 will retain items for 14 days, but you can change this setting. In fact, the Exchange server will perform both soft and hard deletions.

Control Soft Deletions   Soft deletions do not actually remove an object from the Exchange mailbox database. Instead, Exchange maintains a table called MsgFolder. This table maps entries in the folder table and the message table. When a message is soft-deleted, it is marked as such in the MsgFolder table. Items that have been soft-deleted are the items that are available to end users in Deleted Item Recovery.

Microsoft recommends that you set item retention to the default, 14 days. But you can set item retention anywhere from 0 to 24,855 days. When you set it to 0, all items are immediately deleted. You can set item retention at both the mailbox database level and the user level. To set item retention for a database, you must have the Exchange Organization Administrator role. To set item retention for a user, you need the Exchange Recipient Administrator role.

- To set the retention for mailbox databases, use the Exchange Management Console or the **set-mailboxDatabase** cmdlet. In the Console, use the Server Configuration | Mailbox | Database Management tab to go to the storage group that contains the mailbox database you want to configure. Then, when you locate the database, right-click it and select Properties. Use the Limits tab to set Deletion settings.

With the cmdlet, identify the database to modify and use the *−ItemRetention* switch. Days are listed in whole integers.

- To set the retention for a particular user, you can use the Console or the **set-mailbox** cmdlet. In the Console, go to Recipient Configuration | Mailbox to locate the user account. Right-click the user account and select Properties, and then click the Mailbox Settings tab. Double-click Storage Quotas. Under Deleted Item Retention, clear the Use Mailbox Database Defaults check box. In the Keep Deleted Items For (Days) box, enter the number of days to retain data. Click OK and close the Properties dialog box.

  With the cmdlet, identify the account to modify and use the *−ItemRetention* switch. Days are listed in whole integers.

Control Hard Deletions   Messages are hard-deleted when they meet the following conditions:

- The user uses Shift+Delete in Outlook to delete a message. Using Shift+Delete permanently deletes an item and does not move it to the Deleted Items folder.
- The item retention is set to zero.
- Mailbox or public folder databases are set to force hard deletes. This is done by setting the registry value *Force Hard Deletes* for the database.
- The account that requests the deletion is either a gateway or a system account.

IMPORTANT   Retaining hard-deleted items in Outlook

You can still retain items that users have hard-deleted by setting the *DumpsterAlwaysOn* value in the registry. For more information on how to set this value, refer to Knowledge Base article 246153 at *http://support.microsoft.com/?kbid=246153*.

Messages that are hard-deleted are immediately removed from the MsgFolder table and the reference count for the message is checked. When this reference count falls to zero—which occurs when no other mailbox database has a copy of the message—an entry is made in the DeletedMessages table in Exchange. Entries in this table are examined and the corresponding messages are deleted when Exchange performs its next background cleanup process. By default, this process occurs every hour. Of course, you can modify this value by editing the following registry keys. (Values are entered in milliseconds.)

- HKEY_LOCAL_MACHINE\SYSTEM\CurrentControlSet\Services\ MSExchangeIS\ParametersPublic\Background Cleanup
- HKEY_LOCAL_MACHINE\SYSTEM\CurrentControlSet\Services\ MSExchangeIS\ParametersPrivate\Background Cleanup

Keep in mind that modifying these values will have a direct impact on your storage capacity planning. You should modify these entries only if you feel you must meet an essential business requirement.

Control Mailbox Retention   You can also configure how long an entire mailbox will be retained after it is deleted. When you delete a mailbox, it is flagged for deletion and users cannot access it. By default, deleted mailboxes are retained for 30 days. Only when the retention period ends will the mailbox actually be deleted.

If you delete a mail-enabled user object by mistake, you can recreate the object and then reattach its mailbox during the retention period. Of course, if you delete an Active Directory user object, you will want to restore it from Active Directory first. See "Recovery Strategies for Windows Server 2003" later in the chapter for more information.

Mailbox retention is also configured at the mailbox database level. You need the Exchange Organization Administrator role to perform this operation.

To set mailbox retention duration, use either the Console or the **set-mailbox-Database** cmdlet. In the Console, go to Server Configuration | Mailbox| Database Management tab to go to the storage group that contains the mailbox database you want to configure. When you locate the database, right-click it and select Properties. You will use the Limits tab to define the Deletion settings and use the Keep Deleted Mailboxes For (Days) setting to define how long to keep a deleted mailbox.

With the cmdlet, first identify the database to modify, and then use the *−Mailbox Retention* switch. Days are listed in whole integers.

Protect Exchange Server Roles

The next level of protection is the actual backup you will perform. The components you need to back up differ with each Exchange server role. Table 5-2 outlines what you need to back up based on the server role. When server roles are combined on the same system, you need to protect the contents for each of the installed server roles.

Table 5-2   **Components to Protect by Server Role**

Server Role	Components	Description
Mailbox Server	Mailbox storage groups, including mailbox databases and their transaction logs Public folder databases if they exist and their transaction logs MB system settings	With the MB role, the most important data to protect is the end-user data, which is stored inside Exchange databases. Settings are stored within Active Directory and can be recovered using the **Setup/m:RecoverServer** command.
Hub Transport Server	Configuration data Queue database Message tracking and protocol logs	Configuration data is stored in the Active Directory configuration container and does not need to be backed up locally. Queues are transient and can be rebuilt with the server. Message tracking and protocol logs record transactions that occur on the server. Message tracking logs provide historic forensic data on message paths. Protocol logs track conversions on all of the connectors. You need to protect the logs with file system backups.
Client Access Server	Configuration data Web and virtual directory data	Configuration data is in Active Directory and can be recovered using the **Setup/m:RecoverServer** command. Web data is in the IIS metabase and is protected by metabase exports and System State backups.
Unified Messaging Server	Configuration data Transient message queues Server-specific configuration data Custom audio files	Configuration data is in Active Directory and does not need local protection. Server-specific configuration is in XML format in the \bin folder and audio files are in the \Unified Messaging\Prompts folder. Protect both with a file system backup.

Table 5-2   **Components to Protect by Server Role**

Server Role	Components	Description
Edge Transport Server	Configuration data Queue database Message tracking and protocol logs	Like the HT, there is little information to protect, but note that configuration data is not stored in Active Directory, but in Active Directory Application Mode (ADAM). This is the most important information to protect. Exchange includes two Windows PowerShell scripts that can clone configurations: ExportEdgeConfig.ps1 and ImportEdgeConfig.ps1.
Support Service: Active Directory	NTDS.DIT	Replicated on each domain controller. Use System State backup in NT Backup. Without Active Directory, Exchange servers cannot function.
Support Service: DNS	NTDS.DIT or zone files	In Active Directory, DNS data should be stored within the directory database. Protect it through replication to DCs or through System State backups. If DNS data is not in Active Directory, use file system backups.
Support Service: Certificate Authority	Certificate Stores	Use Certification Authority console to back up the entire CA.
Client Data	Personal Storage (.pst) files Offline Storage (.ost) files Configuration files MAPI profiles POP3 or IMAP4 clients	Personal storage files are local and are not backed up by default. Use file system backup. Offline storage files can be re-created by connecting to Exchange and do not need backing up; unsynchronized changes can be lost. MAPI profiles can be regenerated by the Autodiscover service. Configuration or data files for POP3 or IMAP4 clients must be protected through file system backups.

As you can see, each role has its particular components to protect.

MORE INFO   **Cloning Edge configuration data**

For more information on how to use the Edge configuration protection scripts, go to *http://technet.microsoft.com/en-us/library/bb125150.aspx*.

MORE INFO   **Protecting UM data**

For more information on protecting the UM role, go to *http://technet.microsoft.com/en-us/library/ aa996875.aspx*.

MORE INFO   **Protecting Certificate Authorities**

For more information on protecting CAs, go to *http://technet2.microsoft.com/windowsserver/en/ library/0f1a31e4-8bc1-45ef-987f-c3e1a904eabe1033 .mspx?mfr=true*.

Mailbox Server   Because you must protect user data on the MB role, you should be aware of the folder paths where this data is stored. Table 5-3 outlines the various folder paths for Exchange data as well as a recommended backup strategy.

IMPORTANT   **Default Exchange file paths**

By default, all Exchange data and configuration information is stored in the C drive under Program Files. You would very rarely use these paths for user data because you must place database files on independent storage. Table 5-3 assumes that database files are on a volume named D: and that log files are on a volume named E:.

Table 5-3   MB Data and Configuration Folder Paths

Data	Folder Path	Backup Strategy
Database files, both mailbox and public folders	D:\Mailbox\ *storagegroup-foldername*	Exchange-Aware Backup Tool.
Transaction log files	D:\Mailbox\ *storagegroup-foldername*	Exchange-Aware Backup Tool.
Search information specific to a mailbox database	D:\Mailbox\ *storagegroup-foldername*	None

Table 5-3 MB Data and Configuration Folder Paths

Data	Folder Path	Backup Strategy
Offline Address Book	D:\ExchangeOAB on MB D:\ExchangeOAB on CAS (optional)	File system backup. Backing up the CAS OAB is optional but can speed up CAS recovery by eliminating replication.
Offline Address Book (public folder)	Public folder	Public folder replication or backup.
Windows registry	HKLM\ SOFTWARE\ Microsoft\Exchange HKLM\SYSTEM\ currentcontrolset\ Services	System State backup. You can also export the registry.

You will remember that databases are stored in ESE files with the .edb extension and transaction logs are stored in .log files. The .edb files cannot exceed 16 terabytes, but you should keep them much smaller or they will take forever to restore in the event of a disaster.

Log files are used to store every change made to Exchange data. Changes are first written to the log file, then committed to the cached database. They are moved from the cached database in RAM to the actual database when server workload permits.

Backup type can affect how your databases function. Remember that when your transaction logs are not committed to a database and deleted through database maintenance, they can easily and quickly fill up the entire disk volume they are assigned to. This is why you must carefully select the backup method you use. Backup tools can perform three different types of backups:

- *Full* takes a complete copy of all data. It also resets the archive bit on each file it backs up.

- *Incremental* will take only changed data since the last full or incremental backup. It also resets the archive bit.

- *Differential* will take only changed data since the last full backup.

Organizations often choose to perform a full backup during weekends and either incremental or differential backups during the week. If you take incremental backups, you must restore the full backup plus each incremental backup that was performed until the failure. If you take differential backups, you must restore the full backup plus the last differential before the failure. This is because differentials store all changed data since the full backup. They make restores easier, but continue to grow as time goes by: A Thursday differential, for example, would include all of the days since the full backup, while a Thursday incremental would include only Thursday's changed data.

When you perform a full or incremental backup with an Exchange-aware tool such as Windows Server Backup, transaction logs are committed and then deleted from the file system. Transaction logs are not deleted when you perform a differential backup because the differential backup does not reset the archive bit on the transaction log file. If you have a high volume of change to your Exchange databases and you use differential backups, you can potentially run out of space. When you run out of space, Exchange dismounts the database and stops accepting any changes until more space is available on the disk. You do not want to be stuck in this situation.

IMPORTANT   Database and Dial Tone Portability

In Exchange 2007, mailbox databases are portable. This means they can be mounted on any MB server. This facilitates recovery and allows you to provide access to data from any existing MB server. The Autodiscover service automatically links a user with a moved database.

Note that public folder databases are not portable and must be remounted on the same or rebuilt server. For this reason, you should replicate your public folder databases to more than one server.

In Exchange 2007, you also have Dial Tone Portability. This allows you to provide a user whose data is on a damaged server with a temporary mailbox on another server. Dial Tone Portability lets you move the user's mailbox without having access to the mailbox data. Once again, the Autodiscover service will automatically link the user with the new mailbox. Find out more at *http://technet.microsoft.com/en-us/library/aa997656.aspx*.

As you can see, running Office Outlook 2007 on client systems is a significant part of a disaster recovery solution because of its ability to work with the Autodiscover service.

Client Access Server   Much of the configuration data in a CAS system is stored within either Active Directory or the IIS metabase. But some data is not protected by default. For example, if you use the **Setup /m:RecoverServer** command, you restore your CAS computer to its default state and any custom configuration you performed will be lost. This is why you must protect this information as much as possible. However, a CAS computer must be synchronized with others through Active Directory, therefore restoring custom configuration information can be complex because the CAS will experience errors if it is not synchronized properly.

Table 5-4 outlines where CAS configuration data is stored as well as which data to protect; it assumes that folder paths are located under the C:\Program Files\Microsoft\ Exchange path.

Table 5-4   CAS Configuration Folder Paths

Data	Folder Path	Backup Strategy
OWA Web site and web.config file	\Client\owa	File backup.
POP3 and IMPA4 protocol settings	\ClientAccess \ClientAcces\PopImap	File backup.
Availability Service	\ClientAccess\exchweb\ews Active Directory configuration container Web.config file	File backup. Active Directory replication or backup.
Autodiscover	IIS metabase	System State backup or metabase export.
ActiveSync	\ClientAccess\Sync Active Directory configuration container IIS metabase	File backup. Active Directory replication or backup. Metabase export.
OWA virtual directories	\ClientAccess\Sync Active Directory configuration container	File backup. Active Directory replication or backup.
Registry settings	Windows registry (optional)	Rebuild by using the **Setup /m:RecoverServer** command. If backed up, use System State backup or registry export.
Web services configuration	IIS metabase	System State backup or metabase export.

MORE INFO   IIS metabase backup script

Microsoft provides a script that can back up the IIS metabase for a CAS role at *http://technet.microsoft.com/en-us/library/bb124359.aspx*.

MORE INFO   Information on the *Setup /m:RecoverServer* command

More information on the **Setup /m:RecoverServer** command can be found at
http://technet.microsoft.com/en-us/library/aa998656.aspx.

Recovery Strategies for Windows Server 2003

When it comes to servers and server configuration protection, you are really dealing with the protection of a Windows server. Recovery strategies for Windows Server 2003 depend, of course, on the type of problem you encounter, but they include:

- **Driver Rollback**   If you install an unstable driver on your system, you can use the driver rollback feature to restore the previous version of a driver, as long as you can still log on to your system. You do this by viewing the device properties in the Device Manager (System Properties, Hardware tab), clicking the Driver tab and selecting Roll Back Driver.

- **Disabling Devices**   You can also disable devices that are not operating properly. Again, you do this by moving to the Device Manager, locating the device, right-clicking it and selecting Disable from the shortcut menu.

- **Last Known Good Configuration**   Just like Windows NT and 2000, WS03 includes a Last Known Good Configuration startup choice. This reverts to the last configuration saved in the registry before you applied changes. This is done by pressing the F8 key during system startup. This will also give you access to a number of different startup modes, Safe Mode, Safe Mode with Networking, and so on. These are also operation modes you can use to repair WS03 installations.

- **Recovery Console**   This console allows you to perform recovery operations such as disabling services, copy device drivers or other files to the system, and otherwise repair an installation. Installing the console saves you from requiring the Windows Server 2003 original installation CD to perform a repair because the Recovery Console is listed as an operating system in your startup choices.

- **Windows Preinstallation Environment**   You can use Windows PE to create a bootable CD that will boot into a character-based Windows environment. This is also an excellent recovery tool because Windows PE will give you access to both network drives and local NTFS drives during your repair process. Download it from the Windows Automated Installation Kit at *http://www.microsoft.com/downloads/details.aspx?FamilyID=c7d4bc6d-15f3-4284-9123-679830d629f2&DisplayLang=en*.

- **Emergency Management Services**   If you have appropriate hardware, you can use Windows Server 2003's Emergency Management Services (EMS) to remotely manage and administer servers when problems arise. EMS is mostly oriented to "headless" servers—servers without monitors or human interface devices such as keyboards and mice.

BEST PRACTICES   **Protect server access**

Anyone who has physical access to a server and the administrator password for that server can use these tools and technologies to severely damage the server. Make sure that physical access to servers is tightly controlled.

- **Automated System Recovery**   The Automated System Recovery (ASR) option is a tool that allows you to reconstruct a non-working system. It is composed of two portions: ASR Preparation Wizard and ASR Restore. The Preparation Wizard captures everything on a system, from disk signatures to system state and other data. It also creates an ASR Boot Floppy disk. If you need to restore the system because none of the other strategies outlined in this section work, you simply start system setup by using the proper Windows Server 2003 installation CD, pressing F2 when prompted, and inserting the ASR floppy. ASR Restore will restore the disk signatures, install a minimal version of Windows, and restore all system and data files. It is not 100 percent perfect, but it is the best recovery tool to date to come with Windows.

- **Third-Party Backup and Restore Tools**   A number of different third-party tools are designed for backup and restore for Windows Server 2003 and Exchange. When selecting a third-party product, you must consider three key elements: integration to the Volume Shadow Copy Service APIs, complete system recovery from diskette (comparable to the ASR), and integration to Active Directory. The latter is the most important aspect because so much of the Exchange configuration is stored within the directory.

Of course, when all else fails, you should rely on backup and recovery.

System Recovery Strategies

When issues occur, you usually go through specific steps to resolve them. Take the following scenario:

- Service interruption is detected.

- The interruption type is identified and has been categorized through your troubleshooting strategy.

- Risk has been evaluated and the level of response identified.

- The recovery plan for this problem and level of risk is put into action.

- A plan B is ready in case the main recovery plan does not work for some reason.

- The results of recovery actions are fully tested to ensure that everything is back to normal.

- Secondary recovery actions are performed. For example, broken servers that were taken offline are repaired, or users are notified that their files are back online.

- The incident is documented and the procedure is updated, if required.

You may not have time to document recovery processes for every single disaster situation, but if you have taken the time to evaluate risks, you can ensure that the most critical situations are documented.

System Protection Strategies

Backing up your systems will mean backing up several types of information: user data, corporate data, databases, documents, system state information for your servers, and Active Directory data. As mentioned earlier, you can use either the Windows Server 2003 Backup Utility (in either graphical or command-line mode) or a third-party backup tool to perform these backups. Whichever one you use, make sure that you will use a standard backup strategy, creating backup sets of specific data types; for example, create only user data backups in one backup set and only system data in another. This will simplify the restoration process. If you keep system and data disk volumes separate, it is possible that if one disk set fails, the other will remain intact. For example, if the system disk set fails, data is still protected. Rebuild the system and the data will still be there. Separating disk sets at the onset is part of your overall protection strategy.

To protect systems, you must protect the system volume and the System State. You should also perform Automated System Restore backups on an ongoing basis. ASRs allow you to recover systems in one single step and are therefore very valuable in any recovery strategy.

When you prepare your backup schedules, consider the following:

- Both data and System States should be backed up at least on a daily basis.

- ASRs should be taken on a weekly basis.

- System States and data backups can be incremental or differential during weekdays—differentials are preferred; they take more space, but are faster to restore because they include all the new data on the same backup set.

Make sure you have enough disk space to use them, however—then on weekends, you can take full backups of both. ASR backups are full backups by default.

BEST PRACTICES   System State backups

Your System State backups should include both the System State as well as system and boot volumes. In most cases, this means backing up the System State and drive C:.

You need to support your backup strategy with offsite media storage. You will need to ensure that you have a safe offline storage space for media. You should rotate offsite media on a regular basis. For example, every second complete backup should be stored offsite in a controlled environment.

Many organizations rely on schedules with a four-week retention strategy. This means that you retain backup media for a period of four weeks. If you keep every second copy offsite, you always have access to copies that are only a week old. In addition, your archiving schedule and compliance policies will outline which copies you should keep offsite on a permanent basis.

System State Backups

System State backups are more complex for administrators because these are the tools that protect the operating system itself. It is important to fully understand what a System State backup consists of. A System State backup has nine potential elements. Some are always backed up and others depend on the type of server you are backing up. They are identified as follows:

- The System Registry
- The COM+ Class Registry Database
- Boot and System Files
- Windows File Protection System Files
- Active Directory database (on Domain Controllers)
- SYSVOL Directory (on DCs)
- Certificate Services Database (on Certificate Servers)
- Cluster Service Configuration Information (on Failover Clusters)
- IIS Metadirectory (on Web Application Servers)

System State data is always backed up as a whole; it cannot be segregated. The System State backup is performed by selecting System State in the Backup dialog box, under the Backup tab (see Figure 5-1).

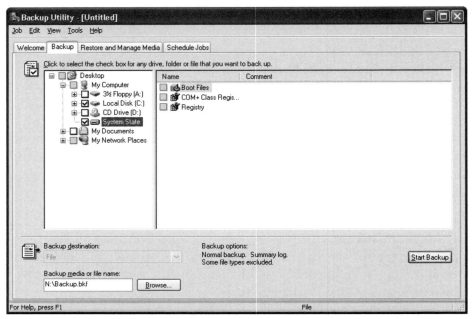

Figure 5-1   Backing up the System State with the system drive

---

BEST PRACTICES   **Using NTBackup**

Launch NTBackup through the shortcut in All Programs | Accessories | System Tools from the Start Menu. By default, the backup tool starts in wizard mode. To ensure that you always start in Advanced mode, clear the Always Start In Wizard Mode check box.

Selecting Third-Party Backup Tools

Many organizations find NTBackup too limiting and opt for third-party tools. Consider the following when selecting this third-party tool. A number of third-party backup solutions on the market are specifically designed for Windows Server 2003 and Exchange 2007. Many meet specific criteria, which must include:

- Being aware of System State data.
- Being integrated to the Volume Shadow Copy Service, triggering a VSS snapshot before launching a backup operation.
- Enabling complete system recovery from a simple process comparable to the ASR.
- Being Active Directory-aware and supporting single-object restores in Active Directory.
- Being Exchange-aware and supporting single-object restores in Exchange.

- Providing a simple but efficient restore process.

- Supporting data duplication or the ability to use pointers to store similar data in the protected backup repository. This greatly reduces required backup storage space.

Meeting these basic criteria is essential. Some criteria, of course—such as integration with the massive storage products—are supported by Windows, including special drivers for SQL Server. But the ones listed here are the core requirements for an intelligent, third-party backup solution for Microsoft Exchange 2007.

IMPORTANT Data retention

Today, organizations must retain data for much longer periods than ever before because of compliance regulations. When you select a third-party backup tool, you should ensure that it will support the restoration of data to any new or upgrade version of Exchange. This way, your archived backups will also support your compliance policies.

Using NTBackup

The Backup utility found in Windows Server 2003, NTBackup, has greatly improved with this edition of Windows. It now includes a comprehensive graphical interface (see Figure 5-2) with three operating modes:

- The Backup Wizard, which takes users through a backup or restore operation

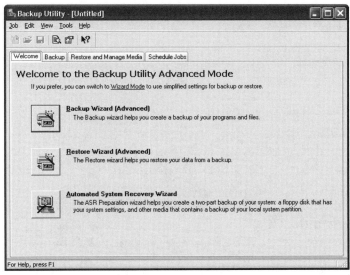

Figure 5-2 The NTBackup Advanced Mode interface

- The Advanced Backup interface, which is more appropriate for enterprise system administrators
- The command-line backup tool

The Advanced Backup interface has changed the most. The startup screen now includes an ASR button instead of the Emergency Repair Disk button found in Windows 2000.

In addition, the interface includes the Scheduled Jobs tab. This tab allows you to schedule backups directly within the graphical interface, making it much easier than in previous versions of Windows, where you had to create a command-line script and integrate the script with Scheduled Tasks.

NTBackup also includes the Automated System Restore feature which creates a comprehensive system backup and supports system restoration from a single restore diskette. Creating an ASR backup is simple. Just click the ASR button on the Advanced Backup startup screen.

When the backup is complete, you can view a report of the backup operation. In fact, this displays the backup log. You should store these logs in a safe place because they are very useful for quickly locating files that need to be restored. They are simple text files that can be searched much faster than a restore through the Backup utility. With the addition of the ASR, NTBackup becomes a much more viable backup solution than ever before, but it is not, by far, an enterprise backup solution.

MORE INFO   **NTBackup and Exchange 2007**

More information on using NTBackup for Exchange can be found at
http://technet.microsoft.com/en-us/library/aa998870.aspx.

Authoritative Active Directory Restores

One of the most significant issues with NTBackup and Windows Server 2003 in general in terms of backup and especially restoration is Active Directory. Active Directory is a complex database. Often, the best way to restore a downed domain controller (DC) is to rebuild the DC to a certain level, and then let multi-master replication take over to bring the server up to date. The impact of this recovery strategy is that it taxes the network, especially if the DC is a regional server. It all depends on the level to which you rebuild the server and the obsolescence of the data it contains.

Fortunately, Windows Server 2003 lets you stage DCs with offline media. This means that you can create an Active Directory database backup—through the System State backup—on CD and use it to stage or restore DCs. The more recent the CD, the less replication will be required. Recoveries of this type are not too complex. These recoveries assume that the data within the other replicas of the directory database is *authoritative*—that it is valid data. It also means that the disabled DC contained no critical and unreplicated data.

Issues arise when there is critical data within a downed DC, data that is not within the other replicas, or when an error occurs and data within the directory is damaged and must be restored. In this case, you must perform an authoritative restore. This is where you begin to find the limitations of NTBackup.

Active Directory manages directory replication through the update sequence number (USN), which you can think of as change counters and represent the number of modifications on a domain controller since the last replication. Values for objects and properties that have the highest USN are replicated to other domain controllers and replace the values that are in the copies of the directory database located on the target DCs. USNs are also used to manage replication conflicts. If two domain controllers have the same USN, a timestamp determines the latest change. When you perform a normal Active Directory restore, data that is restored from backup is updated according to the information in other domain controllers; in fact, it is overwritten if the USN for the data in other DCs is higher than the USN for the data in the restored DC.

When you need to restore data from a crashed DC that included critical data—data that is not found in the current version of the directory (for example, if someone deleted an entire OU and the deletion has been replicated to all DCs), you need to perform an authoritative restore. In this restore, the information you will recover from backup will take precedence over the information in the directory even if the USNs are of a lower value.

To perform an authoritative restore, you must begin by taking the DC offline and entering the Directory Services Restore Mode. Then you perform a normal restore. When the data is restored and the domain controller is still offline, you use the NTDSUTIL tool to make the restore authoritative. The authoritative restore can include all or just a portion of the restored Active Directory data.

To perform an authoritative restore, follow these steps:

1. Repair the server if required and start it. During startup, press F8 to view the startup modes.
2. Select the Directory Services Restore Mode and press Enter, which will boot into Windows.
3. Log on to the local administrator's account.
4. Launch the backup utility and perform the restore.

5. When the restoration is finished, reboot the server.

6. Press F8 once again to select Directory Services Restore Mode and press Enter.

7. Log on to the local administrator's account.

8. Launch the command prompt and type **ntdsutil**.

9. In the NTDSUTIL tool, type the following commands:

    ```
    authoritative restore
    restore database
    ```

10. Type **quit** and restart the server in normal mode.

When the server is restarted, the replication process will start and the restored information will be replicated to other domain controllers.

If you want to restore only a portion of the directory, use the following restore command:

```
restore subtree ou=ouname,dc=dcname,dc=dcname
```

For example, in the Services OU in the LucernePublishing.com domain, you would use the following command:

```
restore subtree ou=services,dc=lucernepublishing,dc=com
```

As you can see, restoring information that can be deleted from a simple operator error can be quite complex when using the default Windows Server 2003 backup utility. This is one of the key reasons why you would consider using a comprehensive third-party backup technology specifically designed to integrate and support all of Windows Server 2003's features.

MORE INFO   **Free Active Directory restore utilities**

When you delete information in Active Directory, it is actually tombstoned for a default period of time, usually 60 days. During this period, you can recover the information from the tombstone container. Recovering this information without a custom utility is very complex, but fortunately, two such utilities exist. Microsoft provides a command-line ADRestore utility at *http://www.microsoft.com/ technet/sysinternals/Networking/AdRestore.mspx*. Quest also offers a free and better utility for restoring tombstoned objects: the Quest Object Restore for Active Directory at *http://www.quest.com/object-restore-for-active-directory/*. This utility lets you access tombstoned data through the graphical interface, making it much easier to restore content. For example, if you inadvertently delete a mail-enabled user, you can recover it from the tombstone data much faster than if you try to recover it through an authoritative restore.

Finalize Your Backup Strategy

Choosing the right data protection technology is a core element of your resiliency strategy, but as you have seen here, it is not the only element. You need to design and implement the proper system protection processes and ensure that they are followed. In addition, you must ensure that your data protection strategies complement your system redundancy strategies. One of the key elements of data protection is integrated and regular testing: your backup tapes or other media must be tested on a regular basis.

Practice: Prepare Exchange Backups

In this practice, you will perform a backup of Exchange data. This will let you become familiar with the different options available for backup. This practice consists of a single exercise.

▶ **Exercise: Perform an Exchange Backup**

Backing up Exchange data is one of the key concepts related to system and data protection. In this exercise, you back up the data on your Exchange server by completing the following steps:

1. Make sure your Active Directory server, TreyDC.treyresearch.net, is running. Also make sure ExchangeOne.treyresearch.net is running.

2. Log on to ExchangeOne with the EXAdmin account. Backups require either Local Administrator or Backup Operators access rights. The EXAdmin account provides both.

3. Launch NT Backup. Use Start Menu | All Programs | Accessories | System Tools | Backup.

4. If NTBackup launches in Wizard mode, clear the Always Launch In Wizard Mode check box, click Cancel, and start it again. This will launch NT Backup in Advanced mode.

5. Click the Backup tab.

6. In the tree pane, expand the Microsoft Exchange Server section, expand the ExchangeOne section, and then expand Microsoft Information Store.

7. Select the First Storage Group. This selects all mailboxes within this storage group.

8. Move to the bottom of the page and select Browse to change the backup destination.

9. Move to My Computer and select drive E:. Normally you would not back up to this destination, but for the purpose of this exercise, this will be fine.

10. Name the backup **FirstExchangeBackup.bkf** and click Save.

11. Click Start Backup.

12. In the Backup Job Information window, keep the defaults and click Start Backup. Note that Windows performs a Shadow Copy and then starts the backup.

13. When the backup is complete, click Report to view the results of the backup. Close the Report window when done.

14. Open Windows Explorer and select drive E:. Verify that your FirstExchange-Backup.bkf file exists.

15. Close the NT Backup window.

You have performed your first backup.

Quick Check

1. What are the items that a backup strategy should include?

2. What are the two key factors that are addressed by the disaster recovery service level agreements?

3. What are the available technologies that can be used for backup purposes?

4. What data needs to be addressed in the data protection strategy?

5. What are the two types of deletions that Exchange Server will perform? Describe each.

6. How are database files and transaction logs stored?

Quick Check Answers

1. The backup strategy should include the following items:

   ❑ E-mail data

   ❑ All configuration settings

   ❑ System components

   ❑ Everything else that you need to re-create an Exchange server

   ❑ Information from all of the supporting systems that make up the Exchange implementation (Active Directory, DNS, certificate authorities, and so on)

2. The two key factors addressed by the disaster recovery SLA are:

   ❑ **Maximal Recovery Time (MRT)** How long will it take to recover data or systems based on the SLA you put in place? You need to choose the appropriate backup hardware and software that will satisfy the commitment you make to users in the SLA.

   ❑ **Maximal Acceptable Data Loss (MADL)** How often do you need to perform backups? This factor identifies just how much data loss can be acceptable based on your SLAs. For example, if you have agreed with your end users that two hours is the maximal amount of time you can accept potential data losses, you need to back up your systems every two hours. If you decide that this period of time should be longer or shorter, you must schedule your backups accordingly.

3. The available technologies are:

   ❏ Legacy streaming backup

   ❏ Volume Shadow Copy Service

   ❏ Tape backups

   ❏ Disk-to-disk backups

   ❏ Storage Area Network (SAN) backups

4. The data addressed in the protection strategy includes:

   ❏ Individual messages

   ❏ Data on the Exchange server

   ❏ Exchange server role configuration information

5. Exchange Server will perform both soft and hard deletions:

   ❏ Soft deletions do not actually remove an object from the Exchange mailbox database. Instead, Exchange maintains a table called Msg-Folder. This table maps entries in the folder table and the message table. When a message is soft-deleted, it is marked as such in the Msg-Folder table. Items that have been soft-deleted are the items that are available to end users for Deleted Item Recovery.

   ❏ Messages are hard-deleted when they meet the following conditions: The user uses Shift+Delete in Outlook to delete a message. Using Shift+Delete permanently deletes an item and does not move it to the Deleted Items folder. The item retention is set to zero. Mailbox or public folder databases are set to force hard deletes. This is done by setting the registry value *Force Hard Deletes* for the database. The account that requests the deletion is either a gateway or a system account.

6. The database files are stored in ESE files with the .edb extension and the transaction logs are stored in .log files.

Lesson 2: Plan a Recovery Solution Implementation

Estimated lesson time: 30 minutes

As stated earlier, disaster recovery solutions must first take backup copies of the vital information you want to protect, but more important, they must also support the ability to restore information. You can back up all you want, but if you cannot restore the information, all your backup efforts will be useless.

As you saw in Lesson 1, you need to protect data at several levels when working with Exchange systems. You need to work with four core components:

- Exchange data, which consists of messages, mailboxes, and public folders.
- Exchange systems, which consist of the server software and configuration information.
- Supporting systems, which consist of Active Directory, DNS, certificate authorities, and so on.
- Client systems, which host most Exchange data in the form of a local cache from the server.

Disaster Recovery Concepts

Your recovery strategy must provide protection mechanisms for each of these four components. As you have seen, in the perfect Exchange 2007 environment two of these four items are very easy to deal with. The perfect Exchange 2007 environment includes only Exchange 2007 servers and Outlook 2007 clients. When you have this configuration, user data is protected in many ways, including:

- Users can restore their own data even after they empty their Deleted Items folder.
- You can restore data from the Dumpster for users if they no longer have access to it. For example, if a mailbox is lost, you can restore it from the Dumpster without having to resort to backups. By default, mailboxes are kept for 30 days in the Dumpster before being removed. Note that the Dumpster is automatically emptied when you perform a full backup. This means that if you perform full backups every week, the Dumpster retention period will be 7 days, not 30 days.
- If users are running Outlook 2007 and you have provided them with sufficient storage space on the servers, the loss of their computers will not be catastrophic because of the following:
  - ❑ All data is only cached locally within an .ost file and can be rebuilt from the server.

❏ MAPI configuration data can be automatically restored to a client through the Autodiscover service.

Thus when you have this configuration, you have fewer items to consider in your protection strategy.

Recover a Single Mailbox

You can recover mailboxes from two locations: the Dumpster or backups. Ideally, you recover them from the Dumpster because you identify the problem before the Dumpster is emptied. This also saves you from having to locate the backup that contains the mailbox.

To recover a mailbox from the Dumpster, you must have the Exchange Organization Administrator role. Then you can use either the Exchange Management Console or the Exchange Management Shell. In the Console, go to Recipient Configuration | Disconnected Mailbox. In the Action pane, click Connect To Server, right-click the name of the server to connect to, and click Connect. This will list all of the disconnected mailboxes on that server. Then use the Connect Mailbox Wizard to complete the process.

In the Exchange Management Shell, use the **get-MailboxStatistics** cmdlet. For information on the actual syntax to use, go to *http://technet.microsoft.com/en-us/library/ aa997182.aspx.*

If the mailbox is no longer in the Dumpster, you must restore it from backup first. When you do so, you will need to proceed through the use of a recovery storage group (RSG). First you must create the recovery storage group. To do so, you will need the Exchange Server Administrator role and local Administrators rights on the server where you will create the RSG. Then you will need the Exchange Recipient Administrator role to recover the mailbox. Mailbox recovery is performed through the **restore-Mailbox** cmdlet. There is no graphical interface to restore a mailbox. See *http://technet.microsoft.com/en-us/library/aa997694.aspx* for more information.

IMPORTANT   Recovering mailboxes

Exchange mailboxes can only be recovered within the same Active Directory forest they originated from. You cannot use the **restore-Mailbox** command to move mailboxes between forests.

Work with Recovery Storage Groups

Recovery storage groups are special storage groups that allow you to mount mailbox databases and extract information from those databases. You can use RSGs to recover data from either a backup or a database copy (using LCR or CCR, see Lesson 1 in

Chapter 6). Because you mount these databases into the RSG, they do not affect existing user databases or existing user mailbox data.

In Exchange 2007, RSGs include the following features:

- You use two tools to work with and create RSGs: the Exchange Management Shell or the Exchange Server Disaster Recovery Analyzer Tool (Exchange DRA).
- After you create and populate them, RSGs will not appear in the Exchange Management Console.
- If you use the Exchange DRA tool, it will guide you through the recovery process using an RSG.

You can use RSGs in the following situations:

- In the event of a complete database loss, you can set up a temporary database using Dial Tone Recovery and then use an RSG to restore mailbox content. This way, your users have immediate access to e-mail even though it takes a bit longer to give them access to their e-mail history. You can set up dial tones on the original or alternate servers.
- You can also use an RSG to repair a secondary copy of a database and then merge this new copy with the original database when it is ready.
- If you need to recover a mailbox database and the original server is not available, you can mount it into an RSG on a different server and then move it to an existing storage group.
- When performing content recovery from a mailbox, you can mount it into an RSG and copy content from the RSG to a mailbox folder in a production database.
- When you need to locate historical information—for example, for compliance purposes—you can use an RSG to locate it.

RSGs differ from normal storage groups because several normal storage group functions are disabled in the RSG. The only protocol an RSG will support is the MAPI protocol. You cannot use SMTP, POP3, or IMAP4 to communicate with the RSG. This stops the RSG from inserting unwanted e-mail into your system. And, even though MAPI is enabled, an RSG cannot be accessed via Outlook or OWA.

When you mount a mailbox database into an RSG, the mailboxes cannot connect to Active Directory user accounts and therefore cannot corrupt existing mailbox content. RSG content is also exempted from normal system and mailbox policies, preventing the deletion of content while you are trying to recover it. RSGs are also exempt from online maintenance tasks, which prevents them from impacting server performance.

All databases mounted in an RSG must be mounted manually, preventing them from impacting production databases. You cannot change data paths or move files after you create the RSG. To make such changes, you must delete and re-create the RSG.

RSGs cannot contain public folder databases. You must use a different strategy, such as public folder replication, to protect public folder content. In addition, you can only mount a single RSG per server. Finally, you cannot use RSGs in conjunction with LCR or CCR, and you cannot use them as a source for a data backup. As their name implies, RSGs are only used for data recovery, and if you must work with multiple databases, they must all be from the same original storage group. If you need to recover mailbox databases from several storage groups, you must use more than one MB system.

As you can see, RSGs are useful only for specific situations where you need to recover data from one mailbox database at a time. If you have lost a complete MB system, do not use an RSG to recover it because you will need to recover multiple storage groups as well as the system itself.

However, when you do use an RSG, you can extract any mailbox information, including normal or hidden folders, notes, tasks, calendar events, contacts, and of course, e-mail messages. Any restored special content in the mailbox—search folders, calendar items, or Dumpster content—will be automatically converted to avoid loss of functionality or duplicate data. When you recover data, you can either merge it with an existing mailbox or copy it to a subfolder. Data can be filtered before merges or copies to restore selected content only. Note that merges will not include rules, search folders, or any items that already exists because Exchange deems that what is in the mailbox is the best version. If you want to restore a copy of a message that already exists, you must copy it to a subfolder.

MORE INFO   Recovery storage groups

More information on RSGs can be found at *http://technet.microsoft.com/en-us/library/aa997260.aspx*.

Perform a Dial Tone Recovery

As you know, the MB role is the most complex to recover. This is why Microsoft included the Dial Tone Recovery (DTR) feature in Exchange 2007. When you use a DTR, you create an empty database on a server to replace the failed database. This provides users with the ability to use e-mail, but not the ability to have access to their historical databases. Obviously, using a DTR is an emergency procedure that you use when nothing else is available.

You can use DTRs on the actual server that has the failed database or on an alternate server. Then you can repair and recover the failed database on either the original or the alternate server. When you perform a DTR, you use the same basic steps whether you recover the content on the same server or on an alternate server:

1. Create the DTR database. This uses the Dial Tone Portability (DTP) feature of Exchange. Users are redirected to the dial tone database through the Autodiscover service. If the DTR database is placed on an alternate server, you must move the mailbox configuration to this new server.

2. Restore the failed database. You can restore it to either the same or another server. If you restore it to the same server, you must place it within the recovery storage group so that it does not interfere with the DTR database.

3. After you restore the failed database, you swap the dial tone from the DTR database for the repaired database. If your DTR database was on an alternate server, move the mailbox configuration back to the original server.

4. Merge the two databases using the Exchange DRA tool.

You must consider two factors when determining where to place the DTR database. If you place it on the server where the database failed, you will have faster recovery times because you will not need to move data from one server to another, but there will be a performance impact on all of the databases of that server. If you place the DTR database on an alternate server, you will have better performance, but longer recovery times. Also, using an alternate server involves more steps, which can leave room for error.

IMPORTANT   Using legacy versions of Outlook

If you are not using Outlook 2007, you cannot use the Autodiscover service. In this case, place the DTR database on the original server. This does not require you to modify user configurations in legacy versions of Outlook.

MORE INFO   Dial Tone Recovery procedures

More information on DTR procedures can be found at *http://technet.microsoft.com/en-us/library/bb310765.aspx*.

Recover Exchange Systems

Every once in a while, you will lose an entire Exchange system. When this happens, you need to be prepared to recover it. As discussed earlier, the recovery procedure you use depends on the system role. Edge and Hub Transport servers include more automated recovery procedures because their configuration is stored within directory containers. The HT stores its configuration within Active Directory and the ET stores it within ADAM. Recovering one of these server roles is relatively simple as long as you have ready access to either directory container.

MORE INFO Recovering Edge Transport servers

Remember that you can recover ET systems using Cloned Configuration. More information on this procedure, which is based on two custom Shell scripts included with Exchange, can be found at *http://technet.microsoft.com/en-us/library/bb125150.aspx.*

UM systems also store their configuration within the Active Directory directory service, but because of their nature, they also have audio files that are stored locally. To recover these files, you must have access to a server backup.

CAS systems are more complex to recover because they host Web sites and virtual directories that support client functions. The best way to protect CAS systems is to use the two custom scripts provided with Exchange 2007. Table 5-5 outlines how to recover different content for a CAS system. It assumes that folder paths are located under the C:\Program Files\Microsoft\Exchange path.

Table 5-5 CAS Configuration Folder Paths

Data	Folder Path	Restore Strategy
OWA Web site and web.config file	\Client\owa	File restore.
POP3 and IMAP4 protocol settings	\ClientAccess \ClientAcces\PopImap	File restore.
Availability Service	\ClientAccess\exchweb\ews Active Directory configuration container Web.config file	File restore. Configure using Management Scripts.
Autodiscover	IIS metabase	System State restore or metabase import.
ActiveSync	\ClientAccess\Sync Active Directory configuration container IIS metabase	File restore. Metabase import. Configure using Management Scripts.

Table 5-5 CAS Configuration Folder Paths

Data	Folder Path	Restore Strategy
OWA virtual directories	\ClientAccess\Sync	File restore.
	Active Directory configuration container	Configure using Management Scripts; folders will lose all customizations.
Registry settings	Windows registry (optional)	If backed up, use System State restore or registry import
Web services configuration	IIS metabase	System State restore or metabase import.

The MB role is the most complex to rebuild because it hosts mailbox databases and may also be placed within a Failover Cluster, which provides failure protection, but complicates the restoration process in the event of a complete cluster loss. If you are running mailbox servers in a Failover Cluster, you can rebuild their configuration using the **Setup /RecoverCMS** command.

MORE INFO Rebuild a lost mailbox cluster

For more information on the **Setup /RecoverCMS** command, go to *http://technet.microsoft.com/en-us/library/bb124095.aspx*.

Table 5-6 outlines the various folder paths for Exchange data as well as its configuration and the restore method to use.

Table 5-6 MB Data and Configuration Folder Paths

Data	Folder Path	Restore Strategy
Database files, both mailbox and public folders	D:\Mailbox\ *storagegroupfoldername*	Exchange-aware Backup Tool.
Transaction log files	D:\Mailbox\ *storagegroupfoldername*	Exchange-aware Backup Tool.
Search information specific to a mailbox database	D:\Mailbox\ *storagegroupfoldername*	Rebuild it.

Table 5-6   MB Data and Configuration Folder Paths

Data	Folder Path	Restore Strategy
Offline Address Book	D:\ExchangeOAB on MB	Rebuild or restore through file system.
Offline Address Book (public folder)	Public folder	Public folder replication, rebuild or backup.
Windows registry	HKLM\SOFTWARE \Microsoft\Exchange HKLM\SYSTEM\ currentcontrolset\Services	System State restore. You can also import the registry.

In any case, if you completely lose a server role, you can always use the **Setup /m: RecoverServer** command, although it will not necessarily recover all lost information. If you need to use this command to recover a server role, you will need to reset the computer account for the server in Active Directory first. Because you rebuild the server with the same name, the original account will not work until it is reset.

MORE INFO   Rebuild a lost server

For more information on the **Setup /m:RecoverServer** command, go to *http://technet.microsoft.com/en-us/library/bb123496.aspx*.

Special Exchange Role Considerations

Each server role has its own particularities when being restored, including the following factors.

Recover Databases   When restoring databases to MB systems, you can restore them to the original server or alternate servers, as with the Dial Tone Recovery procedure outlined earlier. Depending on the type of backup tool you use, you will have to use different procedures.

If you use a legacy streaming backup technology such as Windows Server Backup or NTBackup, you use the standard restore procedure to recover the database to its original server. When you want to recover the database to an alternate server, you must use a special procedure outlined in the following steps:

1.   You must create a storage group using the same name as the original storage group that contained the database you want to restore onto the new server.

2. Create a new database with the original name and set it so that it can be overwritten.

3. Use your legacy streaming backup tool to restore the database files onto the new server into the new storage group and into the new database folder.

4. Mount the database.

5. Set the database to mount at startup.

Your database is ready to use.

MORE INFO **Restoring a database from legacy streaming backups**

More information on restoring databases through legacy streaming backup tools can be found at *http://technet.microsoft.com/en-us/library/aa995898.aspx*.

If you are using a more modern backup technology, you do not need to use the legacy streaming procedure. You can use database portability instead. Database portability allows you to move a database from one server to another. Before you can move a database, it must be in what is considered a Clean Shutdown state. This means that all of its transaction logs have been emptied and committed to the database. To force the commitment of all logs to the database, use the following command:

```
Eseutil /R LogFilePrefix
```

Note that this command is run through the command prompt, not the Exchange Shell. The *LogFilePrefix* value is required and can be obtained with the following Shell command:

```
Get-StorageGroup <Server_Name>\<StorageGroup_Name> | fl LogFilePrefix
```

When this is done, you can move the mailbox database from server to server. This move process is fairly straightforward:

1. Create a new database on the target server and make sure its database files can be overwritten.

2. Move the original database files, including the .edb and .log files as well as the Search catalog, into the folder containing the new database.

3. Mount the moved database.

4. Modify user configurations by using the **move-Mailbox -ConfigurationOnly** cmdlet.

5. Delete the database files on the original server.

The result is a moved database and updated user configurations.

MORE INFO **Moving a database**

More information on using database portability to move a database can be found at
http://technet.microsoft.com/en-us/library/aa998340.aspx.

Repair the Transport Queue   Transport servers use a single Exchange database to
manage the transport queue. All SMTP messages move through this queue at some
point in time. The queue is stored in a single file called mail.que. In some cases, messages located in this queue are not transmitted because of a transport server failure.
This can occur when the database is fragmented and takes up all available space or
when the server fails completely.

In this situation, you can move the queue database to another location on the same
server, repair it, replace it, and then restart it. Queue databases can also be moved
from one server to another in the same Active Directory domain, in the same Active
Directory forest, or even in different Active Directory forests. To repair a transport
queue, complete the following steps:

1. Move the database to a temporary folder. Databases are stored in the \Transport-
   Roles\data\Queue folder under Program Files\Microsoft\Exchange by default.
   You can change this location by modifying the *QueueDatabasePath* and *QueueDa-
   tabaseLoggingPath* values in the EdgeTransport.exe.config file. You must stop the
   transport service before you can move the database.

2. Use the Exchange Server Database Utility (Eseutil.exe) to recover the database.

3. While the database is offline, defragment it.

4. Modify the original database so that it can be replaced with the newly defrag-
   mented database.

5. Restart the repaired database.

Perform this operation only if you know that unsent messages are contained within
the damaged server.

MORE INFO **Repairing transport queues**

More information on transport queue recovery operations can be found at
http://technet.microsoft.com/en-us/library/bb124343.aspx.

Repair Exchange Search   Search data for each mailbox database is stored within the
same folder as the database itself. Search data is mostly a full-text index of the contents of the database. This index data can become unsynchronized with the database
contents when the database is restored from either the Dumpster or from a backup

file. This can happen especially if transaction log files are played into the recovered database because the search engine does not read played log files and therefore does not include them in the index.

To rebuild the search catalog and resynchronize it with database contents, you must stop the Exchange Search Service, delete the old catalog files, and then restart the service. Restarting the service will force the catalog to re-index the database contents.

MORE INFO   Rebuild the search index catalog

More information on how to rebuild the search index catalog can be found at *http://technet.microsoft.com/en-us/library/aa995966.aspx*.

Recover Lost Mail-Enabled Accounts

Active Directory is the container that stores all supplemental e-mail information. As mentioned in Lesson 1, recovering data from Active Directory can be daunting. This is why it is so important to have access to the tools that let you restore information from the Tombstone container. When this does not work, you can use other methods to recover accounts without having to resort to Directory Services Restore Mode.

For example, you can recover a user account from information stored within the mailbox for that user. Previous versions of Exchange used a special tool, the Mailbox Reconnect (Mbconn.exe) tool, to perform this operation. This tool does not work in Exchange 2007. The Exchange 2007 procedure relies on a completely different strategy.

IMPORTANT   Recovering user accounts

While you can use some mailbox data to recover a user account into Active Directory, you should always look to other means to perform this operation first. When you recover an account from a mailbox, you only recover information related to Exchange and not information related to any other aspect of the user account. For this reason, users with lost accounts may also experience a significant loss of functionality within the domain.

To recover a lost mail-enabled account, follow these steps:

1. Use Exchange Management Shell scripts to gather the information from the mailbox.

2. Store this information in a file that uses the Lightweight Directory Access Protocol Data Interchange Format (LDIF).

3. Import the LDIF file into Active Directory using the LDIF Data Exchange (LDIFDE) tool.

To perform this operation, you must have both the Exchange Recipient Administrator and the Account Operator role in Active Directory.

Note that this process will fail if user accounts with the same name as the account you are trying to re-create already exist in the forest.

MORE INFO **Recover user accounts from mailbox data**

More information on this procedure can be found at *http://technet.microsoft.com/en-us/library/bb430758.aspx*.

Work with Exchange's Disaster Recovery Tools

Exchange 2007 includes several tools that are aimed at disaster recovery. Four tools in particular can assist you when you run into issues with Exchange 2007 systems:

- **Database Recovery Management Tool**   Relies on the Exchange Troubleshooting Assistant engine to execute a set of troubleshooting steps against databases you specify. When the problem is identified, it displays a wizard to help you repair the problem.

- **Database Troubleshooter**   Also uses the same engine as the Exchange Troubleshooting Assistant to help identify why databases will not mount. It collects a set of data on the problem and then provides guidance for possible solutions through a set of repair wizards.

  Both the Database Recovery Management and the Database Troubleshooter are found in the Exchange Management Console Toolbox.

- **Exchange Server Database Utility Tool**   Eseutil.exe is a non-Shell tool (it uses the command line) that works with the Extensible Storage Engine, database files, and transaction logs to verify, modify, or repair them. It will repair corrupt databases, thereby avoiding the need to restore them from backups.

- **Information Store Integrity Checker Tool**   Isinteg.exe is also a non-Shell tool that is used to locate and remove errors from public folder and mailbox databases. This tool works at a different level than Eseutil.exe, the application level, and therefore can sometimes recover information that Eseutil.exe cannot. Use this tool only when you must restore a database. This tool will update the information store when a database is restored from an offline backup. Then it will test the information store and if errors are found, repair it.

MORE INFO **Learn more about these tools**

More information about these tools can be found at *http://technet.microsoft.com/en-us/library/aa998611.aspx*.

Finalize Your Recovery Solution

As with backup, you must run a series of tests to validate and document all of the potential recovery strategies for Exchange 2007. Make sure you run through any potential situation before you completely finalize your recovery solution. It is very important to test every aspect of the solution before you begin moving data into your new Exchange 2007 infrastructure. Testing is usually performed in a lab and solutions are validated and fully documented before being moved into production.

Testing not only proves that the solution will work, but is also used to outline the administrative policies and practices you will use when the solution is in place. You should also test backup and restore performance. You may need to update your SLAs based on the results of these tests. Finally, you should test every aspect of the solution—normal operations as well as emergency situations—so that you know what to do when the unexpected occurs.

Practice: Prepare for Recovery

In this practice, you will perform a database recovery. This practice consists of a single exercise. This will let you review the procedures for a recovery operation.

▶ **Exercise: Perform a Mailbox Database Recovery**

In this exercise, complete the following steps using the backup you performed earlier to recover a mailbox database:

1. Make sure your Active Directory server, TreyDC.treyresearch.net, is running. Also make sure ExchangeOne.treyresearch.net is running.

2. Log on to ExchangeOne with the EXAdmin account. Backups require either Local Administrator or Backup Operators access rights. The EXAdmin account provides both.

3. Open Windows Explorer and move to the E: drive. Create a folder called **Temp** in the root of E: drive. You will use this folder to temporarily store data during the restore operation.

4. Before you can perform a restore, you must set the database so that it can be overwritten by the restore. Use the following cmdlet in the Exchange Management Shell:

```
set-mailboxdatabase "mailbox database" -allowfilerestore $true
```

5. Open the Exchange Management Console and navigate to Server Configuration | Mailbox.

6. Right-click Mailbox Database in the details pane and select Dismount Database from the shortcut menu. Confirm your operation by clicking Yes. Your database is ready to be restored.

7. Launch NT Backup. Use Start Menu | All Programs | Accessories | System Tools | Backup.

8. Click the Restore And Manage Media tab.

9. Use the tree pane to expand File and then expand FirstExchangeBackup.bkf.

10. Select ExchangeOne. Note that because you are on the same server that the backup originated from, you cannot change the restore location.

11. Click Start Restore.

12. In the Restoring Database Store window, note that you now have the option to restore the database to a different server. Because you only have one Exchange server at this time, you will restore to the original server. Type **E:\Temp** in the Temporary Location For Log And Patch Files entry.

13. Select Last Restore Set, and then select Mount Database After Restore.

14. Click OK to begin the restore. You can view the report when the restore is complete. Close NTBackup when done. You can review the status of the database in the Exchange Management Console.

15. Reset the database so that it will automatically mount at startup. Use the following cmdlet:

```
set-mailboxdatabase "mailbox database" -mountatstartup $true
```

The restore operation is complete.

Quick Check

1. What are the two locations where you can recover mailboxes?

2. How do you recover a mailbox from the Dumpster?

3. How do you recover a mailbox from a backup?

4. What are recovery storage groups and why do you need to use them?

5. When can you use the Recovery Storage Groups tool?

6. What tools does Exchange 2007 provide for disaster recovery?

Quick Check Answers

1. The two locations are the Dumpster and offline backups.

2. To recover a mailbox from the Dumpster, you must have the Exchange Organization Administrator role. Then, you can use either the Exchange Management Console or the Shell. In the Console, go to Recipient Configuration | Disconnected Mailbox. In the Action pane, click Connect To Server, right-click the name of the server to connect to, and click Connect. This will list all of the disconnected mailboxes on that server. Then use the Connect Mailbox Wizard to complete the operation. In the Shell, you use the **get-MailboxStatistics** cmdlet.

3. You will need to proceed through the use of a recovery storage group (RSG). But, first you must create the RSG. To do so, you will need the Exchange Server Administrator role and local Administrators rights on the server where you will create the RSG. Then you will need the Exchange Recipient Administrator role to recover the mailbox. Mailbox recovery is performed through the **restore-Mailbox** cmdlet. There is no graphical interface to restore a mailbox.

4. Recovery storage groups are special storage groups that allow you to mount mailbox databases and extract information from those databases. You can use RSGs to recover data from either a backup or a database copy (using LCR or CCR, see Lesson 1 in Chapter 6). Because you mount these databases into the RSG, they do not affect existing user databases or existing user mailbox data.

5. You can use RSG tools in the event of a complete database loss, to repair a secondary copy of a database, to recover a mailbox database if the original server is not available, to perform content recovery from a mailbox, or to locate historical information.

6. Exchange provides the database recovery management tool, database troubleshooter, the Exchange server database utility tool and, the information store integrity checker tool for recovery purposes.

Chapter Summary

- When you do create your backup strategy, you will need to plan for the following:
  - ❑ Identify what you need to back up based on the type of system or data you are backing up.
  - ❑ Select the appropriate backup solution for the content to back up.
  - ❑ Plan backup schedules, backup types, and retention duration for each backup category.
  - ❑ Plan for media management.
  - ❑ Test the overall backup solution to ensure that it meets your objectives.
  - ❑ Implement your backup solution in production.

- You will remember that databases are stored in ESE files with the .edb extension and transaction logs are stored in .log files. The .edb files cannot exceed 16 terabytes, but you should keep them much smaller or they will take forever to restore in the event of a disaster.

- To protect systems, you must protect the system volume and the System State. You should also perform Automated System Restore backups on an ongoing basis. ASRs allow you to recover systems in one single step and are therefore very valuable in any recovery strategy.

- You can recover mailboxes from two locations: the Dumpster or from backups. Ideally, you will recover them from the Dumpster because you will identify the problem before it is emptied. This also saves you from having to locate the backup that contains the mailbox.

- Exchange mailboxes can only be recovered within the same Active Directory forest they originated from. You cannot use the **restore-Mailbox** command to move mailboxes between forests.

- Recovery storage groups are special storage groups that allow you to mount mailbox databases and extract information from those databases. You use two tools to work with and create RSGs: the Exchange Management Shell or the Exchange Server Disaster Recovery Analyzer Tool (Exchange DRA).

- To perform a Dial Tone Recovery (DTR), you create an empty database on a server to replace the failed database. This provides users with the ability to use e-mail, but not the ability to have access to their historical database. Obviously, using a DTR is an emergency procedure that you use when nothing else is available.

■ To rebuild the search catalog and resynchronize it with database contents, you must stop the Exchange Search Service, delete the old catalog files, and then restart the service. Restarting the service will force the catalog to re-index the database contents.

Case Scenarios

In the following case scenarios, you will apply what you have learned about Exchange disaster recovery. You can find answers to the questions in this scenario in the "Answers" section at the end of this book.

Case Scenario 1: Plan a Backup Schedule for Exchange Datasets

The Graphics Design Institute has been planning their Exchange migration for some time. They are ready to install their first Exchange 2007 servers, but before they do so, they want to make sure they have a proper system and data protection policy in place. They are trying to decide whether they need a third-party backup tool or whether the default backup tool in Windows Server 2003 will be sufficient. Because they plan to implement a Simple Organization type of medium size, they will have one main Exchange server running all four coexistence roles. The Edge Transport server they intend to use will be hosted by an application service provider.

They turn to you, the messaging professional, to assist them in their choice. Specifically, they ask you the following questions:

1. What do they need to protect on their internal Exchange server?
2. What, if anything, do they need to protect elsewhere?
3. Do they need to protect information on the Edge server?

What do you answer?

Case Scenario 2: Plan a Recovery Solution for Exchange Mailboxes

The Graphics Design Institute is almost ready to deploy Exchange 2007, but before they do so, they want to be fully prepared with their disaster recovery solution. Their Exchange administrator is having a hard time understanding the concept of the recovery storage group. One question in particular is bothering her: How does an RSG differ from a normal storage group? She turns to you, the messaging professional, in an attempt to clarify the differences between these two storage group types. What do you answer?

Case Scenario 3: Protect Client Access Servers

The Graphics Design Institute is concerned about the protection of their Client Access Server role. They know that this role will host a series of Web sites and virtual folders that will provide all client-facing services. Their Exchange administrator read somewhere that it will be difficult to retain customization data if the CAS role is lost. Being a graphics design institute, they are very concerned about the presentation of the Web sites users will interact with. Therefore, they want to customize sites such as the OWA site to have their own look and feel.

They turn to you, the messaging professional, to help them understand just what they can customize and how they need to protect the customized data on their Web sites. What do you respond?

Suggested Practices

It is difficult to practice backup and recovery with Exchange Server without access to a full infrastructure, but you can do so if you prepare a virtual environment as outlined in the Introduction. You should then use the ExchangeOne.treyresearch.net server to practice backup and restore operations for each of the different services it runs.

Chapter 6
Plan for Business Continuity

For many organizations both small and large, Exchange systems have become mission-critical systems. This is not surprising, because users are so focused on e-mail and communications in general. For many users, the inbox is the sole repository for any and all information they work with.

As a system administrator, your responsibility is to make sure the e-mail systems are always up and running, If they are not, do not worry—you will be the first to know. And then you will have to rebuild or repair the system while everyone is nagging you because they cannot get anything done without e-mail.

This is understandable in a way; you might even agree that it is hard to do any business today without e-mail. That is why Microsoft has put so much effort into making Exchange even more resilient in Exchange Server 2007. You have already seen how to protect both Exchange systems and Exchange data in Chapter 5, "Plan for High Availability Implementation." Now you will discover how to make Exchange downtime a thing of the past and turn it into nothing more than a bad memory by using Exchange's new high availability features—features that can be implemented by organizations large and small.

Organizations traditionally rely on the built-in measures Microsoft provides through the Windows Server operating system to protect Exchange servers. With Exchange Server 2007, some of these traditional measures have changed to help provide better support for high availability and business continuity. In addition, Exchange itself offers new availability features that, together with those Windows Server offers, can provide even better results. In fact, each server role relies on a different feature set to provide high availability, data protection, and system redundancy:

- **Edge Transport Servers** Can be protected through round robin Domain Name System (DNS) strategies. This means the DNS server will provide load balancing by rotating the load between multiple DNS Mail Exchanger (MX) records targeting different ET systems.

■ **Hub Transport Servers** Provide their own redundancy through new built-in role features and through the Active Directory service where their configuration is stored. The same redundancy feature has been built into the Mail Submission Service on Mailbox servers. All you need to do is deploy more than one HT in your organization. In Service Pack 1, you can also use NLB to make client connections to HT systems redundant.

■ **Client Access Servers** Use the Network Load Balancing (NLB) service or third-party hardware-based network load balancing. This service transforms a series of identical servers into one single set of resources and automatically redirects users to the best available resource in the set.

■ **Mailbox Servers** Use either new built-in features or Microsoft Failover Clusters (MFC) for data storage protection.

■ **Unified Messaging Servers** Use more than one server deployed into the same dial plan. Then you use round robin DNS to provide load balancing for the Voice over IP (VoIP) gateways that route calls to the UM, but this only provides load balancing for the initial connection. After a client is connected, it remains on the same server until the connection is severed. In addition, VoIP gateway can use DNS to retrieve the list of names of all the servers in a dial plan. When the call is routed, if the initial UM does not accept it, the VoIP gateway will automatically move on to the next server in the list.

As you can see, each server role uses its own protection mechanism. But, the most important features for Exchange 2007 protection are focused on the Mailbox Server role. Exchange 2007 offers three new scenarios for mailbox protection, and with the release of Service Pack 1 adds one more data protection capability:

■ Data protection for single servers through the Local Continuous Replication (LCR) model. LCR uses asynchronous transaction log shipping to generate and maintain a second copy of the storage groups contained on the server to a second set of disks. The features that make LCR work include log shipping, log replay, and a manual switch from the production to the copy of the storage group data.

■ Data and service protection for clustered servers through the Cluster Continuous Replication (CCR) model. CCR relies on the Failover Cluster capability of Windows Server 2003 or Windows Server 2008 to create one of two clustered solutions: a two-node cluster in a single site or a geographically dispersed two-node cluster. It then relies on log shipping to generate and maintain a second copy of the storage groups contained on the source server to a set of disks located on a second or target server. Therefore, CCR can provide site resiliency as well as service and data protection when the cluster nodes are located in different sites. Note that CCR uses direct-attached storage in its cluster configuration.

- Additional data protection for continuous replication models through the Transport Dumpster. When either LCR or CCR is configured on an MB system, Hub Transport servers will automatically defer the deletion of e-mails in their queues. This applies only to e-mails that are destined for storage groups located on either LCR- or CCR-enabled MB systems. In the event of a replica failure, e-mail in the Transport Dumpster can be redelivered if replication could not be completed.

- Data protection for either single or clustered servers through the Standby Continuous Replication (SCR) model. SCR is new with Service Pack 1, but it continues to rely on log shipping to generate and maintain a second copy of the storage groups contained on the source server to a set of disks located on a second, standby server.

Exam Tip   Like the original release of Exchange, the original release of the exam does not include the Standby Continuous Replication model. However, SCR is an important new feature that must be included in any environment that wants to make the most of Exchange 2007 business continuity.

Along with these data protection scenarios, Exchange 2007 offers two service protection scenarios.

- Service protection for clustered servers through the Single Copy Cluster (SCC) model. SCC relies on the traditional Failover Cluster model, linking server nodes together to provide service continuity. SCCs rely on shared storage and maintain a single copy of the storage groups. You can, however, use the SCR from SP1 to create and maintain a second, standby copy of the storage groups maintained by an SCC.

- Service protection for clustered servers through the Standby Cluster model. In a Standby Cluster, the MB role is not clustered, but is instead hosted on a cluster node. In the event of a failure, you can provision another node into the cluster and therefore fail over the service.

To make the right decision to protect your MB and other server roles, you need to fully understand what each protection model offers as well as understand the native protection features built into Windows Server.

Exam Tip   The new protection features of Exchange 2007—LCR, CCR, SCC, and SCR—only apply to the MB role. No other role can be protected by these features. When MB systems use either SCC or CCR, they are referred to as clustered mailbox servers (CMSs). CMS configurations using CCR support a maximum of 2 nodes in a cluster even though Windows Server can support up to 8- or 16-node clusters. You can, however, create a 3-node cluster when you introduce a voting node to a CCR configuration. SCC configurations can include up to 8 or 16 nodes. Most organizations use only two nodes in an Exchange cluster.

Data Protection

Data protection in Exchange 2007 is provided through Continuous Replication, which is based on log shipping. Microsoft has built asynchronous replication of transaction logs into Exchange 2007, which works like this:

1. Two data stores are created, one active and one passive. Both need to use redundant disk access hardware to provide true resiliency. In addition, each should have separate physical disks for both the logs and the database. In the best configuration, four disk sets are required. (See Chapter 2, "Planning Deployments," for RAID configuration recommendations.)

2. Transactions are recorded in the transaction log of the active store and then committed to the database. When this process is complete, the transaction logs are closed.

3. The passive store pulls the active store's closed transaction log to get a copy. In Exchange 2007, transaction log size has been reduced to 1 MB instead of the 5 MB of previous releases to support this. This copy is placed into an inspection folder.

4. The passive copy inspects the log for consistency and then moves it to its final destination.

5. The log is committed to the passive store's database, keeping it in tune with the active copy within a slight delay.

That is it in a nutshell. In the Local Continuous Replication model, the active and passive stores are located on the same server using redundant disk access hardware. In the Cluster Continuous Replication model, the active and passive stores are attached to different servers, providing redundancy for the service as well as for the data. When the CCR servers are in a different site, they also provide site-level redundancy.

Using continuous replication means changes in the way you configure the hardware for your Mailbox servers. In previous releases, Exchange Server was mostly focused on writing to transaction logs and not reading them; read/writes were focused on the actual database. With Exchange 2007 and continuous replication, transaction logs are written and read, creating much more input and output than with previous releases (see Figure 6-1). This means you need to have very fast hardware, which explains in part the move to 64-bit. The x64 servers provide much faster I/O than their 32-bit counterparts. You also need to reconsider your random array of independent disks (RAID) configurations. Many people use RAID 5 or RAID 6 for Exchange data stores, but both suffer in performance in Exchange 2007. Microsoft has found that RAID 10—a combination of striped and mirrored disk sets—provides much better performance for Exchange 2007.

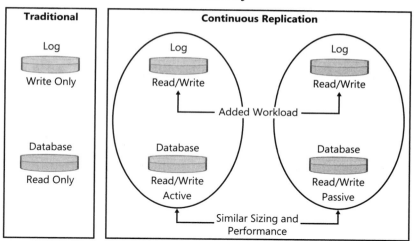

Figure 6-1   Traditional versus continuous replication disk sets

---

IMPORTANT   Recovery Objectives

When you prepare your protection strategy, you need to keep two objectives in mind. The first is the recovery time objective (RTO) which is the amount of time within which a failed service must be brought back online before there is a serious consequence for the organization. The second will be your recovery point objective (RPO) which refers to the amount of time since the last good backup was created. With Continuous Replication, the RPO can seriously be reduced which can help your organization limit the impact of outages. Consider this when you plan your protection strategy.

Design for High Availability

As you can see, redundancy in Exchange 2007 is based on both data protection and service continuity. When you plan your Exchange deployment, you should plan to integrate both features within each site in your network where Exchange server roles will be deployed. In some cases, you can provide redundancy by including an additional server role in a remote site; in other cases, you might want to include redundancy within the remote site itself.

In the best redundancy configurations, you will also include site-level redundancy in the deployment plan. Site-level redundancy can be based on your own resources or on hosted resources provided by application service providers (ASPs). Everything depends on the number of users you must support in your Exchange Organization, your Organization type, the criticality of the e-mail service to your business, and the resources you have at your disposal when you create your Exchange architecture.

For this reason, the lessons in this chapter will cover the following scenarios:

- High availability concepts comparing NLB with Failover Clustering
- Single Copy Clusters for local service continuity
- DNS round robin configurations
- Data redundancy strategies
- Local Continuous Replication for local data protection
- Cluster Continuous Replication for local or remote data protection and service continuity
- Standby Continuous Replication
- Upgrading existing back-end mailbox server clusters to Exchange 2007

When you complete this chapter, you should be able to plan for redundancy at any level for any Exchange Organization type.

Exam objectives in this chapter:
- Plan the service's high availability implementation.
- Plan a data redundancy implementation.

Before You Begin

To complete the lessons in this chapter, you must have the following:

- A virtual machine setup as outlined in the Introduction under "Virtual Machine Environments."

- Use the Exchange Server 2007 virtual machine from Microsoft to review the configuration options for pre-installed computers.

- Use the newly created virtual environment you set up to test high availability operations. For the exercises in this chapter, you will need access to the Active Directory server and the multi-disk Exchange server, ExchangeLCR.

Additionally, if you have the required resources, you should create enough virtual machines to test each of the high availability measures discussed in this chapter.

Lesson 1: Plan for Service Continuity

Estimated lesson time: 40 minutes

When you plan for highly available systems, you must first determine which situations can cause systems to become unavailable. Most often, people think of some form of system failure as a cause for unavailability, and while it is true that system failures–hardware, software, power, networking, storage, or other components–are often the cause of a system becoming unavailable, they are not they only causes. For example, maintenance–both scheduled and unscheduled–can cause system unavailability. Software updates can also cause system unavailability because many of them require a system reboot. Maintenance-related service shutdowns are usually referred to as scheduled outages. Failures are usually referred to as unscheduled outages.

You have already seen how to plan for some forms of continuity–for example, with device redundancy in the form of redundant disk subsystems, as discussed in Chapter 2. You have also seen how to protect both systems and data through backup technologies in Chapter 5. Now you need to plan for high availability, making sure that no matter the cause, your systems will remain available as much as possible. Of course, you will have to consider your actual requirements and realistically compare them to the budget you have access to to help determine which level of availability you can aim for. For example, few organizations have the means to avoid a complete site loss and maintain system availability during such a loss, but given the right budget, you could create redundant sites that would provide such levels of availability no matter which situation you face.

The first step in configuring and budgeting for availability is to learn which features Exchange provides to support it. As soon as you have a better understanding of these capabilities, you can design and deploy the appropriate solution for your environment. Table 6-1 outlines examples of availability goals and the feature set that Exchange 2007 offers to support it.

Exam Tip Several features in Exchange 2007 are completely different from previous versions in terms of availability. Keep this in mind as you read this chapter.

Throughout the planning and deployment process, your goal will be to eliminate single points of failure as much as possible.

Table 6-1   Availability Goals and Exchange 2007 Features

Availability Goal	Supporting Exchange Feature
Data archival	Archival is supported through backup, along with long-term tape archival.
Data Loss in individual mailbox	Data loss is protected by the Dumpster on the server, and can be retrieved by the user over the default 14-day period.
Individual mailbox loss	Mailbox loss is protected by the Dumpster on the server, and can be retrieved by an administrator over the default 30-day period or until the next full backup.
Mail-enabled account loss	Lost accounts can be recovered from tombstone data in Active Directory or through Active Directory backup, or they can be regenerated through Exchange Management Shell scripts.
Individual mailbox disk failure	Disk failures are protected through RAID implementations on the local disk set.
Mailbox database failure	Database failures can be protected through continuous replication—either local or cluster-based—as well as standby replication in SP1. You can also rely on the Dial Tone feature if no replica set is available, and then restore the database from backup.
Mailbox disk set failure	Disk sets can be protected through continuous replication, either local or cluster-based as well as standby replication in SP1.
Server failure—hardware or software: any role	To protect from hardware and software failures, rely on Windows Server high availability features or rely on high availability features that are built into the server role.

Table 6-1   Availability Goals and Exchange 2007 Features

Availability Goal	Supporting Exchange Feature
Server failure—hardware or software: Mailbox server	Mailbox servers can be protected from failures through the Single Copy Cluster or Cluster Continuous Replication with local or remote site targets.
Site failure: Mailbox server	Entire sites can be protected through Cluster Continuous Replication with a remote site target. You can also use a Dial Tone in an alternate site while restoring the database with the portability feature. You can also rely on Standby Continuous Replication to a remote site in SP1.

Plan Single Site Service Availability

When you plan for high availability, you should start by ensuring that the e-mail service will be available at all times in your organization. Within a single site, service availability for the ET, HT, UM, and CAS roles relies on creating several servers that have the same or similar configuration and are ready to continue providing the service if one of them fails or is taken offline for maintenance purposes.

For the MB server, single site service availability relies on the Single Copy Cluster, creating two or more server nodes in a clustered environment to take over the service workload if the node offering the service fails or is taken down for maintenance.

You also need to ensure that redundancy is built into your supporting services. To ensure redundancy for UM servers, you should ensure that more than one IP gateway is available so that there is no single point of failure. For Active Directory, you should have more than one domain controller. Ideally, you will also have at least two domain controllers running the Global Catalog Service. Therefore, to provide full service redundancy, your single site should include at least two servers running each role within the site (see Figure 6-2). The overall number of servers you plan to deploy will depend on the size of the organization and the number of users you need to service. Keep in mind that MB systems running in an SCC cannot host any other roles. Therefore, if the size of your organization dictates that you must co-host services on the same server and you intend to run an SCC, you will only be able to co-host three roles: HT, CAS, and UM.

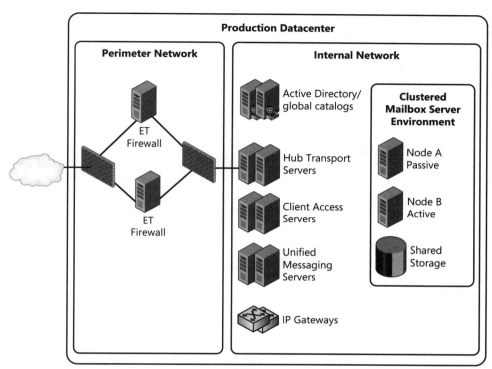

Figure 6-2   Providing single site service redundancy

Use Windows Server High Availability Services

One of the areas that can add service resiliency is service clustering. Windows Server 2003 includes built-in support for two types of clusters:

- **Network Load Balancing (NLB)**   This service provides high availability and scalability for IP-based services (both TCP and UDP) and applications by combining up to 32 servers into a single cluster. Clients access the NLB cluster by accessing a single IP address for the entire group. NLB services automatically redirect the client to the first available server. Members of an NLB cluster are usually servers that include identical configurations and use direct-attached storage. Each member runs identical services at the same time. NLB clusters are often referred to as front-end clusters.

- **Windows Server Failover Clusters (WSFC)**   This service provides resilience through resource failover: If a node fails, the client is automatically transferred to another node in the cluster. Windows Server 2003 supports up to 8 nodes while Windows Server 2008 supports up to 16 nodes. Nodes or member servers are linked to shared storage. The service is installed on each node, but usually runs from only one node at a time. If an issue occurs, the service is moved or failed over from one node to another to continue providing service to users. The failover process is transparent to users. Standby Failover Clusters include several nodes, but the service is installed only on one node. In the case of a failure, the service must be installed on another node before service can resume for end users. Failover Clusters are often referred to as back end-clusters.

These two clustering services work together to provide a complete service structure (see Figure 6-3).

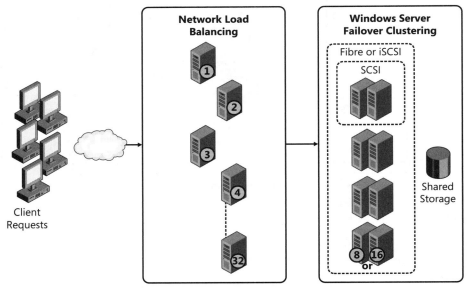

Figure 6-3   Protecting n-tier services with Windows Server

You build resiliency solutions based on these two technologies along with technologies included within the service you want to protect. Keep the following in mind:

- When protecting stateless systems or systems that provide read-only services, use Network Load Balancing. For example, CAS roles provide read-only services.

- When protecting stateful systems or systems that provide read-write services, use Failover Clustering. For example, MB roles provide read-write services.

The formula is simple: systems that do not persist data rely on NLB and systems that persist data rely on Failover Clustering.

Exam Tip   Remember that in Exchange 2007, Failover Clustering is not installed through the Windows interface, but through Exchange setup. Therefore, no manual tasks are required for cluster setup as with previous versions of Exchange. Also note that Failover Clusters can only be installed on either Windows Server Enterprise or Datacenter Editions.

MORE INFO   Failover Clusters in depth

For more information on Failover Clusters and their configuration, see *Windows Server 2008: The Complete Reference* by Ruest and Ruest (McGraw-Hill Osborne, 2008). This book outlines how to build a complete service redundancy solution based on built-in Windows features.

Implement the Single Copy Cluster

The Single Copy Cluster represents the traditional approach used in previous versions of Exchange to protect back-end mailbox services. As with previous versions, an SCC only provides protection for the mailbox service itself. Because members of the SCC access shared storage and only a single copy of the storage groups is on the shared storage, the SCC does not provide data protection services.

In an SCC, the Failover Cluster service from Windows Server moves the network identity of the MB from one node to another. This is because during the SCC creation process, you create a network identity for the MB that is independent of the nodes that make up the cluster. You can then move this independent network identity from one node to another without interrupting the service for end users. Because storage is shared, you do not need to move storage groups from one node to another; instead, the Failover Cluster service disconnects the resources from one node and reconnects them to another during the failover process.

Failover occurs when a service failure is detected by the Failover Cluster service. Failures can be related to hardware components for the node, network connectivity, or even maintenance purposes. In the case of a failure, the active node—the node providing the service—is taken offline. Then the passive node—the node waiting to provide service—is activated. Failback occurs when the service is returned to the original node. Cluster configurations normally assign a principal node as the active node. When this is done, the Failover Cluster service will endeavor to assign the service to this principal node whenever possible.

As with the installation of the SCC, operation of the SCC has been moved from the Windows Cluster Administrator to the Exchange Management Shell and, in Service Pack 1, to the Exchange Management Console. In previous versions, all cluster administration was performed from the Cluster Administrator. Although you can run an SCC with up to 8 or 16 nodes in various active and passive node configurations, you must have at least 1 passive node in each SCC cluster. Note that even in multi-node cluster configurations, Exchange 2007 supports only one active and one passive node for the SCC. Therefore, most organizations create two-node SCC configurations, with one active node and one passive node (see Figure 6-4).

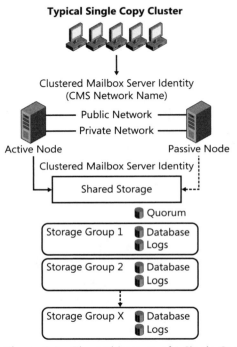

Typical Single Copy Cluster

Clustered Mailbox Server Identity
(CMS Network Name)

Public Network
Private Network

Active Node   Passive Node

Clustered Mailbox Server Identity

Shared Storage

Quorum

Storage Group 1   Database
Logs

Storage Group 2   Database
Logs

Storage Group X   Database
Logs

Figure 6-4   The architecture of a Single Copy Cluster

Multiple CMS Installations per SCC   You can create quite a few different cluster configurations for SCCs. Use the following rules:

- Windows Server Failover Clusters can host a maximum of 8 nodes in Windows Server 2003 and 16 nodes in Windows Server 2008.
- Each Single Copy Cluster requires at least one passive node.
- You need a minimum of two nodes each time you install a clustered mailbox server.
- Each instance of a CMS requires an active node and a passive node.
- A passive node can be shared between two CMS installations.

- Shared passive nodes can only provide failover for a single CMS installation at a time.

- If you share a passive node between two or more CMS installations, it can become a single point of failure for that installation of CMS.

To avoid all single points of failure, design configurations that pair active nodes and passive nodes for each CMS installation, with a maximum of four installations per cluster. This gives you the best availability option in a multiple-installation SCC, but it is also the most expensive option. You could have a slightly lower level of availability in a cluster that has six active nodes and two shared passive nodes, but it would be considerably less expensive because you would have two more nodes working on an ongoing basis. In the end, your availability requirements, the number of users you need to service, and your budget will determine which configuration, if any, you will select.

IMPORTANT   Potential multi-CMS installation issues

When you create an SCC with multiple instances of CMS, you may run into a known issue related to the ability to create mailbox databases on any but the first instance of CMS. You can create the new mailbox on the first instance and then move it to another instance. For more information, please read Knowledge Base article 928811 at *http://support.microsoft.com/?kbid=928811*.

Single Copy Cluster Requirements   Single Copy Clusters are composed of all of the elements of a Failover Cluster. All of the hardware components selected to create a Failover Cluster must be listed in the Cluster Solution category of the Microsoft Windows Server Catalog of Tested Products. You can find the catalog at *http://go.microsoft.com/fwlink/?linkid=17219*.

You must install the Failover Cluster service before you can perform the Exchange SCC installation. When the cluster is ready, install Exchange on the nodes selected for this service. This will automatically install the cluster-aware version of Exchange 2007. SCC components should include:

- At least two server nodes configured with identical components, including number of processors and cores, amount of memory, number of network interface cards (NIC), and local and/or remote disks. Cluster nodes can boot off remote storage, but are usually configured with direct-attached disks for system drives. Both nodes must be running at least Windows Server 2003 Enterprise Edition and must be joined to the same Active Directory domain. You can use Windows Server 2008 Enterprise Edition if you are installing Exchange 2007 SP1. These nodes cannot be running the domain controller role and must have the Failover Cluster service installed.

- In Windows Server 2003, you will need to create a domain account for the cluster service. This service account must also be local administrator on each node of the cluster. In Windows Server 2008, the cluster service runs under the Local-System account; therefore, you do not need to pre-create a custom service account.

- Shared storage accessed either through SCSI, iSCSI, or Fibre Channel connectivity. All disk sets must be available to the cluster before the installation of Exchange. The shared storage should be partitioned into multiple disk sets that include:

  ❑ One small—usually no more than 1 gigabyte (GB)—disk set for the cluster's quorum resource, which is the resource that maintains the cluster's configuration data in the quorum log. It also includes the cluster database checkpoint and resource checkpoints. The volume this disk set creates is usually named Quorum. You can also use a Majority Node Set (MNS) quorum or an MNS quorum with File Share Witness (FSW) to create the cluster. In this case, the quorum does not have to reside on shared storage. Most organizations rely on a shared storage quorum because it is the traditional configuration for single-site clusters. However, if the quorum resource fails, the entire cluster will fail.

  ❑ Two disk sets per storage group if you are following best practices and assigning one mailbox database per storage group. The first, smaller disk set will store the transaction logs; the second, larger disk set will store the mailbox database. Both disk sets should be empty before installation and installation should be performed into appropriate folders. Refer to Lesson 1 in Chapter 2 for more information on disk set configurations.

- At least two network interface cards (NICs) per server. The first provides end-user access to the clustered service through a public network connection. The second provides cluster heartbeat services through a private, intra-cluster network connection. You can create multiple public connections by adding NICs to each system, but only one private connection is required. It is, however, a best practice to create at least one public connection as a mixed network, supporting both the public and the private connection to ensure complete component redundancy.

❑ Private network connection addresses must be static IP addresses and must be on a different subnet than public network connections. Organizations usually use 10.10.10.x as the base address for private NICs with a subnet mask of 255.255.255.0—unless, of course, they use the 10.x.x.x network for their public addresses, in which case they must use a different range for the private network. Private NICs do not require DNS settings or a gateway to function. If more than one private network connection is created on the cluster, use different network addresses for each.

❑ Public network addresses should be static as well and should be part of your standard public internal IP address scheme.

❑ One additional public internal IP address will be required for the cluster itself as well as one for each instance of SCC in the cluster.

❑ In Windows Server 2008 running Exchange 2007 SP1, you can use dynamic IPv6 addresses for both the private and the public networks.

BEST PRACTICES **Windows Server 2003 geographically dispersed clusters**

SCC is usually deployed in a single site. However, Windows Server 2003 also supports *geoclusters*, or clusters that are geographically dispersed into different sites. You can install SCC into this cluster configuration, but when you do, your cluster must have round-trip latency of fewer than 0.5 seconds. All network connections must be configured in a virtual LAN (VLAN) switch. In addition, the link between the nodes making up the cluster must appear as a single point-to-point connection to the Windows operating system otherwise, the cluster installation will fail. Finally, all server nodes must be within the same Active Directory site—a site that spans all of the physical locations hosting a cluster node—for the cluster to work.

■ A network name for the clustered service—in this case the Mailbox Server role. This network identity is called a clustered mailbox server. This network name must be recorded within DNS as a Host (A) record and must not include more than 15 characters to provide NetBIOS naming compatibility for the CMS. One Host (A) record is required for each CMS. In addition, an independent Host (A) record is required for the cluster itself. If you are using the Windows dynamic DNS service, these records will be created automatically during setup.

MORE INFO **Exchange and DNS**

More information on the interaction of Exchange and DNS can be found in Knowledge Base article 322856 at *http://support.microsoft.com/?kbid=322856*. In addition, Knowledge Base article 240942 provides information on how to configure node host names properly at *http://support.microsoft.com/?kbid=240942*.

■ Installed code for the shared service—in this case MB. This installed code will also install a custom component for communication between Exchange and the cluster service: Exres.dll. This dynamic-link library (DLL) is part of the cluster-aware version of Exchange 2007.

■ Installation on each cluster node must use identical file and folder paths for the cluster to work.

IMPORTANT Exchange Single Copy Cluster requirements

You cannot install SCC into a cluster if that cluster already includes Exchange Server 2003, Exchange 2000 Server, or any version of SQL Server. You can run either SQL Server Express Edition or Microsoft Access on the cluster provided that either of these applications is not clustered and runs as a stand-alone application.

In addition, previous versions of Exchange required the Microsoft Distributed Transaction Coordinator (MSDTC) to be installed as a cluster resource along with Exchange for the cluster to work. Exchange 2007 eliminates this requirement and has no dependencies on MSDTC at all.

■ During the Exchange installation process a cluster group containing all of the resources tied to the clustered Exchange installation will automatically be created. For example, the quorum resource—a core component of the cluster itself— will not be within this Exchange group, but it will be within the default cluster group. The default cluster group will also include the cluster IP address and the cluster Network Name. Grouped resources failover from one node to another as one single unit. The Exchange group will include network resources such as the clustered mailbox server network identity and its corresponding IP address, shared disk resources, and the Exchange System Attendant and Exchange Information Store services. The Exchange group will also include Exchange storage groups and a new cluster resource called the Microsoft Exchange Database Instance.

■ When the installation is complete, you must use Cluster Administrator to configure the dependencies of the Exchange database instances on physical disk resources for the cluster to work properly. See *http://technet.microsoft.com/ en-us/library/aa997696.aspx* for more information.

Windows clusters rely on the shared nothing disk model. This means that when a node is the active holder for the clustered service, it has exclusive access to the shared disks. The passive node cannot access the disks until it is given control of the clustered service. This occurs in the failover process. During this process, disks are disconnected from the failing node and reconnected to the node taking over the service.

When administrators perform the failover procedure, it is called a handoff. In Exchange 2007 SCCs, handoffs are performed through the **move-ClusteredMailbox-Server** cmdlet and only through this cmdlet. Do not use the Cluster Administrator to perform these handoffs. In Service Pack 1, you can also use the Exchange Management Console through the Manage Clustered Mailbox Server Wizard to perform this operation. In either case, you will be given the opportunity to provide a reason for the move, allowing you to track managed changes in your Exchange environment.

The Makeup of a Single Copy Cluster Resource Group   Once installed, the SCC group will consist of several resources, including:

- **The Microsoft Exchange Information Store**   Represents the CMS in the cluster resource group. When this resource is online, it enables MAPI traffic to the CMS. Because it is the interface to MAPI traffic for the SCC, this resource can take the entire cluster group offline when it is not available.

- **The Microsoft Exchange System Attendant**   Represents the System Attendant service for the SCC. If it is offline, it does not affect the resource group as a whole. Note that in Exchange 2007, the Information Store no longer has dependencies on the System Attendant.

- **The CMS Network Name**   The DNS name used to reach the clustered resource. If the Network Name is not available, the entire resource group is taken offline.

- **The CMS IP Address**   The IP address linked to the Network Name for the resource group. If the IP address is offline, the entire resource group is offline.

- **The Microsoft Exchange Database Instance**   Represents a database hosted by the cluster. Mounted databases appear as online cluster resources. Offline database resources are dismounted. Database instances cannot be mounted unless the Exchange Information Store is online therefore these instances are dependent on the Information Store. Each database instance must be linked to the appropriate physical disk resource to set appropriate dependencies. Because of their nature, database instances do not affect the Exchange group of resources as a whole.

- **Physical Disk Resources**   Linked to database instances. If a physical disk resource is offline, the database that is linked to it is offline, but the entire resource group continues to provide services. Therefore, you must ensure that physical disk resources are not configured to affect the group as a whole.

As you can see, there are several dependencies in an SCC resource group. The IP address is the starting point for these dependencies, which work as follows:

1. If the IP address is not available, the Network Name is not available.

2. If the Network Name is not available, the Microsoft Exchange Information Store is not available.

3. If the Microsoft Exchange Information Store is not available, the clustered mailbox server is not available.

4. If a specific physical disk resource is not available, the Microsoft Exchange Database Instance linked to that physical disk resource is not available. However, the CMS is still available as a whole.

Therefore, three resources are critical to the group as a whole and one resource type is critical to each database instance.

Recovering from SCC Failures Remember that SCC provides protection for the service only. If the service fails on one node for some reason, it will automatically fail over to its corresponding passive node. In addition, disk set failures affecting physical disk resources only affect their corresponding database instance, allowing the server to continue managing mail, but losing access to any mailboxes within this database instance. According to Microsoft, failure of the entire storage subsystem on an SCC results in outages of one day and average data loss of 12 hours, assuming that you have daily full backups. This is due to the fact that the shared storage configurations required for an SCC is more complex to set up and prepare than the direct-attached storage required by other mailbox service availability configurations such as Cluster Continuous Replication.

But these are not the only outages that can affect the SCC. Table 6-2 outlines some typical outages related to Single Copy Clusters and their potential resolutions.

Because you design SCCs to provide service continuity, you should make sure that you test failover for every instance of CMS you install on the cluster before you provide end-user connections to the instance.

MORE INFO **Performing SCC installations**

More information on the SCC and its installation process can be found at *http://technet.microsoft.com/en-us/library/bb124899.aspx*. Information on how to create an SCC with Windows Server 2008 can be found at *http://technet.microsoft.com/en-us/library/bb629581.aspx*. Information on installing Exchange 2007 SP1 prerequisites on Windows Server 2008 can be found at *http://technet.microsoft.com/en-us/library/bb691354.aspx*.

Table 6-2   Potential SCC Outages

Source of Outage	Triggered Action
Complete failure of active server node	Automatic failover to passive node. Databases mount when their storage comes online.
Complete failure of shared storage for a CMS instance	Service will continue, but no e-mail will be stored. You need to manually rebuild the shared storage.
Complete site failure	Require a third-party replication solution or a CCR installation to protect data.
Node operating system disk failure	Because many node operating system partitions are on direct-attached storage, the cluster will not detect this failure unless it stops the operating system. Then an automatic failover will occur.
Complete failure of public network	The cluster stops responding and you must provide corrective action.
Complete failure of the quorum	Automatic failover to passive node if it can form a quorum. If not, the cluster stops responding and you must provide corrective action.
Complete information store failure	Automatic restart of information store resource. May require manual move if resource fails to restart.
Partial information store failure	No action unless it becomes a complete failure.
Node application disk failure	Because many node application partitions are on direct-attached storage, the cluster will not detect this failure unless it stops the application. Then an automatic failover will occur.
Complete storage group or database access failure	Database instances linked to the storage group are dismounted, but the service continues if other storage groups are available. You must manually repair the storage group.

Table 6-2 Potential SCC Outages

Source of Outage	Triggered Action
Corrupted storage group logs	No automatic action. The corresponding database is broken and must be re-seeded.
Any drive sets in a storage group is out of space	Database instances linked to the drive set are dismounted, but the service continues if other drive sets running other databases are available. You must manually repair the drive set.

MORE INFO   Uninstalling an SCC

Information on removing an SCC from your Exchange infrastructure can be found at *http://technet.microsoft.com/en-us/library/bb124928.aspx.*

MORE INFO   Managing SCC installations

More information on managing an SCC after it is installed can be found at *http://technet.microsoft.com/en-us/library/aa996753.aspx.*

Upgrade an Existing Mailbox Cluster to SP1   You cannot upgrade a clustered back-end mailbox server installation from a legacy version of Exchange to Exchange 2007 because there is no direct upgrade path for any previous version of Exchange. You must create a new cluster and move the mailbox databases from the legacy cluster to the new cluster. This is also the process you must use to upgrade the server nodes to Windows Server 2008 because, again, there is no direct upgrade path from a Windows Server 2003 cluster to one running Windows Server 2008.

You can however upgrade an Exchange 2007 cluster to one running Service Pack 1. Clusters that will be upgraded to SP1 must be running a minimum of Windows Server 2003 Service Pack 2. If not, you must upgrade them to SP2 first.

To perform the upgrade to Exchange SP1, you must install the service pack on a node running the passive role. Because active nodes are actually running the Information Store service, they cannot be upgraded. Therefore, you must begin the upgrade process with the passive node, failover the service to the newly upgraded node, and then install it on the next node. Make sure that each passive node is not only passive for the CMS, but also passive for all other processes, such as the clustering service itself.

To upgrade the passive node to SP1, you must use the command-line version of Setup.com. You cannot perform the upgrade with the graphical version of Setup. Performing this upgrade will cause some downtime on the SCC. If several passive nodes are in the cluster, upgrade them all first. After you upgrade all passive nodes, begin moving the service from the active nodes to the newly upgraded passive nodes. Before you can move the service, you must take all of its components offline. Only then can you move the service. After you move the service, you can bring it online on the newly upgraded node. Then you can upgrade the rest of the nodes. Downtime occurs each time you take the service offline on an active node to move it to an upgraded passive node.

MORE INFO **Upgrade steps for SCCs**

More information on the upgrade process can be found at *http://technet.microsoft.com/en-us/library/bb691226.aspx*.

Implement Load Balancing for CAS and HT Roles

The Mailbox Server role is the only role that relies on the Failover Cluster service for high availability. Other roles require other methods to ensure that they are always available. For example, the Client Access Server role and, with the release of Service Pack 1, the client connections for the Hub Transport Server role, use the Network Load Balancing service to provide service continuity.

Plan for Network Load Balancing Network Load Balancing clusters differ from Failover Clusters in that they do not require special hardware. Each cluster member usually is a system of similar design and configuration, though this is not a requirement for the cluster to work. Any computer that plays a server role and includes at least two network interface cards can be a member of an NLB cluster. However, most organizations implement NLB clusters with identical computers to simplify the configuration and management of the cluster.

Like Failover Clusters, NLB clusters provide service to end users by presenting one IP address that represents a group of computers. Clients connect to this virtual IP address and the NLB service redirects them to a cluster member. Cluster members present stateless information—information that is read-only—to end users. For this reason, a front-end Web service is often the best type of system to include in these clusters, though Terminal Services servers are also good candidates.

If one of the cluster members is taken offline, the NLB service will automatically redirect requests to other members. The redirection process usually takes fewer than 10 seconds because there are no resources to fail over as in the Failover Cluster. Because nothing needs to go offline and then be brought online, the NLB failover process is much faster than its back-end counterpart. When cluster members become available to rejoin the cluster again, NLB simply adds them to the pool of servers and starts redirecting clients to them.

NLB systems usually use a minimum of two NICs each. The first is dedicated to cluster network traffic and the second is for communications with clients and other normal network communications. Cluster network traffic from the member is mostly in the form of a heartbeat signal that is emitted every second and sent to the other members of the cluster. If a member does not send a heartbeat within a time span of five seconds, the other members automatically perform a convergence operation to remove the failed member from the cluster and eliminate it from client request redirections. If the cluster faces a heavy load, you can add additional client-facing NICs to provide better throughput.

NLB clusters can either be based on the Windows Server NLB service or third-party, hardware-based load balancers. The latter usually include additional traffic acceleration logic to help improve speeds over WAN links. The NLB service does not include acceleration logic. Its core process is based on a network driver that sits between the network interface card and network traffic. It filters all NLB communications and sets the member server to respond to requests if they have been directed to it.

NLB is very similar to round robin DNS, but provides better fault tolerance. Round robin DNS relies on multiple DNS entries for a specific service. When clients require a connection, the DNS service provides the first address, and then the second, and then the third, and so on. Its main failing is that it cannot check to see whether the address actually resolves. This is one reason why NLB is better. NLB always checks destination addresses to ensure that the server is available when redirecting clients. And, because the NLB service is hosted by every cluster member, there is no single point of failure. There is also immediate and automatic failover of cluster members.

NLB Cluster Modes   NLB clusters operate in either multicast or unicast mode. The default mode is unicast. In this mode, the NLB cluster automatically reassigns the MAC address for each cluster member on the NIC that is enabled in cluster mode. Members that have only one NIC cannot perform member-to-member communications. This is one reason why it is best to install two NICs in each server.

When using the multicast mode, NLB assigns two multicast addresses to the cluster adapter. This mode ensures that all cluster members can automatically communicate with each other because there are no changes to the original MAC addresses. However, some Cisco routers cannot function in this mode because they reject the address resolution protocol (ARP) response sent out by a cluster host. If you use multicast mode in an NLB cluster with Cisco routers, you must manually reconfigure the routers with ARP entries mapping the Cluster IP address to its MAC address.

Another advantage of using two NICs per server is that it allows you to configure one card to receive incoming traffic and the other to send outgoing traffic, making your cluster members even more responsive. In addition, because NLB clusters are often front-end systems communicating with back-end servers, you can configure the NIC that is not bound to the cluster to perform all back-end communications, again improving cluster speeds. Note, however, that most Exchange 2007 NLB implementations rely on unicast mode.

NLB Cluster Affinity Modes   NLB clusters work in affinity modes. Each affinity mode refers to the way NLB load balances traffic and how each cluster member handles that traffic. The three possible affinity modes are:

- Single affinity, which performs load balancing based on the IP address and automatically redirects all requests from the same incoming address to the same cluster member. This means that a user linking to the cluster will be linked to the same cluster member for the duration of the operation—unless, of course, the cluster member fails for some reason. If you use an NLB cluster to provide VPN connections using either L2TP/IPSec or PPTP sessions, you must configure your cluster in single affinity mode to ensure that client requests are always redirected to the same host. Single affinity should also be used for any application that uses sessions lasting over multiple TCP connections to ensure that the entire session is mapped to the same server. You must use single affinity if your client sessions use the secure sockets layer (SSL) to connect to NLB servers.

- No affinity, which performs load balancing based on both the incoming IP address and its port number. With no affinity, clients are redirected to any member in the cluster. No affinity is very useful when supporting calls from networks using network address translation (NAT) from IPv4 transmissions because these networks only present a single IP address to the cluster but rely on TCP ports to control each connection they manage. If you use single affinity mode and you receive a lot of requests from NAT networks, these clients will not profit from the cluster experience because all of their requests will be redirected to the same server. Because a host of clients can sit behind a NAT connection, all of their requests would be serviced by only one cluster member and performance would be poor.

- Class C affinity, which also relies on the IP address only, but is even more granular than single affinity. It ensures that clients using multiple proxy servers to communicate with the cluster are redirected to the same cluster member at all times. You can use Class C affinity in the same situations as single affinity. The difference lies in the granularity of the connection.

Ideally, you will use single affinity for Exchange NLB clusters.

MORE INFO NLB clusters in depth

For more information on NLB clusters and their configuration, see *Windows Server 2008: The Complete Reference* by Ruest and Ruest (McGraw-Hill Osborne). This book outlines how to build a complete service redundancy solution based on built-in Windows features.

Using NLB with Client Access Server Roles   In Exchange 2007, you can use NLB with the Client Access Server role and, if you are running SP1, with the Hub Transport Server role to help persist client connections to HT systems. To use NLB with CAS systems, proceed as follows:

1. Obtain an IP address for the NLB cluster. Several IP addresses can be used, but one is the minimum.

2. Select a fully qualified domain name (FQDN) for the cluster, such as **Mail .Contoso.com**.

3. Create NLB Host (A) records in the Forward Lookup Zone on both internal and external DNS servers.

4. Decide on unicast or multicast modes for the cluster. Unicast provides simpler configuration, but multicast provides easier long-term management.

5. On each cluster member, configure and rename each network connection with appropriate settings. For example, the NLB connection(s) could be named **NLB** and the other could be named **Public**. The NLB NIC should only include an IP address and a subnet mask; for example, you could use 10.10.10.x with 255.255.255.0 as the subnet mask. Gateway and DNS addresses are not required.

6. Configure the binding order for the network interface cards on each member of the NLB cluster. Binding orders are configured in the Advanced Settings in the Network Connections window. Ensure that the public connection(s) appear first

on the list before the NLB connection. This will ensure that public connections link to the servers and that NLB will not interfere with these connections.

7. Use the Network Load Balancing Manager to enable the cluster. On the first CAS server, launch NLB Manager. Use the Create NLB Cluster Wizard to create the cluster. Use the values you prepared earlier to configure the cluster name, IP address, unicast or multicast mode, host parameters, and port rules. Port rules should use single affinity and should be set to support only those ports that support the operation of the CAS role. All other port rules should be deleted. Port rules must be created for the following ports:

   ❑ Port 80 for internal requests that do not require secure communications.

   ❑ Port 443 for external requests that require secure communications.

   ❑ Optionally, port 110 for POP3 requests if they are enabled on your CAS systems.

   ❑ Optionally, port 995 for secure or SSL-enabled POP3 requests if they are enabled on your CAS systems.

   ❑ Optionally, port 143 for IMAP4 requests if they are enabled on your CAS systems.

   ❑ Optionally, port 993 for secure or SSL-enabled IMAP4 requests if they are enabled on your CAS systems.

   ❑ In addition, create appropriate rules to disable all other ports. For example, if you are using only ports 80 and 443, create disable rules for ports 1–79, 81–442, and 444–65,535.

   The last rules ensure that the servers will not respond to requests on ports other than those you have authorized.

8. Add the additional cluster hosts to complete the cluster configuration. Make sure you use the same settings for each host.

BEST PRACTICES   Cluster remote control

It is a best practice not to enable cluster remote control because this control is based on a single password that is not stored in a secure container, but simply assigned to the cluster. If the password is compromised, the operation of the cluster can be in jeopardy.

MORE INFO   TCP/IP port information

For more information on the ports used by Exchange, see Knowledge Base article 176466 at *http://support.microsoft.com/kb/176466*.

The cluster is now operational and can begin accepting requests on the ports you have enabled. However, each cluster member will require an additional public key infrastructure (PKI) Web server certificate to be able to service requests on port 443 through the SSL without generating errors on client systems.

CAS systems have a self-signed certificate installed by default, but this self-signed certificate does not include the new NLB cluster name. Because of this, clients trying to connect through port 443 using the NLB FQDN will get an error. They will still be able to access Outlook Web Access, but Outlook Anywhere and ActiveSync will not work. Therefore, you need to obtain or generate a second certificate, one that will include the NLB cluster name.

BEST PRACTICES **PKI Certificates**

It is always best to obtain PKI certificates from commercial PKI Certificate Authorities because, as part of the trusted roots included in each computer configuration, these certificates are automatically trusted by your client systems. For a list of commercial CAs that provide SAN certificates, see Knowledge Base article number 929395 at *http://support.microsoft.com/kb/929395*. If you choose to generate your own certificate, you will have to add your CA as a trusted authority to each client system that will use your CAS systems. If you choose to generate the certificate internally, use the **New-ExchangeCertificate** cmdlet because the Internet Information Server Manager cannot generate requests for this type of certificate. For more information on working with an internal CA, go to *http://technet2.microsoft.com/windowsserver/en/library/e3d396dd-c141-432b-9e69-50f597061e471033.mspx?mfr=true*.

Because each host in the cluster services two system names—the cluster name and its own server name—you must create a special subject alternative name (SAN) certificate that will include all of the required names to be able to function properly. To facilitate the installation of the certificate, you should include the following names:

- The FQDN of the NLB cluster
- The NetBIOS name of each server in the cluster
- The FQDN of each server in the cluster

After you obtain the new certificate, import it onto each CAS server by using the **Import-ExchangeCertificate** cmdlet. To verify the available certificates on each server, use the **Get-ExchangeCertificate** cmdlet. Finally, you must enable the certificate for each service you need to support. Use the following cmdlet to do so:

```
Enable-ExchangeCertificate -Thumbprint thumbprintID -Services "IIS"
```

This enables the certificate for the OWA, ActiveSync, and Outlook Anywhere. Use the **Get-ExchangeCertificate** cmdlet to obtain the *thumbprintID* for the new certificate.

Add POP and/or IMAP in comma-separated format in the quotation marks to enable the certificate for these additional services.

Export the certificate from the first host server and repeat this process on each other host in the NLB cluster. Use the Certificates Snap-in in a custom Microsoft Management Console to export the certificate from the first host.

To test your new NLB cluster, open a browser on a client and type the FQDN for the NLB cluster. Test both the open and the secure channels by using both HTTP and HTTPS connections. Use NLB Manager to stop each host one at a time while you test client connections to ensure that the cluster is working properly. You can also use Office Outlook 2007 to test Outlook Anywhere connections and the Autodiscover service. To test only the Autodiscover service, open Outlook, and then right-click the Outlook icon in the System Tray while holding down the Ctrl key. Select Test E-Mail AutoConfiguration from the shortcut menu. Finally, use a mobile device to test ActiveSync connectivity. If you do not have a mobile device on hand, use the **Test-ActiveSyncConnectivity** cmdlet.

Using NLB with Hub Transport Server Roles   Hub Transport servers can also rely on the NLB service, but only for client connections because the high availability structure of the HT is built into the role itself. In addition, using NLB for HT roles is only supported in SP1 of Exchange 2007.

The structure of your NLB cluster should be identical to that of a CAS NLB cluster. Basically, you must ensure that your port rules exclude the SMTP, Secure SMTP, and Message Submission ports (25, 465, and 587 respectively); otherwise, the base Send and Receive Connectors for the HT will not work. If you use other ports for SMTP traffic, you must exclude them as well.

Ideally, you would use an NLB cluster for the HT role only when it is hosted on the same server as the CAS role. This way, you can use the NLB configuration (as described earlier) to ensure that the port rules disabling all non-CAS ports are enforced and implemented. In this scenario, your HT role will provide its own load balancing services and the NLB will provide load balancing for the CAS role.

Use DNS Round Robin for Other Exchange Roles

Three other roles require high availability: the Hub Transport Server role, the Edge Transport Server role, and the Unified Messaging Server role. Each uses the Domain Name System round robin system for high availability. In this system, you create multiple servers for each role. Each server's fully qualified domain name is recorded within the DNS service through dynamic update—as long as you are using the built-in Windows Server DNS service, of course. When requests are sent to DNS for connection to any of these three services, DNS will automatically provide a list of all of the corresponding systems to the requester.

For example, say you have four Hub Transport server systems in a site: HTOne, HTTwo, HTThree, and HTFour. When a system requests the address of the HT systems, DNS will provide them in the following order:

- First request: HTOne, HTTwo, HTThree, HTFour
- Second request: HTTwo, HTThree, HTFour, HTOne
- Third request: HTThree, HTFour, HTOne, HTTwo
- Fourth request: HTFour, HTOne, HTTwo, HTThree

As you can see, DNS provides the complete list of all HT systems in a site as a response to an SMTP request, rotating through the list at each request. This does not provide the same level of high availability as an NLB cluster, but as long as you have more than one HT available, your SMTP requests will be serviced.

The same approach is used for both the ET and the UM roles. Each of the three roles supported by DNS round robin requires slightly different approaches for complete high availability.

Provide Availability for the Hub Transport Server Role   As you know, Hub Transport Server role configuration is stored within Active Directory. This means that each time you install another HT system after the first one has been installed and configured in your environment, the new server will automatically pick up its configuration from Active Directory. This is the first part of the availability structure of your HT systems.

The second part is tied to the DNS round robin system. Each time you add a new HT system in your network, its FQDN is stored within DNS. When more than one HT system is present in a site, DNS will automatically provide a list of all of the HT systems to any requester. This ensures that your SMTP requests are always fulfilled.

Provide Availability for the Edge Transport Server Role   The Edge Transport Server role is different from the HT in that it is not part of Active Directory. Its configuration is stored within Active Directory in Application Mode (ADAM) instances. However, the configuration information for these systems can be updated automatically through Edge Subscriptions, ensuring that each ET system can take over for the other(s) if they become unavailable.

Lesson 2 in Chapter 2 outlines how Edge Subscriptions work, but here is a recap: You must export the Edge Subscription file from each of the ET systems you deploy and then import these files into an HT system. This system will store the information in Active Directory and therefore make it available to all other HT systems. From that point on, your ET configurations will be fault tolerant because they rely on the Edge-Sync service to update their configuration from the internal Active Directory through Edge Subscriptions with your HT systems.

Provide Availability for the Unified Messaging Server Role   The UM role also relies on multiple installations with multiple FQDNs in DNS for service continuity. As with the transport servers, DNS will round robin the list of UM systems when requests come in. For true service availability, however, you must create multiple links between your UM servers and the VoIP gateways you use for incoming and outgoing calls routed to the UM systems. Only then will your dial plans provide service continuity if one of your UM systems becomes unavailable.

Table 6-3 summarizes the various strategies you must use to ensure service continuity within the same site.

Table 6-3   Single Site Service Continuity

Exchange Server Role	Service Continuity Strategy
Mailbox Server	Within a single site, you must rely on the Single Copy Cluster running on the Windows Server Failover Cluster service. Failover Clusters require custom hardware and must use shared storage. In an SCC, only one server provides service for a given set of storage groups at a time. Upon failure, the storage group connection is transferred to a passive node of the cluster, which then becomes the active owner of this collection of storage groups.
Client Access Server	Use the Network Load Balancing service to create NLB clusters. NLB clusters do not require custom hardware, but should include identical configurations for each member of the cluster. When servicing requests, each active member of the cluster responds to requests. If one member fails, requests will automatically be redirected to the remaining cluster members.

Table 6-3   **Single Site Service Continuity**

Exchange Server Role	Service Continuity Strategy
Hub Transport Server	Use two availability components: DNS round robin and Active Directory. Configurations are stored in Active Directory to make them available to any HT system. Connections are made highly available through DNS round robin as soon as you have more than one HT in a site. If an HT system fails, connections are automatically redirected towards the remaining HT systems in the site.
Edge Transport Server	Also on two availability components: DNS round robin and Edge Subscriptions. Configurations are stored in ADAM instances on each ET system and are updated automatically through Edge Subscriptions with internal HT systems. Connections are made highly available through DNS round robin as soon as you have more than one ET in a perimeter network. If an ET system fails, connections are automatically redirected toward the remaining ET systems.
Unified Messaging Server	Use two availability components: DNS round robin and multiple VoIP gateway links. Connections are made highly available through DNS round robin as soon as you have more than one UM in a site. If a UM system fails, connections are automatically redirected toward the remaining UM systems. For VoIP gateway links, you should have fault tolerance in your VoIP gateway installations. If you only have one VoIP gateway in your site, it could become a single point of failure.
Active Directory	The Active Directory service provides storage for all aspects of the Exchange configuration. It also includes the Global Address List (GAL) and configuration for each e-mail-enabled user. Active Directory service redundancy is provided by creating multiple domain controllers within the same site.

Table 6-3   Single Site Service Continuity

Exchange Server Role	Service Continuity Strategy
Global Catalog	The Global Catalog includes all of the information related to the GAL as well as Universal Group Memberships, which may double as distribution lists. Provide Global Catalog redundancy by assigning the Global Catalog role to multiple domain controllers within the same site.
DNS	Both internal and external DNS servers must exist for your e-mail system to function properly and for the round robin system to support service continuity. Internally, your DNS servers should be married to your domain controllers and DNS data should be contained within the Active Directory database. This will provide service continuity so long as you have multiple domain controller servers running DNS within the same site. Externally, you must ensure that more than one DNS server is available to service e-mail requests to your systems.

Use this table to prepare service availability within single sites.

Practice: Plan a High Availability Strategy for Exchange Services

In this practice, you will prepare for service continuity through non-Exchange services. This practice consists of a single exercise. Your job is to configure DNS to support Exchange service high availability.

▶ **Exercise: Prepare DNS Round Robin**

Many Exchange services use DNS round robin to provide high availability. DNS round robin works through the inclusion of multiple addresses for the same service. If one address does not respond, the client is directed to another and so on until all addresses have been provided. This task is performed in the DNS console on the Trey Research DC as follows:

1. Make sure the TreyDC.treyresearch.net server is up and running.

2. Log on with the EXAdmin account. This will give you domain administrator credentials.

3. Launch the DNS console using Start Menu | Administrative Tools | DNS.

4. Enable round robin, by clicking TreyDC in the tree pane to select it, right-clicking it, and then selecting Properties.

5. Click the Advanced tab.

6. Verify that the Enable Round Robin option is selected. This option is normally selected by default, but it is always best to be sure. Close the Property sheet.

   You can configure DNS round robin using two methods. The first method relies on multiple Mail Exchanger (MX) records all using the same priority. This lets you address SMTP requests through several addresses. The second method relies on using Host (A) records with multiple IP addresses. This method also lets you address client requests with multiple potential responses. Begin with the first method.

7. Expand the tree pane content to view the Forward Lookup Zones. Right-click TreyResearch.net and then choose New Mail Exchanger (MX).

8. In the New Resource Record dialog box, leave the Host Or Child Domain entry blank and type **ExchangeOnetreyresearch.net** in the Fully Qualified Domain Name (FQDN) Of Mail Server box. Set a mail server priority of 10. Click OK.

9. Repeat the procedure with ExchangeLCR.treyresearch.net and use the same priority setting.

   This creates two records with the same priority. When SMTP requests come in, users will be directed to either server.

10. Use the second configuration method to create multiple Host (A) records. Right-click TreyResearch.net and then select New Host (A).

11. In the New Host dialog box, type **Mail** in the Name (Uses Parent Domain Name If Blank) box and then type the IP address you assigned to ExchangeOne.treyresearch.net, such as **192.168.1.92**. Select the Create Associated Pointer (PTR) Record check box and leave all other options blank.

12. Click Add Host to create the record.

    Note that if you did not configure the Reverse Lookup Zone for this domain, you will get an error message because of the PTR record. This record cannot be created because the zone does not exist.

13. Use the dialog box again to repeat the operation with the IP address of ExchangeLCR.treyresearch.net, such as **192.168.1.94**.

14. Click Done to close the dialog box.

You should now have two Mail.TreyResearch.net records pointing to two different addresses.

15. Review the records you created in DNS and close the DNS console.

Your DNS round robin configuration is complete. Normally, in a production environment, you would not use both methods but would choose one of the two.

Quick Check

1. Your client insists on using the Single Copy Cluster and also wants to minimize the number of servers that will be deployed. Which server role is supported in an SCC and cannot host any other roles?

2. Which cluster implementation does not provide data protection services and why? How many nodes does Exchange 2007 support in this cluster mode?

3. Which resources are part of the SCC group after you install it? Name at least four.

4. What are the three possible affinity modes for the NLB cluster and which is recommended for Exchange 2007?

5. What are the three server roles that rely on the DNS round robin system for high availability?

Quick Check Answers

1. The MB role is supported in an SCC and cannot host any other roles.

2. The Single Copy Cluster represents the traditional approach used in previous versions of Exchange to protect back-end mailbox services. As with previous versions, an SCC only provides protection for the mailbox service itself. Because members of the SCC access shared storage and there is only a single copy of the storage groups on the shared storage, the SCC does not provide data protection services. Exchange 2007 requires at least one passive node in an SCC. This means that because the Failover Cluster service supports clusters of up to 8 or 16 nodes, the maximum number of clustered mailbox servers on an SCC in Windows Server 2003 is 7; in Windows Server 2008 it is 15.

3. These resources include:

    ❑ The Microsoft Exchange Information Store

    ❑ The Microsoft Exchange System Attendant

- ❑ The CMS Network Name
- ❑ The CMS IP Address
- ❑ The Microsoft Exchange Database Instance
- ❑ Physical Disk Resources

4. The three affinity modes are:

- ❑ Single affinity, which performs load balancing based on the IP address and automatically redirects all requests from the same incoming address to the same cluster member.

- ❑ No affinity, which performs load balancing based on both the incoming IP address and its port number. It does not link clients to any particular host in the cluster.

- ❑ Class C affinity, which also relies on the IP address only, but is more granular than single affinity. Class C is the recommended affinity mode for Exchange 2007.

5. The three roles are: the Hub Transport Server role, the Edge Transport Server role, and the Unified Messaging Server role.

Lesson 2: Plan a Data Redundancy Implementation

Estimated lesson time: 70 minutes

Now that you have seen how to prepare for service availability, you can begin to look at data availability. Chapter 5 outlined how you can protect data through backup technologies, but restoring data from a backup can be cumbersome and take a considerable amount of time. That is why Microsoft added new data protection features in Exchange 2007 through continuous replication scenarios. In single sites—sites where you want to have local access to a redundant copy of your e-mail data—you rely on Local Continuous Replication (LCR) to protect the data.

Plan Single Site Data Redundancy

LCR is a solution that is implemented on a single server. This server is attached to two storage containers. Each storage container includes a similar disk configuration. The first disk set, or production disk set, contains the storage groups managed by the MB system. The second disk set is used to create a replica of the production storage groups managed by this MB system (see Figure 6-5). The production disk set is called the active copy. The replica disk set is the passive copy. Exchange uses log shipping and then log replay to create and maintain the replica. *Log shipping* is sending a copy of each transaction log from the active to the passive copy; *log replay* is reading the copied logs into the passive copy of the storage group databases.

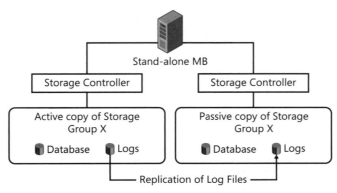

Figure 6-5   A Local Continuous Replication configuration

If damage occurs to the active copy, the Exchange administrator must manually switch to the passive copy of the e-mail storage groups to provide relatively rapid access to the data for end users. This is called replica activation: The administrator must activate the replica and mount the replica databases to complete the switch.

LCR is designed to meet several redundancy goals:

- It reduces the recovery time for disasters related to data storage. In fact, you can recover data within minutes instead of the hours it usually takes to recover data from backup. All you need to do is activate the passive copy and you have immediate access to the data.

- It can help reduce the number of backups, especially full backups, you require for complete data protection. LCR does not replace backups, however—especially off-site backup storage—because LCR replicas are usually contained within a single site. For example, because you have near-time access to a live replica of the data, you can reduce full backups to a weekly schedule, performing incremental or differential backups on weekdays. This lets you create a two-part service level agreement, providing fast near-time recoveries through LCR and longer, full-system recoveries from backup.

- It can increase performance levels, especially during backup operations, because you can generate backups using the replica instead of the active copy. You must, however, use a backup solution that works with the Volume Shadow Copy Service (VSS) and is Exchange-aware. This also reduces the input/output impact on the active copy because it can be dedicated to servicing end-user requests as well as shipping logs to the passive copy. The passive copy disk sets are then dedicated to replica generation and backup operations.

- It can easily be activated to recover from disasters or data corruption. Replica activation is a two-step operation that can be performed at either the Exchange or the operating system level. At the Exchange level, you change the active storage group and database paths through a configuration change. At the operating system level, you can change the mount points tied to the log and database volumes. You must, however, use volume mount points to be able to use the operating system-level operation.

- Administrators can selectively determine which storage groups to protect through LCR, providing protection for high-risk data only. For example, you could configure a system containing five storage groups, each with a single mailbox database and log set, to protect only three of its storage groups—those that require the highest level of protection. The other two storage groups could contain data that is less at risk and could rely on a backup solution for data protection.

- LCR is available in all editions of Exchange 2007, making it a viable solution for organizations of any size and supporting any Exchange Organization type.

- You can manage LCR either through the Exchange Management Console or the Exchange Management Shell, making it easy for novice as well as expert Exchange administrators to use it.

IMPORTANT   LCR disk structures

Because of the read/write operations inherent in log shipping and log replay, LCR disk configurations require faster I/O than traditional Exchange disk configurations. This is one more reason why Microsoft now recommends RAID 10 configurations for Exchange 2007. See Lesson 1 in Chapter 2 for more information.

Unlike the Single Copy Cluster, LCR implementations do not require special disk configurations such as shared storage. In fact, any supported disk configuration for Windows Server will work with LCR, but ideally you will use the fastest possible disk configuration. Because of this, you should favor direct-attached storage (DAS) over serially attached SCSI (SAS), Internet SCSI (iSCSI) or Fibre Channel storage configurations. DAS provides faster disk I/O than any of the other solutions because it is contained within the server itself, whereas all other configurations are a remote form of storage.

Keep in mind that LCR is a data redundancy solution only. LCR disk sets are tied to a single MB system that must be a stand-alone, unclustered system. Because of this, LCR does not provide service redundancy. If the MB system fails, having a replica of the data will not assist the Exchange administrator in bringing the service back online.

Plan for Local Continuous Replication

You can perform LCR configuration for a storage group after you create the storage group or during the storage group creation process. After the LCR pairing is created, Exchange begins a process called *seeding*, which creates a seed copy of the database that is then maintained in a replica state through log shipping. Although you can create an LCR on the disk set that stores the active copy, you should endeavor to create the replica on a separate disk set, ideally using a separate disk controller. This isolates the replica from potential failures related to the production disk set and disk controller.

LCR will apply an additional load on the MB system because it will have to maintain two disk operations per LCR-enabled storage group. You must take this into consideration when planning the capacity of the server. CPU and memory capacity, for example, are two aspects that will be affected. In addition, storage configurations will require careful planning.

Configure Storage Groups   Configuring LCR is relatively straightforward. It mostly involves configuring disk sets and storage groups. Follow the guidelines outlined in Lesson 1 of Chapter 2 and keep the following guidelines in mind when preparing for LCR:

- Remember to use a single database per storage group. This makes it easier to manage and to recover if problematic events occur.

- Use volume mount points instead of drive letters. This lets you create many more volumes than the base 26 letters of the alphabet. Considering that you can have up to 50 storage groups with the enterprise edition and each storage group requires at least two drive sets as well as the corresponding drive sets required for LCR, you could find yourself with a configuration that involves more than 200 drive sets. Drive letters will not work.

- Keep to the separate disk set rule for databases and log files. Keeping these on separate disk sets can protect your data in the event of a failure. If one drive set fails, you can use the other to recover from the failure.

- Use different volumes and assign them to separate drive sets to increase system performance. For example, if your configuration allows it, you should also place the operating system files and the Exchange application files on separate disk sets along with the logs and databases.

- Use separate disk controllers for the active and passive copies. This ensures that one does not impact the performance of the other.

- Make sure each disk set uses its own redundancy configuration. Remember that the best configuration for Exchange 2007 is RAID 10.

- Make sure each disk set has sufficient storage space for the data it will host. Size your database copy disk sets similarly and do the same for the log copy disk sets.

- If you cannot use direct-attached storage, make sure the technology you do use—Fibre Channel or iSCSI—is configured appropriately. iSCSI in particular must provide low latency and high bandwidth. The advantage of iSCSI is that it is easy to add more network interface cards to the system to increase bandwidth and decrease latency. However, iSCSI is discouraged in the release version of Exchange because the passive copies can require up to two or three times the input and output per second required for the active copies. This has been changed in SP1 so that both active and passive copies require equivalent storage, but if you are not up to SP1 yet, this can have an impact on iSCSI configurations.

Exam Tip Keep in mind that the original exam is not on SP1; therefore, you must remember that in the release version of Exchange, passive copies can require up to two or three times the I/O per second required for the active copies.

- Use the Exchange Jetstress tool to validate your storage configurations before deploying LCR onto them. Using this tool, you can validate storage independently for active and passive copies. More information on Jetstress can be found at *http://technet.microsoft.com/en-us/library/bb738152.aspx*.

In addition, you should ensure that the configuration of processor and memory is adequate for the load LCR adds to the server. Normally, MB systems running LCR will run all of the services associated with the MB role as well as the Exchange Replication tool. This puts an additional 20 percent load on the processor and requires at least 1 GB of additional RAM to operate at peak efficiency; keep this in mind when configuring resources for the MB system running LCR.

Configure Mailbox Database Size Because LCR is a near-time data access solution, you can usually configure databases in an LCR pair to be double the size of those in non-LCR configurations. Larger databases require more maintenance, but because you have access to two copies of the data, you can increase the size of your maintenance windows and manage larger databases more easily.

When you do size your databases, keep in mind that in the event of a failure, you will no longer have access to two copies of the data. Take the following scenario: You have two copies of a database—the active copy and the passive copy. While both copies work, you have access to a near-time backup. But as soon as a failure occurs and you must activate the passive copy, you lose the LCR pair. When this loss occurs, you are again vulnerable to data loss, at least during the time it takes you to effect repairs on the failed copy and reactivate LCR for this storage group.

As outlined in Lesson 1 in Chapter 2, Microsoft recommends that you keep databases without LCR to a maximum of 100 GB in size and databases with LCR to a maximum of 200 GB. Use this rule of thumb when planning your database sizes.

Plan for Public Folder Database Replication LCR is designed to protect mailbox databases. Public folder databases are automatically protected as soon as you have two systems hosting them. When two MB systems host public folder databases with the same content, Exchange automatically initiates replication between the two. The more replicas of public folders you have, the safer the data will be. This is very much like domain controllers in Active Directory.

The engines used for public folder databases and LCR are not the same. You should not enable LCR for storage groups containing public folders, but only for storage groups containing mailbox databases. To protect public folder storage groups, you should endeavor to have at least two MB systems hosting them. But if you cannot, and if you only have one MB system in the network—such as for the Simple Organization type—you can enable LCR for the public folder storage group because in this case, LCR will not conflict with public folder replication.

Similarly, if you have multiple MB systems and only one hosts public folder storage groups, you can also enable them for LCR. You can also use public folder replication to migrate data from one system to another, and as soon as the data is migrated you can shut down the originating system. At that time, you can enable LCR for the system.

Ideally, you should avoid enabling both LCR and public folder replication at the same time on the same storage groups.

Use the Transport Dumpster in SP1   Microsoft has provided several enhancements to LCR in Service Pack 1. One of the most interesting for organizations implementing LCR is the use of the Transport Dumpster on the Hub Transport Server role. HT systems include a special dumpster, the Transport Dumpster, which is designed to help protect messages that have been sent to a potentially corrupted database.

In the event of a database or active copy failure, administrators can use the **Restore-StorageGroupCopy** cmdlet in Exchange Server 2007 SP1 to request resubmission of messages from the HT server to the newly activated passive copy of an LCR pair. This takes messages that have been moved from the HT queue to its dumpster—including any message that is delivered to a storage group contained within a continuous replication system—and replays them to update potentially missing information in the LCR passive copy. This task is performed on each HT server in the same site as the affected MB system. To avoid duplication, the MB will automatically purge any messages that are replayed but that already exist in the passive copy of the database. In SP1, the **Restore-StorageGroupCopy** cmdlet has been updated so that when the administrator activates the passive copy, it automatically triggers a Transport Dumpster replay as well.

This system only protects actual messages that have been sent. It does not protect messages that have been drafted but not sent, or calendar, contact, and task information. In addition, messages that are in transit but have not yet been received by the HT system are not included in the messages protected by a Transport Dumpster.

However, the Transport Dumpster must have been configured prior to the failure. Although the Transport Dumpster feature is enabled by default, you should configure two values to meet the requirements of your environment:

- **MaxDumpsterSizePerStorageGroup**   The setting that determines the maximum size of the Transport Dumpster for each storage group protected by a continuous replication strategy. You should configure this setting to be at least 1.5 times the maximum size of messages in your environment. For example, if you set the maximum message size to 20 MB, you should configure this value to be 30 MB. By default, this value is set to 18 MB.

- **MaxDumpsterTime**   The setting that determines how long an e-mail message should remain in the Transport Dumpster queue. This value is set to seven days by default, which gives you enough time to recover from an extended outage. If you decide to modify this value, you need to use a full value. For example, the value for seven days is 07.00:00:00.

Keep in mind that you must allow for additional storage on each HT system where you configure the Transport Dumpster: You must allow for the value of the *MaxDumpsterSizePerStorageGroup* multiplied by the number of storage groups you are protecting. When the values for each setting is reached, messages are removed from the dumpster on a first in, first out basis.

You can configure these settings in either the Exchange Management Console or the Exchange Management Shell. See *http://technet.microsoft.com/en-us/library/bb629500.aspx* for detailed commands to modify these settings.

Exam Tip   Remember that the original exam does not include SP1 information.

Manage Continuous Replication with SP1   In addition to the ability to work with the Transport Dumpster with LCR, Service Pack 1 provides enhancements to the administration of continuous replication. Specifically, SP1 includes enhancements and new commands for:

- **Get-StorageGroupCopyStatus**   The command that provides you with information on the status of your replication pairs. It has been enhanced in SP1 to overcome known deficiencies such as misleading reports on the status of a replication group. For example, some replication pairs do not report status until a log has been replayed—or when replication is initiated do not report status until it has been completed. Another issue is related to the dismounting of storage groups.

In this situation, the value of the *LastLogGenerated* field can be erroneous. The changed cmdlet also addresses other issues.

- **Test-ReplicationHealth**   A new command that provides feedback on replication itself. For LCR, this command checks all aspects of replication status. It also provides value for the Cluster Continuous Replication (CCR) scenario because it includes support for the cluster portion of this continuous replication strategy. But for LCR, it covers replication service status, storage group copy status, storage group replication queue lengths, and status of databases after copy activation.

Although these commands will not be on the original exam, any messaging professional planning for LCR should be aware of them and be able to include them in a strategy definition.

Use Standby Continuous Replication with LCR in SP1   Another new feature of Exchange 2007 SP1 is Standby Continuous Replication (SCR). SCR is a new replication model that relies on the same log shipping and log replay technologies as LCR, but without the limitations of LCR. For example, LCR must be deployed on a stand-alone server, whereas CSR must not. It can be deployed between two separate stand-alone servers or even between members of a cluster, even a Single Copy Cluster.

The activation process for SCR is like that of LCR: It is a manual process that must be initiated by the Exchange administrator when a failure is noticed. It does not use the same strategy, however. SCR can be activated in one of three ways:

- Enable database portability along with the dial tone service.
- Enable the passive copy through the recovery option in Setup (**Setup /m:Recover-Server**).
- Enable the passive copy in a cluster through the recovery option in Setup (**Setup /RecoverCMS**).

The option you use depends on your system configuration.

Plan for LCR Management   While management is not related to deployment, it is still essential for the messaging professional planning for LCR to make allowances for the additional management overhead LCR will cause once it is in production. Introducing LCR to any Exchange deployment will increase the management workload because of the activities associated with LCR administration. In fact, administrators will have the following tasks in addition to day-to-day Exchange administration:

- Managing additional disk volumes
- Managing LCR pairings

- Managing replication and verifying replication status
- Ensuring replay operates properly when replication issues arise between LCR pairs
- Additional database activities such as mounting, dismounting, and adding or removing the databases
- Managing mount points for storage group disk sets
- Activating passive copies

The additional workload will vary with the number of LCR pairings to manage and the number of systems running LCR.

MORE INFO **Managing LCR**

More information on additional LCR management activities can be found at *http://technet.microsoft.com/en-us/library/aa998823.aspx*.

Plan Multi-Site Data Redundancy and Service Availability

So far, you have seen how to protect data in a single site. These strategies are appropriate for organizations deploying Exchange in the Simple and perhaps the Standard Organizations, but as soon as you have multiple sites, especially multiple sites with considerable numbers of users, or you have high-risk data that must be protected at all times, you need to implement a solution that will provide multi-site redundancy for both the e-mail service and the data it manages.

Of course, you could simply plan to have backup tapes located at a secondary site and use this site as a recovery site in the event of a disaster, but relying on backup tapes, while an essential part of any disaster recovery solution, takes time and does not provide very good service levels. In fact, many have found that if they do not test their recovery procedures on a regular basis, they can end up with no recovery at all if they elect to rely on backup tapes alone.

With previous versions of Exchange, organizations needing more near-time site redundancy solutions often opted to implement third-party replication solutions. These solutions installed agents on mailbox database servers. These agents replicated each modification to the mailbox databases to another Mailbox server located within a remote site. In addition, these solutions provided immediate failover to the remote site in the event of a disaster.

With the release of Exchange Server 2007, Microsoft has added new features that provide similar functionality. You have already seen how continuous replication can use log shipping and log replay to protect data within the same site. You have also seen how the Failover Cluster service of Windows Server can provide service redundancy within a local site. You use these two features—replication and clustering—to provide multi-site data and service redundancy using the built-in features of Windows and Exchange, but with modifications. You use the new Cluster Continuous Replication (CCR) feature in Exchange.

Like the Single Copy Cluster, CCR is based on the MCS service, but relies on the Majority Node Set (MNS) cluster model instead of the Shared Quorum model. MNS clusters are often called geoclusters or stretch clusters because each node of the cluster is located in datacenters in different sites. In addition, MNS clusters do not require shared storage. In fact, because MNS clusters are located in different datacenters, it is often best to build them with direct-attached storage because it provides faster I/O. Keep in mind that like LCR implementations, you still need separate physical disk systems for the transaction log and database for both the active and passive stores. CCR configurations for Exchange 2007 only support two node clusters.

What is different in the MNS cluster is that you now rely on a File Share Witness (FSW) feature that is included with Windows Server 2008 but that has been released as a hotfix for Windows Server 2003. The File Share Witness serves as an additional voting node to allow the cluster to determine whether failover is required. It serves as a tie-breaker if each node loses communications with the other. This avoids the split-brain syndrome where both nodes lose communication with each other and want to become the active node. To protect even further against this syndrome, you might optionally place the file share witness in a third datacenter, avoiding potential networking issues tied to location.

MORE INFO   **Windows Server hotfix for CCR**

The hotfix for Windows Server to support CCR can be found at *http://support.microsoft.com/kb/921181*. Make sure you get the version for x64 editions of Windows Server. This hotfix requires Windows Server 2003 x64 Edition with SP1 or version R2. This hotfix supports two new Failover Cluster features: the file share witness and configurable cluster heartbeats. Both are designed to reduce false positives in cluster failures. Note that this hotfix is already included in Service Pack 2 for Windows Server.

This hotfix is not required for Windows Server 2008. In Windows Server 2008, the cluster mode you select for CCR is called Node And File Share Majority Quorum.

Replication between the nodes is performed in much the same way as it is with Local Continuous Replication, but in this case it is over the WAN. For replication to work, all members of the MNS cluster, including the File Share Witness—which is usually located on a Hub Transport server—must be part of the same Active Directory site forcing them to use high-speed replication instead of delayed replication (see Figure 6-6). Active Directory sites using this structure are called stretched Active Directory sites.

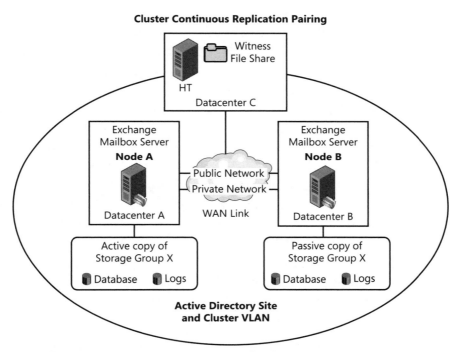

Figure 6-6   A typical Cluster Continuous Replication structure

Plan for Service and Data High Availability

Several configurations are possible for CCR implementations; each depends on the budget you have access to and the service level agreements (SLAs) you need to support. For example, you can have one of three different remote backup sites: hot, warm, or cold. In a hot backup site, the remote datacenter that hosts the paired CCR server is immediately ready to provide service if a disaster occurs. In a warm backup site, activation of the paired CCR server requires a manual intervention. In a cold backup site, operators need to perform several tasks to bring the paired CCR server online.

In addition, paired CCR servers can either be dedicated, or completely devoted to the CCR pair, or non-dedicated (also called shared), sharing the CCR pair function with others or other functions. As you can see, you can create several paired CCR configurations: hot-dedicated, warm-dedicated, warm-shared, cold-shared, and so on. In fact, the industry often uses custom terms to address the type of continuity solution you can put together. For example, you could configure the following continuity solutions with CCR:

- In a Production: Cold (Dedicated) site, you simply ship your backup tapes to an offsite location. In the event of a disaster, you must deploy new hardware and software and restore all backups to get the system up and running again.

- In a Production: Warm (Dedicated) site, you have deployed hardware and software that is maintaining dedicated copies of your data, but you must perform a manual operation to activate the center in the event of a disaster. For example, you might have a Cluster Continuous Replication pair within the site to protect e-mail data and mailbox services, but you would use another strategy to protect other server roles as well as supporting services such as DNS and Active Directory.

- In a Production: Warm (Non-Dedicated) using a two Active Directory site structure, you have deployed hardware that services users in each site and deployed hardware that provides backup for the resources in the other site. Again, because the structure is warm, a manual operation is required to activate the backup site.

- In a Production: Production (Non-Dedicated) using a single Active Directory site structure, resources in both datacenters provide active service to end users, but act as backups for the resources in the other center. Activation is automatic and does not require manual intervention.

Keep this in mind when planning your CCR configurations. Also keep in mind that the hotter your solution, the more expensive it will be because you will have more hardware dedicated to recovery that provides no other service.

Exam Tip   Keep in mind that the CCR is not the only implementation that can let you build backup sites. You can also use backup alone, Standby Continuous Replication (with SP1), multiple Single Copy Clusters, multiple Local Continuous Replication pairs, and so on. Be creative when you consider which availability elements a solution requires.

MORE INFO   **Defining backup site strategies**

More information on each backup site strategy can be found at *http://technet.microsoft.com/en-us/library/bb201662.aspx*.

Understand Cluster Continuous Replication Concepts

Cluster Continuous Replication offers the best possible solution for service and data availability using Exchange's built-in feature set. That is because it is first based on the

Failover Cluster service, which provides automatic failover if a problem occurs on the active node. In addition, because it includes continuous data replication, it ensures that there is no data loss when this failover occurs. In fact, CCR provides the following availability features:

- No single point of failure because the cluster service is in constant communication with each node through the heartbeat pulse.

- No special hardware requirements because unlike the SCC, the CCR can rely on direct-attached storage.

- Can provide single site or multiple site redundancy because it can be deployed in a single site or in two sites.

- Because it uses the Exchange Replication Engine, CCR provides the possibility of reducing the full backup window as with LCR.

- Unlike LCR, each storage group that is managed by a CCR node is replicated. This occurs automatically. Each database in each storage group is seeded as soon as the pairing is created. This is because storage groups are linked together through the Failover Cluster service. In an LCR pair, you can determine which storage group is paired on a one-by-one basis as well as remove pairings as you like.

The main feature that makes the CCR possible in Exchange 2007 is database portability—the ability to reassign a database from one MB system to another. In a CCR pair, this feature is automatically activated in case of a failure because both the service and the data are protected. In an LCR configuration, there is no automatic activation because an LCR configuration only protects the data and not the service. In a CCR pair, when the service fails, it is automatically failed over to the second node in the cluster, which automatically fails over data connections as well.

Understand Cluster Continuous Replication Requirements

Special conditions must be met to implement a CCR pairing, including:

- The Failover Cluster service requires 0.5 second network latency between each site; otherwise, the cluster nodes will not detect each other's heartbeats. Set up a virtual LAN between the two nodes and place them into the same Active Directory site to ensure high-speed replication.

- Bandwidth requirements are not as considerable as they could be because Microsoft has reduced the log size to 1 MB. Because replication is based on log shipping, transmitting 1 MB logs has less impact than transmitting the logs of previous versions, which were 5 MB in size. Use a minimum of Gigabit Ethernet to ensure appropriate bandwidth and speeds. For example, you will need the following speeds and bandwidth:

- ❏ Single database reseed: about 25 MB/second.
- ❏ Multiple database reseed: about 100 MB/sec. but will be limited by available bandwidth.

- Both cluster nodes require a minimum of two network interface cards for both public and private cluster communications. Both seeding and replication occur over the public NIC. Ideally, you will add several NICs to the system to create several public links and increase replication speeds. This has a particular impact when one node of the pair has been down for a significant period of time and requires resynchronization of a large number of transaction logs. This also avoids public NIC failures. These issues are limited in SP1 because SP1 allows the administrator to specify multiple mixed-mode or public NICs as well as identifying which NIC is to be used for seeding. Mixed-mode NICs can be used as both public or private carriers in Failover Clusters. Keep the following in mind when setting up the network connections:

  - ❏ Private network connection addresses must be static IP addresses and must be on a different subnet than public network connections. Organizations usually use 10.10.10.x as the base address for private NICs with a subnet mask of 255.255.255.0—unless of course, they use the 10.x.x.x network for their public addresses. Private NICs do not require DNS settings or a gateway to function. If more than one private network connection is created on the cluster, use different network addresses for each.

  - ❏ Public network addresses should be static as well and should be part of your standard public internal IP address scheme.

  - ❏ One additional public internal IP address will be required for the cluster itself as well as one for each instance of SCC in the cluster.

  - ❏ In Windows Server 2008 running Exchange 2007 SP1, you can use dynamic IPv6 addresses for both the private and the public networks.

  - ❏ Make sure the binding order is properly designed for the private NICs to be bound first and public NICs last.

- The traffic that moves over the link between the two sites includes:

  - ❏ Shipped logs.
  - ❏ Active Directory replication traffic.
  - ❏ Client traffic if services are offered at both locations.

- ❑ Cluster heartbeat traffic.

- ❑ Cluster configuration information.

- ❑ Other traffic related to other, non-Exchange applications.

- Other factors including performance are related to:

  - ❑ File system notifications, which tell the Exchange Replication Engine when new logs are ready to be shipped.

  - ❑ Cluster database updates on each member of the CCR pair.

  - ❑ The active node has little additional overhead because log replay is performed on the passive node.

- Log shipping is asynchronous in a CCR pair. The only time that databases are up-to-date on each system is when a failover occurs either manually or automatically.

- Unlike an LCR pair, replication between CCR pairs automatically reverses direction when the active/passive roles are switched by the Failover Cluster service.

- Failover—whether manually activated for maintenance purposes or automatically in case of failures—should only take about two to four minutes to occur. During this time, users will experience a small loss of service, but service will continue automatically as soon as the failover is complete.

- The CCR automatically makes use of the Transport Dumpster on the HT systems in each site. Be sure to configure the Transport Dumpster settings as described at the beginning of this lesson.

- A file share witness is required to ensure that cluster state information is available to both members of the cluster at all times. Ideally, this file share witness will be located in a third site. In any case, it should be on an HT system. Configure the host name for the file share witness server as a CNAME in DNS instead of a Host (A) record. This makes it easier to replace it if a problem occurs.

- Replication is performed by creating a hidden share on the folder containing the transaction logs for the replicated storage group. This share is created automatically at setup. The passive node connects to this share and pulls the logs from it to update its own copy of the database. Roles are reversed in the case of a failover.

- Replication traffic is not encrypted by default. If you need to encrypt the traffic because it travels over a WAN link, create an IPsec tunnel between the paired nodes in the CCR cluster. You can also use an isolated network for replication that does not require the creation of an IPsec tunnel.

- Each storage group should only contain a single database as per best practice recommendations. As with LCR, you can double the size of your databases from 100 to 200 GB because they are protected by replication.

- Your DNS server must accept dynamic updates. This is a core requirement of the Failover Cluster service because it depends on these updates to provide failover services. Use the Microsoft DNS and marry it to the Active Directory service.

- As with the SCC, both cluster nodes must be members of the same Active Directory domain.

- You must create the cluster before you can install CCR. Remember that you must use either the Enterprise or the Datacenter editions of Windows Server to create a Failover Cluster. Cluster node names should be 15 characters or fewer to provide legacy support. In addition, the cluster service account must have all appropriate permissions both on the local system and in Active Directory.

- As with the SCC, the cluster cannot include any previous version of Exchange or any full version of SQL Server. Running unclustered databases such as SQL Server Express or MS Access is supported, but as a best practice, your CCR node pairs should only run CCR and nothing else. Also, make sure you use the same version of Exchange 2007 on each node. Remember that only the MB role is supported in a Failover Cluster.

- Storage group data must be placed inside a folder structure on each disk set. In addition, these folders must be completely empty before installation.

- All resources must be located in the cluster resource groups created by the installation. Do not move any of these resources and do not place Exchange resources within the default cluster group. Also, previous versions of Exchange required the installation of the Microsoft Distributed Transaction Coordinator (MSDTC). Exchange 2007 does not require MSDTC at all.

- Remember that CCR has the same limitations as LCR in terms of public folders and public folder replication. Try to avoid situations where public folder replication will be enabled at the same time as the Exchange Replication Engine. For this reason, host public folders on CCR pairs only if there is a single copy of the public folder in your network.

Your CCR configuration also requires the deployment of HT and CAS systems in each location. Remember that in each location where you deploy an MB, you also need to deploy an HT and a CAS. This is because both the HT and the CAS must have a local area network link to the MB to function. You would ideally have both domain controllers and Global Catalog servers in each site to ensure true redundancy (see Figure 6-7).

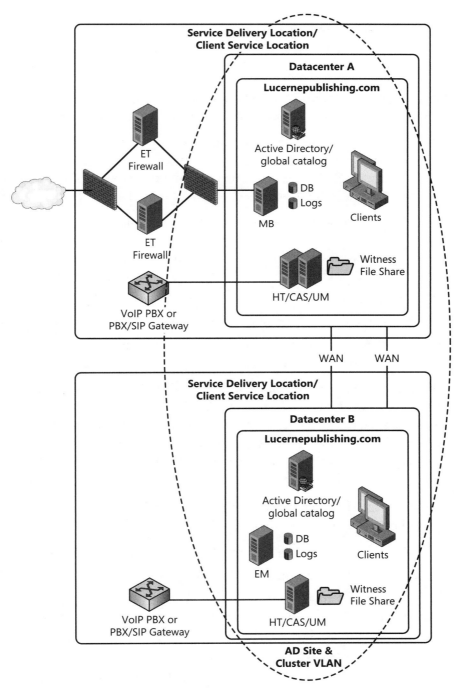

Figure 6-7   Using a CCR to provide continuity services

MORE INFO   **Use the Exchange CCR planning checklist**

Microsoft has provided a planning checklist for CCR preparation. Find it at
http://technet.microsoft.com/en-us/library/aa996568.aspx.

The Make-up of a Cluster Continuous Replication Resource Group   Once installed, the CCR resource group will consist of several resources. These include:

- **The Microsoft Exchange Information Store**   Represents the clustered mailbox server in the cluster resource group. When this resource is online, it enables MAPI traffic to the CMS. Because it is the interface to MAPI traffic for the CCR, this resource can take the entire cluster group offline when it is not available.

- **The Microsoft Exchange System Attendant**   Represents the System Attendant service for the CCR. If it is offline, it does not affect the resource group as a whole. Note that in Exchange 2007, the Information Store no longer has dependencies on the System Attendant.

- **The CMS Network Name**   The DNS name used to reach the clustered resource. If the Network Name is not available, the entire resource group is taken offline.

- **The CMS IP Address**   The IP address linked to the Network Name for the resource group. If the IP address is offline, the entire resource group is offline.

- **The Microsoft Exchange Database Instance**   Represents a database hosted by the cluster. Mounted databases appear as online cluster resources. Offline database resources are dismounted. Database instances cannot be mounted unless the Exchange Information Store is online. Therefore, these instances are dependent on the Information Store. Because of their nature, database instances do not affect the Exchange group of resources as a whole.

As you can see, there are several dependencies in a CCR resource group. The IP address is the starting point for these dependencies, which work as follows:

1. If the IP address is not available, the Network Name is not available.

2. If the Network Name is not available, the Microsoft Exchange Information Store is not available.

3. If the Microsoft Exchange Information Store is not available, the clustered mailbox server is not available.

4. If a specific Microsoft Exchange Database Instance is not available, only that resource is not available. However, the CMS is still available as a whole.

Therefore, three resources are critical to the group as a whole and one resource type is critical to each storage group.

Recovering from CCR Failures   Remember that CCR provides protection for both the data and the mailbox service. If the service fails on one node for some reason, it will automatically fail over to the passive node. In addition, database failures will only affect the corresponding database instance, allowing the server to continue managing mail, but losing access to any mailboxes within this database instance. According to Microsoft, failure of a node in a CCR pair does not result in significant outages. However, when one node is down, you are no longer protected by the CCR pairing, therefore you must repair broken nodes as fast as possible.

These are not the only outages that can affect the CCR. Table 6-4 outlines some typical outages related to Single Copy Clusters and their potential resolutions.

Table 6-4   Potential CCR Outages

Source of Outage	Triggered Action
Complete failure of active server node	Automatic failover to passive node, if available. Operator can force failback if the failure was only temporary.
Complete failure of storage on an active node	Service will continue, but no e-mail will be stored. You need to manually force failover to the passive node.
Complete site failure	Automatic failover to passive node, if available.
Node operating system disk failure	The cluster will not detect this failure unless it stops the operating system. Then an automatic failover will occur.
Complete failure of public network	Automatic failover to passive node, if available.
Complete failure of the quorum	Automatic failover to passive node if it can form a quorum. If not, the cluster stops responding and you must provide corrective action.
Complete information store failure	Automatic restart of information store resource. Automatic failover if resource fails to restart.
Partial information store failure	No action unless it becomes a complete failure.

Table 6-4 **Potential CCR Outages**

Source of Outage	Triggered Action
Node application disk failure	The cluster will not detect this failure unless it stops the application. Then an automatic failover will occur.
Complete storage group or database access failure	Database instances linked to the storage group are dismounted, but the service continues if other storage groups are available. You must manually repair the storage group or force failover and then repair the storage group.
Corrupted storage group logs	No automatic action. The corresponding database is broken and must be re-seeded.
Any drive sets in a storage group is out of space	Database instances linked to the drive set are dismounted, but the service continues if other drive sets running other databases are available. You must manually repair the drive set.

Because you design CCR to provide service and data continuity, you should make sure that you test failover for the CCR when you install on the cluster before you provide end-user connections to it.

Work with Scheduled and Unscheduled Outages Because a CCR provides both data and service continuity, you can perform management tasks on each node without loss of service or data. These maintenance windows are called scheduled outages. When unscheduled outages or unexpected failures occur, you must determine the status of your databases before restoring service from the broken node. Exchange 2007 provides a special attribute, *AutoDatabaseMountDial*, which you can set to control database operation in this instance:

- **Lossless** When you set the *AutoDatabaseMountDial* attribute to the *Lossless* value, no transaction logs are lost. This forces the CCR nodes to wait for each other to mount database instances so that replication can continue. In this situation, the failed system must have a complete set of uncorrupted logs for service to continue.

- **Good Availability** When you set the *AutoDatabaseMountDial* attribute to the *Good Availability* value, up to three logs can be lost. This provides automatic failover in most instances.

- **Best Availability** When you set the *AutoDatabaseMountDial* attribute to the *Best Availability* value, up to six logs can be lost. This is the default setting and supports higher replication latency levels than the previous setting. Use this value unless you have a pressing need for different cluster behavior.

MORE INFO Tuning failover behavior in a CCR pair

More information on each behavior can be found at *http://technet.microsoft.com/en-us/library/bb124389.aspx*.

Scheduled outages provide more predictable behavior. Use the **Move-ClusteredMailboxServer** cmdlet to cause a failover from one node to the other. Avoid using the Windows Server Cluster Manager to cause failovers because it will not use Exchange-specific components to validate the health or state of the passive node before failover and may cause replication to be left in a broken state.

Migrating Previous Version Clusters to CCR As with the SCC, you cannot use a direct path to migrate existing legacy version Exchange clusters to a CCR implementation. This is because there is no direct upgrade path from legacy versions to Exchange 2007. Therefore, you must first, create your CCR cluster and then use the **Move-Mailbox** cmdlet to migrate mailboxes or mailbox databases from existing instances to the new cluster.

Refer to Chapter 3, "Planning Exchange 2007 Upgrades and Migrations," for more information on migration or transition scenarios from legacy versions of Exchange.

MORE INFO Performing CCR installations

More information on the CCR and its installation process can be found at *http://technet.microsoft.com/en-us/library/aa997144.aspx*. Information on how to create a CCR with Windows Server 2008 can be found at *http://technet.microsoft.com/en-us/library/bb629714.aspx*. Information on installing Exchange 2007 SP1 prerequisites on Windows Server 2008 can be found at *http://technet.microsoft.com/en-us/library/bb691354.aspx*.

MORE INFO Uninstalling a CCR

Information on removing a CCR from your Exchange infrastructure can be found at *http://technet.microsoft.com/en-us/library/bb123709.aspx*.

MORE INFO Managing CCR installations

More information on managing a CCR once it is installed can be found at *http://technet.microsoft.com/en-us/library/aa997676.aspx*.

MORE INFO   **Exchange SP1 upgrade steps for CCRs**

More information on the upgrade process can be found at *http://technet.microsoft.com/en-us/library/bb676320.aspx*.

Plan for the Integration of Exchange SP1 Features

With the release of Service Pack 1 for Exchange 2007, Microsoft has introduced new features and enhanced existing features to make the Exchange e-mail service even more resilient. One feature in particular, the Standby Continuous Replication feature, has a significant impact on the configurations you can use to create resiliency. While this is not on the original exam, it is important for anyone planning to deploy Exchange Server 2007 to understand the impact of this feature on high availability deployments.

You can run SCR on a variety of configurations. For example, you can apply it to a stand-alone MB, a CMS within an SCC, a Standby Cluster, and a CMS within a CCR. This means that you can mix and match configurations to provide the best availability according to both your budget and required service levels. For example, you can perform the following configurations:

- If you are running stand-alone MB systems, you can use SCR to replicate the data onsite or offsite, thereby protecting the data within each stand-alone server.

- If you are running an SCC, you can protect the data along with the service through the use of SCR. SCR replicas can be local or remote.

- If you are running a Standby Cluster, you can use SCR to replicate the data either onsite or offsite and therefore provide data as well as potential service availability.

- If you are running a CCR, you can configure the CCR to provide local site resilience and avoid latency or bandwidth issues related to CCR replication, and use SCR to replicate data offsite and provide additional data protection.

Each of these scenarios costs less and provides more protection than if you use the feature set included in the release version of Exchange 2007 on its own. Remember that SCR replicas must be activated manually, much as with the LCR model. Include this manual activation in your recovery plans.

MORE INFO   **Working with SCR**

More information on SCR can be found at *http://technet.microsoft.com/en-us/library/bb676502.aspx*.

Practice: Build Data Redundancy Systems

In this practice, you will perform a Local Continuous Replication installation to prepare for data protection with Exchange 2007. This practice consists of a single exercise.

▶ **Exercise: Install a Local Continuous Replication System**

LCR provides single site data redundancy. To deploy it, you must have several disk systems linked to a single server. This is the reason for the preparation of the ExchangeLCR.treyresearch.net computer. In this exercise, you will use this computer to install a new LCR system to protect mailbox data. Proceed as follows:

1. Make sure the TreyDC and the ExchangeLCR computers are both running.

2. Log on to the ExchangeLCR.treyresearch.net computer with the EXAdmin account from the domain. This will give you local administrator privileges.

3. Open Windows Explorer and select the DVD drive. Double-click Setup.exe to launch the Exchange Setup.

4. Click Install Microsoft Exchange.

5. Click Next.

6. Accept the License Agreement and click Next.

7. Configure Error Reporting according to your organizational standards and click Next.

8. Under Installation Type, select Custom Exchange Server Installation. Leave the installation defaults and click Next.

9. Under Server Role Selection, select Mailbox Role. This also automatically selects Management Tools. Leave the installation defaults and click Next.

10. Review the Readiness Checks and click Install.

11. Click Finish when the installation is complete.

12. Return to the Setup window and click step 5: Get Critical Updates For Microsoft Exchange. This launches Microsoft Update. Click Custom to obtain the list of applicable updates. Apply the proposed updates.

13. Close the Internet Explorer window when done and then close the Setup window. You may have to restart the system if updates were available.

14. Launch the Exchange Management Console (Start Menu | All Programs | Microsoft Exchange Server 2007 | Exchange Management Console).

15. Expand the Server Configuration section in the tree pane of the console.

16. Click Mailbox.

17. When the mailbox section has been updated in the details pane, right-click First Storage Group and select Move Storage Group Path. This opens the Move Storage Group Path dialog box.

18. Note that you cannot change the name of the storage group. Select the Log Files Path section and click Browse. Navigate to the E: drive and click Make New Folder. Call the new folder **FSGLogsOne for First Storage Group logs** and click OK.

19. Move to the System Files Path and click Browse. Navigate to the D: drive and click Make New Folder. Call the new folder **FSGTempOne for First Storage Group Database** and click OK.

20. You are ready to move the storage group. Click Move.

21. Exchange warns you that moving the database and logs will automatically render them inaccessible for a temporary period. Click Yes.

22. Return to the Move Storage Group Path dialog box and click Finish.

23. Right-click Mailbox Database and select Move Database Path.

24. Click Browse. Navigate to the D: drive and click Make New Folder. Call the new folder **FSGDataOne for Mailbox Database** and click Save.

25. Click Move.

26. Exchange warns you that moving the database will automatically render it inaccessible for a temporary period. Click Yes.

27. Click Finish.

28. Prepare the Local Continuous Replication configuration. Right-click First Storage Group and select Enable Local Continuous Replication.

29. Click Next. Move to the Log Files Path section and click Browse. Navigate to the G: drive and click Make New Folder. Call the new folder **FSGLogsTwo** and click OK.

30. Move to the System Files Path and click Browse. Navigate to the F: drive and click Make New Folder. Call the new folder **FSGTempTwo** and click OK.

31. Click Next. Click Browse. Navigate to the F: drive and click Make New Folder. Call the new folder **FSGDataTwo for Mailbox Database** and click Save.

32. Click Next. Verify your paths and click Enable.

33. Remember that you can copy the contents of this window to Notepad to create scripts for repeated operations.

34. Click Finish.

Your LCR configuration is now ready. You can use Windows Explorer to review the existence of the log and database files on each drive.

Quick Check

1. In an LCR solution, what is the required disk configuration for the two storage containers?
2. What do you need to protect public folder storage groups in an LCR?
3. The Cluster Continuous Replication (CCR) feature of Exchange is based on which service and uses which model?
4. What are the different possible continuity solutions with CCR?
5. Which resources are included in the CCR resource group?

Quick Check Answers

1. The first disk set, or production disk set, contains the storage groups managed by the MB system. The second disk set is used to create a replica of the production storage groups managed by this MB system.
2. To protect public folder storage groups, you should endeavor to have at least two MB systems hosting them. But, if you cannot, and if you only have one MB system in the network, such as for the Simple Organization type, you can enable LCR for the public folder storage group because in this case, LCR will not conflict with public folder replication.
3. CCR is based on the MCS service and relies on the Majority Node Set (MNS) cluster model instead of the Shared Quorum model.
4. Potential solutions include:

   ❑ In a Production: Cold (Dedicated) site, you simply ship your backup tapes to an offsite location. In the event of a disaster, you must deploy new hardware and software and restore all backups to get the system up and running again.

   ❑ In a Production: Warm (Dedicated) site, you have deployed hardware and software that is maintaining dedicated copies of your data, but you must perform a manual operation to activate the center in the event of a disaster. For example, you might have a Cluster Continuous Replication pair within the site to protect e-mail data and mail box services, but you would use another strategy to protect other server roles as well as supporting services such as DNS and Active Directory.

❑ In a Production: Warm (Non-Dedicated) using a two Active Directory site structure, you have deployed hardware that services users in each site and deployed hardware that provides backup for the resources in the other site. Once again, because the structure is warm, a manual operation is required to activate the backup site.

❑ In a Production: Production (Non-Dedicated) using a single Active Directory site structure, resources in both datacenters provide active service to end users, but act as backups for the resources in the other center. Activation is automatic and does not require manual intervention.

5. The CCR resource group includes:

❑ The Microsoft Exchange Information Store

❑ The Microsoft Exchange System Attendant

❑ The CMS Network Name

❑ The CMS IP Address

❑ The Microsoft Exchange Database Instance

Chapter Summary

- The LCR, CCR, SCC, and SCR protection features apply only on the MB role. The transaction log size has been reduced to 1 MB instead of the 5 MB in Exchange 2007 to support log shipping.

- You must install the Failover Cluster service before you can perform the Exchange SCC installation. In Exchange 2007 SCCs, handoffs are performed only through the **move-ClusteredMailboxServer** cmdlet.

- You cannot upgrade a clustered back-end Mailbox server installation from a legacy version of Exchange to Exchange 2007 because there is no direct upgrade path for any previous version of Exchange. You must create a new cluster and move the mailbox databases from the legacy cluster to the new cluster.

- CAS systems have a self-signed certificate installed by default, but this self-signed certificate does not include the new NLB cluster name. Because of this, clients trying to connect through port 443 using the NLB FQDN will get an error.

- Hub Transport servers can also rely on the NLB service, but only for client connections because the high availability structure of the HT is built into the role itself. In addition, using NLB for HT roles is only supported in SP1 of Exchange 2007.

- In single sites—sites where you want to have local access to a redundant copy of your e-mail data—you rely on Local Continuous Replication (LCR) to protect the data. Microsoft recommends that you keep databases without LCR to a maximum of 100 GB in size and databases with LCR to a maximum of 200 GB. Use this rule of thumb when planning your database sizes.

- Remember that CCR provides protection for both the data and the mailbox service. The CCR configuration requires the deployment of HT and CAS systems in each location. Remember that in each location where you deploy an MB, you also need to deploy an HT and a CAS. The reason for this is that both the HT and the CAS must have a local area network link to the MB to function.

- Exchange 2007 provides a special attribute, *AutoDatabaseMountDial*, that you can set to different values to control database operation in Cluster Continuous Replication configurations: *lossless*, *good availability*, and *best availability*.

- As with the SCC, you cannot use a direct path to migrate existing legacy version Exchange clusters to a CCR implementation. This is because there is no direct upgrade path from legacy versions to Exchange 2007. Therefore, you must first, create your CCR cluster and then use the **Move-Mailbox** cmdlet to migrate mailboxes or mailbox databases from existing instances to the new cluster.

Case Scenarios

In the following case scenarios, you will apply what you have learned about Exchange high availability. You can find answers to the questions in this scenario in the "Answers" section at the end of this book.

Case Scenario 1: Protect Exchange Data

The Phone Company (TPC) is moving to Exchange 2007 but they must ensure that Exchange data is available at all times. They have already consulted you on the various features that are available for Exchange 2007 data protection. Now they want you to assist them in planning their data availability strategy, but because they have never performed such an implementation before, they are not sure which elements they must include in their solution.

Your job is to help them determine which elements must be considered for their solution as well as help them identify how they should structure their service level agreements (SLAs) in relation to data availability. How do you proceed?

Case Scenario 2: Build Multi-Site Data Redundancy Plans

The Phone Company plans to move to Microsoft Exchange 2007, but they are concerned about data availability. Specifically, they do not fully understand which options are available for data protection in Exchange 2007 and what the difference is between each option. As such, they turn to you, the messaging professional, to ask that you provide them with a summary of the various options available in Exchange for data availability. Because they are deploying Exchange after Service Pack 1 has been released, they want to make sure you include SP1 features in your summary. Therefore, they ask two questions:

- What are the data availability options in Exchange 2007 SP1?
- How do the data availability options affect disk set configurations?

How do you respond?

Case Scenario 3: Plan to Protect Exchange Services

Now The Phone Company wants to establish a full strategy for Exchange high availability. Each level of the Exchange service and data must have high availability. They turn to you, the messaging professional, to help them identify which elements must be protected and at which level each element requires protection.

You must therefore outline responses to two questions:

- What needs to be protected to make Exchange highly available?
- In the elaboration of the protection strategy, which elements require a recovery time objective and a recovery point objective?

How do you respond?

Case Scenario 4: Plan High Availability for Exchange Services

Lucerne Publishing wants to move to Exchange Server 2007, but for them, e-mail is a mission-critical application. Therefore it is highly important for them to ensure that the e-mail service will be available at all times. They outline how their network is structured (see Figure 6-8) and ask you what they need to do and which technologies they need to rely on if they want to ensure service availability in their most important sites, which include New York and Los Angeles.

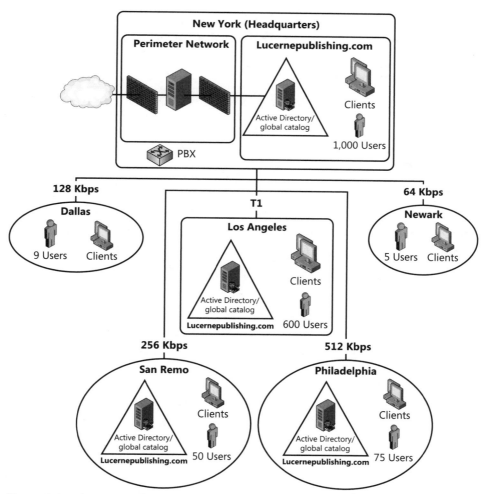

Figure 6-8   The Lucerne Publishing network structure

They turn to you, the messaging professional, to request an explanation of the technologies they will need to implement to provide the level of availability they need. Specifically, they request the following:

1. What are the service availability features they need to put in place for Exchange 2007?

2. What type of availability can they provide in the perimeter network?

3. What type of availability can they provide in the two main sites, New York and Los Angeles?

4. What should they do for users in Dallas and Newark?

5. Will they need additional third-party software to provide the levels of service they are looking for?

How do you respond?

Suggested Practices

It is difficult to practice high availability with Exchange Server without access to a full infrastructure, but you can do so if you prepare a virtual environment as outlined in the Introduction. You should then use the ExchangeLCR.treyresearch.net server to practice data protection operations for the Mailbox Server role and ExchangeOne. treyresearch.net to work with the other server roles.

If you want to work with the other high availability features, you will need at least four more Exchange 2007 servers: one more with the ET role to practice ET protection; two with the three coexistence roles to practice HT, CAS, and UM protection; and two with MB to practice CCR. Then you can run through the high availability strategies for each role to see what is needed and how you should configure it. As you can see, this can require significant resources.

Chapter 7

Plan Messaging Security and Compliance Implementation

Few technological deployments can occur without including a significant security element. And the same applies to Exchange Server 2007. In fact, security is a critical element of the Exchange deployment because e-mail has become so critical to the operation of many businesses and organizations. In addition, with new compliance rulings in place, organizations must not only ensure that their e-mail systems are secure, but they must also ensure that they have proper retention capabilities for all e-mail data. Compliance and privacy regulations also have impositions on what kind of information can be transmitted in an e-mail.

This is why you must plan for both security and compliance in your messaging platform deployments. This chapter will focus on the security portion of this combination. Chapter 8, "Work with Transport Rules and Compliance," will focus on compliance. When considering your Exchange 2007 deployment, each of the following security components should be included:

- The first component you must consider is antivirus and anti-spam protection. E-mail systems are traditional vectors for infiltration and must therefore provide significant defenses against the introduction of malicious content into the e-mail stream.

- The second component should cover the actual server deployment itself including server positioning and core operating system security.

- The third should cover the assignment of security roles to e-mail administrators within your organization.

- The fourth should focus on securing both client and server communications and mail flow in general.

You must examine each of these elements in depth before you begin your deployment to ensure that you can properly protect all data as soon as the e-mail system is up and running and data begins to flow through it.

Exam Tip   Because of the objectives of the exam and in the interest of conserving space, only the first and the last bullet points are covered in this chapter. However, to properly plan your deployment, you should consider both of the other elements. The best place to start is with the "Exchange 2007 Security Guide," found here: *http://technet.microsoft.com/en-us/library/ bb691338.aspx*.

Exam objectives in this chapter:

- Plan the antivirus and anti-spam implementation.
- Plan the network layer security implementation.

Before You Begin

To complete the lessons in this chapter, you must have the following:

- A virtual machine setup as outlined in the Introduction under "Virtual Machine Environments."
- Use the Exchange Server 2007 virtual machine from Microsoft to review the configuration options for pre-installed machines.
- Use the virtual environment you set up to test the implementation of security strategies with Exchange Server. For the exercises in this chapter, you will need access to the Active Directory server and the all-in-one Exchange server, ExchangeOne, as well as the Edge Transport server, ExchangeETOne.

Lesson 1: Plan the Antivirus and Anti-spam Implementation

Estimated lesson time: 40 minutes

Security threats abound, as do threat vectors. Malicious attackers are now moving to blended threats, using multiple vectors and multiple attacks all at once to try to get past organizational defenses. As a messaging professional, you need to protect critical systems, especially e-mail, from these unwanted threats. IT administrators in small to medium-sized organizations are already swamped with work. This is why it is so important to plan defenses before you put new systems in place. The first place to start is to identify the nature of the potential threats. Only then can you prepare appropriate defenses.

Identify Potential Threats and Threat Vectors

You must consider a number of potential security vulnerabilities. Some of the most common include:

- **Accidental Security Breach**   These attacks are usually caused accidentally by users or system operators. They stem from a lack of awareness of security issues. For example, users who do not protect their passwords because they are not aware of the consequences can be the cause of accidental attacks. Operators who place users in the wrong security groups and assign them the wrong privileges can also cause accidental security breaches. Users should know that they should never give out their passwords, and operators need to be careful when given such a responsibility.

- **Internal Attack**   Internal attacks are a major source of attacks. In fact, they are still the major source of attacks, but with the proliferation of Internet-based attacks, their importance in proportion to all other attacks has diminished. Internal attacks stem from within the internal network. Their source can be the organization's personnel or other personnel that are allowed access to the internal network—consultants, outsourced workers, and so on. These attacks are often the result of a lack of vigilance. Internal personnel often assume that because the internal network is protected from the outside, everyone that has access to it can be trusted. This is not the case. Make sure all access to your network is protected.

- **Social Engineering**   These attacks also stem from a lack of awareness. They are caused by external sources trying to impersonate internal personnel and thereby trick users into divulging compromising information. For example, an attacker might call a user while impersonating the Help desk and ask for the user's password. It is common practice even today for Help desk personnel to ask users for their password. This behavior is completely unacceptable. Help desk personnel should never have reason to have access to a user's password. Users should know never to divulge their passwords.

- **Organizational Attack**   These attacks stem from competitive organizations who want to penetrate your internal network and discover your trade secrets.

- **Automated Attacks**   These are one of the most common attack types. An external computer scans Internet addresses until it finds a response. When it finds a working address, it scans this address to identify potential vulnerabilities. These attacks have become extremely sophisticated today and protecting yourself from them has now become a full-time occupation. For example, many administrators do not know they have the Simple Network Management Protocol (SNMP) enabled on their systems. A simple SNMP scan can provide details such as the computer's name, IP address, domain partnership, and much more.

- **Denial of Service (DoS)**   These attacks are designed to stop the operation of a service on your network. Attacks that target generic Microsoft technologies instead of specifically targeting your organization are excellent examples of DoS attacks.

- **Viral Attacks**   These attacks are in the form of viruses, worms, or Trojan horses and are designed to infiltrate your systems to perpetrate some form of damage on either services or data. Viruses seek to infect a computer, replicate, and then infect as many other computers as possible as quickly as they can. The goal of malicious code is often destruction.

- **Spyware Infiltrations**   These infiltrations are typically in the form of hidden code bundled with freeware or shareware programs users download from the Internet. Once installed, spyware will monitor user activity and transmit data about this activity to another location. The most malicious spyware will gather data about user identities such as passwords or even credit card numbers. Rootkits are also a most virulent form of spyware because they are nearly unidentifiable by the operating system and require special tools for removal. Spyware and rootkits tend to be made of complete programs that integrate themselves into the system and go as far as making specific entries into the registry. The intent of spyware is to gather data and send it to a remote location. Unlike viruses, spyware is often motivated by profit.

- **Phishing** Phishing is another form of social engineering. It usually takes the form of an e-mail message. The objective is to fraudulently obtain sensitive information from users. For example, many phishing schemes attempt to impersonate banks or other trusted account sources. In the messages, they tell the user they need confirmation for account information and instruct the user to click the included link to confirm the information. The link usually redirects the user to a phisher's Web site in an attempt to collect account information from the user.

- **Spam** Spam is comparable in some ways to a DoS attack because it overloads your e-mail system with unwanted traffic. Each time a user leaves his or her e-mail address on a Web site, this e-mail address becomes subject to becoming a spam recipient. What is worse, some reputable Web sites sell their e-mail lists, so even if you think you have dealt with someone you trust, your address falls into some spam bucket somewhere.

Of these, the threats that affect e-mail systems the most are viral attacks, spyware infiltrations, and spam. In addition, threats are becoming blended, using multiple attack vectors to carry multiple attack payloads. Blended threats include several different threat characteristics: viruses, worms, Trojan Horses, spyware, and/or rootkits. The blended approach makes these threats more pervasive than any others. They use multiple attack vectors to try to reproduce themselves as much as possible and perform as much damage as possible.

One thing is clear: whether you are facing blended or single threats, you need a comprehensive defense system. And because the e-mail system is one of the most important threat vectors you will have in place, you need to pay special attention when deploying it to ensure that you have taken a layered approach to defending your systems and as little unwanted e-mail will get through as possible.

Protect E-mail Systems

One of the best ways to get protection for e-mail is to filter out all unwanted noise. Filtering reduces potentially dangerous content from your e-mail traffic. The best filtering techniques include the following capabilities:

- **Spam protection** Despite the fact that spam is not as dangerous as viruses, organizations generally receive more spam and have more nefarious impact from spam than from viruses. That is because spam clogs the pipeline and reduces the level of service you get from your e-mail servers.

- **Virus protection**   Antivirus engines need to be completely integrated to your e-mail server system to identify and quarantine any potential threat. Each message must be scanned without affecting e-mail server performance.

- **Content filtering**   Ideally, your protection system would be able to scan the content of e-mail messages to filter out anything you just do not want in your systems. You need to scan attachments and their contents, message bodies, and—especially with the new approach to graphical spam—perform some form of character recognition on images.

- **Blocked senders**   Your system should also let you block senders by generating Blocked Senders lists. Of course, you also need to make sure partners and other people you actually deal with are on a corresponding safe recipients list.

- **Notifications**   Your protection system needs to send you proper notifications of suspicious events as they occur so that you are up to date on how well you are protected.

- **Message classification**   With the advent of new compliance regulations that affect pretty well every organization with access to the Internet, you need to make sure your system will be able to classify messages and route them to appropriate locations.

- **Archiving**   Because compliance is an issue, you need a proper archiving system so that you can go back to retrieve important information when you need it.

These are a few of the most important aspects of the e-mail protection system you need to have in place. Exchange 2007 offers support for each and every one of these items. One of its strongest features is the protection it offers from unwanted noise through the Edge Transport Server role and the new filtering capabilities built into its transport mechanisms.

Reduce Unwanted Noise with Edge Transport Servers

Spammers use a variety of different techniques to try to get unwanted noise into your e-mail system. This is why you need to stop it at the gate. This is exactly what you can do with Exchange 2007's new antivirus and anti-spam features. Generally, the Exchange 2007 features for the control of malware include:

- **Connection Filtering**   Exchange can identify the IP address of the server that is trying to send messages to your organization. Based on this identification, Exchange can perform filtering actions. These actions are based on IP Block or

Allow lists, which help the Exchange server receiving the message to determine whether the messages from this source are trusted or untrusted. Untrusted messages are stopped at the gate and do not enter your organization's e-mail system, but only after all of the RCPT TO: headers—the headers that include the potential recipients of the message—are processed in case there is an exception for this message. Because this filter acts at the SMTP gateway level, it only runs on Edge Transport Server roles and usually runs on the Internet-facing connection of these systems.

The Connection Filter agent processes IP addresses against administrator-configured allow and block lists, but it also uses block and allow lists from list providers. Local lists are configured through either the Exchange Management Console or the Shell and can be entered as individual addresses, address ranges, or address and subnet mask. Block list entries can have an expiration time or date assigned when they are configured to automatically remove them after a given period of time. Use these lists to allow or block IP addresses that are not in the lists provided by real-time block list (RBL) providers. Note that in Exchange, RBLs are referred to as IP Block Lists and lists originating from safe list providers (SLP) are referred to as IP Allow Lists.

RBLs from providers are useful especially when spammers rely on dial-up connections—connections that provide dynamic IP addresses—to send spam. Good RBL providers will include ISPs that allow SMTP traffic over dynamic connections into their lists, blocking this threat. Exchange supports multiple subscriptions to RBL providers. ET systems first verify their own lists, and then verify the IP address against any provider list you have configured. Multiple list provider connections are the best practice because Exchange administrators would be overwhelmed trying to keep their own lists up to date on their own. However, legitimate senders can be found within provider RBLs by mistake. For example, this can occur when SMTP relays are misconfigured as open relays and relay any SMTP message. Spammers love to take advantage of these misconfigurations, which leaves the legitimate sender out in the cold. Configuring IP Allow lists avoids this issue if it occurs on your systems because local lists are always processed before provider lists.

MORE INFO   Real-Time block Lists

More information on real-time block list providers can be found at *http://www.email-policy.com/spam-black-lists.htm*.

- **Sender Filtering**   Exchange can use the MAIL FROM: SMTP command on incoming messages to identify the sender of an e-mail and determine which action to take based on defined lists of trusted and untrusted senders or sender domains. Exchange administrators can block single senders (such as John.Kane@lucernepublishing.com); block entire e-mail domains (such as *@lucernepublishing.com); or block e-mail domains and any subdomains they contain (such as *@*.lucernepublishing.com). Resulting actions are also configurable. For example, you can set rejected senders to receive a 554 5.1.0 Sender Denied message, or you can accept the message and mark it as a message originating from a blocked sender and move it up the chain. This value will be added to the computations the Content Filtering agent will perform when determining the spam confidence level for the message. Make sure you combine the Sender Filter with the Sender ID filter to avoid spoofing of the MAIL FROM: SMTP header. Spoofing relies on the modification of this header to pretend the message originates from a different location than its actual location.

- **Recipient Filtering**   Exchange can use the RCPT TO: SMTP command on incoming messages to identify the recipients of an e-mail and determine which action to take based on defined lists of untrusted recipients. This filter can also determine whether the recipient is valid or not to block invalid recipients at the gate. Three possible scenarios can be used to filter at this level:

  - ❏ Recipients can be nonexistent and therefore are blocked by default. Good examples of recipients that should be blocked at this level are administrator@lucernepublishing.com or support@lucernepublishing.com.

  - ❏ Special distribution lists that are for internal e-mail purposes only can be blocked to ensure that no message originating on the Internet can be sent to these lists.

  - ❏ Special mailboxes that are for internal use only can also be included here to prevent messages from the Internet to be delivered to them.

  This filter uses either its block list or recipient lookups against the GAL to verify whether recipients are allowed or denied. The ET system does not have access to the GAL because it is within Active Directory, so it is important to set up Edge Subscriptions to ensure that GAL information is located within the ADAM instance on each ET. If the recipient is in a block list or does not exist, Exchange sends a 550 5.1.1 User Unknown message to the sending server. If the recipient is approved, Exchange sends a 250 2.1.5 Recipient OK message to the sending server.

If your organization manages multiple e-mail domains—for example, lucernepublishing.com and graphicsdesigninstitute.com—you must make sure your ET systems are configured as authoritative for both domains; otherwise, recipient lookup will fail for all non-authoritative domains.

IMPORTANT Tarpitting within the Recipient Filtering Agent

Because the Recipient Filtering Agent returns the 250 2.1.5 Recipient OK message to the sending server each time a recipient is approved, your organization could be at risk. For example, spammers could use this information to enter valid e-mail IDs into a spam database, bypassing the Recipient Filter. This is called a *directory harvest attack* because spammers harvest approved recipient names and sell them to others through automated programs. Because of this, Exchange includes tarpitting functionality to artificially delay responses—specifically the 550 5.1.1 User Unknown response—to sending servers when specific conditions indicating potential spam attacks are detected. Because of these delays, harvest attacks become too expensive to sustain properly. Tarpitting is configured to a five-second interval by default, but you can change this setting by changing the *TarpitInterval* value on the Receive connector.

- **Sender ID**   Sender ID is a new validation method for e-mails. It relies on the identification of the IP address of the sending server along with the Purported Responsible Address (PRA) of the sender to validate that the sender's address is not spoofed. The agent requests PRA information from the DNS server that includes the record for the sending server and sending e-mail domain. This information is usually published within sender policy framework (SPF) records on the DNS server. PRA calculations include four elements drawn from the message headers: Resent-Sender:, Resent-From:, Sender:, and From:. PRA and Sender ID are based on request for comment (RFC) number 4407. Sender ID should be used in conjunction with Sender Filtering to avoid spoofing. Three actions can be taken should the message seem spoofed: stamp the message with its status, reject it, or delete it. Stamping the message adds a MAPI property to the message. The Outlook Junk E-mail Filter relies on this MAPI property to evaluate the spam confidence level for the message once it reaches the Inbox. Rejected e-mails return an SMTP error message to the sender. Deletion does not inform the sender and can often be the best action to take. Remember that any form of confirmation of the reception of a message can also be used by spammers.

- **Sender Reputation**   Over time, as messages are received from specific sources, Exchange uses the Protocol Analysis agent to build a sender reputation from the originating IP address of the server delivering the mail. This agent uses a variety of factors to determine the sender's reputation level (SRL). If this level exceeds a specific threshold, the messages it delivers will be blocked. In addition, the Protocol Analysis agent will rely on updated IP Reputation updates that are provided through Microsoft Update to supplement its own SRL analyses. The factors used to determine the SRL include:

❑ The first test involves the HELO and EHLO SMTP commands, which are normally used to return the sending e-mail domain name or IP address, but which are often forged by spammers. Potential forgeries can include constantly wrong IP addresses in the header, local e-mail domain names—for example, the same domain as the ET system—or constantly changing domain names.

❑ The second test involves a reverse DNS lookup based on the information in the HELO or EHLO SMTP commands. This is much like the Sender ID verification, but in this case, the lookup simply verifies that the IP address associated with the message returns the proper domain name.

❑ The Content Filter continually generates spam confidence level ratings on messages from various senders. Sender reputation will rely on these ratings to determine the reputation of a sender.

❑ The last test verifies whether the message originates from an open proxy. A proxy server is often used to share Internet connections traversing a firewall among multiple users. Open proxies are configured to accept connection requests from anyone anywhere and forward the traffic as if it originated from the proxy itself. This can happen when proxies are misconfigured or when Trojans are used to provide the proxy link.

Sender reputation can be used to reject, delete, and archive or accept and mark a message. It acts at two levels of a transmission: when the MAIL FROM: SMTP command is processed and when the _EOD or end of data SMTP command is processed. Sender reputation works in conjunction with other connection filters to block or allow SMTP traffic.

■ **Content Filtering**   Content filtering relies on Microsoft SmartScreen technology and the Intelligent Message Filter (IMF) to examine the body of a message. The IMF learns to distinguish valid from non-valid information in a message. In addition, IMF is updated regularly through the Microsoft Anti-spam Update Service when it is run to ensure that it will capture as many positives as possible. Suspicious messages are quarantined instead of blocked to reduce the risk of false positives. Administrators review these messages to see whether they should be forwarded on or rightly deleted.

Content filtering also acts as the engine for safelist aggregation by collecting lists managed by users in Outlook and Outlook Web Access to make this information available to the Content Filter agent on ET systems. This includes not only the messages from contacts users have in their Inbox, but also from Outlook Safe Senders and other trusted source lists. When safelist aggregation is used, messages marked as safe by the Content Filter agent do not undergo additional processing—except for anti-virus processing—and are automatically delivered within the organization's e-mail system.

Content Filtering also uses other techniques for evaluation, including:

- ❑ Allowed or denied words or phrases
- ❑ Outlook E-mail Postmark validations
- ❑ Recipient, sender, or sender domain bypasses

Each technique provides a pass or fail test. Passes are moved up the chain and fails are not.

Overall, the Content Filtering Agent assigns a spam confidence level (SCL) rating to the message. Messages are deleted, rejected, quarantined, or delivered based on their SCL rating. Low ratings are good; high ratings are bad. Administrators can configure the rating threshold to determine which messages are rated as good or bad. Messages are, however, also filtered based on size. Messages of 11 MB or greater are not scanned by the IMF and are moved up the chain unchecked. Note that the default maximum message limit on Exchange Receive connectors is 10 MB, so if you do not change the default, this should not be an issue. Messages that are deemed safe are moved on to antivirus processing within the processing chain.

- ■ **Attachment Filtering**   Like content filtering, attachment filtering will examine not the body of a message, but the type of attachment included with a message. Attachment filtering is performed based on filenames, file extensions, or MIME content type, determining what type of attachment it is. The Attachment Filtering agent can even determine whether a file name or extension has been modified to pass as an approved format. You can use the **Get-AttachmentFilterEntry | FL** cmdlet on a transport server—using at least local administrative rights—to get a full list of both file extensions and MIME types Exchange addresses.

When suspicious attachments are found, this filter can block the message, remove the attachment, and send the message on—or the filter can simply delete the message and the attachment. When messages are blocked, the sender will receive a delivery status notification message telling him or her the attachment was blocked. When attachments are removed, they are replaced with a text message stating that the attachment was removed. If the message is deleted, neither sender nor recipient will be notified. Note that deleted messages or removed attachments are not recoverable. Also, consider putting in exceptions for messages that are digitally signed; modifying these messages automatically invalidates their signature.

MORE INFO   Forefront Security for Exchange Server

Organizations choosing to use Forefront Security for Exchange Server or another third-party security filter will be able to scan attachments contained within container files such as compressed or zipped files. The default Exchange agent can only scan for filenames within compressed files. Third-party tools can scan for filename or extension changes within the compressed file. In addition, these tools can quarantine messages and notify either senders or recipients.

More information on Forefront Security for Exchange can be found at *http://go.microsoft.com/fwlink/?linkid=96630*.

- **Outlook Junk E-mail Filtering** Outlook also filters e-mail on a local basis if any potentially malicious message gets through the various Exchange filters. Trapped messages are moved to the Junk E-mail folder to be reviewed by the end user before deletion.

- **Antivirus Engines** Exchange also has special virus scanning application programming interfaces (VSAPI) that are designed to work with commercial antivirus engines. Exchange itself however, does not include an antivirus engine. Microsoft offers Forefront Security for Exchange Server, while other manufacturers offer their own third-party antivirus engines for Exchange. No Exchange implementation should move forward without at least one of these engines deployed on the ET and/or the HT roles.

- **Spam Confidence Level Rating** When messages are analyzed by the various anti-spam filtering technologies included in Exchange, they are stamped with evaluation metadata called the Spam Confidence Level Rating. This metadata details the logic used to analyze a specific message and outlines why it was either blocked or accepted. When accepted, this metadata is then used to allow message processing on other Exchange servers within the organization.

- **Anti-spam Updates** For the first time, Exchange 2007 can benefit from the Microsoft Update service or an internal deployment of Windows Server Update

Services (WSUS) to obtain updates related to spam identification. Two levels of updates are available:

❏ The standard update service offers updates on a bimonthly basis (every two weeks). Updates are obtained from the Microsoft Update Web sites.

❏ The premium service, called Forefront Security for Exchange Server anti-spam updates, provides daily updates for the content filter. It can also provide point-in-time Spam Signature to identify recent spam campaigns as well as IP Reputation Service updates if the need arises. These point-in-time updates can even occur several times a day. To have access to the premium update service, organizations must acquire the Exchange Enterprise Client Access License (CAL).

MORE INFO Anti-Spam updates

For information on available anti-spam updates, go to *http://technet.microsoft.com/en-us/library/bb124241.aspx*.

■ **Hosted Services** Organizations that do not have the facilities to host their own ET systems can take advantage of services hosted by application service providers (ASPs). Microsoft itself offers an Exchange Hosted Services, which provides filtering. Other vendors also offer this type of service.

IMPORTANT Using Windows Server 2008 and IPv6

Organizations deploying Windows Server 2008 with Exchange 2007 SP1 will also have access to IPv6 because it is installed by default with the operating system. Microsoft recommends against configuring Receive connectors to accept anonymous IPv6 connections from unknown sources. If you need to receive mail from IPv6 sources, configure a specific Receive connector that is bound to the source addresses of these senders. This will help protect you from potentially harmful messages transported over this carrier. IPv6 adoption is still in its infancy and there are as yet no standards for its use for message delivery.

Exchange Filtering Strategies

As you can see, several different filtering technologies work together to protect your systems from unwanted traffic. By default, Exchange uses the filtering technique that requires the least amount of server resources first. Then, if the message passes this level of filter, Exchange escalates it up through the other filters until it is deemed authorized or rejected, using more and more resources as the message moves up the escalation path.

Because of this, the logic used by Exchange 2007 on Edge Transport servers to evaluate messages uses the following steps once an SMTP session is initiated with a sending server:

1. The Connection Filter uses the IP Allow, IP Block, Safe Provider, and IP Block Provider real-time block lists (RBL) to determine whether the message should be blocked or allowed.

IMPORTANT   The Bypass Anti-Spam Permission

Microsoft Exchange includes the ability to set a special trusted attribute to trusted SMTP senders (*Ms-Exch-Bypass-Anti-Spam*). If an administrator sets this value for partner SMTP servers, anti-spam processing is skipped and message filtering moves to step 5 to perform content filtering.

---

2. The Sender Filter examines the SMTP source of the message to see whether the sending domain or the sender itself is on a block list. This occurs before a user's own Safe Senders List is evaluated and may block messages from senders that are approved by end users but not at the organizational level.

3. The Recipient Filter examines the recipient list in the message to see whether they are trusted or untrusted or whether they even exist. If there are multiple recipients and only some are blocked, those recipients are removed and the message moves on. Blocked messages are returned to the sender and the sender's reputation is updated.

4. The Sender ID Filter determines the PRA of the message based on a standard PRA algorithm. The resulting value is the SMTP address of the sender—for example, John.Kane@lucernepublishing.com. The filter then uses the domain section of the address (lucernepublishing.com) to query the DNS server for that domain. If this domain has a sender policy framework (SPF), it will be returned to the Exchange agent who will use it in its evaluation. If there is no SPF, the message is stamped accordingly and processed further along the chain. If the sender's domain or IP address is in a blocked list, the message will be processed according to the rules set by the Exchange administrator. In this case, the message can be rejected, deleted, or simply stamped with the results and moved along the chain.

5. The Content Filter first reviews the results of the previous connection filtering actions to make sure there are no missed rejections, and applies the antivirus scan. When the antivirus has scanned the object, content filtering is applied.

Content filtering assigns a spam confidence level (SCL) rating to the message. If the SCL rating exceeds the threshold, the message can be deleted, rejected, or quarantined. If not, it moves on through the processing chain. Note that if safelist aggregation has been configured, this level of filtering will also rely on Outlook Safe Sender lists to process the message.

6. The Attachment Filter will evaluate the message if it includes an attachment. If not, the message moves on up the chain. This level of filtering will once again perform one of three actions if the attachment meets the blocking criteria: reject the message, delete the message, or strip the attachment and send the message on up the processing chain.

7. If Forefront Security for Exchange Server is in place, another level of antivirus scanning is performed on the message. If a virus is found at this stage, the message is deleted and a notice is send to the recipient.

8. The last filtering stage is the Outlook Junk E-mail Filter, which is performed when the message arrives in the user's Inbox. If the message meets a condition set by the user but not set at the organizational level, it is placed into the user's Junk E-mail folder. If not, it is placed into the Inbox.

Each message received by an ET system is processed according to this flowchart (see Figure 7-1). Administrators must enable several levels of configuration to obtain full functionality from the Exchange anti-spam filters.

IMPORTANT   Edge Transport server location in message path

The Microsoft Exchange architecture assumes that the ET role will be the first SMTP gateway to receive messages from the external world. In some cases, organizations place additional, non-Exchange SMTP gateways before the ET role. Because Exchange evaluates messages based on source IP address, it is important for these organizations to include the IP addresses of these third-party SMTP gateways in the InternalSMTPServer property of the *TransportConfig* object on the ET systems to avoid false positives. Use the **Set-TransportConfig** cmdlet to perform this activity.

MORE INFO   Anti-spam settings migration from Exchange 2003

Although the anti-spam capabilities of Exchange 2007 go far beyond those of Exchange 2003, that is no reason for anyone to lose all of the hard work they have done in configuring anti-spam settings in the legacy Exchange version. Fortunately, Microsoft has released an Anti-spam Migration Tool, which you can use to recover your settings. For information on this tool, go to *http://technet.microsoft.com/en-us/library/bb508835.aspx*.

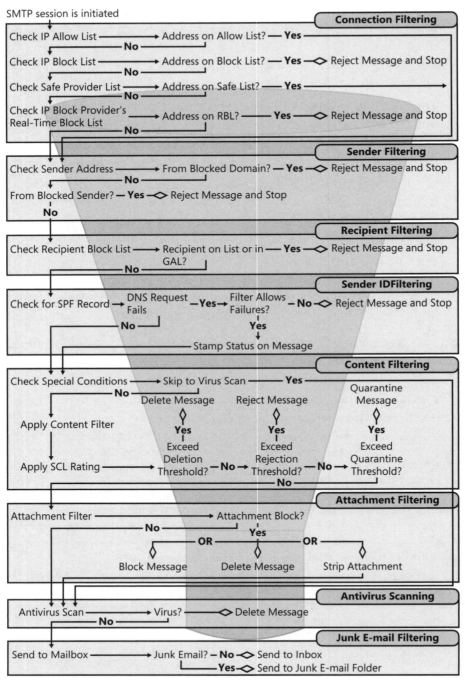

Figure 7-1 The Exchange e-mail filtering funnel

Understand Anti-Spam Stamping

When a message is processed through the various filters on an ET, it is stamped with the results of the analysis it goes through. Messages are stamped whether they succeed or fail to get through the system and actions are taken accordingly. Four stamps are possible:

- The anti-spam report
- The phishing confidence level
- The spam confidence level
- The Sender ID

Stamps are added to messages in the form of metadata that is inscribed into the header of a message. For example, you can view the stamp on a message through Office Outlook 2007. Open a message and click Message Options in the Options group on the Message tab. This displays message options. (See Figure 7-2.) Scroll through the Internet Header to view the content of the stamp.

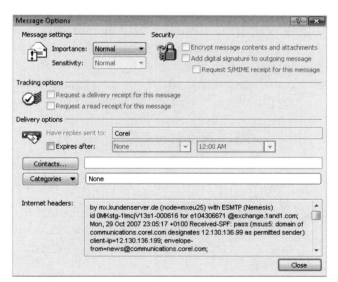

Figure 7-2 Viewing anti-spam stamps on a message—in this case, the SPF passed from the sending server

The anti-spam report can be made up of a considerable series of different information blocks. It usually begins with the X-MS-Exchange-Organization-Antispam-Report: heading and includes the anti-spam report itself along with the other three stamping items listed earlier. This information is inscribed by the Content Filter into the message header. Note that anti-spam reports will only include those elements that were actually applied to a message. For example, if a message is rejected at the content filtering level, its report will not include any information about attachment filtering.

Table 7-1 describes the potential values in an anti-spam report.

Table 7-1   Potential Information in an Anti-Spam Report

Stamp	Comments
AllRecipientsBypassed	AllRecipientsBypassed refers to the fact that the recipients are approved for bypass. This is set in one of three ways: by changing the *AntispamBypassedEnabled* parameter on the recipient's mailbox to $True, by placing the sender in an Outlook Safe Senders List and enabling safelist aggregation, or if another exception has been applied to this recipient.
CW	CW refers to custom weight of a message. Custom weight is determined based on keyword or phrase searches within message body. As with the SCL, values between 0 and 9 are used: Unapproved words or phrases are set to 9 and approved words or phrases are set to 0. Evaluation is based on the Allow or Block phrases you configure on your servers.
DV	DV relates to the DAT version stamp and is used to indicate which version of the definition file was used to scan the message.
IPOnAllowList	IPOnAllowList refers to the fact that the sender's IP address is on the IP Allow List you configure on your servers.
MessageSecurity-AntispamBypass	MessageSecurityAntispamBypass refers to the fact that the sender is on the bypass list and that anti-spam filtering was not applied to the message.
MIME: MIME-Compliance	MIME: refers to whether the message format is MIME compliant or not.

Table 7-1 Potential Information in an Anti-Spam Report

Stamp	Comments
P100: PhishingBlock	P100: refers to the fact that the message contains a URL that is listed in a phishing definition file.
PCL	PCL refers to the phishing confidence level of the message. Outlook uses this stamp to block or unblock message content. Values can range from 1 to 8 and are processed as: Neutral if the value is 1 to 3, meaning that the content is not considered to be phishing. Suspicious if the value is 4 to 8, meaning that the content is considered to be phishing.
PP	PP refers to the pre-solved puzzle value of the message. PP messages use an Outlook E-mail Postmark. The filtering agent performs a computation against the Postmark to determine whether it is valid. If yes, the agent will lower the SCL rating and allow the message through. If the computation fails for some reason, the SCL rating stays the same for the message.
SA	SA refers to signature action that was used when a signature was found in the message. Actions can include deletion or rejection.
SCL	SCL refers to the spam confidence level of the message content. Ratings can range from 0 to 9. 0 ratings means the content is not spam; 9 means that it is. Actions performed on messages depend on the SCL threshold you set on your servers.
SenderBypassed	SenderBypassed refers to the fact that the sender is on a bypass list you configured and that the Content Filtering agent did not process this message.

Table 7-1   Potential Information in an Anti-Spam Report

Stamp	Comments
SID	SID relates to the Sender ID and is based on the sender policy framework (SPF) that is used to authorize the use of domains in e-mail. Several status values can be included in this stamp:
	Pass means that the message has passed the SID verification.
	Neutral means that the results were not conclusive.
	Softfail means that the results were less than conclusive. For example, the IP address of the sender may not be in the SPF.
	Fail means that the IP address is not in the SPF.
	None means that the DNS query did not provide any SPF data.
	TempError means that the filter agent was not able to contact a DNS server.
	PermError means that the DNS information was not valid.
SV	SV refers to the signature DAT version of the file used to scan the message.
TIME: TimeBased-Features	TIME: refers to the duration of the travel time for the message, evaluating the time when it was sent against the time it was received. This rating determines the final SCL rating for the message.

Plan Exchange Mail System Protection

Several steps are required to plan and prepare for mail system protection, especially protection from unwanted e-mail traffic. First, you must configure your Edge Transport servers, then you put in place the Edge Subscription between Hub Transport servers and the ET systems you deployed (see Lesson 2 in Chapter 2, "Planning Deployments"), and only then can you begin to configure the various filtering agents that run on the transport servers.

Several transport filtering agents are designed specifically to run on Internet-facing connections and as such have been designed to run only on the Edge Transport server. However, in some situations—for example, in a Simple Organization that has no ET systems—you may need to run anti-spam features on Hub Transport servers. Table 7-2 outlines which agents run only on the ET role and which can be made to run on the HT role.

Table 7-2   Filtering Agents and Transport Roles

Agent	Runs on ET	Runs on HT
Connection Filter	☑	☑
Sender Filter	☑	☑
Recipient Filter	☑	☑
Sender ID	☑	☑
Sender Reputation	☑	☑
Content Filter	☑	☑
Attachment Filter	☑	☐
Antivirus Filter	☑	☑

You should not enable filtering on both the ET and HT systems if they both exist in your network. Also, you will notice that even when you configure the anti-spam filters on HT systems, attachment filtering will not occur. This is because attachment filtering is a function of the antivirus engine and the antivirus filter does not run by default on an HT system. Instead, you must purchase a third-party antivirus engine and configure it to run on the HT as you would on an ET.

Anti-spam features are installed on HT systems through a custom Exchange Shell script, but once installed they are configured in the same manner as those on ET systems.

MORE INFO   Installing anti-spam features on HT roles

For more information on the installation of anti-spam features on HT roles, go to *http://technet.microsoft.com/en-us/library/bb201691.aspx*.

Configure all your filters in the order they will apply to incoming messages. Each filter is configured independently.

Keep in mind that the higher you set your filtering thresholds, the more messages you will discard and, unfortunately, the more likely it will be that many of these messages are false positives. For example, many users do not enter a subject in the Subject field of a message. Is this enough justification to reject the message? Chances are that spammers will not forget the subject line in their messages, but does that mean that messages without subject lines are valid? Only careful monitoring of rejected messages will tell you. In addition, you can be sure to hear from your users if they expect messages from outside your organization and the messages do not arrive because your spam filters are set to an aggressive level.

Microsoft recommends that when messages are rejected by one of three key filters—the Connection, Recipient, or Sender filters—you should consider it spam by default and reject it. Because of this, the first two filters, Connection and Recipient, block bad messages by default. Only the Sender Filter is configurable. These filters provide the best spam identification levels because they rely on lists that are either managed directly by you or by organizations that specialize in spam prevention.

Based on this recommendation, you can plan to keep these three filters at fairly aggressive levels and adjust any other filters to a low or medium threshold. Whatever you do, you should plan to monitor your spam filtering levels closely, at least at first, once they are deployed. Only then will you be able to adjust them appropriately for your organization's needs.

Configure the Connection Filter

Configuring the Connection Filter is performed through either the Exchange Management Console or the Exchange Management Shell. Because this task is performed on the Edge Transport server, you must have local administrative rights to perform it. Configuring this filter involves four (or possibly five) steps:

1. Enable the filter.
2. Populate the IP Allow and Block lists.
3. Populate the IP Allow and Block List providers.
4. If the ET is not the first point of contact for inbound SMTP traffic, configure the filter accordingly.
5. Test the configuration.

Also, because the ET system is not linked to an Active Directory forest, configuration changes are stored locally. Therefore, you must perform these configuration activities on each ET system in your perimeter network.

The Connection Filter is enabled by default on ET systems for inbound messages that originate from the Internet and are not authenticated. These messages are categorized as external messages and are automatically examined. You should always use this filter on external sources, but never on internal or authenticated sources to avoid generating false positives.

Because you should configure several providers to increase the value for the lists you obtain, Exchange allows you to configure a custom SMTP 550 message for each provider. When a message is blocked by a list from particular provider, you can configure the SMTP 550 message to identify the provider in the message returned to the sender. This way, legitimate senders can contact the provider to have their names removed from the list. When configuring these messages, however, you must be able to properly identify which provider rejected a message. Two types of identification systems exist: bitmask and absolute value. You should verify the documentation from your providers to see which method they use and which values they return.

Potential bitmask and absolute values are listed in Table 7-3. These values are returned based on the message evaluation.

Table 7-3   **Potential Bitmask and Absolute Values**

Value Type	Value	Status
Bitmask	127.0.0.1	IP address is in a block list.
	127.0.0.2	Originating SMTP server is an open relay.
	127.0.0.4	IP address supports dial-up and therefore dynamic IP addresses.
Absolute	127.0.0.2	IP address is a direct source of spam.
	127.0.0.4	IP address is a bulk mailer.
	127.0.0.5	Originating SMTP is known to support multistage open relays.

Use these values to properly configure the return message for blocked e-mails.

When the ET is not the first SMTP gateway between your organization's e-mail system and the Internet, you must modify its configuration to ensure that Connection Filtering works properly. This is done by including the list of each SMTP server's IP address in your perimeter network in the ET configuration. Use the **set-TransportConfig** cmdlet with the *InternalSMTPServers* parameter to do this. If you do this on a Hub Transport server, EdgeSync or the Edge Subscription will automatically populate the information to the ET systems.

From then on, the Connection Filter will look up each IP address in the Received header of the messages it receives, compare it to the IP addresses of your internal SMTP servers, and be able to properly identify the originating sender's IP address to properly process the message.

When your configuration is complete, use the **Test-IPAllowListProvider** and **Test-IPBlockListProvider** cmdlets along with the appropriate IP addresses provided by your list providers to run tests against the Connection Filter and ensure that it is operating properly.

MORE INFO   Configure the Connection Filter

For information on the commands used to configure the Connection Filter, go to *http://technet.microsoft.com/en-us/library/bb124376.aspx*.

For information on populating IP Allow and Block Lists, go to *http://technet.microsoft.com/en-us/library/bb123801.aspx*.

For information on populating IP Allow and Block List Providers, go to *http://technet.microsoft.com/en-us/library/bb124369.aspx*.

Configure the Sender Filter

Configuring the Sender Filter is performed through either the Exchange Management Console or the Shell. Because this task is performed on the Edge Transport server, you must have local administrative rights to perform it. Configuring this filter involves four steps:

1. Enable the filter.
2. Populate blocked senders and e-mail domains.
3. Enable blocking of blank senders.
4. Identify the blocking action.

Because the ET system is not linked to an Active Directory forest, configuration changes are stored locally. Therefore, you must perform these configuration activities on each ET system in your perimeter network.

The Sender Filter is enabled by default on ET systems for inbound messages that originate from the Internet and are not authenticated. These messages are categorized as external messages and are automatically examined. You should always use this filter on external sources, but never on internal or authenticated sources to avoid generating false positives.

You should also configure this filter to block messages that do not include information in the MAIL FROM: SMTP header. Messages of this type are often used in non-delivery report (NDR) attacks against SMTP servers. In these attacks, multiple messages are sent to the server, which tries to respond with non-delivery messages and can be overwhelmed by this attack/response scenario. Most organizations that send legitimate messages will include information in this header.

Microsoft recommends that you reject all messages blocked by this filter because you configure the blocked entries yourself on this filter. If you choose to use this approach, you must be very careful not to mistype entries to avoid false positives. In addition, if you add a domain to the blocked list and this domain is later reregistered by a legitimate organization, you may be blocking valid content. If you are careful, it will make sense to reject all blocked messages.

MORE INFO   **Configure the Sender Filter**

For information on the commands used to configure the Sender Filter, go to *http://technet.microsoft.com/en-us/library/bb124087.aspx*.

For information on how to add Blocked Senders and Domains, go to *http://technet.microsoft.com/en-us/library/bb123706.aspx*.

For information on how to configure Sender Filter Actions, go to *http://technet.microsoft.com/en-us/library/aa997235.aspx*.

Configure the Recipient Filter

Configuring the Recipient Filter is performed through either the Exchange Management Console or the Exchange Management Shell. Because this task is performed on the Edge Transport server, you must have local administrative rights to perform it. Configuring this filter involves four steps:

1. Enable the filter.
2. Populate the Recipient Block list.
3. Configure ADAM for recipient lookup.
4. Configure tarpitting.

Also, because the ET system is not linked to an Active Directory forest, configuration changes are stored locally. Therefore, you must perform these configuration activities on each ET system in your perimeter network.

The Recipient Filter is enabled by default on ET systems for inbound messages that originate from the Internet and are not authenticated. These messages are categorized as external messages and are automatically examined. You should always use this filter on external sources, but never on internal or authenticated sources to avoid generating false positives.

ADAM configuration means linking the ADAM instance to an Active Directory Global Catalog server for GAL replication. This is done through the Edge Subscription between HT and ET systems. This also means opening specific outgoing ports in the internal firewall to ensure proper traffic flow for the subscription.

The tarpitting value is set to five seconds by default. You can, of course, increase or decrease this value. Decreasing it is not recommended, but you can increase it if you discover directory harvest attacks against your SMTP servers. In most cases, the five-second interval is adequate.

MORE INFO   Configure the Recipient Filter

For information on the commands used to configure the Recipient Filter, go to *http://technet.microsoft.com/en-us/library/bb125187.aspx.*

For more information on how to add recipients to the Recipients Block List, go to *http://technet.microsoft.com/en-us/library/bb123992.aspx.*

Configure Sender ID and Sender Reputation

Configuring Sender ID is performed through either the Exchange Management Console or the Shell. Because this task is performed on the Edge Transport server, you must have local administrative rights to perform it. Configuring this filter involves four steps:

1. Modify your DNS configuration to support Sender ID.
2. Enable the filter.
3. Populate the list of excluded recipients and sender domains.
4. Identify the blocking action.

Also, because the ET system is not linked to an Active Directory forest, configuration changes are stored locally. Therefore, you must perform these configuration activities on each ET system in your perimeter network.

Sender ID depends on data obtained from DNS servers; therefore, it is important to configure them properly to provide appropriate responses. This means putting in place a sender policy framework record on Internet-facing DNS systems.

MORE INFO   Generate the SPF record

For more information on Sender ID in general, go to *http://www.microsoft.com/mscorp/safety/ technologies/senderid/technology.mspx*. To create an SPF record for your organization, go to *http://www.microsoft.com/mscorp/safety/content/technologies/senderid/wizard/*.

Sender ID is enabled by default on ET systems for inbound messages that originate from the Internet and are not authenticated. These messages are categorized as external messages and are automatically examined. You should always use this filter on external sources, but never on internal or authenticated sources to avoid generating false positives.

If, for some reason, your partners do not use SPF records of their own, you can exclude them from Sender ID processing. You can also exclude specific recipients from this processing if you feel it is necessary. The more organizations that use SPF records, the more effective Sender ID will become. Try to avoid exclusions and suggest to your partners that they should include these records in their DNS servers.

When you configure actions for the Sender ID Filter, you face two situations: spoofed messages and transient errors. Exchange supports different actions for each situation. Spoofed message actions can be configured in the Exchange Management Console, while transient error behavior must be configured with the **Set-SenderIdConfig** cmdlet. In both cases, actions can stamp the message, reject the message with an SMTP error response, or delete the message without any response. By default, messages are stamped because the stamp is used by other filters to process the spam confidence level for the message.

MORE INFO   Configure Sender ID

For information on the commands used to configure Sender ID, go to *http://technet.microsoft.com/en-us/library/aa997136.aspx*.

For information on how to exclude recipients or sender domains, go to *http://technet.microsoft.com/en-us/library/bb124506.aspx*.

For information on configuring Sender ID actions, go to *http://technet.microsoft.com/en-us/library/bb124414.aspx*.

Configuring Sender Reputation is performed through either the Exchange Management Console or the Exchange Management Shell. Because this task is performed on the Edge Transport server, you must have local administrative rights to perform it. Configuring this filter involves five steps:

1. Enable the filter.
2. Set the blocking threshold.
3. Set sender blocking duration times.
4. Enable open proxy detection.
5. Identify the action when open proxies are detected.

Also, because the ET system is not linked to an Active Directory forest, configuration changes are stored locally. Therefore, you must perform these configuration activities on each ET system in your perimeter network.

Sender Reputation is enabled by default on ET systems for inbound messages that originate from the Internet and are not authenticated. These messages are categorized as external messages and are automatically examined. You should always use this filter on external sources, but never on internal or authenticated sources to avoid generating false positives.

Setting the sender reputation level determines the threshold when sender reputation values will be used to allow or block messages. When senders reach this threshold, their IP addresses are added to the IP Block list for the Connection Filter for a specific duration period. By default this period is 24 hours. After this period the sender is removed from the Block list and can send messages again. Each time the IP address is added to the block list, the reputation agent deletes all reputation information for the sender to give it a clean slate when its IP address is released from the Block list.

In addition, Sender Reputation is set to detect open proxies by default. This detection is performed through the use of several common proxy protocols—for example, SOCKS4, SOCKS5, HTTP, Telnet, Cisco, and Wingate. When a connection is created, Exchange tries to send an SMTP request from the proxy itself. If this request is received by the ET, the originating sender is listed as an open proxy and incoming e-mails are blocked.

MORE INFO   **Configure Sender Reputation**

For more information on configuring Sender Reputation, go to *http://technet.microsoft.com/en-us/library/bb125186.aspx.*

For information on how to set the Sender Reputation Level Threshold, go to *http://technet.microsoft.com/en-us/library/bb124510.aspx.*

For information on how to configure Open Proxy Detection, go to *http://technet.microsoft.com/en-us/library/aa995974.aspx.*

Configure the Content Filter

Configuring the Content Filter is performed through either the Exchange Management Console or the Exchange Management Shell. Because this task is performed on the Edge Transport server, you must have local administrative rights to perform it. Configuring this filter involves seven steps:

1. Enable the filter.
2. Identify the mailbox to use to quarantine spam.
3. Configure the spam confidence level threshold and threshold actions.
4. Configure postmark validation.
5. Identify exceptions.
6. Identify allow or block phrases or words.
7. Configure the rejection response.

Also, because the ET system is not linked to an Active Directory forest, configuration changes are stored locally. Therefore, you must perform these configuration activities on each ET system in your perimeter network.

Content Filtering is enabled by default. When you configure it, you should enable it only for inbound messages that originate from the Internet and are not authenticated. These messages are categorized as external messages and are automatically examined. You should always use this filter on external sources, but never on internal or authenticated sources to avoid generating false positives.

Once the filter is enabled, you must configure a quarantine mailbox if you want to use the quarantine threshold. Using a quarantine mailbox is valuable because it lets you review potential false positives instead of simply deleting or rejecting them. Configure the quarantine mailbox and identify it on the ET system by adding its address to the *QuarantineMailbox* parameter within the Content Filter configuration.

When the quarantine mailbox is configured, you can configure the spam confidence level thresholds. Three thresholds are configurable and each is tied to a blocking action: deletion, rejection, or quarantine. These thresholds are important because Content Filtering is the last anti-spam action performed on a message before it is delivered. Ideally, you will configure settings according to the action. For example, because SCLs range from 0 to 9, you might use 8 to 9 as the basis for the deletion action, 7 as the basis for rejection, and 6 as the basis for quarantine.

You can also rely on the Outlook E-Mail Postmark validation process to validate legitimate messages. This validation process is enabled by default once you enable

Content Filtering. Outlook 2007 postmarks e-mail messages by default. Postmarked messages are not identified as spam by the Content Filter as long as the postmark returns a valid computation when calculated by the filter.

In some cases, you may want to exclude specific recipients, such as an external customer support e-mail alias, or specific senders as well as sender domains from Content Filtering. You can do this by listing these recipients or senders in the Content Filter configuration. You can also obtain these exceptions automatically from the Safe Senders Lists generated by your users in Outlook. This is done through safelist aggregation.

Because Content Filtering scans the actual content of a message, you should also configure Allow or Deny words or phrases so that the filter will recognize them automatically and perform the appropriate action based on these values. For example, a hospital may want to accept messages with the word *sex* in their body, whereas a religious organization may want to reject them outright. Messages with accepted words or phrases are granted a 0 rating and messages with unacceptable content are granted a 9 rating. The filter initiates the corresponding action based on these ratings.

Finally, you need to enable the rejection response on your servers. This response is sent to the originator of a rejected message. By default, this response returns "Message rejected due to content restrictions" to the sender. You can customize this message to return a proper value to senders.

MORE INFO   **Configure Content Filtering**

For more information on configuring Content Filtering, go to *http://technet.microsoft.com/en-us/library/bb123737.aspx*.

Adjust the Spam Confidence Level   Spam confidence levels in Exchange 2007 work in conjunction with the SCL Junk E-Mail folder in Outlook to provide a more comprehensive anti-spam strategy for organizations running these systems. You should, however, endeavor to adjust the SCL thresholds properly on your servers so that you can control spam identification more precisely. After all, no Content Filter is infallible, and false positives can occur in several situations. As you know, three thresholds are configurable for the SCL: delete, reject, and quarantine.

In Exchange 2007, these thresholds can be configured in two locations:

- On the Content Filter itself on each ET system. This sets organization-wide thresholds.

- On each individual user mailbox. This is done through the **set-Mailbox** cmdlet and configures the SCL for the Junk E-Mail folder on the mailbox. Each time you set one of the thresholds on a mailbox, its configuration is stored within Active Directory and then transported to the ET through EdgeSync. If per-user thresholds are set, the Content Filter will use these settings instead of the organization-wide settings when it detects messages targeted to this user.

Begin by using the default values for each threshold on the ET systems. Then set additional values for each user mailbox. Begin with the same values as the default settings. Monitor the results of your configuration changes and adjust them accordingly. In most cases, the default values will prove adequate for your organization.

MORE INFO Configure SCL thresholds on user mailboxes

For more information on configuring SCL thresholds on user mailboxes, go to *http://technet.microsoft.com/en-us/library/bb123559.aspx.*

Configure Safelist Aggregation To configure safelist aggregation, you must use the **Update-Safelist** cmdlet against user mailboxes. This cmdlet can scan for both Safe Senders and Safe Recipients; however, safelist aggregation only relies on the sender information. Therefore, you should make sure you use the default cmdlet. This will only return the Safe Senders list. Because all aggregated data is stored within the Active Directory and then propagated to ET systems through Edge Subscriptions, you want to keep the amount of data generated by this command as small as possible. Data within Active Directory will replicate to all domain controllers, which could have a negative impact on DC performance. It will also have an impact on the amount of data sent through EdgeSync.

When the cmdlet has been run the first time, you should schedule regular updates. Use the Exchange Management Shell **AT** cmdlet to create this schedule and regularly update safelist aggregation on your servers. Use a daily schedule on each mailbox.

MORE INFO Schedule safelist aggregation

Go to *http://technet.microsoft.com/en-us/library/aa998280.aspx* for a sample command to schedule safelist aggregation and for more information on safelist aggregation in general.

To then verify that ADAM has been updated through EdgeSync on each ET system, use the ADSIEdit snap-in in a custom MMC console on the ET itself. Look for user objects and then verify that new values exist for the *msExchSafeSendersHash* value. If no value exists, the ET server has not been updated.

Finally, verify that safelist aggregation is being used by the Content Filter to allow or deny e-mails. Use a free e-mail provider such as Hotmail.com to create a temporary address, add this address to your Safe Senders list in Outlook, wait one day, and then try to send yourself a message from this address. Make sure the message includes a word or phrase that you know is blocked by your Content Filter. If the message gets through, everything is working fine.

Configure Spam Quarantines   While you might think that quarantines are not worth your while and that you prefer to reject all messages, think again. Because of new regulations that bind organizations of all types (see Chapter 8), you may find yourself in a situation where you are forced to retain all valid e-mail messages, no matter what. This means quarantines are not only necessary, but are obligatory because you must trap all false positives to ensure that you comply to the letter of the law.

To set up a quarantine mailbox, you need to create a custom mailbox and then designate it as a quarantine mailbox. Messages that are flagged as potentially malicious are wrapped in a non-delivery report by the Content Filter and then delivered to the quarantine mailbox. Make sure you size this mailbox appropriately because it may come to contain a lot of messages.

The size of the quarantine mailbox is determined by the spam confidence level thresholds you set. The lower the thresholds, the more mail you will have in the quarantine mailbox and vice versa. Monitor these thresholds carefully to determine which thresholds work best for you.

By its very nature, the spam quarantine may contain private and confidential messages that may be viewed by the quarantine administrator. Be sure that you use a highly trustworthy person in this role because it is so sensitive.

Configuring the spam quarantine is part of the Content Filter activation process. Two of the steps in this process are related to spam quarantine set up. The first involves the actual creation of the spam mailbox and the second involves indicating to the Content Filter agent where the spam mailbox is found. Use the following best practices when creating the quarantine mailbox:

- Use a special Active Directory user account for the quarantine mailbox. This will let you apply custom recipient policies to this user.

- Use a dedicated storage group. Remember that the best practice is to create a single mailbox database per storage group. Ideally, you would contain all potential spam into a single mailbox database to avoid contamination of valid mailboxes.

Give this database a large amount of space to ensure that even if the quota is reached for the mailbox, it will still accept messages.

■ Use a new mailbox tied to the special user account you created. Make sure you apply the appropriate recipient policies and mail retention schedule to this mailbox.

■ Use a custom Outlook profile to view and retrieve messages from the mailbox. Make sure this profile is set to display Sender, Recipient, Copied Recipients, and Blind Copied Recipients.

After you create these items, you can assign the mailbox as the quarantine within the Content Filter. Use the **set-ContentFilterConfig** cmdlet with the *QuarantineMailbox* parameter to do this. Remember that you have to do this on each ET system in your perimeter network because each uses an independent configuration.

MORE INFO Assign the quarantine mailbox

Go to *http://technet.microsoft.com/en-us/library/bb123746.aspx* for more information on how to assign the quarantine mailbox.

Now you are ready to manage the quarantine. Use the following best practices:

■ Keep a close eye on the size of the mailbox. In some cases, this means checking the mailbox on a daily basis.

■ Delete all messages that appear as actual spam.

■ Verify false positives and forward them to original recipients. Make sure that sent items are released quickly from the mailbox to release space.

In the end, you will discover what works best for your organization and determine which are the best SCL thresholds for quarantine.

MORE INFO Recover quarantined messages

Go to *http://technet.microsoft.com/en-us/library/aa998920.aspx* for more information on how to manage the content of the quarantine mailbox.

Configure the Attachment Filter

Unlike the other filters, Attachment Filtering cannot be managed through the Exchange Management Console. You can only manage it through the Exchange Management Shell. As usual, when you make configuration changes for Attachment

Filtering, you must repeat them on each ET system in your perimeter network. In addition, keep in mind that Attachment Filter is the only filtering technique that does not work on Hub Transport servers if you need to set up filtering on these systems instead of ET systems. You must be a local system administrator to perform this action.

Like many other filters, Attachment Filtering is enabled by default on the ET system. You can verify this status through the **get-TransportAgent** cmdlet. As you know, Attachment Filtering relies on filenames, file extensions, and MIME content type to perform filtering. The filename and file extension component is smart enough to know whether a filename or extension has been modified to try to get it past the filter. MIME content types include a lot of different document types. For more information on each content type, look up RFC 1341 at *http://www.ietf.org/rfc/rfc1341.txt*. By default, all MIME types are scanned by the Attachment Filter, but you can add more content types as well as adding custom filenames and file extensions.

MORE INFO   **Add content types to the Attachment Filter**

Go to *http://technet.microsoft.com/en-us/library/aa997139.aspx* for more information on how to modify the content types managed by the Attachment Filter.

In addition to content types, you can modify several other parameters for the Attachment Filter:

- You can modify the rejection response of the non-delivery report generated when messages are rejected because of attachment type.

- You can modify the action taken by the filter based on attachment type. Three actions are possible: reject with response, strip the attachment and forward the message, and delete the message without any warnings.

- You can exclude specific connectors from filtering. For example, you could create a connector that is designed to manage partner e-mails only and exclude it from attachment filtering. Exclusions should be rare occurrences because Attachment Filtering is the first line of defense against viruses.

You change the configuration of the Attachment Filter by using the **set-Attachment-FilterListConfig** cmdlet.

Configure Antivirus Scanning

The last line of defense before the message leaves the Edge Transport server and enters your internal mail flow is virus scanning. Exchange does not offer antivirus scanning on its own. It does, however, offer virus scanning application programming interfaces (VSAPIs), which allow third-party antivirus vendors to develop Exchange-aware antivirus engines. Keep in mind that you cannot reuse the same antivirus engine you used with legacy versions of Exchange because Exchange 2007 runs on a 64-bit platform. Because virus scanning is a low-level system function, 32-bit AV engines will not work on 64-bit architectures.

In addition, Exchange 2007 provides a new architecture for e-mail transport—an architecture that is different from previous versions. For these reasons, you will need to acquire an AV engine that is designed specifically for the Exchange 2007 platform.

When you plan any defense system, you should always work toward a multi-layered, or defense-in-depth, strategy. For this reason, you should look to deploy your antivirus engine on at least three levels for Exchange:

■ The first level is to scan items as they enter your network. This means scanning on the ET systems. Exchange's anti-spam strategy works well with the antivirus strategy because it first eliminates unwanted or unneeded messages so that by the time your antivirus engine scans them, fewer messages are left and, one hopes, only valid messages are left. Note that if you are running a Simple Organization and you do not have ET systems—either through hosted services or even through your own systems—you must ensure that the Internet-facing Hub Transporter servers are running this antivirus engine. As a best practice, you should run SMTP-enabled virus scanning on every transport server in your network—both Hub and Edge. This will protect any items that are in transit through your systems.

■ The second level should be within the Exchange Mailbox server systems you deploy inside your internal network. Antivirus vectors include much more than simply e-mail. Therefore, you must make sure every mailbox is protected at the database level. Two types of antivirus scanning can be performed here:

  ❑ The first type performs only file-level scanning. Most generic antivirus engines can perform this type of scanning. In many cases, this may be adequate because e-mail is transferred from the HT system to the MB through a custom shared folder and then picked up by the Store Driver. Make sure, however, that you do not run file level scanning against the store databases because this will impact their performance and can cause issues with Exchange operation.

  ❑ The second type uses the Exchange VSAPI version 2.5—the version in Exchange 2007—to scan e-mail as it enters the mailbox database itself. VSAPI-enabled engines run directly within the Information Store process itself. Only a few engines on the market offer this functionality. Using this type of antivirus engine will protect all of the contents of a mailbox, including content that does not transit through the transport layer of Exchange, such as public folder contents, sent items, and calendar or contact items. In addition, it will protect content that does not enter the database through traditional vectors such as the transport or the client structures. Therefore, this type of scanning addresses content added through custom applications relying on the Collaboration Data Objects (CDO) interface, WebDAV (for example, SharePoint Portal Server), or Exchange Web Services. Finally, VSAPI scanners are often the best place to start when cleaning up a viral infection that was transmitted into your e-mail system.

■ The third level is on the client itself. Make sure you have an antivirus engine that supports scanning Outlook items so that users and potential user personal stores (.pst) are protected along with all of the other e-mail deposits in your organization. In addition, you should update your clients if you are running anything other than Outlook 2003 or Outlook 2007, because older clients use an outdated attachment handling behavior and are not as secure by default as the newer versions. For this reason, Exchange 2007 only accepts client-enabled connections from the two latest versions of Outlook.

MORE INFO Protecting Outlook

For more information on how newer versions of Outlook protect from virus infections, go to *http://go.microsoft.com/fwlink/?linkid=77565.*

Of course, you also need antivirus scanners on each server in your organization no matter which role they play, but for Exchange, your best defense is to address each of the three levels mentioned here and to ensure that at least file-level scanning is performed on all of the other Exchange server roles you deploy. Keep in mind that costs increase as you add virus scanning capabilities, so budget considerations will have an impact on your final strategy.

In most situations, you will at least run file-level scanning on your Exchange 2007 servers. File-level scanners perform two types of scans: in-memory scans—which are real-time scans—and scheduled scans. The latter can be manually generated or automatically generated. But because Exchange 2007 uses some custom processes, you must ensure that the file-level scanning engine you install on each server is configured properly—especially to omit certain folders and files—to have the scanning be as effective as possible and to ensure that the scanning engine and the Exchange processes cohabitate properly on the system. For example, when file-level scanning is enabled against mail stores, it is possible for the antivirus engine to lock a file—such as a log file—that is required by Exchange. When this occurs, Exchange cannot access the file and may stop and generate -1018 read errors. Table 7-4 outlines what to omit from file-level scanning on each server role.

MORE INFO   Understand -1018 errors

For more information on -1018 and other errors that can cause Exchange failures, go to *http://support.microsoft.com/kb/314917*.

Table 7-4   Configure File-Level Scanning per Exchange Server Role

Exchange Server Role	Exclusions	Supporting Cmdlets
Exchange Mailbox Server	Exchange storage groups including databases, logs, checkpoint files, and content indexes. Storage group-related file extensions.	Use **get-StorageGroup –server** *ServerName* **| fl *path*** to obtain the file paths to your storage groups. Exclude *.chk, *.log, *.edb, *.jrs and *.que for storage groups. Exclude *.ci, *.wid, *.000, *.001, *.002 and *.dir for content indexes.
	General activity logging files.	Use **get-MailboxServer** *ServerName* **|fl *path*** to obtain the logging paths.
	The Offline Address Book and its file extension.	The OAB is located in %ProgramFiles%\Microsoft\Exchange Server\ExchangeOAB by default. Also exclude *.lzx.
	IIS system files.	IIS system files are in %SystemRoot%\System32\Inetsrv.

Table 7-4   Configure File-Level Scanning per Exchange Server Role

Exchange Server Role	Exclusions	Supporting Cmdlets
	Temporary folders used by offline maintenance utilities.	Offline utilities such as Eseutil.exe usually create temporary files in their own folder.
	Other temporary folders that are used to perform conversions.	Content conversions are in the TMP folder. OLE conversions are in %ProgramFiles%\Microsoft\Exchange Server\Working\OleConvertor. The mailbox database temporary folder in %ProgramFiles%\Microsoft\Exchange Server\Mailbox\MDTEMP.
	System files and Exchange-aware antivirus program folders.	System files such as the paging file should be except from scanning as should be the program files for the anti-virus itself.
Clustered Mailbox Server	The same as the MB plus the cluster-specific files.	The quorum disk. The %Winnt%\Cluster folder. The File Share Witness (FSW) folder (usually on a HT).
Hub Transport Server	General activity logging files.	Use **get-TransportServer** *ServerName* **|fl *logpath*,*tracingpath*** to obtain the logging paths.
	Message folders.	Use **get-TransportServer** *ServerName* **|fl *dir*path*** to obtain the message folder paths.
	Transport queue database, logs, and checkpoint files.	These files are in the %ProgramFiles%\Microsoft\Exchange Server\TransportRoles\Data\Queue folder by default.

Table 7-4 Configure File-Level Scanning per Exchange Server Role

Exchange Server Role	Exclusions	Supporting Cmdlets
	Sender Reputation database, log, and checkpoint files.	These files are in the %ProgramFiles%\Microsoft\Exchange Server\TransportRoles\Data\SenderReputation folder by default.
	IP filter database, log, and checkpoint files.	These files are in the %ProgramFiles%\Microsoft\Exchange Server\TransportRoles\Data\IPfilter folder by default.
	Temporary folders that are used to perform conversions.	Content conversions are in the TMP folder. OLE conversions are in %ProgramFiles%\Microsoft\Exchange Server\Working\OleConvertor.
	System files and Exchange-aware antivirus program folders.	System files such as the paging file should be except from scanning, as should be the program files for the antivirus itself.
Edge Transport Server	Same files and folders as the HT, plus the ADAM database and log files.	These files are in the %ProgramFiles%\Microsoft\Exchange Server\TransportRoles\Data\Adam folder by default.
Client Access Server	IIS system files.	IIS system files are in %SystemRoot%\System32\Inetsrv.
	The IIS compression folder used by OWA.	These files are in the %SystemRoot%\IIS Temporary Compressed Files folder by default.
	CAS Internet-related files.	These files are in the %ProgramFiles%\Microsoft\Exchange Server\ClientAccess folder by default.

Table 7-4   Configure File-Level Scanning per Exchange Server Role

Exchange Server Role	Exclusions	Supporting Cmdlets
	The temporary folder that is used to perform conversions.	Content conversions are in the TMP folder.
	System files.	System files such as the paging file should be except from scanning.
Unified Messaging Server	Grammar files.	These files are in the %ProgramFiles%\Microsoft\Exchange Server\UnifiedMessaging\grammars folder by default.
	Voice prompts.	These files are in the %ProgramFiles%\Microsoft\Exchange Server\UnifiedMessaging\Prompts folder by default.
	Voicemail files.	These files are in the %ProgramFiles%\Microsoft\Exchange Server\UnifiedMessaging\voicemail folder by default.
	Bad voicemail files.	These files are in the %ProgramFiles%\Microsoft\Exchange Server\UnifiedMessaging\badvoicemail folder by default.
	Unified Messaging-related file extensions.	Exclude *.cfg and *.grxml.
	System files.	System files such as the paging file should be except from scanning.

Table 7-4   Configure File-Level Scanning per Exchange Server Role

Exchange Server Role	Exclusions	Supporting Cmdlets
All roles	Application-related file extensions.	Exclude *.config, *.dia, and *.wsb.
	Database-related file extensions.	Exclude *.chk, *.log, *.edb, *.jrs and *.que.

If your antivirus engine can scan processes as well as files, you should exclude specific processes from scanning. If your antivirus is truly Exchange-aware, it will automatically exclude all of these items at installation.

Finally, your antivirus strategy should make sure it covers automatic deployment of updated signature files to all endpoints. Most modern solutions will do this automatically, but you should still ensure that it is done. Today, daily updates are the most common schedule used. Many organizations that are in sensitive industries will perform updates several times a day and even go as far as downloading and distributing beta signatures to protect from viral outbreaks. Choose the schedule that is appropriate for your organization's needs.

MORE INFO   Detailed exclusion lists for Exchange

For detailed exclusion list information for Exchange 2007, go to *http://technet.microsoft.com/en-us/library/bb332342.aspx*.

There you have it. Make sure you thoroughly test your Exchange anti-spam and antivirus strategy when you have it ready to go. Then you should be ready to deploy it. Monitor its effects closely as you run it and update it as needed.

Practice: Prepare for Communication Protection

In this practice, you will explore message filtering operation on Edge Transport servers. This practice consists of three exercises. First, you will create a dedicated storage group to contain the quarantine mailbox. Next, you will create and configure a quarantine mailbox. Last, you will work with the Edge Transport server to configure content filtering.

▶ **Exercise 1: Create a Custom Storage Group**

In this exercise, you will create and configure a custom storage group. This group will be dedicated to quarantine and will only contain the quarantine mailbox.

1. Begin by making sure the ExchangeOne.treyresearch.com server is running.

2. Log on with the EXAdmin account. This will grant you local administrative privileges.

3. Launch the Exchange Management Console (Start Menu | All Programs | Microsoft Exchange Server | Exchange Management Console).

4. Drill down to Server Configuration | Mailbox in the tree pane. Make sure ExchangeOne is selected in the details pane.

5. Click New Storage Group in the Action pane.

   Here you will assign the storage group to an existing drive set to limit the resources required for this practice. Normally, you would assign it to its own drive set.

6. Name the storage group **Quarantine** and assign its log files path to E:\QLogs, its system files path to D:\QTemp, and leave the LCR paths empty. Create new folders as needed. Click New.

7. Click Finish when the operation is complete.

8. Right-click the Quarantine storage group and select New Mailbox Database.

9. Name the new database **Quarantine** and store it in D:\QMBDB. Create the folder as needed. Make sure the Mount This Database option is selected and click New.

10. Click Finish when the operation completes.

Your new storage group is ready.

▶ **Exercise 2: Create the Quarantine Mailbox**

In this exercise, you will create and configure a quarantine mailbox.

1. Launch the Exchange Management Console if it is not already open (Start Menu | All Programs | Microsoft Exchange Server | Exchange Management Console).

2. Move to Recipient Configuration | Mailbox in the tree pane.

3. Click New Mailbox in the Action pane.

4. Select User Mailbox and click Next. Select New User and click Next.

5. Assign **Quarantine** as the First Name and **Mailbox** as the Last Name, Quarantine as the Logon Names and **P@ssw0rd** as the Password. Make sure you do not select User Must Change Password At Next Logon. Click Next.

6. Make sure Quarantine is the Alias, select ExchangeOne as the host server, Quarantine as the storage group, and Quarantine as the mailbox. Do not assign a managed folder or ActiveSync policy. Click Next.

7. Review the information and click New. Click Finish to complete the operation.

The quarantine mailbox is ready.

▶ **Exercise 3: Configure Exchange Content Filtering**

In this exercise, you will configure content filtering on the Edge Transport server.

1. Make sure the ExchangeETOne.treyresearch.com server is running.

2. Log on with the EXAdmin account. This will grant you local administrative privileges.

3. Launch the Exchange Management Shell (Start Menu | All Programs | Microsoft Exchange Server | Exchange Management Shell).

4. Begin by specifying the quarantine mailbox. Use the following cmdlet:

```
set-contentfilterconfig -quarantinemailbox quarantine@treyresearch.net
```

5. This will send all retained and potential spam messages to the quarantine mailbox. Minimize the Exchange Management Shell.

6. Launch the Exchange Management Console (Start Menu | All Programs | Microsoft Exchange Server | Exchange Management Console).

7. Move to the Edge Transport section in the tree pane.

8. Notice that the Content Filter is enabled by default. Right-click the Content Filter and choose Properties.

9. Click the Action tab and select Quarantine Messages That Have A SCL Rating Greater Than Or Equal To. Set the value to **6**. Type in the Quarantine Mailbox Address as **quarantine@treyresearch.net**. Click Apply.

10. Take the time to review the content of both the Custom Words and the Exceptions tabs. You will not configure them now, but it is good practice to see what options these tabs contain. Click OK to close the Properties dialog box.

11. Minimize the Console.

12. Move to configure the rejection response. Return to the Shell and use the following cmdlet:

```
set-contentfilterconfig -rejectionresponse "Your Message has been rejected due to its content. If your message is valid, please contact the intended recipient directly."
```

13. Close the Shell and the Console.

Content filtering is now configured. This is an example of a simple content filtering configuration.

Quick Check

1. Which filter do you have to combine with the Sender ID Filter to avoid spoofing of the MAIL FROM: SMTP header?
2. What are the scenarios that you can use to validate or block invalid recipients at the gate?
3. What are the two levels of updates from Microsoft Update that are related to spam identification?
4. What are the four stamps used by the anti-spam filters?
5. Which steps are used to configure the Connection Filter?

Quick Check Answers

1. The Sender Filter.
2. There are three scenarios:
   ❑ Recipients can be nonexistent and therefore are blocked by default.
   ❑ Special distribution lists that are for internal e-mail purposes only can be blocked to ensure that no message originating on the Internet can be sent to these lists.
   ❑ Special mailboxes that are for internal use only can also be included here to prevent messages from the Internet to be delivered to them.
3. Two levels of updates are available:
   ❑ The standard update service offers updates on a bimonthly basis (every two weeks). Updates are obtained from the Microsoft Update Web sites.

❏ The premium service, called Forefront Security for Exchange Server anti-spam updates, provides daily updates for the content filter. It can also provide point-in-time Spam Signature to identify recent spam campaigns as well as IP Reputation Service updates should the need arise. These point-in-time updates can even occur several times a day. To have access to the premium update service, organizations must acquire the Exchange Enterprise Client Access License (CAL).

4. The four stamps are anti-spam report, the phishing confidence level, the spam confidence level, and the sender ID.

5. Configuring the Connection Filter involves four (or possibly five) steps:

❏ Enable the filter.

❏ Populate the IP Allow and Block lists.

❏ Populate the IP Allow and Block List providers.

❏ If the ET is not the first point of contact for inbound SMTP traffic, then configure the filter accordingly.

❏ Test the configuration.

Lesson 2: Plan the Network Layer Security Implementation

Estimated lesson time: 30 minutes

The core of any e-mail delivery system is the communications infrastructure that underlies it and Exchange, especially Exchange 2007, is no exception. Chapter 1, "Plan the Exchange Topology Deployment," presented the Exchange mail flow once e-mail was inside the organization, but when you work with Exchange and you transmit and receive e-mail from the Internet, the mail flow and the general communications flow involved in Exchange transactions can become much more complicated, especially because it must traverse firewalls to both get in and to get out (see Figure 7-3).

Protect Exchange Communications

When you plan to work with Exchange communications and secure them as much as possible, you must cover the following elements:

- Server-to-server communications, which involve internal server-to-server communications as well as internal-to-external communications and vice versa. Each Exchange internal network server role installs a self-signed PKI certificate by default. These certificates are managed by Active Directory so that they are trusted by both servers and clients within the Active Directory domain and forest. In addition, external SMTP links can also rely on Transport Layer Security (TLS) through the STARTTLS SMTP command. If the destination or the originating server supports TLS encryption, Exchange Edge Transport servers will automatically encrypt the session.

- Client-to-server communications, which also involve internal client connections to servers as well as external connections from a variety of client devices to servers that are located in a perimeter network. Internal connections are automatically encrypted either through Remote Procedure Calls (RPC) or through the Secure Sockets Layer (SSL). External connections can also rely on SSL or the RPC over HTTP protocol (now called Outlook Anywhere).

- Firewall exceptions for internal server-to-external server communications and vice versa as well as exceptions to allow client communication links to server services. The latter can take several forms:
  - Secure Sockets Layer connections to Exchange services
  - IPsec communications to Exchange services
  - Virtual private network (VPN) communications to Exchange services

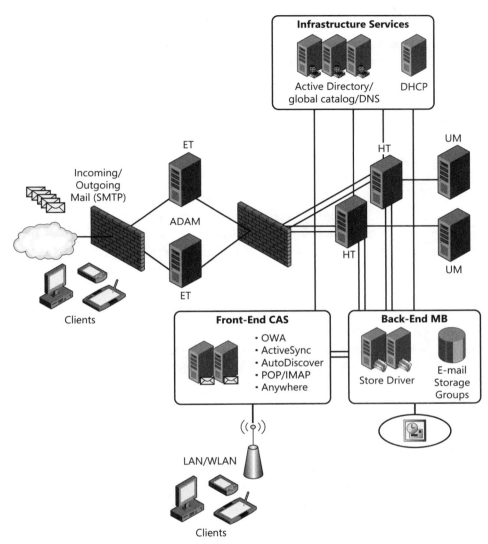

Figure 7-3 Exchange internal and external communication paths

Microsoft has provided several enhancements to secure communications within the Exchange 2007 infrastructure. For example, all communications between Exchange server roles are secure by default and internal communications between clients and servers are also encrypted by default. This leaves external server and client communications to configure. First, you need to understand how communications are secured by default.

Protect Server-to-Server Communications

By default, Exchange servers communicate with each other over encrypted communication paths. Internal servers rely on mutual Kerberos authentication and authorization as well as TLS encryption for confidentiality and integrity. This process is completely automatic and is configured by Exchange during setup of each server role.

For TLS communications, Exchange server roles rely on self-signed certificates that are generated during the installation. These certificates are linked to the server account in Active Directory so that they are automatically maintained by the directory service and there is no requirement for a Public Key Infrastructure installation to control and manage them. This is because Exchange does not rely on X.509 validation for the certificate. X.509 validation requires moving up the trust chain until you get to the appropriate certificate authority to validate the certificate. It is based on obtaining Certificate Revocation Lists and verifying the certificate against these lists. But, because Exchange generates self-signed certificates, there is no certificate authority to validate against.

Instead, Exchange relies on direct trust to authenticate certificates. With direct trust, the system relies on a trusted storage mechanism to maintain the certificate. Both Active Directory and ADAM are considered trusted stores. Certificates for each internal server are stored within Active Directory by default. Certificates for Edge Transport servers are stored in ADAM by default.

External communications—or rather, internal-to-perimeter communications—rely on mutual TLS authentication. This means that server-to-server communications authenticate through the TLS certificates located on each server role. For this process to be automatic there must be an exchange of the keys from each server, internal and external. This exchange of keys is generated through the Edge Subscription and then maintained through EdgeSync when it is established. Remember that Edge Subscriptions require exporting the configuration of each ET system in the perimeter and then importing them onto an HT system with a direct link to the ET systems. When imported, the ET configuration will be propagated to other HT systems through Active Directory (see Lesson 2 in Chapter 2 for more information). At this point the ET certificates are contained within Active Directory, thereby allowing the HT systems to trust the ET systems. Conversely, the Edge Subscription will push the HT certificates into each ADAM instance on the ET systems so that they will trust the internal HT systems.

Exchange relies on direct trust because only direct trust allows multiple systems to work with self-signed certificates. Direct trust enables encrypted and trusted communications without requiring the expense or complication of putting a PKI in place.

MORE INFO   **Exchange and PKI certificates**

To learn how Exchange works with certificates, go to *http://technet.microsoft.com/en-us/library/bb851505.aspx.*

Trusted communications can even cross forest boundaries. If you want mutual Kerberos authentication and authorization between Exchange servers across forests, you must implement a forest trust between the forests. If for some reason you cannot implement a forest trust, you can use Basic Authentication without a trust. To protect Basic Authentication traffic, you can ensure that TLS is used between servers in each forest. The TLS encryption tunnel that is created will ensure that Basic Authentication data will be protected while in transit. Note that ET communications are always encrypted between two different Exchange Organizations. The ET systems try to use TLS communications by default with any SMTP sender or receiver if it is supported. Because TLS is supported in ET roles, when two ET systems communicate with each other, they always encrypt the communication.

Hub Transport servers also use encryption when communicating with Exchange Mailbox servers. The trusted path for these communications differs according to your deployment type. When HT and MB roles are deployed on the same server, mail submission is local and authentication is based on Kerberos. When the roles are deployed on separate servers, mail submission is over the network. In this case, NTLM authentication is used. NTLM is not as secure as Kerberos, but because it is within an internal network and only runs on a local area network, it provides an acceptable level of security in this case. (Remember that you must always deploy a local HT in each site you deploy a local MB.)

Communications are also secured between other server roles, such as Client Access servers and Unified Messaging servers and all other server roles. Because the various Exchange server roles must interact with Active Directory to update their configuration and retrieve mail-enabled user information as well as distribution lists, communications between these systems are also encrypted (see Figure 7-4).

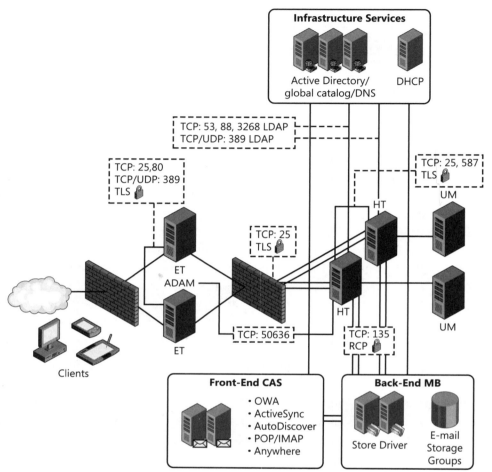

Figure 7-4   Main traffic paths in Exchange 2007 and supported encryption methods

Table 7-5 outlines the various protocols and authentication methods used by Exchange server roles during server-to-server communications. In most cases, ports used are TCP ports. UDP ports are indicated when required.

Several additional ports can be in use. Table 7-5 outlines only the ports used by Exchange 2007 systems. When legacy systems are in place, such as when you have legacy mailbox servers, much of the communication occurs over port 135, some of which may not be encrypted by default. Ideally, you will transition to a complete Exchange 2007 server infrastructure as soon as possible to ensure the most secure communications possible.

Table 7-5   Exchange Server-to-Server Communication Protocols

TCP Port	UDP Port	Purpose	From Server Role	To Server Role	Comments and Authentication Method	Encryption Method
25		SMTP	HT	HT	Kerberos by default	TLS by default
		SMTP	HT	ET	Direct Trust with Edge Subscription	TLS by default
		SMTP	UM	HT	Kerberos	TLS by default
		SMTP	ET	HT	Direct Trust with Edge Subscription	TLS by default
		SMTP	ET	ET	Anonymous Certificate	TLS by default
53		DNS Lookups	HT or MB	Active Directory	Kerberos	Kerberos by default
80		HTTP certificate lookup	ET	ET	n/a	n/a
		WebDAV to Web Service	CAS	MB	Basic, NTLM, Negotiate	HTTPS by default
		Exchange ActiveSync	CAS	CAS	Certificate or Kerberos, but Kerberos by default	HTTPS by default

Table 7-5 Exchange Server-to-Server Communication Protocols

TCP Port	UDP Port	Purpose	From Server Role	To Server Role	Comments and Authentication Method	Encryption Method
		Outlook Web Access	CAS	CAS	Kerberos	HTTPS by default
88		Kerberos validations	HT or MB	Active Directory	Kerberos	Kerberos by default
135		RPC using Exchange Mail Submission Service	MB	HT	NTLM on separate servers Kerberos on same server or using LocalSystem account	RPC by default
		RPC using MAPI	HT	MB	NTLM on separate servers Kerberos on same server or using LocalSystem account	RPC by default
		Netlogon service	MB	Active Directory	Kerberos	Kerberos by default
		Exchange Active Directory Topology Service	MB	Active Directory	NTLM or Kerberos	RPC by default
		Offline Address Book updates	MB	Active Directory	Kerberos	Kerberos by default
		Mailbox assistants	MB	MB	NTLM or Kerberos	Local, not required

Table 7-5 Exchange Server-to-Server Communication Protocols

TCP Port	UDP Port	Purpose	From Server Role	To Server Role	Comments and Authentication Method	Encryption Method
		Voicemail transmissions	UM	MB	NTLM on separate servers Kerberos on same server or using LocalSystem account	RPC by default
		Remote Registry access	Management Console	MB	NTLM or Kerberos	IPsec can be used, but not encrypted by default
		SCC Clustering	CMS	CMS	NTLM or Kerberos	Local, not required
		CCR Clustering	CMS	CMS	NTLM or Kerberos	Should use IPsec
	389	LDAP for ADAM lookups	ET	ET	n/a	n/a
389		LDAP Active Directory lookups	HT or MB	Active Directory	Kerberos	Kerberos by default
		LDAP Active Directory lookups	HT	Active Directory	Kerberos	Kerberos by default
443		WebDAV to Web Service	CAS	MB	Basic, NTLM, Negotiate	HTTPS by default

Table 7-5 Exchange Server-to-Server Communication Protocols

TCP Port	UDP Port	Purpose	From Server Role	To Server Role	Comments and Authentication Method	Encryption Method
		Exchange ActiveSync	CAS	CAS	Certificate or Kerberos, but Kerberos by default	HTTPS by default
		Outlook Web Access	CAS	CAS	Kerberos	HTTPS by default
445		SMB LCR Log shipping but port can be random	MB	MB	NTLM or Kerberos	Not required
		SMB CCR Log shipping but port can be random	CMS	CMS	NTLM or Kerberos	Should use IPsec
		SMB remote admin access to hidden shares	Management Console	MB	NTLM or Kerberos	IPsec can be used, but not encrypted by default
587		Secure SMTP	HT	HT	Kerberos by default	TLS by default
3268		Global Catalog lookups through LDAP	HT or MB	Active Directory	Kerberos	Kerberos by default

Table 7-5 Exchange Server-to-Server Communication Protocols

TCP Port	UDP Port	Purpose	From Server Role	To Server Role	Comments and Authentication Method	Encryption Method
	3343	SCC heartbeat	CMS	CMS	Over private network	Local, not required
		CCR heartbeat	CMS	CMS	Over private network	Should use IPsec
5060		SIP Voicemail lookups	CAS	UM	IP Address authentication	TLS by default
		SIP fax or voicemail transmissions	UM	IP gateway or IP PBX	IP Address authentication	TLS by default, but media is not encrypted
5061		SIP Voicemail lookups	CAS	UM	IP Address authentication	TLS by default
		SIP fax or voicemail transmissions	UM	IP gateway or IP PBX	IP Address authentication	TLS by default, but media is not encrypted
5062		SIP Voicemail lookups	CAS	UM	IP Address authentication	TLS by default
		SIP fax or voicemail transmissions	UM	IP gateway or IP PBX	IP Address authentication	TLS by default, but media is not encrypted
50389		EdgeSync without SSL	HT	ET	Basic	LDAPS by default

Table 7-5 Exchange Server-to-Server Communication Protocols

TCP Port	UDP Port	Purpose	From Server Role	To Server Role	Comments and Authentication Method	Encryption Method
50636		EdgeSync with SSL	HT	ET	Basic	LDAPS by default
		ADAM lookups	ET	ET	NTLM or Kerberos	None
Random		RPC client communications through CAS	CAS	MB	NTLM or Kerberos, Kerberos by default	RPC by default
		Legacy backup tool	MB	BU Server	NTLM or Kerberos	IPsec can be used, but not encrypted by default
		SIP Voicemail lookups	CAS	UM	IP Address authentication	TLS by default
		SIP fax or voicemail transmissions	UM	IP gateway or IP PBX	IP Address authentication	TLS by default, but media is not encrypted

Also, whenever unsecured communications occur over wide area network links, you should put in place an IPsec tunnel to ensure that the transmission contents are encrypted. For example, establishing an IPsec tunnel is the recommended practice when preparing a Cluster Continuous Replication geographically dispersed cluster.

MORE INFO   **Complete port description**

Microsoft offers a more complete port description, including legacy server ports at *http://technet.microsoft.com/en-us/library/bb331973.aspx.*

Protect Client-to-Server Communications

Client communications to Exchange server roles are also encrypted in most situations by default. Once again, Exchange server roles rely on their self-signed certificates to perform the encryption. As such, internal clients are able to work with the self-signed certificates because they are members of the Active Directory domain that hosts the servers, but as soon as you exit the network and try to access Exchange services from the other side of a firewall, self-signed certificates no longer work.

One good example is when you try to configure a Network Load Balancing cluster for Client Access servers. In this case, a real certificate originating from a third-party Certificate Authority (CA) is required for two reasons. First, the existing self-signed certificate does not include the name of the cluster and therefore will cause an error when clients try to connect and second, using a real certificate avoids having to deploy additional trusted CAs to end points because the CAs will already be included in the trusted sources located on each client. See Chapter 6, "Plan for Business Continuity," for more information on certificates and NLB.

In addition, self-signed certificates on Client Access servers only allow validation of some of the features the CAS role supports. While both ActiveSync and OWA will work with the self-signed certificate, Outlook Anywhere will not. It is always best to rely on certificates obtained from trusted third-party CAs because you do not have to change the configuration of the client for them to work. You can, of course, use a trusted internal PKI CA, but this will only work when you have control of the client. When you do not, as often happens when client systems are not located within your premises, using an internal PKI CA will simply not work. And, as you know, you simply cannot rely on the end users themselves to update their trusted authorities because the operation is often complex and can cause a massive number of calls to your Help desk. Best practice: use a third-party CA.

Table 7-6 outlines the various ports used by clients to access Exchange Client Access servers. Note that because all of the features supported by the CAS rely on Web sites to publish information to users, you can configure them to use different security methods, one for each feature.

Secure Outlook Web Access   As listed in Table 7-6, several different authentication methods can be used with Outlook Web Access. In Exchange 2003, the preferred method was forms-based authentication, but in Exchange 2007, you can also use Basic, Digest, or Integrated Windows authentication. By default, OWA still relies on forms-based authentication and requires SSL encryption for client communications. Forms-based authentication is the default because it relies on a cookie on both private and public computers to store a user's credentials during the OWA session. Exchange can track this cookie to determine user behavior. If the session is idle for too long, Exchange can force the user to reauthenticate. This cookie is cleared as soon as the user either closes the browser session or uses the Log Off button in OWA.

By default, the cookie lifetime is managed by the user's original selection when the user signs into OWA. If, as a user, you indicate that you are using a public computer, the session times out after 15 minutes of inactivity. The time-out is eight hours if you choose the private option. For this reason, you should educate your users about the importance of these options. If you feel your users will not use these options properly, you can always modify these default time-out values.

Other authentication methods are either too weak—such as Basic, which uses clear text passwords—or require a specific client operating system—such as Integrated Windows authentication. This is one more reason why forms-based authentication is often best; it works with multiple browsers, it is secure, and it is configured by default.

MORE INFO   Working with OWA authentication methods

For more information on how to work with OWA's different authentication methods, go to *http://technet.microsoft.com/en-us/library/bb430796.aspx*.

When you assign a new SSL certificate to OWA, you must ensure that it is assigned to each of the four virtual directories created by the OWA installation: \owa, \exchange, \public, and \exchweb. In addition, you must enable it for each new virtual directory you create. This is done by first installing the certificate on the CAS system and then editing the properties of the Web site in IIS.

Table 7-6 Exchange Client-to-Server Communication Protocols

TCP Port	UDP Port	Purpose	From Client Role	To Server Role	Comments and Authentication Method	Encryption Method
80		HTTP Offline Address Book access	Outlook	MB	NTLM or Kerberos	None
		WebDAV access	OWA	CAS	Basic or OWA forms-based authentication	HTTPS by default
		Autodiscover service	Outlook or mobile device	CAS	Basic, Digest, NTLM, or Negotiate (Kerberos), but Basic/Integrated Windows Authentication is used by default	HTTPS by default
		Availability Service	Outlook, OWA or mobile device	CAS	NTLM or Kerberos	HTTPS by default
		Outlook Web Access	Web Browser	CAS	Basic, Digest, Forms-based, NTLM (v2 only), Kerberos or Certificate, but Forms-based authentication is the default	HTTPS by default
		Exchange ActiveSync	Mobile device or Windows PC	CAS	Basic or Certificate, but Basic is the default	HTTPS by default
		Outlook Anywhere	Remote Outlook	CAS	Basic or NTLM, but Basic is the default	HTTPS by default

Table 7-6 Exchange Client-to-Server Communication Protocols

TCP Port	UDP Port	Purpose	From Client Role	To Server Role	Comments and Authentication Method	Encryption Method
110		POP3	Outlook or other client	CAS	Basic, NTLM or Kerberos	SSL or TLS, depends on client
143		IMAP4	Outlook or other client	CAS	Basic, NTLM or Kerberos	SSL or TLS, depends on client
135		RPC Availability Web Service	Outlook or OWA (through CAS)	MB	NTLM or Kerberos	RPC by default
443		HTTPS Offline Address Book access	Outlook	MB	NTLM or Kerberos	HTTPS
		WebDAV access	OWA	CAS	Basic or OWA forms-based authentication	HTTPS by default
		Autodiscover service	Outlook or mobile device	CAS	Basic, Digest, NTLM, or Negotiate (Kerberos), but Basic/Integrated Windows Authentication is used by default	HTTPS by default
		Availability Service	Outlook, OWA or mobile device	CAS	NTLM or Kerberos	HTTPS by default

Table 7-6 Exchange Client-to-Server Communication Protocols

TCP Port	UDP Port	Purpose	From Client Role	To Server Role	Comments and Authentication Method	Encryption Method
		Outlook Web Access	Web Browser	CAS	Basic, Digest, Forms-based, NTLM (v2 only), Kerberos or Certificate, but Forms-based authentication is the default	HTTPS by default
		Exchange ActiveSync	Mobile device or Windows PC	CAS	Basic or Certificate, but Basic is default	HTTPS by default
		Outlook Anywhere	Remote Outlook	CAS	Basic or NTLM, but Basic is the default	HTTPS by default
993		Secure IMAP4	Outlook or other client	CAS	Basic, NTLM or Kerberos	SSL or TLS, depends on client
995		Secure POP3	Outlook or other client	CAS	Basic, NTLM or Kerberos	SSL or TLS, depends on client

MORE INFO Assigning an SSL certificate to OWA

For more information on how to assign a new SSL certificate to OWA virtual directories, go to *http://technet.microsoft.com/en-us/library/bb123583.aspx.*

In addition, you can limit user access to either OWA in general or to only specific OWA features. OWA access can be disabled completely for all users in your organization or it can be done on a per-user basis. To restrict OWA features, you use either the Exchange Management Console on the CAS itself or run the **set-OwaVirtualDirectory** cmdlet.

OWA now supports several methods for users to view attachments. Each provides its own risk. For example, when you use WebReady Document Viewing, users will be able to read but not modify documents. This is the most secure document viewing feature. When you give users direct file access, they will have direct access to the documents in attachments. Of course, this requires the appropriate client application on the system they use to access OWA, but in this case, you can still control user interaction with these files through Allow, Block, or Force Save actions you set on file access. Users can also access either SharePoint Services or Windows File Shares through OWA. This lets them send links in an e-mail instead of sending the attachment, saving e-mail space. Fortunately, you can control which servers are available for these options, letting you block access to sensitive servers and allowing access to more open systems. Note that all access in this case is read-only access.

MORE INFO Configuring file access in OWA

For more information on how to configure file or data access in OWA, go to *http://technet.microsoft.com/en-us/library/bb430754.aspx.*

Note that OWA disables Web Beacons automatically. Web Beacons are often placed in the form of images within specific Web pages. When a user opens a junk e-mail through OWA, it is possible that this junk e-mail will place a Web Beacon on the computer the user is working with. Once this happens, the Web Beacon returns a notification to the junk e-mail sender that the e-mail address is valid. But, because Web Beacons are disabled in OWA by default, your users will be protected from them even if they make the mistake of opening a junk e-mail in OWA.

MORE INFO Web Beacon behavior in OWA

For more information on Web Beacon behavior in OWA, go to *http://technet.microsoft.com/en-us/library/bb430788.aspx.*

Secure Outlook Anywhere Unlike OWA, Outlook Anywhere is not a feature that can be used from any computer or any browser. That is because it is designed to provide RPC over HTTP access to Exchange mailboxes from Outlook clients that are not necessarily in a LAN connection with the CAS system. You can use Outlook Anywhere in several situations. For example, when the number of clients in a remote office does not warrant their own Exchange server, you can let them connect to servers in other sites through Outlook Anywhere. A second example is when users are on the road and they want to use Outlook without having to first initiate a complex virtual private network connection through the firewall. Outlook Anywhere is ideal in this example because it encrypts communications between the client and the server without requiring complex configurations and relying on common ports that are usually already open on the firewall.

Microsoft recommends using NTLM authentication for Outlook Anywhere. This authentication mode works because users will have an account within your Active Directory and they will also already have the Outlook client on their systems.

Also, you must put in place an SSL certificate for Outlook Anywhere to function. Because users of Outlook 2007 rely on the Autodiscover service to configure their mailboxes on their systems, you must design this SSL certificate to support the Autodiscover URLs (see Lesson 2 in Chapter 2). To ensure that everything works properly together, you will need to have a certificate that uses a subject alternate name so that it can include both the name of the servers and the names of all of the URLs required for both Outlook Anywhere and Autodiscover to function properly. Using SAN certificates avoids the need to deploy multiple certificates—one for each service—on CAS systems.

MORE INFO Configuring Outlook Anywhere security

For more information on how to configure Outlook Anywhere security, go to *http://technet.microsoft.com/en-us/library/bb430792.aspx*.

IMPORTANT Use a reverse proxy firewall with Exchange 2007

Exchange 2007 is an application that must expose specific client services such as Outlook Anywhere to the Internet. In addition, these applications often require authentication. Reverse proxies are application-level firewalls that expose application interfaces to the Internet without exposing the application itself. Microsoft's Internet Security and Acceleration Server (ISA) is specifically designed to support outward-facing applications such as Exchange 2007. Find out more about ISA and Exchange at *http://technet.microsoft.com/en-us/library/bb430749.aspx*.

Secure Exchange ActiveSync   Exchange ActiveSync provides a host of e-mail functionality to users of Windows Mobile devices, especially users of Windows Mobile 6. But,
as with Outlook Anywhere and OWA, you must secure both authentication and the
communications channel used by ActiveSync to ensure that this service is secure.
Once again, you should deploy a proper third-party certificate to allow users to
automatically encrypt communications.

You should also select a proper authentication method for this service. By default,
when you configure ActiveSync, Exchange assigns Basic authentication with SSL. The
SSL tunnel secures the clear text password because the communication is encrypted.
But ActiveSync supports other, more secure, authentication methods. You should
consider using either certificate-based or token-based authentication instead of Basic.
Certificate-based authentication requires the deployment of a certificate to the device.
Often the best way to do this is to put in place an internal PKI that is linked to Active
Directory for automated user provisioning. In this case, the certificate is installed on
the device only when it is linked to a computer that is part of a domain. This ensures
that certificates do not travel over the air.

Another authentication method is the token-based authentication method. This is a
two-factor authentication method that requires that the user have both the token and
a pin to authenticate. You can use a hardware or software token with mobile devices.
Each one will display a special pin that will be valid for a period of 60 seconds. A good
example of a token-based system is RSA's SecureID.

Finally, you should configure mailbox policies so that each and every mobile device
user will be required to use proper complex passwords when logging on. Mailbox policies also let you wipe data from the device remotely if an incorrect password is
entered a specific number of times. Note that if a device is wiped and it contains
unsynchronized data, this data will most likely be lost because it is very hard to
recover data from mobile devices when the device has been wiped. In fact, most
organizations do not have the means to recover data after it has been wiped.

MORE INFO   **Configuring Exchange ActiveSync security**

For more information on how to configure Exchange ActiveSync security, go to
http://technet.microsoft.com/en-us/library/bb430761.aspx.

Secure POP3 and IMAP4   If you end up using POP3 or IMAP4 on your CAS servers,
you should also configure them for secure operation. Both e-mail services are open for
use by a variety of clients and make it easy for your users to access a limited functionality
mailbox from almost anywhere. But both rely on the SSL for secure communications.

Once again, this involves obtaining a third-party certificate, and once again this validates the use of a SAN certificate because it can be used for multiple purposes instead of obtaining a single certificate for each feature you activate on your CAS systems.

MORE INFO   **Configuring POP3 or IMAP4 security**

For more information on how to configure POP3 or IMAP4 security, go to *http://technet.microsoft.com/en-us/library/bb430779.aspx.*

Rely on a Firewall to Protect Exchange

The most common configurations of Exchange 2007 rely on Edge Transport servers located in a perimeter network. This usually means placing the ET systems between two firewalls: an internal and an external firewall. The external firewall is exposed to the Internet and requires stricter rules than the internal firewall. The internal firewall is used to separate the perimeter network from the internal network. This way, the perimeter acts as a buffer zone between the Internet and your network.

Firewalls are systems, either hardware or software, that protect access to a network through the control of the TCP and UDP ports in the TCP/IP protocol. The most basic firewall will close all ports and then let you open only those ports you need to communicate with the external world. Because the external firewall is open to the Internet, you must make the ports you open available to all IP addresses. But, because your internal firewall is designed to control access to internal resources only, you can configure it in a much more secure manner, including:

- Creating point-to-point connections that let traffic through only if it originates from known IP addresses in the perimeter. For example, you create an ET system with at least two NICs: an Internet or external-facing NIC and an intranet or internal-facing NIC. Traffic flowing through the internal firewall would only be allowed from the internal-facing NIC's IP address and no other.

- Creating one-way connections that originate from the internal network only. By creating one-way connections that originate from the internal network, you can control the traffic that goes through the firewall. This assumes, of course, that when a connection is initiated from the internal network, it is a trusted connection. A good example of this is EdgeSync, which originates from an internal HT system and is directed to the ET systems in the perimeter network.

In an Exchange 2007 configuration, you must consider opening ports for several items. Table 7-7 outlines the various ports you need to open depending on the functionality you want to make available through your firewalls.

Table 7-7 Potential Firewall Configurations for Exchange 2007

Firewall	Direction	TCP Port	Purpose	Comments
External	Inbound and Outbound	25	SMTP	Inbound e-mails to ET systems.
		53	DNS	Name resolution for externally exposed services.
		80	Read-only HTTP	Static Web site viewing
		443	Secure HTTP	Outlook Web Access Outlook Anywhere Exchange ActiveSync Autodiscover service
		587	Secure SMTP	Accept and respond to STARTTLS SMTP command
		993	Secure IMAP	IMAP4 e-mail service (optional)
		995	Secure POP	POP3 e-mail service (optional)
Internal	Inbound and Outbound (point-to-point only)	443	Secure HTTP	Outlook Web Access Outlook Anywhere Exchange ActiveSync Autodiscover service
		587	Secure SMTP	Accept and respond to STARTTLS SMTP command
		993	Secure IMAP	IMAP4 e-mail service (optional)
		995	Secure POP	POP3 e-mail service (optional)
	Outbound (point-to-point only)	50636	Secure LDAP	EdgeSync from HT to perimeter ET systems.

As you can see from Table 7-7, more ports are open on the external firewall than on the internal firewall. In addition, internal firewall connections are point-to-point connections only, and in Exchange 2007, you can also configure the Send and Receive Connectors on the ET and HT systems to require authentication. This means that each connection from the ET to an HT or vice versa can be authenticated accepting traffic only from approved partner servers.

To avoid publishing DNS information from the internal network, you should use a Hosts file on each ET server. The Hosts file can include the IP addresses of the direct-connect HT systems the ET systems are allowed to use. This way, name resolution works, but you do not need to expose internal DNS information into the perimeter network.

In addition, your internal firewall should be a reverse proxy; a server that can publish internal services without exposing the service itself. Microsoft ISA Server is a good example of a reverse proxy and it is also designed specifically to work with Exchange services. The overall configuration of your firewalls should provide more external connections than internal connections (see Figure 7-5).

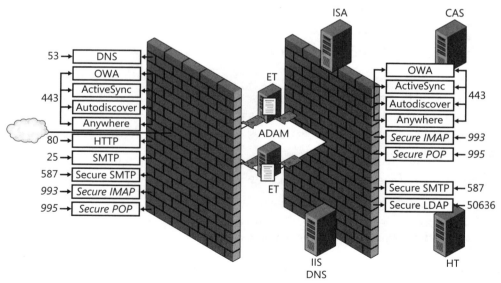

Figure 7-5   A typical Exchange 2007 firewall configuration

IMPORTANT Simple Organization firewall configurations

Simple Organizations do not include ET systems because they are based on Small Business Server (SBS). This means that they expose the Hub Transport server to the Internet. What is worse, the HT is colocated on the same server as the Mailbox server. Fortunately, SBS also includes ISA Server, which protects the HT. Despite this, the best Simple Organization configuration is one that uses a Hosted Filtering linking the HT to an external, hosted ET instead of linking it directly to the Internet. For more information on Exchange Hosted Filtering, go to *http://www.microsoft.com/exchange/services/filtering.mspx*.

Implement Domain Security

As mentioned earlier, Exchange Edge Transport servers always try to create a secure SMTP connection through Transport Layer Security. If sending or receiving servers can work with the STARTTLS SMTP command, the ET will create a secure connection. However, this leaves the connection to chance because you can never guarantee that sending or receiving SMTP servers will accept the secure connection.

When you work with partner organizations, you might want to implement a more consistent strategy. This can be done through Domain Security. Domain Security lets you create secured message paths over the Internet. Once a secured path has been created, any message that is transmitted through the path will automatically be displayed as a Domain Secured message in both Outlook and OWA.

Domain Security relies on TLS with mutual authentication to encrypt and authenticate SMTP session between your servers and those of your partner organizations. With mutual authentication, servers on both ends of the communication tunnel will authenticate each other's certificate before they begin to transmit data.

Once again, you should rely on third-party certificates to reduce the management overhead of Domain Security. This way certificates on each end will automatically be trusted.

MORE INFO Working with Domain Security

To learn more on Domain Security in general, go to *http://technet.microsoft.com/en-us/library/bb124996.aspx*. To learn how Exchange works with TLS certificates, go to *http://technet.microsoft.com/en-us/library/bb430764.aspx*.

Practice: Design a Protected Messaging Solution

In this practice, you will use a policy to protect Exchange ActiveSync users. This practice consists of a single exercise. You will create a single policy.

▶ **Exercise: Create an ActiveSync Policy**

In this exercise, you will create an ActiveSync user policy on a CAS system.

1. Make sure the DC (TreyDC) and the all-in-one Exchange server (ExchangeOne) are up and running.

2. Move to ExchangeOne.treyresearch.net and log on with the EXAdmin account from the domain. This will give you local administrator privileges.

3. Launch the Exchange Management Console (Start Menu | All Programs | Microsoft Exchange Server | Exchange Management Console).

4. Move to Organization Configuration | Client Access in the tree pane.

5. Click New Exchange ActiveSync Mailbox Policy in the Action pane.

6. Name the policy **Main ActiveSync Policy** and choose the following options:

   ❑ Do not select Allow Non-Provisionable Devices. This policy applies to Windows Mobile Devices only.

   ❑ Select Allow Attachments To Be Downloaded To Device.

   ❑ Select Require Password.

   ❑ Select Require Alphanumeric Password.

   ❑ Select Enable Password Recovery.

   ❑ Select Require Encryption On Device.

   ❑ Do not select Allow Simple Password.

   ❑ Select Minimum Password Length and set the value to **6**.

   ❑ Select Time Without User Input Before Password Must Be Re-entered (In Minutes) and set the value to **15**.

   ❑ Select Password Expiration (Days) and set the value to **45**.

   ❑ Type **5** in the Enforce Password History setting.

7. Click New to create the policy. Click Finish when the operation completes.

Your new ActiveSync policy is now in place. Note its settings in the details pane.

Quick Check

1. Where are the certificates for each internal Hub Transport and the Edge Transport servers stored by default?

2. What are the TCP ports and the encryption methods used between Hub Transport servers?

3. When should you use IPsec tunnels?

4. You want to configure a Network Load Balancing cluster for Client Access servers in your network. Why do you need a real certificate published by a third-party Certificate Authority?

5. What was the preferred method of authentication in Exchange 2003 for Outlook Web Access and what is the one used in Exchange 2007?

Quick Check Answers

1. The certificates for the internal servers are stored within Active Directory, and the certificates for Edge Transport servers are stored in ADAM.

2. The HT uses TCP port 25 or port 587 and TLS encryption by default.

3. IPsec tunnels can be used between Exchange Management Console and Mailbox servers, between Clustered Mailbox servers in multi-site CCR deployments, and between Mailbox servers and Backup servers.

4. First, the existing self-signed certificate does not include the name of the cluster and therefore will cause an error when clients try to connect; second, using a real certificate avoids having to deploy additional trusted CAs to end points because the CAs will already be included in the trusted sources located on each client.

5. In Exchange 2003, the preferred method was forms-based authentication, but in Exchange 2007, you can also use Basic, Digest, or Integrated Windows authentication. By default, OWA still relies on forms-based authentication and requires SSL encryption for client communications. Forms-based authentication is the default because it relies on a cookie on both private and public computers to store a user's credentials during the OWA session. Exchange can use this cookie to monitor session duration and therefore protect the session when it is inactive for long periods of time.

Chapter Summary

- The ET system does not have access to the GAL because it is within Active Directory, so it is important to set up Edge Subscriptions to ensure that GAL information is located within the ADAM instance on each ET.

- If your organization manages multiple e-mail domains—for example, lucerne-publishing.com and graphicsdesigninstitute.com—you must make sure your ET systems are configured as authoritative for both domains; otherwise, recipient lookup will fail for all non-authoritative domains.

- The Purported Responsible Address (PRA) calculations include four elements drawn from the message headers: Resent-Sender:, Resent-From:, Sender:, and From:. PRA and Sender ID are based on request for comment (RFC) number 4407.

- Messages of 11 MB or greater are not scanned by the Intelligent Message Filter and are moved up the chain unchecked. Note that the default maximum message limit on Exchange Receive connectors is 10 MB; if you do not change the default, this should not be an issue.

- Note that deleted messages or removed attachments are not recoverable. Also, consider putting in exceptions for messages that are digitally signed; modifying these messages automatically invalidates their signature.

- When the ET is not the first SMTP gateway between your organization's e-mail system and the Internet, you must modify its configuration to ensure that Connection Filtering works properly. This is done by including the list of each SMTP server's IP address in your perimeter network in the ET configuration.

- For the quarantine mailbox, three thresholds are configurable and each is tied to a blocking action: deletion, rejection, and quarantine. These thresholds are important because Content Filtering is the last anti-spam action performed on a message before it is delivered. They can be configured on the Content Filter itself on each ET system and configured on each individual user mailbox.

- Keep in mind that you cannot reuse the same antivirus engine you used with legacy versions of Exchange since Exchange 2007 runs on a 64-bit platform. Because virus scanning is a low-level system function, 32-bit AV engines will not work on 64-bit architectures.

- Each Exchange internal network server role installs a self-signed PKI certificate by default. These certificates are managed by Active Directory so that they are trusted by both servers and clients within the Active Directory domain and forest. Internal connections are automatically encrypted either through Remote Procedure Calls (RPC) or through the Secure Sockets Layer (SSL). External connections can also rely on SSL or the RPC over HTTP protocol (now called Outlook Anywhere).

■ When you assign a new SSL certificate to OWA, you must ensure that it is assigned to each of the four virtual directories created by the OWA installation: \owa, \exchange, \public, and \exchweb. In addition, you must enable it for each new virtual directory you create.

■ Microsoft recommends using NTLM authentication for Outlook Anywhere. This authentication mode works because users will have an account within your Active Directory and they will also already have the Outlook client on their systems. Also, you must put in place an SSL certificate for Outlook Anywhere to function.

■ The most common configurations of Exchange 2007 rely on Edge Transport servers located in a perimeter network. This usually means placing the ET systems between two firewalls: an internal and an external firewall. The external firewall is exposed to the Internet and requires stricter rules than the internal firewall. The internal firewall is used to separate the perimeter network from the internal network.

■ When you work with partner organizations, you might want to implement a more consistent strategy. This can be done through Domain Security, which lets you create secured message paths over the Internet. When a secured path has been created, any message that is transmitted through the path will automatically be displayed as a Domain Secured message in both Outlook and OWA.

Case Scenarios

In the following case scenarios, you will apply what you have learned about Exchange system security. You can find answers to the questions in this scenario in the "Answers" section at the end of this book.

Case Scenario 1: Explore Malware Protection

The Phone Company has been working toward their Exchange 2007 deployment and is starting to become very familiar with its topology and capabilities. One of their potential Exchange administrators, Sara Davis, is concerned about malware protection and has been claiming that Exchange may not be the right platform to move to because it does not offer sufficient protection against malware. The project manager, Karin Lamb, has turned to you, the messaging professional, to help overcome this hurdle in their deployment plans. Karin thinks it is just a matter of understanding which features are available to protect against malware, so she asks you to put together a table outlining these features. She will use this table with your support in an upcoming project meeting to discuss the issue.

What information do you provide in the table?

Case Scenario 2: Understand Anti-Spam and Antivirus Mail Flow

The Phone Company now understands which anti-spam and antivirus functions are available in Exchange 2007, but they want to make sure they also understand the anti-spam/antivirus mail flow within their Edge Transport servers. They turn to you, the messaging professional, once again and request that you draw up a flowchart demonstrating how mail flows through the various anti-spam and antivirus features so that they can better diagnose potential problems and also better understand the cumulative effect of multiple anti-malware levels within Exchange.

Specifically, they ask you two questions:

- In which order do the various anti-spam and antivirus functionalities work?
- Can you draw a flowchart demonstrating how mail flows through these functionalities?

How do you answer?

Case Scenario 3: Understand Client-to-Server Communications

The Phone Company intends to implement Exchange Server 2007 as well as Outlook 2007 in its corporate network. The network includes both remote offices that will include Exchange services and remote offices that will not. When planning the deployment, The Phone Company discovers are a series of services that the Client Access server can provide to end users running Outlook 2007. The company wants to know how those services communicate with the CAS—especially which TCP ports are used in the communication—so that they can plan their internal network routing and switching strategy.

Not being familiar enough with the various Exchange capabilities, they turn to you, the messaging professional, and ask you to clarify this issue for them. Specifically, they want you to build a table that outlines the various communication ports client systems can use to work with Exchange 2007.

How do you respond?

Case Scenario 4: Understand Exchange Firewall Requirements

The Phone Company has been working toward their Exchange 2007 deployment and is getting very close to being ready. But the project is continually facing resistance to change. One potential Exchange administrator in particular, Sara Davis, has been known to foster this resistance because she prefers the existing e-mail system, which is based on both POP3 and IMAP4. She claims the existing systems are easier to manage and lately has been going around claiming that if Exchange is deployed, it will perforate the firewall.

The project manager, Karin Lamb, is getting fed up with this and has turned to you, the messaging professional, once again to help overcome this hurdle in their deployment plans. Karin hopes you can squash this resistance once and for all, so she asks you to be very direct and to the point in your explanation. Specifically, she wants you to put together a table that outlines which ports Exchange will require for operation in each of the external and internal firewall.

What information do you provide in the table?

Suggested Practices

It is difficult to practice security with Exchange Server without access to a full infrastructure, but you can do so if you prepare a virtual environment as outlined in the Introduction. Rely on both the ExchangeOne and the ExchangeETOne computers to run through the security strategies for each role detailed in this chapter to see what is needed and how you should configure it.

Chapter 8

Work with Transport Rules and Compliance

Microsoft Exchange Server 2007 has become a mission-critical application for many organizations around the world. In some cases, users exclusively rely on Exchange for document management, task and appointment scheduling, and managing their day-to-day workloads. Many users have Outlook Inboxes that include thousands of messages and do not bother to classify them because they find it simpler to have everything in one place.

Microsoft has made both Outlook and Exchange evolve with the goal of making it easier for these users to flag items, assign tasks from e-mail messages, and generally simplify message classification. However, you simply cannot force a user to take up these habits. Message management is a very personal activity and just cannot be imposed.

The result is that mailboxes are often repositories of information that is vital to the organization. This is one more reason why the backup strategies outlined in Chapter 5, "Plan for High Availability Implementation," are so important: When users lose their e-mail, they lose their life's work! But, in addition to backup, you must plan and prepare for several other activities just because e-mail has become so much more important in most organizations' work:

- You need to ensure that your systems rely on appropriate transport rules. For example, you do not want users to rely on the e-mail system to send vital organizational information in unencrypted formats. Transport rules ensure that messages with specific content will not transit through your Exchange infrastructure.

- You need to ensure that messages are properly recorded and archived. This is done through message journaling. Journaling lets you identify messages that require special handling and then record them into special containers for later access.

- You need to plan for message classification, which ensures that messages are tagged with the appropriate information. When you need to return to these messages because of industry regulations or compliance requirements, you can rely on the classification information to locate the messages you need.

■ You need to secure message content, ensuring that it is not tampered with during transit. Otherwise, you will never be able to meet compliance requirements. In many cases, this is done through message protection with digital rights management.

Overall, message records management has become an important part of e-mail systems management just because of new regulations and new compliance requirements organizations need to meet. For example, in the United States alone, several regulations have come into effect over the last few years. Similar regulations have been put in place in other countries such as Canada, Australia, and New Zealand. And while the regulations are different in Europe, they must still be complied with. The goal of these regulations is to protect the disclosure of personal and financial information as well as corporate intellectual property.

Your job as a messaging professional is changing because of these regulations, and you now need to be aware of their consequences and of the actions you must take into consideration when preparing your Exchange 2007 deployment.

Regulations in the United States

In the United States, new legal obligations have emerged in light of recent events. Four key acts affect the type of documentation organizations are now responsible for:

■ 21 CFR Part 11

■ Gramm-Leach-Bliley Act (Financial Modernization Act)

■ Sarbanes-Oxley Act (SOX)

■ HIPAA (Health Insurance Portability and Accountability Act)

Each act has its own requirements. For example, the first three are focused on securing and protecting the privacy of your financial and personal information on an individual basis, especially when it is collected by organizations you are involved with. The fourth is aimed at protecting information that belongs to the beneficiaries of group health plans.

21 CFR Part 11

Part 11 of Title 21 of the Code of Federal Regulations; Electronic Records; Electronic Signatures (21 CFR Part 11) is part of the Food and Drug Association's guidelines for trustworthy electronic records and requires organizations to employ procedures and controls that are designed to ensure the authenticity, integrity and, if necessary, the confidentiality of electronic records. If called upon to validate a system, you have to provide documentation on the way your systems have been installed and configured to prove that three specific processes were completed:

- Installation Qualification
- Operation Qualification
- Performance Qualification

These processes are necessary to support the FDA's regulations, which require the following controls and requirements for closed systems:

- Limiting system access to authorized individuals
- Use of operational system checks
- Use of authority checks
- Use of device checks
- Determination that persons who develop, maintain, or use electronic systems have the education, training, and experience to perform their assigned tasks
- Establishment of and adherence to written policies that hold individuals accountable for actions initiated under their electronic signatures
- Appropriate controls over systems documentation
- Corresponding controls for open systems
- Requirements related to electronic signatures

Evaluation is based on five factors. Each one must be met for compliance to these guidelines.

- **Validation**   You must be able to prove that you have evaluated the potential of a system to affect product quality and safety, and record integrity.

- **Auditing**   You must be able to trace the changes that have been applied to the systems.

- **Legacy systems**   According to 21 CFR Part 11, a legacy system is one which was in place before the regulation became effective. Unfortunately, that was August 20, 1997. With the rate of change in IT, few systems that were put in place in 1997 are still operational today.

- **Copies of records**   You must be able to provide valid copies of your records.

- **Record retention**   You must store records of your system changes and you must be able to prove that these records have not been tampered with.

While you may or may not be affected by this rule, you do not want to learn the hard way that as far as an auditor is concerned, if you do not have an item documented or recorded, it has not happened in real life. In this regard, it is always better to be prepared beforehand.

The Gramm-Leach-Bliley Act (GLB Act)

If you are in a financial institution, you need to safeguard the confidentiality and integrity of your customer information. This is no longer just a best practice—it is now a legal requirement, one that is enforced by the Financial Modernization Act of 1999, also known as the Gramm-Leach-Bliley Act. This act mandates that your institution establish appropriate security standards to protect private customer and employee data from internal and external threats. This data also has to be completely protected from unauthorized access.

This means a complete and accurate auditing trail of all events related to this data as well as well-documented configuration information on the systems you put in place to protect it.

The GLB Act gives authority to some federal agencies and each state to administer and enforce two regulations: the Financial Privacy Rule and the Safeguards Rule. These rules apply to financial institutions which, according to the Federal Trade Commission, include not only banks, securities firms, and insurance companies, but also companies providing other types of financial products and services to consumers. These products and services include lending, brokering, or servicing any type of consumer loan, transferring or safeguarding money, preparing individual tax returns, providing financial advice or credit counseling, providing residential real estate settlement services, collecting consumer debts, and an array of other activities.

If you are involved in any of these products and services, you need to properly document how you protect this data and what measures you have taken to ensure that it remains protected.

The Sarbanes-Oxley Act

Probably the single most important act affecting information technology in publicly-traded companies is the Sarbanes-Oxley Act enforced by the Security and Exchange

Commission. This act outlines that all public organizations demonstrate due diligence in the disclosure of financial information. In addition, organizations are responsible for the implementation of internal controls and procedures that ensure that the data is protected at all times. This includes protection of the data during transmission as well as where and how the data is stored.

Section 404 of this act applies particularly to IT controls. This section, entitled "Management Assessment of Internal Controls," requires that each annual report of any publicly traded organization contain an internal control report. This report must:

- State the responsibility of management for establishing and maintaining this internal control structure and the procedures for financial reporting.
- Contain an assessment of the effectiveness of the internal control structure and procedures used for financial reporting.

You must also indicate whether you have adopted a code of ethics for senior financial officers. If you have, you must disclose the contents of that code.

In the event of an audit, you must give auditors documented evidence of data storage and protection mechanisms, and you must identify the internal controls you have applied to this data. Once again, this is a specific requirement for documentation and records management, one that you have to comply with.

The Sarbanes-Oxley Act went into effect for larger organizations with market capitalization of $75 million on November 15th, 2004. Compliance for all other publicly traded companies began with the production of their first annual report after July 15th, 2005.

Health Insurance Portability and Accountability Act (HIPAA)

The Health Insurance Portability and Accountability Act (HIPAA) has had a major impact on how health care providers do business electronically. The implications of this act are not limited to the providers themselves—their business partners are also affected. This act addresses four particular areas of electronic health care provision:

- Electronic transactions and code sets
- Security of the systems
- Use of unique identifiers for patients
- Privacy of patient and other critical information

Not all operations need to be performed electronically, but if they are, they must be performed in accordance to the standard format outlined in the act. If you contract a third-party organization to conduct a service for you, such as electronic billing, it is your responsibility as the health care provider to ensure that this third-party organization complies with the requirements of the act.

HIPAA applies to any organization involved in any of the following areas in relation to health care:

- Claims
- Payment or Remittance Advice
- Claims Status Inquiry or Response
- Eligibility Evaluations
- Referral Authorizations

This means that if your organization falls into any of these categories, you need to fully document your systems and how your systems and processes protect the information outlined here. In fact, you must do the following:

- Notify patients about their privacy rights and how their information may be used
- Adopt and implement privacy procedures
- Train employees in your privacy procedures
- Designate an individual as the privacy agent responsible for overseeing how these rules are adopted and followed
- Secure patient records containing information pertaining to specific individuals

This act has a lot to do with standards, documentation, and records management.

In addition to these four acts, the United States put in place the Uniting and Strengthening America by Providing Appropriate Tools Required to Intercept and Obstruct Terrorism Act of 2001 (commonly referred to as the Patriot Act). While this act does not specifically address records management and documentation, it does broaden the authority of U.S. law enforcement agencies to fight acts of terrorism.

Other Compliance-Oriented Regulations

As mentioned earlier, other countries and world regions have implemented similar legislations to those in the United States. For example, in Europe, organizations must comply with the European Union Data Protection Directive (EUDPD), which standardizes how they must protect the privacy of data for citizens in each and every country that is a member of the European Union.

In Canada, two acts work together to protect personal information: the Privacy Act, which was put in place in 1983, and the Personal Information Protection and Electronics Documents Act (PIPEDA). PIPEDA sets out the guidelines and rules organizations must follow when collecting, using, or disclosing personal information. Originally, this act was directed to federally regulated private sector organizations such as banks, airlines, and telecommunications firms, but today it has been expanded to include the retail sector, publishing companies, the service industry, manufacturers, and provincially regulated organizations. All governmental institutions in Canada are also under the aegis of PIPEDA.

The Federal Privacy Act in Australia and the Personal Information Protection Act in Japan both work the same way as the Canadian, U.S., and European regulations to protect personal information.

Compliance in Exchange 2007

As you can see, few organizations are exempt from compliance or privacy regulations. These regulations are fast becoming the worldwide norm. In addition, organizations themselves are making a best practice of implementing their own internal rules about information management and recordkeeping.

Therefore, as a messaging professional you should be aware of the features in Exchange that support compliance. This means developing proper messaging standards and policies for each deployment. Here you need to deal with message retention periods, disclaimers in the body of e-mail messages, and e-mail deletion policies. In the past, it has been difficult to put these policies in place, but with the release of Exchange 2007, Microsoft specifically invested in compliance-related features and tools. With 2007, you can determine which type of information can be sent through e-mail, automatically retain messages that meet specific conditions, and determine which type of e-mail can be sent outside your organization.

Exchange now supports three types of policies:

- Transport Policies apply rules and settings through the transport mechanism and as such are focused on the Hub Transport Server and the Edge Transport Server roles.

- Journaling Policies apply rules and settings on messages themselves, allowing you to save copies of messages that meet specific criteria. Like Transport Policies, Journaling Policies apply rules to messages either sent or received in your organization. Journaling sends messages to a specific SMTP address as journal reports. These reports are special e-mail messages that include Subject, Message ID, Sender, and Recipient as well as an attachment containing the original message itself.

- Messaging Records Management Policies are used to control message retention on users' mailboxes. This lets you configure how long messages in the Inbox are retained and when they should be deleted or archived in any folder of users' mailboxes. These policies are automatically applied as soon as messages are moved to the folders they are linked to.

These three policies support compliance and add significant control over the e-mail flow in general.

Exam objectives in this chapter:
- Plan the transport rules implementation.
- Plan the messaging compliance implementation.

Before You Begin

To complete the lessons in this chapter, you must have the following:

- A virtual machine setup as outlined in the Introduction under "Virtual Machine Environments."

- Use the Exchange Server 2007 virtual machine from Microsoft to review the configuration options for pre-installed computers.

- Use the virtual environment you set up to test transport rules and message compliance. For the exercises in this chapter, you will need access to the Active Directory server and the all-in-one Exchange server, ExchangeOne.

Lesson 1: Plan the Transport Rules Implementation

Estimated lesson time: 60 minutes

To meet compliance both at the regulatory level and at the organizational level, you must be able to control the flow of data within your e-mail system. In Exchange 2007, you do this through transport rules. Transport rules are designed to apply specific conditions to e-mail messages as they traverse through the Exchange transport mechanism. When messages are transported, they are examined to see whether they meet the conditions set out in a specific rule. If so, the actions that are tied to the rule are triggered and operations occur against the message. Transport rules can also include exceptions so that even if a message meets the conditions of a rule, it can be excluded from the actions if it also meets one of the exceptions.

Transport Rule Application

Generally, transport rules are designed to provide specific functionality:

- You can use transport rules to control what information enters or exits your organization. For example, the Edge Transport Server Anti-spam Content Filter can use key words or phrases within the body of a message to block messages at the gate.

- You can use a transport rule to control which users or groups can or cannot communicate with each other, either within your organization or outside your organization.

- You can use a transport rule to determine how a message is handled based on the classification a user has assigned to the message.

- You can use a transport rule to ensure that a copy of a message is always sent to a special mailbox whenever it is directed to specific recipients.

- You can use a transport rule to protect yourself from a specific viral outbreak even if your antivirus vendor does not have an updated signature yet. You do this by placing the rule on an Edge Transport server and you use the conditions that best describe the attack vector the virus is using.

- You can use a transport rule to create custom disclaimers that are either prepended or appended into the body of the messages that leave your organization and meet specific conditions.

■ You can also use transport rules to create an *ethical wall*. Ethical walls are special buffer zones that are created between departments in an organization so that they cannot communicate with each other. For example, to keep trade secrets secret, you might not want the research department to directly link to the marketing department. By putting in place an ethical wall, you ensure that when members of these departments try to send messages to each other, the messages are rejected and a non-delivery report is returned to the sender. Mailboxes from members of the ethical wall can still reside on the same Mailbox server because whenever messages are sent, they always go through a transport server where rules will be applied.

Because transport rules are structured the way they are, the possibilities are quite vast. Transport rules always have the same three components:

■ **Conditions** Outline which elements of the e-mail—sender, recipient, header, message body, message attributes—will be used to identify when the rule should be applied. Conditions are cumulative. This means that if more than one condition is set on a rule, all conditions must be met for the rule to apply. If no condition is set, the rule applies to all messages.

■ **Exceptions** Outline when the rule should not apply even if the conditions are met. In a way, exceptions are the opposite of conditions because they identify when the rule should not apply instead of when it should. And unlike conditions, if multiple exceptions are listed, only one match is required for the message to be excluded from rule application.

■ **Actions** The result of the application of a rule. Actions determine what happens to a message when it meets the conditions outlined in the rule and does not meet any of the exceptions.

Transport rules apply to the following message types:

■ **Anonymous messages** Messages transiting through an ET or an HT but sent from an unauthenticated sender or server.

■ **Interpersonal messages** Messages that contain a message body in Rich Text Format (RTF), HTML, plain text or include multiple or alternative message bodies.

■ **Opaque messages** Messages that are encrypted.

■ **Clear-Signed messages** Messages that are signed but not encrypted.

- **Unified messaging messages**   Messages that are either created or processed by a UM role and will include voicemail, fax, missed call notifications, or messages originating from Outlook Voice Access.

- **IPM.Note. messages**   Messages with a message class prefix of IPM.Note. Generated by applications or custom forms.

Note that the last two message types—Unified Messaging and IPM.Note.—are only supported in Exchange 2007 Service Pack 1.

Transport Rule Structures

Because these rules are transport rules, they work on the transport server roles within Exchange, but because of the structure of the Hub Transport server versus that of an Edge Transport server, and because of their respective functions, not all of the same rules will work on both roles. This is because each server role has a specific purpose.

HT systems usually run within an organization's internal network. Therefore, the available rules are designed to control policy and compliance-related conditions. In addition, the conditions or exceptions of a rule can query Active Directory to identify recipients and the members of distribution groups, or even identify message classifications that are also stored in the directory. And because all HT configuration is stored within the directory itself, as soon as you create one rule, it becomes available to all of the HT systems in your network, or at least as soon as Active Directory replication has occurred to the sites where your HT systems are located.

ET systems usually run in perimeter networks and do not rely on Active Directory, but rather on Active Directory in Application Mode (ADAM). Because of this, ET configurations do not replicate to each other and changes must be performed on each ET system individually. In addition, because ET systems are at the edge of your organization's network, most of the rules available to run on these systems are oriented toward protection from unwanted message traffic. Also, rules can run on both incoming and outgoing traffic in case of a compromised system or systems within your internal network. For example, ET systems would be the ideal place to create a rule to protect from antivirus outbreaks while you wait for new definitions.

Transport Rule Conditions and Exceptions

Table 8-1 outlines the various properties you can use on either HT or ET systems to build rules. In Exchange 2007, conditions and exceptions are called *predicates* because they precede the action in the rule.

Table 8-1   Transport Rule Condition and Exception Properties

Property	Format	HT	ET	Comments
		Runs on		
Addresses and Addresses2	Comma-delimited array	☑	☑	Accepts a mailbox, mail-enabled user, contact, distribution group object.
				Use **$Condition.Addresses = @((Get-Mailbox "John Kane"), (Get-MailContact "Kim Ralls"), (Get-DistributionGroup "Marketing"))** to obtain multiple values.
				Note that on ET systems, addresses must be in SMTP format, while on HT systems, they must use the real address name because they are drawn from Active Directory.
Classification	Classification object	☑	☑	Use **$Condition. Classification = (Get-MessageClassification ClassificationName).Identity** to obtain the object, where *ClassificationName* is the name you gave to the classification.
Importance	Single value	☑	☑	Values can be High, Normal, Bulk, and must be in double quotes.
Message-Header	String	☑	☑	Values must be a string of words or characters to match in a message header and must be in double quotes. Often used in combination with Patterns or Words.

Table 8-1 **Transport Rule Condition and Exception Properties**

Property	Format	Runs on HT	ET	Comments
Patterns	Expression array	☑	☑	Values must be a phrase, must be in array format (as with Addresses) and must be in double quotes.
SCL Value	Integer	☑	☑	The spam confidence level is a value between 0 and 9. Use double quotes.
Scope	InOrganization or NotInOrganization	☑	☑	Used to identify where the message originated, inside or outside your organization. It also identifies whether the recipient(s) are within or outside of the organization. Use double quotes. Compares domain portion of e-mail against accepted domains list. Can work on mail-enabled user, distribution group, or public folder.
Size	Integer with quantifier	☑	☑	Use an integer with either B for bytes, KB, MB, GB, or TB.
Words	String array	☑	☑	Values must be individual words, must be in array format (as with Addresses) and must be in double quotes.

Table 8-2 outlines how you can use the properties in Table 8-1 to create conditions and exceptions you can apply on HT or ET systems.

Table 8-2 Transport Rule Conditions and Exceptions

Predicate	Property 1	Property 2	Runs on HT	ET	Comments
AnyOfTo-Header-MemberOf	Addresses	n/a	☑		Use to identify recipients that are members of a distribution list in To: field only.
AnyOfCC-Header	Addresses	n/a	☑		Use to identify message recipients. Matches mailbox, mail-enabled user, or contact in CC: field only.
AnyOfCC-Header-MemberOf	Addresses	n/a	☑		Use to identify recipients that are members of a distribution list in CC: field only.
AnyOf-Recipient-Address-Contains	Words	n/a		☑	Use to find messages that contain specific words in To:, CC:, or BCC: fields.
AnyOf-Recipient-AddressMatches	Patterns	n/a		☑	Use to find messages that contain specific expressions in To:, CC:, or BCC: fields.

Table 8-2   Transport Rule Conditions and Exceptions

Predicate	Property 1	Property 2	Runs on		Comments
			HT	ET	
AnyOfTo-CCHeader	Addresses	n/a	☑		Use to identify message recipients. Matches mailbox, mail-enabled user, or contact in To: or CC: fields.
AnyOfToCC-Header-MemberOf	Addresses	n/a	☑		Use to identify recipients that are members of a distribution list in To: or CC: fields.
AnyOfToHeader	Addresses	n/a	☑		Use to identify message recipients. Matches mailbox, mail-enabled user, or contact in To: field only.
Attachment-NameMatches	Patterns	n/a	☑		Use to find messages with specific patterns in attachment filenames.
AttachmentSize-Over	Size	n/a	☑	☑	Use to find messages with attachments equal to or over a given size.

Table 8-2   Transport Rule Conditions and Exceptions

Predicate	Property 1	Property 2	Runs on HT	Runs on ET	Comments
Between-MemberOf	Addresses	Addresses2	☑		Use to identify messages sent between members of two distribution lists.
From	Addresses	n/a	☑		Use to identify people. Matches mailbox, mail-enabled user, or contact sending the message.
FromAddress-Contains	Words	n/a	☑	☑	Use to find messages with specific words in From field.
FromAddress-Matches	Patterns	n/a	☑	☑	Use to find messages with specific patterns in From field.
FromMemberOf	Addresses	n/a	☑		Use to identify members of a distribution list sending a message.
FromScope	Scope	n/a	☑	☑	Use to identify sending scope of a message (inside or outside the organization).

Table 8-2   **Transport Rule Conditions and Exceptions**

Predicate	Property 1	Property 2	Runs on HT	Runs on ET	Comments
Has-Classification	Classification	n/a	☑		Use to find messages matching a specific classification.
HeaderContains	Message-Header	Words	☑	☑	Use to find messages with specific message Header field values.
HeaderMatches	Patterns	n/a	☑	☑	Use to find messages with specific patterns in Header field.
SCLOver	SCLValue	n/a	☑	☑	Use to find messages with spam confidence level equal to or over specific value.
SentTo	Addresses	n/a	☑		Use to identify message recipients. Matches mailbox, mail-enabled user, or contact in To:, CC:, or BCC: fields.
SentToMember-Of	Addresses	n/a	☑		Use to identify recipients that are members of a distribution list in To:, CC:, or BCC: fields.

Table 8-2   Transport Rule Conditions and Exceptions

Predicate	Property 1	Property 2	Runs on		Comments
			HT	ET	
SentToScope	Scope	n/a	☑		Use to identify receiving scope of a message.
SubjectContains	Words	n/a	☑	☑	Use to find messages with specific words in Subject field.
SubjectMatches	Patterns	n/a	☑	☑	Use to find messages with specific patterns in Subject field.
SubjectOrBody-Contains	Words	n/a	☑	☑	Use to find messages with specific words in Subject field or message body.
SubjectOrBody-Matches	Patterns	n/a	☑	☑	Use to find messages with specific patterns in Subject field or message body.
WithImportance	Importance	n/a	☑		Use to find messages with a specific importance level.

IMPORTANT Recipient caches

Keep in mind that Hub Transport servers include a recipient cache so that they do not need to query Active Directory each time they need to locate recipient information. You cannot configure the cache update, but at least the presence of the cache will increase transport rule processing speeds.

Transport Rule Actions

Actions are applied when e-mail messages meet the conditions and do not meet the exceptions outlined in a rule. Table 8-3 outlines the properties you can apply to actions when creating a rule.

Table 8-3 Transport Rule Action Properties

Property	Format	Runs on HT	Runs on ET	Comments
Addresses	Comma-delimited array	☑	☑	Accepts a mailbox, mail-enabled user, contact, distribution group object.
				Use **$Condition.Addresses = @((Get-Mailbox "John Kane"), (Get-MailContact "Kim Ralls"), (Get-DistributionGroup "Marketing"))** to obtain multiple values.
				Note that on ET systems, addresses must be in SMTP format, while on HT systems, they must use the real address name because they are drawn from Active Directory.
Classification	Classification object	☑	☑	Use **$Condition.Classification = (Get-MessageClassification** *ClassificationName***).Identity** to obtain the object, where *ClassificationName* is the name you gave to the classification.

Table 8-3   **Transport Rule Action Properties**

Property	Format	Runs on		Comments
		HT	ET	
Enhanced-StatusCode	Single value	☑	☑	Use to determine which message to display and include in non-delivery report when messages are rejected by RejectMessage rule.
				Relies on delivery status notification (DSN) code of 5.7.1 or any value between 5.7.10 and 5.7.999.
				Use the **New-SystemMessage** cmdlet to create custom messages.
Event-Message	String	☑	☑	Requires event number to store in local system Event Log.
FallBack-Action	Single value	☑	☑	Use when disclaimer text cannot be added to a message, such as with an encrypted message. Can be one of three values:
				■ *Wrap* (the default) places the unchanged original message into a new one.
				■ *Ignore* lets the message continue unchanged.
				■ *Reject* returns an NDR to the sender.
				Note that when messages are wrapped, all other rules are applied to the wrapper and not the original message. Also, if wrapping does not work, the default fallback is Reject.

Table 8-3 Transport Rule Action Properties

| Property | Format | Runs on | | Comments |
		HT	ET	
Font	Single value	☑	☑	Specifies the font of the disclaimer text. Values include Arial (default), CourierNew, or Verdana. Use in double quotes.
FontColor	Single value	☑	☑	Specifies the color of the disclaimer text. Values can be Gray (default), Black, Blue, Fuchsia, Green, Lime, Maroon, Navy, Olive, Purple, Red, Silver, Teal, White, or Yellow. Use in double quotes.
FontSize	Single value	☑	☑	Specifies the font size of the disclaimer text. Values include Smallest (default), Smaller, Normal, Larger, or Largest. Use in double quotes.
Header-Value	String	☑	☑	Use with MessageHeader property. Applies single string to message header.
Location	Single value	☑	☑	Specifies the location of the disclaimer text. Values can be Append (end of message) or Prepend (beginning of message). Use in double quotes.
Message-Header	String	☑	☑	Works with HeaderValue to determine which values to insert in a message header. Use in double quotes.

Table 8-3   Transport Rule Action Properties

Property	Format	Runs on HT	Runs on ET	Comments
Prefix	String	☑	☑	Inserts string before existing subject in Subject field. Use in double quotes. Use with SubjectContains exception to prevent addition of Prefix each time the message passes through a transport server.
Reject-Reason	String	☑	☑	Use to insert custom information in NDRs when messages are rejected. Use in double quotes.
SCLValue	Integer	☑	☑	The spam confidence level is a value between 0 and 9. Use double quotes.
Separator	Single value	☑	☑	Specifies whether a separator is inserted between a disclaimer and the original message body. Values include WithSeparator or WithoutSeparator. Use in double quotes.
Text	String	☑	☑	Specifies the disclaimer text to insert. Use in double quotes.

Table 8-4 outlines how you can use the properties in Table 8-3 to create actions you can apply on HT or ET systems.

Table 8-4 **Transport Rule Actions**

Predicate	Property 1	Property 2	Runs on		Comments
			HT	ET	
AddTo-Recipient	Addresses	n/a	☑	☑	Adds additional recipient(s) to the To: field. Original recipients view the change.
Apply-Classification	Classification	n/a	☑		Adds a classification to the message.
Apply-Disclaimer	Text	Font, Font-Color, FontSize, Location, Separator, FallBackAction	☑		Applies disclaimer text to a message.
BlindCopy-To	Addresses	n/a	☑	☑	Adds additional recipient(s) to the BCC: field. Original recipients cannot view the change.
CopyTo	Addresses	n/a	☑	☑	Adds additional recipient(s) to the CC: field. Original recipients view the change.
Delete-Message	n/a	n/a	☑	☑	Deletes a message without notification to sender or recipient(s).

Table 8-4 **Transport Rule Actions**

Predicate	Property 1	Property 2	Runs on		Comments
			HT	ET	
Disconnect	n/a	n/a		☑	Terminates connection from sending server with no NDR.
LogEvent	Event-Message	n/a	☑	☑	Adds an event to the Application Log.
Prepend-Subject	Prefix	n/a	☑	☑	Adds a string at the beginning of the Subject field.
Quarantine	n/a	n/a		☑	Redirects message to quarantine mailbox. Quarantine mailbox must exist first.
Redirect-Message	Addresses	n/a	☑	☑	Redirects message to specified recipient(s). Senders are not notified and original recipients are removed.
Reject-Message	RejectReason	Enhanced-StatusCode	☑		Rejects a message with an NDR. Intended recipient(s) do not receive the message.

Table 8-4   Transport Rule Actions

Predicate	Property 1	Property 2	Runs on HT	Runs on ET	Comments
Remove-Header	Message-Header	n/a	☑	☑	Removes Header field.
SetHeader	Message-Header	HeaderValue	☑	☑	Creates or modifies Header field.
SetSCL	SCLValue	n/a	☑	☑	Sets spam confidence level on a message.
SMTP-Reject-Message	StatusCode	RejectReason		☑	Deletes message and sends notification to sender. Also includes delivery status notification code.

Use Regular Expressions

Expressions are important in transport rules because they are used to identify strings of characters. For example, you could use a string of text such as "Contract details" to ensure that messages containing contract details would always have a special disclaimer ensuring that your organization is not tied to any contract details sent by e-mail. But, when it comes to identifying strings of text that vary, for example, bank account numbers that are always in 123-45678-90123 format, you need to use special expressions—in Exchange they are called regular expressions—to identify text or numerical positions. Regular expressions are used through the Exchange Management Shell and are applied with the Patterns predicate property. In the Exchange Management Console, you can use them with any condition or exception that includes the words "with text patterns".

Table 8-5 lists the pattern strings you can use in this case.

Table 8-5 Transport Rule Regular Expressions

String	Usage
\S	Matches any single character that is not a space.
\s	Matches any single white space character including spaces.
\D	Matches any non-numeric digit—for example, when specifying IPv6 addresses that include both numeric and non-numeric digits such as 3ffe:501:8:0:260:97ff:fe40:efab.
\d	Matches any single numeric digit.
\w	Matches any single letter (a–z or A–Z), numeric digit (0–9) or any Unicode character.
|	Performs an OR action (pipe character).
*	Matches any instance of the previous letter from none to multiple instances (wildcard). For example, 12*3 matches 13, 123, 1223, 12223, and so on.
( )	Act as grouping delimiters (parentheses). For example, 1(23)*4 matches 14, 1234, 123234, 12323234, and so on.
\\	Means that the following character is the real character you are looking for (backslash). For example, \\a means you are looking for the character "a".
^	Means that the following string of characters must exist at the beginning of an expression (caret). For example, ^John.Kane@ will match all of the SMTP addresses for John.Kane.
$	Means that the preceding string of characters must exist at the end of an expression (dollar). For example, lucernepublishing.com$ matches any SMTP address as well as any Web URL that ends with the expression *lucernepublishing.com*.
^ $	Using both the caret at the beginning and the dollar sign at the end of a string of characters will only locate matches for that particular string. For example, ^John.Kane@lucernepublishing.com$ will only find the expression *John.Kane@lucernepublishing.com*.

You combine these regular expressions together to determine what you are looking for in a transport rule. Rely on the following examples for more information:

- $(\d\d\d)^*(\s|.)^*(\d\d)^*(\s|.)^*\d\d\d\d\d(\s|.)^*\d\d\d(\s|.)^*\d\d\d$
  is an expression that looks for a phone number from the UK. UK phone numbers are five digits followed by two strings of three digits. The expression can find the following values:
  07700 954 321 (where $(\s|.)$ locates the space character between digit strings)
  07700.954.321 (where $(\s|.)$ locates the period character between digit strings)
  44 07700 954 321 (where $(\d\d)^*$ found the country code)
  011 44 07700 954 321 (where $(\d\d\d)^*$ found the international dialing code)
  44.07700.954.321 (where $(\s|.)^*$ found a period instead of a space)
  011.44.07700.954.321 (where $(\s|.)^*$ found a period instead of a space)
  0114407700954321 (where there are no spaces or periods)
  4407700954321 (where there are no spaces or periods and no international dialing code)
  07700954321 (where there are no spaces or periods and no country code)

- ^$
  The caret character (^) delimits a string at the beginning of an expression while the dollar ($) delimits the end of an expression. When there are no characters between the two, they automatically identify empty strings. For example, you could use this regular expression to locate messages that have empty subject lines.

As you can see, you have a lot of possible combinations to work with.

Configure Transport Rules

Transport rules can be configured in either the Exchange Management Console or the Shell. For example, you might configure them with the Console on HT systems because you only need to configure them once, which automatically stores them in Active Directory and makes them available to all other HT systems after replication has occurred. But you might prefer to configure them with the Shell on ET systems: You can create scripts that you can run on each ET system because ET systems do not share configurations.

In the Exchange Management Console, go to Organization, then Hub Transport or Edge Transport and select New Transport Rule to launch the New Transport Rule Wizard (see Figure 8-1). This wizard will step you through the creation of the rule, the assignment of conditions and exceptions, and the generation of the action assigned to

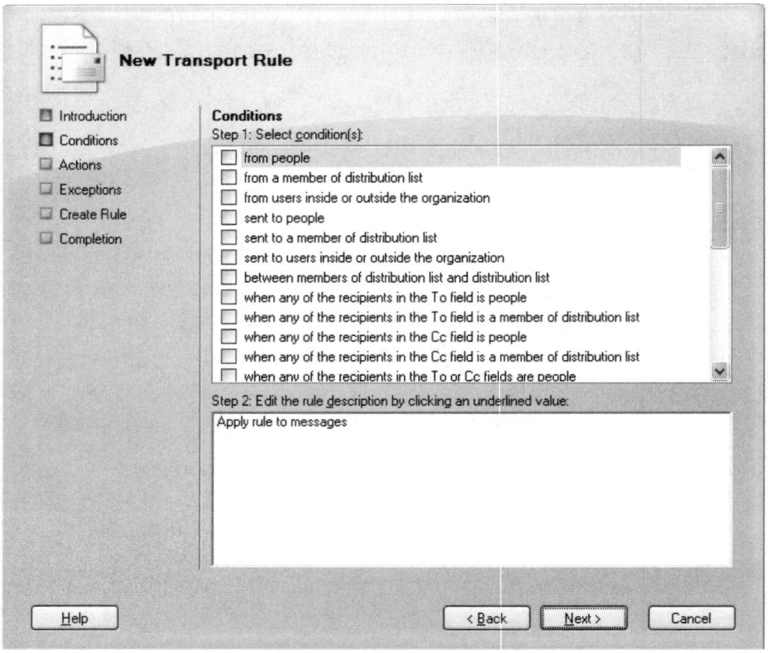

Figure 8-1   Assigning conditions to a transport rule

the rule. The Review page will display a summary of the rule. You can use Ctrl+C to copy the rule to the clipboard, paste it into a Notepad document, and save it. This will make it easier to document the rule.

The last page of the wizard includes the Shell cmdlet that you used to create the rule (see Figure 8-2). You can use Ctrl+C to copy the rule to the clipboard, paste it into a Notepad document, and save it with a .ps1 extension. You can then use this new Shell script to run the same rule on Edge Transport servers to make sure each ET runs the same rules.

If you prefer to generate the rule directly through the Shell, you can use the following cmdlets:

```
New-TransportRule
Get-TransportRule
Set-TransportRule
Enable-TransportRule
Disable-TransportRule
Remove-TransportRule
Get-TransportRuleAction
Get-TransportRulePredicate
```

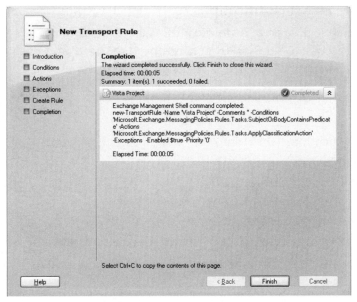

Figure 8-2   Using the console to generate a transport rule script

The last two cmdlets will produce the list of available rule actions or predicates. Two more cmdlets let you import or export a set of rules from one server to another:

```
Import-TransportRuleCollection
Export-TransportRuleCollection
```

Be aware that when you import a rule collection, it automatically overwrites all pre-existing rules, so use this cmdlet with caution. Using this cmdlet on an HT system will overwrite all of the rules in the entire Exchange Organization. Using it on an ET system only affects that particular system.

You might prefer to use the Shell when configuring rules on ET systems because you can trap Shell cmdlets into scripts and simply run the same scripts on each ET system to ensure that they have the same rule configuration. You can also use the Export and Import cmdlets to get the same result. For example, you could configure the following rule to avoid the transmission of international phone numbers from the UK through your e-mail system:

```
$Condition = Get-TransportRulePredicate SubjectMatches
$Condition.Patterns = ("(\d\d\d)*(\s|.)*(\d\d)*(\s|.)*\d\d\d\d(\s|.)*\d\d\d(\s|.)*\d\d\d")
$Action = Get-TransportRuleAction RejectMessage
$Action.RejectReason = "Transmitting UK phone numbers is not allowed."
New-TransportRule -Name "UK Phone Number Prohibition Rule" -Condition
$Condition -Action $Action
```

Associate Delivery Status Notifications to Transport Rules

When you apply the RejectMessage action to a message, Exchange associates a delivery status notification code to the NDR that is returned to the sender of the message and then deletes the message. The NDR is also called a *bounce* message.

As indicated in Table 8-3 earlier, the RejectMessage action is associated with two properties:

- RejectReason, which inserts text into the "Diagnostic information for administrators" section of an NDR.

- EnhancedStatusCode, which actually refers to the DSN. The value used for the EnhancedStatusCode can be 5.7.1 or any value between 5.7.10 and 5.7.999. Only two values already have DSNs associated with them:

  - 5.7.0, which is the default DSN Exchange sends if no DSN value is specified.
  - 5.7.1, which is a standard message including the same text as 5.7.0.

Messages between the values 5.7.10 and 5.7.999 are not defined and are messages you can customize. This lets you create a series of NDR messages for use in special compliance situations. For example, if you build an ethical wall, you might want to create a custom DSN to indicate to the sender that the message could not be delivered because it breaches the ethical wall your organization has put in place.

You create new DSN messages by using the **New-SystemMessage** cmdlet on a Hub Transport server. For example, if you wanted to create a new DSN message for an ethical wall at Lucerne Publishing, you might use the following cmdlet structure:

```
New-SystemMessage –DsnCode 5.7.10 –Language En –Internal $True –Text 'You are not allowed to
send messages to this recipient. For more information, see
<a href = "http://intranet.lucernepublishing.com/policy.html#514">Internal Policy 514</a>.'
```

This cmdlet creates a new DSN number 5.7.10 and points the refused sender to a URL for more information on the violated policy.

MORE INFO **Manage delivery status notifications**

For more information on managing DSNs, go to *http://technet.microsoft.com/en-us/library/ bb124571.aspx.*

Guidelines for Transport Rule Implementation

Transport rules can include a whole series of different conditions, exceptions, and actions. Remember that if a rule has no conditions, it applies to each and every message that is transmitted through your mail flow. And, because having a series of different rules that are applied at different levels of the organization can become quite confusing, you should always endeavor to use the following guidelines when applying and managing rules:

- Consider the impact of a rule as you design it. A rule that adds a disclaimer to all messages that are sent outside your organization will have little impact, but a rule that sends copies of messages to recipients in other sites may have an impact on bandwidth.

- Document each rule you create. Include the conditions, the exceptions, the actions, the scope (internal or external), the location (HT or ET), and the reason or regulation this rule applies to. Also include the potential impact of the rule on the e-mail system itself.

- Obtain approval for each rule. Rules are often applied to conform to regulations or legal obligations. Therefore, it is a good practice to obtain approval for the rule before its implementation. Approval should stem from various sources, but should include at least:
  - Project Management in the Exchange Deployment Project
  - Project Management Committee, including Project Sponsors, in the Exchange Deployment Project
  - Legal authorities within or outside of your organization
  - Corporate management

  Rely on the documentation you created for the rule to obtain approval. This will also act as a good quality assurance test for the documentation itself.

- Validate and test each transport rule in a lab environment before you deploy it in your Exchange Organization. You should have a series of different test levels, progressively increasing in scope and complexity as you graduate your tests through them until you reach production. This ensures that you can trap errors you might have missed if you only use one level of tests.

MORE INFO **Learn to use graduated test environments**

For a description of the various testing levels you should use to graduate tests, see Chapter 3 of the free e-Book *The Definitive Guide to Vista Migration* by Ruest and Ruest at *www.realtime-nexus.com/dgvm.htm*.

Practice: Begin to Build a Messaging Privacy Strategy

In this practice, you will begin to prepare a compliance strategy in relation the protection of confidential client information in an Exchange 2007 deployment. This practice consists of a single exercise. This exercise will help you understand transport rule functionality.

▶ **Exercise: Create a Transport Rule**

In this exercise, you create a transport rule by defining its conditions, exceptions, and the actions to undertake when the rule is applied. In this case, you want to make sure customer phone numbers are never sent out of your organization through e-mail. The situation you need to control is the following: Any messages with North American phone numbers in the 123-456-7890, (123) 456-7890, or 1234567890 formats cannot be transmitted.

Because there is only one condition to meet, you only need to implement a single rule. The rule should be a rejection rule that will stop any e-mail that contains any of the possible combinations of text within the body of the message.

To create the rule, follow these steps:

1. Make sure both the TreyDC and the ExchangeOne servers are running.

2. Log on to the ExchangeOne.treyresearch.net server with the EXAdmin account. This will grant you local administrator privileges.

3. When you are logged on, launch the Exchange Management Shell. Use Start Menu | All Programs | Microsoft Exchange Server | Exchange Management Shell.

4. Begin the preparation of your rule. Start with the condition. Use the following cmdlets:

   ```
   $Condition = Get-TransportRulePredicate SubjectMatches
   $Condition.Patterns = ("(\\()*\d\d\d(\\))*(\s|-)*\d\d\d(\s|-)*\d\d\d\d")
   ```

5. Because this rule has no exceptions, move on to set the action to undertake. Use the following cmdlets:

   ```
   $Action = Get-TransportRuleAction RejectMessage
   $Action.RejectReason = "Transmitting client phone numbers is not allowed."
   ```

6. To apply the rule, use the following cmdlet:

   ```
   New-TransportRule -Name "Client Phone Number Prohibition Rule" -Condition
   $Condition -Action $Action
   ```

7. The rule is set. Close the Exchange Management Shell.

This rule will find all of the combinations displayed at the beginning of the exercise, reject messages, and send a rejection reason to the sender. You might also consider adding a condition to this rule to forward messages that match this rule to an administrator so that your organization can be aware of attempts to transmit client information through e-mail. In some cases, the transmissions are unintended, but in others, these could be malicious attempts; therefore, tracking these messages is very important to your organization.

Quick Check

1. What are transport rules?

2. What is an ethical wall?

3. What are the specific purposes of transport rules based on transport server type?

4. What are the two properties that are associated with RejectMessage?

5. Which two values already have a DSN associated with them?

Quick Check Answers

1. Transport rules are designed to apply specific conditions to e-mail messages as they traverse through the Exchange transport mechanism. When messages are transported, they are examined to see if they meet the conditions set out in a specific rule. If so, the actions that are tied to the rule are triggered and operations occur against the message. Transport rules can also include exceptions, so that even if a message meets the conditions of a rule, it can be excluded from the actions if it also meets one of the exceptions.

2. Ethical walls are special buffer zones that are created between departments in an organization so that they cannot communicate with each other. You ensure that when members of these departments try to send a message to each other, the messages are rejected and an NDR is returned to the sender. Mailboxes from members of the ethical wall can still reside on the same Mailbox server because whenever messages are sent, they always go through a transport server where rules will be applied.

3. The rules that are available for the HT servers are designed to control policy and compliance-related conditions. The rules on the ET servers are oriented toward protection from unwanted message traffic.

4. The two properties are RejectReason, which inserts text into the "Diagnostic information for administrators" section of an NDR, and EnhancedStatus-Code, which refers to the DSN.

5. The two values are 5.7.0, which is the default DSN Exchange sends if no DSN value is specified, and 5.7.1, which is a standard message including the same text as 5.7.0.

Lesson 2: Plan the Messaging Compliance Implementation

Estimated lesson time: 40 minutes

Compliance is also a factor that Exchange administrators must now take into consideration when they plan Exchange 2007 deployments. No matter where you are in the world, chances are very good that you will be responsible for putting in place a compliance strategy when you prepare your Exchange deployment. When considering compliance strategies, you must consider the following items:

■ **Message Classification**   Ensures that messages are properly classified as they are transported through your mail flow.

■ **Messaging Records Management (MRM)**   Manages messages users store in their mailboxes. This lets you determine how long these messages can be retained and what should be done with them when the retention period expires.

■ **Message Journaling**   Ensures that you preserve copies of important e-mail messages for posterity. This ensures that you have them on hand when you need to produce them for compliance purposes. Journaling also involves Message Lifecycle Management (MLM) or managing messages that are at rest and not in transit.

■ **Secure/Multipurpose Internet Mail Extensions (S/MIME)**   Protects messages sent to external recipients to ensure that they are not tampered with.

■ **Digital Rights Management (DRM)**   Protects documents from tampering, much like the S/MIME feature.

Each of these features plays a part in meeting compliance regulations along with transport rules. Together, they help you form a complete messaging compliance strategy.

Classify Messages

When you run both Exchange 2007 and Office Outlook 2007, you can put in place a message classification strategy. Classification adds specific metadata to messages as they are transported through the mail flow. This metadata describes items such as the intended use of a message or its intended audience. Outlook 2007 and Outlook Web Access 2007 can use this metadata to display descriptions about senders or recipients of classified messages to end users. In addition, the Exchange transport mechanism can apply special treatment to classified messages because it can use transport rules to identify them.

Classifications can be added by end users themselves as they prepare an e-mail message. With these messages, transport rules can rely on this classification to act on the message. Transport rules can also add the classification themselves based on specific conditions such as key words in the message body, recipient name, or distribution list. Then, once you add the classification, the rules will act upon the classification you have added. A good example is adding a confidential classification to a message and then ensuring that messages classified as confidential do not go out of the organization. Another example is when the Attachment Filter (see Lesson 1 in Chapter 7, "Plan Messaging Security and Compliance Implementation") removes an attachment, it adds the Attachment Removed classification to the message before sending it on to the recipient.

One of the best examples of classification is Attorney-Client Privilege (A/C Privileged). In most jurisdictions, attorneys and clients are allowed privileged discussions where they can openly discuss a case in complete privacy. When they use an e-mail system to do so, they must be absolutely sure that their conversations will not be listened in on in any way; otherwise, they could not discuss the case openly. Clients can send A/C Privileged messages to their attorneys and vice versa, and attorneys can only forward these messages under the strictest rules. Messages classified as A/C Privileged are treated in a confidential manner by the transport rules legal organizations put in place.

Because the A/C Privileged classification is so important, it is one of the default classifications included in Exchange 2007. However, by default, it is informational only—that is, it only displays the classification message. In most organizations requiring this classification, administrators should set up a special transport rule that if an A/C Privileged message is sent to recipients that are not lawyers, it will be returned to the sender.

Default message classifications include:

- ExACPrivileged
- ExAttachmentRemoved
- ExCompanyConfidential
- ExCompanyInternal
- ExPartnerMail

These default settings include default content. You might want to customize the content of each classification if you choose to use it.

Set Message Classifications

Exchange administrators can set message classifications to be used in the Exchange Organization. Classifications are tied to specific message fields, which include:

- **Display Name** The name of the classification. This appears in the Permission menu in Outlook and is how users select the classification.

- **Sender Description** The description that tells senders why they should be using this classification.

- **Recipient Description** The description recipients see on the Outlook InfoBar of a message when it has been classified.

- **Locale** The ability to have classification messages appear in different languages based on the user's language settings.

Users rely on these fields to select the appropriate classification before sending the message. Administrators enter specific description text as they prepare each classification. Locale is used to regionalize the classifications.

Administrators must enable classifications in their Exchange Organization before users can assign them. Deploying classifications involves three (sometimes four) tasks:

1. You must create or customize the classifications on an Exchange server. Use the **New-MessageClassification** cmdlet to create new classifications. Use the **Set-MessageClassification** to modify existing classifications.

2. You must create localized versions of the classification messages if you are running a multilingual organization.

3. You must deploy the message classification configuration file (Classifications.xml) to end-user computers running Outlook 2007. You create this file by exporting it from the Exchange server on which you create the classifications. Use the Export-OutlookClassification.ps1 script to do so.

4. You must create a custom registry key on these same computers. No special configuration is required to display message classifications in OWA.

After you deploy the classifications, users can click the Set Permissions button in the Options group on the Message tab in a new message to set classifications. After the classification is applied, a special display message is added to the message. This display message can be viewed by users of either Outlook or OWA 2007.

If your organization is multilingual, you can use Exchange's localization features to create classifications in multiple languages. Then classifications in appropriate languages are displayed in Outlook and OWA based on the user's language settings. However, you must make sure that classifications apply to users in each locale before you do this. For example, users in Europe may not be subject to the same limitations as those in Canada because of the different legislatures involved. Make sure you understand the implications before you localize classifications for one particular region of the world.

Note that the Classifications.xml file must be updated each time you modify the classifications on an Exchange server. Because of this, you might consider placing the file on a central share that each connected system can access, and then enabling offline caching of the file so that mobile systems can transport a copy with them. Because the file is centrally located, you would only have to update it in a single location and offline caching would automatically synchronize the file on each client computer. Make sure you reference the appropriate path in the Registry when you create the registry keys required to activate classification on client computers.

MORE INFO   Manage classifications

For more information on how to manage classifications, go to *http://technet.microsoft.com/en-us/library/bb124705.aspx*.

Use Precedence in Classifications

After you assign classifications to a message, they will stay with the message until the message leaves the organization. In addition, a message may have multiple classifications. For example, if a message that is assigned an A/V Privileged classification has an attachment that must be removed, you want to make sure that the A/V Privileged classification appears before the Attachment Removed classification because of its importance. You do this by using the Precedence setting on a classification.

In this scenario, the A/V Privileged classification would have a Precedence setting of Highest while the Attachment Removed classification would be set to Medium. This would ensure that the A/V Privileged message would appear first. Then, because of the nature of the two classifications, if the lawyer forwarded the message, only the A/V Privileged would be retained because only this classification is required to stay with the message for its lifetime.

Records Management

Another aspect of compliance is designing a records management strategy that allows you to globally manage message age and retention on individual mailboxes. With Exchange 2007, you can control quite a few mailbox features from a central location. For example, you can control retention of messages in users' mailboxes based on message type or message age. You can automatically delete messages; you can move them to a special, managed folder; or you can mark them for future actions. In addition, you can put policies in place that will manage custom folders and let you control archiving of the content of these folders from users' mailboxes.

Managed folders can be applied to both the default folders—folders such as Inbox, Sent Items, Deleted Items, and Calendar—or custom folders, which are folders created by administrators when they create the records management policy. As with default folders, users cannot delete, move, or rename custom managed folders. Custom folders have the added advantage of being able to support maximum size limits set by the administrator. These settings apply to the custom folder and any subfolder it contains. Default folders do not support maximum size settings.

Records management policies apply at two different levels. First, you can configure a retention policy directly on users' mailboxes. Second, you can configure Journaling Policies to take messages from a specific folder and forward them to another recipient. Journaling recipients can be any e-mail address including an actual mail-enabled user or even a Windows SharePoint Services library. When you do this, classifications are preserved to ensure that you are retaining an actual copy of the original message. Journaling is covered further later in the chapter.

To set up the first type of message records management policies—policies you apply on user folders—you use a five-step process:

1. Determine which folders you want to manage, including both default and custom folders. All default folders are displayed in the Exchange Management Console. You might prefer to use custom folders rather than the defaults. After all, keeping 1,000 messages in the Inbox is not a good practice. For example, if your users are working on a special project such as the deployment of a new technology like Windows Vista, you might want to create a custom folder called Vista Project and have messages in this folder retained for the duration of the migration project.

2. Determine which settings you want to base your policy on. A good example is when you want to empty the Deleted Items folder of any item that is more than 60 days old. Configurable settings include:

   ❑ Message type

   ❑ Length of retention

   ❑ Action to perform

   ❑ Journaling settings to save a copy of the contents of the folder

3. Create a managed folder policy based on the settings you determined. One policy can apply to a single folder or to multiple folders.

4. Apply the policy to users by linking the policy with user properties in the Exchange Management Console or through the Shell. Using the Shell, you can assign the policy to multiple users at once. No policies exist in a default Exchange configuration.

5. Use the Managed Folder Assistant to schedule the change on user folders. This assistant does not run in a default Exchange configuration.

When a policy is in place, all users need to do to interact with it is to move messages into the appropriate folders in their mailboxes. As soon as a message is placed into a managed folder, it falls under the sway of the managed folder policy. In addition, if users want to make it easier for themselves, you can show them how they can create rules in Outlook to automatically move messages into the managed folder as soon as they arrive in the mailbox. You can, of course, also set policies on mailboxes where users do not have to do anything because all mailbox content is managed.

The Managed Folder Assistant provides all records management as soon as you set a schedule for it to run. Normally, administrators select which folders are managed in which mailboxes, but Exchange also provides the ability to create a custom Web service that allows users to select their own managed folders.

Implement Managed Folders

Managed folders are set up through either the Exchange Management Console or the Shell. In the Console, go to Organization | Mailbox and choose New Managed Default Folder or New Managed Custom Folder. When you create the rule, you need to specify the following:

- Folder name and display name if it is a custom folder. In a default folder, you must select which default folder you want the rule to apply to.

- Storage limit. Applies only to custom folders.

- Comment to display in Outlook when users view the folder. Note that these comments should be short and to the point because they are limited to only 255 characters.

This creates the folder (see Figure 8-3). Note that the folder policy will not apply to user mailboxes until you have assigned it and scheduled the assistant to run. To perform the same operation with the Shell, use the **New-ManagedFolder** cmdlet.

Figure 8-3   Creating a managed folder

After you have designated or created the folder, you need to modify the content settings you want to apply to the folder. In the Console, either right-click the new folder to modify its settings or click New Managed Content Settings in the Action pane. In the Shell, use the **New-ManagedContentSettings** cmdlet. When you modify content settings, you need to specify the following information:

- Name of the settings object.
- Message type to apply the settings to. This can be any mailbox object or only a specific object type.
- Length of retention in days.

- When the retention should start. Two options are available. For messages, this can be when it is delivered; for calendar and recurring task items it is the end date for the item or when the object is moved to the managed folder.

- Journaling settings, which include whether the object should be forwarded and to whom, whether a label is required, and in which format the object should be delivered. The default is the Exchange MAPI Message Format (TNEF); the format can also be Outlook message format (.msg).

The first dialog box sets the managed content settings (see Figure 8-4) and the second sets journaling features. You can apply multiple settings to the same folder. For example, you could create one settings configuration to journal all e-mails and another to simply delete calendar items.

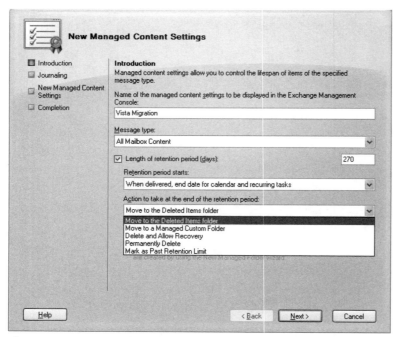

Figure 8-4   Applying managed content settings

Implement Managed Mailbox Policies

Next, you must create the managed folder policy. Policies can be applied to one or multiple managed folders and managed folders can have one or more policies applied to them. Policies are created under Organization | Mailbox using the **New Managed**

Folder Mailbox Policy command. You can also use the **New-ManagedFolderMailboxPolicy** cmdlet. A managed folder mailbox policy includes a display name and the folder or folders it applies to.

After you create the policy, you can apply it to user mailboxes. Keep the following in mind when you are ready to assign a mailbox policy to users:

- You can only use the console to assign a managed mailbox policy to a new user mailbox as you create it (see Figure 8-5). This means that you must plan mailbox management policies *before* you mail-enable your user accounts if you want to do it through the Console.

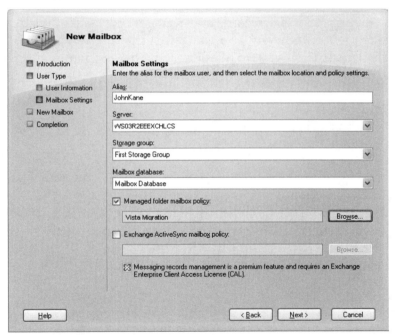

Figure 8-5 Assigning a managed mailbox policy to a newly created mailbox

- If users already exist, you must use the **set-Mailbox** Shell cmdlet along with the ManagedFolderMailboxPolicy property. However, you can easily script this to assign a policy to multiple users.

- You can only apply one policy per mailbox. If you want to apply several policies to a single mailbox, you must plan your settings configurations and include the proper managed folders all in the same mailbox policy. Once again, this means planning mailbox policies carefully before deploying them.

- Policies are applied only to Mailbox Server roles because they manage user mailboxes.

- Custom managed folders are a premium feature of MRM and can only be applied in organizations that have an Exchange Server Enterprise Client Access License (CAL). In Exchange 2007 SP1, you can apply MRM to default folders with a Standard CAL.

- Mailbox policies can only be applied to mail-enabled users, not to contacts or distribution lists.

Schedule the Managed Folder Assistant

The last step in the message records management process is to enable a schedule for the managed folder assistant to run against mailboxes with managed mailbox policies. By default, this assistant does not run. This assistant performs several tasks:

- It creates all custom managed folders in users' mailboxes.

- It removes all expired items.

- If journaling has been applied, it journals messages according to the configured settings.

In the Console, drill down to Server | Mailbox, right-click the Mailbox server you want to apply the schedule to, and then select Properties. Click the Message Records Management tab, select Custom Schedule from the drop-down list, click Customize and create a custom schedule to run the assistant. In the Shell, use the **set-Mailbox** cmdlet with the ManagedFolderAssistant property. Your records management strategy is now in place.

Use managed folders to control how users manage their e-mails. In organizations where users keep everything in the Inbox, you can create rules that either move the contents out of the Inbox after a specific time period, or simply delete them. If users are e-mail gluttons and do not want to discard anything, you can create a settings configuration that is applied to a special folder called Entire Mailbox. The settings applied to the Entire Mailbox apply to every content type in the mailbox and can help users keep it empty of clutter when otherwise they would fill it up. Make sure you communicate to users any settings rule you create; otherwise, you could end up with some very irate users.

MORE INFO Manage records management

For more information on managing records management, go to *http://technet.microsoft.com/en-us/library/bb123507.aspx*.

Work with Message Journaling

As with message records management, you can create journaling rules to ensure the retention of special messages for compliance purposes. In Exchange 2007, you can journal messages sent to or from a specified mailbox, contacts, or even distribution lists. Journaling captures these messages and automatically forwards a copy of the message to a special collection mailbox. Journaled messages are wrapped into a journal report that includes information on the sender, the recipient(s), the subject, and other data. The message itself is inserted as an object inside the journal report.

Journaling is very much like transport rules because it works on transport servers only. As mentioned earlier, you can journal messages to any valid SMTP address, including Windows SharePoint Services sites or e-mail addresses used by special, third-party e-mail archiving solutions. In legacy versions of Exchange, you had to journal messages based on mailbox stores. This means that you had to plan stores carefully and make sure that every mailbox you wanted to journal was in the same store. In Exchange 2007, you use journaling rules, which are much like transport rules, to determine which messages are journaled.

Exchange 2007 provides two levels of journaling:

- Standard journaling relies on the journaling agent to act on messages that are sent to or sent from mail-enabled users whose mailboxes are located in a specific mailbox database. To address a standard rule to all users, you need to set it on each of the mailbox databases in your organization. Standard journaling is very much like legacy Exchange journaling. Note that each time you enable journaling on a mailbox database, all mailboxes in the database are journaled.

- Premium journaling relies on Hub Transport servers to process journaling rules against any message that is transmitted through them. To use premium journaling, you must have an Exchange Enterprise CAL. Premium journaling supports three journaling operations:

  - Per recipient or per distribution list journaling, which identifies which mail-enabled user, contact, or distribution list you want to journal against.

  - Journaling rule scope lets you determine which message type you want to journal—internal, external, or both.

  - Journaling replication. As with transport rules, once you create a premium journaling rule on an HT, it will automatically be available to every other HT system as soon as Active Directory replication has completed.

Both standard and premium journal reports contain quite a bit of information about the message. Table 8-6 lists the potential content of a journal report.

Table 8-6   Potential Journal Report Contents

Field	Field Type	Comment
Version	Basic	Lists the version of Exchange that created the report.
Sender	Basic	In SMTP format. Displays the name of the sender.
Subject	Basic	Lists the MIME subject header value.
Message-ID	Basic	Lists the internal Exchange message ID.
Recipient	Basic	In SMTP format. Lists external recipients or recipients that do not have an e-mail address in your Exchange Organization.
On-Behalf-of	Extended	In SMTP format. Displays the name of the purported sender if the user used the On Behalf of feature in Outlook.
To	Extended	In SMTP format. Lists the address of recipients. If the recipient is a distribution list, expands list members into Expanded field. If expanded, the To field will include Expanded. If forwarded, the To field will include Forwarded.
CC	Extended	In SMTP format. Lists recipients in the CC: field.
BCC	Extended	In SMTP format. Lists recipients in the BCC: field.
Expanded	Extended	In SMTP format. Lists the members of a distribution list from either the To:, CC:, or BCC: fields.
Forwarded	Extended	In SMTP format. Lists forwarder if message was forwarded in either the To:, CC:, or BCC: fields.

As you can see, there are two types of journaling fields. The Basic type is always included in a report. The Extended type is included if recipient addressing can be determined in the message. This occurs if the message meets the following requirements:

- It has been sent as a MAPI submission through an HT. Messages that meet this requirement are sent from Outlook 2007 or Windows Mobile.
- It has been sent through an authenticated SMTP submission to an HT. In this case, the sender cannot have the Send-As-Anyone permission because this indicates that the sender is a server.

If either of these conditions can be met, your journaling reports will include much more information.

MORE INFO   Understand journal reports

More information on the contents of journal reports can be found at *http://technet.microsoft.com/en-us/library/bb331962.aspx*.

Plan Journal Rules

When you plan for the implementation of journaling, you should keep the following in mind:

- Be aware of the legal and privacy impact of journaling on e-mail messages. Make sure you have documented corporate support for the implementation of these rules.
- Document your configuration plan well to ensure that everyone involved fully understands what will happen when the rules are put in place.
- List which messages will be journaled in detail. Make sure there are no omissions.
- Identify where journal reports will be kept and which protection measures are in place to protect these containers.
- Identify how journal reports will be secured while in transit.
- Identify who will have access to journal containers, whether they are mailboxes, Windows SharePoint Services document libraries, or third-party archives.

Of all of these guidelines, the first is by far the most important. Journaling is probably the most important aspect of compliance. Make sure you implement it properly and make sure you get counsel from your internal officers to ensure that you are meeting whichever regulations affect your organization.

Note that you might want to limit the type of message you want to journal. Although Exchange 2007's journaling lets you journal voice, fax, and e-mail communications, you may decide that you do not need either the voice or the fax messages because they will significantly add to the hard disk space required in your journaling containers. However, make sure you verify with the proper authorities to ensure that your journaling strategy meets corporate compliance requirements before you make this decision.

Exam Tip   Messages that are generated by a UM system and that contain faxes are always journaled, even if you set an exception on voicemail and missed call notifications. Do not be fooled by questions that state the opposite.

Configure Standard Journal Rules

Standard journaling is very much like legacy journaling because it is based on the entire mailbox database and journals every mail-enabled user in that database without exception. But, even though it is a legacy feature, it still requires proper preparation to work well. When you prepare to enable journaling, you need to follow these steps:

1. Prepare the journaling mailbox(es).
2. Protect the journaling mailbox(es).
3. Enable journaling.
4. Enable the journaling agent on Hub Transport servers because they are responsible for transmitting journal reports on behalf of the Mailbox server.

Of course, this takes into consideration the fact that you have planned your journaling rules ahead of time and that you have proper approval for your journaling strategy.

To prepare standard journaling, use the following steps. You will need the Exchange Recipient Administrator role to perform this task.

1. Prepare the mailbox or mailboxes you need. You might consider using a single-purpose mailbox database for journaling reports, much as you would for the quarantine database. It is not necessary to do so, but because standard journaling is a mailbox database feature, you could exclude this database from journaling by default. In addition, having a database that is exclusively restricted to journaling makes it easier to protect and manage securely. Keep in mind that the best practice is one mailbox database per storage group. When the database is ready, create a new mail-enabled user to host the journaling mailbox.

2. Protect the mailbox. In Exchange, journaling mailboxes are protected through three features:

   ❏ Secure transport links between Hub Transport servers and Mailbox servers.

   ❏ Authenticated senders to transport journal reports. The sender is Exchange itself so it can always be authenticated.

   ❏ When you send journal reports internally, only authenticated connections are used.

   However, you must configure secure connections. In fact, you must set the mailbox to accept messages only from itself. You can only do this with the Exchange Management Shell. In the release version of Exchange, use the following cmdlet:

   ```
   Set-Mailbox JournalingMailbox -AcceptMessagesOnlyFrom JournalingMailbox
   -RequireSenderAuthenticationEnabled $True
   ```

   where *JournalingMailbox* is the name of the mailbox to configure. In Exchange 2007 SP1, you can change this cmdlet to set Exchange as the authenticated sender:

   ```
   Set-Mailbox JournalingMailbox -AcceptMessagesOnlyFrom "Microsoft Exchange"
   -RequireSenderAuthenticationEnabled $True
   ```

   Your mailbox is ready.

3. Enable journaling on mailbox database(s). In the Console, go to Server | Mailbox, locate the database you want to configure, right-click it, select Properties and set the Journal Recipient on the General tab (see Figure 8-6). Repeat for each mailbox database you want to journal. You can use a different journaling mailbox for each mailbox database if you need to. To configure this setting using the Exchange Management Shell, use the **set-MailboxDatabase** cmdlet with the JournalRecipient property.

4. Ensure that the journaling agent is enabled on HT systems. Because the HT configuration is stored in Active Directory and replicated to all other HT systems, you only need to do this on one HT system. You can only do this through the Shell. Use the following cmdlets. First, find out whether the journaling agent is enabled; if it is not, enable it.

   ```
   Get-TransportAgent
   Enable-TransportAgent -Identity "Journaling agent"
   ```

Make sure you continue to secure the access to the journaling mailbox(es) you create. The information they contain is very important.

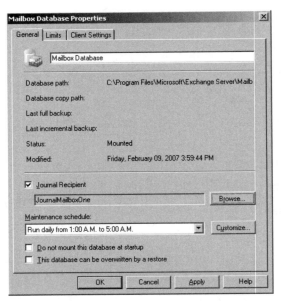

Figure 8-6 Configuring standard journaling

Note that if you decide to send your reports to a third-party storage system, you should secure it in the same way you would with Exchange. Specifically, you must do the following:

- Use Transport Layer Security to communicate between systems so that communications are secure.

- Set up authenticated communications on the receiving end.

- Set up the recipient to accept e-mail only from the MS Exchange contact.

- Create a mail-enabled contact that will be used to relay messages to the third-party system. Configure journaling to send e-mail to the contact.

Remember, journaling reports can contain sensitive if not confidential data. Keep them secure at all times.

Configure Premium Journal Rules

Remember that you need Enterprise CALs to use premium journaling. Make sure you prepare the journaling repositories as per the instructions in the preceding section on standard journaling section, and then prepare the rules themselves.

When you configure premium journal rules, your rules should always contain the following elements:

- **Journal Rule Scope**   Determines which messages to journal. Can be one of three values:

  - ❏ Internal, which processes messages that are sent or received by members of your own Global Address List.

  - ❏ External, which processes messages that are sent or received by e-mail addresses that are not in your own Global Address List.

  - ❏ Global, which processes all messages that pass through a Hub Transport server, regardless of origin. Global processing occurs after the Internal or External scopes have been addressed.

- **Journal Rule Recipients**   Can include mailboxes, contacts, or distribution lists and are in SMTP format.

- **Journal E-mail Address(es)**   The address(es) to which journal reports are sent. The address must be in the GAL and therefore must be internal. You can send all reports to a single address or send reports to different addresses based on message type. Addresses can be a mail-enabled user, a contact, or a distribution list—as long as they exist in the GAL. When you use a contact, you can redirect the journal reports to a Windows SharePoint Services document library.

Be sure to secure the repositories you use for your journal reports because they often contain sensitive or even confidential information. Also, be sure to provide enough space for the containers you use for journal reports because they tend to multiply at an exponential rate when you journal many messages.

You configure premium journal rules either through the Console or the Shell. In the Console, you go to Organization | Hub Transport and choose New Journaling Rule (see Figure 8-7). In the Exchange Management Shell, you use the following cmdlets:

```
New-JournalRule
Get-JournalRule
Set-JournalRule
Enable-JournalRule
Disable-JournalRule
Remove-JournalRule
```

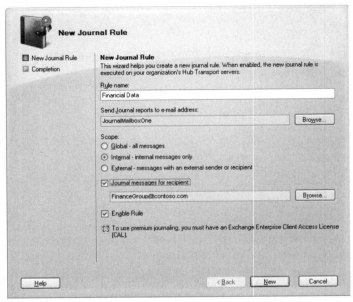

Figure 8-7   Configuring premium journaling

Remember that journaling can also be part of the settings configuration for managed folders through messaging records management. In fact, you have the option of setting up journaling rules on managed folders in the second window of the New Journal Rule Wizard (see Figure 8-8).

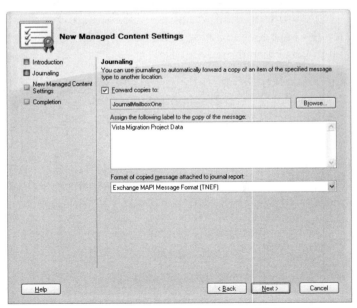

Figure 8-8   Configuring journaling in managed folder settings

That is it. Your journaling should now be configured and should start sending reports to the journaling mailbox.

MORE INFO   **More on journaling**

More information on journaling can be found at *http://technet.microsoft.com/en-us/library/bb124382.aspx*.

Work with S/Mime

Another level of protection you should put in place is protection for messages that exit from your network. Messages have a life cycle of their own, and never seem to die because original messages are embedded into responses and messages simply grow and grow. Therefore, you want to make sure that original content is not tampered with, especially when it is outside your control.

You have three ways to protect message content that leaves your internal organization. The first is through the implementation of Domain Security—a point-to-point authentication scheme that lets messages travel between partners. Domain Security was covered in Lesson 2 in Chapter 7. The second way is to secure messages through S/MIME—digitally signing or encrypting messages. S/MIME is covered in this topic. The third way is to use Digital Rights Management—controlling content through digital rights mechanisms. Digital Rights Management is covered in the next topic.

Like Domain Security, S/MIME relies on digital Public Key Infrastructure (PKI) certificates to protect data. S/MIME is more expensive than Domain Security because in Domain Security you only need two certificates: one for your receiving and sending servers and one for your partner's receiving and sending servers. With S/MIME, certificates are assigned to each user that needs to protect e-mail content. Because of this, you need to consider the following when planning for S/MIME:

- Which certificate authority will you use? Remember that messages are sent outside your organization. Therefore, it is unlikely that you will be able to use an internal certification authority unless, of course, your internal authority is validated by an external, third-party root certificate. This approach is by far the least expensive because you only need to purchase a root certificate for your organization. This root certificate is then embedded into each of your own certificates ensuring that they are trusted by outside sources without having to modify their trusted roots. You can also use individual third-party certificates for each user. Some organizations offer free e-mail certificates for individuals. If you are designing a corporate S/MIME policy, you should acquire proper certificates for each user.

MORE INFO   Outsource your root certificate

For information on how to design an internal PKI structure that is validated by a third party, see "The Case for Outsourcing PKI" in the "Advanced PKI" section at *http://www.reso-net.com/ articles.asp?m=8#c*.

MORE INFO   Obtain free personal e-mail certificates

Some third-party Certificate Authorities offer free, individual e-mail certificates. One such organization is Thawte, Inc. Obtain a free Thawte personal e-mail certificate at *http://www.thawte.com/secure-email/personal-email-certificates/index.html?click=main-nav-products-email*.

■ Determine how to distribute certificates to your users. The key point of a Secure Sockets Layer certificate is that it absolutely represents who the person is. This means you will need to use a validation process to ensure that the certificates you issue are delivered to the person to whom you issue them and to no one else. For example, never, ever give an executive's certificate to his or her assistant. Always ensure that the certificate is given directly to the person for whom it is intended; otherwise, you cannot guarantee that it was delivered to the right person. If you use the outsourcing strategy mentioned previously, you can use the Active Directory auto-enrollment feature to distribute these certificates.

■ Prepare a policy that outlines which message types need to be signed and which ones need encryption. Communicate this policy to all intended users.

■ Prepare your users to know how to work with S/MIME. A short training course is always a good idea. Also, showing them how to create template messages with either signatures or encryption will save them time when they use these features.

■ Implement the S/MIME policy. Verify that all required messages are properly protected.

S/MIME is supported by Outlook, Outlook Web Access, and Windows Mobile devices. S/MIME in Exchange Server 2007 works in the same way as it did in Exchange 2003. Updates were included in Service Pack 1, but only to add support for higher encryption levels.

MORE INFO   Learn more about S/MIME in Exchange

To learn more about S/MIME and Exchange, go to *http://technet.microsoft.com/en-us/library/ aa995740.aspx*.

MORE INFO **Configure S/MIME in Windows Mobile**

For information on how to configure S/MIME on Windows Mobile devices, go to
http://msexchangeteam.com/archive/2007/06/07/440445.aspx.

Rights Management Services

The last element you should consider when preparing to protect message content is
Digital Rights Management (DRM). The original release of Exchange 2007 provides
minimal support for DRM, but Exchange Server 2007 Service Pack 1 includes much
more. This is because Microsoft has updated its DRM engine with the preparation of
Windows Server 2008. In Windows Server 2008, DRM is provided by Active Directory Rights Management Services (AD RMS). As such, the new AD RMS Prelicensing
client is now installed by default on Hub Transport servers that run SP1. If your
servers are not running Windows Server 2008, you need to update them to the
Windows Rights Management Services Client with Service Pack 2 to work properly
with AD RMS.

The problem with original releases of RMS features was that you had to retain access
to your original RMS infrastructure for the DRM to remain effective. Now, however,
with the release of AD RMS, you can use persistent usage policies. Persistent usage
policies remain with the data even when they are no longer in touch with the original
RMS source.

Implementing rights management strategies relies on implementing a complete RMS
infrastructure, which is beyond the scope of this book. Suffice it to say that RMS is
supported in Exchange and in the various clients that can link to it.

MORE INFO **Learn more about AD RMS and Exchange**

To learn more about AD RMS and Exchange, go to *http://technet.microsoft.com/en-us/library/
bb123950.aspx*.

Exam Tip Remember that the original copy of the exam does not include information about
Service Pack 1.

Practice: Build a Message Compliance Solution

In this practice, you will prepare a records management strategy, especially in relation
to the e-mail life cycle in your organization. This practice consists of a single exercise.
You will use Exchange 2007's new records management functionality to perform this
exercise.

▶ **Exercise: Prepare for Message Records Management**

In this exercise, you will use a specific process to apply records management in Exchange. You will configure a retention policy directly on users' mailboxes.

1. Make sure the TreyDC and the ExchangeOne computers are running.

2. Log on to ExchangeOne.treyresearch.net with the EXAdmin account. This will grant you local administrator rights.

   Determine which folders you want to manage, including both default and custom folders. All default folders are displayed in the Exchange Management Console. You might prefer to use custom folders instead of the defaults. After all, keeping 1,000 messages in the Inbox is not a good practice. For example, if your users are working on a special project such as the deployment of a new technology like Windows Vista, you might want to create a custom folder called Vista Project and have messages in this folder retained for the duration of the migration project.

3. Open the Exchange Management Console (Start Menu | All Programs | Microsoft Exchange Server | Exchange Management Console).

4. Move to Organization Configuration | Mailbox in the tree pane.

5. Click New Managed Custom Folder in the Action pane.

6. Name the new folder **Vista Project** and assign it a storage limit of 100,000 KB or 100 MB.

7. In the Display The Following Comment When The Folder Is Viewed In Outlook section, type **This folder is used for the new Vista Migration Project**.

8. Do not select the Do Not Allow Users To Minimize This Comment In Outlook check box. Click New, and then click Finish when you are done.

You now have a managed folder and can move on to the creation of a managed folder policy. Keep the following items in mind when you do create the policy:

■ Determine which settings you want to base your policy on. A good example is when you want to empty the Deleted Items folder of any item that is more than 60 days old. Configurable settings include:

   ❑ Message type

   ❑ Length of retention

   ❑ Action to perform

   ❑ Journaling settings to save a copy of the contents of the folder

- Create a managed folder policy based on the settings you determined. One policy can apply to a single folder or multiple folders.

- Apply the policy to users by linking the policy with user properties in the Exchange Management Console or through the Shell. Using the Shell, you can assign the policy to multiple users at once. No policies exist in a default Exchange configuration.

- Use the Managed Folder Assistant to schedule the change on user folders. This assistant does not run in a default Exchange configuration.

When the policy is in place, all users need to do to interact with it is to move messages into the appropriate folders in their mailboxes. As soon as a message is placed into a managed folder, it falls under the sway of the managed folder policy. In addition, if users want to make it easier for themselves, you can show them how they can create rules in Outlook to automatically move messages into the managed folder as soon as they arrive in the mailbox. You can, of course, also set policies on mailboxes where users do not have to do anything because all mailbox content is managed.

Quick Check

1. How does message classification work?
2. Which specific message fields are tied to classifications?
3. What are the two types of records management polices?
4. What do you need to specify when you create a managed folder rule?
5. Which steps do you need to perform when you enable journaling?

Quick Check Answers

1. Classification adds specific metadata to messages as they are transported through the mail flow. This metadata describes items such as the intended use of a message or its intended audience. Outlook 2007 and Outlook Web Access 2007 can use this metadata to display descriptions about senders or recipients of classified messages to end users. In addition, the Exchange transport mechanism can apply special treatment to classified messages because it can use transport rules to identify them.

2. The specific message fields are:
   - Display Name, which is the name of the classification. This appears in the Permission menu in Outlook and is how users select the classification.

❑ Sender Description, which is the description that tells senders why they should be using this classification.

❑ Recipient Description, which is the description recipients see on the Outlook InfoBar of a message when it has been classified.

❑ Locale, which is the ability to have classification messages appear in different languages based on the user's language settings.

3. First, you can configure a retention policy directly on users' mailboxes. Second, you can configure Journaling Policies to take messages from a specific folder and transmit it to another recipient. Journaling recipients can be any e-mail address including an actual mail-enabled user or even a Windows SharePoint Services library.

4. You need to specify the folder name and display name if it is a custom folder, the storage limit, and the comment to display in Outlook when users view the folder.

5. To enable journaling, you need to do the following: prepare the journaling mailbox(es), protect them, enable journaling, and enable the journaling agent on the HT.

Chapter Summary

■ Transport rules apply to the following message types: anonymous messages, interpersonal messages, opaque messages, clear-signed messages, unified messaging messages, and IPM.Note.messages. Note that the last two message types are only supported in Exchange 2007 Service Pack 1.

■ Expressions are important in transport rules because they are used to identify strings of characters. In Exchange they are called regular expressions—to identify text or numerical positions. Regular expressions are used through the Exchange Management Shell and are applied with the Patterns predicate property. In the Exchange Management Console, you can use them with any condition or exception that includes the words "with text patterns".

■ When the RejectMessage action is applied to a message, Exchange associates a delivery status notification code to the non-delivery report (NDR) that is returned to the sender of the message and then deletes the message. The NDR is also called a bounce message.

- Default message classifications include: ExACPrivileged, ExAttachmentRemoved, ExCompanyConfidential, ExCompanyInternal, and ExPartnerMail.

- The Classifications.xml file must be updated each time you modify the classifications on an Exchange server. Because of this, you might consider placing the file on a central share that each connected system can access, and then enabling offline caching of the file so that mobile systems can transport a copy with them.

- In Exchange 2007, you can journal messages sent to or from a specified mailbox, contacts, or even distribution lists. Journaling captures these messages and automatically forwards a copy of the message to a special collection mailbox. Journaled messages are wrapped into a journal report that includes information on the sender, the recipient(s), the subject, and other data.

- Exchange 2007 provides two levels of journaling: Standard journaling relies on the journaling agent to act on messages that are sent to or sent from mail-enabled users whose mailboxes are located in a specific mailbox database; premium journaling relies on Hub Transport servers to process journaling rules against any message that is transmitted through them.

- S/MIME is more expensive than Domain Security because in Domain Security you only need two certificates: one for your receiving and sending servers and one for your partner's receiving and sending servers. With S/MIME, certificates are assigned to each user that needs to protect e-mail content. S/MIME in Exchange Server 2007 works in the same way as it did in Exchange 2003. Updates were added in Service Pack 1, but only to add support for higher encryption levels.

Case Scenarios

In the following case scenarios, you will apply what you have learned about Exchange feature support for compliance. You can find answers to the questions in this scenario in the "Answers" section at the end of this book.

Case Scenario 1: Understand Transport Rules

Ever since 2001, when an employee was discovered sending vital organizational information including customer contact names and private customer information to a competitive firm, The Phone Company has been very concerned about controlling e-mail transport. Before they deploy Exchange 2007, they want to understand which functionality it includes to control mail flow based on mail content. They turn to you, the messaging professional, to explain to them what they will be able to do in

Exchange when it is in place to control this message flow. They want to know how transport rules are structured and to which message types they can be applied.

How do you respond?

Case Scenario 2: Identify Message Journaling Best Practices

The Phone Company has historically been challenged with e-mail Inbox management. Their users, though savvy on other technologies, just cannot seem to grasp how to manage their Inboxes correctly. TPC has heard that with Exchange 2007, they can create records management strategies that will solve this issue for many users automatically. They turn to you, the messaging professional, to tell them what they can expect in terms of records management capabilities after Exchange 2007 is deployed.

Specifically, they want to know which best practices they should use when they implement managed folder policies. How do you respond?

Case Scenario 3: Implement Message Journaling

The Phone Company has already asked you about how they can manage Inboxes through the records management features of Exchange 2007. They were quite pleased with the answer you gave them, but they were intrigued by the first portion of the answer when you mentioned that records management could also involve message journaling. Now, they turn to you, the messaging professional, to discover what journaling is and which features in Exchange will support it.

Specifically, they want to have a complete description of the journaling features in Exchange and which elements they need to consider before putting a journaling strategy in place. How do you respond?

Suggested Practices

It is difficult to practice compliance with Exchange Server without access to a full infrastructure, but you can do so if you prepare a virtual environment as outlined in the Introduction. Use both the ExchangeOne and the ExchangeETOne computers to run through the compliance strategies detailed in this chapter to see what is needed and how you should configure it.

Chapter 9

Plan for Messaging Environment Maintenance

Enterprise messaging environment management and administration can be quite complex, especially when you have to do it while it is in use on a 24/7 basis. Even smaller environments relying on the Simple Organization type can find it challenging to properly manage their systems since their administrators are often overworked. This is one reason why hosted services can be quite a boon for these types of organizations: Professionals manage the hosted service and these professionals can help small organizations learn how to structure their administrative activities and reduce their workloads.

In larger environments—meaning environments that run either the Standard, Large, or Complex Organization types—you do not have the luxury of performing administrative tasks on an ad hoc basis. Everything must be structured and controlled. Worse, everything must be documented at all times if you want to be able to support any of the changes you make in your environment.

When you run complex Exchange systems, you are often faced with several maintenance and administration issues that must be addressed either to improve system performance or to ensure that systems run continuously. Potential issues you might face include:

- Change management, such as determining the right time to update components without disrupting business operations.

- Infrastructure improvements and configuration changes, such as adding unused services, removing obsolete services, adding additional features, adding new servers, protecting data, and so on. This also includes update management, such as deploying fixes or upgrades such as service packs into your Exchange infrastructure.

Whichever situation you are faced with, you should know by now that you must *always* use a structured change management approach to perform any modifications in your e-mail environment, or any IT environment for that matter. The last thing you want is a bunch of your users irate because you caused something that disrupted their critical e-mail service. That is the bottom line. When everything runs great, it seems you never hear about it or get any thanks for it, but when something goes wrong, you will be the first to know. So your best bet is to get it right the first time and the only way to do that is to use a structured change management process.

Exam objectives in this chapter:
- Plan for Exchange infrastructure improvements.
- Plan for configuration changes.
- Plan for change management.
- Plan for update and service pack implementation.

Before You Begin

To complete the lessons in this chapter, you must have the following:

- A virtual machine setup as outlined in the Introduction under "Virtual Machine Environments."
- Use the Exchange Server 2007 virtual machine from Microsoft to review the configuration options for pre-installed computers.
- Use the virtual environment you set up to test the administration and change management procedures discussed in this chapter. For the exercises in this chapter, you will need access to the Active Directory server, the all-in-one Exchange server, ExchangeOne, and the LCR server you created, ExchangeLCR.

Lesson 1: Plan for Change Management

Estimated lesson time: 20 minutes

Change is the very nature of IT. It seems as though you have barely finished doing something when it is already time to modify it. Exchange infrastructures are no exception. Moving to Exchange 2007 is a significant change in and of itself—new server architectures, 64-bit operating systems, new features, new administrative console, new management shell, and more. And you have barely time to deploy it when a new service pack, chock full of new features, is available and must be deployed. That is the nature of IT.

Use a Structured Change Management Process

The only way to achieve stability within change is to develop a series of management processes that can be applied to change situations. A structured approach allows us to adapt to change or, even better, adapt the change to our needs. A common approach to change management includes five distinctive phases (see Figure 9-1):

■ **The Diagnostics Phase**   This is when you identify and describe the unsatisfactory situation the change aims to modify. It also describes the situation the change is to bring. It identifies the resources that can be applied to support this change and predicts the different types of resistance you should expect, especially resistance that can be influenced or mitigated. The diagnostics phase is an evaluation and comprehension of needs at various levels. In fact, it focuses on a situation review and needs analysis.

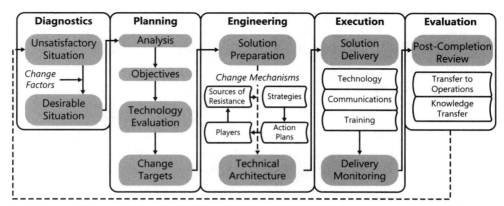

Figure 9-1   The elements of a structured change management process

- **The Planning Phase**   This phase serves to define and structure the objectives to be attained. It is designed to identify appropriate actions or strategies to attain each objective, identify positions to be taken, and the solutions to adopt. It ends with a complete plan including deadlines, milestones, and task definitions for each person who is implicated. Here, you create partnerships with the appropriate players who will have to act upon the change. The focus of this phase is to understand the impact of the coming change.

- **The Engineering Phase**   This phase is designed to prepare the coming change. In IT, each change—such as deploying a new e-mail technology—requires considerable preparation. This preparation is the focus of the engineering phase. It is designed to prepare all of the technological components of the solution you plan to put in place to resolve the issues you discovered in the diagnostics phase. It follows the plan you created in the planning phase to prepare a configured technical implementation.

- **The Execution Phase**   This phase focuses on the implementation or the deployment of the change and ensures that appropriate follow-ups are undertaken throughout this implementation. The follow-ups use defined criteria to evaluate the change as it is being implemented. This phase focuses on the introduction of technologies and techniques that aim to facilitate the way people can adapt to the change. Ideally, the technologies implemented or the way the technologies are implemented will resolve issues as the implementation proceeds.

- **The Evaluation Phase**   This phase completes the cycle with a thorough post-completion review—in fact, a renewed situation review—to ensure that all objectives have been met with minimum impact.

When performing maintenance and implementing change in your e-mail infrastructure this is the goal you should aim for: Ensure that all change is controlled so that you can manage impact as well as expectations. Each controlled change strategy focuses on two key elements: documentation of the change and appropriate change approvals. Then, when the change is in place, you continue to monitor it to ensure that it meets expectations.

Structured change management processes will differ based on organization size. Organizations running the Simple or even the Standard Organization type may use a less formal but still structured change management process based on a simple approval process. But organizations running the Large or Complex Organization types will most certainly have a more formal approval process where all changes must go through an approval committee and must be fully documented before being implemented. Whether your process is formal or informal, you should always endeavor to provide documentation on the change—documentation lets you track the change and helps quickly correct issues if they arise because of the change.

MORE INFO **Understand the five-step change management process**

For a detailed description of a structured five-step change management process, look up Chapter 2, "Preparing the Migration," from the *Definitive Guide to Vista Migration*, by Ruest and Ruest, a <u>free</u> e-Book published by Realtime Publishers at *www.realtime-nexus.com/dgvm.htm*.

Using a standard change management process, whether formal or informal, has several benefits:

- When change is structured, all stakeholders are made aware of the coming change and its potential positive or negative impact.

- If multiple changes occur at the same time, they can be coordinated to minimize their impact. In addition, coordinating changes can reduce the costs involved with a change because efforts are also coordinated.

- Standard change management processes reduce the possibility of mistakes and ensure better change quality control.

- Because it is structured, a change management process will give you more time to implement a change and, therefore, give you more time to think it through and identify all of the potential consequences. When you identify consequences, you can deal with them ahead of time. When they are not identified, consequences become "surprises" that pop up at the most inconvenient times.

- Structured change management processes always provide a Plan B, or a rollback plan if the proposed change does not work out as expected.

Everyone knows that change management processes can help diminish the impact of change. Take, for example, changes that affect every user in your organization, or even a change that affects only the organization's executive: If no change management process is in place, and things go awry, it is probably a good time for you to begin looking for a new position elsewhere.

But your change management process must be flexible. Sometimes situations arise in which you must fast-track change to immediately correct a problematic situation. In this case, you still want to rely on a structured approach, but your testing and strategy development timelines will be much shorter. For example, you might only get summary approval for the change and then go back for formal approval once the situation has been corrected.

Make the change strategy work for you and adapt it to your environment. Change management does not have to be complex; it just has to be a standard, repeatable process.

Work with Industry-Specific Change Management Strategies

If you are in an organization that requires a more formal change management process, you can look to industry-specific strategies and adapt them to your own needs. Two major sources of information are available:

- The Information Technology Infrastructure Library (ITIL), published by the United Kingdom's Office of Government Commerce (OGC), provides a complete technology-independent datacenter and IT infrastructure guidance. The OGC found that they needed to document their internal change management processes and discovered that this documentation could also be useful to other organizations. Therefore, they made it available to all to foster an industry standard in structured change control for more organizations running complex IT infrastructures. More information on ITIL can be found at *http://www.itil-officialsite.com/home/home.asp*.

- The Microsoft Operations Framework (MOF) is guidance produced by Microsoft but widely based on ITIL. The difference between the two is that MOF specifically focuses on Microsoft-based infrastructures and includes guidance and best practices from the Microsoft operations groups, partners, and customers. MOF is based on four quadrants: It is designed to support the changing, operating, supporting, and optimizing activities in IT infrastructures. More information on MOF and Exchange can be found at *http://technet.microsoft.com/en-us/library/bb232042.aspx*.

Another excellent source of infrastructure information is the Windows Server System Reference Architecture (WSSRA), which has now become the Infrastructure Planning and Design (IPD). The IPD is a detailed reference architecture outlining how various products from the Microsoft Windows Server System, including Exchange, should fit together at the technical level. It provides complete architectural blueprints as well as blueprints for every architectural level such as network, storage, application, management, and security. More information on the IPD can be found at *http://www.microsoft.com/technet/solutionaccelerators/wssra/raguide/default.mspx*. The IPD is a must for any organization that must implement complex infrastructures and does not want to have to discover the details of each implementation on their own. Updated IPD information can be found at *http://www.microsoft.com/downloads/details.aspx?familyid=AD3921FB-8224-4681-9064-075FDF042B0C&displaylang=en.*

Formal change management systems such as ITIL and MOF may be too rigid for most organizations. Our recommendation is that you look up both MOF and ITIL and only use what works best for you and your organization. It is relatively easy to rely on these formal processes to derive a less rigid but still structured change management strategy. Ideally, your change management strategy will include the following elements:

1. Structured change requests, which are used to initiate a change. They document what is to be included in the change and why the change is necessary. This usually outlines the business requirement for the change.

2. A classification for the change. This can be as simple as a ranking system for the priority of the change such as High, Medium, or Low. This ranking system will help determine the timeline for the change. It should also include a category for the change, such as whether it affects the infrastructure itself, a specific feature, or a specific component of a feature. The classification will serve to link the requested change with its business requirements.

3. An authorization for the change. Authorizations can be obtained from different levels of the organization and will depend on the complexity of the change. For example, implementing a new Hub Transport server to increase processing speeds has less impact than implementing new custom managed folders because the first change will improve service levels transparently, while the second will directly affect all users. Because of the difference in scope, different authorizations are required.

4. Engineering the change will focus on preparing its actual implementation. Engineering involves the examination of a feature, the design of the implementation, and lab testing to ensure that it works as expected. Engineering often involves the largest effort because of the enhanced testing involved.

5. Releasing the change involves the actual deployment of the planned modification. All testing is done and final approvals have been obtained. The modification is deployed and the progress of the deployment is monitored.

6. When the change is deployed, you need to review it to ensure that everything went as expected throughout the process. The objective of the review is to determine whether the change actually produced the outcomes that were documented in step 1.

7. Signoff on the change completes the process. All documentation is in and the change has achieved the objectives that were set for it.

This process is generic, but you should run through these steps for each change so that you can know what to expect when it occurs.

Work with Internal Change Management Strategies

Internally, you should also put in place infrastructures that support change management. Four elements are important:

- Using an internal documentation plan.
- Using an internal knowledge base.
- Providing technology-specific documentation.
- Relying on a standard set of tools.

Each element helps support structured operations.

Use Internal Documentation

Although manufacturers endeavor to provide documentation that is as complete as possible on the various products they release, it is still important for you to create documentation of your own. For example, Microsoft's installation documentation on Exchange Server 2007, while fairly comprehensive, will never fulfill your needs if you have to reinstall one of your Mailbox servers because it does not detail the settings you used in your internal configuration.

You need to create your own documentation on configurations and technical architectures. When you document your systems, you should consider including the following elements:

- Server physical location
- Server type: rack-mounted, blade, stand-alone, or virtual
- Server hardware manufacturer make and model
- Hardware BIOS and firmware levels
- Hardware configuration including processor(s), RAM, disk configuration, network interface card(s), and any other hardware component
- Operating system version and update level
- Installed operating system features and components
- Network configuration for the server, including domain or workgroup configuration

- Configured server role, including installed applications
- Backup schedule and backup types

Although this list is not exhaustive, it demonstrates the type of information that is specific to your own server configurations and requires documentation. In addition, you should maintain a change log for the server to ensure that you capture any modifications that are made to the documented configuration. Maintaining this type of documentation will make it easier for you and your peers to troubleshoot, repair, and otherwise maintain each component in your IT infrastructure.

Maintain an Internal Knowledge Database

Whether you use a formal Help desk management tool or not, you should still maintain a database of all of the issues you run into and document their solutions. Having a database of this type lets you quickly resolve issues if they occur again. It also lets you resolve related problems even if they do not arise from the same initial issue.

Several tools are available for this, including simple homemade databases running in Microsoft Access as well as complex, full-fledged Help desk systems such as Microsoft System Center Service Manager. Another excellent knowledge base tool is Windows SharePoint Services, which is a free component in Windows Server and provides an infrastructure for collaboration. In addition, Microsoft provides seed SharePoint sites or templates, many of which are ideal to begin your own internal documentation repository. More than 40 template sites are available. The most useful templates for IT administration include the Change Request Management, the Compliance Process Support Site, the Bug Database, the Document Library and Review, the Help Desk, the IT Team Workspace, the Knowledge Base, and the Physical Asset Tracking and Management sites. For information on the various site templates you can use with Windows SharePoint Services, go to *http://technet.microsoft.com/en-us/windowsserver/sharepoint/bb407286.aspx.*

Maintain Exchange-Specific Documentation

When it comes to Exchange, you should have documentation that covers your entire implementation. Not only should you detail the configuration of each server in your infrastructure, but you should also have information on how Exchange itself is deployed to provide service to your organization. Table 9-1 outlines the documentation you would typically include on Exchange.

Table 9-1 Documentation for Exchange Configurations

Exchange Component	Information to Include
Exchange Organization	Organization type
	Organization name and structure
	Administrator roles and administrative assignations
	Managed folder policies and locations
	Mailbox policies, including ActiveSync
	Global transport rules
	Accepted and remote domains, including rejected domains
	E-mail address policies
	Journaling policies
	Number and location of Mailbox servers
	Number and location of Hub Transport servers
	Number and location of Client Access servers
	Number and location of Unified Messaging servers
	Number and location of Edge Transport servers
	Antivirus configuration on each server
Mailbox servers	Storage groups, including databases contained in the group as well as database and log location
	Database purpose, including database type and type of users it contains
	Disconnected mailboxes
	Data protection implementation, including Local Continuous Replication, Cluster Continuous Replication, or Standby Continuous Replication
	Service protection implementation, including Single Copy Cluster, Cluster Continuous Replication, or Standby Cluster

Table 9-1 Documentation for Exchange Configurations

Exchange Component	Information to Include
Hub Transport servers	Send connector purpose, including connector type and associated configuration
	Receive connector purpose, including connector type and associated configuration
	Transport Rules purpose and configuration
	Edge Subscription configuration
	Service redundancy through multiple server deployment
Client Access servers	Outlook Web Access configuration
	Exchange ActiveSync configuration
	Offline Address Book distribution configuration
	Outlook Anywhere configuration
	Service redundancy strategies through Network Load Balancing services
Unified Messaging servers	Dial plan purpose and configuration
	IP Gateway purpose and configuration
	Unified Messaging mailbox policy purpose and configuration
	Auto Attendant configuration
	Service redundancy through multiple server deployment and DNS Round Robin configurations
Edge Transport servers	Send connector purpose, including connector type and associated configuration
	Receive connector purpose, including connector type and associated configuration
	Anti-spam filtering configuration
	Antivirus engine and configuration
	Service redundancy through multiple server deployment and DNS Round Robin configurations

The list in Table 9-1 is not exhaustive, but it does demonstrate the type of information you need to maintain on your Exchange configuration.

Rely on Standard Tool Kits

The last element of your strategy should be based on standard toolkits for infrastructure management. Toolkits include a lot of different components that can range from the simple command line to more sophisticated graphical consoles. But one of the most important aspects of any tool utilization is that you use a standard tool for the modification of any particular component and that each administrator or operator in your organization relies on this same tool when performing the same task.

In Exchange 2007, you already know that the System Manager of yore has been replaced by the new Exchange Management Console. This console is nothing more than a graphical interface to the new Exchange Management Shell because each configuration change is performed by the Shell; the console only provides the ability to determine the configuration of the cmdlet you want to generate. The Exchange Management Shell is based on Windows PowerShell, the new flagship scripting language and shell that is based on the Microsoft .NET Framework. In addition, the Exchange Management Shell includes additional cmdlets that control operations that are not included in the Exchange Management Console. In most instances, these cmdlets are designed to support more advanced configuration changes in Exchange 2007.

IMPORTANT   Automate Exchange tasks

The most powerful feature of the Exchange Console/Shell combination is that it provides a very simple way to automate recurrent tasks. That is because you can run through a wizard in the Console and then copy the resulting script at the end of the operation. Paste the script in Notepad and save it with a .ps1 extension and you have automated the task. No scripting knowledge is required to do this. Now that is powerful automation.

In addition to the Exchange Management Console and the Exchange Management Shell, Exchange 2007 includes the following utilities:

- **Best Practices Analyzer**   Designed to verify the configuration and health of the Exchange topology as well as provide recommendations for problem correction.

- **Database Recovery Management**   Designed to help recover lost data in mailbox databases.

- **Database Troubleshooter**   Helps diagnose mounting and other database-related issues.

- **Mail Flow Troubleshooter** Helps diagnose issues related to mail transport in and out of your organization.

- **Message Tracking** Lets you examine the message tracking logs that capture information about each message that is transmitted through your organization.

- **Queue Viewer** Designed to assist you in managing Exchange mail queues.

- **Performance Monitor** Monitors server performance and overall health.

- **Performance Troubleshooter** Helps you diagnose performance issues on Exchange server roles.

You can also supplement your Exchange infrastructure with additional tools and utilities. Some of these are free, while others are commercial add-ons. Chapter 10, "Monitor and Report on Exchange," will discuss some of these because it focuses on Exchange service monitoring.

Define Change Management for Exchange Server

The first place you should focus on when implementing structured change is in the deployment of Exchange itself. One of the key factors of any migration or technological deployment is the mix between preparation and implementation efforts. Ideally, you would spend 80 percent of your efforts on preparation and testing, running through a laboratory environment and ensuring that the solution works exactly as expected *before* you deploy it. When this phase is complete, you should then spend only 20 percent of your efforts in deploying the technology.

To do this, you should rely on a graduated testing strategy. The best graduated testing technologies use multiple testing levels, which include:

- **Unit Testing** The first level of testing, which is done in an isolated environment. The purpose of Unit Testing is to discover the feature set of the technology you are investigating. Each tester focuses on a specific technical aspect of the solution.

- **Functional Testing** The second level of testing. It is also isolated. The purpose of the Functional Testing level is to obtain a peer review of the initial solutions you designed in Unit Testing. Testers get together to review each other's discoveries.

- **Integration Testing** The third level, which begins to integrate different solution components. This testing level is more complete and more rigid in its control and operations. Solutions introduced here must be documented and must be applied in a controlled manner.

- **Staging Testing**   The fourth level of testing, which is focused on simulating the production environment as much as possible. For example, if remote sites exist in production, at least one remote site will be simulated in the Staging Testing level. Here solutions must be fully documented and must work the first time and every time afterward. This level also obtains technical and subject matter expert acceptance before proceeding to the next level.

- **Pilot Testing**   The fifth and last level of testing. Pilot testing is run in the production environment but only focuses on a subset of users and technological components of production. On average, a pilot project will include up to 10 percent of the user population. This test is an end-to-end test of the solution, including communications, training, and technological deployment. All pilot participants are required to complete a pilot evaluation survey so that the solution can be completely functional before actual deployment begins.

Entry and exit criteria are used at every testing level. Solutions must "graduate" from one level to another to pass up the testing chain. If solutions fail any of the exit or entry criteria, they must return to the previous environment to be updated (see Figure 9-2).

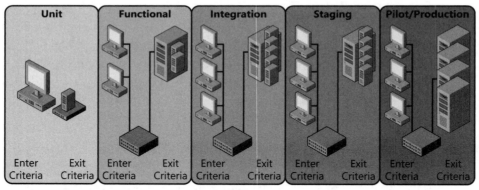

Figure 9-2   Working with graduated testing levels

MORE INFO   **More on graduated testing**

To find out more on graduated testing levels, see Chapter 3, "Creating the Migration Test Bed," from *The Definitive Guide to Vista Migration* by Ruest and Ruest, a free e-Book from *www.realtime-nexus.com/dgvm.htm*.

If you take care in your actual deployment, modifying the Exchange infrastructure to meet changes in your organization will not be a major endeavor. In fact, it should just be an extension of your deployment processes and should only be a repetition of processes you have already used during the deployment. It is true: Organizations that take the time to properly test every facet of their deployment not only document and prepare the implementation of solution components, but also prepare the ongoing procedures that will be used to manage change once the technology is in place.

In fact, when you deploy new technologies such as Exchange 2007, you should ensure that your initial deployment does not include the implementation of every new feature of the technology. Instead, aim to implement the base infrastructure during the initial deployment, and then plan on evolution when the infrastructure is in place. For example, with Exchange 2007, you could plan a deployment that only intends to put the ET, CAS, MB, and HT roles in place and then, as soon as the infrastructure is stable, plan further feature deployments such as Direct Push e-mail to mobile devices, External client access through OWA, and unified messaging services. This breaks down the challenge of putting in place new technologies and keeps them in smaller, more manageable units.

MORE INFO   **Rely on operating system virtualization**

Little has been discussed on operating system virtualization technologies in this book so far, but virtualization is a mainstream technology that cannot go unmentioned. Operating system virtualization provides a way to transform physical server installations into transportable, virtual installations. Physical disk structures are transformed into disk files contained within a folder that regroups all virtual machine (VM) components. Virtualization has been a major factor in server consolidation in 2007 and will continue to be so moving forward. Datacenters around the world are relying on this technology to reduce physical server footprints by a factor of at least 10. This is quite significant.

With the release of Windows Server 2008 and its most dramatic feature, Hyper-V, Microsoft will democratize operating system virtualization This means that virtualization will be within everyone's reach and organizations of all sizes will be able to take advantage of its benefits.

Exchange 2007, with its multiple server roles, is an ideal target for virtualization. Imagine requiring another Client Access server to improve service levels and only having to duplicate a set of files to create this server. Imagine doing the same when you need another Hub Transport server. With virtualization, server deployments can be as quick as 20 minutes! Virtualization is without a doubt transforming the datacenter, and that must be a significant part of any Exchange 2007 deployment, especially when it is running on Windows Server 2008.

Practice: Plan Change Management for Exchange

In this practice, you will prepare for a change that will affect an executive user in your organization. This practice consists of a single exercise. You will move the executive's mailbox from one MB server to another.

▶ **Exercise: Prepare for a Mailbox Move**

Moving a mailbox is a relatively simple operation, but each time you perform an operation of this type and you know it will affect the messaging system for a user, you must prepare your operation carefully. In this case, the employee is an executive officer. While the move should not be any different from a move for any other user, administrators often tend to pay much more attention to detail when the mailbox belongs to someone who can potentially control their salaries.

1. Make sure the TreyDC, ExchangeOne, and ExchangeLCR computers are running.

2. Log on to the ExchangeOne.treyresearch.net computer with the EXAdmin account. This will grant you local administrator access.

3. Launch the Exchange Management Console (Start Menu | All Programs | Microsoft Exchange Server | Exchange Management Console).

4. Move to the Recipient Configuration | Mailbox node in the tree pane.

   You are going to move the John.Kane mailbox from ExchangeOne to ExchangeLCR. Because the move will affect mail reception for the user for a short period of time, you must communicate with him first. Ideally, you would have time to communicate with the user well beforehand and warn him that he will experience some down time in his mailbox, and then you would perform the operation during off hours. When the user has acknowledged your communication, you can proceed with the move.

5. Select the John.Kane mailbox in the details pane and click Move Mailbox in the Action pane.

6. Select ExchangeLCR as the destination server, First Storage Group as the storage group, and Mailbox Database as the database. Click Next.

7. Under Move Options, click Skip The Mailbox. This will skip the move if corrupted messages are found. Click Next.

8. Under Move Schedule, click Immediately and leave all other options cleared. Click Next.

9. Under Move Mailbox, review your information and click Move.

10. Click Finish when the operation completes. Record the change in your log book.

    The Autodiscover Service will automatically re-link to John Kane's mailbox once the operation is complete. Send a message to John.Kane to tell him the operation is finished. Because this is an executive officer, you might follow up with an actual call to make sure everything is all right.

Moving mailboxes is easy, but as you can see, it must be wrapped by an administrative process if you want to manage change correctly within your Exchange configuration.

Quick Check

1. What are the four elements that must be part of the infrastructure that supports change management?

2. Which tools are included in the Exchange Management Console under Toolkits? Name at least four of them.

Quick Check Answers

1. Four elements are important:
   - ❑ Using an internal documentation plan.
   - ❑ Using an internal knowledge base.
   - ❑ Providing technology-specific documentation.
   - ❑ Relying on a standard set of tools.

2. The tools are:
   - ❑ Best Practices Analyzer
   - ❑ Database Recovery Management
   - ❑ Database Troubleshooter
   - ❑ Mail Flow Troubleshooter
   - ❑ Message Tracking
   - ❑ Queue Viewer
   - ❑ Performance Monitor
   - ❑ Performance Troubleshooter

Lesson 2: Plan for Exchange Infrastructure Improvements

Estimated lesson time: 40 minutes

Now that you are familiar with change management strategies, you can begin to look at how you would change existing Exchange configurations in the event of a new requirement. Potential changes fall into different categories, including:

- Hardware modifications such as processor additions, increases in RAM, or network interface card (NIC) additions
- Storage modifications, either for increased demand or for data protection purposes
- Server deployments for redundancy or for improved service levels
- Server configuration modifications to add or remove features
- Server updates through the application of security updates, hotfixes, or service packs

Many of these configuration changes rely on the features and processes outlined in Chapters 1 through 8. In addition, few administrators today are unfamiliar with the application of security updates and service packs, which have become a mainstay of every technology on the market.

Modify Server Hardware

Hardware modifications should be fairly rare for most organizations that move to Exchange 2007. All previous versions of Exchange ran on 32-bit hardware, while Exchange 2007 requires 64-bit hardware in production systems so almost every organization that deploys Exchange 2007 will have purchased new hardware to support the deployment. Because this is the case, most organizations will, or at least should, have used a proper hardware sizing exercise to plan the configuration of the servers they use to run Exchange server roles. When a proper sizing exercise is used, it is rare to have to modify hardware configurations during the first few years of the service operation.

It is, however, important to understand how to proceed when you do face the need to modify the hardware your Exchange services are running on. The best way to determine whether a server is in need of a potential hardware component upgrade is through monitoring. While monitoring itself will be covered in Chapter 10, you can rely on other telltale signs. One of the best is user perception. When you get reports from users that messages are slow to open or take time to be delivered or, even worse, their Outlook clients keep being disconnected from the Exchange server, you know something is wrong. However, if you get these reports soon after the deployment of your new Exchange infrastructure, you know something is *really* wrong.

Even if you know it is unlikely that hardware upgrades will be required soon after your deployment, you should still have a standard hardware upgrade process in place. This process should include the following steps:

1. Rely on user feedback and system monitoring to determine whether upgrades are required. Potential upgrades can include additional processors, additional RAM, additional disk space, or additional network interface cards. Refer to Chapter 1 to make sure you map additional processors and processor cores to the maximum allowed based on server role.

2. Use your laboratory environment to test the upgrade process. Here you can rely on virtualization technologies to see the effect of additional simulated hardware components on server performance. For example, many virtualization products support the addition of virtual processors to virtual machines and, like physical machines, must be stopped before the configuration change can take place. This will let you test the process and its consequences on Exchange services, but you should also have access to physical testing servers so that you can test the actual physical change as well.

3. Perform a full system backup before you make the actual change. Adding RAM and NICs and even processors may not affect server operation, but it is always best to be safe. Operating systems prior to Windows Server 2003 were very sensitive to the number of processors located within a system. This backup will support a back out plan if the change does not work properly.

4. Map out your back out plan. In many cases, you may have to remove the new hardware component and perform a full system restore if the upgrade does not work. Include a back out test in your lab in step 2.

5. Document the process fully and have the documentation on hand when you actually perform the operation. The best documentation format is a checklist. This way you can check off the steps as you perform them. Verify the manufacturer's documentation to see whether you must use special parameters with the new hardware component and include them in your documentation.

6. Implement the hardware change. Use the documentation you prepared to perform the procedure in a step-by-step format.

7. Test the system as it comes up and continue to monitor its behavior as it resumes operation. Continue this special monitoring process for a short period—usually a few days—until you feel confident that everything is working as it should.

When the modification is complete, ensure that you update the server configuration documentation so that it reflects the actual status of the newly updated server.

Modify Storage Configurations

One of the areas that changes the most in the life of an Exchange Organization is storage. Of course, your new Exchange 2007 storage infrastructure will be completely different than the structure you may have used when running legacy versions of Exchange. (See Lesson 1 in Chapter 2, "Planning Deployments.") Not only is Exchange server hardware now updated to 64-bit systems, but the storage structure also now relies much more on RAID 10 than on any other RAID format.

Three factors affect storage and can impact it enough to require modifications in your storage structure:

- E-mail growth. By its very nature, e-mail grows at an exponential rate. You have two choices: either implement a strict archiving policy or add more storage to keep more e-mail content live.

- Backup strategies. As you saw in Chapter 5, "Backup and Recovery," Exchange 2007 has great support for backup and restore. More storage is often required to address the restore capabilities and requirements.

- Data protection. As you work with Exchange 2007, you will find that it might be a good idea to implement the data protection policies discussed in Lesson 2 in Chapter 6, "Business Continuity," running one of the LCR, CCR, or SCR protection models.

These three justifications will warrant significant storage modifications such as adding disks and disk sets. Of course, you should use volume mount points rather than drive letters because mount points will let you access many more disk sets than the 26 letters of the alphabet.

Other modifications you can perform on storage on an ongoing basis include:

- Manage storage group and mailbox databases.
- Maintain and modify storage limits in each database.
- Configure default public folder databases.

- Configure the Offline Address Book for each database.
- Move transaction logs and databases to different locations.
- Mount and dismount databases.

You can perform each of these either through the Exchange Management Console or the Exchange Management Shell. Remember that because database modifications address actual mailboxes and therefore directly affect users, you will need to use your structured processes to effect the modifications. The most important aspect here is to ensure that you inform end users that modifications will be made and that because of this, their mailboxes may not be available for certain periods of time. One good way to do this is to provide users with an Exchange server availability Web page indicating which servers are being worked on and for how long. This will save you a lot of Help desk phone calls when you do perform maintenance activities on Mailbox servers.

Finally, though public folders are no longer necessary in Exchange 2007, you can still put them in place if you need them. For example, the first MB role you deploy will have a public folder database only if you indicate that you still have Outlook 2003 in your network. If not, no public folder database is created by default. Note that public folders are no longer available through OWA, IMAP4, or even the Network News Transfer Protocol (NNTP) because Client Access servers no longer provide access to public folders. To access public folders you must use a MAPI client such as Outlook. However, if public folders are stored on Exchange 2003 servers, users will still be able to access them through OWA.

If you do use public folders, you may be called upon to modify their configuration, including:

- Modify replication schedules.
- Create, modify, or remove public folder replicas.
- Modify public folder size limits.
- Modify public folder hierarchies.
- Move public folder databases.

When you perform management activities on public folders, you will find that the best tools are the Exchange Management Shell, Outlook itself, or even the legacy Exchange System Manager. Because public folders are slowly being deprecated in Exchange 2007, the Exchange Management Console only provides limited functionality for public folder management.

Monitor Transport Configurations

Like the other servers in your Exchange deployment, transport servers, both Hub and Edge, should have been sized properly when they were selected for implementation. But, as time goes by and your organization's reliance on Exchange services increases, you may be facing much more e-mail throughput than you previously anticipated. If this is the case, then your transport servers may turn out to be bottlenecks and may impact the proper flow of messages throughout your Exchange infrastructure.

To help avoid this issue, Exchange 2007 includes a feature called *back pressure monitoring*. This is a system resource monitoring feature that focuses on critical resources on transport servers—resources such as hard disk space and available random access memory (RAM)—to ensure that the system is able to continue to process messages properly. If a resource exceeds a specified threshold, then the transport server will stop accepting new connections or messages until existing messages are delivered. When the resource returns to a normal level of utilization, the transport server begins accepting new connections and processing new messages once again.

The resources included in back pressure monitoring include:

- Hard disk free space including the drive that stores the message queue database as well as the drive that stores the transaction logs for this database.

- Memory resources including the uncommitted message queue database transactions as well as all other processes.

- And, on Edge Transport servers, the memory used by the EdgeTransport.exe process.

For each of these resources, back pressure applies one of three utilization levels. Normal applies when a resource is not over used. In this case, back pressure does not apply any policy to the server. When a resource is slightly overused, back pressure sets it to medium utilization and begins to apply control policies; internal mail is allowed for processing but external mail is not. When resource utilization is high, then back pressure stops accepting any new mail or connections from any source.

You can modify default back pressure settings however it is highly recommended that you retain the settings configured at installation. Keep an eye on system event logs on transport servers to ensure you do not run into issues related to back pressure monitoring as your messaging workload grows.

If you do run into issues related to back pressure, the solution is usually relatively easy to implement. If your issues are related to disk resources, then add more disk volumes. If the issue is related to memory, then add more RAM. This is one more reason why the proper sizing of new Exchange servers is so important. You don't want to have to bring a transport server down once the infrastructure is in place just because you didn't size either the RAM or the hard disks properly.

MORE INFO Back Pressure

For more information on the back pressure monitoring feature, go to
http://technet.microsoft.com/en-us/library/bb201658(EXCHG.80).aspx.

Improve Service Redundancy

Chapter 6 outlined the various strategies you can rely on to improve both data protection and service resilience in Exchange 2007. Some of these changes can be transparent to your end users while others will have more impact. Remember that for most of the services, you often only need to add another server role to increase its availability. Table 9-2 summarizes the approaches you use to increase availability for each server role.

Table 9-2 Availability Strategy Per Server Role

Server Role	Availability Strategy	Comment
Hub Transport Server	Multiple HT Systems	HT configuration is stored within Active Directory. In most cases, to increase availability, all you need to do is add an additional server to the site. The configuration is automatically picked up from Active Directory.
Edge Transport Server	Multiple ET Systems	ET configuration is stored within the Active Directory in Application Mode (ADAM) instance stored on the ET system. Use Cloned Configuration to add a new server with the same configuration.
		Remember that Edge Subscriptions must be deleted and re-created each time you add a new ET system after the initial Edge Subscription has been created.
		Also, remember to add the ET IP address in DNS so that Round Robin can include it in its rotations.

Table 9-2   Availability Strategy Per Server Role

Server Role	Availability Strategy	Comment
Unified Messaging Server	Multiple UM Systems	UM configuration is also stored in Active Directory. However, you should implement multiple dialing plans and multiple links to IP Gateways to increase redundancy.
		Remember to add the UM IP address in DNS so that Round Robin can include it in its rotations.
Client Access Server	Multiple CAS Systems	CAS availability is controlled through the Network Load Balancing cluster. If the NLB cluster does not exist, you must create it. If you create it using the IP address of the original CAS server you deployed, little change is required at the end-user level, but this change will require some downtime for the CAS system because you must change its IP address before you can deploy it into an NLB cluster.
		Remember also that you will need a new Subject Alternate Name (SAN) certificate to install into the cluster.
Mailbox Server	Single Copy Cluster, Standby Cluster or Cluster Continuous Replication	If an MB has been deployed and was not deployed into a cluster to begin with, you must install a new instance of MB to create the cluster because clusters are created at installation. Then, you must move the mailbox databases from the original MB to the new clustered instance. This will have a direct impact on mailbox availability during the time you put your high availability strategy in place.

Table 9-2 provides a quick summary of the strategies you would use to increase system availability. Much more information is available in Chapter 6.

Of course, everything must be prepared and tested in a laboratory so that you have full-fledged instruction sets to follow when you perform the same procedure in production. In addition, you can see that increasing availability for the HT, ET, and UM roles would have little impact on existing operations, but adding availability for the CAS or the MB will have a direct impact on service availability during the implementation. Therefore, if you perform changes related to these two roles, you must use a stricter change management strategy than with the others.

MORE INFO   **Cloning ET configurations**

Adding a new ET requires cloning the configuration from an existing server to the new system. When you clone the configuration, you export the configuration from a source server into an XML file and then load it into the new server. When the cloning process is complete, you must run the Edge Subscription to update additional information on the new ET server. For more information on configuration cloning, go to *http://technet.microsoft.com/en-us/library/aa998622.aspx*.

Add or Remove Services or Features

When you modify services and features—for example, adding managed folders or new transport rules—you must also proceed with care because services and features impact mail flow and will therefore impact users. Several different configurations can be performed when the Exchange 2007 infrastructure is in place. Remember that when you target your original deployment plan, you should focus on those features that will form the core set of services you want in place initially. Then, as time progresses and the infrastructure begins to prove its stability, you can begin to add additional functionality.

Several different aspects of the infrastructure configuration can be modified throughout the life of your Exchange infrastructure. For example, you might decide to implement message throttling, placing limits on your transport servers to make sure that they are not overwhelmed with a storm of e-mail messages. This is one example of the type of change you can make to transport servers.

MORE INFO   **Message throttling**

For more information on message throttling, go to *http://technet.microsoft.com/library/bb232205.aspx*.

But, the one server role that calls for the most modifications in terms of adding features or services is the Client Access Server role. While most of the services the CAS role supports are installed and enabled by default, most organizations do not begin to work with them as they are out of the box. As you saw in Chapter 2, each of these services requires considerable configuration before you should start using it.

Once again, make sure you use the proper change management procedure, test everything in the lab, and deploy it only when you are absolutely sure everything will work.

Apply Updates to Exchange Server

The element that will have the most impact on your Exchange infrastructure in terms of changes impacting its availability is the production of updates and service packs Microsoft will release during its lifecycle. Since its release, Exchange 2007 has had numerous update releases as well as the release of a very significant service pack. In fact, if you have not implemented Exchange 2007 yet, you should make sure you deploy Exchange 2007 with Service Pack 1 instead of relying on the original release of the product. Service Pack 1 provides additional functionality to Exchange as well as making it available to run on Windows Server 2008 operating systems.

Exam Tip   If you are deploying Exchange 2007 and you want to rely on your deployment to study for the exam, you will be in a paradoxical situation. Ideally, you should deploy Exchange with Service Pack 1 to have the latest and greatest infrastructure, but it may be more difficult for you to rely on this infrastructure to study for the exam because the original exam does not include SP1 content. This is one reason we so strongly recommend using virtual machines. You can use a VM to deploy the original release of Exchange 2007 and then rely on this VM to validate your studies, but still use only an updated infrastructure in your production environment.

Deploy Exchange Service Packs

Keep the following items in mind when planning to use service pack updates:

- If you have already deployed Exchange 2007, you must plan for a server-by-server update process. If you have not implemented availability strategies—either because you are not ready to include them in your infrastructure yet or because the size of your organization simply does not warrant them—you will have to plan for service outages. Use the following strategy:
    - If you have availability strategies in place, rely on the availability of multiple copies of each role to update each system. For HT, ET, and UM systems, you can simply work on one system at a time, taking it out of production for a short period, updating it, and then putting it back into production. If you do this during off-peak hours, the impact on users will be limited. Use the same strategy for CAS NLB clusters. For MB clusters, update the passive node first, move the service from the active node to the newly updated passive node, update the second node, and continue on until all nodes are updated. See Chapter 6 for more information.

❑ If you do not have an availability strategy in place, you must plan for service outages. Be sure to communicate the update to your users, perform full system backups, and then update your servers.

■ If you have not deployed Exchange yet, either obtain code that includes the service pack or use the Microsoft service pack slipstreaming capability to update a copy of the installation code so that you deploy updated code directly without having to perform the update when the installation is complete. Slipstreaming lets you inject new updates into the original installation code to create an updated version of the code.

Whichever situation you find yourself in, be sure to fully test all procedures in the lab before you do anything in production.

Deploy Exchange Updates

Microsoft releases updates on a regular schedule and most come out on the second Tuesday of every month. Each update is documented in a corresponding Knowledge Base article that explains which component of a Microsoft product the update applies to. In case of emergencies, for example, such as a specific security issue or a critical problem with a component, Microsoft will release updates in a more punctual manner. In any event, you should subscribe to Microsoft updates so that you are immediately aware when they become available. If you have not done so yet, go to *http://www.microsoft.com/technet/security/bulletin/notify.mspx*.

Deploying updates uses much the same process as service packs because in many cases, updates will require a system reboot and will cause system shutdowns. For this reason, system outages will occur. Once again, having high availability implementations makes it much easier to deploy updates while reducing service outages. Few system administrators today do not have a system update process that follows Microsoft's Tuesday releases.

Use an Update Deployment Process

Whether you deploy updates or service packs, you rely on the same process. In summary, this process should include the following steps:

1. Deploy only required updates. The advantage of dividing Exchange services into different server roles means fewer updates on a per-role basis.

2. Validate the functionality of the update in a lab. Ideally, your lab will meet the exact configuration of your production environment so that your tests provide valid results.

3. Perform a full system backup. This protects the configuration as it exists before the update.

4. Prepare a rollback plan. If the update does not work and the system is broken, will you have to perform a full system restore? Be ready in case this happens.

5. Document the installation process fully so that you have a step-by-step process to follow when performing the update.

6. Implement the update. Rely on your documentation to follow the process.

7. Test the system after the update has been applied and monitor its performance to ensure that it still responds as it should.

As you can see, the update process for service packs is the same process you would use for any update or change in Exchange or any other service infrastructure that has the potential to impact end users and business processes.

In most organizations, a formal update or hotfix deployment tool will already be in place. Many of these exist on the market. Microsoft offers a free add-on to Windows Server called Windows Server Update Services (WSUS). If you do not use a third-party tool or do not have a tool in place, look to WSUS to help you manage this critical change process on your servers. Information on WSUS is available at *http://technet.microsoft.com/en-ca/wsus/ default.aspx.*

MORE INFO Structure your update deployments

For more information on how to manage updates in your environment, look up "The Ultimate Patching Guide" and "A Practical Guide for Patch Testing" at *http://www.reso-net.com/articles.asp?m=8#e.*

Practice: Plan for Exchange Service Evolution

In this practice, you will prepare a change management strategy, in relation to the deployment of updates to Exchange 2007. This practice consists of a single exercise. You will focus on how you should apply updates to Exchange 2007.

▶ **Exercise: Build a Plan for Applying Updates to Exchange**

The Graphics Design Institute wants to move to Exchange 2007, but because they will be using a Simple Organization, they know they will only have a few systems running Exchange. This means that when they perform updates, they will have a loss of service. Therefore, they want to create a strategy that will minimize this loss of service as much as possible. They turn to you, the messaging professional, to assist them in preparing a strategy that will minimize the impact of applying updates.

Because they have a simpler deployment structure for Exchange, GDI does not have a high availability implementation in place and does not have the means to move to a high availability implementation. This means that they will need to have service outages when update installations require system reboots. Therefore, you suggest the following strategy:

1. Determine whether the update is required. Exchange's division into different server roles minimizes the updates you need to apply per system, but in the case of the GDI deployment, all shareable roles are on one single system. As such, most updates that apply to Exchange will have to be deployed on this system.

2. Use the GDI laboratory environment to test the update process. Because of limited resources, the GDI lab environment runs on virtual machines. Fortunately, it does reflect the production installation quite well.

3. Perform a full system backup before you make the actual change. This is part of the test procedure first and will also be duplicated in production.

4. Map out the rollback plan. Once again, the best place to prepare and test this plan is in the lab. Because it relies on virtual machines, you can simply perform the test on a copy of the computer and then discard it if it is broken after the test. This lets you repeat the test as many times as you need to ensure that it works all the time, every time.

5. Document the process fully and have the documentation on hand when you actually perform the operation. The result is a comprehensive checklist to follow.

6. Implement the update. Use the documentation you prepared to perform the procedure in a step-by-step format. Make sure you perform this in a maintenance window and that all users have been informed of the change.

7. Test the system as it comes up and continue to monitor its behavior as it resumes operation. Continue this special monitoring process for a short period—usually a few days—until you feel confident that everything is working as it should.

You can even help them test out this process because they have access to a full-fledged lab.

Quick Check

1. Which steps should a standard hardware upgrade process include? Name at least four.

2. Which modifications can be performed on storage on an ongoing basis? Name at least two.

Quick Check Answers
1. A standard hardware upgrade process should include the following steps:
   - ❑ Rely on user feedback and system monitoring to determine whether upgrades are required.
   - ❑ Use your laboratory environment to test the upgrade process.
   - ❑ Perform a full system backup before you make the actual change.
   - ❑ Map out your rollback plan.
   - ❑ Document the process fully and have the documentation on hand when you actually perform the operation.
   - ❑ Implement the hardware change.
   - ❑ Test the system as it comes up and continue to monitor its behavior as it resumes operation.
2. The possible modifications are:
   - ❑ Storage group and mailbox database management.
   - ❑ Maintain and modify storage limits in each database.
   - ❑ Configure default public folder databases.
   - ❑ Configure the Offline Address Book for each database.
   - ❑ Move transaction logs and databases to different locations.
   - ❑ Mount and dismount databases.

Chapter Summary

- Whether your change management process is formal or informal, you should always endeavor to provide documentation on the change because documentation lets you track the change and helps quickly correct issues if they arise because of the change.

- You have two major sources of information for industry-specific strategies: Information Technology Infrastructure Library (ITIL) and Microsoft Operations Framework (MOF). Another source of infrastructure information is the Infrastructure Planning and Design (IPD).

- Whether you use a formal Help desk management tool or not, you should still maintain a database of all of the issues you run into and document their solution. Having a database of this type lets you quickly resolve issues if they occur again. It also lets you resolve related problems even if they do not arise from the same initial issue.

■ Public folders are no longer necessary in Exchange 2007. You can still put them in place if you need them. For example, the first MB role you deploy will have a public folder database only if you indicate that you still have Outlook 2003 in your network. If not, no public folder database is created by default.

■ Microsoft releases updates on a regular schedule and most come out on the second Tuesday of every month. Each update is documented in a corresponding Knowledge Base article that explains which component of a Microsoft product it applies to.

Case Scenarios

In the following case scenarios, you will apply what you have learned about Exchange feature support for change management. You can find answers to the questions in this scenario in the "Answers" section at the end of this book.

Case Scenario 1: Identify Standard Management Tools

The Graphics Design Institute is preparing to deploy Exchange 2007 in a Simple Organization using the new Medium configuration available with the release of Windows Server 2008. They will have two different Exchange administrators. They have taken your advice on structured change management and have already begun documenting their infrastructure. They also want to implement standard toolkits. One of the tools they think they will use the most is the new Exchange Management Console. Their administrators have used Exchange System Manager in the past. Now they want to know what they will be able to do through the new Console.

How do you respond?

Case Scenario 2: Define an Updating Strategy

Lucerne Publishing is using a Standard Organization with two sites. They have implemented high availability strategies for each of the server roles they have deployed. In fact, they have the following infrastructure (see Figure 9-3):

■ The perimeter network includes two ET systems.

■ Each site has two HT systems.

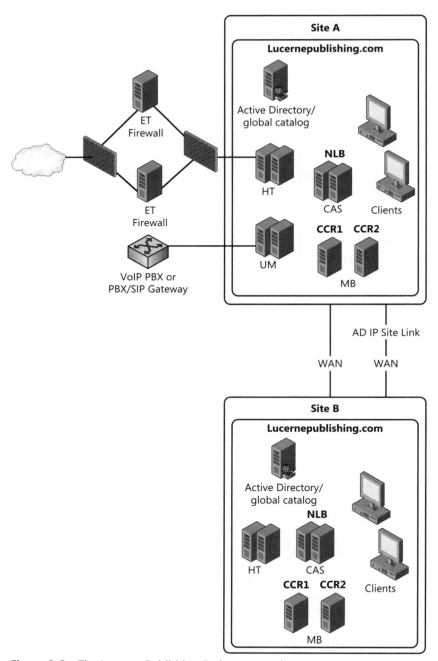

Figure 9-3   The Lucerne Publishing Exchange topology

- The main site has two UM systems.

- Client Access servers in each site are running through Network Load Balancing clusters. Each NLB cluster includes two CAS systems.

- The Mailbox servers are running Cluster Continuous Replication with pair nodes located one in each of the two sites Lucerne runs. Two CCR clusters are in operation.

They turn to you, the messaging professional, to help them determine how system updates will affect their infrastructure.

How do you respond?

Suggested Practices

It is difficult to practice change management with Exchange Server without access to a full infrastructure, but you can do so if you prepare a virtual environment as outlined in the Introduction. Rely on both the ExchangeOne and the ExchangeLCR machines to run through the change management strategies detailed in this chapter. In fact, this environment will provide you with the ideal testing bed to prepare for the move to Exchange Server Service Pack 1.

Chapter 10

Monitor and Report on Exchange 2007

The health of an IT infrastructure is usually determined by its level of responsiveness as well as its stability. As discussed in Chapter 9, "Plan for Messaging Environment Maintenance," the very best way to guarantee that your infrastructure is stable and responsive is to ensure that your deployment strategy responds as well as possible to the business requirements of your organization. In addition, you want to make sure that you test the deployment as fully as possible so that when it comes to the actual implementation, you will be following the strict guidelines you produced in the deployment preparation activities of your implementation project.

If you follow this golden rule, you can be assured that your Exchange infrastructure is going to run well and respond to your needs for a long period of time—barring, of course, any significant change to the structure of your organization, such as a merger or an acquisition. Even then, if your infrastructure update process uses proper change management procedures, you can mitigate the impact of a change even with this massive a scope.

When the system is in place, however, you will still need to perform two activities to ensure that it stays as stable as when you put it in place.

- The first activity is proactive in scope. You maintain the system through regularly scheduled administrative and maintenance activities. This is the only way to ensure that systems run as you expect.

- The second activity is reactive in scope—it is focused on systems monitoring. When you monitor your systems, you can find out how they behave under a variety of circumstances. Monitoring in and of itself can also be proactive because it can proactively make system changes when specific situations are discovered, but it is also reactive because events must occur before you can do anything about them.

Putting both of these activities in place will be the final part of your deployment strategy.

Exam objectives in this chapter:

- Plan for monitoring and reporting.

Before You Begin

To complete the lessons in this chapter, you must have the following:

- A virtual machine setup as outlined in the Introduction under "Virtual Machine Environments."

- Use the Exchange Server 2007 virtual machine from Microsoft to review the configuration options for pre-installed computers.

- Use the virtual environment you set up to test the monitoring procedures discussed in this chapter. For the exercises in this chapter, you will need access to the Active Directory server; the all-in-one Exchange server, ExchangeOne; the LCR server you created, ExchangeLCR; and the ET server, ExchangeETOne.

Lesson 1: Implement Proactive Systems Administration

Estimated lesson time: 60 minutes

The first place to start to ensure system health is with a structured administrative approach. Exchange, like all IT systems, requires maintenance through a series of tasks that must be performed on a consistent schedule. In most cases, this means performing tasks on a daily, weekly, monthly, and often ad hoc basis. Ad hoc tasks are tasks that you must perform only once in a while and may be on a schedule, but the schedule for this particular task does not follow monthly repetitions and may require bimonthly, quarterly, semi-annual, or even annual repetitions. In the interest of clarification, these tasks are all included in the ad hoc schedule. You determine which schedule will fit best for your organization.

Periodic maintenance tasks help you determine what is normal for your organization as well as help you detect any abnormal or unusual activity. You can also establish criteria for how systems should work when they are operating normally. You should rely on your periodic task schedule to capture and maintain data about your Exchange implementation. Data such as regular usage levels, peak hours of operation, performance peaks on a per role basis, potential bottlenecks, and controlled changes will help you get a better overview of the system itself and how it functions.

Table 10-1 outlines which tasks should be performed on which schedule if you want to maintain the health of your system. Refer to the preceding chapters to identify how to perform each task.

Table 10-1   Periodic Exchange Maintenance Task List

Task	Daily	Weekly	Monthly	Ad hoc
Physical Environment				
Check physical environment:	☑			
Physical security: locks, doors, restricted-access rooms				
Temperature and humidity				

Table 10-1 Periodic Exchange Maintenance Task List

Task	Daily	Weekly	Monthly	Ad hoc
Devices and components: routers, switches, hubs, physical cables, connectors				
Test physical environment		☑		
Air conditioning				
Temperature and humidity				
Physical security measures				
Security				
Perform audits of security			☑	
Firewall rules				
User rights				
Group memberships				
Delegate rights				
Perform a full security audit in response to an upgrade or redesign				☑
Check security updates		☑		
Service Pack				
Hotfixes				
Updates				
Updates for IIS, Active Directory, and DNS server				
Critical updates				
Maintain a list of the ones that apply			☑	

Table 10-1 Periodic Exchange Maintenance Task List

Task	Daily	Weekly	Monthly	Ad hoc
Security logs	☑			
Verify security logs and match security changes				
Investigate unauthorized security changes				
Check security news for viruses, worms, and so on				
Update and fix security problems				
Verify SMTP relay				
Verify SSL				
Update virus signatures				
Perform virus scan		☑		
Disaster Recovery				
Back up Exchange data and Active Directory data:	☑			
Server configuration				
Active Directory database				
Exchange Information Store service				
Log event and performance data				
Exchange application software				
Exchange message tracking log files				
Exchange databases and log files				
Check previous night's backup jobs	☑			

Table 10-1   Periodic Exchange Maintenance Task List

Task	Daily	Weekly	Monthly	Ad hoc
Review any errors or warnings	☑			
Test your backups			☑	
Review the procedure and the backup strategy				☑
Test the disaster recovery strategy			☑	
Recover mailbox from dumpster or database backup following the procedure				☑
CPU, Memory, Disk				
Check CPU and memory usage	☑			
% processor time performance counter				
Available MBs performance counter				
% committed bytes in use performance counter				
Check disk usage	☑			
Drives for transactions logs				
Drives with queues				
Other drive				
Available space MB				
Available % free				
Monitor Exchange store statistics (Event ID 1113)				

Table 10-1   Periodic Exchange Maintenance Task List

Task	Daily	Weekly	Monthly	Ad hoc
Event Logs				
Check event viewer	☑			
Application and system logs of Exchange servers				
Services failures				
Replication errors in Active Directory				
Virtual memory warnings				
Disk space warnings				
IIS logs and filters				
Archive and delete event logs		☑		
Performance				
Monitor server performance	☑			
Exchange servers				
Exchange components				
Monitor network performance	☑			
Resource usage				
Network traffic				
Exchange servers				
Exchange messages				
IIS Performance	☑			
Web service counters				

Table 10-1 Periodic Exchange Maintenance Task List

Task	Daily	Weekly	Monthly	Ad hoc
Web service cache counters				
FTP service counters				
Active Server Pages counters				
MAPI Performance	☑			
System monitor counters				
Event viewer logs				
Test account log on Exchange server				☑
Test send/receive capabilities				☑
Mail flow status				
Send messages between internal servers with test accounts			☑	
Verify messages deliveries			☑	
Send outgoing messages to non-local accounts			☑	
Verify outgoing messages deliveries			☑	
Send messages across any connectors			☑	
Verify message transfer across connectors and routes			☑	
Run WinRoute to ensure connectivity		☑		
Service Level Agreements				
Review Service Level Agreements (SLAs) performance		☑		

Table 10-1 Periodic Exchange Maintenance Task List

Task	Daily	Weekly	Monthly	Ad hoc
Previous data for the previous week				
Performance against requirements of SLA				
Trends and items that do not meet targets				
Review capacity for the previous month		☑		
Plan for any upgrades to operating system within the limits of SLAs				☑
Update performance baselines after an upgrade or configuration change				☑
Exchange Database	☑			
Number of transactions logs				
Databases are mounted				
Public folder is up to date				
Indexes are up to date				
Test mailbox				☑
Verify the logon of each database				
Verify Send/Receive capabilities				
Maintain Exchange database				☑
Check public folder replication		☑		
Create public folder following the procedure				☑
Add or remove users following the procedure				☑

Table 10-1   Periodic Exchange Maintenance Task List

Task	Daily	Weekly	Monthly	Ad hoc
Queue Management				
Monitor Mail Queues on HT and ET				☑
Messages queued for extended periods of time to review the performance metrics				
Peaks in queued messages				
Check queues for each server in each admin group	☑			
Record queue size	☑			
Reporting				
Reports		☑		
Note data from event log and system monitor				
Note disk usage				
Note memory and CPU usage				
Note uptime and availability				
Note database and mailbox sizes				
Create capacity reports from messages sent and client logons				
Note queue use, size, and growth				
Incident report		☑		
Note the top-generated, resolved, and pending incidents				
Solution for unresolved incidents				

Table 10-1   Periodic Exchange Maintenance Task List

Task	Daily	Weekly	Monthly	Ad hoc
Update reports with new trouble tickets				
Repository for troubleshooting guides and post-completion reviews following outages				
Status meeting		☑		
Server and network for the overall organization and segments				
Organizational performance and availability				
Review reports and incidents				
Risk analysis and upcoming changes				
Review capacity, availability, and performance				
SLA performance and targets that do not meet target				

By performing these tasks, you will not only ensure that your systems are running properly, but in many cases, you will also identify potential issues before they become problems.

MORE INFO   Periodic task lists for Windows

Periodic tasks do not apply only to Exchange Server. For optimum system health, you should perform periodic tasks on the operating system as well.

For a list of periodic tasks for Windows Server 2003, look up *Windows Server 2003 Pocket Administrator* by Ruest and Ruest (McGraw-Hill Osborne, 2003).

For a list of periodic tasks for Windows Server 2008, look up *Windows Server 2008: The Complete Reference* by Ruest and Ruest (McGraw-Hill Osborne, 2008).

For a list of periodic tasks for Windows Vista, look up *The Deploying and Administering Windows Vista Bible* by Cribbs, Ruest, and Ruest (Wiley, 2008).

Monitor and Report on Exchange Infrastructures

In addition to proactive administration, you should implement some form of monitoring in your solution even if it is nothing more sophisticated than verifying Exchange Event Logs on a regular basis. You should regularly monitor several different classes of objects and aspects of the Exchange infrastructure:

- System performance for each deployed server role
- Resource usage on each server in the e-mail infrastructure
- Server uptime on a per-role basis
- Connections between server roles
- Mail transport and mail flow throughout the system
- Send and receive message timings
- Mail queues both on transport and on mailbox servers
- Messaging Records Management operation and updates
- Offline Address Book and address list availability
- Calendaring and Availability service performance
- Public folder replication, management, and access
- Unified Messaging server access and interactions

This list is not exhaustive, but it points to the type of items you must monitor when running Exchange. As with the hardware upgrade requirements discussed in Chapter 9, one of the best places to obtain performance information is from end users themselves. They are used to working with the system and will be immediately aware if something is not running as it should be.

Of course, you can perform many tasks with both the Exchange Management Console and the Exchange Management Shell. The Exchange Management Console in particular is used to access the Tools node, which links you to the most common monitoring and troubleshooting tools. But the Exchange Management Shell provides access to every single Exchange 2007 command, and is a tool that administrators need to be very familiar with to perform complete life-cycle management of Exchange 2007 infrastructures. In addition, several tools focus on the monitoring and maintenance of specific Exchange infrastructure components. Table 10-2 lists several of these tools.

Table 10-2 Monitoring Tools for Exchange Server 2007

Tool	Monitoring Focus	Comment
Queue Viewer	Mail queues	Set queue thresholds and monitor them with Queue Viewer to see whether they are appropriate.
Event Viewer	System and Application Logs	Use Event Viewer to review event logs for each component of the system running an Exchange server role. In Windows Vista and Windows Server 2008, you can even collect logs centrally through Event Forwarding. For instructions on how to set up Event Forwarding, look up "Collect Vista Events" at *http://www.prismmicrosys.com/ newsletters_june2007.php*.
HTTPMon	Outlook Web Access	HTTPMon is from the Windows Resource Kit. You use it to generate reports about the availability and response times of Web sites and Web applications. HTTPMon can verify several Web sites or applications at once. Reports are generated in comma-separated value (CSV) format.
Windows PowerShell	Entire Exchange infrastructure	Windows PowerShell is the engine for the Exchange Management Shell that exposes the entire Exchange infrastructure.
Network Monitor	Inter-server communications	Network Monitor is a Windows tool that is designed to monitor and capture network traffic. Use it to analyze traffic between servers as well as between clients and servers.
Performance Troubleshooter	Overall system health	Part of the Exchange Console Toolbox; focuses on overall system health.

Table 10-2   Monitoring Tools for Exchange Server 2007

Tool	Monitoring Focus	Comment
Mail Flow Troubleshooter	Overall mail flow	Part of the Exchange Console Toolbox; focuses on overall mail flow health. Requests input on problem and recommends troubleshooting approach.
Database Troubleshooter	Mailbox databases	Part of the Exchange Console Toolbox; helps identify issues related to storage groups as well as database mounting issues.
Database Recovery Management	Mailbox databases	Part of the Exchange Console Toolbox; searches databases and transaction logs for issues that can affect database recoverability. Identifies missing or corrupted log files and recommends repair actions.
Message Tracking	E-mail messages	Part of the Exchange Console Toolbox; requires input criteria to locate specific messages in the mail flow.
Performance Monitor	Overall system health	Part of the Exchange Console Toolbox; uses the Windows Performance Monitor with special Exchange counters to determine the overall performance of the system.
Best Practices Analyzer	Single server, Servers in an Administration Group, or all servers in the Organization	Gathers configuration information from Active Directory, Windows Management Instrumentation, the registry, and the IIS metabase to validate the configuration of the systems against proven best practices. Recommends modifications if modifications are required.

Table 10-2   Monitoring Tools for Exchange Server 2007

Tool	Monitoring Focus	Comment
Exchange Troubleshooting Assistant	Overall Organization configuration	Downloadable tool that includes Performance Troubleshooting, Database Recovery Management, and Mail Flow Troubleshooter in one tool. Download from: *http://technet.microsoft.com/en-us/ exchange/bb288481.aspx.*
Exchange Server Jetstress	Disk subsystems	Verifies the performance and stability of a disk subsystem. Usually used before the disk system is put into production.
Exchange Load Generator	MAPI messaging	Simulates the delivery of multiple MAPI client messaging requests against an Exchange system. Use in lab testing environments to validate server configurations.
Exchange Server Stress and Performance	Exchange protocols	Simulates a large number of client sessions against Exchange infrastructure. Use in lab testing environments to validate server configurations.
Exchange Server Profile Analyzer	Mailbox servers	Collects statistical information from either the single mailbox store or the entire Organization to analyze performance and health of MB systems.
Exchange ActiveSync Certificate-based Authentication Tool	ActiveSync	Supports the validation and configuration of client certificate authentication for Exchange ActiveSync. Obtain it from *http://www.microsoft.com/downloads.*
Exchange Server User Monitor	User connections	Use to gather real-time data from client connections to help understand client connection workloads. Obtain it from *http://www.microsoft.com/downloads.*

MORE INFO   Obtain more tools

Many of the Exchange troubleshooting tools listed in Table 10-2 are available for download. Locate them at *http://go.microsoft.com/fwlink/?linkid=50259*.

Many of the tools discussed in Table 10-2 are available in the Tools section of the Exchange Management Console (see Figure 10-1). This is the first place you should look when you begin putting your monitoring strategy in place.

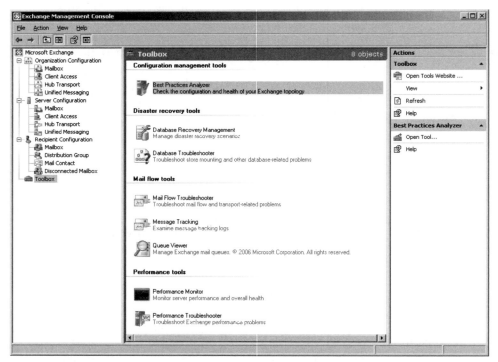

Figure 10-1   Accessing Exchange tools through the Exchange Management Console

Rely on a Commercial Monitoring Tool

You can put in place a monitoring tool that is specifically designed to support Microsoft Exchange. Several third-party tools are available from companies such as Quest Software, NetIQ, and many more. Microsoft also makes available System Center Operations Manager (SCOM, formerly Microsoft Operations Manager, or MOM), which relies on management packs to provide monitoring and proactive management support for specific Microsoft products. The advantage of using SCOM is that each management pack is written by the developers of the product group itself. For example, the Exchange 2007 management pack for SCOM has been written by the Exchange product team.

This ensures that the management pack covers all of the required services for the intended product. For example, the SCOM Exchange Management Pack covers the following items:

- All Exchange services
- Mailbox and public folder databases
- Available disk space on all disks
- Office Outlook 2007 connectivity and performance
- Mail flow within the Exchange Organization
- Overall system performance and configuration
- Backup status

In addition, SCOM can load a special management pack for the Exchange Best Practices Analyzer and rely on this component to perform continual validations of your Exchange infrastructure.

Because SCOM is a proactive monitoring tool, you can set it up to perform specific actions when issues arise. For example, if a disk set fills up, SCOM can delete all temporary files to free up disk space as it advises you of the issue.

IMPORTANT   Obtain a monitoring tool

It is highly recommended that you obtain an official, and most likely commercial, monitoring tool for Exchange 2007. As you know, e-mail infrastructures are becoming more and more essential to business, and trying to manage them without a real monitoring tool is well-nigh impossible.

MORE INFO   Learn about Exchange and MOM

For more information about Microsoft Operations Manager and Exchange, go to *http://technet.microsoft.com/en-us/library/bb201735.aspx*.

Review Exchange Monitoring Best Practices

When you plan to keep an eye on your Exchange infrastructure, you should begin by preparing your monitoring strategy. Monitoring strategies are based on structured approaches much like the change management processes discussed in Chapter 9 and should include the following:

1. Begin by determining what should be monitored. Gather information about the Exchange infrastructure itself such as organization type and deployed infrastructure, as well as number of users, locations, and average e-mail flow on a daily basis.

2. Use the Exchange Best Practices Analyzer to determine whether your configuration is working properly and whether changes are required.

3. Determine which tools you want to use to perform the monitoring. Keep in mind that not all tools must be specific to Exchange. For example, you may want to add non-Exchange tools for the verification of your PBX gateways, SMS gateways, or Fax gateways and include them in your overall messaging infrastructure monitoring plan.

4. Establish the parameters you need to monitor. Do this for each aspect of the infrastructure.

5. Establish baselines to determine how systems perform with no workload, with low workloads, with medium workloads, and with high workloads.

6. Document the baselines and establish baseline thresholds.

7. Periodically monitor the entire infrastructure to identify its overall performance levels. Compare these levels to your baselines and then determine whether action is required.

This approach will provide the best results because it helps you identify how systems are working at specific points in time.

Establish a Best Practices Configuration

As part of your monitoring strategy, you should begin by scanning all of your systems with the Exchange Best Practices Analyzer (BPA) to determine the health of your existing configuration, and then perform any required modifications. This will set your configuration on its best behavior and should form the basis of any infrastructure you deploy.

The Exchange Best Practices Analyzer can be accessed through the Tools node in the Exchange Management Console. When you start the Exchange BPA, you will have the opportunity to select the type of scan you want it to perform (see Figure 10-2). Several scans are available:

- The Health Check identifies issues related to general system health.
- The Permission Check validates all permissions and account access rights in relation to the Exchange configuration.
- The Connectivity Test validates the communication paths used by the mail flow.
- The Baseline option allows you to generate a baseline from your systems.

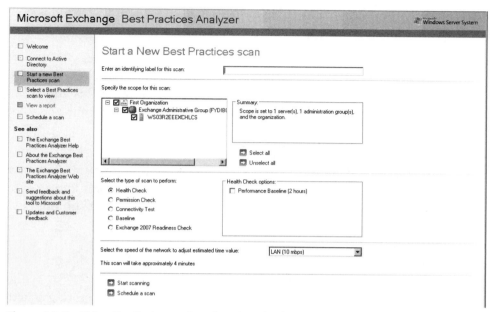

Figure 10-2 Using the Exchange Best Practices Analyzer

- The Exchange 2007 Readiness Check validates that an Exchange Organization is ready for operations.

Each scan is then stored within a BPA report that you can view through the BPA tool. Reports should be stored in secure locations because they include sensitive information about your e-mail configuration.

Build Baselines and Thresholds

When you build a baseline to establish your monitoring thresholds, you rely on the Exchange Performance Monitor because it is automatically configured to monitor the most important counters related to Exchange service operation. You need to perform three steps to create the baseline:

1. Identify the resources to be monitored. These include resources such as disk, memory, processor, network, and paging files.
2. Capture the data. Data captures should be run on a regular basis during off hours as well as during peak hours. For example, you might capture data at 5:00, 8:00, 10:00, 12:00, 15:00, and 18:00 for at least 45 minutes per time frame for at least one week. This should give you a valid sample set of data on which to establish your baseline.

3. Store the data for long-term validation. This data becomes your baseline and should therefore be stored in a safe location.

Taking performance snapshots such as these also affects system performance. The object with the most severe impact on performance is the logical disk object, especially if logical disk counters are enabled. But because this affects snapshots at any time, even with major load changes on the server, the baseline should still be valid.

Deploy the Monitoring Plan

Deploying your monitoring plan will put the finishing touches on your Exchange deployment. When everything is in place, you will be ready and able to host users and run a full messaging system. To deploy your monitoring solution, use the following steps:

1. Identify the selected tool(s).
2. Deploy the tool in a lab environment.
3. Validate all of the objects to monitor as well as monitoring schedules.
4. Train all affected personnel using the lab environment.
5. Deploy the tools used to monitor in the production environment.
6. Establish all baselines from production systems.
7. Establish the monitoring and verification schedule.

Ideally, the monitoring tools you select will be deployed on client workstations and not on servers. Administrators should perform all system tasks from their workstations and use standard user accounts for everyday work. Administrator accounts should be used only when administrative tasks are performed. Use the Run As command in Windows XP or the Run As Administrator command in Windows Vista.

Many monitoring tools are also agentless, which may be the best configuration because it does not add loads to the operation of the servers. However, you should rely on the best practices outlined with the tool to use the best possible configuration.

When this process is in place, you will be ready to run your Exchange infrastructure and make sure it is as healthy as possible on an ongoing basis.

Practice: Define an Exchange Monitoring Plan

In this practice, you will assist the Graphics Design Institute (GDI) in preparing their monitoring strategy for Exchange 2007 when it is implemented. This practice consists of a single exercise. Your job as a messaging professional will be to help GDI understand how to prepare baselines to use as the initial thresholds for measurement.

▶ **Exercise: Plan for the Monitoring of Mailbox Sizes within Exchange Storage Groups**

The Graphics Design Institute is almost ready to finalize their Exchange deployment, but before they do so, they want to make sure they have a proper monitoring solution in place. Because they are running a Simple Organization, they do not want to acquire a third-party monitoring tool; they expect to be satisfied with the standard Exchange toolset. However, they are not familiar enough with Exchange to create the baseline—the sample set of data against which they can validate ongoing performance—and they have asked you, the messaging professional, to assist them. Specifically, they want you to tell them how to establish the baseline.

GDI has decided to rely on the standard tools available within Exchange to monitor their systems. Therefore, to build a baseline to establish monitoring thresholds, GDI should rely on the Exchange Performance Monitor because it is automatically configured to monitor the most important counters related to Exchange service operation. Basically, GDI will need to perform three steps to create their baseline:

1. Identify the resources to be monitored. These include resources such as disk, memory, processor, network, and paging files.

2. Capture the data. Data captures should be run on a regular basis during off hours as well as during peak hours. For GDI, you create the following data capture schedule:

   ❑ Start at 5:00; end at 5:30.

   ❑ Start at 8:00; end at 8:30.

   ❑ Start at 10:00; end at 10:30.

   ❑ Start at 12:00; end at 12:30.

   ❑ Start at 15:00; end at 15:30.

   ❑ Start at 18:00; end at 18:30.

   In addition, you have them run these captures each day for an entire week (seven days). This will give them a valid sample set of data on which to establish their baseline.

3. Have them store the data for long-term validation. This data becomes GDI's baseline and should therefore be stored in a safe location.

When the baseline is established, GDI will need to devise a standard monitoring schedule using the same data sets to ensure that all is working well.

Quick Check

1. Which are the classes of objects and aspects of the Exchange infrastructure you should monitor regularly? Name at least four.
2. What can you verify with the Exchange Server Jetstress tool?
3. Which tool would you use to collect statistical information from either the single mailbox store or the entire organization to analyze performance and health of Mailbox servers?
4. Which kind of scans can you perform when using Exchange Best Practices Analyzer?

Quick Check Answers

1. The classes of objects are:
   - ❑ System performance for each deployed server role
   - ❑ Resource usage on each server in the e-mail infrastructure
   - ❑ Server uptime on a per-role basis
   - ❑ Connections between server roles
   - ❑ Mail transport and mail flow throughout the system
   - ❑ Send and receive message timings
   - ❑ Mail queues both on transport and on mailbox servers
   - ❑ Messaging Records Management operation and updates
   - ❑ Offline Address Book and address list availability
   - ❑ Calendaring and Availability service performance
   - ❑ Public folder replication, management and access
   - ❑ Unified Messaging server access and interactions
2. The Exchange Server Jetstress tool verifies the performance and stability of a disk subsystem and is usually used before the disk system is put into production.
3. The Exchange Server Profile Analyzer.
4. The available scans are: health check, permission check, connectivity test, baseline option, and the Exchange 2007 Readiness check.

Chapter Summary

- You should rely on your periodic task schedule to capture and maintain data about your Exchange implementation. Data such as regular usage levels, peak hours of operation, performance peaks on a per-role basis, potential bottlenecks, and controlled changes will help you get a better overview of the system itself and how it functions.

- When you plan to keep an eye on your Exchange infrastructure, you should begin by preparing your monitoring strategy.

- Monitoring strategies are based on structured approaches and should include the following:
  - Determine what should be monitored.
  - Use Exchange Best Practices Analyzer to determine whether the configuration works properly.
  - Determine which tools should be used for monitoring.
  - Establish the parameters to be monitored.
  - Establish baselines.
  - Document the baselines and establish baseline thresholds.
  - Monitor periodically the entire infrastructure to identify the overall performance levels.

- As part of your monitoring strategy, you should begin with a scan of all of your systems with the Exchange Best Practices Analyzer (BPA) to determine the health of your existing configuration and perform any required modifications.

- To create the baseline, you need to perform three steps:
  - Identify the resources to be monitored.
  - Capture the data.
  - Store the data for long term validation.

- Ideally, the monitoring tools you select will be deployed on client workstations and not on servers.

Case Scenario

In the following case scenario, you will apply what you have learned about Exchange monitoring. You can find answers to the questions in this scenario in the "Answers" section at the end of this book.

Case Scenario: Learn to Rely on Proactive Management

John Kane has just been hired to assist Lucerne Publishing with their Exchange 2007 infrastructure. He meets up with the Exchange administrator, Jeff Price, on a Friday afternoon. At first, John is impressed because the office is very clean and there is no clutter anywhere. After an hour, John begins to notice that the office is very quiet, especially the desks located immediately beside him and Jeff. Phones are not ringing often and Jeff's Blackberry has not gone off once for the entire hour.

After another hour, John is beginning to wonder what is going on. Things are as quiet as ever. Jeff still has not once picked up his Blackberry and the phones still are not ringing. Have they staged this quiet afternoon just for his benefit? How could an entire staff dedicated to Exchange administration be so laid-back, especially on a Friday afternoon when everything should be ringing off the hook as users get ready to leave for the weekend and want to make sure they have access to e-mail from any location? Finally, John cannot take it anymore and asks Jeff point-blank what is going on.

Jeff smiles, and even laughs, as he responds, "Not to worry, John. Lots of people who come to visit us have the same question. I guess we do not have your typical Exchange deployment. In fact, things are like this every day and you can look forward to enjoying exactly the same type of workload as we do when you come on board."

How do you think Lucerne could have defined a deployment where things just work? Which approaches do you think they used to get to this point?

Suggested Practices

It is difficult to practice monitoring Exchange Server without access to a full infrastructure, but you can do so if you prepare a virtual environment as outlined in the Introduction. Rely on all of the virtual machines you created to run through the monitoring strategies detailed in this chapter.

Appendix A

Update for Microsoft Certified IT Professional (MCITP) Enterprise Messaging Administrator: Microsoft Exchange Server 2007 Service Pack 1

— Danielle Ruest and Nelson Ruest

Normally, a service pack does not include new features. Its main purpose is to provide a single source for the correction of known issues with the software it is intended for. But, once in a while, Microsoft must divert from this policy and include significant new features within a service pack. This is the case with Service Pack 1 for Exchange Server 2007.

Exchange 2007 SP1 includes a considerable selection of new features for two reasons:

1. To allow Exchange Server 2007 to run and operate with Windows Server 2008, the latest release of Microsoft's flagship server operating system. Windows Server 2008 is a substantial improvement over Windows Server 2003 because it is based on the latest NT kernel provided within Windows Vista SP1.

MORE INFO **Windows Server 2008**

For detailed information on Windows Server 2008 as well as implementation instructions, see *Windows Server 2008, The Complete Reference* by Ruest and Ruest (McGraw-Hill Osborne, 2008).

---

2. Because Exchange Server 2007 has the distinction of being the first Microsoft product to rely fully on Windows PowerShell as the execution engine for all administrative and operational tasks. This makes Exchange Server 2007 the first of all Microsoft tools to fully integrate automation at the very core of its operational model—you simply run through an operation within the graphical user interface and copy the script the operation generates when it is complete to repeat the same operation on one or one hundred servers in an automated fashion. This

model is very powerful and helps justify the use of a graphical interface in the first place. With Exchange Server 2007, you no longer need to be a scripting expert to automate procedures. Because this model was first introduced in the original release of Exchange Server 2007, Microsoft has increased the interaction between the Exchange Management Console and the Exchange Management Shell in this product's first service pack.

Because of the new features the service pack contains, messaging professionals undertaking any of the exams included within the Microsoft Certified IT Professional (MCITP) Enterprise Messaging Administrator program should take the time to learn and understand the new and changed feature set offered in Exchange Server 2007 Service Pack 1. The exams in this program include:

- Exam 70-236, Technical Specialist: Configuring Exchange Server 2007

- Exam 70-237, PRO: Designing Messaging Solutions with Microsoft Exchange Server 2007

- Exam 70-238. PRO: Deploying Messaging Solutions with Microsoft Exchange Server 2007

Exam Tip   Note that the original exams for this series do not include Service Pack 1 content . This appendix is provided as a source of additional information and serves two specific purposes: First, readers will be able to include Exchange SP1 information in their Exchange deployments moving forward. Second, when Microsoft performs a second pass on exam content and updates the exams to include SP1 content, readers will be able to rely on this appendix to update their skills to include SP1 information. This appendix will serve this purpose whether you undertake one exam or all of the exams within the Enterprise Messaging Administrator certification program.

Table A-1 lists the various exam objectives covered by each of the three exams. Objectives have been regrouped into specific categories to facilitate their organization.

Table A-1   Exchange Enterprise Messaging Administrator Exam Skill Matrix

Skills Measured by the Exam	Exam 70-236	Exam 70-237	Exam 70-238
Prepare Messaging Services			
Configure client connectivity.	☑		
Configure connectors.	☑		
Configure Exchange server roles.	☑		

Table A-1   Exchange Enterprise Messaging Administrator Exam Skill Matrix

Skills Measured by the Exam	Exam 70-236	Exam 70-237	Exam 70-238
Configure mail-enabled groups.	☑		
Configure public folders.	☑		
Configure recipients.	☑		
Configure resource mailboxes.	☑		
Design and plan for new Exchange features.		☑	
Design organization configuration to meet routing requirements.		☑	
Evaluate and plan server deployment based on best practices, budget, and other business factors.		☑	
Evaluate and recommend Active Directory configuration.		☑	
Evaluate network topology and provide technical recommendations.		☑	
Implement bulk management of mail-enabled objects.	☑		
Install Exchange.	☑		
Move mailboxes.	☑		
Plan the deployment of optional Exchange services.			☑
Plan the deployment of required Exchange services.			☑
Plan the server role deployment.			☑
Plan the storage group deployment.			☑
Prepare the infrastructure for Exchange installation.	☑		
Prepare the servers for Exchange installation.	☑		

Table A-1   Exchange Enterprise Messaging Administrator Exam Skill Matrix

Skills Measured by the Exam	Exam 70-236	Exam 70-237	Exam 70-238
Plan for Server High Availability			
Configure backups.	☑		
Configure high availability.	☑		
Define a high availability solution based on client types and client loads.		☑	
Design a disaster recovery, backup, and restore solution.		☑	
Design and recommend a strategy for dependent services that impact high availability.		☑	
Evaluate existing business requirements to define supporting infrastructure.		☑	
Evaluate role availability requirements and design solutions.		☑	
Plan a backup solution implementation.			☑
Plan a data redundancy implementation.			☑
Plan a recovery solution implementation.			☑
Plan the service's high availability implementation.			☑
Recover messaging data.	☑		
Recover server roles.	☑		
Upgrades and Migrations			
Design a migration strategy.		☑	
Design and plan for migration of legacy Exchange features.		☑	

Table A-1 Exchange Enterprise Messaging Administrator Exam Skill Matrix

Skills Measured by the Exam	Exam 70-236	Exam 70-237	Exam 70-238
Plan the Exchange Server 2007 migration implementation.			☑
Plan the Exchange Server 2007 upgrade implementation.			☑
Prepare for Coexistence			
Plan coexistence with Exchange 2000 Server and Exchange Server 2003 in a single organization.			☑
Plan for coexistence (management tools for Exchange Server 2003 and Exchange Server 2007).		☑	
Prepare for Interoperability			
Plan interoperability with Exchange in separate organizations.			☑
Plan interoperability with third-party messaging systems.			☑
Policies and Security Procedures			
Configure policies.	☑		
Configure the antivirus and anti-spam system.	☑		
Configure transport rules and message compliance.	☑		
Design a solution to address regulatory and legal requirements.		☑	
Design procedures for message content filtering.		☑	
Design secure messaging.		☑	
Plan policies to handle unsolicited e-mail and virus outbreaks.		☑	

Table A-1   Exchange Enterprise Messaging Administrator Exam Skill Matrix

Skills Measured by the Exam	Exam 70-236	Exam 70-237	Exam 70-238
Plan the antivirus and anti-spam implementation.			☑
Plan the messaging compliance implementation.			☑
Plan the network layer security implementation.			☑
Plan the transport rules implementation.			☑
Messaging Environment Maintenance			
Plan for change management.			☑
Plan for configuration changes.			☑
Plan for Exchange infrastructure improvements.			☑
Plan for patch and service pack implementation.			☑
Manage, Monitor, and Report			
Create server reports.	☑		
Create usage reports.	☑		
Monitor client connectivity.	☑		
Monitor mail queues.	☑		
Monitor system performance.	☑		
Perform message tracking.	☑		
Plan for monitoring and reporting.			☑

Exchange Service Pack 1 Feature Categories

Exchange Server 2007 Service Pack 1 includes new features that fit within 12 different categories. Each of these new features also fits within the specific categories covered by each of the three exams that make up the Enterprise Messaging Administrator certification program. However, the new features only affect four of the eight exam categories. Affected exam categories include the following. Each new Exchange SP1 feature is assigned to the exam category it affects:

1. Prepare Messaging Services
   - ❑ Exchange ActiveSync Improvements
   - ❑ Outlook Web Access Improvements
   - ❑ Manage POP3 and IMAP4 Protocols
   - ❑ Exchange Web Services Improvements
   - ❑ Transport Server role Improvements
   - ❑ Mailbox Server role Improvements
   - ❑ Unified Messaging Server role Improvements
2. Plan for Server High Availability
   - ❑ High Availability Improvements
3. Upgrades and Migrations
   - ❑ Transition from an Exchange server running Windows Server 2003 to Windows Server 2008
   - ❑ Install Exchange Server 2007 SP1 on Windows Server 2008
   - ❑ Use IPv6 with Exchange Server 2007 SP1
4. Prepare for Coexistence
5. Prepare for Interoperability
6. Policies and Security Procedures
7. Messaging Environment Maintenance
   - ❑ Update to Exchange Server 2007 Service Pack 1
8. Manage, Monitor, and Report

The information in this appendix addresses the specific exam objectives that are affected by the release of Exchange Server 2007 SP1; however, they have been restructured to meet the order in which messaging professionals should approach them.

Messaging Environment Maintenance

For those of you who have already deployed Exchange Server 2007, the first and foremost activity you will need to undertake regarding Service Pack 1 is to evaluate and prepare the upgrade of your Exchange servers to this service pack. Exam 70-238 includes a specific focus on messaging environment maintenance, which includes service pack applications. The affected exam objective is outlined in Table A-2.

Table A-2   Affected Exam Objective

Skills Measured by the Exam	Exam 70-236	Exam 70-237	Exam 70-238
Messaging Environment Maintenance			
Plan for patch and service pack implementation.			☑

Update to Exchange Server 2007 Service Pack 1

The Training Kit for Exam 70-238 outlines a specific structure for the implementation of a service pack within existing Exchange Server 2007 infrastructures. In fact, it outlines a five-step process that helps you manage change in your Exchange infrastructure. This is the process you need to use to move on to Exchange Service Pack 1. It includes the following phases:

- **The Diagnostics Phase**   Identify and describe the unsatisfactory situation the change aims to modify. In this case, you want to apply corrections and fixes to the existing Exchange environment.

- **The Planning Phase**   Define and structure the objectives to be attained. The focus of this phase is to understand the impacts of the coming change. This means you need to perform some level of testing to identify the impact of moving to the service pack.

- **The Engineering Phase**   Prepare the coming change. Perform further tests and outline a specific implementation strategy. This strategy includes detailed steps for the implementation of the service pack.

- **The Execution Phase**   Focus on the implementation or the deployment of the change and ensure that appropriate follow-ups are undertaken throughout this implementation. This is where you apply the change and deploy the service pack.

- **The Evaluation Phase**   Complete the cycle with a complete post-completion review—in fact, a renewed situation review—to ensure that all objectives have been met with minimum impact.

Throughout this change process, you must ensure that key elements of change management are implemented. For example, with regards to the implementation of Service Pack 1, you must ensure that users are informed of the coming change and that administrators and operators are trained in the new features the change will bring.

In addition, when you deploy service packs, you must keep the following items in mind:

- If you have already deployed Exchange 2007, you must plan for a server-by-server update process. If you have not implemented high availability strategies—either because you are not ready to include them in your infrastructure yet or because the size of your organization simply does not warrant them—you will have to plan for service outages. Use one of the following strategies:
  - ❑ If you have high availability strategies in place, rely on the availability of multiple copies of each role to update each system. For HT, ET, and UM systems, you can simply work on one system at a time, taking each one out of production for a short period, updating it, and then putting it back into production. Doing this during off-peak hours will limit the impact on users. Use the same strategy for CAS NLB clusters. For MB Failover Clusters, update the passive node first and then move the service from the active node to the newly updated passive node, update the second node, and continue on until all nodes are updated. Even though the impact will be limited, you must still communicate the upcoming change to end users.
  - ❑ If you do not have an availability strategy in place, you must plan for service outages. Be sure to communicate the update to your users, perform full system backups, and then update your servers.
- If you have not deployed Exchange yet, either obtain code that includes the service pack or use the Microsoft service pack slipstreaming capability to update a copy of the installation code so that you deploy updated code directly without having to perform the update after the installation is complete. Slipstreaming lets you inject new updates into the original installation code to create an updated version of the code.

Whichever situation you find yourself in, be sure to fully test all procedures in the lab before you do anything in production.

MORE INFO   Obtain Service Pack 1

Download Service Pack 1 for Exchange 2007 from *http://www.microsoft.com/downloads/details.aspx? FamilyID=44c66ad6-f185-4a1d-a9ab-473c1188954c&displaylang=en*. Be sure to select the x64 version.

Exchange Server Role Upgrade Order

Microsoft recommends that you upgrade the servers in your Exchange topology in a specific order. Table A-3 outlines the order you should consider using when upgrading servers to Exchange 2007 Service Pack 1. Upgrading servers in this order should avoid potential service outages.

Table A-3   Exchange Server Role Upgrade Order

Server Role to Upgrade	Comments
Management Tool Workstations	■ Workstations that include the Exchange Management Tools can be updated at any time during the upgrade process. You might consider updating them at the very beginning of the process to ensure that you can manage any part of the Exchange infrastructure at all times.
Client Access (CAS)	■ Begin with the CAS role. ■ Begin with CAS systems that are outward-facing or linked to the Internet before you perform the upgrade of inward-facing or intranet CAS systems. For example, say your organization has two Active Directory sites, Site A and Site B. Site A is linked to the Internet and Site B uses a path through Site A to connect to the Internet. You would upgrade the CAS systems in Site A first.
Unified Messaging (UM)	■ Systems running the Unified Messaging role tend to be smaller in number than systems running other Exchange server roles. Because of this, it makes sense to upgrade these systems before the others.
Edge Transport (ET)	■ Servers running the ET role often rely on Edge Subscriptions to obtain information about internal transport servers. If you have an Edge Subscription in place, you must update all transport servers—Edge and Hub—in the same update group. All transport servers must run the same version of Exchange to work. Because of this, all transport servers that participate in Edge Subscriptions must be updated within 15 days of the upgrade of any transport server in your Exchange Organization. If your EdgeSync process runs between ET servers in your perimeter network and HT servers in Site A, update the servers in the perimeter, then the servers in Site A, and then move on to transport servers in other Active Directory sites.

Table A-3   Exchange Server Role Upgrade Order

Server Role to Upgrade	Comments
Hub Transport (HT)	■ Transport servers control the mail flow in your Exchange Organization. Therefore, you want to make sure all systems with this role are updated together as much as possible. You also want to make sure they are updated before the Mailbox server role; otherwise, mail may not be delivered properly. ■ Changes in the credential renewal process used in the EdgeSync process may affect the operation of this process. Therefore, all HT servers must be updated to SP1 together.
Mailbox (MB)	■ MB servers that are not clustered should be updated with care because users will face a temporary service outage. ■ MB servers that are clustered should start with upgrades of the passive node. Make sure the node is completely passive and does not contain any of the cluster groups, even the default cluster group, before you perform the upgrade. Then, to move the service from the active node to the newly updated node, stop all clustered Exchange components, move them, and then start them again. This will incur a service outage, but this outage is much shorter than for Mailbox servers that do not use a high availability strategy.
All-in-one servers (CAS, HT, UM, MB)	■ Shops that run servers with combined roles usually have very few Exchange systems. Update all-in-one servers all at once. The Setup program for Service Pack 1 does not allow you to choose which role to update. All roles are updated together.

Required Permissions for the Upgrade

You will need the following permissions in order to perform the upgrade:

■ Active Directory Schema Administrator to update the Active Directory schema to Exchange SP1.

■ Exchange Organization Administrator to update the first Exchange server in your network. This also updates the entire organization.

- Exchange Server Administrator for every other internal server role after the first server has been updated.

- Local Administrator for each ET server upgrade.

Upgrade Caveats

In addition, keep the following in mind before performing the upgrade:

- You must begin with the preparation of Active Directory before you can upgrade any server within the Exchange Organization. This means updating the forest schema and then each domain in the forest that contains Exchange objects.

- Windows Server 2003 must be updated to Service Pack 2 before you can install Exchange 2007 SP1. Make sure all servers running Exchange roles as well as all domain controllers are updated to this service pack.

- Exchange SP1 does not support uninstallation. To remove SP1 and return to the original release of Exchange 2007, you must remove Exchange and then reinstall the original release version.

- Setup.exe (graphical version) and Setup.com (command-line version) of SP1 must be run from a local resource. Both versions of Setup are .NET Framework applications and therefore require local access to the setup files to perform a trusted operation. If you install from a network share, Setup will first copy all files locally before it upgrades the system. Keep this in mind when you calculate available space for the upgrades.

- If you have third-party applications that support Exchange operations, such as an antivirus engine installed on your systems, you must disable them prior to the upgrade. Make sure you enable them as soon as the upgrade is complete.

IMPORTANT Third-party applications and SP1

You should check with your vendor to ensure that the third-party application you are running is compatible with Exchange 2007 SP1. For example, the original version of Microsoft Forefront Security for Exchange does not work with Exchange 2007 SP1 and must be upgraded to the latest version before you can upgrade Exchange.

- Exchange 2007 SP1 will not work within a network that relies solely on single-label DNS names. For example, with Windows Server 2008, you can replace the Windows Internet Naming Service (WINS)—the original single-label naming service for Windows networks—with DNS GlobalNames Zones (GNZ). If your network uses single-label DNS names—names that do not end in .com, .net, .biz, or other suffixes—Exchange SP1 will not work.

- Updating clustered Mailbox Server roles must be performed through the command-line version of Setup.

- After SP1 is installed, you must use SP1 Setup to add or remove a server role on an Exchange server. In previous releases, you added the role with the original setup and then ran the service pack installation again. With Exchange 2007, the setup for the service pack replaces the original installation logic.

As you can see, Exchange 2007 SP1 changes many aspects of the Exchange installation process.

Perform the Exchange Upgrade

With SP1, the Exchange service pack upgrade involves three major phases:

1. Active Directory updates.

2. Exchange Organization updates, which are performed through the update of the first Exchange server.

3. Exchange server updates, which include any Exchange server after the first server has been updated.

The procedure for each is outlined in the following section. Make sure you download and expand the appropriate version of the Exchange Service Pack file before you proceed. You can expand these files to a network share, but remember that Setup will copy them locally to perform the update. Therefore, it is best to copy the expanded files to the server you want to update before you proceed.

Upgrade the Active Directory Forest

To perform the Active Directory update, you must be a logged on as a member of the Schema Administrators group, and then complete the following steps:

1. Because Exchange service pack binaries are in x64 format, you must log on to a 64-bit installation of Windows Server 2003 to run the Active Directory preparation commands. You can, of course, download the x86 version of the service pack, but this means downloading two different files. Instead, log on to an x64 computer with Schema Administrator credentials. Ideally, this computer will also include Exchange 2007 because the Exchange prerequisites are required for the service pack installation.

2. Load the Exchange 2007 service pack media into the DVD reader of the server or copy it to a folder on a disk drive, open a command prompt, and change to the drive containing the update. Make sure the core prerequisites for Exchange—.NET Framework 2.0, MMC 3.0, and Windows PowerShell—are already available on this computer.

3. If you downloaded the service pack, expand the service pack media by double-clicking the service pack executable and extracting the files to a new folder on a local drive. Name the folder **EX07SP1**.

4. After the files are extracted, open a command prompt and change to the EX07SP1 folder.

5. Type the following commands. Wait for the completion of each command and verify its results before moving on to the next one.

    ```
    setup /PrepareSchema
    setup /PrepareAD
    setup /PrepareDomain
    ```

    You do not need to indicate the name of the Exchange Organization in the /**PrepareAD** command because the organization already exists.

6. You can also prepare all domains in a forest with a single command, but be sure you have high-speed links to each domain for the command to work:

    ```
    setup /PrepareAllDomains
    ```

7. If you do not use the /PrepareAllDomains switch and more than one domain in your network will host Exchange server roles, you must repeat the **Setup /PrepareDomain** command in each domain.

Your Active Directory Forest is ready to run Exchange SP1. You can now proceed to updating your server installations.

Update the First Exchange Server in the Organization

Now that your Active Directory is ready to host Exchange services, you can install your first Exchange server. You perform this installation on any server that hosts internal Exchange server roles. Ideally, this computer will be located in the Active Directory site that is connected to the Internet and it will host the Client Access Server role.

1. Log on to the Exchange server computer using Exchange Organization Administrator credentials. Stop all third-party services, including the antivirus engine.

2. If you have not already done so, copy the expanded Exchange 2007 SP1 files to a local drive. Change to the EX07SP1 folder and double-click Setup.exe.

3. This screen will list three options (see Figure A-1):

    ❑ *Plan* will lead you to more information on Exchange 2007 SP1.

    ❑ *Install* will upgrade your Exchange installation.

❑ *Enhance* will let you install Forefront Security for Exchange Server. Remember: if you are running Forefront Security for Exchange, you must update this component and then stop it before you can run the Exchange Service Pack update.

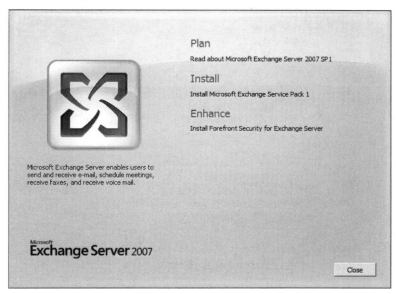

Figure A-1   Running Exchange 2007 Service Pack 1 setup

4. Click Install Microsoft Exchange Service Pack 1. This opens the Introduction screen. Click Next.

5. Accept the License Agreement and click Next. Choose how you want to report errors to Microsoft and click Next.

6. Exchange then runs the readiness checks for the service pack. If any test fails, click Cancel to cancel the installation and then confirm the cancellation. Perform the corrective action and relaunch Setup. Run through steps 1 through 6 again. If no test fails, click Upgrade.

7. Exchange begins the installation of the service pack and displays progress information in the graphical interface. The upgrade prepares Setup, removes existing Exchange files, copies new files, updates each role on the server as well as the Management Tools, and then finalizes the update (see Figure A-2). Click Finish when done and click Close to close the SP Setup window when it reappears.

There you are. Your first Exchange server has been updated to Exchange 2007 SP1.

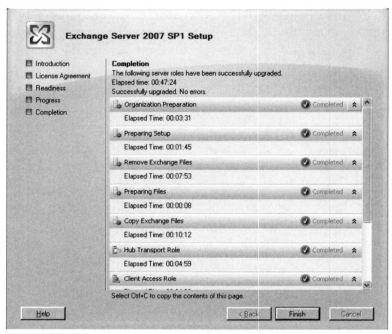

Figure A-2   Completing the Exchange Service Pack 1 update

Update Other Exchange Servers and Management Workstations in the Organization

Now that your Active Directory Forest and the first Exchange server have been updated, you can proceed to the update of all other servers in the organization. Use the recommendations provided earlier in Table A-3 to choose an upgrade order for all server roles.

Remember that you will need Exchange Server Administrator credentials to update the servers within your Active Directory Forest, and you will need Local Administrator credentials for all of the Edge Server roles in your perimeter network.

Your update is complete when all Exchange 2007 servers, as well as all client workstations that include the Management Tools, have been updated.

Upgrades and Migrations

Another potential process organizations that have already deployed Exchange will face is the upgrade of your server operating systems from Windows Server 2003 to Windows Server 2008. This process also involves the evaluation and preparation of a deployment using Exchange 2007 Service Pack 1 because this is the only version of

Exchange 2007 that will run on the new version of Microsoft's new server operating system. The affected exam objectives are outlined in Table A-4.

Table A-4   Affected Exam Objectives

Skills measured by the Exam	Exam 70-236	Exam 70-237	Exam 70-238
Upgrades and Migrations			
Design a migration strategy.		☑	
Design and plan for migration of legacy Exchange features.		☑	
Plan the Exchange Server 2007 upgrade implementation.			☑

Organizations may want to run Exchange Server 2007 on Windows Server 2008 for several reasons. For example, the original release of Exchange 2007 provides minimal support for digital rights management (DRM), but Exchange Server 2007 Service Pack 1 includes much more. This is because Microsoft has updated its DRM engine in Windows Server 2008. In Windows Server 2008, DRM is provided by Active Directory Rights Management Services (AD RMS). As such, the new AD RMS Prelicensing client is now installed by default on Hub Transport servers that run SP1. If not all of your servers are running Windows Server 2008, you need to update them to the Windows Rights Management Services Client with Service Pack 2 to work properly with AD RMS.

In addition, Windows Server 2008 offers a host of new features and services that make it a compelling platform for security-conscious organizations. For example, the inclusion of built-in Network Access Protection (NAP) features lets you protect your network from connections by unhealthy systems and can help remediate this unhealthy state before a connection is authorized. Windows Server 2008 also offers full support for IPv6, the next version of the TCP/IP protocol.

These are only a few of the reasons why you might opt for Exchange Server 2007 running on Windows Server 2008.

Transition from an Exchange Server Running Windows Server 2003 to Windows Server 2008

Just as there is no direct upgrade path from any of the legacy versions of Exchange Server to Exchange Server 2007, there is no direct upgrade path for servers running Exchange

Server 2007 on Windows Server 2003 to Windows Server 2008. First of all, Exchange Server 2007 must include Service Pack 1 to run or install on Windows Server 2008. Second, Microsoft does not support the upgrade of a server running Exchange 2007 on Windows Server 2003 to Windows Server 2008. This means that you must use the standard transition process to move from an organization running Exchange 2007 on Windows Server 2003 to Exchange 2007 SP1 running on Windows Server 2008.

The process is as follows:

1. Begin by installing an x64 version of Windows Server 2008 on a new server. You cannot use Server Core—the new minimalist version of Windows Server 2008—to run Exchange Server. You must use the full installation of Windows Server 2008 because Server Core does not support the core prerequisites for Exchange: the .NET Framework, MMC version 3, and Windows PowerShell.

2. Use a version of Exchange 2007 that includes SP1 to install Exchange onto the Windows Server 2008 server.

3. After the new Exchange server is installed, use the **move-mailbox** cmdlet to move mailboxes from your existing Exchange 2007 on Windows Server 2003 servers to the new Exchange 2007 SP1 server on Windows Server 2008.

4. Repeat this process until all existing Exchange servers have been migrated to Windows Server 2008 with SP1.

5. Decommission all Windows Server 2003 versions of your Exchange servers when all services and mailbox content have been transitioned to the new infrastructure.

Rely on the Transition sections of each of the Exchange Server Training Kits to identify the actual steps to use for each operation.

Install Exchange Server 2007 SP1 on Windows Server 2008

In other circumstances, you may decide to move directly to Exchange Server 2007 SP1 running on Windows Server 2008 when you create a new Exchange Organization. Because—just like the move from any legacy version of Exchange—the move from Windows Server 2003 to Windows Server 2008 involves a transition, you might consider moving directly to the latest platform to reduce your workload. However, this option has some effects:

- If you create an infrastructure based on Windows Server 2008 and Exchange 2007 SP1, you will not have the required environment for the practices or for the support of your preparation for each exam—at least, not until Microsoft updates the corresponding exams. The differences between Exchange 2007 on Windows

Server 2003 and Exchange 2007 SP1 on Windows Server 2008 are significant enough to affect your performance on the exams.

■ As you know, you cannot install the original release of Exchange Server 2007 on Windows Server 2008 because it is not supported by Microsoft. Support for Windows Server 2008 is only available in Exchange 2007 Service Pack 1.

■ If you are currently running Windows NT and Exchange 5.5, you may be best off moving directly from Windows NT Server to Windows Server 2008 and creating new networks based on the very latest operating system Microsoft has to offer. This should stabilize your environments and last you almost as long as your NT and Exchange 5.5 implementations have lasted. If you decide to do so, you will need to implement Exchange 2007 with Service Pack 1 because the original release of Exchange 2007 does not run on Windows Server 2008.

■ If you are running Windows Vista as a client and you need access to the Management Tools, you will need to run Exchange Server 2007 with SP1. Exchange 2007 with Service Pack 1 supports both new platforms: Windows Vista and Windows Server 2008. For client tools, you can install either the x86 or the x64 version of Exchange.

■ If your organization includes Windows 2000 domain controllers (DC), you can rely directly on the graphical setup of Exchange Server 2007 with SP1. Before SP1, you had to run the Active Directory setup portions of the Exchange installation through the command line when Windows 2000 domain controllers were present and specify the /DomainController switch. If you are deploying Exchange 2007 with SP1 in an environment running Windows 2000 DCs, you can use the graphical setup tool because you no longer need to specify this parameter.

■ If you are deploying a new Exchange Organization, you should deploy Exchange 2007 SP1 on either Windows Server 2003 or Windows Server 2008. Since its release, Exchange 2007 has had numerous update releases. If you have not implemented Exchange 2007 yet, you should make sure you deploy Exchange 2007 with Service Pack 1 instead of relying on the original release of the product. Service Pack 1 adds considerable functionality to Exchange.

If you decide to install Exchange 2007 SP1 on Windows Server 2008, you should rely on the installation instructions included in the Training Kits for Exchange because the installation process has not changed.

MORE INFO   **Preparing to install Exchange 2007 SP1 on Windows Server 2008**

For information on preparing the Exchange Server 2007 SP1 prerequisites on Windows Server 2008, go to *http://technet.microsoft.com/en-us/library/bb124558.aspx*.

Use IPv6 with Exchange Server 2007 SP1

The original version of Exchange Server 2007 will only work with an IPv4 addressing scheme. To support IPv6, you need to deploy Exchange Server 2007 with Service Pack 1 and run it on Windows Server 2008. Most organizations will deploy Exchange initially on Windows Server 2003 with IPv4.

Any organization deploying Windows Server 2008 with Exchange 2007 SP1 will also automatically have access to IPv6 because it is installed by default with the operating system. Deploying IPv6 is considerably different than deploying IPv4. For one thing, you must make sure all your network infrastructure services will support IPv6. This means routers, switches, network intrusion detection systems, and any other component that is part of your overall network layer services.

In addition, Microsoft recommends against configuring Receive connectors to accept anonymous IPv6 connections from unknown sources. If you need to receive mail from IPv6 sources, configure a specific Receive connector that is bound to the source addresses of these senders. This will help protect you from potentially harmful messages transported over this carrier. This is a cumbersome method for the user of these Receive connectors because you must first communicate with your sender to obtain the address, and then add the address to a specific Receive connector. Because IPv6 adoption is still in its infancy and as yet no standards exist for its use for message delivery, you should put this manual verification process in place. This also means that while you are using IPv6, you will have to communicate with any potential recipients of messages from your organization to tell them the address of your sending servers.

Keep in mind, however, that most organizations implementing IPv6 will also continue to use IPv4 for a transition period. With Service Pack 1, you can also configure connectors to support IPv6 if the Hub Transport (HT) computer is running Windows Server 2008. In this configuration, you can support IPv4, IPv6, or both. Using both will help you transition from one to the other.

IMPORTANT   Exchange 2007 SP1 and IPv6

Exchange 2007 SP1 will only work with IPv6 on Windows Server 2008, not Windows Server 2003, even though you can add the protocol to this operating system. In addition, you must run both IPv6 and IPv4 for Exchange to operate. If you remove the IPv4 protocol, Exchange will stop working. Make sure you keep both protocols active in your Windows Server 2008 configurations.

Currently, there is no broadly accepted industry standard protocol for looking up IPv6 addresses. In addition, most IP Block List providers do not support IPv6 addresses.

Therefore, if you decide to move to IPv6, you will have to work closely with your IP Block List provider to ensure that IPv6 addresses are included in their lists.

As you can see, it may still be early to begin implementing IPv6 with Exchange 2007 SP1.

MORE INFO   Running IPv6 with Exchange 2007 SP1 on Windows Server 2008

For information on running IPv6 with Exchange Server 2007 SP1 on Windows Server 2008, go to *http://technet.microsoft.com/en-us/library/bb629624.aspx*.

Prepare Messaging Services

Exchange Server 2007 has the distinction of being the first Microsoft product to rely fully on Windows PowerShell as the execution engine for all administration tasks. That made it the first of all Microsoft tools to fully integrate automation at the very core of its operational model, and it is even better in SP1 because many more operations have been added to the Exchange Management Console. These changes affect several different aspects of Exchange operation. The affected exam objectives are outlined in Table A-5.

Table A-5   Affected Exam Objectives

Skills Measured by the Exam	Exam 70-236	Exam 70-237	Exam 70-238
Prepare Messaging Services			
Configure client connectivity.	☑		
Configure connectors.	☑		
Configure Exchange server roles.	☑		
Configure mail-enabled groups.	☑		
Configure public folders.	☑		
Configure recipients.	☑		
Design and plan for new Exchange features.		☑	
Design organization configuration to meet routing requirements.		☑	
Evaluate and plan server deployment based on best practices, budget, and other business factors.		☑	

Table A-5 **Affected Exam Objectives**

Skills Measured by the Exam	Exam 70-236	Exam 70-237	Exam 70-238
Prepare Messaging Services			
Plan the deployment of optional Exchange services.			☑
Plan the deployment of required Exchange services.			☑
Plan the server role deployment.			☑
Plan the storage group deployment.			☑

Exchange ActiveSync Improvements

Client access is one of the most important parts of the configuration of Exchange Server. If clients cannot access their mailboxes, administrators will be the first to know and will be told in no uncertain terms what the client thinks of their administrative skills. It is therefore always best to be proactive and make sure client access always works.

With this in mind, Microsoft has included the following changes in the ActiveSync feature of the Client Access Server role:

- A default policy is created for ActiveSync. In the release version of Exchange 2007, no such policy was created. And, once created, the new policy had to be manually assigned to all users. Now, the policy is created by default at the installation of the CAS feature and automatically assigned to all users. Because an ActiveSync policy is necessary for the use of this feature, this is one additional step administrators will not need to plan for. You should, however, plan to review and potentially modify the contents of this default policy.

- New ActiveSync policy settings have been integrated in SP1. For example, you can control mobile device settings such as locking the use of remote storage devices, locking the use of the camera, turning Wi-Fi on or off, blocking Internet sharing, or even blocking the use of mail services such as POP/IMAP and making sure users only access Exchange mailboxes. In fact, three new tabs have been added to the policy settings Property dialog box: Sync Settings, Device, and Advanced. Sync Settings controls how messages are synchronized to the device. Device controls specific device components (see Figure A-3). Advanced controls which applications are allowed or blocked on the device.

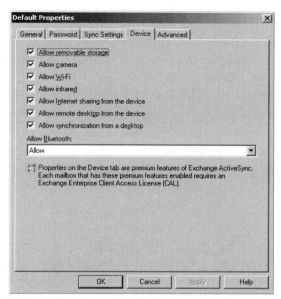

Figure A-3   The new Default Properties dialog box for ActiveSync policy

- ActiveSync includes the ability to remotely wipe the contents of a lost or stolen mobile device. In the release version of Exchange 2007, no confirmation was sent when you used this feature. In SP1, a new confirmation e-mail message has been added to ensure that when you do wipe devices, they have been wiped. Users can wipe devices through Outlook Web Access; administrators can do so through the Exchange Management Console. If a user initiates the wipe, he or she receives a confirmation e-mail. If the administrator initiates the wipe, the confirmation e-mail is sent to both the administrator and the affected user.

- Direct Push—the ability to automatically receive messages on a mobile device as soon as the message arrives in the inbox—has been enhanced to improve performance. In fact, the amount of information sent during Direct Push connections has been reduced, thereby reducing the length of the Internet connection required for updates.

These changes are implemented mostly through the Exchange Management Console. You can review them by going to the appropriate locations. Rely on the original Training Kit to identify these locations.

MORE INFO   **ActiveSync improvements**

For more information on ActiveSync improvements in SP1, go to
http://technet.microsoft.com/en-us/library/bb684907.aspx.

Outlook Web Access Improvements

Outlook Web Access (OWA) is one of the most powerful client access features in Exchange 2007. As you know, OWA comes in two flavors: OWA Light and OWA Premium. OWA Light was designed to minimize the footprint accessing Exchange information can leave on a computer. But, because OWA Light was designed with high security in mind, it had a tendency to time out when users were typing in long messages. Because of the duration of the operation, OWA Light would log off the user, thinking there was no activity. As you can imagine, this was not well received by users. In SP1, Microsoft has changed the behavior of OWA Light so that it monitors activity and does not simply assume that because activity is light, no one is at the terminal. In addition, messages are saved to the Drafts folder so that they can be recovered if the session times out anyway.

But the biggest change to OWA in SP1 involves OWA Premium. Microsoft added several additional features to OWA Premium with Service Pack 1. Using these features, users can:

- Recover deleted items.
- View calendar months.
- Control personal distribution lists.
- Create and manage server-side rules.
- View Microsoft Office Word 2007, Microsoft Office Excel 2007, and Microsoft Office PowerPoint 2007 documents in WebReady Document Viewing. This has limitations, however. Smart Art graphics will not display properly, many chart graphics will not display properly, equations cannot be seen in Office Word 2007 documents, and some shapes will not appear in Office PowerPoint 2007. In addition, documents are not indexed and cannot be searched unless you have updated the Exchange Search Service with the filters for the 2007 Microsoft Office system. To obtain these filters and the procedure to install them, look up Microsoft Knowledge Base article 944516 at *http://support.microsoft.com/kb/944516*.
- Recover messages from the dumpster using Recover Deleted Items.
- Use S/MIME to protect message contents, letting users view and send encrypted e-mails. Note that to use S/MIME on shared or kiosk computers, the user must run Internet Explorer with local administrator credentials. Because of this limitation, it is unlikely that users will be able to access this feature through shared or kiosk computers because by default, these computer types are completely locked down.

- Work with public folders. Note that users should access OWA through the /owa virtual folder to access this feature. Also, no legacy Exchange servers are required for this feature to work because it is integrated directly within the Exchange 2007 Mailbox server.

- Move or copy items through context menus.

- Work with custom message types and with custom applications integrated directly into OWA.

As you can see, these features mostly affect user interaction with OWA and have little impact on how administrators need to manage the OWA feature itself.

MORE INFO   OWA improvements

For more information on OWA improvements in SP1, go to *http://technet.microsoft.com/en-us/library /bb684907.aspx.*

Manage POP3 and IMAP4 Protocols

The release version of Exchange included limited management capabilities for the POP3 and IMAP4 protocols. In SP1, Microsoft has added more controls in the Exchange Management Console to simplify the management of these two protocols through the graphical interface and, correspondingly, generate Exchange Management Shell scripts for later user.

You can now configure port settings to include either Transport Layer Security (TLS) or Secure Sockets Layer (SSL) encryption. The Console also lets you configure settings such as logon type and certificate name for authentication. You can now control time-out values and maximum number of connections as well as configure message and calendar retrieval settings for users of these protocols.

To manage these settings, first enable the service—either POP3, IMAP4, or both—by setting the respective service to automatic start and starting the service in Computer Management. Then, switch to the Exchange Management Console and expand the Server Configuration | Client Access node. Click POP3 and IMAP4 in the lower part of the details pane and select the service you want to configure. Then, either right-click the service name to choose Properties or click Properties in the Action pane under the service's name. The result is a new dialog box with five tabs (see Figure A-4). Browsing through these tabs will give you access to all of the new configuration settings. Note that each time you change the configuration of the service, you must recycle or stop and restart it manually.

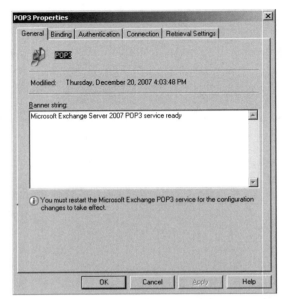

Figure A-4 Configuring POP3 settings in the Exchange Management Console

---

MORE INFO   POP3 and IMAP4 management improvements

For more information on POP3 and IMAP4 management improvements in SP1, go to
http://technet.microsoft.com/en-us/library/bb684907.aspx.

Exchange Web Services Improvements

Because of the changes in the client access features included in SP1, Microsoft has also
improved the Exchange Web Services application programming interface (API). For
example, developers can now access the improved public folder features through this
API. This means that you can now control public folders discretely and programmat-
ically, letting you integrate their features into your Exchange applications. The API
also provides new support for the following:

- Management of delegates within Exchange and better access for delegates
  themselves
- Folder permission controls
- Automatic redirection to the most responsive Client Access server for proxy
  access to Exchange features

These features support better programming and integration with Exchange 2007.

MORE INFO   Web Services improvements

For more information on Exchange 2007 Web Services improvements in SP1, go to *http://msdn2.microsoft.com/en-us/exchange/default.aspx.*

Transport Server Role Improvements

Service Pack 1 includes a series of improvements in terms of transport functionality. These improvements are focused on two different aspects of this functionality. The first improves basic transport functionality and affects the core transport service. The second affects message processing and routing and is specifically focused on the Hub Transport Server role.

Core Transport Improvements

Core transport improvements are focused on two components:

- Back pressure in the transport mechanism. Back pressure basically monitors resource utilization on the transport servers (Edge and Hub). Back pressure will stop accepting new connections or messages if critical resources such as memory and disk space are too low. To increase transport server responsiveness, Microsoft has decreased the fixed constant the back pressure algorithm uses to calculate required free disk space from 4 gigabytes (GB) to 500 megabytes (MB).

  MORE INFO   Back pressure

  For more information on back pressure, go to *http://technet.microsoft.com/en-us/library/ bb201658.aspx.*

- Management and configuration of core transport functionality. In fact, Microsoft has added functionality to the Exchange Management Console so that you can rely on it to configure transport settings instead of having to rely exclusively on the Exchange Management Shell.

  MORE INFO   Transport configuration

  For more information on transport feature configuration, go to *http://technet.microsoft.com/ en-us/library/aa997166.aspx.*

These two changes will make it easier to manage transport servers as well as improve the quality of service you can expect from this critical Exchange 2007 role.

Message Processing and Routing Improvements

Processing and routing improvements are addressed in both the Hub and the Edge Transport roles. Changes are more significant in the HT server than in the ET server, however. The Edge Transport feature improvements are mostly limited to changes in two Exchange Management Shell cmdlets:

- You can now run the **Start-EdgeSynchronization** cmdlet remotely by using the *-Server* parameter.

- The **Test-EdgeSynchronization** cmdlet lets you now use the *-VerifyRecipient* parameter to test synchronization results for individual users.

Each of these changes improves your ability to validate Edge Subscriptions between your ET and HT servers.

MORE INFO   **The EdgeSync process**

For more information on the EdgeSync process, go to *http://technet.microsoft.com/en-us/library/bb232180.aspx.*

But the biggest improvement of transport features addresses the Hub Transport role. For example, before Service Pack 1, Exchange 2007 did not support setting maximum message size limits on Active Directory IP site links or routing group connectors that relied on HT systems as either source or destination servers. Therefore, Exchange 2007 also did not recognize message size limits set on routing group connectors by earlier versions of Exchange. When a message was sent from Exchange 2007 to legacy versions of Exchange, it could be reevaluated for delivery by the legacy systems and, because of existing restrictions, could be sent back to the Exchange 2007 server. This could cause message loops and result in the message never being delivered.

Therefore, Microsoft recommended that all message size restrictions be removed from every routing connector in the organization when Exchange 2007 is installed along with legacy Exchange servers. Now you can use the **Set-ADSiteLink** cmdlet along with the *-MaxMessageSize* parameter to restrict the maximum size of messages relayed between Active Directory sites. The *-MaxMessageSize* parameter is also now included in the **New-RoutingGroupConnector** and the **Set-RoutingGroupConnector** cmdlets to let you correct the potential message loops that could be caused in the release version of Exchange 2007 when coexisting with legacy servers.

Also, before Service Pack 1, Exchange 2007 did not recognize non-SMTP connectors as routing connectors. They were always ignored when routing path calculations were made. Now non-SMTP connectors can be part of any Exchange configuration. In addition, Exchange 2007 SP1 supports the use of X.400 authoritative domains and X.400 long addresses. Keep in mind, however, that Exchange 2007 must either rely on an Exchange 2003 server or a third-party connector to route to X.400 message transfer agents (MTAs).

MORE INFO X.400 improvements

For more information on X.400 improvements in SP1, go to *http://technet.microsoft.com/en-us/library/bb676307.aspx.*

Exchange 2007 SP1 also supports priority queuing. In the original release of Exchange 2007, all messages were treated with the same priority. As you can imagine, this was less than optimal behavior: Messages assigned with a High priority were treated in exactly the same manner by HT servers as messages with a Low priority setting. Now in SP1, HT servers can properly recognize the priority rating users assign to messages and process them according to their relative importance.

MORE INFO Priority queuing

For more information on priority queuing in SP1, go to *http://technet.microsoft.com/en-us/library/bb691107.aspx.*

In some cases, you may want to create Send connectors that are limited to a specific Active Directory site. In the release version of Exchange 2007, you did not have this option, but in SP1, not only can you scope a connector to a single site, but the scoping operation is also greatly simplified. A new option is available in the Exchange Management Console through a check box item on connector properties (see Figure A-5) and you can use a new option, the *-IsScopedConnector*, with the connector cmdlets in the Exchange Management Shell.

Finally, changes have been made to transport rules behavior in SP1. Two additional message types—Unified Messaging and IPM.Note.—are now supported in Exchange 2007 Service Pack 1. The first change is self-explanatory and lets you apply messaging rules to the Unified Message type including voice mail, fax messages, and missed call notifications. The second change refers to programmatic messages or messages and forms generated by applications programmed through the Exchange Web Services API. This extends the control of messages to all of the message types controlled by Exchange 2007.

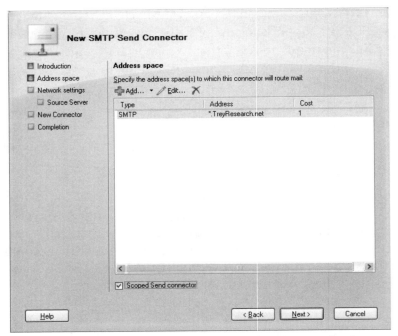

Figure A-5 Setting the Scoped Connector option on a new Send connector

In addition, when dealing with rules for content protection, you might want to consider the use of digital rights management (DRM). The original release of Exchange 2007 provides minimal support for DRM, but Exchange Server 2007 Service Pack 1 includes much more. This is because Microsoft has updated its DRM engine with the preparation of Windows Server 2008. In Windows Server 2008, DRM is provided by Active Directory Rights Management Services (AD RMS). As such, the new AD RMS Prelicensing client is now installed by default on Hub Transport servers that run SP1. If, however, not all of your servers are running Windows Server 2008, you will need to update them to the Windows Rights Management Services Client with Service Pack 2 to work properly with AD RMS. Obtain this client from *http://www.microsoft.com/downloads/details .aspx?FamilyId=02DA5107-2919-414B-A5A3-3102C7447838&displaylang=en.*

MORE INFO   Transport server improvements

For more information on transport server improvements in SP1, go to *http://technet.microsoft.com/ en-us/library/bb684905.aspx*.

Mailbox Server Role Improvements

Several changes have also been applied to the Mailbox (MB) Server role. As mentioned earlier, in the section on Client Access servers, new features have been added in support of public folders. For example, you can now manage public folder referral strategies through the Exchange Management Console. In the original release, all referral management capabilities were reserved to the Exchange Management Shell.

SP1 also sports three new features for public folder management:

- A new Public Folder Administrator group that now lets you delegate public folder management.

- Mail-enabled public folders now appear properly in address lists, e-mail address policies, and in group memberships.

- A new Public Folder Management Console (PFMC), which is located in the Exchange Server Toolbox under the Configuration Tools section and includes the ability to create, configure, and generally manage public folders through a graphical interface (see Figure A-6).

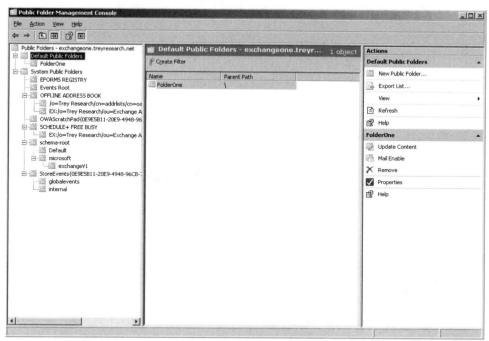

Figure A-6   Managing public folders through the graphical interface

In fact, the Exchange Toolbox includes several new tools in addition to the PFMC:

- Under Configuration Tools, the Details Templates Editor lets you graphically manage and edit details templates in any of the supported languages. Default details templates include the Search Dialog as well as the User, Group, Public Folder, Mailbox Agent, and Contact dialog boxes.
- Under Mail Flow Tools, the Routing Log Viewer lets you examine routing table logs through the graphical interface. This tool lets you view log contents from any server in the organization.

These tools also add to your ability to control your Exchange Organization.

Mailbox management has also been improved. For example, you can now import and export mailboxes through the use of .pst files. This makes it easier to transport mailbox contents as well as recover content when you move from POP3, IMAP4, or non-Exchange messaging systems. In addition, you can now create mailboxes for multiple users in one single operation by selecting each new mailbox user within the New Mailbox Wizard (see Figure A-7). The Exchange Management Console also includes two new wizards. The Manage Full Access Permission Wizard lets you graphically

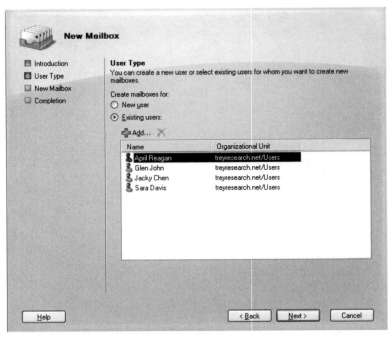

Figure A-7   Creating mailboxes for several users at once

grant or remove Full Access permissions on mailboxes. The Manage Send As Permission Wizard lets you manage Send As permissions through a graphical interface. These new tools simplify mailbox management.

One change that affects licensing more than mailbox functionality regards Exchange managed folders and Message Records Management (MRM). To manage default or custom folders in the original release of Exchange 2007, you needed the Enterprise client access license (CAL). With Service Pack 1, you still need the Enterprise CAL to create custom managed folders, but now you can manage default folders with the Standard CAL. Also, the **Set-Mailbox** cmdlet includes a new parameter, *-RemoveManagedFolderAndPolicy*, which lets you quickly and easily remove MRM policies from any mailbox.

Microsoft has also modified the journaling feature. As part of your journaling security strategy, you should ensure that all connections are secure. In fact, you should set the mailbox to accept messages only from itself. You can only do this with the Exchange Management Shell. In the release version of Exchange, you had to use the following cmdlet, where *JournalingMailbox* is the name of the mailbox to configure:

```
Set-Mailbox JournalingMailbox -AcceptMessagesOnlyFrom JournalingMailbox
-RequireSenderAuthenticationEnabled $True
```

In Exchange 2007 SP1, you can change this cmdlet to set Exchange as the authenticated sender:

```
Set-Mailbox JournalingMailbox -AcceptMessagesOnlyFrom "Microsoft Exchange"
-RequireSenderAuthenticationEnabled $True
```

This simplifies the application of the secure connection to your journaling mailbox.

Finally, new information has been added for mailbox database online defragmentation. Event 703 in the Event Log includes additional information that makes it easier to identify defragmentation pass completions. In addition, the Performance Monitor includes new counters for Extensible Storage Engine (ESE) monitoring.

MORE INFO   **Mailbox server improvements**

For more information on Mailbox server improvements in SP1, go to *http://technet.microsoft.com/en-us/library/bb684903.aspx*.

Unified Messaging Server Role Improvements

Unified Messaging is a new role added to the Exchange infrastructure with the release of Exchange 2007. In Service Pack 1, the UM role has been enhanced significantly. As you know, many of the features for the UM role are not available unless you also deploy the Microsoft Office Communications Server 2007 (MOCS) in your network. Feature updates are therefore listed in two sections. The first section lists updates that do not require MOCS; the second section lists features that require MOCS to function properly.

Exam Tip   Remember that the original versions of the three Exchange exams do not include questions on Unified Messaging. In fact, none of the exam objectives mentions Unified Messaging (see Table A-1). Therefore, unless Microsoft changes the exam objectives when they update the exams to include Service Pack 1 information, you can expect that the exams will continue to exclude the Unified Messaging role. You should, however, rely on Table A-1 to verify that the exam objectives have not changed before you prepare to take the updated exams so that you will not be caught unawares.

New features that are enabled without the deployment of MOCS include:

■ Exchange Management Console improvements for configuring dial plans that rely on mutual TLS. Other improvements include the ability to add Session Initiation Protocol (SIP) or E.164 addresses to user accounts through the Enable Unified Messaging Wizard and the ability to modify extension numbers for both values after the user has been UM-enabled.

■ UM supports the Secure Realtime Transport Protocol (SRTP), which provides better communications security.

■ UM supports Quality of Service (QoS), which lets you guarantee better communications throughput during the use of UM features.

■ UM can now properly detect inband fax tones when using IP PBXs. This lets UM properly detect the type of call coming into the infrastructure. Without this feature, the UM role relies on the IP PBX or the IP gateway to properly detect the type of incoming call.

New features that require the deployment of MOCS include:

■ Microsoft Office Communicator improvements such as the ability to access Outlook Voice Access directly without the use of a personal identification number (PIN) as well as more control of voice messages. In addition, Office Communicator can now receive missed call notifications. Play on Phone calls are also now exempt from call-forwarding rules.

■ New logic for resolving internal calling numbers.

■ The ability to leave notices when a call is being sent to a location that already includes call forwarding.

- Better voice recording quality.
- Support for media streams that traverse firewalls.

All of these features provide significant improvements to the UM role.

MORE INFO   **Unified Messaging server improvements**

For more information on Unified Messaging server improvements in SP1, go to *http://technet.microsoft.com/en-us/library/bb691398.aspx*.

Plan for Server High Availability

Perhaps the most significant feature update in Exchange 2007 Service Pack 1 is the feature set that deals with high availability. High availability changes affect several server roles, but the role most affected is the Mailbox Server role. Rely on Table A-6 to identify the exam objectives affected by these changes.

Table A-6   **Affected Exam Objectives**

Skills Measured by the Exam	Exam 70-236	Exam 70-237	Exam 70-238
Plan for Server High Availability			
Configure high availability.	☑		
Define a high availability solution based on client types and client loads.		☑	
Design and recommend a strategy for dependent services that impact high availability.		☑	
Evaluate existing business requirements to define supporting infrastructure.		☑	
Evaluate role availability requirements and design solutions.		☑	
Plan a data redundancy implementation.			☑
Plan the service's high availability implementation.			☑
Recover server roles.	☑		

High Availability Improvements

New improvements to high availability include:

- The introduction of a Standby Continuous Replication (SCR) model.

- New support for high availability features in Windows Server 2008, including the ability to create Failover Clusters that span multiple subnets, support for IPv6 and Dynamic Host Configuration Protocol (DHCP) on IPv4, and support for the new quorum models—disk quorums or File Share Witness quorums—included in the Failover Cluster service in Windows Server 2008.

- Cluster Continuous Replication (CCR) support over redundant cluster networks, improving the replication model.

- Performance, reporting, and monitoring improvements for high availability services.

- Improvements in the Exchange Management Console for graphical administration of high availability features.

- Improved transport dumpster high availability.

Each of these changes has an impact on how you implement high availability in Exchange.

Upgrading a Cluster

In the first topic of this appendix, you learned about changes included in SP1 regarding updating or upgrading your servers. One topic not covered extensively is the upgrade of servers running a clustered configuration. You can upgrade an Exchange 2007 cluster to one running Service Pack 1. You cannot, however, upgrade a cluster running Windows Server 2003 and Exchange 2007 to Windows Server 2008 and Exchange 2007 SP1. To do so, you must create a new cluster running Windows Server 2008 and Exchange 2007 SP1 and then move the mailboxes from the original cluster to the new one.

Clusters running Windows Server 2003 that you plan to upgrade to SP1 must be running a minimum of Windows Server 2003 Service Pack 2. If not, you must upgrade them to SP2 first.

To perform the upgrade to Exchange SP1, you must install the service pack on a node running the passive role. Because active nodes are actually running the Information Store service, they cannot be upgraded when they are active. Therefore, you must begin the upgrade process with the passive node, failover the service to the newly upgraded node, and then install it on the next node. Make sure that each passive node is not only passive for the Clustered Mailbox Server (CMS) service, but also passive for all other processes, such as the clustering service itself.

To upgrade the passive node to SP1, you must use the command-line version of Setup.com. You cannot perform the upgrade with the graphical version of Setup. Performing this upgrade will cause some downtime on the cluster. If it is a Single Copy Cluster (SCC) and several passive nodes are in the cluster, upgrade them all first. After you have upgraded all passive nodes, begin moving the service from the active nodes to the newly upgraded passive nodes. Before you can move the service, you must take all of its components offline. Only then can you move the service. After you move the service, you can bring it online on the newly upgraded node and then upgrade the rest of the nodes. Downtime occurs each time you take the service offline on an active node to move it to an upgraded passive node. Therefore, you need to plan the upgrade during scheduled downtime for the Mailbox service.

Use the following command to upgrade each passive node:

```
Setup.com /mode:upgrade
```

Remember that after you upgrade the nodes, you will not be able to remove the service pack unless you remove Exchange itself from the clustered servers.

Changes in Single Copy Clusters

In Exchange 2007, you can provide service protection for clustered servers through the Single Copy Cluster model. SCC relies on the traditional Failover Cluster model, linking server nodes together to provide service continuity. SCCs rely on shared storage and maintain a single copy of the storage groups. SCCs are designed to provide protection for the Mailbox service only, not mailbox data. You can, however, use Standby Continuous Replication (SCR). This is a new high availability feature of Service Pack 1 that allows you to create and maintain a second, standby copy of the storage groups maintained by an SCC. This provides reliability for both the service and the data it maintains.

Exam Tip Windows Server 2008 supports up to 16 nodes in a Failover Cluster compared to the 8 nodes supported by Windows Server 2003. However, you can create a maximum of eight nodes in an SCC even on Windows Server 2008. Be sure to remember this fact—it will certainly show up on the updated exams.

In addition, you can now manage Clustered Mailbox Servers (CMS) through the Exchange Management Console. Remember that with Exchange 2007, installation and operation of clusters has been moved from the Windows Cluster Administrator to the Exchange Management Shell and, with Service Pack 1, to the Exchange Management Console. You can now rely on the Exchange Management Console through the Manage Clustered Mailbox Server Wizard to perform all cluster management operations. This includes starting and stopping cluster components, moving services from active to passive nodes, and other general administrative activities related to Exchange clusters.

Continuous Replication Management

Another significant change in high availability with SP1 is the ability to provide continuous replication for the transport dumpster. Remember that the transport dumpster maintains the queue of messages that were recently delivered to mailboxes located on Cluster Continuous Replication (CCR) systems. In SP1, you can now provide Local Continuous Replication (LCR) for the transport dumpster queue, ensuring even higher levels of data availability.

In the event of a database or active copy failure, administrators can use the **Restore-StorageGroupCopy** cmdlet in Exchange Server 2007 SP1 to request resubmission of messages from the HT server to the newly activated passive copy of a continuous replication pair. This takes messages that have been moved from the HT queue to its dumpster—including any message that is delivered to a storage group contained within a continuous replication system—and replays them to update potentially missing information in the passive copy of the pair.

You must perform this task on each HT server in the same site as the affected MB system. To avoid duplication, the MB will automatically purge any messages that are replayed but already exist in the passive copy of the database. In SP1, the **Restore-StorageGroupCopy** cmdlet has been updated so that when the administrator activates the passive copy, it automatically triggers a transport dumpster replay as well.

In addition to the ability to work with the transport dumpster with LCR, Service Pack 1 provides enhancements to the administration of continuous replication. Specifically, SP1 includes enhancements and new commands for:

- **Get-StorageGroupCopyStatus** The command that provides you with information on the status of your replication pairs. It has been enhanced in SP1 to overcome known deficiencies such as misleading reports on the status of a replication group. For example, some replication pairs did not report status until a log had been replayed, or when replication was initiated did not report status until it had been completed. Another issue was related to the dismounting of storage groups. In this situation, the value of the *LastLogGenerated* field could be erroneous.

- **Test-ReplicationHealth** A new command that provides feedback on replication itself. For LCR, this command checks all aspects of replication status. It also provides additional value for the Cluster Continuous Replication scenario because it includes support for the cluster portion of this continuous replication strategy. For LCR, this command covers replication service status, storage group copy status, storage group replication queue lengths, and status of databases after copy activation.

Messaging professionals planning for continuous replication scenarios should be aware of these commands so as to include them in their strategy definition.

Use Standby Continuous Replication

Exchange 2007 with SP1 adds one more data protection capability: Data protection for either single or clustered servers through the Standby Continuous Replication model. SCR is new with Service Pack 1, but it continues to rely on log shipping to generate and maintain a second copy of the storage groups contained on the source server to a set of disks located on a second, standby server. SCR uses the same technologies as LCR, but without the limitations of LCR. For example, LCR must be deployed on a stand-alone server, whereas SCR must not. You can deploy SCR between two separate stand-alone servers or even between members of a cluster, such as a Single Copy Cluster.

The activation process for SCR is like that of LCR—it is a manual process that must be initiated by the Exchange administrator when a failure is noticed. It does not rely on the same strategy, however. You can activate SCR in one of three ways:

- Enable database portability along with the dial tone service.
- Enable the passive copy through the recovery option in Setup (**Setup/m: RecoverServer**).
- Enable the passive copy in a cluster through the recovery option in Setup (**Setup /RecoverCMS**).

The option you use depends on your system configuration.

You can run SCR on a variety of configurations. For example, it can be applied to a stand-alone MB, a CMS within an SCC, a Standby Cluster, and a CMS within a CCR. This means that you can mix and match configurations to provide the best availability according to both your budget and required service levels. For example, you can perform the following configurations:

- If you are running stand-alone MB systems, you can use SCR to replicate the data onsite or offsite, thereby protecting the data within each stand-alone server.
- If you are running an SCC, you can protect the data along with the service through the use of SCR. SCR replicas can be local or remote.
- If you are running a Standby Cluster, you can use SCR to replicate the data either onsite or offsite and therefore provide data as well as potential service availability.

- If you are running a CCR, you can configure the CCR to provide local site resilience and avoid latency or bandwidth issues related to CCR replication; then you can use SCR to replicate data offsite and provide additional data protection.

Each of these scenarios costs less and provides more protection than if you use the feature set included in the release version of Exchange 2007 on its own. Remember that SCR replicas must be activated manually, much as with the LCR model. You should include this manual activation in your recovery plans.

Also keep in mind that both active and passive copies in an SCR pair require equivalent storage, the same path for Exchange application files and require the same operating system on each node of the pair. For example, you cannot create an SCR pair with one server running Windows Server 2003 and the other running Windows Server 2008. Keep this in mind when you plan to implement SCR to protect your mailbox data.

Working with Streaming Backups in SP1

By default, remote streaming backups have been disabled in Exchange 2007 SP1. This is done to protect Exchange information because when enabled, any member of the Backup Operators group can generate a backup. Because these backups contain highly sensitive information, Microsoft elected to disable this feature.

With the use of continuous replication, you must re-enable this feature to support local streaming restores on Clustered Mailbox Servers. To enable this feature, you must set the following registry value:

- Key: HKEY_LOCAL_MACHINE\System\CurrentControlSet\Services\MSExchange IS\ParametersSystem
- Name: Enable Remote Streaming Backup
- Type: DWORD
- Value: 1 (Remote backup enabled; use 0 to disable the feature. 0 is the default.)

Set this value if you need to use backups to seed continuous replication copies with the **Update-StorageGroupCopy** cmdlet or if your third-party backup tool needs to rely on remote streaming backups.

Changes in Network Load Balancing

Another technology that you can use to provide high availability for non-mailbox services is the Network Load Balancing (NLB) service. Unlike Failover Clusters, NLB clusters are created by linking independent servers running identical service configurations. In the original release of Exchange, you rely on NLB clusters to provide high availability for the Client Access Server role. With Service Pack 1, you can also rely on NLB to make client connections to Hub Transport servers redundant. This helps persist client connections to HT systems. Using NLB for HT roles is only supported in SP1 of Exchange 2007.

Rely on the instructions in the corresponding Exchange training kit to learn how to implement NLB clusters for HT server roles.

MORE INFO **High availability improvements**

For more information on high availability improvements in SP1, go to *http://technet.microsoft.com/en-us/library/bb676571.aspx.*

Final Recommendations

Rely on this appendix to update your exam skills to include Service Pack 1 information. Take the time to look up the additional information that is included in each topic. For your convenience, each of these references has been collated in the last section of this document, "References."

In addition, take the time to look up and read the Release Notes for the Service Pack. These include last-minute details about the functionalities included in the service pack and outline special procedures you must use to ensure its proper implementation. Find the SP1 Release Notes at *http://www.microsoft.com/downloads/details .aspx?FamilyId=5770BD59-376E-42EC-B940-BE6225CD97FF&displaylang=en.*

Good luck with your exams!

References

The following references are useful to better understand the exam objectives for this update.

- Windows Server 2008: *Windows Server 2008, The Complete Reference* by Ruest and Ruest (McGraw-Hill Osborne, 2008)

- Obtain SP1: *http://www.microsoft.com/downloads/details.aspx?FamilyID=44c66 ad6-f185-4a1d-a9ab-473c1188954c&displaylang=en*

- SP1 Release Notes: *http://www.microsoft.com/downloads/details.aspx?FamilyId= 5770BD59-376E-42EC-B940-BE6225CD97FF&displaylang=en*

- Preparing to install Exchange 2007 SP1 on Windows Server 2008: *http://technet .microsoft.com/en-us/library/bb124558.aspx*

- Running IPv6 with Exchange 2007 SP1 on Windows Server 2008: *http://technet .microsoft.com/en-us/library/bb629624.aspx*

- Client Access server improvements: *http://technet.microsoft.com/en-us/library/ bb684907.aspx*

- Web Services improvements: *http://msdn2.microsoft.com/en-us/exchange/default .aspx*

- Back pressure: *http://technet.microsoft.com/en-us/library/bb201658.aspx*

- Transport configuration: *http://technet.microsoft.com/en-us/library/aa997166 .aspx*

- EdgeSync process: *http://technet.microsoft.com/en-us/library/bb232180.aspx*

- X.400 improvements: *http://technet.microsoft.com/en-us/library/bb676307.aspx*

- Priority queuing: *http://technet.microsoft.com/en-us/library/bb691107.aspx*

- Transport server improvements: *http://technet.microsoft.com/en-us/library/bb68 4905.aspx*

- Mailbox server improvements: *http://technet.microsoft.com/en-us/library/bb68 4903.aspx*

- Unified Messaging server improvements: *http://technet.microsoft.com/en-us/ library/bb691398.aspx*

- High availability improvements: *http://technet.microsoft.com/en-us/library/bb67 6571.aspx*

Answers

Chapter 1: Case Scenario Answers

Case Scenario 1: Build a Plan for a Multi-site Server Role Deployment

Given Lucerne's network topology and available bandwidth, you decide to implement a Standard Organization. Exchange server roles will be located in four locations, as listed in Table CS-1. Clients in the last two locations do not have enough available bandwidth to support the placement of any server roles within their sites. As such they will use RCP over HTTPS to communicate with an Exchange Server in other sites. The resulting configuration is illustrated in Figure CS-1.

Table CS-1   Lucerne Publishing Exchange Server Role Positioning

Site Name	Number of Users	Server Roles	Client Connectivity
Headquarters (New York)	1,000	ET in the Perimeter Network CAS, HT, MB, and UM in the site itself	MAPI RPC over TCP
Site 2 (Los Angeles)	600	CAS, HT, and MB	MAPI RPC over TCP
Region 1 (San Remo)	50	CAS, HT, and MB	MAPI RPC over TCP
Region 2 (Philadelphia)	75	CAS, HT, and MB	MAPI RPC over TCP
Region 3 (Dallas)	9	None	MAPI RPC over HTTPS
Region 4 (Newark)	5	None	MAPI RPC over HTTPS
Total	1,739		

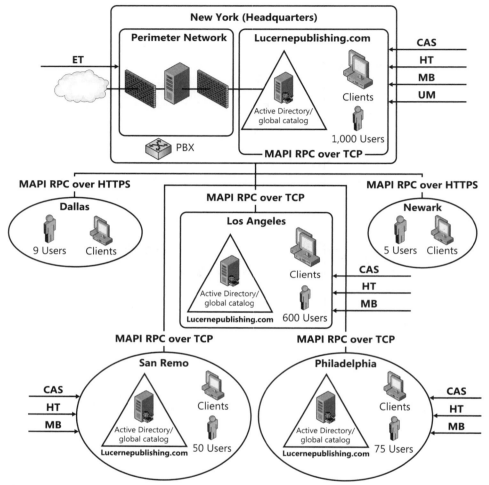

Figure CS-1   Correctly identified Exchange server role positions

Case Scenario 2: Deploying Unified Messaging

1. Because each office has a PBX, some offices may have different language requirements. For example, San Francisco and Los Angeles will want both English and Spanish on their telephone systems. London may want more languages than that. Because of this, you should suggest they deploy the UM role in each location that includes a PBX. This will give them the most freedom for local configurations.

2. As you know, four server roles can coexist on the same server: CAS, HT, MB, and UM. The simplest answer would be to have each of these roles coexist on the

same servers in each location. But you should also tell TPC that role coexistence depends on server load. If the expected load is fairly light, one server can host all roles. If server loads are heavier, TPC will have to think about separating the roles onto different servers.

3. TPC will only be able to install a single role into a Failover Cluster: the MB role. All other roles use different technologies for high availability. Given that TPC wants to cluster the MB role, it will not be able to host this role on the same servers as the other roles as it requested in question number 2. No other roles can be installed with the MB role when it runs on Failover Clusters.

4. Since TPC has its own perimeter network, they should deploy the Edge Transport Server role to manage Internet-facing messaging. To provide high availability for the ET service, TPC should deploy at least two ET computers in the perimeter network.

5. Since TPC wants to run unified messaging in its Exchange organization, they will require both the Standard and the Enterprise CAL. The Standard CAL will give them access to the basic e-mail functions of Exchange Server 2007 while the Enterprise CAL—a cumulative CAL that builds on features available in the Standard CAL—will give them access to the features required for client access to unified messaging. Note that they cannot buy retail versions of Exchange Server 2007 if they want to have both of these CALs.

Chapter 2: Case Scenario Answers

Case Scenario 1: Plan for a New Messaging System Implementation

You create a standard MB role configuration for them. You know that they will be using CCR, so you can create a simpler server configuration.

1. Each server should use two quad-core AMD Opteron x64 processors. This will give you the maximum number of cores for the MB role. You can also use Intel EM64T processors, but you know that AMD processors require less power and generate less heat so you recommend them.

2. Each server needs a minimum of 2 GB of RAM, but because each will host no more than 20 storage groups, you only need to add 10 GB of RAM overall to each server.

3. Each server should rely on RAID 10 storage types. Each system will need multiple disk sets, two for each storage group plus two for the recovery storage group for a total of 22 disk sets, not counting the operating system.

4. The partners did not give you enough information to determine the disk set sizing for each system because you have no idea of mailbox quotas or mailbox profiles. However, you can recommend that each disk set should have at least 200 GB of space because the partners intend to use CCR.

5. Disk configurations should be direct-attached if at all possible. This will let the partners have the best possible speed and, because they are relying on CCR, the best performance ratio, because all storage groups will be replicated to another site. Replication of this type requires fast read and write access for the disk sets storing transaction logs, therefore your configuration recommendation is best.

Case Scenario 2: Work with Transport Servers

1. The problem resides in the fact that while Edge Subscriptions are propagated to all of the existing HT computers when you first set it up in Active Directory, it does not propagate to new computers that are added after the original subscription was set up.

2. To correct the problem, you must remove the existing subscription from the Active Directory site as well as from the ET computers. Then, when the new HT computers are added, regenerate the subscription files from the two Edge Transport servers and import them again into the Active Directory site where the HT computers reside. You need to do this each time a new HT computer is added. For this reason, you should plan HT computers carefully before you create your Edge Subscription.

Case Scenario 3: Design a Storage Group Strategy in a SAN Environment

The result of your storage recommendations should be as displayed in Table CS-4. Commentary on each choice follows the table. To determine the number of mailboxes per server, you need to use the mailbox calculation formula:

```
Mailbox Size=MailboxQuota+Whitespace+(WeeklyIncomingMail*2)
```

All other values are assumed to be at defaults.

Based on the Table 2-17 values in Chapter 2, "Planning Deployments," your initial formulas should be:

```
Mailbox Size=1024+12+120=1156
Mailbox Size=2048+20+200=2268
Mailbox Size=4096+30+300=4426
```

For example, in New York, there are 1,000 users. Given the ratios of 50-25-25 in terms of usage, this means that the total mailbox size in New York would be:

```
500x1156=578000
250x2268=567000
250x4426=1106500
```

This gives you a total of 2,251,500 MB or 2.3 terabytes for New York alone. To calculate totals for each site, you should create a matrix with required values. This matrix is displayed in Table CS-2.

Table CS-2   Lucerne Publishing Mailbox Sizing Matrix

Site Name	Users	Quotas	Whitespace	Dumpster	Total
New York	1000	500x1024	500x12	500x120	578000
		250x2048	250x20	250x200	567000
		250x4096	250x30	250x300	1106500
Los Angeles	600	300x1024	300x12	300x120	346800
		150x2048	150x20	150x200	340200
		150x4096	150x30	150x300	663900
San Remo	50	25x1024	25x12	25x120	28900
		13x2048	13x20	13x200	29484
		12x4096	12x30	12x300	53112
Philadelphia	75	38x1024	38x12	38x120	43928
		18x2048	18x20	18x200	40824
		17x4096	17x30	17x300	75242
Dallas	9	5x1024	5x12	5x120	5780
		2x2048	2x20	2x200	5670
		2x4096	2x30	2x300	11065
Newark	5	3x1024	3x12	3x120	3468
		1x2048	1x20	1x200	2268
		1x4096	1x30	1x300	4426

Total mailbox sizes are listed in Table CS-3.

Table CS-3 Lucerne Publishing Mailbox Sizing Matrix

Site Name	Total in MB	Total in GB	Total in Terabytes
New York	2,251,500	2,251.5	2.3
Los Angeles	1,350,900	1,351	1.4
San Remo	111,496	112	0.12
Philadelphia	156,890	157	0.16
Dallas	17,120	17	0.02
Newark	10,162	10	0.01

Because both Dallas and Newark are hosted in New York, you will need to add their requirements to the New York requirements. Storage recommendations are outlined in Table CS-4.

Table CS-4 Lucerne Publishing Exchange Storage Recommendations

Site Name	Number of MB	Storage Groups Per Server	Databases Per Storage Group	Mailboxes Per Database	Number of Disk Sets
Headquarters (New York)	2	12	1	85	26
Site 2 (Los Angeles)	2	7	1	86	16
Region 1 (San Remo)	1	1	1	50	4
Region 2 (Philadelphia)	1	1	1	75	4
Region 3 (Dallas)	n/a	n/a	n/a	n/a	n/a
Region 4 (Newark)	n/a	n/a	n/a	n/a	n/a

- Each site that hosts the MB role will have at least one server. Though each server can host up to 50 storage groups with the Enterprise Edition, you decide to place two servers in both New York and Los Angeles to protect database access.

- You know Lucerne wants to use LCR eventually; therefore, your disk set size for databases should be 200 GB even if LCR is not to be configured right away.

- You want to use the best practice of placing only a single database per storage group to simplify backup and recovery as well as administration.

- All transaction logs will be placed on different disk sets than their corresponding databases.

- Each site will have a recovery storage group; therefore, each site requires two additional disk sets beyond the number required for normal production operations.

- In determining required disk sets, you must calculate the number of required databases, multiply it by two to separate transaction logs from databases, and then add two more to include the two disk sets required for the recovery storage group.

Case Scenario 4: Design a Deployment Strategy for the Autodiscover Service

Hosted environments have special requirements when it comes to Exchange Server 2007 and the configuration of the Autodiscover service. Because they host multiple Exchange Organizations, ASPs must configure the original Autodiscover connection to be unencrypted. Then, when the connection is established, users are redirected to the encrypted Autodiscover settings file. This is done through a redirect of the Autodiscover Web site in IIS.

Once the redirect is set up, users who try to connect will get the appropriate HTTP 302 response from the ASP over port 80. When they try to connect the first time, using Auto Account Setup, the original encrypted connection will fail, but when they try again using an unencrypted connection, IIS will redirect them to the appropriate Autodiscover Web site, encrypt the communication and send them the appropriate configuration file.

You set up a meeting with the ASP and the Coho Winery officials, and using virtual machines, demonstrate to them how this should be set up and work. After the demonstration, everyone agrees that this was no more than a misconfiguration issue. Coho is happy because they can move on to use their new unified messaging service and the ASP is happy because they now know how to host Exchange 2007 properly.

Case Scenario 5: Prepare the Design for a Mobility Solution

As you know, there will be significant differences between the two phones and special requirements on the CAS configuration to support both. First, deal with the configuration of the CAS.

The CAS configuration has the following requirements:

- ActiveSync must be enabled.
- Direct Push must be enabled.
- The client's mailbox must be enabled for ActiveSync and Direct Push.
- The CAS must include a public PKI certificate for SSL encryption.
- The firewall should support long-lived HTTPS requests.
- Port 443 must be opened on the firewall.
- Clients should have unlimited data plans.
- Autodiscover must be configured properly.
- Ideally, an ActiveSync policy will be enabled to facilitate its management.
- IMAP4 must be enabled on the CAS to support the non-Windows Mobile phone and the service must be started and set to automatic.

In terms of the different supported features for both devices, Table CS-5 displays the results.

Table CS-5   Features for the Touch Pocket PC Compared to a non-Windows Mobile Phone

Feature	Touch Pocket PC	Non-Windows Mobile Phone
Direct Push	Yes	No
E-mail, Calendar, and Contact Synchronization	Yes	No
Task Synchronization	Yes	No
HTML E-mail Support	Yes	Yes
Message Flags	Yes	No
Meeting Attendee Information	Yes	No

Table CS-5   Features for the Touch Pocket PC Compared to a non-Windows Mobile Phone

Feature	Touch Pocket PC	Non-Windows Mobile Phone
Out-of-Office Management	Yes	No
Exchange Search	Yes	No
Windows SharePoint Services and UNC document access	Yes	No
Inline Message Fetch	Yes	No
Exchange ActiveSync Policy Support	Yes	No
Remote Device Wipe	Yes	No
SSL Encryption	Yes	Yes
Device Certificate for Authentication Management	Yes	No
Recovery Password	Yes	No
Attachment Download	Yes	Yes (view only)

In short, the Touch Pocket PC is a better choice for GDI because it also offers the touch interface that makes the other phone so popular and yet supports many more enterprise-level features.

Chapter 3: Case Scenario Answers

Case Scenario 1: Create a Migration Lab

1. The best way to set up the lab to simulate the existing environment is to reproduce a core set of existing computers. Often, 10 percent of the existing systems will be enough to let the lab produce a valid proof of concept. You can stage all of the existing computers from scratch if you want to, but you can also rely on tools such as the Virtual Server Migration Toolkit to transform an existing physical computer into a virtual machine. This creates an exact duplicate of the existing computer and can save a lot of time.

2. The transition scenario is cross-forest to cross-forest.

3. Exchange 2007 virtual machines should be set up from scratch as 64-bit virtual machines. This will provide the most realistic scenario testing.

4. Ideally, the two companies should rely on Microsoft Identity Lifecycle Manager 2007 because it provides the best support for Exchange 2007. But if they decide to do so and they are currently using another technology for cross-forest replication, they will have to include a replication engine upgrade as part of their testing scenarios.

Case Scenario 2: Move from Lotus Notes to Exchange Server 2007

1. Use the information from Table 3-12 in Chapter 3, "Planning Exchange Server 2007 Upgrades and Migrations," to size the new Mailbox Server Storage Groups. This gives you an idea of the amount of storage required for these servers.

2. Plan the construction of their new Exchange Server 2007 forest. You have the opportunity to prepare a pristine forest, so you use best practices everywhere.

3. Because you know that using Microsoft tools would involve a multi-step migration including an intermediary step using Exchange 2003, you propose the companies buy a third-party migration tool. Otherwise, they must rely on the Lotus Notes Connector for Exchange 2003 to perform the initial migration. They cannot use the Microsoft Transporter Suite because it only works with Domino and not Lotus Notes.

4. Work with the companies to implement the third-party tool and perform the migration.

5. As a last step, you can help them decommission their Lotus Notes environment and train them in the further uses of Exchange 2007.

Chapter 4: Case Scenario Answers

Case Scenario: Manage Exchange Server 2007

You need two tables to answer their questions. The first (Table CS-6) must cover the different Exchange management tools. The second (Table CS-7) must cover non-Exchange administration tools.

Table CS-6 Managing Mixed Exchange Systems

Legacy Exchange Feature	Corresponding Exchange 2007 Feature	Manage in		Description
		Exchange 2007 Management Tools	Exchange System Manager	
Organizational Settings: Delegate Control	n/a	☞	☞	Legacy delegation rights must be managed from ESM.
Internet Mail Wizard	n/a	☞	☞	If ET servers exist, this feature will not work.
Stop Public Folder Content Replication	n/a	☞	☞	Only for Exchange 2003 SP2.
Internet Message Format	Remote Domains	☞	☞	Can be managed from both, but after it is modified in Exchange 2007, it is upgraded and can no longer be modified by ESM.
Message Delivery Properties: Sender or Recipient Filtering	Sender or Recipient Filtering	☞	☞	Replaced by new entries in Exchange 2007. On ET, manage through the Console. On HT, manage through the Exchange Management Shell.

Table CS-6   Managing Mixed Exchange Systems

Legacy Exchange Feature	Corresponding Exchange 2007 Feature	Manage in		Description
		Exchange 2007 Management Tools	Exchange System Manager	
Message Delivery Properties: Connection Filtering	IP Allow or Block Lists, IP Allow or Block List Providers	☞	☞	Replaced by new entries in Exchange 2007. On ET, manage through the Console. On HT, manage through the Exchange Management Shell.
Intelligent Mail Filter: Gateway Blocking Threshold	ET Content Filtering: Actions	☞	☞	Configurations are stored in different locations in Exchange 2007. Each threshold must be managed independently for both systems.
Intelligent Mail Filter: Store Junk E-mail Configuration settings	**Set-Organiza-tionConfig** *SCLJunkThreshold*	☞	☞	Can be maintained from both systems.
Sender ID Filtering	n/a	☞	☞	No interoperability. Must be managed independently for both systems.

Table CS-6 Managing Mixed Exchange Systems

Legacy Exchange Feature	Corresponding Exchange 2007 Feature	Manage in		Description
		Exchange 2007 Management Tools	Exchange System Manager	
Mobile Services	n/a	👉	👉	Features such as Always-up-to-date (AUTD) System Management Server SMS, Exchange ActiveSync, and Direct Push are now located in the appropriate section of the Exchange Management Console. Must be managed independently for both systems.
Recipient Details and Address Templates	n/a	👉	👉	Maintained as separate items.
GAL/Address Lists	n/a	👉	👉	Can be edited in either tool, but after it is modified in Exchange 2007, it is upgraded and can no longer be modified by ESM.

Table CS-6 Managing Mixed Exchange Systems

Legacy Exchange Feature	Corresponding Exchange 2007 Feature	Manage in		Description
		Exchange 2007 Management Tools	Exchange System Manager	
Offline Address Book	n/a	☞	☞	Can be edited in either tool, but to edit it in Exchange 2007, you must move it to an Exchange 2007 server. After it is moved, it can no longer be edited by ESM.
Offline Address Book: Rebuild Action	Update-OfflineAdressBook	☞	☞	Can be managed from either tool.
Recipient Update Service	Update-AddressList and Update-EmailAddressPolicy	☞	☞	This service does not exist in Exchange 2007. However, Exchange 2007 servers will appear in the list because the filter only looks for non-front-end servers. *Do not assign a 2007 server to this service.* If you do, it will break. Make sure you name your servers appropriately to avoid this issue.

Table CS-6   Managing Mixed Exchange Systems

Legacy Exchange Feature	Corresponding Exchange 2007 Feature	Manage in		Description
		Exchange 2007 Management Tools	Exchange System Manager	
Recipient Policies	E-mail Address Policy and Accepted Domains	👆	👆	Separated in Exchange 2007. If any mailbox is modified, either through Move-Mailbox or Set-Mailbox, policies are reapplied even though they were never applied in legacy systems. To avoid this, turn off automatic update on e-mail accounts (see Figure 4-7 in Chapter 3).
Recipient Policies	Accepted Domains	👆	👆	Because they are separated in Exchange 2007, accepted domains must be added manually in both systems to make them routable. The Exchange Best Practices Analyzer can tell you whether objects are mismatched.
Recipient Policies	E-mail Address Policy	👆	👆	If modified in Exchange 2007, the policy is upgraded and can no longer be modified in ESM.

Table CS-6   Managing Mixed Exchange Systems

Legacy Exchange Feature	Corresponding Exchange 2007 Feature	Manage in		Description
		Exchange 2007 Management Tools	Exchange System Manager	
Recipient Policy: Apply this policy now	E-mail Address Policy or **Update-EmailAddress-Policy**	☞	☞	If the change is made in ESM, you must wait for the Recipient Update Service to process it. If it is made in Exchange 2007, it is applied immediately.
Mailbox Policy Manager	n/a	☞	☞	Does not take place in Exchange 2007 even though the property is applied to the mailboxes.
Queues	Queue Viewer	☞	☞	ESM will not be able to manage Exchange 2007 objects even though it displays them. If you try, you will receive an error message.
Storage Group	n/a	☞	☞	Must be managed through ESM.
Mailbox Store	n/a	☞	☞	Must be managed through ESM.

Table CS-6   Managing Mixed Exchange Systems

Legacy Exchange Feature	Corresponding Exchange 2007 Feature	Manage in		Description
		Exchange 2007 Management Tools	Exchange System Manager	
Public Folder Store	n/a	☞	☞	Must be managed through ESM.
X.400 Connectors and Mail Transfer Agent objects	n/a	☞	☞	Neither object exists in Exchange 2007. Must be managed by ESM.
SMTP Virtual Server	Receive Connector	☞	☞	This object does not exist in Exchange 2007. Must be managed by ESM.
SMTP Virtual Server: Resolve anonymous e-mail	Receive Connector	☞	☞	To provide the same functionality in Exchange 2007, configure a Receive Connector on an HT and assign the Exchange Servers permission group as well as using Externally Secured as the authentication.

Table CS-6   Managing Mixed Exchange Systems

Legacy Exchange Feature	Corresponding Exchange 2007 Feature	Manage in		Description
		Exchange 2007 Management Tools	Exchange System Manager	
Routing Group	n/a	☞	☞	Exchange 2007 does not use routing groups. Placing mixed Exchange 2007 and legacy servers in routing groups is not supported.
Routing Group Connectors	Routing Group Connectors	☞	☞	Any routing group that contains an Exchange 2007 server must be managed in Exchange 2007.
SMTP Connectors	Send Connectors	☞	☞	Must be managed in the tool where they are created.

Remind TPC administrators that they cannot modify Exchange 2007 objects such as servers in Exchange System Manager even though they are displayed through the console.

Some objects and properties from legacy e-mail systems are also managed in Active Directory Users and Computers. Table CS-7 outlines which objects and properties can be managed in Active Directory Users And Computers in mixed Organizations. This applies to both User Accounts and *InetOrgPerson* objects. Operations applied to Contact and Group objects are listed at the end of the table.

Table CS-7   Managing Mixed Exchange Active Directory Objects

Legacy Active Directory Feature	Corresponding Exchange 2007 Feature	Manage in	
		Exchange 2007	Legacy Exchange
Outlook Mobile Access: Enable or Disable	ActiveSync	👎	👍
ActiveSync and Up-to-Date Notifications	ActiveSync	👎	👍
OWA, POP3, or IMAP4: Enable or Disable	n/a	👎	👍
Mailbox Rights	**Set-MailboxPermission**	👎	👍
Delivery Restrictions	**Set-MailboxPermission**	👎	👍
Delivery Options	**Set-MailboxPermission**	👎	👍
Storage Limits	**Set-MailboxPermission**	👎	👍
Establish E-mail Address	**Enable-Mailbox**	👎	👍
Enable Mailbox	**Enable-Mailbox**	👎	👍
Delete Mailbox	**Disable-Mailbox**	👎	👍
Configure Exchange Features	**Set-Mailbox** or **New-Mailbox**	👎	👍

Table CS-7   Managing Mixed Exchange Active Directory Objects

Legacy Active Directory Feature	Corresponding Exchange 2007 Feature	Manage in	
		Exchange 2007	Legacy Exchange
Remove Exchange Attributes	**Disable-Mailbox**	👎	👍
Contact: Establish E-mail Address	**Enable-MailContact**	👎	👍
Contact: Delete E-mail Addresses	**Disable-MailContact**	👎	👍
Contact: Remove Exchange Attributes	**Disable-MailContact**	👎	👍
Group: Add E-mail Addresses	n/a	👍	👍
Group: Delete E-mail Addresses	n/a	👍	👍
Group: Add Query-based Distribution Group to a Group	n/a	👍	👍
Group: Add Public Folder to a Group	n/a	👍	👍

Chapter 5: Case Scenario Answers

Case Scenario 1: Plan a Backup Schedule for Exchange Datasets

After having considered their upcoming architecture, you determine that they will need to protect the information in their internal network only. As such, you respond to questions number 1 and 2 with the information in Table CS-8.

In response to their third question, you state the following:

- Because the Edge server is provided by an ASP, they will not need to protect data within it, because that is part of the service they are paying for. They should, however, make sure that this is part of the contract they engage in with the ASP.

Table CS-8   Components for GDI to Protect

Server Role	Components	Description
Mailbox Server role	Mailbox storage groups including mailbox databases and their transaction logs	With the MB role, the most important data to protect is the end user data, which is stored inside Exchange databases.
	Public folder databases if they exist and their transaction logs	Settings are stored within Active Directory and can be recovered using the **Setup /m:RecoverServer** command.
	MB system settings	
Hub Transport Server role	Configuration data Queue database Message tracking and protocol logs	Configuration data is stored in the Active Directory configuration container and does not need to be backed up locally. Queues are transient and can be rebuilt with the server. Message tracking and protocol logs record transactions that occur on the server. Message tracking logs provide historic forensic data on message paths. Protocol logs track conversions on all of the connectors. You need to protect the logs with file system backups.
Client Access Server role	Configuration data Web and virtual directory data	Configuration data is in Active Directory and can be recovered using the **Setup /m:RecoverServer** command. Web data is in the IIS metabase and is protected by metabase exports and System State Backups.
Unified Messaging Server role	Configuration data Transient message queues Server-specific configuration data Custom audio files	Configuration data is in Active Directory and does not need local protection. Server-specific configuration is in XML format in the \bin folder and audio files are in the \Unified Messaging\Prompts folder. Protect both with a file system backup.

Table CS-8   Components for GDI to Protect

Server Role	Components	Description
Support Service: Active Directory	NTDS.DIT	Replicated on each domain controller. Use System State Backup in NT Backup. Without Active Directory, Exchange servers cannot function.
Support Service: DNS	NTDS.DIT or zone files	In Active Directory, DNS data should be stored within the directory database. Protect it through replication to DCs or through System State Backups. If DNS data is not in Active Directory, use file system backups.
Client Data	Personal Storage (.pst) files Offline Storage (.ost) files Configuration files MAPI profiles	Personal storage files are local and are not backed up by default. Use file system backup. Offline storage files can be re-created by connecting to Exchange and do not need backing up; unsynchronized changes can be lost. MAPI profiles can be regenerated by the Autodiscover service.

Case Scenario 2: Plan a Recovery Solution for Exchange Mailboxes

You prepare your answer carefully, and provide your client with the following information:

RSGs differ from normal storage groups because the following normal storage group functions are disabled in the RSG:

- The only protocol an RSG will support is the MAPI protocol. You cannot use SMTP, POP3, or IMAP4 to communicate with the RSG. This stops the RSG from inserting unwanted e-mail into your system. And even though MAPI is enabled, an RSG cannot be accessed via Outlook or OWA.

- When you mount a mailbox database into an RSG, the mailboxes cannot connect to Active Directory user accounts and therefore cannot corrupt exiting mailbox content.

- RSG content is also exempted from normal system and mailbox policies, preventing the deletion of content while you are trying to recover it.

- RSGs are exempt from online maintenance tasks, preventing RSGs from impacting server performance.

- All databases mounted in an RSG must be mounted manually, preventing them from impacting production databases.

- You cannot change data paths or move files after the RSG is created. To make such changes, you must delete and re-create the RSG.

- RSGs cannot contain public folder databases. You must use a different strategy, such as public folder replication, to protect public folder content. In addition, you can only mount one RSG per server.

- Finally, RSGs cannot be used in conjunction with LCR or CCR and cannot be used as a source for a data backup. As their name implies, RSGs are only used for data recovery.

Case Scenario 3: Protect Client Access Servers

You realize that it is important for this customer's Web sites to have their own look and feel, and you want to reassure them that they can still have custom Web sites. First, you outline what needs to be backed up on the CAS role and how to protect it. You prepare Table CS-9 to outline where CAS configuration data is stored as well as which data to protect. In this table, you assume that folder paths are located under the C:\Program Files\Microsoft\Exchange path.

Table CS-9   CAS Configuration Folder Paths

Data	Folder Path	Backup Strategy
OWA Web site and web.config file	\Client\owa	File backup.
POP3 and IMPA4 protocol settings	\ClientAccess \ClientAcces\PopImap	File backup.
Availability Service	\ClientAccess\exchweb\ews Active Directory configuration container Web.config file	File backup. Active Directory replication or backup.
Autodiscover	IIS metabase	System State Backup or metabase export.

Table CS-9 CAS Configuration Folder Paths

Data	Folder Path		Backup Strategy
ActiveSync	\ClientAccess\Sync		File backup.
	Active Directory configuration container		Active Directory replication or backup.
	IIS metabase		Metabase export.
OWA virtual directories	\ClientAccess \Sync		File backup.
	Active Directory configuration container		Active Directory replication or backup.
Registry settings	Windows registry (optional)		Rebuild by using the *Setup /m: RecoverServer* command. If backed up, use System State Backup or registry export
Web services configuration	IIS metabase		System State Backup or metabase export.

You also explain that Microsoft provides a script that can back up the IIS metabase for a CAS role and explain how they can use this script to further protect their Web sites.

Finally, you explain that the very best protection strategy is to create a script that exports Web site-specific configuration details from the IIS metabase on a regular basis. You set this script up as a Scheduled Task and make sure it runs every week to provide the best protection levels.

Chapter 6: Case Scenario Answers

Case Scenario 1: Protect Exchange Data

Because The Phone Company needs to prepare SLAs for data availability, you must begin with obtaining information from them. The values you need to determine include:

- **Allowed Downtime** What is the maximum allowed downtime that is acceptable to TPC? For example, if you are allowed a two-hour downtime window for data availability, perhaps a dial-tone recovery solution is sufficient, letting users continue to send and receive e-mail while repairs are performed on the actual mailbox store. If less than two hours is acceptable, a different data availability solution will be required.

- **Allowed Recovery Time**   What is the maximum allowed recovery time that is acceptable to TPC? For example, how long can TPC allow for operators to effect repairs on data stores? Find out this value for a single mailbox, for a single database, and for an entire storage container.

- **Tolerance for Data Loss**   What is the maximum allowed data loss that is acceptable to TPC? Each outage can lead to data loss. If TPC cannot accept any data loss at all, you will need to devise the appropriate solution to ensure that all data is protected at all times.

These three factors will help define the SLAs that will be acceptable to TPC. These SLAs will determine which combination of data protection, service protection, and recovery strategies TPC will use to ensure the availability of Exchange e-mail. Other factors include the daily hours of operation for TPC. Because TPC is a nationwide organization, they operate in several time zones and may also provide services outside the United States. If so, they will need to extend their hours of operation to support worldwide operations.

When planning for SLAs, you need to consider several factors. Table CS-10 outlines the main factors you should have TPC consider for the elaboration of their SLAs.

Table CS-10   Factors Defining Enterprise Service Level Agreements

SLA Factor	Key Reflections
Hours of operation	When is the messaging service required by users?
	How many hours are reserved for scheduled downtime?
	How much advance notice do you need to provide to users when planning downtime?
Service availability	What percentage of time should Exchange be available during a typical year?
	What percentage of time should mailboxes be available?
	What percentage of time should domain controllers be available?

Table CS-10 Factors Defining Enterprise Service Level Agreements

SLA Factor	Key Reflections
System performance	How many users does the e-mail system support?
	How many of these users rely on internal connections?
	How many rely on external connections?
	How many messaging transactions does your system need to support on an hourly basis?
	What is the acceptable latency users will be able to live with?
Disaster recovery	How much time is allowed to recover from a typical failure?
	Should the service be available during this recovery time?
	Should data be available during recovery times?
	Would users accept a period of time where they have access to e-mail functions, but not to their historical data? If so, how long is the acceptable period of time?
	How much data loss is acceptable, if any, to the organization?
Help desk and support teams	Which methods should be used to allow users to contact the Help desk?
	What is an acceptable Help desk response time for a typical user issue?
	How is the Help desk structured to support issue escalation?
User feature set	How much data and storage space will the average user require?
	Do users require special features such as mobile data access or Direct Push? If so, how many users in the organization require these special features?

Answers to the questions in this table will vary, as will the questions themselves, but when you design a set of SLAs for messaging systems or any other system for that matter, you need to first identify organizational requirements, operating factors for the service, operating factors for any data attached to the service, budget levels, and, of course, supported feature sets for the technology to be implemented.

Case Scenario 2: Build Multi-Site Data Redundancy Plans

Because they are concerned about data protection, The Phone Company only needs you to talk about the protection mechanisms for data stored by the MB role. Exchange 2007 offers two new scenarios for mailbox protection, and with the release of Service Pack 1 adds one more data protection capability:

- Data protection for single servers through the Local Continuous Replication (LCR) model. LCR uses asynchronous transaction log shipping to generate and maintain a second copy of the storage groups contained on the server to a second set of disks. The features that make LCR work include log shipping, log replay, and a manual switch from the production to the copy of the storage group data.

- Data and service protection for clustered servers through the Cluster Continuous Replication (CCR) model. CCR uses the Failover Cluster capability of Windows Server 2003 or Windows Server 2008 to create one of two clustered solutions: a two-node cluster in a single site or a geographically dispersed two-node cluster. CCR then uses log shipping to generate and maintain a second copy of the storage groups contained on the source server to a set of disks located on a second or target server. Because of this, CCR can provide site resiliency as well as service and data protection when the cluster nodes are located in different sites. Note that CCR uses direct-attached storage in its cluster configuration.

- Additional data protection for continuous replication models through the Transport Dumpster. When either LCR or CCR is configured on an MB system, Hub Transport servers will automatically defer the deletion of e-mails in their queues. This applies only to e-mails that are destined for storage groups located on either LCR- or CCR-enabled MB systems. In the event of a replica failure, e-mail in the Transport Dumpster can be redelivered if replication was not able to complete.

- Data protection for either single or clustered servers through the Standby Continuous Replication (SCR) model. SCR is new with Service Pack 1, but it continues to use log shipping to generate and maintain a second copy of the storage groups contained on the source server to a set of disks located on a second, standby server.

For the second question, you explain to The Phone Company that data protection in Exchange 2007 is provided through Continuous Replication, which is based on log shipping and log replay. Microsoft has built asynchronous replication of transaction logs into Exchange 2007. Here is how it works:

1. Two data stores are created, one active and one passive. Both need to use redundant disk access hardware to provide true resiliency. In addition, each should have separate physical disks for both the logs and the database. In the best configuration, four disk sets are required.

2. Transactions are recorded in the transaction log of the active store and then committed to the database. When this process is complete, the transaction logs are closed.

3. The passive store pulls or reads the active store's closed transaction log to get a copy. In Exchange 2007, transaction log size has been reduced to 1 MB instead of the 5 MB of previous releases to support this. This copy is placed into an inspection folder.

4. The passive copy inspects the log for consistency and then moves it to its final destination.

5. The log is committed to the passive store's database, keeping it in tune with the active copy within a slight delay.

In the Local Continuous Replication model, the active and passive stores are located on the same server using redundant disk access hardware. In the Cluster Continuous Replication model, the active and passive stores are attached to different servers providing redundancy for the service as well as for the data. When the CCR servers are in a different site, CCR also provides site-level redundancy.

Case Scenario 3: Plan to Protect Exchange Services

The focus of any high availability strategy must be the removal of any single point of failure in the Exchange architecture. This means that you must protect the following items:

- Active Directory
- Domain Name System
- TCP/IP network

- Storage subsystem
- Backup services
- Monitoring services
- Datacenter infrastructure (power and air conditioning)

These components must be protected in each site where the Exchange service has been made available.

Now that you understand which items require protection, you can create a list that will include a general class of failure and its expected RTO. For elements that are data-dependent, you should also indicate the potential impact on the data itself. By establishing an RPO for these items, you will be able to identify the data impact by clarifying the amount of data that will be available when the recovery process is complete. The items in this list include:

- Loss of single mail item
- Loss of single mailbox
- Loss or corruption of single database
- Loss of a single disk
- Loss of an entire disk volume
- Loss of an entire storage unit
- Loss of an entire server
- Loss of network connectivity either at the client or the server level
- Loss of an entire datacenter

You should also categorize these items on a per user type basis because not all users require the same level of service. Users for whom messaging is a critical service should have shorter RTOs and RPOs, whereas casual messaging users can live with longer RTOs and RPOs.

Case Scenario 4: Plan High Availability for Exchange Services

The first thing you need to do is provide Lucerne with an overview of how service availability works in Exchange 2007. To do this, you provide them with the following information on availability support for each role:

- **Edge Transport servers** Can be protected through round robin Domain Name System (DNS) strategies. This means the DNS server will provide load balancing by rotating the load between multiple DNS Mail Exchanger (MX) records targeting different ET systems.

- **Hub Transport servers**   Provide their own redundancy through new built-in role features and through the Active Directory service where their configuration is stored. The same redundancy feature has been built into the Mail Submission Service on Mailbox servers. All you need to do is deploy more than one HT in your organization. In Service Pack 1, you can also rely on NLB to make client connections to HT systems redundant.

- **Client Access servers**   Use the Network Load Balancing (NLB) service or third-party, hardware-based network load balancing. This service transforms a series of identical servers into one single set of resources and automatically redirects users to the best available resource in the set.

- **Mailbox servers**   Use either new built-in features or Microsoft Failover Clusters (MFC) for data storage protection.

- **Unified Messaging servers**   Use more than one server deployed into the same dial plan. Then you use round robin DNS to provide load balancing for the Voice over IP (VoIP) gateways that route calls to the UM, but this only provides load balancing for the initial connection. When a client is connected, the client remains on the same server until the connection is severed. In addition, VoIP gateways can use DNS to retrieve the list of names of all the servers in a dial plan. When the VoIP gateways try to route a call, if the initial UM does not accept it, the VoIP gateways will automatically move on to the next server in the list.

The answer to the second question is easy. The company must ensure that they have more than one ET system deployed in the perimeter network. The FQDNs of these servers must be contained in more than one external DNS server. And, to make their ET configurations redundant, they should use Edge Subscriptions with the internal HT systems.

The third question focuses on larger sites. Each large site should deploy more than one server playing each role. Roles can be combined, but this can only include the CAS, HT, and UM roles because the MB role uses a different strategy—the Microsoft Failover Cluster service—to provide high availability. If the CAS, HT, and UM roles are combined, Lucerne engineers will have to be very careful to ensure that they set up the proper deny port rules in the NLB cluster they prepare in each site.

For the fourth question, users in Dallas and Newark do not warrant a local Exchange server, let alone multiple Exchange servers, because of their numbers. They should connect to another site, perhaps New York, and have redundant WAN connections.

For the fifth question, you can tell Lucerne that organizations traditionally rely on the built-in measures Microsoft provides through the Windows Server operating system to protect Exchange servers. With Exchange Server 2007, some of these traditional measures have changed to help provide better support for high availability and business continuity. In addition, Exchange itself offers new availability features that, together with those Windows Server offers, can provide even better results. Therefore, it will not be necessary for Lucerne to obtain a third-party solution.

Chapter 7: Case Scenario Answers

Case Scenario 1: Explore Malware Protection

You produce Table CS-11 to provide a summary of the various features available against malware in Exchange 2007. You also make sure you have Internet access so that you can supplement the information in the table with the Microsoft Exchange TechNet Web site if content questions arise during the meeting.

Table CS-11   Exchange Anti-Malware Features

Exchange Anti-Malware Feature	Description
Connection Filtering	The Connection Filter agent processes IP addresses against administrator-configured allow and block lists, but it also uses block and allow lists from list providers. Local lists are configured through either the Exchange Management Console or the Shell and can be entered as individual addresses, address ranges, or address and subnet mask. Block list entries can have an expiration time or date assigned when they are configured to automatically remove them after a given period of time. Use these lists to allow or block IP addresses that are not in the lists provided by real-time block list (RBL) providers. Note that in Exchange, RBLs are referred to as IP Block Lists and lists originating from safe list providers (SLP) are referred to as IP Allow Lists.

Table CS-11   Exchange Anti-Malware Features

Exchange Anti-Malware Feature	Description
Sender Filtering	Exchange can use the MAIL FROM: SMTP command on incoming messages to identify the sender of an e-mail and determine which action to take based on defined lists of trusted and untrusted senders or sender domains. Exchange administrators can block single senders, such as John.Kane@lucernepublishing.com; block entire e-mail domains, such as *@lucernepublishing.com; or block e-mail domains and any sub-domains they contain, such as *@*.lucernepublishing.com. Resulting actions are also configurable. For example, you can set rejected senders to receive a 554 5.1.0 Sender Denied message or you can accept the message and mark it as a message originating from a blocked sender and move it up the chain. This value will be added to the computations the Content Filtering agent will perform when determining the spam confidence level for the message. Make sure you combine this filter with the Sender ID filter to avoid spoofing of the MAIL FROM: SMTP header. Spoofing relies on the modification of this header to pretend the message originates from a different location than its actual location.
Recipient Filtering	This filter uses either its block list or recipient lookups against the GAL to verify whether recipients are allowed or denied. The ET system does not have access to the GAL because it is within Active Directory, so it is important to set up Edge Subscriptions to ensure that GAL information is located within the ADAM instance on each ET. If the recipient is in a block list or does not exist, Exchange sends a 550 5.1.1 User unknown message to the sending server. If the recipient is approved, Exchange sends a 250 2.1.5 Recipient OK message to the sending server.

Table CS-11   Exchange Anti-Malware Features

Exchange Anti-Malware Feature	Description
Sender ID	Sender ID is a new validation method for e-mails. It relies on the identification of the IP address of the sending server along with the Purported Responsible Address (PRA) of the sender to validate that the sender's address is not spoofed. The agent requests PRA information from the DNS server that includes the record for the sending server and sending e-mail domain. This information is usually published within sender policy framework (SPF) records on the DNS server. PRA calculations include four elements drawn from the message headers: Resent-Sender:, Resent-From:, Sender:, and From:. PRA and Sender ID are based on request for comment (RFC) number 4407. Sender ID should be used in conjunction with Sender Filtering to avoid spoofing.
Sender Reputation	Over time, as messages are received from specific sources, Exchange uses the Protocol Analysis agent to build a sender reputation from the originating IP address of the server delivering the mail. This agent uses a variety of factors to determine the sender's reputation level (SRL). If this level exceeds a specific threshold, the messages it delivers will be blocked. In addition, the Protocol Analysis agent will rely on updated IP Reputation updates that are provided through Microsoft Update to supplement its own SRL analyses.
Content Filtering	Content filtering relies on Microsoft SmartScreen technology and the Intelligent Message Filter (IMF) to examine the body of a message. The IMF learns to distinguish valid from non-valid information in a message. In addition, IMF is updated regularly through the Microsoft Anti-spam Update Service when it is run to ensure that it will capture as many positives as possible. Suspicious messages are quarantined instead of blocked to reduce the risk of false positives. Administrators review these messages to see whether they should be forwarded on or rightly deleted.

Table CS-11 Exchange Anti-Malware Features

Exchange Anti-Malware Feature	Description	
	Overall, the Content Filtering Agent assigns a spam confidence level (SCL) rating to the message. Messages are deleted, rejected, quarantined, or delivered based on their SCL rating. Low ratings are good; high ratings are bad. Administrators can configure the rating threshold to determine which messages are rated as good or bad.	
Attachment Filtering	Like content filtering, attachment filtering will examine not the body of a message, but the type of attachment included with a message. Attachment filtering is performed based on filenames, file extensions, or MIME content type, determining what type of attachment it is. The Attachment Filtering agent can even determine whether a filename or extension has been modified to pass as an approved format. You can use the **Get-Attachment-FilterEntry	FL** cmdlet on a transport server—using at least local administrative rights—to get a full list of both file extensions and MIME types Exchange addresses. When suspicious attachments are found, this filter can block the message, remove the attachment, and send the message on or simply delete the message and the attachment. When messages are blocked, senders receive a delivery status notification message telling them the attachment was blocked. When attachments are removed, they are replaced with a text message stating that the attachment was removed. If the message is deleted, neither sender nor recipient will be notified.	
Outlook Junk E-mail Filtering	Outlook also filters e-mail on a local basis for any potentially malicious message attempting to get through the various Exchange filters. Trapped messages are moved to the Junk E-mail folder to be reviewed by the end user before deletion.	

Table CS-11   **Exchange Anti-Malware Features**

Exchange Anti-Malware Feature	Description
Antivirus Engines	Exchange also has special virus scanning application programming interfaces (VSAPI) that are designed to work with commercial antivirus engines. Exchange itself, however, does not include an antivirus engine. Microsoft offers Forefront Security for Exchange Server, while other manufacturers offer their own third-party antivirus engines for Exchange. No Exchange implementation should move forward without at least one of these engines deployed on the ET and/or the HT roles.

Case Scenario 2: Understand Anti-Spam and Antivirus Mail Flow

You begin with the first question and outline the following sequence of events:

1. The Connection Filter uses the IP Allow, the IP Block, the Safe Provider, and the IP Block Provider real-time block lists (RBL) to determine whether the message should be blocked or allowed.

2. The Sender Filter examines the SMTP source of the message to see whether the sending domain or the sender itself is on a block list. This occurs before a user's own Safe Senders List is evaluated and may block messages from senders that are approved by end users, but not at the organizational level.

3. The Recipient Filter examines the recipient list in the message to see whether the recipients are trusted or untrusted—or whether they even exist. If there are multiple recipients and only some are blocked, they are stripped from the message and the message moves on. Blocked messages are returned to the sender and the sender's reputation is updated.

4. The Sender ID Filter determines the PRA of the message based on a standard PRA algorithm. The resulting value is the SMTP address of the sender, such as John.Kane@lucernepublishing.com. The filter then uses the domain section of the address (lucernepublishing.com) to query the DNS server for that domain. If there is a sender policy framework (SPF) for this domain, it will be returned to the Exchange agent who will use it in its evaluation. If there is no SPF, the message is stamped accordingly and processed further along the chain. If the

sender's domain or IP address is in a blocked list, the message will be processed according to the rules set by the Exchange administrator. In this case, the message can be rejected, deleted, or simply stamped with the results and moved along the chain.

5. The Content Filter first reviews the results of the previous connection filtering actions to make sure there are no missed rejections, and applies the antivirus scan. When the antivirus engine has scanned the object, content filtering is applied. Content filtering assigns a spam confidence level (SCL) rating to the message. If the SCL rating exceeds the threshold, the message can be deleted, rejected, or quarantined. If not, it moves on through the processing chain. Note that if safelist aggregation has been configured, this level of filtering will also rely on Outlook Safe Sender lists to process the message.

6. The Attachment Filter will evaluate the message if it includes an attachment. If not, the message moves on up the chain. This level of filtering will once again perform one of three actions should the attachment meet the blocking criteria: reject the message, delete the message, or strip the attachment and send the message on up the processing chain.

7. If Forefront Security for Exchange Server is in place, another level of antivirus scanning is performed on the message. If a virus is found at this stage, the message is deleted and a notice is send to the recipient.

8. The last filtering stage is the Outlook Junk E-mail Filter, which is performed when the message arrives in the user's Inbox. If the message meets a condition set by the user but not set at the organizational level, it is placed into the user's Junk E-mail folder. If not, it is placed into the Inbox.

The second question draws on your talents as an illustrator. Because Exchange funnels all e-mail through the various anti-spam and antivirus filters it maintains, you put together the following illustration for TPC (see Figure CS-2).

Case Scenario 3: Understand Client-to-Server Communications

TPC can deploy several services in their Exchange topology, but not all are required services. Therefore, you prepare Table CS-12, which you use to list all of the potential ports that can be in use when running client-to-server communications from Outlook 2007 to Exchange 2007.

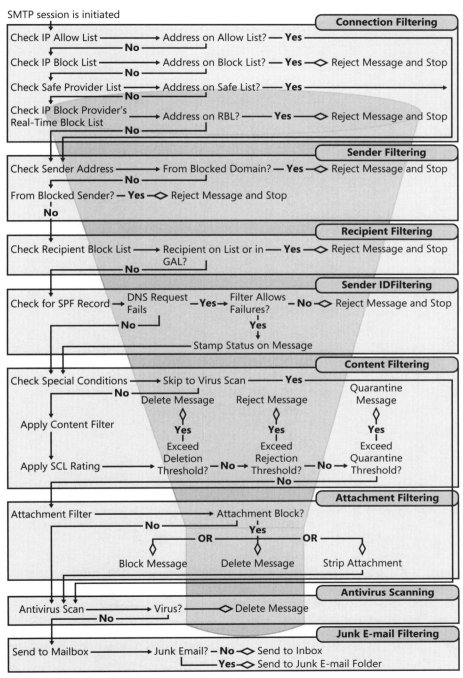

Figure CS-2   The Exchange E-mail filtering funnel

Table CS-12 Exchange Client-to-Server Communication Protocols

TCP Port	UDP Port	Purpose	From Client Role	To Server Role	Comments and Authentication Method	Encryption Method
80		HTTP Offline Address Book access	Outlook	MB	NTLM or Kerberos	None
		WebDAV access	OWA	CAS	Basic or OWA forms-based authentication	HTTPS by default
		Autodiscover service	Outlook or mobile device	CAS	Basic, Digest, NTLM, or Negotiate (Kerberos), but Basic/Integrated Windows Authentication is used by default	HTTPS by default
		Availability Service	Outlook, OWA, or mobile device	CAS	NTLM or Kerberos	HTTPS by default
		Outlook Web Access	Web Browser	CAS	Basic, Digest, Forms-based, NTLM (v2 only), Kerberos or Certificate, but Forms-based authentication is the default	HTTPS by default
		Exchange ActiveSync	Mobile device or Windows PC	CAS	Basic or Certificate, but Basic is the default	HTTPS by default

Table CS-12   Exchange Client-to-Server Communication Protocols

TCP Port	UDP Port	Purpose	From Client Role	To Server Role	Comments and Authentication Method	Encryption Method
		Outlook Anywhere	Remote Outlook	CAS	Basic or NTLM, but Basic is the default	HTTPS by default
110		POP3	Outlook or other client	CAS	Basic, NTLM or Kerberos	SSL or TLS, depends on client
143		IMAP4	Outlook or other client	CAS	Basic, NTLM or Kerberos	SSL or TLS, depending on client
135		RPC Availability Web Service	Outlook or OWA (through CAS)	MB	NTLM or Kerberos	RPC by default
443		HTTPS Offline Address Book access	Outlook	MB	NTLM or Kerberos	HTTPS
		WebDAV access	OWA	CAS	Basic or OWA forms-based authentication	HTTPS by default
		Autodiscover service	Outlook or mobile device	CAS	Basic, Digest, NTLM, or Negotiate (Kerberos), but Basic/Integrated Windows Authentication is used by default	HTTPS by default

Table CS-12 Exchange Client-to-Server Communication Protocols

TCP Port	UDP Port	Purpose	From Client Role	To Server Role	Comments and Authentication Method	Encryption Method
		Availability Service	Outlook, OWA, or mobile device	CAS	NTLM or Kerberos	HTTPS by default
		Outlook Web Access	Web Browser	CAS	Basic, Digest, Forms-based, NTLM (v2 only), Kerberos or Certificate, but Forms-based authentication is the default	HTTPS by default
		Exchange ActiveSync	Mobile device or Windows PC	CAS	Basic or Certificate, but Basic is default	HTTPS by default
		Outlook Anywhere	Remote Outlook	CAS	Basic or NTLM, but Basic is the default	HTTPS by default
993		Secure IMAP4	Outlook or other client	CAS	Basic, NTLM or Kerberos	SSL or TLS, depending on client
995		Secure POP3	Outlook or other client	CAS	Basic, NTLM or Kerberos	SSL or TLS, depending on client

Case Scenario 4: Understand Exchange Firewall Requirements

Because they are using POP3 and IMAP4 today and they will not need to use these systems anymore when Exchange is deployed, TPC will actually be reducing the number of ports that are open in their firewalls. First, you provide them with Table CS-13, which outlines which ports are required for Exchange to function. Then, you supplement the table with specific bullet points.

Table CS-13 Potential Firewall Configurations for Exchange 2007

Firewall	Direction	TCP Port	Purpose	Comments
External	Inbound and Outbound	25	SMTP	Inbound e-mails to ET systems.
		53	DNS	Name resolution for externally exposed services.
		80	Read-only HTTP	Static Web site viewing
		443	Secure HTTP	Outlook Web Access Outlook Anywhere Exchange ActiveSync Autodiscover service
		587	Secure SMTP	Accept and respond to STARTTLS SMTP command
		993	Secure IMAP	IMAP4 e-mail service (optional)
		995	Secure POP	POP3 e-mail service (optional)
Internal	Inbound and Outbound (point-to-point only)	443	Secure HTTP	Outlook Web Access Outlook Anywhere Exchange ActiveSync Autodiscover service

Table CS-13   Potential Firewall Configurations for Exchange 2007

Firewall	Direction	TCP Port	Purpose	Comments
		587	Secure SMTP	Accept and respond to STARTTLS SMTP command
		993	Secure IMAP	IMAP4 e-mail service (optional)
		995	Secure POP	POP3 e-mail service (optional)
	Outbound (point-to-point only)	50636	Secure LDAP	EdgeSync from HT to perimeter ET systems

Right now, TPC's external firewall uses ports 53, 80, 110, 143, 443, 993, and 995. In the new configuration, the external firewall will use ports 25, 53, 80, 443, and 587. This reduces the number of open ports by two, making it even more secure than it is right now. In addition, most of the traffic through the firewall will run through ports 443 and 587, which are both secure connection ports based on both SSL and TLS. Communications will be vastly more secure, not to mention that users will have vastly improved services with the availability of Outlook Anywhere, Autodiscover, Outlook Web Access, and ActiveSync.

There is no comparison between the service levels and the improved security that Exchange will provide compared to the existing systems. Yes, Exchange will be more complex to manage, but if TPC manages their implementation properly, maintenance will be reduced because things will just work.

Chapter 8: Case Scenario Answers

Case Scenario 1: Understand Transport Rules

First, you need to tell them how transport rules are structured. Transport rules always have the same three components:

- **Conditions**   Outline which elements of the e-mail—sender, recipient, header, message body, message attributes—will be used to identify when the rule should be applied. Conditions are cumulative. This means that if more than one condition is set on a rule, all conditions must be met for the rule to apply. If no condition is set, the rule applies to all messages.

- **Exceptions** Outline when the rule should not apply even if the conditions are met. In a way, exceptions are the opposite of conditions because they identify when the rule should not apply instead of when it should. And unlike conditions, if multiple exceptions are listed, only one match is required for the message to be excluded from rule application.

- **Actions** Result from the application of a rule. Actions determine what happens to a message when it meets the conditions outlined in the rule and does not meet any of the exceptions.

Next, you need to tell the rules where they apply. Transport rules apply to the following message types:

- **Anonymous Messages** Messages transiting through an ET or an HT but sent from an unauthenticated sender or server.

- **Interpersonal Messages** Messages that contain a message body in Rich Text Format (RTF), HTML, plain text, or include multiple or alternative message bodies.

- **Opaque Messages** Messages that are encrypted.

- **Clear-Signed Messages** Messages that are signed but not encrypted.

- **Unified Messaging Messages** Messages that are either created or processed by a UM role and will include voicemail, fax, missed call notifications, or messages originating from Outlook Voice Access.

- **IPM.Note. Messages** Messages with a message class prefix of IPM.Note. Generated by applications or custom forms.

Remember to indicate that the last two message types—Unified Messaging and IPM.Note.—are only supported in Exchange 2007 Service Pack 1.

Case Scenario 2: Identify Message Journaling Best Practices

Records management policies apply at two different levels. First, you can configure a retention policy directly on users' mailboxes. You have already seen how to do that. Second, you can configure journaling policies to take messages from a specific folder and transmit them to another recipient. Journaling recipients can be any e-mail address including an actual mail-enabled user or even a Windows SharePoint Services library. When you do this, classifications are preserved to ensure that you are retaining an actual copy of the original message.

The way you perform journaling really depends on the version of the Exchange CAL the organization is using. TPC should keep the following conditions in mind when they are ready to assign a mailbox policy to users:

- You can only use the console to assign a managed mailbox policy to a new user mailbox as you create it. This means that you must plan mailbox management policies *before* you mail-enable your user accounts if you want to do it through the Console.

- If users already exist, you must use the **set-Mailbox** Shell cmdlet along with the ManagedFolderMailboxPolicy property. However, you can easily script this to assign a policy to multiple users.

- Only one policy can apply per mailbox. If you want to apply several policies to a single mailbox, you must plan your settings configurations and include the proper managed folders all in the same mailbox policy. Once again, this means planning mailbox policies carefully before deploying them.

- Policies are applied only to Mailbox Server roles because they manage user mailboxes.

- Custom managed folders are a premium feature of MRM and can only be applied in organizations that have an Exchange Server Enterprise Client Access License (CAL). In Exchange 2007 SP1, you can apply MRM to default folders with a Standard CAL.

- Mailbox policies can only be applied to mail-enabled users, not to contacts or distribution lists.

This should satisfy their curiosity about messaging journaling.

Case Scenario 3: Implement Message Journaling

You explain to The Phone Company that in Exchange 2007, they can journal messages sent to or from a specified mailbox, contacts, or even distribution lists. Journaling captures these messages and automatically forwards a copy of the message to a special collection mailbox. Journaled messages are wrapped into a journal report that includes information on the sender, the recipient(s), the subject, and other data. The message itself is inserted as an object inside the journal report.

Journaling is very much like transport rules because it works on transport servers only. You can journal messages to any valid SMTP address including Windows SharePoint Services document libraries or e-mail addresses used by special, third-party e-mail archiving solutions. In legacy versions of Exchange, you had to journal messages based on mailbox stores. This means that you had to plan stores carefully and make sure that every mailbox you wanted to journal was in the same store. In Exchange 2007, you use journaling rules, which are much like transport rules, to determine which messages are journaled.

Exchange 2007 provides two levels of journaling:

- Standard journaling relies on the journaling agent to act on messages that are sent to or sent from mail-enabled users whose mailboxes are located in a specific mailbox database. To address a standard rule to all users, you need to set it on each of the mailbox databases in your organization. Standard journaling is very much like legacy Exchange journaling. Note that each time you enable journaling on a mailbox database, all mailboxes in the database are journaled.

- Premium journaling relies on Hub Transport servers to process journaling rules against any message that is transmitted through them. To use premium journaling, you must have an Exchange Enterprise CAL. Premium journaling supports three journaling operations:

  - Per recipient or per distribution list journaling, which identifies which mail-enabled user, contact, or distribution list you want to journal against.

  - Journaling rule scope, which lets you determine which message type you want to journal: internal, external, or both.

  - Journaling replication. As with transport rules, as soon as you create a premium journaling rule on an HT, it will automatically be available to every other HT system after Active Directory replication has completed.

Both standard and premium journal reports contain quite a bit of information about the message. When you plan for the implementation of journaling, you should keep the following in mind:

- Be aware of the legal and privacy impact of journaling on e-mail messages. Make sure you have documented corporate support for the implementation of these rules.

- Document your configuration plan well to ensure that everyone involved fully understands what will happen when the rules are put in place.

- List which messages will be journaled in detail. Make sure there are no omissions.

- Identify where journal reports will be kept and which protection measures are in place to protect these containers.

- Identify how journal reports will be secured while in transit.
- Identify who will have access to journal containers, whether they are mailboxes, Windows SharePoint Services document libraries, or third-party archives.

Of all of these guidelines, the first is by far the most important. Journaling is probably the most important aspect of compliance because it creates a message archive. Make sure you implement it properly and make sure you get counsel from internal officers to ensure that you are meeting whichever regulations affect TPC.

Chapter 9: Case Scenario Answers

Case Scenario 1: Identify Standard Management Tools

It is true that the Exchange Management Console is considerably different than the previous Exchange System Manager. After considerable thought, you decide that the best way to provide this information to GDI's administrators is to create a table and list the functions the Exchange Management Console exposes to them. Table CS-14 is the results of your efforts.

Table CS-14 Exchange Management Console Functionality

Feature	Description	
Configuration Level	Organization Configuration contains all objects of organizational scope and manages all settings for the entire organization.	
	Can do the following tasks at the first node:	
	■ Modify Configuration Domain Controller	
	■ Add Exchange Administrator	
	■ Configure administrative access roles for users or groups	
	Includes the following sub-nodes:	
	■ Mailbox	
	■ Client Access	
	■ Hub Transport	
	■ Unified Messaging	

Table CS-14   Exchange Management Console Functionality

Feature	Description
Mailbox	■ New Address List ■ New Managed Default Folder ■ New Managed Custom Folder ■ New Managed Folder Mailbox ■ New Offline Address Book
Client Access	■ New Exchange ActiveSync
Hub Transport	■ New Remote Domain ■ New Accepted Domain ■ New Email Address Policy ■ New Transport Rule ■ New Journal Rule ■ New SMTP Send Connector ■ New Edge Subscription
Unified Messaging	■ New UM Dial Plan ■ New UM IP Gateway ■ New UM Mailbox Policy ■ New UM Auto Attendant
Server Configuration	Displays a list of all the servers in the Exchange organization to perform specific tasks on server roles and can modify the configuration of domain controller.
Mailbox	Storage Group ■ Move Storage Group Path ■ New Mailbox Database ■ New Public Database ■ Enable Local Continuous Replication ■ Remove

Table CS-14   Exchange Management Console Functionality

Feature	Description
	Database
	■ Dismount Database
	■ Move Database Path
Client Access	■ Outlook Anywhere
	■ Outlook Web Access
	■ Exchange ActiveSync
	■ Offline Address Book
Hub Transport	■ Enable, disable, or remove Receive Connectors
Unified Messaging	■ Enable or disable unified messaging
Recipient Configuration	In this node you can do the following tasks:
	■ Modify recipient scope
	■ Modify the maximum number of recipients to display
	■ Create a new:
	❑ Mailbox
	❑ Mail contact
	❑ Mail user
	❑ Distribution group
	❑ Dynamic distribution group
	■ Disable m ail-enabled object
	■ Remove mail-enabled object
	■ Move mail-enabled object
	■ Enable unified messaging
Mailbox	■ Modify the maximum number of recipients to display
	■ New mailbox
	■ Disable mail-enabled object

Table CS-14   Exchange Management Console Functionality

Feature	Description
	■ Remove mail-enabled object
	■ Move mail-enabled object
	■ Enable unified messaging
Distribution Group	■ Modify the maximum number of recipients to display
	■ New distribution group
	■ New dynamic distribution group
	■ Disable mail-enabled object
	■ Remove mail-enabled object
Mail Contact	■ Modify the maximum number of recipients to display
	■ New mail contact
	■ New mail user
	■ Disable mail-enabled object
	■ Remove mail-enabled object
Disconnected Mailbox	■ Connect to server
Toolbox	Regroups the additional tools that are provided with Exchange Server 2007.
Configuration Management	■ Best Practices Analyzer
Disaster Recovery Tools	■ Database Recovery Management
	■ Database Troubleshooter
Mail Flow Tools	■ Mail Flow Troubleshooter
	■ Message Tracking
	■ Queue Viewer
Performance Tools	■ Performance Monitor
	■ Performance Troubleshooter

Armed with this table, the Exchange administrators should have a good idea of what they will be able to do through the console.

Case Scenario 2: Define an Updating Strategy

The best way to respond to this question is to produce a table that outlines how each server role is affected by the update process. Table CS-15 is the result.

Table CS-15   **Availability Strategy Per Server Role**

Server Role	Comment
Hub Transport Server	HT systems dynamically update their naming information in DNS when DNS is integrated to Active Directory. DNS then uses the Round Robin process to load-balance the HT systems. If a system is down, DNS will automatically connect the requestor with another available system. All Lucerne must do to make sure that they have HT service continuity during updates is to apply updates on one HT server only, bring it back up, verify that it works properly, and then move on to the next HT system.
Edge Transport Server	ET systems work in much the same way as HT systems. Once again, all that is needed is to ensure that one system is up while the other is being updated and then to ensure that the newly updated system is fine before moving on to the next one.
Unified Messaging Server	UM systems also rely on Round Robin, so their update strategy would be the same as with the HT and ET systems.
Client Access Server	CAS availability is controlled through the Network Load Balancing cluster. First, the administrator must perform a drain stop to keep one of the CAS nodes from responding to NLB requests. Once this is done, the administrator performs the update on the stopped node, brings it back up without rejoining the NLB cluster, ensures that the node is working properly and rejoins it to the NLB cluster. The administrator repeats the process with the second node.

Table CS-15   Availability Strategy Per Server Role

Server Role	Comment
Mailbox Server	Because the MB systems are running CCR, both data and service availability are protected. The administrator should begin with the passive node, update it, bring it back up and verify its proper operation, and then use the Exchange Management Shell to force a failover from the active node to the newly updated passive node and repeat the process with the second node.

The administrator should repeat the process for each server role that is duplicated in the remote site.

Chapter 10: Case Scenario Answers

Case Scenario: Learn to Rely on Proactive Management

Answers will vary, but should resemble the following.

Lucerne undoubtedly had to perform a structured deployment to ensure that their e-mail systems just work. Typically, such deployments will rely on the following strategies:

- First, they use a structured change management process. A five-step process, as outlined in Chapter 9, is usually the right approach to take.

- Second, they use structured project management to first prepare activity lists and then track all activities as the project progresses.

- Third, they probably rely on graduated test levels. Normally, five levels of testing are sufficient. The testing strategy outlined in Chapter 9 would be adequate.

- Fourth, they put in a commercial monitoring tool as soon as they validated that their configuration met all suggested best practices. The commercial monitoring tool lets them know of potential problems before issues occur.

- Finally—though this is not likely the only other element they used to create a best practice deployment—they relied on the right team of players to perform the deployment. Within this team, they relied on the right technical architect—you, the messaging professional—to provide them with essential knowledge of the inner workings of Exchange 2007 as well as support them in the preparation of their deployment plan, outlining what should be done and in which order.

Best practices deployment should not aim to do everything at once, and should take small steps, implementing one component at a time and validating that it is working well before moving on to the next stage. Every deployment project will require a savvy technical architect to provide this essential role, and that is where you come in. By taking this exam, you prove to others that you know what it takes to deploy Exchange. Good job and good luck!

Glossary

Active copy   The master, mountable copy for the storage group.

ActiveSync   This service allows the transfer of messaging and calendaring data to a mobile device from an Exchange Server 2007 mailbox.

Address list   A collection of recipient addresses that can be accessed when a client is connected to Exchange.

Attack surface   The port, services, and applications that can respond to requests from the network. Shutting down ports, services, and applications reduces attack surface.

Autodiscover   This service allows Outlook 2007 and Windows mobile clients to be automatically configured given an e-mail address and password.

Availability service   This service provides up-to-date calendaring information.

Backup job   The act of backing up a set of files at the same time.

Backup set   The set of files created by a backup job.

Baseline   A set of readings (typically performance counter values) that define the normal operating parameters of a system. You take baselines for quiet, normal, and busy periods, whenever there is a significant system change, and regularly to determine if the load on your resources is increasing over time.

Block list   A block lists is a list of items that you do not want to allow. This list can consist of senders, recipients, or domains.

Bottleneck   The resource that is under most stress. You can never eliminate bottlenecks. If you allocate more resources to a bottleneck, the next most stressed resource becomes the bottleneck.

Bulk management   Performing the same operation on more than one Exchange entity at the same time—for example, configuring or moving several mailboxes.

Categorizer   An Exchange transport component that processes all inbound messages and determines what to do with them on the basis of information about their intended recipients.

Checkpoint file   A file that tracks the progress of transaction logging. The checkpoint file has a pointer to the oldest log file that contains data that has not yet been written to the database.

Circular logging   Helps control the hard disk space that is used to store log files by overwriting older data in logs.

Cluster continuous replication (CCR)   A high availability feature of Microsoft Exchange Server 2007 that combines the asynchronous log shipping and replay technology built into Exchange 2007 with the failover and management features provided by the Microsoft Windows Cluster service. The CCR process achieves high availability by using separate servers with separate storage devices to replicate storage group and mailbox data.

Comma-separated value (CSV) file   An implementation of a delimited text file that uses commas to separate values. CSV files can be read by most report-generating software packages.

Compliance   A set of legal requirements or policies that must be implemented through Exchange Server configuration.

Consistent state   If the database is in a consistent state, the database can be remounted without any kind of transaction log replay. Changing a database from an inconsistent state to a consistent state generally involves two processes: restoring the database from a backup that was completed while the database was online and replaying the transaction log files into the restored database.

Contact   An entity in Active Directory that is not a user account. Contacts cannot log on to the domain. A contact is typically mail-enabled, and its purpose is to allow users to send e-mail (typically to an external e-mail address) by specifying the contact's name in the To: or Cc: lines.

Custom attribute   An attribute that describes an object in Active Directory other than standard attributes, such as Location or Employer. You can use custom attributes, for example, to define membership of a dynamic distribution group.

Database   In the context of disaster recovery, database is a generic term that refers to either a mailbox store or a public folder store.

Dynamic distribution group   A mail-enabled group that does not have a fixed membership and whose members are identified dynamically using filters and conditions each time e-mail is sent to the group.

E-mail address policy   A policy that determines the format of an e-mail address.

Equipment mailbox   A resource mailbox used to identify items of equipment that typically do not have a fixed location and can be used anywhere in an organization's premises.

Exchange ActiveSync mailbox policy   A policy, applied to users, that is used to manage a Windows Mobile device.

Extensible storage engine (ESE)   The database engine that Exchange uses.

Failover   The process by which the passive component becomes active when the existing active component fails.

Hard recovery   The process that changes a restored database back to a consistent state by playing transactions into the database from transaction log files.

Inconsistent state   If the database is in an inconsistent state, it cannot be remounted, and transaction log replay needs to be performed.

Link state   Routing protocol used by previous versions of Exchange.

Local continuous replication   A process by which high availability is achieved using separate storage devices attached to the same Mailbox server.

Mail-enabled user   A user that has a user account in Active Directory but does not have a corresponding mailbox. E-mail sent to this user is forwarded to the user's mailbox in another organization. Mail-enabled users have external e-mail addresses.

Mailbox database   A database for storing mailboxes. The mailbox database manages the data in mailboxes, tracks deleted messages and mailbox sizes, and assists in message transfers. A mailbox database is stored as an Exchange database (.edb) file.

Mailbox-enabled user   A user that has both a user account and a mailbox in an Active Directory domain.

Mailbox server   An Exchange Server 2007 server that has the Mailbox Server role installed.

Mailbox statistics   Values for parameters associated with a mailbox, such as item count, last logon time, last logoff time, total item size, and whether a valid account exists in Active Directory.

Message queue   A temporary location that holds e-mail messages that are waiting to enter the next stage of processing. Message queues exist on Exchange Server 2007 servers that have the Edge Transport or Hub Transport role.

Message subject logging   Storing the subject line of an SMTP e-mail message in the message tracking log. Message subject logging is enabled by default, but you can disable it if required.

Message tracking log   Records message activity when messages are transferred to and from a Microsoft Exchange Server 2007 server that has the Hub Transport Server role, the Mailbox Server role, or the Edge Transport Server role installed.

Mounting a database   The process of preparing a database for use. A public folder database needs to be mounted before public folders can be stored in it.

MX record   A special type of record that defines the hosts in a DNS zone that can accept mail.

Network load balancing   A process by which client load is shared between identically configured servers using a virtual address.

Offline address book   A point-in-time collection of recipient addresses based on an existing address list.

Offline backup   A backup made while the Exchange services are stopped. When you perform an offline backup, users do not have access to their mailboxes.

Online backup   A backup made while the Exchange services are running.

Out-of-office message   An automatic message that informs senders that the recipient is currently unavailable. These messages are almost always configured by recipients prior to their going on leave.

Outlook anywhere   This service replaces RPC over HTTP and allows external Outlook 2007 clients to access a protected Exchange Server 2007 infrastructure without requiring a VPN.

Performance counters   Counters related to a performance object that monitor aspects of performance associated with that object. For example, the Messages Delivered/sec counter in the MSExchangeIS performance object monitors the rate that messages are delivered to all recipients.

Performance log   A file that records (logs) counter values that indicate resource usage.

Performance object   An entity that describes an aspect of server performance and provides performance-related counters. For example, the MSExchangeIS Mailbox object provides counters that monitor the performance of mailboxes in the information store.

Perimeter network   A network location between the Internet and your organization's network. This network location is bounded by two firewalls.

Protocol logging   Can be enabled on Send and Receive connectors to monitor SMTP conversations that occur between Exchange Server 2007 servers that have the Hub Transport Server role or the Edge Transport Server role installed.

Public folder   A folder that users can access directly with client applications such as Microsoft Outlook. Users can place files in public folders so that other users can access them.

Public folder database   A dedicated database in a storage group used to store public folders. There can be only one public folder database on an Exchange Server 2007 server.

Public folder hierarchy   Sometimes known as the public folder tree or the IPM_Subtree. A structured list of the public folders in a public folder database showing parent/child relationships.

Public folder replication   The process by which public folder databases replicate public folder information to Exchange servers that hold content replicas of the folder. Information about the public folder hierarchy and public folder permissions can be replicated in addition to public folder content.

Receive connector   This type of connector handles incoming SMTP traffic.

Recipient template   A recipient object (e.g., a mailbox) that is used as a template or pattern for creating similar objects. Using this technique allows you, for example, to configure the mailbox template with nondefault settings (e.g., you could alter the storage quota or the maximum message size from the database defaults).

Replay   A process in which Exchange examines the transaction log files for a storage group to identify transactions that have been logged but have not been incorporated into the databases of that storage group. The replay process then uses the information in the transaction logs to bring the database to a consistent state.

Resource forest   A forest that contains mailboxes but not their associated user accounts. Typically, you create a resource forest when an organization wants to outsource the administration of e-mail and retain the administration of Windows user accounts.

Resource mailbox   A mailbox that enables users to identify and schedule a resource within an organization, for example, a room or a piece of equipment, by including the resource mailbox in a meeting request.

Restore   To return the original files that were previously preserved in a backup to their location on a server.

Retention   The period of time that data is kept before it is irrevocably deleted.

Retry   The status of a delivery queue when Exchange Server 2007 attempts to resend the queued messages at regular intervals. You can force a retry so that an attempted resend occurs immediately.

Room mailbox   A resource mailbox that enables users to identify a room and schedule its use (if scheduling is enabled). Custom attributes associated with a room mailbox can identify equipment and facilities permanently located in the room.

Root public folder   The folder at the top of the public folder subtree, also known as the IPM_Subtree. The root public folder is denoted by a backslash (\). Top-level public folders are children of the root public folder.

Schema   A set of definitions for all object classes that can exist within an Active Directory forest.

Security group   A group in Active Directory that can be used to grant or deny permissions to its members. A universal security group can be mail-enabled, although many are not.

Send connector   This type of connector handles outgoing SMTP traffic.

Sender reputation level   A score assigned to a sender's address based on analysis of the message traffic.

Server availability   A level of service provided by applications, services, or systems on a server.

Server health   An indication of the stress that is placed on server resources and on major applications that run on a server, such as Exchange Server 2007.

Single copy cluster   A process by which high availability is achieved using two Mailbox servers that share the same storage device.

Site   A collection of IP subnets defined within Active Directory.

Soft recovery   An automatic transaction log file replay process that occurs when a database is remounted after an unexpected stop. Soft recovery uses the checkpoint file to determine which transaction log file to start with when it sequentially replays transactions into databases. In hard recovery, the checkpoint file is deleted, and all available transaction files are played against a recovered database.

Spam   Unsolicited advertising and other unwanted e-mail messages.

Spam confidence level (SCL)   Indicates the likelihood of a message being spam. The higher the SCL, the higher the likelihood of spam. The SCL value is an integer from 0 through 9.

SSL (Secure Sockets Layer)   A method of establishing identity and of encrypting communication using a digital certificate.

Storage group   An Exchange feature that allows you to group databases into a common container that shares a single transaction log set.

Storage quota   A size limit for a public folder (or a mailbox). Several quota levels can be specified, for example, Warning and Prohibit Post.

System folder   A folder that users cannot access directly with client applications such as Microsoft Outlook. Client applications such as Outlook use system folders to store information such as free/busy data, offline address lists, and organizational forms. Other system folders hold configuration information that is used by custom applications or by Exchange itself.

Threshold   A value for an operational parameter above or below which you need to be notified so that you can take appropriate action.

Top-level public folder   A public folder that is a child of the root public folder. Users cannot create top-level public folders by using Microsoft Outlook.

Top users   Users who have the most number of messages or the largest total message size in their mailboxes.

Transport server   An Exchange Server 2007 server that has the Hub Transport or Edge Transport Server role installed.

Universal distribution group   A group with a fixed membership used to facilitate sending e-mail to its members. A single e-mail sent to the group mailbox goes to every member of the group.

Virus   Executable content that can infect a computer after being executed by a user.

References

The following references offer more information about all the objective domains for Exam 70-238.

Planning Microsoft Exchange Server 2007 Upgrades and Migration

- GALSync configuration for cross-forest interoperability: *http://technet.microsoft .com/en-us/library/bb124363.aspx*
- Exchange MAPI client libraries: *http://go.microsoft.com/fwlink/?linkid=94800*
- Exchange Inter-Organization Replication Tool: *http://go.microsoft.com/fwlink/ ?linkid=22455*
- Upgrading from legacy versions of Outlook: *http://technet2.microsoft.com/ Office/en-us/library/8a060469-bbe7-4f09-80f3-24201e6ac4ef1033.mspx?mfr=true*
- Cross-forest Availability Service configuration: *http://technet.microsoft.com/ en-us/library/bb125182.aspx*
- IORepl configuration information: *http://support.microsoft.com/?kbid=238573*
- Cross-forest connector configurations: *http://technet.microsoft.com/en-us/ library/bb123546.aspx*
- Cross-forest and legacy connector configurations: *http://technet.microsoft.com/ en-us/library/bb123546.aspx*
- Administering a mixed environment: *http://technet.microsoft.com/en-us/library/ aa995972.aspx*
- Microsoft Migration Tools for Lotus Notes: *http://go.microsoft.com/fwlink/ ?linkid=57194*
- Migrate from Novell GroupWise: *http://technet.microsoft.com/en-us/library/ aa998380.aspx*
- Unsupported legacy system interoperability: *http://technet.microsoft.com/en-us/ library/bb124132.aspx*

Planning for High Availability Implementation

- Microsoft Software as a Service (SAAS) offerings: *http://technet.microsoft.com/en-us/exchange/bb288501.aspx*
- Retaining hard-deleted items in Outlook: *http://support.microsoft.com/?kbid=246153*
- Cloning Edge configuration data: *http://technet.microsoft.com/en-us/library/bb125150.aspx*
- Protecting UM data: *http://technet.microsoft.com/en-us/library/aa996875.aspx*
- Protecting certificate authorities (CAs): *http://technet2.microsoft.com/windowsserver/en/library/0f1a31e4-8bc1-45ef-987f-c3e1a904eabe1033.mspx?mfr=true*
- Dial Tone Portability: *http://technet.microsoft.com/en-us/library/aa997656.aspx*
- NT Backup and Exchange 2007: *http://technet.microsoft.com/en-us/library/aa998870.aspx*
- Recovery storage groups: *http://technet.microsoft.com/en-us/library/aa997260.aspx*
- Dial Tone Recoveries: *http://technet.microsoft.com/en-us/library/bb310765.aspx*
- Edge Transport server recovery: *http://technet.microsoft.com/en-us/library/bb125150.aspx*
- Rebuilding mailbox clusters: *http://technet.microsoft.com/en-us/library/bb124095.aspx*
- Rebuilding a lost server: *http://technet.microsoft.com/en-us/library/bb123496.aspx*
- Repairing transport queues: *http://technet.microsoft.com/en-us/library/bb124343.aspx*
- Rebuilding search indexes: *http://technet.microsoft.com/en-us/library/aa995966.aspx*
- Multi-CMS installations: *http://support.microsoft.com/?kbid=928811*
- Exchange and DNS: *http://support.microsoft.com/?kbid=322856*
- Exchange cluster dependencies: *http://technet.microsoft.com/en-us/library/aa997696.aspx*
- Perform an SCC installation: *http://technet.microsoft.com/en-us/library/bb124899.aspx*
- Upgrade SCCs: *http://technet.microsoft.com/en-us/library/bb691226.aspx*

- TCP/IP port information: *http://support.microsoft.com/kb/176466*
- Internal Certificate Authority installations: *http://technet2.microsoft.com/windowsserver/en/library/e3d396dd-c141-432b-9e69-50f597061e471033.mspx?mfr=true*
- Manage LCR: *http://technet.microsoft.com/en-us/library/aa998823.aspx*
- Define backup site strategies: *http://technet.microsoft.com/en-us/library/bb201662.aspx*
- CCR planning checklist: *http://technet.microsoft.com/en-us/library/aa996568.aspx*
- CCR installations: *http://technet.microsoft.com/en-us/library/aa997144.aspx*
- SCR operations: *http://technet.microsoft.com/en-us/library/bb6765*

Plan the Exchange Topology Deployment

- Microsoft Exchange Server 2007 on TechNet: Getting Started at *http://technet.microsoft.com/en-us/library/bb124265.aspx*
- Microsoft Exchange Server 2007 on TechNet: Planning and Architecture at *http://technet.microsoft.com/en-us/library/aa998636.aspx*
- Microsoft Exchange Server 2007 on TechNet: Deployment at *http://technet.microsoft.com/en-us/library/bb123895.aspx*
- Look up Exchange Server 2007 Deployment at *http://msexchange.org/*
- Microsoft Exchange Server 2007 Storage Concepts on TechNet: *http://technet.microsoft.com/en-us/library/bb124518.aspx*
- Exchange 2007 storage considerations: *http://msexchangeteam.com/archive/2007/01/15/432199.aspx*
- Exchange ESE architecture: *http://technet.microsoft.com/en-us/library/bb310772.aspx*
- Affinity configuration information: *http://technet.microsoft.com/en-ca/library/aa998575.aspx*
- Multi-forest mailbox moves: *http://technet.microsoft.com/en-ca/library/bb201665.aspx*
- Configuring cross-forest availability: *http://technet.microsoft.com/en-us/library/bb125182.aspx*
- Foreign Send Connector configuration: *http://technet.microsoft.com/en-us/library/aa996779.aspx*

- Microsoft Active Directory preparation white paper: *http://technet.microsoft.com/en-us/library/bb288907.aspx*
- Move mailbox operation: *http://technet.microsoft.com/en-us/library/aa997961.aspx*
- Public folder scripted operations information: *http://technet.microsoft.com/en-us/library/aa997966.aspx*
- GAL configurations to support transitions: *http://technet.microsoft.com/en-us/library/bb124363.aspx*
- Single- to cross-forest transitions: *http://technet.microsoft.com/en-us/library/aa996926.aspx*
- Migrate from Exchange 5.5 to Exchange 2003: *http://technet.microsoft.com/en-us/library/84fd1f06-cf90-43fe-b836-f21b2fa88d4d.aspx*
- Exchange 5.5 migration tools: *http://go.microsoft.com/fwlink/?linkid=96684*
- Lotus Notes migration tools: *http://go.microsoft.com/fwlink/?linkid=82688*
- Novell to Exchange migration: *http://technet.microsoft.com/en-us/exchange/bb288526.aspx*

Planning Messaging Security and Compliance Implementation

- Exchange Security Guide: *http://technet.microsoft.com/en-us/library/bb691338.aspx*
- Real-time Block List Providers: *http://www.email-policy.com/spam-black-lists.htm*
- Forefront for Exchange: *http://go.microsoft.com/fwlink/?linkid=96630*
- Migrate anti-spam settings: *http://technet.microsoft.com/en-us/library/bb508835.aspx*
- Install anti-spam on Hub Transport servers: *http://technet.microsoft.com/en-us/library/bb201691.aspx*
- Manage Delivery Status Notifications: *http://technet.microsoft.com/en-us/library/bb124571.aspx*
- Configure Connection Filters: *http://technet.microsoft.com/en-us/library/bb124376.aspx*
- Configure Sender Filters: *http://technet.microsoft.com/en-us/library/bb124087.aspx*
- Configure Recipient Filters: *http://technet.microsoft.com/en-us/library/bb125187.aspx*

- Configure Sender ID: *http://technet.microsoft.com/en-us/library/aa997136.aspx*

- Configure Sender Reputation: *http://technet.microsoft.com/en-us/library/bb125186.aspx*

- Configure Content Filtering: *http://technet.microsoft.com/en-us/library/bb123737.aspx*

- Configure SCL Thresholds on User Mailboxes: *http://technet.microsoft.com/en-us/library/bb123559.aspx*

- Schedule Safelist Aggregation sample: *http://technet.microsoft.com/en-us/library/aa998280.aspx*

- Assign a quarantine mailbox: *http://technet.microsoft.com/en-us/library/bb123746.aspx*

- Detailed Exclusion Lists for Exchange: *http://technet.microsoft.com/en-us/library/bb332342.aspx*

- Exchange and PKI: *http://technet.microsoft.com/en-us/library/bb851505.aspx*

- OWA Authentication: *http://technet.microsoft.com/en-us/library/bb430796.aspx*

- Assign an SSL certificate to OWA: *http://technet.microsoft.com/en-us/library/bb123583.aspx*

- Configure Exchange ActiveSync security: *http://technet.microsoft.com/en-us/library/bb430761.aspx*

- Configure POP3 or IMAP4 Security: *http://technet.microsoft.com/en-us/library/bb430779.aspx*

- Work with Domain Security: *http://technet.microsoft.com/en-us/library/bb124996.aspx*

- Manage classifications: *http://technet.microsoft.com/en-us/library/bb124705.aspx*

- Manage records management: *http://technet.microsoft.com/en-us/library/bb123507.aspx*

- Understand journal reports: *http://technet.microsoft.com/en-us/library/bb331962.aspx*

- More information on journaling: *http://technet.microsoft.com/en-us/library/bb124382.aspx*

- Learn more about S/MIME in Exchange: *http://technet.microsoft.com/en-us/library/aa995740.aspx*

- AD RMS and Exchange: *http://technet.microsoft.com/en-us/library/bb123950 .aspx*

- Manage Delivery Status Notifications: *http://technet.microsoft.com/en-us/ library/bb124571.aspx*

Planning for Messaging Environment Maintenance

- More information on ITIL: *http://www.itil-officialsite.com/home/home.asp*

- More information on MOF: *http://technet.microsoft.com/en-us/library/ bb232042.aspx*

- More information on the WSSRA: *http://www.microsoft.com/technet/ solutionaccelerators/wssra/raguide/default.mspx*

- Site templates for Windows SharePoint Services: *http://technet.microsoft.com/ en-us/windowsserver/sharepoint/bb407286.aspx*

- Clone ET Configurations: *http://technet.microsoft.com/en-us/library/aa998622 .aspx*

- More information on message throttling: *http://technet.microsoft.com/library/ bb232205.aspx*

- For instructions on how to set up Event Forwarding, look up "Collect Vista Events" at *http://www.prismmicrosys.com/newsletters_june2007.php*

- Locate Exchange troubleshooting tools at *http://go.microsoft.com/fwlink/ ?linkid=50259*

- For more information about Microsoft Operations Manager, go to *http://technet .microsoft.com/en-us/library/bb201735.aspx*

Index

Additional Windows (R2) Resources for Administrators

Published and Forthcoming Titles from Microsoft Press

Microsoft® Windows Server™ 2003 Administrator's Pocket Consultant, Second Edition
William R. Stanek • ISBN 0-7356-2245-0

Here's the practical, pocket-sized reference for IT professionals supporting Microsoft Windows Server 2003—fully updated for Service Pack 1 and Release 2. Designed for quick referencing, this portable guide covers all the essentials for performing everyday system administration tasks. Topics include managing workstations and servers, using Active Directory® directory service, creating and administering user and group accounts, managing files and directories, performing data security and auditing tasks, handling data back-up and recovery, and administering networks using TCP/IP, WINS, and DNS, and more.

MCSE Self-Paced Training Kit (Exams 70-290, 70-291, 70-293, 70-294): Microsoft Windows Server 2003 Core Requirements, Second Edition
Holme, Thomas, Mackin, McLean, Zacker, Spealman, Hudson, and Craft • ISBN 0-7356-2290-6

The Microsoft Certified Systems Engineer (MCSE) credential is the premier certification for professionals who analyze the business requirements and design and implement the infrastructure for business solutions based on the Microsoft Windows Server 2003 platform and Microsoft Windows Server System—now updated for Windows Server 2003 Service Pack 1 and R2. This all-in-one set provides in-depth preparation for the four required networking system exams. Work at your own pace through the lessons, hands-on exercises, troubleshooting labs, and review questions. You get expert exam tips plus a full review section covering all objectives and sub-objectives in each study guide. Then use the Microsoft Practice Tests on the CD to challenge yourself with more than 1500 questions for self-assessment and practice!

Microsoft Windows® Small Business Server 2003 R2 Administrator's Companion
Charlie Russel, Sharon Crawford, and Jason Gerend • ISBN 0-7356-2280-9

Get your small-business network, messaging, and collaboration systems up and running quickly with the essential guide to administering Windows Small Business Server 2003 R2. This reference details the features, capabilities, and technologies for both the standard and premium editions—including Microsoft Windows Server 2003 R2, Exchange Server 2003 with Service Pack 1, Windows SharePoint® Services, SQL Server™ 2005 Workgroup Edition, and Internet Information Services. Discover how to install, upgrade, or migrate to Windows Small Business Server 2003 R2; plan and implement your network, Internet access, and security services; customize Microsoft Exchange Server for your e-mail needs; and administer user rights, shares, permissions, and Group Policy.

Microsoft Windows Small Business Server 2003 R2 Administrator's Companion
Charlie Russel, Sharon Crawford, and Jason Gerend • ISBN 0-7356-2280-9

Here's the ideal one-volume guide for the IT professional administering Windows Server 2003. Now fully updated for Windows Server 2003 Service Pack 1 and R2, this *Administrator's Companion* offers up-to-date information on core system administration topics for Microsoft Windows, including Active Directory services, security, scripting, disaster planning and recovery, and interoperability with UNIX. It also includes all-new sections on Service Pack 1 security updates and new features for R2. Featuring easy-to-use procedures and handy work-arounds, this book provides ready answers for on-the-job results.

MCSA/MCSE Self-Paced Training Kit (Exam 70-290): Managing and Maintaining a Microsoft Windows Server 2003 Environment, Second Edition
Dan Holme and Orin Thomas • ISBN 0-7356-2289-2

MCSA/MCSE Self-Paced Training Kit (Exam 70-291): Implementing, Managing, and Maintaining a Microsoft Windows Server 2003 Network Infrastructure, Second Edition
J.C. Mackin and Ian McLean • ISBN 0-7356-2288-4

MCSE Self-Paced Training Kit (Exam 70-293): Planning and Maintaining a Microsoft Windows Server 2003 Network Infrastructure, Second Edition
Craig Zacker • ISBN 0-7356-2287-6

MCSE Self-Paced Training Kit (Exam 70-294): Planning, Implementing, and Maintaining a Microsoft Windows Server 2003 Active Directory® Infrastructure, Second Ed.
Jill Spealman, Kurt Hudson, and Melissa Craft • ISBN 0-7356-2286-8

For more information about Microsoft Press® books and other learning products,
visit: **www.microsoft.com/mspress** *and* **www.microsoft.com/learning**

Prepare for Certification with Self-Paced Training Kits

Official Exam Prep Guides—
Plus Practice Tests

Ace your preparation for the skills measured by the MCP exams—and on the job. With official *Self-Paced Training Kits* from Microsoft, you'll work at your own pace through a system of lessons, hands-on exercises, troubleshooting labs, and review questions. Then test yourself with the Readiness Review Suite on CD, which provides hundreds of challenging questions for in-depth self-assessment and practice.

- **MCSE Self-Paced Training Kit (Exams 70-290, 70-291, 70-293, 70-294): Microsoft® Windows Server™ 2003 Core Requirements.** 4-Volume Boxed Set. ISBN: 0-7356-1953-0. (Individual volumes are available separately.)

- **MCSA/MCSE Self-Paced Training Kit (Exam 70-270): Installing, Configuring, and Administering Microsoft Windows® XP Professional, Second Edition.** ISBN: 0-7356-2152-7.

- **MCSE Self-Paced Training Kit (Exam 70-298): Designing Security for a Microsoft Windows Server 2003 Network.** ISBN: 0-7356-1969-7.

- **MCSA/MCSE Self-Paced Training Kit (Exam 70-350): Implementing Microsoft Internet Security and Acceleration Server 2004.** ISBN: 0-7356-2169-1.

- **MCSA/MCSE Self-Paced Training Kit (Exam 70-284): Implementing and Managing Microsoft Exchange Server 2003.** ISBN: 0-7356-1899-2.

For more information about Microsoft Press® books, visit: **www.microsoft.com/mspress**

For more information about learning tools such as online assessments, e-learning, and certification, visit: **www.microsoft.com/mspress** *and* **www.microsoft.com/learning**

System Requirements

To use the book companion CD-ROM, you need a computer running Microsoft Windows Server 2008, Windows Vista, Windows Server 2003, or Windows XP. The computer must meet the following minimum requirements:

- 1 GHz 32-bit (x86) or 64-bit (x64) processor (depending on the minimum requirements of the operating system)
- 1 GB of system memory (depending on the minimum requirements of the operating system)
- A hard disk partition with at least 700 MB of available space
- A monitor capable of at least 800x600 display resolution
- A keyboard
- A mouse or other pointing device
- An optical drive capable of reading CD-ROMs

The computer must also have the following software:

- A Web browser such as Internet Explorer version 6 or later
- An application that can display PDF files, such as Adobe Acrobat Reader, which can be downloaded at *http://www.adobe.com/reader*
- Microsoft Word or Word Viewer

These requirements will support use of the companion CD-ROM. To perform the practice exercises in this training kit, we recommend that you use a test workstation, test server, or staging server and a virtual machine technology. See the Introduction to the book for detailed hardware and software information.

Note that you will need Exchange Server 2007 to complete the practice exercises included with each chapter. Although Exchange can be installed on a production server, it is not recommended that you do so. Instead, install Exchange and execute the practices in each chapter in a testing environment (detailed information is in the book Introduction).

Evaluation DVDs for Exchange Server 2007 are supplied with this book. Complete Exchange 2007 System Requirements are here: *http://technet.microsoft.com/en-us/library/aa996719.aspx*.

What do you think of this book?

We want to hear from you!

Do you have a few minutes to participate in a brief online survey?

Microsoft is interested in hearing your feedback so we can continually improve our books and learning resources for you.

To participate in our survey, please visit:

www.microsoft.com/learning/booksurvey/

...and enter this book's ISBN-10 or ISBN-13 number (located above barcode on back cover*). As a thank-you to survey participants in the United States and Canada, each month we'll randomly select five respondents to win one of five $100 gift certificates from a leading online merchant. At the conclusion of the survey, you can enter the drawing by providing your e-mail address, which will be used for prize notification only.

Thanks in advance for your input. Your opinion counts!

* Where to find the ISBN on back cover

ISBN-13: 000-0-0000-0000-0
ISBN-10: 0-0000-0000-0

0 000000 000000

Example only. Each book has unique ISBN.

Microsoft® *Press*

No purchase necessary. Void where prohibited. Open only to residents of the 50 United States (includes District of Columbia) and Canada (void in Quebec). For official rules and entry dates see:

www.microsoft.com/learning/booksurvey/